Advances in Technology, Education and Development

Edited by
Wim Kouwenhoven

Advances in Technology, Education and Development
Edited by Wim Kouwenhoven

Republished by InTech
Janeza Trdine 9, 51000 Rijeka, Croatia

Technical Editor Melita Horvat

Cover Designer Dino Smrekar

Additional hard copies can be obtained from orders@intechopen.com

Advances in Technology, Education and Development, Edited by Wim Kouwenhoven
p. cm.
ISBN 978-953-307-011-7

For EU product safety concerns:
IN TECH d.o.o., Prolaz Marije Krucifikse Kozulić 3, 51000 Rijeka, Croatia, info@intechopen.com or visit our website at intechopen.com.

Preface

From 3rd to 5th March 2008 the International Association of Technology, Education and Development organised its International Technology, Education and Development Conference in Valencia, Spain. Over a hundred papers were presented by participants from a great variety of countries.

This book, the first one in a series of two, presents a selection of the papers that have been transformed by the authors into book chapters. The 29 chapters contain descriptions of research, policy or good practice in areas where, in most cases, technology, education and development overlap.

The first two chapters emphasise the growing importance of domain-specific and generic skills or competencies in education and training for professionals. The innovation of Higher education is addressed in a number of chapters and particularly the Spanish authors refer to the objective of the Bologna process to create more comparable, compatible and coherent systems of Higher Education, through the European Higher Education Area.

Naturally the growing role of ICT in education is highlighted in this book. Two chapters deal with ICT applications in the classroom that facilitate teaching and learning processes. Six chapters are grouped under the theme of the use of ICT in the curriculum, three of these discuss the use of ICT in distance education or the mix of distance and face-to-face learning in blended learning.

Innovation in higher education concerns more attention for the professions that graduates will assume, acknowledging that not all students will end up in academia as researchers. So, together with more competence-based approaches more student-centred, constructivist forms of teaching and learning are appearing in the lecture rooms, labs and practice rooms. Seven chapters describe various aspects of the "new learning", from assessment to cooperative work and multidisciplinary approaches.

The last ten chapters are more difficult to group, but all address fascinating facets of technology, education and development. They also represent with their great variety in origin of the authors a proof of the growing globalisation in education and research. There is a contribution from Iran in the field of "the learning brain", signifying the growing attention for the application of findings from neuro-biological research. There is a contribution from Slovakia on the education of materials research. The role of technology networks in learning organisations is addressed by Austrian authors, while a chapter from Botswana reports research on the role of intrinsic and extrinsic motivation in setting career goals.

Summarising, this book provides a kaleidoscopic view of work that is done, all over the world in (higher) education, characterised by the key words 'Education" and 'Development'. I wish the reader an enlightening experience.

Wim Kouwenhoven
Centre for International Cooperation
VU University Amsterdam
The Netherlands

Contents

Professional Prerequisites for Japanese Sea Officers – Professional Training School Requirements –

Olivia C. Ogawa
Kinki University
Japan

1. Introduction

Traditional Japanese-style management, including life time employment and seniority systems has collapsed and instead, alternative achievement-oriented systems have been implemented. As a result, many Japanese people have come to believe that skills are required to secure job opportunities, thus they try to get licenced. However, some of them withdraw from professional training schools even before graduating, and rookie licenced professionals give up continuing their professional career paths, despite making technical improvements because the completion of work itself requires more than just acquiring techniques and licences. The purpose of this reseach is to explore the professional prerequisites for students who are launching careers as Japanese sea officers. In the following sections, previous literature relating to skills will be summarized, and previous research results and qualitative reserch data will be analyzed.

2. Literature

According to the literature about professionalism, professionals have two features, "specific knowledge" and "professional norms" (Macdonald, 1995; Wilensky, 1964). Members of the professional team are convinced that they should agree with their occupational norms and rules which serve as guidelines for the assignment of meaning in their actions. Such norms are described in their cultural contexts, focusing on the consistency rather than the originality of the individuals in the group, even though ideologies are not consistent with one another. These norms justify and explain the behaviors of the group members (Trice and Bayer, 1993).

On the other hand, it is accepted that each individual has his/her own unique ideology and stance in the career-based occupational realization (Katz, 1955; Ogawa, 2001, 2008, 2009).

Ogawa (2001) investigated the professionalism of Japanese sea officers and discovered that it contained two important aspects: knowledge and professional spirit integrating knowledge (intensive work). In this paper, professional spirit is the ideology that explains the reasons why Japanese sea officers work in a profession which contributes to the society.

Katz (1955) describes the skills for administrators, which can be referred to as professional skills. Katz (1955) suggests three basic developmental skills on which effective administration rests. It assumes that a successful administrator is required to obtain technical, human (interpersonal), and conceptual skills.

Technical skill implies an understanding of, and proficiency in, a specific kind of activity, particularly one involving methods, processes, procedures, or techniques. It is evident in many occupations such as surgery, engineering, accounting when each is performing its own specialized knowledge, analytical ability within that speciality, and the use of the tools and techniques of the specific discipline. Technical skill is the most familiar of the skills because it is concrete and required of the greatest number of people. For this reason, our vocational training and on-the-job training programs are largely concerned with developing this skill.

Human skill is a vital part of everything the business person does. This is the ability to work effectively as a group member and to build cooperative effort within a team. It is primarily concerned with working with people. The person with highly developed human skill is aware of his own attitudes, assumptions, and beliefs about other individuals and groups. In accepting the different viewpoints, perceptions and beliefs of others, the person must be skilful in understanding what the others really mean by their words and behaviors, and in communicating to others in their own contexts, what the person means by his/her behavior. In addition, the person can work to create an atmosphere of approval and security in which subordinates feel free to express themselves without fear of censure or ridicule, by encouraging them to take part in the planning and executing of things. The person must be sensitive to the needs and motivations of others. It must become a natural, continuous, unconscious activity, since it involves sensitivity not only in on-the-spot decision making but also in the day-by-day behavior of the individual.

Conceptual skill, as used in the context of this research, involves the ability to see things in one's career as a whole and to choose what one wants to be. It includes recognizing how various functions of the organizations, occupations, and stakeholders depend on each other, and how changes in any one part, affect all the others. It extends to visualizing the relationship of the individual to the industry, the community, and the political, social and economic forces of the nation as a whole. Therefore, the success of any decision depends on the conceptual skill of the people who make that decision and those who put it into action. Not only does the effective coordination of the various parts depend on the conceptual skill of the people involved, but also on the whole future direction and tone of the profession and organization. The attitudes of professionals with conceptual skills color the whole character of the occupational response and determine '(occupational) personality' which distinguishes one occupational practice. These attitudes are a reflection of professional conceptual skill- the way the professional perceives and responds to business growth, occupational objectives and policies, and stakeholders' and students' interests. To whit, conceptual inadequacy leaves professionals at a serious disadvantage.

This research supports Katz (1955) and Ogawa (2001), because it is natural that an individual has his/her own recognition of a profession and its functions to the society, even though professionals share their occupational culture. One can create ideological significance to launch his/her own professional career.

According to Ogawa (2009), knowledge and professional spirit as discussed in Ogawa (2001), are equivalent to technical skill and conceptual skill in Katz (1955). Although human skill

(Katz, 1955) is not mentioned as a characteristic of professionalism in Ogawa (2001), it is recognized as a culturally embedded professional behavior. In this research, it is taken for granted that human skill is a required element in professional relationships.
In the following sections, professional training school prerequisites for students who want to become Japanese sea officers will be analyzed, from the viewpoint of three skills (technical, human and conceptual skills) in Katz (1955). This research will closely discuss the conceptual aspects of professionals, for the purpose of exploring what is more important than acquiring techniques or licences for professional careers.

3. Method

3.1 Measure

Semi-structured interviews and participation observations were conducted between 1998 and 2008.
This research was conducted with students and teachers in professional training schools in Japan. They were chosen to examine a variety of skills influenced by the inferential factors such as occupational characteristics (living and working together 24/7) and school systems (classes and practices).
The purpose of the interviews was to explore all dimension of skills by examining the participants' responses to open-ended questions about learning, lectures and practices since they entered the university. Counseling style interviews were conducted in an effort to build a rapport with the participants, and to have them share their true thoughts and feelings about various issues. Responses to open-ended questions provided qualitative data for analysis. Questions were constructed on the basis of Professionalism literature emphasizing the events of realizing the importance of knowledge, working spirit, and relationships (e.g. Katz, 1955, Ogawa, 2001).
Face-to-face interviews were conducted for approximately forty to sixty minutes, the longest being two hours. All interviews were recorded and transcribed in Japanese, and all the data that has been used in this paper was translated from Japanese to English.
In addition, situation-oriented data was gathered by observation at sea. The researcher was onboard, and remained at the bridge of the ship depending on the students' shifts.

3.2 Respondents and organizations

The number of participants who were interviewed was 60 (55 students and 5 teachers). Students were studying a special course in maritime science at a Japanese national university and on the training ship owned by the National Institute for Sea Training (NIST). These research projects have been conducted since 1998, and some of the respondents have participated in more than one of our projects.
The professional training schools in which this research was conducted, covered the majority of maritime sciences including the government accredited training course for professional ship officers and engineers.
Japanese students attend the maritime academy post-secondary school rather than the post-tertiary schools which is different from the Western system.
The school environment simulated the intended future working situations. It recommended that students, especially those wishing to become sea officers, live at the dormitory adjacent to the campus or the apartments near the campus, even though students preferred to live at

home with their families for personal reasons. Students had to attend practical ship training provided for one month, 24 hours a day by NIST. They attended this training until their third year, and for three months at the end of their senior year. They needed to complete one year of practical training (6 months during university and 6 months in NIST after graduation) before acquiring the license of Third officers. Therefore, students ended up living together throughout their schooldays.
Most of the teachers and students were well acquainted, saying hello whenever they met one another, remembering each other's names easily. Teachers and senior students taught younger students how to communicate with each other, and how to maintain discipline. Small-sized classes facilitated more effective communication. The school enrollment was limited to 90 students for professional training in each grade.
Students were encouraged to study harder by teachers and friends, taking up many core courses as well as preparing for the national examinations to get licenses. Some students were able to pass the paper-based examinations during their schooldays despite the fact that the licenses could be obtained during their practical career after graduation.

3.3 Procedure

This research has initially highlighted the professionalism of sea officers (Ogawa 1999, 2001), from Katz (1955). However, some of the dimensions (human and conceptual skills) in Katz (1955) were explained by analyzing the interview data after 2005, because the interview guidelines after 2005 were reconstructed based on previous research projects and therefore more detailed information was obtained.
Educational systems, unique cultural conventions and students' needs were targeted in order to analyze prerequisites for Japanese sea officers. Data referring to thoughts and feelings were analyzed from a psychological viewpoint in order to interpret the background or underlying reasons for students' behavior.
Also evident, as shown by the interviewees' responses in this paper, is the state of confusion created by thought provoking interview questions that required interviewees to engage in self analysis and reflection throughout the interviews. Hence, the responses may appear to be ambiguous. However, this provides a true image of the interview situation.

4. Results

4.1 Technical skills

Ogawa (1999) summarized the educational programs for students in the professional training school (Fig.1). Classroom lectures and practical trainings are included. Theory and basic disciplines, which are considered to be the basic guidelines for acquiring technical skills, are learned mainly in the classroom. Students can put the knowledge into practice and learn more practical technical skills including procedures, techniques and methods in specific maritime situations.
In this research, businesses and professional organizations have paid great attention in developing technical skills of students throughout their four years of university because the industry requires work-ready graduates. However, Ogawa (1999) found that technical skills learned in the professional training school only covered basic patterns which could be applied in industrial situations after graduating from university. Sea officers had to continue to learn, and to acquire many more technical skills after entering shipping companies.

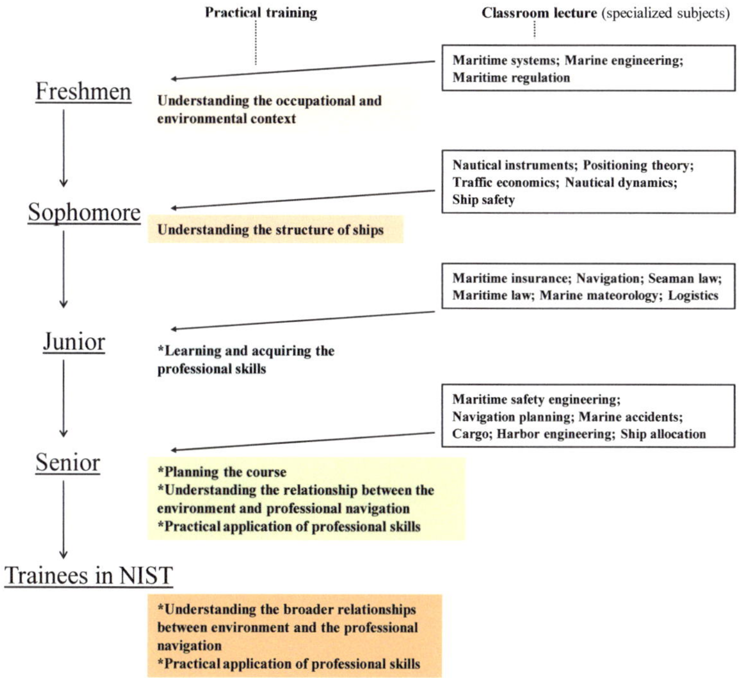

Fig. 1. Academic Transition between Practical Trainings and Classroom Lectures (Courses for Navigators) (Ogawa, 1999) (Translated from Japanese)

4.2 Human Skills

According to Ogawa (2008), human skills in the professional training school are strongly connected to those used by the team at sea and in business groups on the land[1] to create trust within the team. Based on the participation observations that started in 1999, a top-down order system is evident in industry and school. Higher-ranked officers make decisions and give orders to other members. Subordinates are required to follow their superiors' orders. Furthermore, subordinates are required to report the tasks' completion once they have been assigned to them. Senior students strive to teach the top-down system to freshmen during their initial phase in the university.

Moreover, senior students teach freshmen how to communicate and get along with higher-ranked people, and with peers. They are together 24/7 during practical training, and cannot leave the ship once they board the ship. For example, they are in close quarters when doing many activities together including meals and drinking parties. Students are learning these kinds of highly developed human skills as mentioned in Katz (1955), by living together in the dormitory and the training ship. They tend to accept different viewpoints and beliefs of other students and members, and tend to recognize messages and behaviors of others.

[1] Japanese sea officers are moved off to another section on the land, and go back to the sea every several years.

Teachers interact enthusiastically with students and they try to remember each person's name. In addition, students appear to trust teachers and students because they express their real feelings including problems and individual matters.

> We are strongly connected in this school. Everyone knows each other like family. Not in public, but somewhere in a private group…off course, it might give both merits and demerits. Anyway, we rely on each other. I have never had such a connection to friends and teachers in high school. I can speak about my personal issues to my friends or teachers here. (student 1, 2005 spring)

Student 1 indicates that there is a valuable communication and a strong connection between teachers and students that make them feel relaxed and trust each other; rapport is built between the members.
Human skills as mentioned in Katz (1955) are developed at the beginning of university, in parallel with their traditional top-down communication system in the workplace. However, human skills are not taught formally. Teachers and students develop human skills through daily communication.

4.3 Conceptual skills

4.3.1 Conceptual skills of Japanese sea officers and students

The conceptual skills of many respondents in this research have been developed through **the realization of their responsibilites and beliefs**, that by carrying products and natural resources, they are supporting Japanese people's living. From the result in Ogawa (2001), many maritime students and teachers on the training ship showed a strong compassion to others and sometimes sacrificed themselves to support others. They had the strengths to overcome the rigidity of the maritime environment and training. On the other hand, Fujiwara (2005/2006) mentions that 'the Samurai spirit' incorporates charity, sincerity, endurance, justice, courage, and compassionate empathy [2]. This Samurai spirit has functioned as the traditional criteria for actions and morality of many Japanese people since the Samurai emerged. Ogawa (2009) says that "Seamen's spirit" as called, is considered to have originated from "the Japanese Samurai spirit".
One student recounted her experience of building the concept as a freshman,

> I could often feel the professional spirit, that was seamen's spirit, when I was staying with upper levelled officers in the training ships. I hadn't had any friend involved in the maritime society before I entered this university, so it was the unknown world. When I went to the practical training in the ship which was operated by NIST, it was the first time for me to take one-month practical training. During the training, I talked with the teacher who was temporally sent from the Japanese shipping company. He talked me that the sea officers had to work at the risk of their lives. They put their lives in danger! I don't deny that the usual works on the land are at risk, but it is not compared to the workplace on the sea. I had never realized that I was bound by myth of safety. On the other hand, sea

[2] Fujiwara (2005/2006) agreed with the interpretation by Nitobe (1899/1998), which introduced "Bushido" to outside of Japan.

> officers always make their living at a risk for almost whole year! It was no less than astounding and beyond all imagination. He had operated the oil tanker conducted by a Japanese shipping company, so he was vividly aware of responsibility that he and his colleagues carried oil and supported livings for Japanese people. He said that he delivered their happiness, had to eliminate unhappiness such as death which happened in the ship. He mentioned, 'we delivers happiness from which variety goods are made. Someone presents one of them to his girlfriend. On the other hand, someone are waiting for and wishing to give the significant other the goods which we carried from abroad. ' When I listened to his story, I was surprised to his strong concept toward the work and the difference between his recognition and ours at that times. I had thought as a layman that sea officers were only the people who carried the stuffs before I talked with him. I understood that the people like truck drivers also deliver goods, but I was strongly impressed his concept to work as a sea officer who carries across the sea. I was overwhelmed by his tremendous pride and policy as a professional, at the same time I realized that I was tiny and powerless. I was greatly influenced by him because it was the first time, during the practical training in freshman, to see the person with such highly-developed concept to the occupation. [snip] I was deeply influenced by the worldview of the sea officers who was on loan to the educational deck. So would my friends be. It was rare to meet such a kind of officers from companies. I had not had a strong desire to become a sea officer before I met him, but I started to have a strong notion that I wanted to be a sea officer. Now I positively participate in the training in order to absorb everything. (student 2, 2003 spring)

On the other hand, student 4 said that the sea officer's career is built upon the accumulation of worries, which are related to her desire and interests.

> To get a job as a navigation officer means I'll do what I want to do. That's really what I want. It came about after thinking it over and over again. (student 4, 2008 summer)

Conceptual skill of student 4 here could offer the direction of how to be a sea officer. Student 2 has an understanding of the responsibility and beliefs. This demonstrates that the conceptual skill here is defferent from each individual.

4.3.2 Factors developing conceptual skills

According to figure 1[3], the educational program in this training school includes both classroom lectures and practical training. **The practical training** introduces the things inside and around the ship, and assists young students to understand the maritime environmental context, and to give an image of the ideal future workplace and career. As already shown, student 2 talked about her experience that happened during the practical training.

In addition, student 4 discussed that her practical training in her freshman year has encouraged her to create her own conceptual skill that she wanted to be a sea officer. She did not feel as much physical and psychological difficulties as other students, although she went through many difficult situations in the practical environment. Moreover, she was able

[3] The relating parts were highlighted in Figure 1.

to build confidence to launch her career and to take actions by her own decision in the maritime environment.

> I can't do well and easily get intimidated even on a part-time job. I felt confident, however, when I was on board Taisei-maru. I felt the operation was good. I had thought before that it would be just for fun. But now I want to do everything on board a ship. When I had to choose the seminar, I made up my mind for taking it by myself. Although other people talked to each other so that they can be enrolled in the same seminar with their friends. I was kind of independent, thinking like "I really want to study in this seminar, so I sign up for it even if the others don't. I was supposed to take part in this training with a friend of mine. She eventually cancelled but I didn't. It had seemed interesting so I thought I would join alone. I could feel I would do it alone. Isn't it uncomfortable to be alone? I don't know, though. But I could do it. In the former training ship, the other people I signed up with didn't seem to like boarding the ship. They did things sloppily. I liked boarding the ship and wanted to do things right. I got annoyed when I saw someone doing exercises with disoriented attitude in the workout period. I wanted to tell them to do things right. Being with people like them, I thought I should do everything right. I didn't feel sick in Taisei-maru while others did. I think I'm suited to boarding the ship. I could do many things during the practical training. (student 4, 2008 summer)

As a result, doing practical training from an early stage at the university helps students visualize the ideal future workplace. This means that students can acquire conceptual skills by being in a real situation at sea.

The data of student 2 also shows that conceptual skill was deeply influenced by the input and skills of **guiding figures**. Student 2 began creating her own conceptual skill, which was influenced by the story relating to the conceptual skill of the sea officer from a company.

On the other hand, the data of student 4 below revealed one aspect of the skills of guiding figure. She reconstructed the future direction of her career by talking about her career problems with guiding figures. Student 4 considered who to share her opinions with. In addition, student 4 chose the guiding figure depending on the types of issues and career stages.

> When preparing for an interview, I didn't tell my teachers everything in my mind. I wondered if I should tell them things like my future or family. Actually, I've been talking with one of my fellow students about it. She aims at becoming a navigation officer like I do and also wants to get married. We're in the same position. I asked her for some advice. Besides her, I talked about my worries and problems to some other students when I thought they could understand them. To my teachers, I talked a lot about other matters. They taught me various things and encouraged me to keep trying. But I couldn't tell them all. (student 4, 2008 summer)

The student 4 also indicated in the above data that professionals, including teachers and her peers could be guiding figures. Seniors are more suitable to be role models.

4.3.3 Update conceptual skills at the career stages

This research obtained longitudinal data from student 4, starting from the early stage at the university. Student 4 participated in some of the research projects, giving stories about her conceptual skills in her freshman and senior years. According to the analysis, she **validated the core conceptual skills** which were acquired in her freshman year, and she **updated them incrementally** when she struggled with problems and realized important things in her career.

As already shown, when student 4 was a freshman, she shared that being a sea officer was what she really wanted to be, because she could gain confidence and could make independent decisions. Through practical training, she realized that she could handle difficult situation in maritime environment.

Two and a half years later, she reflected on her experiences at the training school in the last three years.

In her freshman year, student 4 wanted to be a teaching officer at the national training school. When she became a sophomore, she participated in the internship program there. Desk work was assigned to her, and realized that job at sea was more appealing than the tedious work provided at the national training school.

> I had a great time training on the ship as a freshman. I got fond of the operation at the navigation training school. I wanted to be an officer at the school. It has been my dream since I was a freshman. Everytime the training ship called on port in Kobe, I went to chat with crews. I asked them if they enjoyed their work or how I could enter the school. I became friends with many of them. Some of them took me out for dinner. Since I felt linked with them after listening to their stories, I got motivated to enter the training school.
> In my sophomore year, I chose to do an internship at the training school. They let me do various on shore duties there. But honestly, those duties were boring because all I did was to sort and file documents. The work at the training ship was more interesting. Ground works were a little boring. (student 4, 2008 summer)

In her junior year, student 4 started job-hunting, and thought more deeply about her career as a sea officer than before. She has met a teaching officer in the practical training. It was difficult for this officer to develop both teaching and maritime skills. Due to this, student 4 has started to wonder about her own future as well. This resulted in a change of interest in becoming a teacher in the training shool. She eventually decided to operate ships and develop skills as a sea officer in a shipping company.

> In the training for juniors, I saw a young officer whose skill was as poor as ours. In fact, we students were better at doing the difficult skill of cross-bearing. This officer was often scolded. I knew this officer really worked very hard even when exhausted. But I became aware of the situation where young officers like this officer can't get enough on-the-job training on board because senior officers are tied up with training students. As a result, the young officers in training can't get a chance to brush up their skills without being coached by their superiors who mainly watch and take care of students. I know we should make efforts on our own, but we need coaching to build up the experience. I thought it might be hard to acquire enough skills as a navigator if I get a job as an officer in the

> training school. I'm not a competent person. I have worry about what it would be like to work with students in the training school. This image affects my thinking. It made me think I would work for a shipping company to get adequate skills and then I'd go back to the training school if I still wish. I can't take care of students as a senior when my skills are not good enough. It might be better to enter the shipping company for brushing up my skills. It was at the training session in October and November in my junior that I came up with the idea that I should be an officer for a company and not for the training school. (student 4, 2008 summer)

In addition to that, student 4 was struggling during the job-hunting stage because she had some doubts about launching her maritime career, which is related to her gender and family.

> When I started job-hunting and took it seriously, I heard some rumors about the school. Since I have wanted to become a navigation officer, I took various tests. I passed the written test for the 1st level. I got all levels of the license to be a wireless operator. I took the liberty to get the license for handling the navigation hazards. I've got enough licenses and have worked hard. I thought it was worthwhile applying for shipping companies including major ones, which were said to be difficult to pass. I wanted to have a baby, as well as to work on board a ship. The shipping companies offer the wide range of on-shore duty. Only 4 or 5 years have passed since they began recruiting female officers. So, I thought I could create a system suitable for female officers. It would be interesting to challenge on things in the new environment under which we have no established systems for female sea officers. This is one of the main reasons why I decided to be an officer for a shipping company. The event which gave me the greatest push was the "Career café". It was a group for working women. In my junior year, I attended it and talked with two people, one is a researcher studying female sea officers in Cardiff, UK, and the other one is a female officer who will soon be a second mate. I thought she was cool. Around the same time, I was inclined to get a job for on-shore duty. I was wondering which job to apply for. The conversation with these women gave me a great motivation. The researcher said, "You should list up what you can't decide to do and link them together like a grape vine to identify what the problems are. Put down the benefits for being a sea officer. Why don't you try something that you think is the most suitable for you." When I got home, I did what I was advised to do. In the end, I realized I really wanted to be a sea officer. I thought I shouldn't worry too much about my current problems or that, I should tackle them. It could be that I'd rather do on-shore duty just because I don't want to be separated from my loved one. But I knew it wasn't the right decision. I didn't want to sacrifice what I really want to do. I thought I would break up with him if he didn't understand me. I know he saw me make the effort to get the job I wanted. I told him my idea and he agreed with me. I thought working on the ship would suit me better. I thought I would quit the job if I got on-shore duty against my will. Besides, many people encouraged me to work on board a ship. That's how I decided to be a sea officer.
>
> I got confused. I cried over the phone. I couldn't decide which way to go. I just let it all out to him. I couldn't say what I really wanted to do when he asked me. I didn't want him to decide, either. I knew I had to decide by myself, but I couldn't right away. That was when I got a chance to talk with the female sea officer and the researcher. They made me think I

> should listen to my heart and do whatever it says. Even if I fail, I can bounce back myself and wait until I find a new way. (student 4, 2008 summer)

She talked with her guiding figures (sea officers, peers, teaching officers, and working women) several times, summarizing her problems and opinions on a sheet of paper. At the end, she decided to go to a more challenging stage which is considered to be very difficult by other student and teachers, and passed the most dificult national examination. In addition, she believed that the guiding figures prayed for her success to overcome hardships and to develop both technical and conceptual skills. This shows that the concept of developing skills and taking on challenges are more inevitable in her career and life.

Focusing on the transition in data by student 4, conceptual skills could be updated at some important events throughout the training and contacts with guiding figures. In addition, conceptual skills had **motivated students to acquire technical knowledge and human skills** everytime they were validated and updated. Student 2, as mentioned earlier, began creating her own conceptual skills and career image which was deeply influenced by the story related to the conceptual skill of the sea officer from a company. As a result, she also became more motivated to develop other skills. Therefore, conceptual skills could be the reasons why professionals integrate a variety of technical and human skills.

On the other hand, student 3 mentioned that he did not have a concept of what a career is, even though he participated in the practical training. He shared that he felt that he had to obey the authority and that did not develop an understanding of the responsibility to the occupation and society.

> I didn't feel the seaman spirit still now, because I am a trainee and ordered and supported by more responsible officers. I have never taken practical training to abroad. But after launching as a sea officer or in tall ship training, we could feel special feeling like the professional spirit. I think that the upper levelled officers, such as captain and chief officer in the ministry of transport, could image such kind of concept to the work. (student 3, 2003 spring)

The excerpt above indicates that sea officers and students need time to build and update their conceptual skills.

The interviews in this section highlighted some important findings. First, conceptual skills in the society of sea officers could be related to the understanding of responsibility and beliefs for Japanese people's living, which originated from Japanese people's traditional aspects. Second, conceptual skills, learned from an early stage at the university, were important for students to choose the maritime career. Third, conceptual skills are built not only in the practical environment, but also by the influence and skills of guiding figures. Fourth, students validate and update their conceptual skills at the developmental stages of their maritime career. Fifth, students become strongly motivated to incorporate technical and human skills when they begin to understand and renew conceptual skills. Finally, it requires more time to obtain conceptual skills. Students could not always acquire conceptual skills from practical training and contacts with sea officers because more time was needed to do so.

5. Discussion

This research investigated professional prerequisites for students wishing to become sea officers from the viewpoint of Katz. Previous researches about sea officers' knowledge (Ogawa, 1999, 2001) and additional qualitative data drawn from the interviews and observations demonstrated each dimension of skills in Katz (1955).

Professional training school teaches technical knowledge to students both through classroom lectures and practical training from their freshmen year. At the beginning of university, the emphasis is in the acquisition of theories and disciplines. Methods, processes, procedures, and techniques, which Katz (1955) pointed out in the definition of technical skills are taught mainly in the junior and senior years. In addition, technical skills acquired in professional training school are only basic patterns for use in limited situations. However, much more complex technical skills are acquired through experiences in business. Moreover, human skills strongly related to the working environment and the building of conceptual skills are fundamental to the accumulation of technical knowledge.

Conceptual skills are strongly based on career stages and various events. Consistent with qualitative research data about students and teachers for Japanese sea officers indicated that they developed conceptual skills throughout their training. Introductory conceptual skills were far more important for students to make the initial decision in launching their maritime career, and to assimilate into the practical Japanese workplace, despite the fact that many Japanese people including some maritime students, concentrate on the basic technical skills for obtaining a license. Therefore, the building of conceptual skills is fundamental from an early stage at university. Practical training and the influence and skills of guiding figures are factors required for understanding the importance of conceptual skills. However, more time is required to acquire conceptual skills because students or younger sea officers need to update their conceptual skills, integrating the ongoing updates with their core values.

In order for students to continue their professional career paths and develop their skills, the updating of conceptual skills are far more important at every developmental stage. People around them such as teachers or administrators, should not become obsessed with the idea that making a decision for students to launch their maritime career or obtaining the licences, is not the end of their voyage.

Figure 2 summarizes the relationship between developmental stages and prerequisites from the Katz's point of view.

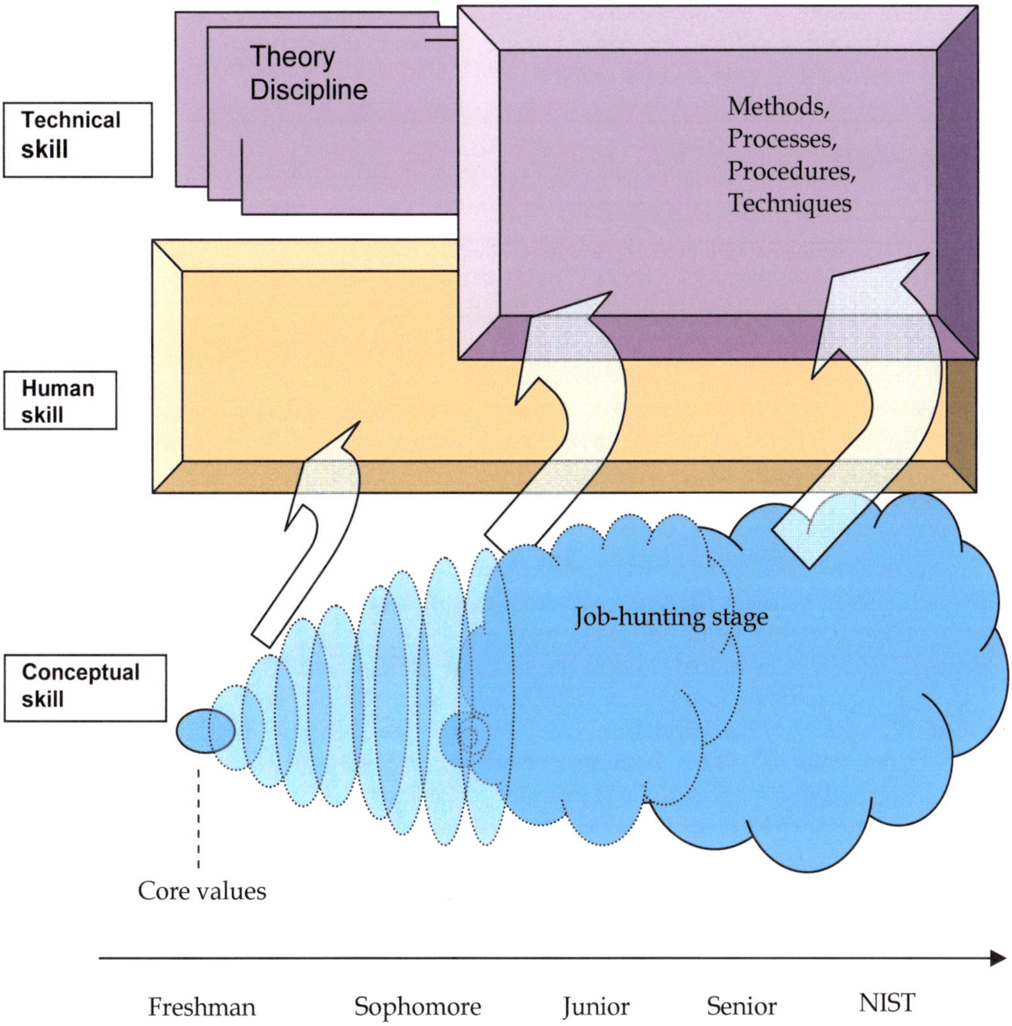

Fig. 2. Prerequisites for Japanese Sea Officers[4]

6. Conclusion

This research demonstrated the professional prerequisites for Japanese Sea Officers from the viewpoint of Katz literature. Consistent with Katz (1955), conceptual, human, and technical skills were revealed from the analysis of qualitative research data. Introductory conceptual skills at the early stage and updating them constantly are far more important for the students to assimilate into the practical careers of Japanese sea officers, despite the fact that most Japanese people try to focus more on technical skills to obtain a license. The teachers

[4] Figure 2 in this paper was updated from the figure 2 in Ogawa (2008).

and administrators in the professonal training organizations should realize that younger professionals need both time and skilful guiding figures to develop their conceptual skills in order to continue their career as sea officers.

7. References

Fujiwara, M. (2007). *The Dignity of the Nation* (G, Murray, Trans.), Tokyo, Japan, IBC publishing. (Original work published 2005)

Glaser, B.G. & Strauss, A.L. (1967). The discovery of grounded theory: strategies for qualitative research, New York. Aldine Pub. Co..

Goode, W. J. (1960). The Profession, Reports and Opinion, *American Sociological Review*, vol.25, pp.902-914.

Greenwood, E. (1957). Attributes of a Profession, *Social Work*, vol.2, No.3, pp.45-55.

Katz, R.L. (1955). Skills of an Effective Administrator, *Harvard Business Review*, January-February, pp.33-42.

Krumboltz, J.D. & Levin, A.S. (2004). *Luck is no Accident*. Atascandero, CA. Impact Publishers.

Macdonald, K. M. (1995). *The Sociology of Professions*, Sage Publications.

Nitobe, I. (1998). *Bushido: The soul of Japan* (T, Suchi, Trans.), Philadelphia, The Leeds and Bible. (Original work published 1900)

Ogawa, C. (1999). Professional skills in the training school -comparing school and business- (in Japanese), *Monograph series* #9909, 108 pages, Kobe University.

Ogawa, C. (2001). Professionalism of Japanese Sea officers in Japanese Shipping Companies.-The Link between School and Industry- (in Japanese), Unpublished doctoral dissertation, Kobe University, Kobe, Japan.

Ogawa, C. (2006). The Career Development of Young Japanese People: The Attainment of Self-confidence in career development, *proceedings of the 46th Congress of the European Regional Science Association,* August 30-September 3, 2006. Volos, Greece.

Ogawa, C. (2008). Professional Training School Prerequisites for Students Wishing to Become Sea Officer, *proceedings of International Technology, Education and Development Conference,* March 3-5, 2008. Valencia, Spain.

Ogawa, C. (2009). The Career-Based Conceptual Skills for Students Wishing to Become Japanese Sea Officers, *Proceedings of the Mediterranean Conference for Academic Disciplines,* February 23-26, 2009. Gozo, Malta.

Schein, E. H. (1972). *Professional Education, Some New Directions,* Mc Graw-hill, New York.

Schein, E. H. (1984). Coming to a New Awareness of Organizational Culture, *Sloan Management Review,* vol.25, pp.3-16.

Schein, E.H. (2006). *The Career Anchors (3rd edition)*. San Francisco, CA. Pfeiffer & Co.

Trice, H. & Beyer, J. (1993). *The Cultures of Work Organizations,* Prentice-Hall.

Wilensky, H. L., (1964). The Professionalization of Everyone?, *The American Journal of Sociology,* vol.70, pp.137-158.

2

Improving General Cross-Curricular Skills in Attendance and Virtual Environments

Guadalupe Ortiz
University of Extremadura Spain

1. Introduction

The different European Union countries try to get closer to the Sorbone (Allegre et al., 1998) and Bologna (Einem et al., 1999) declarations in 1998 and 1999, respectively, in the area of education. In this regards, recent adaptations of educational curricula to the European Higher Education Space (EHES) enabled many education professionals to adopt new teaching methodologies into their daily practice. Although the transmission of the main theoretic and practical concepts of the subject in question must remain the main focus, the improvement of students' general skills claims for special attention not only in the EHES but also with a view to business requirements.

A varied range of activities and methodologies can be used in order to promote general cross-curricular skills such as addressing an audience, team work, preparing documentation, etc. Including new methodologies aimed at promoting these skills into classroom practice can prove challenging, not only in the sense of being able to integrate such activities within the current development of the subject, but also in terms of motivating students to deviate from their traditional passive way of learning.

On the other hand, the mobility of teachers and students among European universities has increased notably: regarding the teachers they often have to attend several conferences to exchange their research ideas with other experts in the matter and it is also becoming quite common for teachers to go for research or teaching stays abroad for several months. In the case of students, the most common situation is that they are awarded an Erasmus scholarship and spend at least one year in a foreign university. Both positions are very positive for teachers and students and shouldn't be avoided for the sake of not missing lectures. Furthermore, it is also quite common that students start working before they have finished the degree, or even that they start studying a new one once they have started working. These students, although they are not abroad may not be able to attend lectures on a regular basis due to their work commitments.

In this regard, we also have to look for new alternatives under the scope of the EHEA, so that education can be followed up without a mandatory requirement of attendance to lectures, and which, at the same time lets us improve students' cross-curricular capabilities. Both tasks are already a challenge, but when faced together the challenge is even bigger. Education through e-learning environments was already approached by several authors in various interesting approaches - (Bitterberg et al., 2008), (Gerval et al., 2003), (Jalobeanu,

1996), (Popovici et al., 2005), (Comai et al., 2007) -; however, most of them do not consider cross-curricular capabilities.

In this chapter, we are going to see how this problem was tackled under the sphere of the *Telematic Engineering* degree at the University of Extremadura, specifically in a mandatory subject called *Data Transmission* and in an optional one called *Web Services,* an attendance and a virtual non-attendance subject, respectively. We will describe the experience of the author and what the results obtained were.

2. Context

In this section we are going to describe the subjects in which the e-learning experience has being carried out and are their curricular and cross-curricular skills in order to analyse in the following sections how new activities in the classroom and in virtual environments could be used to improve such skills and carry out lectures virtually.

2.1 Data Transmission

Data Transmission is particularly connected to two professional profiles: on the one hand to *planning and management of networks* and, on the other, it is linked to *auditing and design of networks.*

The *capabilities specific to the qualification* which are mainly linked to this subject are *design, installation and management of telecommunication networks* and *planning and evaluation of networks, systems and telematic services.*

The *cross-disciplinary capabilities* related to the professional profiles to which this subject is normally linked are the following: *appropriate application of the learned technologies and their integration into the socioeconomic structure, Interaction with users* and *responsibility for own learning.*

Based on these capabilities, the objectives established with regards to the academic and disciplinary abilities are the followings:

- To introduce the student to the spectral theory of signals and the understanding of the different types of signal and their representation in the frequency domain.
- To know the behaviour of physical devices when signals go through them, to know Matlab and Simulink and apply their theoretical knowledge to practical tasks with them.
- To master the mechanisms of error control and flow control at link level.

After studying the general personal capabilities of the degree and the specific disciplinary ones considered in this subject we concluded that suitable objectives with regards to personal and professional capabilities are the following:

- To develop the ability to differentiate several types of signal in communications and their codification.
- To be able to identify and decide on the type of transmission medium to be used in an installation and the consequences of that choice.
- To know how to solve a problem according to a set of requirements.
- To be able to work as a team effectively and to improve the ability to address an audience.

2.2 Web Services

Web Services is particularly connected to three professional profiles: *design and development of telecommunication services, design of distributed applications oriented to the administration and electronic commerce* and *teaching and research for the development of new technologies and services.* The *capabilities specific to the qualification* which are mainly linked to this subject are *to know and design tools related to security in communications and networks, designing communication software incorporating the new technologies TIC to productive processes in the business* and *knowing and applying scientific and technological base knowledge to adapt to technological changes.* The *cross-disciplinary capabilities* related to the professional profiles to which this subject is normally linked are the following: *development I+D+I, design and analysis of telematics applications and services, managing telematics products and services, application of the learned technologies and their integration into the socioeconomic structure, interaction with users* and *responsibility for own learning.*

Based on these capabilities, the objectives established with regards to the academic and disciplinary abilities are the following:

- To introduce the student to the Web service technology, their standards and their development tools as well as the way to model and compose them.
- Besides, students have to be able to research on the named technologies and to be able to acquire and apply new knowledge in the area.

After studying the general personal capabilities of the degree and the specific disciplinary ones considered in this subject we concluded that suitable objectives with regards to personal and professional capabilities are the following:

- To develop the ability to understand, and enable others to understand, knowledge related with Web service technology, to be able to learn themselves about the named technology.
- To be able to work as a team effectively.
- To be able to acquire Web service related knowledge when provided in English.

3. Classifying and Selecting the activities

Before trying to discern what kind cross-curricular activities can be carried out when teaching the subjects described in the previous section, we have to decide what general types of working group are suitable for them: some subjects are mainly theoretical, other more practical ones require work in a laboratory, whereas others may require work in small groups or to do field work. In our case, we can affirm the following considerations:

- Theoretical lessons are completely necessary. In the case of *Data Transmission* this is because the contents covered by the subject are completely new for the student who comes from secondary school and even though the application of the subject content is very practical, we need to provide a wide range of basic theoretical concepts. In the case of *Web Services,* the need of theoretic lessons is due to the concepts of the subject are a completely new domain for the students.
- Practical working groups are also needed. We have just mentioned that the application of *Data Transmission* is mainly practical, therefore the students have to experiment different applications in a laboratory. Besides, the main goal of *Web Services* is to apply the main theoretic concepts in a practical domain.
- Finally, working in small groups may be a questionable decision. We considered that it is important, since this will be the usual situation when they start working in the industry:

they will have to solve relevant-related problems in groups, probably formed by different specialists on the topic. Therefore, this type of working group was also considered when building the plan for these subjects.

Specifically, we divided subject credits by assigning the following percentages to each type of activity.

• Whole class activities, that is, those activities in which all the students who study the subject attend at the same time: 25% percent for *Data Transmission* and 10% for *Web Services.*

• Laboratory activities: in this case we divide the whole class into smaller ones which fit in the laboratory and are small enough to be supervised by the teacher during practical lessons; that is between 15 and 20 students per group. This time we established 10% for *Data Transmission* and 20% for *Web Services.*

• Small groups -also called tutorial activities- are formed for those activities which have to be carried out in small groups and for whose supervision several meetings with the teacher are scheduled. The percentage only measures the time in which the teacher is present and is 2% for *Data Transmission* and 5% for *Web Services.*

• Finally the remainder of the time (60% for *Data Transmission* and 65% for *Web Services)* is allocated for the student to work on his own, or with other students, but without the presence of the teacher.

Once we have all the possible types of working group we have to select what types of activity will be developed by each type of group. After considering the activities developed in previous years and evaluating their success and having attended several courses in order to improve and learn such types of activity, the following ones were selected for each type of working group (each type of activity is thoroughly explained in the following section):

• Whole class activities: magisterial lectures, problem solving competition, discussion and debate, role play, judgement simulation, problem-based learning, mind map elaboration, topic presentation, theoretical exam.

• Laboratory activities: Laboratory lecture, laboratory exam.

• Tutorial activities: problem solving and research in groups.

4. Activities

In this section we are going to describe in depth all the activities carried out during the instruction of *Data Transmission* -that is, in an attendance subject-, in the order they were mentioned in the previous section.

4.1 Whole class Activities

• ***Magisterial lecture.*** *Data Transmission* is taught in the first year of the *Telematic Engineering* degree. Being a first year subject, the magisterial lecture has great importance. A set of basic knowledge on the subject must be acquired by the student, which will help him gain a deeper knowledge of the subject topics, besides being covered from different perspectives. These lectures are more frequent in the first semester and decrease in the second one, being complemented with alternative activities explained throughout the remainder of this section and the following subsections.

• *Problem solving competition.* The main goal of problem solving is the empirical application of theoretical knowledge acquired in magisterial lectures. In the case of *Data Transmission* this is done by a kind of problem-solving competition (see (Ortiz, 2007) for further information), in which the members of a group explain doubts to each other, which is useful for the explainer as it settles her knowledge and for the listener as he obtains new knowledge.

• ***Discussion and debates.*** Any undergraduate student should be able to speak to an audience, arguing her opinions logically and reasoning appropriately about the discussed topic. Moreover, the student needs to learn to listen, not only to hear, and to respect established talking turns. Besides, they must be able to rebut other people's opinions in an argued and reasoned manner.

• ***Role play.*** In the same line as the previous activity, we consider role play a way to improve the ability to talk to an audience and to establish and respect turn taking. Besides, the student has to be able to acquire and defend knowledge and opinions which may be different from her own.

• ***Judgment simulation.*** Also in the same line as the previous activity, professional behaviours can be judged to see how a student can defend professional decisions related to the subject in question firmly and confidently or to judge clearly if other professionals' decisions were right or wrong.

• ***Problem-based learning (PBL).*** One student or a group of them can solve a problem over a week, a month or the whole semester following a set of steps. In order to do so, the student has to search and filter the information necessary to solve a real problem and to face it with her partners by applying the theoretical knowledge. The teacher will set partial submission and revision deadlines in order to help the student.

• ***Mind Map Elaboration.*** It is important to know what are the main concepts to be learned in a subject. In this regard, mind maps help by clarifying the key ideas in a topic. The map may be created by the teacher, by the student or by both. Besides, the student has to be able to infer the whole subject from the information on the mind map.

• ***Topic presentation.*** The student should be able to present the learned topics correctly, creating resources for the presentation when necessary, which may be useful when revising for the exam later.

• ***Theoretical exam.*** Students will also have to sit a theory exam in order to show they have acquired enough knowledge on the subject and their ability to solve problems in their specific scope.

4.2 Laboratory Activities

• ***Laboratory.*** The objective of the laboratory is to apply the knowledge obtained in theoretical classes, both in magisterial lectures and problem solving lessons, in a practical way.

• ***Practical exam.*** Students will also have to sit an exam to show they are able to solve a practical exercise within a reasonable amount of time.

4.3 Tutorial Activities

• ***Problem resolution in group.*** In the first semester, the students will solve a set of problems in groups of about 4. The students will be assisted by the teachers during tutorial hours. The first tutorial will be used to assign the problems and provide indications for their resolution. In the second session, the work developed will be reviewed and if any error is detected more guidance will be provided and the steps to be taken for the presentation will be explained. The problem's solution will be presented in the final tutorial. This activity will be assessed based on a common group mark and an individual one based on each student's performance.

• ***Group research.*** The students will do a research project in groups of about 4 during the second semester. The work will be supervised by the teacher during tutorial hours. The first tutorial will be used to assign the project topic and provide guidance as to where to look for information on the topic. In a second one, the work developed will be discussed and if any error is detected further orientation will be provided together with indications about how to improve the project and steps to be taken for the presentation will be suggested. Finally, the result will be examined during the third tutorial and the presentation slides will be reviewed as well. The students will present the work to the class, improving their capacity of addressing an audience. The project will be assessed based on a common group mark and an individual one based on each student's performance.

4.4 Non Attendance Activities

• ***Bibliographic searches.*** The student's ability to learn by himself and to generate knowledge is specially valued in the convergence process. In this sense, it is important that the student learns how to search for information about the studied subjects and that he is able to acquire new knowledge independently. In this sense not only does the student need to be able to search for information, but also to validate it and extract the concepts in which he is interested. This skill may be developed in tutorial projects, *PBL* or any other activity which requires teacher-given information to be complemented.

• ***Studying.*** The student will have to learn the contents taught during lectures.

5. Virtual Activities

In this section we are going to describe all the activities carried out during the instruction of *Web Services* -that is, in a virtual subject-, in the order they were mentioned in the previous section. Before examining how these activities can be developed under a virtual environment, we are going to describe briefly the virtual platform which was used in the experiment.

At the University of Extremadura we have got a Moodle-based virtual platform available for any subject teaching, among other uses (for further information on Moodle Platform and on the Virtual Campus at the University of Extremadura, see http://docs.moodle.org/en/Main_Page and http://campusvirtual.unex.es/, respectively).

With this tool there are currently several virtual elements available, enumerated in the following lines:

• Files repository: the teacher can upload any file and may or may not make it available for the students at any moment.

• Forums: the teacher can create several forums. For each of them he may decide between three different possibilities: forums in which only the teacher can write, forums in which the teacher is the only person authorized to start a topic and the students can comment on it, and those where both teacher and students can start a topic.

• Wikis: the tutor can create wikis so that students can interact with them. The platform saves the historical data of the wiki so that the teacher can evaluate the students' progress.

• Questionnaires: the teacher can elaborate several types of questionnaire in this platform - true/false, multiple choice, etc- The students can see at the end of their attempt the mark they got and also what would be the right answers. Limited slots of time can also be established for these activities.
• Delivery activities: some tasks may be requested by the students and uploaded onto the platform. They may or may not be set as "visible" for the rest of the students.
There are more activities available but we are not going to describe all of them due to space limitations. The above ones are the most relevant ones for this paper. In fact, in the following lines we are going to explain how this tool can be used to develop the previously described activities.

5.1 Whole Class Activities

• ***Magisterial lecture.*** *Web Services,* being a third year subject, needs fewer magisterial lectures than the subject presented in the previous section. Thus, attendance to magisterial lectures can be replaced by virtual activities: information about the current chapter of the subject can be provided through a virtual platform so that students can download it and read and ask, through the same platform, whichever doubts they may have. Besides, the teacher can elaborate a quiz for the virtual platform which may be taken by the students as many times as they want to check whether the have learned the lesson correctly.
• ***Problem solving competition.*** No problems are solved in the subject *Web Services.* ***Discussion and debates.*** Discussion and debates can be carried out through the virtual forum: the teacher may propose several topics for discussion and then students have to show their arguments for their solutions. Although they do not improve the skill of addressing an audience strictly speaking, since they are not talking to an audience in the virtual environment, they do take the first steps to do so, that is thinking and reasoning about their ideas and using their arguments to rebate others. Later on, they can also use a Webcam to really improve the way to address an audience.
• ***Role play.*** In the same line as the previous activity, once the roles are assigned and the problem is described by the teacher, virtual forums can be used for the performance of their roles in this activity.
• ***Judgment simulation.*** Also in the same line as the previous activity, professional behaviours can be judged through the virtual forum.
• ***Problem-based learning (PBL).*** In order to solve the problem there will be a wiki in which each member of the group can add new information or improve the one that is already inserted. The status of problem solutions will be checked by the teacher through the wiki, so that he can guide students and advice them on how to continue the problem solving exercise.
• ***Mind Map Elaboration.*** For group mind map elaborations we can also use tools such as CMap tool (see http://cmap.ihmc.us/ for further information on CMap), which allows the elaboration of conceptual maps in a collaborative way. The teacher can assign the different maps to be developed by the students and can also access the collaborative map to check how the work is progressing or even to add clues when necessary.
• ***Topic presentation.*** Students should be able to present the learned topics correctly; to do so first of all they can update their slides in the virtual tool so that the teacher can make suggestions about them. Then he can also give a talk using the virtual environment and a

Web cam and at the same time the remaining students and the teacher could visualize the slides in their own computers.

• ***Theoretical exam.*** Ican also be done though the virtual tool. Bearing in mind that the exam will not consist of just repeating the learned theory but on building new knowledge from it, it is even beneficial for them to sit the exam through the virtual environment, where they can also check for previous acquired knowledge to build the new one.

5.2 Laboratory Activities

• ***Laboratory.*** Third year students do not need traditional attendance lectures classes to learn how to use the provided software for lab classes, thus they can deal with laboratory lessons virtually. The teacher can provide them with some helpful information and references at the beginning of the lab task and they can ask any doubts through the virtual environment.

• ***Practical exam.*** The same we have said for the theoretical exam can be applied here.

5.3 Tutorial Activities

• ***Problem resolution in group.*** This activity is developed once the students have received enough lectures through the virtual environment to work on their own. The review meetings can be done through the virtual platform where the students may have elaborated a wiki, for instance, with their resolved problems and the teacher can check it tell them how to continue. Besides, the teacher can evaluate the work each of them has done by following the historic of the wiki.

• ***Group research.*** Analogously to the previous activity, a wiki can be elaborated for this purpose so that the work will be supervised by the teacher at the established dates.

5.4 Non Attendance Activities

• ***Bibliographic searches.*** Obviously this task is perfectly done virtually by the student. He can show his results through the virtual platform, too.

• ***Studying.*** This is another task currently done by the student on his own. However, he can also benefit from virtual platforms where, for instance, several questionnaires can be available so he can check how much he has learned, or frequently asked questions about the subject may have been elaborated and he can consult them, or he may use the forum to ask additional questions, even he can download pre-elaborated conceptual maps so he can organize his knowledge better, etc.

6. Experiences Developing Cross-Curricular Capabilities

Making use of the previous activities we can encourage students to work cross-curricular at the same time, whilst working the main concepts of the subject, as we explain for an attendance and a virtual subject in the following sub-sections.

6.1 Data Transmission

Data Transmission, as previously mentioned, is a first year subject and several attendance lessons had to be developed at the very beginning of the first semester; however, for the reasons explained in the following lines, we had to make use of the virtual scope for particular occasions. For instance, along the first semester in several occasions the teacher had to travel abroad for conferences or stays at other universities. First of all, during these periods, students worked on their own making use of the virtual platform. Several tasks were requested and students had to upload them onto the platform by the given deadline. Besides, they could ask their questions through the teacher's e-mail or through the platform forum available for this purpose.

Secondly, they had to develop problems in group so they had presential meetings among students and reported about them through the virtual environment, where they could also require the help from the teacher.

Thirdly, for lab lessons, students had to update the week practical exercise in the virtual platform each week, where the teacher could check them and provide them with a constructive evaluation. After that, they could also improve and re-upload it. Finally, after every chapter of the subject collaborative mind maps had to be elaborated in teams. The mind maps of the other teams could be examined by the others, so they could improve their own maps with a view to studying for the final exam at a later date. During the second semester, the chapters with the main subject contents reduce their complexity. In this regard, several alternative activities were proposed to work on the subject: documentation about the topic in question could be downloaded by the students from the repository in the platform. In different weeks, diverse activities were proposed to do based on these documents. For instance, several parts of the same chapter were assigned to different students so that they had to do some research on the topic and collect additional information, and after that explain the contents through the virtual environment. Forums were enabled for the remaining students to make questions. Another task was to present a complex problem to be solved in groups over a period of at least a week; first of all they had to collect information related to the topic, then they had to solve it and update it in the platform. Once every group had updated them they could see the solutions of the other groups and, through the use of the forum, discuss which was the best solution and why. The remaining activities previously described -i.e. role play or judgement simulation- would be developed similarly; also mind maps were elaborated during the second semester. On the other hand, the students who were taking the subject from abroad had already taken the subject the year before, so that they had already attended the basic lessons and they also already had some experience in learning independently. Thanks to the virtual platform they could follow the subject and interact with the remaining students at the home university and also be evaluated as any other student.

6.2 Web Services

Since this is a third-year optional subject, as previously mentioned, we can consider that the students are already experienced enough to know how to acquire new knowledge themselves. Besides, since it is an optional subject, we can also assume that the student taking it is really interested in it so he can be motivated to do some research himself. For this subject, at the beginning of every new chapter, basic information on the topic in question was provided by the teacher through the document repository. Afterwards, students had to extend the contents and elaborate a complete document through a collaborative wiki, which was later used for several purposes: firstly, the teacher read the document and asked several questions in a forum in order to start a discussion about key issues; this way the students had to argue about them and thus got a better understanding of the subject. Then, both the wiki and the forum were used for the evaluation of the topic. For the practical part of the subject, teams of two were created. They had to collect information about a topic, which had to be updated in the virtual platform and which showed the results they had obtained so far. The teacher could check the progress of their work and provide them with additional suggestions about how to carry on. Any enquiries could also be done through the virtual platform. For practical enquiries, face to face meetings could be arranged if necessary, however they could still be asked in a virtual manner: depending on the complexity of the questions, several captured screens could be sent to the teacher so he could suggest a solution or even a virtual terminal could be made available for him so he could test the problem himself.

It is also important to notice that this subject is very oriented to work, in a company so many students who choose it are already working, so they cannot attend lectures or do the work related to the subject at the usual hours. In this regard, thanks to the virtual learning environment they can follow the subject as any other student and they do not miss out on the opportunity to learn something else useful for their work.

7. Results of the Learning Experience

Students' first reaction to any change in the educational methodology is always negative since they feel very secure doing what they have always done (mainly attending magisterial lectures and studying on their own for a written exam). From the point of view of the type of activities, these methodologies make them participate more during lessons, being especially encouraged by the virtual format, therefore bringing them back from their passive behaviour. Obviously, this also implies a very negative attitude on their part when moving on to a new methodology. Nevertheless, once they get used to it and once hearsay has run from one year to another, they understand there is no other option and face the subject with a much more positive attitude. However they still have their preferences: it was noticeable that they got used to problem solving in groups after two or three lessons; however those activities which were developed casually (role play, judgements, PBL, etc) still somehow scared them since they are not used to them and feel out of their comfort zone, therefore lacking confidence to complete the tasks naturally. In any case, after the experience one can decide which activities work better for the subject and type of students in question, so some of them may not be used some years, to be included other years when the circumstances are more appropriate. An activity which may result in an interesting experience is to organize a simulation of a research conference and assign the different common roles in conferences to different groups of students (program committee, organizing committee, authors, keynotes and so on), the topics being the contents of the subject. This way, as they learn the main concepts of the subject, they work as part of a team and have to talk to an audience. If the experience works it can also be very fulfilling for them to see how they have been able to organize an event with the whole group.

Eventually, although they have to work harder from the beginning of the academic year, they realize that they learn and acquire more concepts more easily than they used to. They soon feel confident enough to ask any doubts and to make comments in the forums, even to spontaneously rebate about a topic to one of their partners; and this is not quite a usual atmosphere in the university scope, even through a virtual environment. This change of mentality alone would make the effort of improving the teaching methodology worthwhile, however, as we well see in the following section, this is not the only improvement. On the other hand, they seemed to be very surprised when they were told that they did not have to attend lectures regularly in the virtual subject, and they even thought that they might not learn the subject contents properly. However, as soon as they started doing the virtual activities, they realized that they still had to work hard on the subject and that indeed they were going to acquire the correspondent knowledge.

Once the year ended (in this case we are talking about results from the academic year 2006-2007), *Data Transmission* students' marks and aptitudes showed the following general results: the percentage of students who passed the subject increased by approximately 10%, most of the students who passed the subject did so in the June call, not in the September one and the general marks increased by at least 1 point (over 10) in average. Moreover, the students who did not pass the subject felt confident to register for the subject the following year (in the past, many students who did not pass the subject took two or three more years before re-registering for it) and most of the students felt much more confident when talking to an audience at the end of the year than at the beginning. Besides, several problems which the students encountered at the beginning of the year were solved, at least enough to present the group's work at the end of the year successfully.

Concerning *Web Services,* the results showed an improvement of at least 10% compared with the marks the students obtained, plus, I would say, a great improvement in cross-curricular skills and self-learning. Therefore, we can affirm that the methodology piloted with this subject improved not only cross-curricular capabilities, but also efficiency in learning the subject contents through virtual e-learning environments and that the methodology is efficient for students from first to last year.

8. Conclusions

As every education change, adaptation to the European Space has defenders and detractors. The presence in curricula of cross-curricular capabilities as specific targets to be met will no doubt improve our students' training and education. Besides, the decrease in the number of magisterial lectures and their replacement by other more dynamic and virtual activities has been very positive, since these activities motivate students and help them be more active. At the same time, the usual current way of teaching has changed, evolving towards greater mobility for both students and teachers and toward the development of several tasks simultaneously. In this regard, e-learning is also acquiring more importance within the EHEA. Furthermore, with the new activities carried out in the virtual environment we promote supervised work in teams. The resolution of projects without a without the teacher being present makes the student feel able to learn independently; besides, they will learn to abstract the main ideas of a text and to express them should it be necessary for the presentation of their work and of course they will improve both highlighted cross-curricular abilities: addressing an audience properly and working as part of a team successfully. Therefore, we can conclude that with this proposal not only do we work cross-curricular capabilities, but we also dynamize the subjects in an attendance or non-attendance environment, providing the possibility of choosing the subject to those who cannot do it presently, and not interrupting lectures during possible teacher absences. Besides, we complement the student learning experience with activities focused on students' personal work, which are useful for their development both at professional and personal level.

9. References

Allegre, C., Berlinger, L., Blackstone, T. & Ruttgers, J. (1998) *Sorbonne Joint Declaration.* http://www.bologna-berlin2003.de/pdf/Sorbonne_declaration.pdf

Bitterberg T., Hildmann, H., Branki, C.(2008) *UsingResource Management Games for Mobile Phones to Teach Social Behaviour.* Proc of Int. Conf. Techniques and Applications for Mobile Commerce. Glasgow, Uk, 2008.

Einem, C., Ade, J., Schmith, G., Zeman, E., Mmia, A., Lukas, T.Vestager, M., Allegre, C.,Rask, M., Erdsiek-Rave, U., Catenhusen, W-M., Kiss, A., Arsenis, G., Dowling, P., Sigurdardottir, G., Kokek, T., Zecchino, O., Hennicot-Schoepges, E., Platelis, K., Hermans, L., Galea, L., Winkler, W., Lelletun, J., Marga, A., Grilo, E.M., Zgaga, P., Ftacknik, M., Bladh, A., Fernandez Diaz, D.J., Blackstone, T., Kleiber, C. (1999). *The Bologna Declaration of 19 June 1999.* http: / /www.bolognaberlin2003.de/pdf/ bologna declaration.pdf

Gerval, J.-P.; Popovici, D.-M.; Tisseau, J. (2003) *Educative distributed virtual environments for children.* Proc. Int. Conf. on Cyberworlds, Volume 4, Issue , 3-5. 2003.

Jalobeanu, M. Romanian (1996) *Network Resources and Internet Education,* Turkiye First International Distance Education Symposium, Baskent Ogretmenevi, 1996

Ortiz, G. *Alternatives to Lecturing.* (2007) Proc of International, Technology, Education and Development Conference. Valencia, Spain, 2007.

Popovici, D.M, Gerval, J.P. Gueguen, P. (2005) *EVE - An Educational Virtual Environment.*Proceedings of Virtual Reality International Conference, Laval, France, 2005.

Comai, S.; Preciado, J. C.; Linaje, M.; Morales, R.; Sanchez, F. (2007) *An e-Learning collaborative RIA environment for Web Application Modeling and Code Generation.* Proc Int. Conf. Database and Expert Systems Applications, 2007.

3

Smart Classroom Technology

Ciaran O'Driscoll
Dublin Institute of Technology
Ireland

1. Introduction

This chapter presents a range of technologies and examples of Smart classroom technology prototypes and deployed solutions that have been developed as part of current and recent research activities. The educational rationale for developing and using Smart Classroom Technology is also considered. The potential for an emerging digital divide between students and many educators is reviewed in the context of identifying technologies to support educators. A specific case study in the design and deployment of a cost effective smart classroom that is invisible to the users and based on truly pervasive technologies such as Bluetooth is discussed and evaluated. In the conclusion the potential positive contribution of Smart classroom technology is identified.

1.1 Smart Classroom Technologies

A smart classroom is a pseudo intelligent room that can reconfigure itself and its resources automatically based on predefined profiles for specific user groups. This can be done using a predefined schedule or in an event-driven manner based on the arrival of a specific class group and specific lecturer.

Smart classrooms can react automatically to the arrival of staff and students to, for example, set up the space to continue a lecture from a previous session, identify the stakeholders in the room, and record and store material discussed in a session for reflective review. Tedious tasks at the start of, or during, a lecture or laboratory session can be automated, allowing students and lecturers to focus on the learning process. Simple tasks such as providing a list of attendees with associated photographs can enhance the lecturer and student interaction, particularly for large groups or early in the academic term.

Benefits that can be gained from using smart spaces in academic environments are identified. In particular academic institutions can leverage the personal devices of students and staff, in association with standard communications infrastructure, to enable the deployment of smart classrooms in a cost effective manner. For example, the pervasive use of personal mobile phones and PDAs, with significant embedded computing power, provides an opportunity for developing a truly smart environment in a cost-effective manner.

In the case study for a Smart Classroom, based on low cost pervasive technologies is presented, the availability of Bluetooth-enabled personal devices has been used as the core rational for developing the Context Aware Smart Classroom (CASC) within the School of

Electronic and Communications Engineering (SECE) of DIT. Finally the potential for acceptance of the smart classroom by the key stakeholders, educators, has been investigated through semi-structured interviews and the results presented.

2. Why Use Smart Classroom Technologies?

Is there a fundamental educational rational for developing smart classrooms or augmenting existing classrooms? Prior to considering the technical perspective it is a valuable exercise to consider whether there is any educational justification for using smart classroom technologies. In particular can smart classroom technologies fulfill the needs of end-users and stakeholders.

2.1 Technology and Education

Learning styles of students are changing as the environment in which we live changes. Traditional lecturing styles require to be reviewed to determine their suitability to meet the needs of student learning styles. Alternative techniques such as problem based learning and peer instruction provide a significant additional burden on educators during the education session. Enhanced or smart classrooms have the potential to significantly reduce this burden.

As the world around us changes it is essential that educators review their teaching methods to ensure there is an appropriate match to students learning styles. In this section two specific teaching methods are considered and the need to address the digital divide between educators and students is discussed.

2.2 Learning Paradigm Shift

From an educational perspective learning methods and practises are evolving and improving. Traditional deductive approaches that start with the fundamentals in a formal lecture setting and then move onto applications may not address all learning styles of students. Traditional lecturing clearly identifies to students what is required to be known for exam purposes, while this appeals to many students it is not necessarily the best or most appropriate learning style for all students or all subject material. The appropriateness of traditional lecture style teaching, particularly in engineering and physics, has been under challenge for a significant period. Felder and Silverman (Felder and Silverman 1988) developed a comparison of the styles of learning and teaching that identified an incompatibility between students and educators. These incompatibilities require educators to consider alternative teaching approaches such as problem based learning.

2.2.1 Problem Based Learning

Felder (Felder 2002) states that in his experience

> *"the "best" method of teaching – at least below the graduate school level – is induction, whether it be called problem-based learning, discovery learning, inquiry learning, or some variation on those themes".*

Problem based learning involves organizing groups of students to complete a project, or solve a problem, through their own existing knowledge and use research to learn additional material. Educators provide support and guidance to the project groups as required. While this requires additional planning and takes more time the students individual learning styles can be more easily addressed leading to more concrete grasp of the material on completion of the project (Felder and Silverman 1988). While problem based learning requires a significant level of preparatory work by educators (Markham, Mergendoller et al. 2003) it is very practically focused and is accepted as appropriate for many engineering and physics subjects.

There are however fundamental concepts that need to be introduced in a more formal lecturing style, though here it is possible to use Peer Instruction rather than traditional lecturing.

2.2.2 Peer Instruction

Traditional classroom discussion can also use alternative methods such as peer instruction. Peer Instruction is where questions are interspersed through the lecture to reveal common misunderstandings and also to get students to actively engage in the subject material (Mazur 1997). Educators break the lecture into short presentations that focus on a central point, which are each followed by the conceptual questions. Students are asked a conceptual question and they all provide their initial responses, which are noted. Students are then encouraged to work in small groups to discuss their answers and misunderstandings can be addressed through this peer interaction. After some time the concept under review can be posed to the class, though often in a different form, and the responses noted.

This structured questioning method has been found to give significant learning gains with a high level of acceptance among educators who have tried the techniques (Fagen, Crouch et al. 2002). Crouch (Crouch and Mazur 2001) provide a statistical analysis of 10 years of research using Peer Instruction that found a significant improvement in student understanding and that the effort from educators to motivate the students were greeted positively by the students.

There is growing support for such approaches in order to engage students in an active manner in class sessions. There is a perceived difficulty in getting students to be attentive for the time period of an education session.

2.3 Digital Divide between Educators and Students

This is a further driving force in first world developed countries as children get used to immediate gratification through gaming and television that has reduced interest in reading (Prensky 2001a). There is a digital divide that exists between children, who are growing up in a very technologically advanced world, and older people who have not grown up surrounded by the current technologies. Prensky (Prensky 2001a) defines the term Digital Native for students who have been surrounded all their life by digital technology. As a result they are fully conversant with concepts of the internet, hyper text mark-up language (html), mobile phones, multi-media technologies from audio MP3 to digital photography and digital videoing for use on uTube. These digital natives spend more time playing computer games on their televisions using game consoles or with portable game consoles then they spend reading. In this digital habitat the natives are looking for immediate response and interactivity and this has produced a different mind set and way of thinking (Prensky 2001b). Prensky further suggests that the methods used for teaching of the "basics" is legacy teaching and focuses on old teaching rather then teaching for the future.

Educators who have not grown up in such a digital environment are generally able to use and understand digital technologies however it is like a second language as opposed to a native language and these people are referred to as Digital Immigrants (Prensky 2001a). This creates a language barrier, a digital divide, between Digital Natives and Digital Immigrants that cannot be ignored and requires to be considered by educators.

2.3.1 Education for Digital Natives

In order to address the requirements and needs of Digital Natives for immediate response and interactivity Prensky (Prensky 2001a) advocates the use of games for presenting knowledge. Though he accepts educational games or "*Edutainment*" is at an early stage of development and requires further development. Significant levels of additional resources, such as editors, media and scripting experts, etc. and associated costs are required in the move to edutainment. There is reluctance on the part of many educators to become performers to keep students entertained.

Prensky (Prensky 2008) in responding to critiques of his approach identifies that there is a difference between teaching the "basics", which remain the same, and the best practises for teaching, which evolve over time.

As an example he identifies the difference between the "basic" need to know the time and the evolution of methods for telling time:

> *"telling time is a "basic." At one time the best method we had was the sundial. Now we all just strap a machine to our wrist".*

While Prensky accepts that technology does fail on occasions, he questions the value in providing what he calls "backup" teaching as the main education mode (Prensky 2008). Alternative methods and approaches are needed to focus on teaching for the future to entice and excite students who are Digital Natives. However the value and need to convert education materials into a games format in order to interact effectively with Digital natives has yet to be fully vindicated.

Clearly there is a digital divide that needs to be considered and addressed. The author proposes that this can be done through use of alternative learning paradigms with appropriate technological support.

2.4 Interactive Classroom Technologies

There are a significant number of technologies that are available to augment or enhance an existing classroom space. These technologies can be used as components of a smart classroom. In this section the focus will be on technologies identified from literature and from primary research interviews carried out with educational professionals in Ireland.

2.4.1 Interactive Whiteboards

Interactive whiteboards such as from SMART technologies (SMARTBoard 2009) or Promethean (Promethean 2009) are widely used in education in Ireland. Interactive boards use a projector to display material on the board that is generated on a computer. The boards are touch sensitive and can be used as a direct input mechanism for a computer. It is possible to select icons or draw directly onto the board and to store the resultant display.

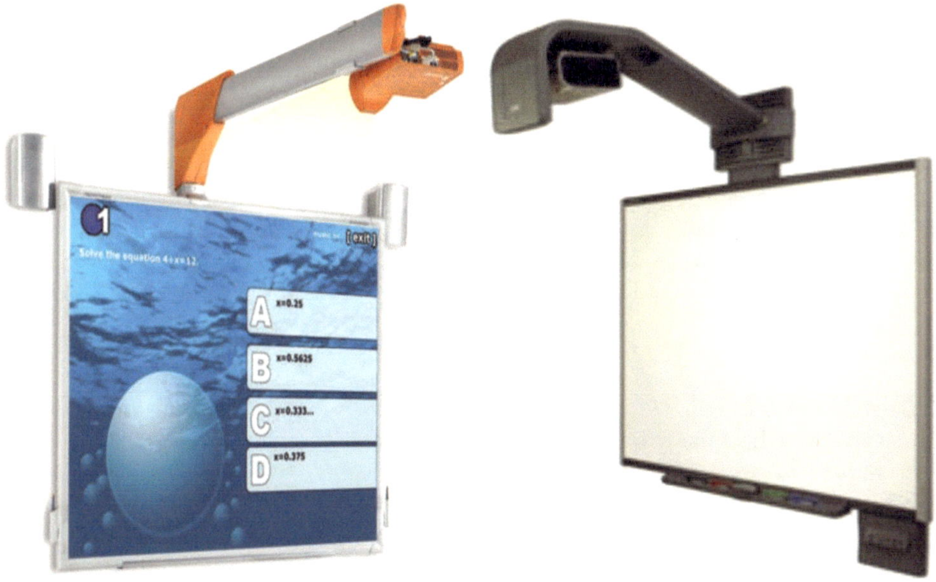

Fig. 1. Fixed Projection Interactive Boards (Promethean 2009) and (SMARTBoard 2009)

In Ireland many primary school level students, ages 5 to 13, have interactive whiteboards. Educators have found them to be an invaluable resource for teaching children. In particular it provides a rich learning environment that is used to channel the creativity of children in a computer medium. It allows different learning styles to be addressed, visualisation, auditory and touch senses to be used in the classroom (Roche 2009). The cost of acquiring and fitting boards is around €5000 per classroom and this cost is covered through fund raising activities of parents and not directly from the Government.

In third level Universities and colleges in Ireland there is a slow uptake in using interactive whiteboards. As in the case of the Dublin Institute of Technology, there are less than ten interactive boards across the campuses of the college, though currently in 2009, there are plans to configure specific classrooms with interactive whiteboards (Harvey 2009).

Interactive whiteboards provide an ideal environment for problem based learning, where each student group can use the board to prepare presentation material or share ideas during the process and later to have an electronic record of the discussions (Bowe 2009).

2.4.2 Interactive Response Systems

Interactive Response systems or voting systems, such as from Quizdom (Quizdom 2009), can be used in the classroom to permit students to respond to questions posed by the lecturer. Each student has a handheld device that can be used for selecting one of a specific number of predefined answers. Each student has an independent remote unit that operate using wireless signals, infra red versions do exist but these require line of sight between transmitter and receiver. It is also possible to implement a classroom response system using existing mobile phones and additional software, though these systems use SMS and there is an associated on-going usage cost.

These are not widely used in the Irish education system, for example in the Dublin Institute of Technology there is currently one set of 60 remote devices that are shared among a number of lecturers who are actively using Peer Instruction techniques (Bowe 2009).
Interactive response systems are ideally suited for Peer Instruction. Student responses are automatically collected and collated and can be displayed in a histogram or tabulated format. In many cases the initial responses are used only by the lecturer to assist in directing the discussions and not displayed to the class group. The supporting software for these interactive voting systems allows educators to readily develop questions and maintain response statistics over an academic period. In particular responses can be exported into the Learning Management System, WebCourses, used in the Dublin Institute of Technology (Bowe 2009).

2.4.3 Capture Systems

Capture systems collect the activities of the classroom environment and store them for later review, either by students or educators. Using display systems such as interactive whiteboards permits the capturing of material presented, modified or generated on a display in electronic format. Audio recording can supplement the captured information, though a time indexing mechanism is required to ensure the material and the audio are synchronised during review. Video recording using single or multiple cameras provides a significant quantity of material for review that also requires careful synchronisation with audio or display information.
The complexity in capturing systems is increased where there is a need for post-processing where educators may require the option to edit audio or video material. These systems shall be discussed in more detail in the Smart classroom section of this chapter.

2.4.4 Interactive Classroom Technologies

Interactive classroom technologies provide an ideal opportunity to enhance the learning environment for students and provide support for alternative learning paradigms to assist educators address the digital divide. Interactive Classrooms provide the capability for users to use technology as a tool to support different learning paradigms, such as peer instruction and problem based learning. This provides a clear educational rationale, with appropriate learning paradigms and suitable technologies, to justify the development of interactive or smart classroom.
Smart Classrooms, in simple terms, are interactive classrooms that provide an additional level of automated response based on the specific situation and are a subset of Smart Spaces.

3. Smart Spaces

Smart spaces are an extension of the Ubiquitous Computing paradigm. The core concept in Ubiquitous Computing is the ability of the technology to disappear and become invisible to users (Russell, Streitz et al. 2005; Streitz and Nixon 2005). In the ubiquitous computing paradigm, if a computer:

> "*knows merely what room it is in, it can adapt its behaviour in significant ways without requiring even a hint of artificial intelligence*" (Weiser 1991).

Smart environments display a degree of autonomy and can adapt to changing situations and communicate with users (Das, Cook et al. 2002). The provision of intelligence based automation enhances ubiquitous computing environments and provides the opportunity for additional features such as detection of anomalous behaviour. Devices can easily be controlled using existing communications infrastructures based on sensor information collected and in particular predictive decision making can be included in the capabilities of the smart environment (Das and Cook 2006). These capabilities allow an environment to exhibit pseudo-intelligent behaviour and so be considered as a smart environment.
Through the collection of relevant data a smart environment is context aware and can use context to inform it's decision process.

3.1 Context Aware Computing

> *"Context-aware computing is a mobile computing paradigm in which applications can discover and take advantage of contextual information such as user location, time of day, nearby people and devices and user activity"* (Chen and Kotz 2000).

This concept has been around for over a decade and it is only the recent availability of suitable portable computing and wireless network resources that make it possible to implement such systems. In the case of smart classrooms the interactive technologies provided significant enhanement capabilities.
The term context is used to describe real world situations, and everything is said to happen in a certain context. This makes it difficult to define context in a precise manner for many different situations. In computing the term "context-aware" was introduced in (Schilit and Theimer 1994) and was applied to location information that could enable software to adapt according to its location of use, the identities of nearby people and objects, and changes to those objects over time.

3.2 Location Aware Computing

Many context aware applications focus on location and these are described as location-aware computing applications (Schilit, Adams et al. 1994; Want, Hopper et al. 1992). A key consideration in location-aware computing is the degree of accuracy required for a particular application and the accuracy that the technology can provide. Many situations do not require a high degree of accuracy such as with "locating a friend" solutions based on who is in a GSM cell. In the case of American legislation governing the location of a person making a 911 call, the requirement for positional accuracy of mobile phone systems is to be better than 50 meters for 67% of calls made (released October 6, 1999). This directive encouraged many mobile phone designers to considering the inclusion of GPS chipsets into their handsets.
There are many location-aware or location based applications such as museum guides (Hsi 2002) and tourist guides (Long, Aust et al. 1996). In these applications a variety of mobile and static technologies have been used to support the provision of environments that respond to users according to their location context. In these systems users choose voluntarily to use the system to get additional information.

3.3 Location and Data Privacy

In developing smart environments, due regard to individuals' privacy is required to be considered. The ability to identify and track the location of specific individuals is covered by EU regulations and cannot be ignored. The collection of electronic location data requires to be protected under the EU data protection directive (1995). Article 6 of the directive demands that:

> *"personally identifiable data are only collected for explicit and legitimate purposes, it must be accurate and up to date or else erased, it must be relevant and not excessive with respect to the purpose of collection and it must be stored for as long as necessary for the purposes for which the data was collected."*

Article 7 of the directive also requires "*explicit consent or demonstration of necessity*" to collect the data.

The preferred approach would be to have students opt-in to using the system and to permit tracking of their location for the purpose of providing enhanced services. Students would get up to date information, such as room changes and current material by opting into the system. Provision of sufficient enhanced services might be enough to encourage them to use the system.

An alternative approach to an opt-in policy is to ensure location data for specific individuals cannot be identified. Anonymity provided by use of pseudonyms could be used to ensure locations and identities are not correlated. This approach is not entirely secure, as when only a few individuals are within an area an observer may be able to identify individuals and their respective pseudonyms (Beresford 2005). This alternative approach provides users with a degree of anonymity; however at some level the system would require to identity individuals in order to provide appropriate services and this would always be a point of concern.

3.4 Context Awareness

Location is an essential element in defining context but it is by no means the only aspect that needs to be considered. Context in computing terms involves a number of different aspects as identified in (Schilit, Adams et al. 1994) a definition for context with 3 elements is presented:

Computing context, made up of nearby computing resources, communications and communications bandwidth.

User context, such as the user's profile, location, people nearby and even the social situation.

Physical context, such as lighting noise levels, traffic conditions and temperature.

To more completely define context for computing time was proposed as a fourth element in (Chen and Kotz 2000):

Time context, where user and physical contexts can be logged to provide a context history that can be useful in certain applications.

These four particular aspects provide sufficient definition of context for the design and development of the context aware smart spaces. Context can be further categorised based on the specific situations under consideration.

3.5 Categories of Context

There are a number of categories of context such as environment, time, temperature or user identity. Location and identity are used to enable software to adapt to the people and objects

that are nearby and to objects that change over time (Schilit and Theimer 1994). In a similar manner, where and who one is, and what resources are available nearby, along with the social situation can be considered as in (Schilit, Adams et al. 1994).
A suitable set of primary categories that coincide with the earlier definition of context are identified in (Dey and Abowd 1999):

> *"Identity: the identity of the relevant entities.*
> *Location: the geographical position of relevant entities.*
> *Activity: the activity or activities being performed.*
> *Time: The period at which the entities perform the activity."*

The category 'activity' is introduced as opposed to 'environment' on the basis that the word environment is used as a synonym for context.
These four primary types are sufficient to fully categorise a specific context, such as the temperature of a location at a particular time. These primary types can also be used as an index to determine secondary information, such as a phone number, which can be determined from the identity of an individual then be used as an index to a phone book. Context data is an essential element for smart classroom enviroenments.

3.6 Smart Classroom Environments

Smart classrooms are specific cases of Smart Spaces in which sensors collect context data that can be used by a decision engine, in association with rules, to reconfigure the environment.

4. Smart Classrooms

There are many types of Smart Classroom that exhibit varying levels of pseudo intelligence to changing the behaviour or configuration of an environment based on decisions related to users, resources and preset rules or policies.

4.1 Classroom 2000 and eCLass

Classroom 2000 (Abowd 1999), renamed as eClass (Brotherton and Abowd 2002), was designed specifically for capturing, through audio and video recording, material presented at a lecture event for later review by students. Multimedia captured material was used to enhance existing class material and web enhanced material to provide a richer review experience. This system involved the development of post-editing facilities to permit lecturers to have comments or sections of the lecture removed prior to distribution via internet access. Lecturers entering the lecture spaces required to log on to the system in order to initiate the capture system (Brotherton and Abowd 2002).
eClass was in use for a period of 3 years and was assessed extensively over that period. An extensive report indicated that access to the recorded material went up significantly before exam times in a repeated manner to indicate general acceptance and use by students. Attendance was not dramatically affected by use of the system. However at under graduate level students did indicate it might cause them to miss more lectures on an occasional basis, while at graduate level where lectures are more discussion based students indicated their attendance was not affected. There was significant positive feedback from students that

used the system however there was no overall statistical improvement on students results during the period of the study (Brotherton and Abowd 2004).

4.2 National Institute of Standards and Technology Smart Space Project

The information access of the National Institute of Standards and Technology, NIST, are interested in developing standards and measurement techniques to address interoperability challenges for pervasive environments that use vast amounts of sensor data. This requires a demonstrator environment that uses pervasive sensors and networks to sense activity and to react appropriately. Current NIST research focuses on a meeting room data collection environment that has multiple cameras and microphone arrays which generate significant volumes of data that have to be handled across networks in this distributed scenario (NIST 2009). An example of the system operation is shown in figure 2 below with multiple camera views and microphone level indicators across the bottom.

Fig. 2. NIST Meeting Room Data Collection Laboratory (NIST 2009)

This NIST project is a capture based environment and while it is not explicitly a smart classroom implementation it is widely referenced and has been used as the basis of alternative smart space projects.

4.3 Tsinghua Smart Classroom for Tele-Education

This project based in the Chinese university of Tsinghua integrates a significant level of technology to provide remote users with an experience close to a real classroom environment. A smart media board is used for the display with a speech recognition system to provide a virtual assistant and to mange the cameras there is a smart camera man that decides which camera to use based on activities in the space. Remote students are projected onto the side wall in order to be able to participate in the lecture. Lecturers are required to login to the system using biometrics based on facial recognition and speaker verification (Shi, Xie et al. 2003).

Fig. 3. Tsinghua Smart Classroom (Shi, Xie et al. 2003)

Similar to the NIST project it is a capture based system. This classroom is highly instrumented with a significant variety of technologies being integrated to provide an enhanced remote learning experience.

4.4 Open Smart Classroom

This prototype system was also developed in Tsinghua and used to support interaction between Chinese and Japanese universities. Similar in facilities to the Tsinghua Smart Classroom it provides support for intercultural exchanges through machine translation of information presented on the Langrid blackboard (Suo, Miyata et al. 2008).

"The two classrooms are connected through the internet with live video shared in both classrooms. The original presentation is in English and translated presentations (in Chinese and Japanese) are showed synchronously in the respective locations .

1) Touch-sensitive SmartBoard screen, displaying presentation for the class; 2) Live video of Kyoto, 3) Support tools helping the students to communicate with each other in different languages, and also giving feedback and questions to the teacher; 4) On-line Chinese translated presentation; 5) The teacher, giving a class in Tsinghua; 6) The Chinese students, using aided tools for discussion. 7)

Presentation of the class material, 8) Live video of Tsinghua University, 9) On-line Japanese translated presentation, 10) The Japanese students, using the support tools for discussion" (Suo, Miyata et al. 2008).

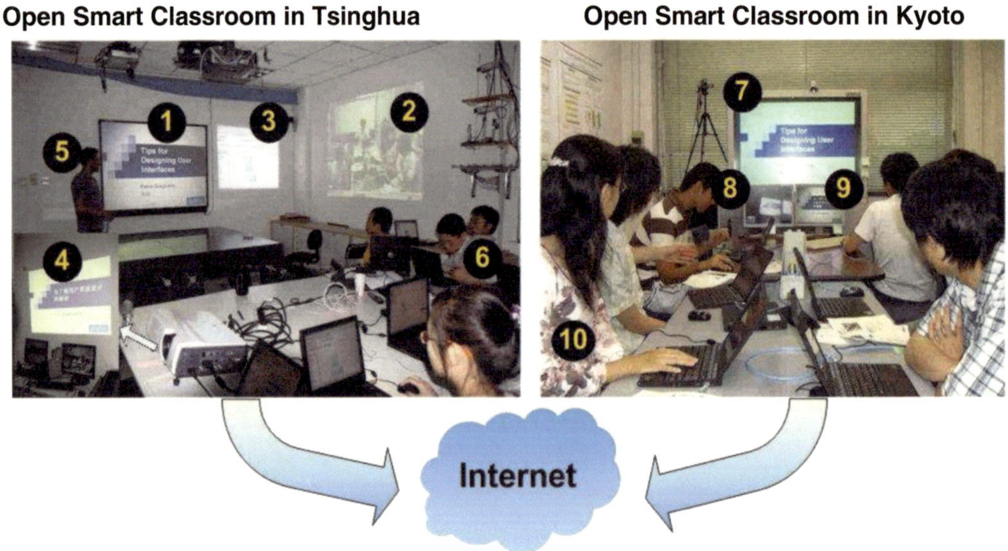

Fig. 4. Open Smart Classrooms systems: Two classrooms in Tsinghua and Kyoto (Suo, Miyata et al. 2008)

As an example of the potential for highly distributed and intercultural support using translation techniques, it will be interesting to see if this prototype can be deployed in a real environment in the future. The level of instrumentation required and the potential issues for network bandwidth makes real world deployment an interesting challenge.

4.5 Network EducationWare

Network EducationWare, NEW, is interesting as it focuses on providing an inexpensive solution to support Smart classrooms and distance learning. In particular is the approach to conserving bandwidth usage to support remote access over low bit rate modems, 56 kb/s.
An interactive white board is used for presentations and annotation, and presentations are converted into PDF format to minimise bandwidth. In the situation that a video or high bandwidth multimedia is to be used during a lecture this requires to be downloaded in advance of the lecture session. Privacy is considered in the system as questions to the lecturer are not visible to all students. This requires the lecturer to restate the question if it is of interest to the class group. This has been in use for three years and claims a student community of 2500(Snow, Pullen et al. 2005).

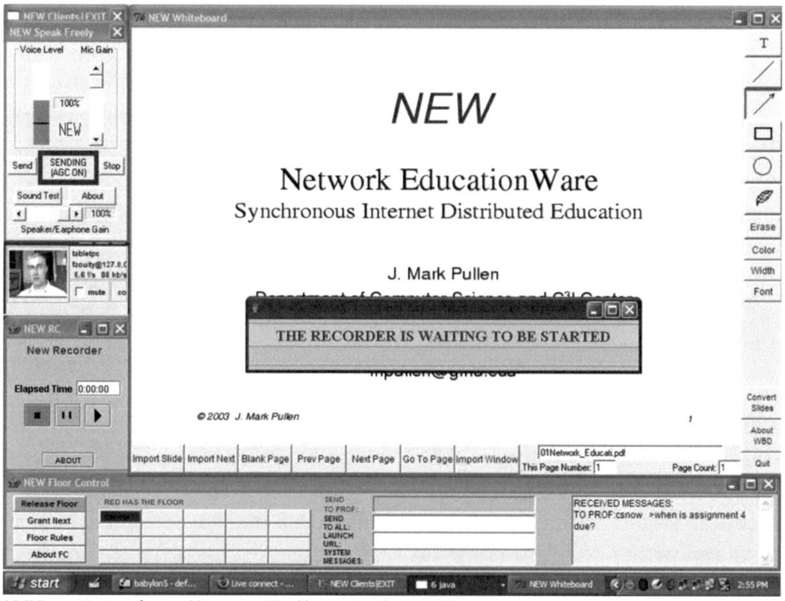

Fig. 5. NEW User Interface (Snow, Pullen et al. 2005)

As a capture system this approach does not require a highly instrumented environment with high cost infrastructure. It permits inexpensive and truly available devices and network infrastructure to be used to deliver an enhanced learning environment to remote users. This system is also available for use under an academic open-source license.

4.6 Ubiquitous Smart Classrooms

Weiser's (Weiser 1991) and Russell's (Russell, Streitz et al. 2005) concepts of ubiquitous computing focuses on the use of devices that become pervasive or technologies that can disappear into the background. In Weiser's vision environments will have sensors for regular operational needs and the development of "*applications are of course the whole point of ubiquitous computing*" (Weiser 1993). In this context the use of highly instrumented spaces that require post-processing or significant computing facilities reduces the potential for the deployment of applications in real world scenarios.

It is from the perspective of developing a smart classroom using currently pervasive devices, with the limitations of existing network capacities that the Context Aware Smart Classroom was designed.

5. Context Aware Smart Classroom: A Case Study

CASC focussed on making, real-time, context aware decisions based on information collected from the environment sensors, policies and rules of the smart classroom for the dissemination of material over WLAN, LAN or email during a class period.

This case study discusses the design and implementation of a Context Aware Smart Classroom, CASC, that focuses on leveraging existing pervasive technologies and infrastructures

5.1 Leveraging Existing Infrastructure

Current education environments, particularly at University level, referred to as third level education in Ireland, support modern Information Technology, IT, infrastructures that can be utilised as a basis for developing smart classrooms. Current IT infrastructures permit rooms and spaces to be used for a variety of different purposes from standard lectures using projectors, to tutorials and practical computer based activities.

The pervasive nature of personal mobile devices permits the investigation of developing low-cost location and identification systems that support development of a smart classroom. Material used during the teaching activity is distributed to students based on students' policies using WLAN, LAN or email. CASC uses the exisiting central scheduling system to determine the teaching activity.

5.2 System Design

Context Aware Smart Classroom, CASC, was designed to react to changes in the environment according to rules preset in the system. A rules algorithm was designed to check information stored in local database tables and makes decisions based on current system context and preset policies. The prototype system implements two main rules:

What should happen when lecturer enters the room?

Which student should the notes transfer to and how?

Delivery of material presented and developed in the lecture session is the initial aim of the prototype system. A block diagram of the key components of CASC is shown in Figure 6.

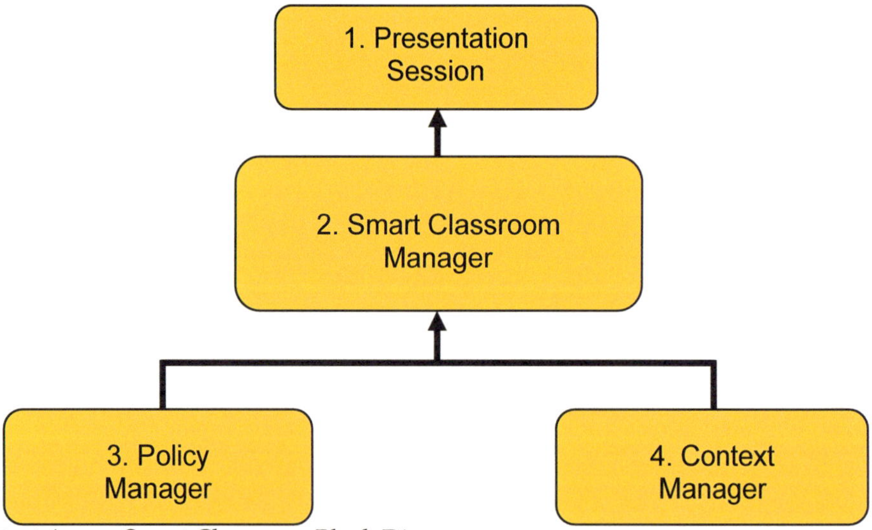

Fig. 6. Context Aware Smart Classroom Block Diagram

5.2.1 Presentation Session

The presentation session component is a client that resides on a local PC in the smart classroom that is responsible for locating the appropriate PowerPoint file and displaying it, starting at the appropriate slide.

5.2.2 Smart Classroom Manager

The core of the CASC system is the smart classroom manager that provides the adaptive behaviour based on a set of system rules. The manager collects the policy settings of the users and the current context by connecting to appropriate database tables and is responsible for transferring material to students according to student specific policies.

5.2.3 Policy Manager

Students and lecturers can log into the system and modify their policies based on the set of options presented. The room operation is set by a room policy that can be modified by the lecturer and the CASC administrator. The notes policy is set by the lecturer and can be used to initiate a change of venue to ensure that appropriate facilities are available in a room.

Lecturer's policy: This policy can request advance notification of lecture times and venues, which is mainly required if room venues are dynamically allocated. The policy informs the CASC client where to access notes, either from the lecturers' desktop machine, wirelessly from a PDA or a central server and they are then displayed on the room projector. The lecturer can set the distribution of material to those present or to all students of the class group.

Students' policy: This policy enables the student to specify how the lecture material is to be transmitted, such as wirelessly to a laptop in the room, or sent to an email address. Also, this policy enables the student to remotely access the smart classroom and receive notes.

Room Policy: The room policy allows the smart classroom to be used for a range of purposes such as a lecture, tutorial, or presentation. Based on the room policy being set as presentation a particular student may take on the role of the lecturer. The room policy ensures the correct activity, such as lecturer and student group, takes place the appropriate room at the right time and date. CASC can send a message to lecturers or students who enter an incorrect room.

Notes Policy: Certain lecture notes may require audio or DVD players and these options can be set by the lecturer. However a room with the appropriate functionality must be requested in advance of the lecture period. This permits the system to find a suitable room and give advance notice to students and the lecturer which room is available. A lecturer can set the notes policy to specify who receives the notes for each of the cases: when a student is present physically in the room; remotely signed in; or not present.

5.2.4 Context Manager

The context manager is responsible for collecting real-time data and storing the information into appropriate tables in a database for use by the smart classroom manager. The context manager relies on a Bluetooth monitoring daemon on the local computer for communicating with user devices.

Identity: Users are identified through the MAC address of their personal devices. When users are added to the system specific device configuration information is also required to be added.

Location: There are two location elements in the system, the smart classroom location and the location and tracking of individuals. The location of individuals is identified using the Bluetooth enabled personal devices and requires to determine if the user is inside the room.

It is possible for CASC to change the room location and generate a Bluetooth broadcast to the appropriate student and lecturer that the venue has changed.
Activity: An academic activity or event is defined in the central scheduling system database and requires a lecturer, class group, venue and activity such as a lecture or tutorial to be identified. The context manager connects to the central database and copies relevant schedules to a local database table for access by the smart classroom manager.
Time: The start time of each activity and the duration is determined from the central scheduling system. This can be used by the smart classroom manager to send out reminders using Bluetooth or email to lecturers and staff in advance of lectures.

5.3 CASC Implementation

In order to provide a scalable solution a client-server architecture was implemented. Each smart classroom requires a local client that manages the classroom space. This client is used to access the Bluetooth device for identification of students and lecturers. Lecture material such as slides and classroom material are managed by the server.
Privacy issues are addressed by having students and lecturers opt-in by registering their own Bluetooth devices and configuring their personal preferences which are used to create profiles for the decision engine. A MySQL database is used on the server to store device, personal information and room configurations. Scheduling information from the central management Information system is transferred into the MySQL database when required by the servers decision engine.

5.4 Managing the Classroom

The local classroom PC is used to run the CASC client, which is responsible for scanning for Bluetooth devices and for retrieving the presentation material for the lecturer. The scanning routine runs continuously and commences a scan every 30 seconds that will identify all Bluetooth devices in the neighbourhood and pass any information collected to the CASC server for the smart classroom manager.
A classroom manager determines if a lecturing event is to take place and updates the client on the current status for the particular room such as no class scheduled. On the arrival of a user, acting in the lecturer role, at the appropriate time the classroom manager will welcome the lecturer, retrieve the appropriate material and present the lecturer with options to commence from a specific slide, change to a different lecturer session or finish the session.

5.5 System Deployment

CASC was deployed in a laboratory in the School of Electronics and Communications Engineering (SECE) at DIT as shown in Figure 7. Currently in SECE, lecture theatres are equipped with LCD projectors and computers connected to the network to enable presentation of material and so CASC can easily be deployed in lecture theatres.
The CASC system uses commonly available personal mobile devices supported by pervasive technologies such as Bluetooth, WLAN and LAN that make system deployment relatively simple and cheap to deploy in a real academic environment. The system is a client-server architecture that makes it easier to set up many smart rooms by adding the CASC client and a Bluetooth dongle to existing theatre or lecture facilities. User interaction is quite straightforward, using applets to setup database tables, although users are required

to find the Bluetooth MAC address of their personal mobile devices. The CASC system effectively managed the retrieval, display and distribution of presentation material as intended.

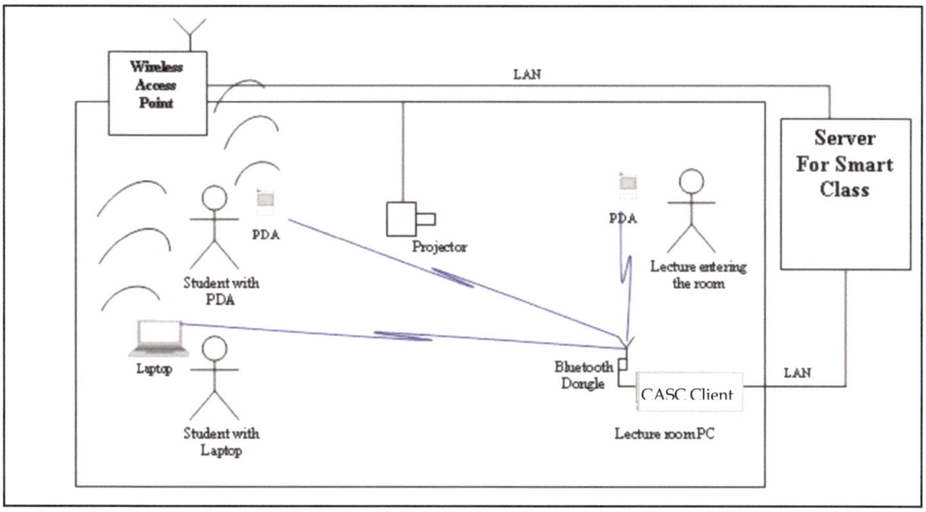

Fig. 7. Context Aware Smart Classroom System configuration

5.6 CASC Limitations

The Bluetooth sensor occasionally scanned extra devices that were not inside the room. This problem depended on the actual positioning of the Bluetooth monitoring sensor. In the case of the local PC being positioned near the door Bluetooth devices outside of the room can be scanned. In this case a student identified as a member of the group would receive the material without attending the session. In the case that the PC was located at an external wall, away from the door, devices outside of the room were not identified by the system.

Performance issues, in terms of system response time, were identified in identifying and transferring material to students when the number of devices in the room was increased. This was due to the time required for Bluetooth to scan the room and collect each devices MAC address, this was observed to take about 5 seconds per device to scan and identify the user.

5.7 Evaluation

Part of the evaluation process is to determine whether users are willing to use the system. Initial feedback from students has been positive and location privacy concerns in relation to system usage have proved to be unwarranted from the student's perspective. In informal discussions students indicated limited concern regarding privacy of their location or data. While research supports this attitude such as Beckwith (Beckwith and Mainwaring 2005) identifyng an array of personal information disclosed on the internet in every day life from credit card numbers to personal addresses. Robles (Robles, Sukumaran et al. 2006) points out the unprecedented self-disclosure through participation in personal home pages, webcams and blogs.

The perceived student perspective requires to be considered in a more formal evaluation approach to determine if it will effect student engagement with the system.

5.7.1 Educator Interviews

Educators require to accept and engage with the proposed solution in order to ensure the technology is fully utilised.

Interviewee	Role	Interview Key Points
J. Kellegher (Kellegher 2009)	Lecturer	Practical laboratories are multi-functional and there is often a delay in starting the sessions. Simplify tedious tasks at the start of practical sessions, such as setting up appropriate applications on student computers. Pre-load laboratory material to individual machines and pre-configure machines. Pre-load lecture material.
D. Clarke (Clarke 2009)	Lecturer	Provide support for peer instruction in classrooms. Display student photographs and names on a lecturer display to assist student interaction, particularly at the start of a semester. Consider voice to text for capturing material discussed in lecture.
D. Gordon (Gordon 2009)	Lecturer	Use the technology to change the habitat for the students who are digital natives. Provide option for peer feedback and peer instruction. Consider accessibility issues, provide auto note taking for students with dyslexia or poor eye sight, text to voice, Also of value to non-native English speakers. Provide management layer to abstract lecturer from the technology
P. Doyle (Doyle 2009)	Lecturer	Consider providing Pod casts, synchronised with material presented and developed during the lecture Limit the capabilities of the system to match available and pervasive technologies.
B. Bowe (Bowe 2009)	Learning & Teaching	Focus on student centred learning approaches, such as peer instruction and problem based learning as they have been successfully implemented. Integrate solution with the learning Management System, WebCourses. Identify suitable interactive response systems to integrate with room, aim to engage and reduce passive listening.
J. Harvey (Harvey 2009)	Learning & Teaching	Interactive classrooms spaces to be deployed with interactive white boards and integrated response system, however only limited number possible. Consider non formal learning spaces with technology support for students outside the classroom.

Table 1. Summary of Interviews Regarding Smart and Interactive Classrooms

As identified previously there is an initial learning curve and time consideration when changing lecture styles. To ensure the next version of the system meets lecturer requirements a number of lecturers were interviewed, during March 2009, in a semi-structured manner to identify the key issues that would encourage system usage. Table 1 summarises the key points in the interviews.

Many of the key points can readily be addressed with minimal extensions to the system, such as providing student photographs on a separate display. However voice to text conversion is not a truly ubiquitous facility and as such will not be considered in the next development phase. In order to perform a more complete evaluation a longitudinal study is currently being planned.

The purpose of developing the CASC system was to leverage existing technologies such as using the personal devices of students and lecturers as Bluetooth tags; to use the existing communications infrastructure provided by WLAN, LAN and email to enhance the students experience in the classroom. The smart classroom manager has been designed to automatically adapt to the behaviour of the room, based on the context, user policies and the core rules of the system. Bluetooth provided an acceptable solution to identifying users within the room although it occasionally identified users outside the room. The time for Bluetooth to identify each user raises concerns about the potential scalability of this identification technique. An alternative technique such as RFID tags in the student cards would probably improve performance and avoid mistaken identification. The CASC system operated as an effective demonstrator for the use of context awareness as a driver for creating a low-cost smart environment that can be developed using existing infrastructure and personal devices.

6. Future Work

Interesting concepts were identified from the primary interviews carried out and these will be evaluated in order to identify which can readily be supported. In particular the concept of pre-configuring machines and pre-loading materials is being considered. To accomplish this, a thin client model is proposed with a single authentication scheme for accessing different operating systems from a single desk-top (Doyle 2008).

Technical limitations of Bluetooth are being addressed by including RFID technologies to address the identification time delays. An interactive response system is being developed that can use mobile phones to permit peer instruction in any classroom.

7. Conclusion

Smart classrooms as in the case of eClass provide an interesting technical solution that does not necessarily guarantee improved student learning, based on grades measured (Brotherton and Abowd 2004). It is necessary to support the technology with appropriate learning styles and pedagogies and then assess the appropriateness of the technical solution.

There is evidence to support the concept of a Digital Divide developing between students and educators. For example students have expressed limited concern about personal data on the internet while educators tend to be more privacy aware. Students seem to be more passive learners and require more effort from educators to get them to engage using traditional lecturing approaches.

Appropriate learning styles, such as Problem Based Learning and Peer Instruction, have been proven to engage students and also gain measurable improvements in student learning. The difficulty for educators is the additional burden in using these methods in classroom environments with large numbers of students.

In certain scenarios, such as large lecture spaces with over a hundred students, all learning paradigms will not be suitable, however Interactive Response Systems could be used in such environments. Peer instruction could be used in such cases, permitting groups of 3 to 5, depending on room configuration, (Limited to 3 in the case of standard lecture theatre with seats organised in a row). The volume of data would be relatively small and could be easily be managed automatically, though there may be time delays due to interference between devices. Smart Classroom technology provides the ability to manage complex environments that contain multiple technologies and pervasive devices.
Smart Classroom technology has the potential to play a supporting role for educators in gaining student engagement and getting measurable gains in student learning and exam performance.

8. References

(1995). Data Protection Directive (95/46/ec) (released October 6, 1999). Revision of the Commission's Rules to Ensure Compatibility with Enhanced 911 Emergency Calling Systems, . Third Report and Order.
Abowd, G. D. (1999). Classroom 2000: An Experiment with the Instrumentation of a Living educational Environment IBM Systems Journal Vol. 38, No.(4), 508-530.
Beckwith, R. and Mainwaring, S. (2005). Privacy: personal information, threats, and technologies. Proceedings of Technology and Society, 2005. Weapons and Wires: Prevention and Safety in a Time of Fear. ISTAS 2005. Proceedings. 2005 International Symposium on, 9.
Beresford, A. R. (2005). Location Privacy in Ubiquitous Computing. Computer Science, University of Cambridge. Ph.D.
Bowe, B. (2009). Learning paradigms and Interactive Classrooms. Interviewed by. C. O'Driscoll. Dublin Institute of Technology, Ireland. (25th March 2009).
Brotherton, J. and Abowd, G. D. (2002). eClass. Sixth Chapter In: The Digital University: Building a Learning Community. R. Hazemi, S. Hailes and S. Wilbur, Ed. 252, Springer Verlag 185233-478-9.
Brotherton, J. A. and Abowd, G. D. (2004). Lessons learned from eClass: Assessing automated capture and access in the classroom. ACM Transactions Computer-Human Interaction. Vol. 11, No.(2), 121-155. ACM. 1073-0516.
Chen, G. and Kotz, D. (2000). A survey of Context-Aware Mobile Computing Research. Technical Report Dartmouth College Computer Science.
Clarke, D. (2009). Reviewing Smart Classroom Technologies. Interviewed by. C. O'Driscoll. Dublin Institute of Technology, Ireland. (12th January 2009).
Crouch, C. H. and Mazur, E. (2001). Peer Instruction: Ten years of experience and results. American Journal of Physics Vol. 69, No.(9). September 2001,
Das, S. K., Cook, D. J., Battacharya, A., Heierman, E. O., III and Tze-Yun, L. (2002). The role of prediction algorithms in the MavHome smart home architecture. Wireless Communications, IEEE Vol. 9, No.(6), 77-84.
Das, S. K. and Cook, D. J. (2006). Designing and modeling smart environments. Proceedings of World of Wireless, Mobile and Multimedia Networks. WoWMoM 5 pp.

Dey, A. K. and Abowd, G. D. (1999). Towards a Better Understanding of Context and Context-Awareness Technical Report Georgia Institute of Technology, College of Computing.

Doyle, P. (2008). Ubiquitous Desktops with Multi-factor Authentication. Third International Conference on Digital Information Management (ICDIM 2008). London.

Doyle, P. (2009). Reviewing Smart Classroom Technologies. Interviewed by. C. O'Driscoll. Dublin Institute of Technology, Ireland. (13th January 2009).

Fagen, A. P., Crouch, C. H. and Mazur, E. (2002). Peer Instruction: Results from a Range of Classrooms. The Physics Teacher Vol. 40, No.(April 2002), 206-209.

Felder, R. M. and Silverman, L. K. (1988). Learning and Teaching Styles In Engineering Education. Journal of Engineering Education Vol. 78, No.(7), 674-681.

Felder, R. M. (2002). Preface to Learning and Teaching Styles In Engineering Education 1988. Journal of Engineering Education Vol. 78 No. (7), 674 - 681 Retrieved 19th March 2009.

Gordon, D. (2009). Smart Classroom Technologies for Digital Natives. Interviewed by. C. O'Driscoll. Dublin Institute of Technology, Ireland. (13th January 2009).

Harvey, J. (2009). Interactive Classrooms in DIT. Interviewed by. C. O'Driscoll. Dublin Institute of Technology, Ireland. (26th March 2009).

Hsi, S. (2002). The Electronic Guidebook: A Study of User Experiences using Mobile Web Content in a Museum Setting. Proceedings of IEEE International Workshop on Mobile and Wireless Technologies in Education, WMTE, pp 48-54.

Kellegher, J. (2009). Reviewing Smart Classroom Technologies. Interviewed by. C. O'Driscoll. Dublin Institute of Technology, Ireland. (12th January 2009).

Long, S., Aust, D., Abowd, G. and Atkeson, C. (1996). Cyberguide: prototyping context-aware mobile applications. Conference companion on Human factors in computing systems: common ground. Vancouver, British Columbia, Canada, ACM.

Markham, T., Mergendoller, J., Larmer, J. and Ravitz, J. (2003). Project Based Learning Handbook, Buck Institute of Education. September 2003.

Mazur, E. (1997). Peer Instruction: A User's Manual, Prentice Hall, Upper Saddle River, NJ, 1997.

NIST. (2009). NIST Smart Space Project. Retrieved 27th March 2009, from http://www.nist.gov/smartspace/.

Prensky, M. (2001a). Digital Natives, Digital Immigrants. On the Horizon Vol. 9, No.(5). 5, October 2001, MCB University Press.

Prensky, M. (2001b). Digital Natives, Digital Immigrants. Part II : Do They Really Think Differently? On the Horizon Vol. 9, No.(6). 6, December 2001, MCB University Press.

Prensky, M. (2008). Backup Education? Too many teachers see education as preparing kids for the past, not the future. Educational Technology Vol. 48, No.(1). Jan-Feb 2008,

Promethean. (2009). Promethean Interactive Whiteboards. Retrieved 26th March 2009, from http://www.prometheanireland.com/.

Quizdom. (2009). Interactive Classroom Voting SystemWhiteboards. Retrieved 27th March 2009, from http://www.qwizdom.co.uk.

Robles, E., Sukumaran, A., Rickertsen, K. and Nass, C. (2006). Being watched or being special: how I learned to stop worrying and love being monitored, surveilled, and assessed. Proceedings of the SIGCHI conference on Human Factors in computing systems. Montr\&\#233;al, Qu\&\#233;bec, Canada, ACM.

Roche, F. (2009). Interactive Whiteboards for Primary Schools. Interviewed by. C. O'Driscoll. Dublin Institute of Technology, Ireland. (27th March 2009).

Russell, D. M., Streitz, N. A. and Winograd, T. (2005). Building disappearing computers. Communications of the ACM Vol. 48, No.(3), 42-48. ACM. 0001-0782.

Schilit, B., Adams, N. and Want, R. (1994). Context-aware computing applications. Proceedings of Workshop on Mobile Computing Systems and Applications, Proceedings., 85.

Schilit, B. N. and Theimer, M. M. (1994). Disseminating active map information to mobile hosts. Network, IEEE Vol. 8, No.(5), 22.

Shi, Y., Xie, W., Xu, G., Shi, R., Chen, E., Mao, Y. and Liu, F. (2003). The smart classroom: merging technologies for seamless tele-education. Pervasive Computing Vol. 2, No.(2), 47-55. IEEE.

SMARTBoard. (2009). SMART Board Interactive Whiteboards. Retrieved 26th March 2009, from http://www.smarttech.com/Products/smartboard/index.asp.

Snow, C., Pullen, J. M. and McAndrews, P. (2005). Network EducationWare: an open-source web-based system for synchronous distance education. Education, IEEE Transactions on Vol. 48, No.(4), 705-712.

Streitz, N. and Nixon, P. (2005). Introduction to The Disappearing Computer. Communications of the ACM Vol. 48, No.(3), 32-35. ACM. 0001-0782.

Suo, Y., Miyata, N., Morikawa, H., Ishida, T. and Shi, Y. (2008). Open Smart Classroom : Extensible and Scalable Learning System in Smart Space using Web Service Technology. IEEE Transactions on Knowledge and Data Engineering Vol. (Accepted for publication in June 2008 for future issue) Available via IEEE eXplore. Accessed 16th March 2009.

Want, R., Hopper, A., Falcao, V. and Gibbons, J. (1992). The active badge location system. ACM Transactions on Information Systems Vol. 10, No.(1), 91-102. ACM. 1046-8188.

Weiser, M. (1991). The computer for the 21st century. Scientific American Vol. 265, No.(3), 94-104. September 1991 (Reprinted in Communications of ACM July 1993. Vol.3 No. (3): p. 3-11),

Weiser, M. (1993). Some computer science issues in ubiquitous computing. Communications of the ACM Vol. 36, No.(7), 75-84. ACM. 0001-0782.

Adaptive M-Learning

Ivan Carlos Alcântara de Oliveira[1] and José Roberto de A. Amazonas[2]
[1]*University of São Paulo and University Cruzeiro do Sul*
[2]*University of São Paulo*
Brazil

1. Introduction

M-Learning is a new education's paradigm that is growing in educational institutions in Brazil and worldwide which encompasses the use of mobile technologies with some data processing capacity as cellular phones, PDAs, notebooks, and wireless Internet access enabling students to break the time and space barriers without class schedules and fixed access points; teaching and learning really at any time, really anywhere, even while in movement (Oliveira & Medina, 2007; Mermelsein & Tal, 2005; Trifonova & Ronchetti, 2006; Mcalister & Xie, 2005).

These technologies can access learning objects that include content and evaluation activities in several formats and media. However, not always the obtained objects are the most indicated to the students' learning styles and to a visualization and usability adequate to the mobile devices.

In addition to that, in a situation in which the content of the objects that can be accessed are already known by the student, he or she may become unmotivated by the need of having to study subjects that are already mastered by him or her. Besides, the student's performance is not always taken into consideration to propose new elements of study.

The present learning environments are systems made of: i) tools for administration and management of content, users and courses; ii) synchronous and asynchronous communication tools; iii) tools for evaluations creation and control. Such environments allow the use of learning objects that cannot always be adequately accessed by mobile devices.

Among these environments we may cite: i) Blackboard Learning System, created by the company Blackboard Inc., disseminated worldwide and not free; ii) MOODLE (Modular Object-Oriented Dynamic Learning Environment), free software of learning support that is largely used; iii) CTELCS (Collaborative Training Environment of the Laboratory of Communications and Signals), a learning environment prototype developed at the LCS-EPUSP laboratory (Oliveira, 2003); the collaborative environment of the TIDIA Ae project (*Tecnologia da Informação no Desenvolvimento da Internet Avançada – Aprendizado Eletrônico*; Information Technology in the Development of the Advanced Internet - Electronic Learning) developed by research laboratories and funded by FAPESP (*Fundação de Amparo à Pesquisa do Estado de São Paulo*), that helps the electronic learning activities, offering support for presencial teaching (Tidia Ae, 2009); and many others.

Presently there are several efforts targeting the development of systems and learning objects that allow the access and visualization by mobile devices in an adequate way.
When the learning environments provide access to content by means of mobile devices, enabling the M-Learning, they allow the access to learning objects, but they do not take into account the technology's characteristics, the learning styles, the students' pre-acquired knowledge and performance.
This chapter presents the proposal of a software architecture to be used for content management that allows to provide learning on mobile platforms considering:

- the selection of learning objects that are best adapted to: i) the mobile device's technological data; ii) learning style information; iii) student's performance; iv) acquired knowledge of the student; v) content associated to a course;
- that the teacher and the student may inform some characteristics of their preference concerning a learning object;
- the interaction of the student with the mobile device and the learning object as well.

The architecture has been elaborated in modules: some modules on the server, a module responsible for the management of learning objects and three modules for the mobile device aiming to provide adaptation.
The modules proposed for the server are:

- the technology module that is in charge of receiving some data concerning the mobile device;
- the student's performance module that is responsible for manipulating the data concerning the students' performance in the proposed activities and content;
- the knowledge module performs the manipulation of the students' pre-acquired knowledge and the acquired knowledge during the students interaction with the activities and content of the on-going course;
- the student's learning styles module that manipulates the data concerning the students' learning styles independently of the enrolled course;
- the adaptation module, that is the focus of the adaptive M-Learning architecture, where the data received from the other modules are processed to determine the adequate content and adapted to the students and mobile devices characteristics;
- the content module that is charge of retrieving the learning object that has characteristics found by the adaptation module.

We can think about this software architecture proposal as part of a learning environment that can also be coupled to an existing environment.
It is worth to emphasize that despite the adaptability treatment is targeted towards mobile devices, due to the generic character of the architecture that performs the adaptation, it can also be directed to non mobile computers.
It is also important to inform that, as an assumption, in real situations the student does not perform the study or all activities of a given course only on mobile devices. Usually, the student employs the mobile device to access content or to perform activities in some stages of his/her study.
This chapter has been organized in sections according to the following description. Section 2 makes a brief summary of related work. Section 3 describes the fundamental concepts related to this chapter's theme. The adaptive M-Learning architecture is depicted in Section 4. Section 5 discusses possible techniques for implementing an algorithm that makes it possible the adaptation of learning objects. Section 6 presents an example of how the

Adaptive M-Leraning works. At last, Section 7 discusses the characteristics of the designed architecture, the needed research to make it complete and summarizes the conclusions.

2. Related Works

Some works along this research line around the world are:

- The KOD "Knowledge on Demand" Project, comprehending the laboratories CERTH-ITI from Greece, FD Learning from England, GIUNTI Interactive Labs from Italy and CATAI from Spain, defines the specification of an e-learning architecture that provides adaptive and reusable content (Sampson et al, 2002);
- MAS-PLANG (MultiAgent System-PLAtaforma de Nueva Generation) Project, that has been developed at the University of Girona in Spain, is an intelligent adaptive tutoring system which uses multi-agents systems with the objective of selecting instructional material for the student in a customized way based on his/her learning style and current knowledge (Peña et al, 2002);
- JADE (Java Agent framework for Distance learning Environments), offers a set of resources that make it easier the development and implementation of computational environments to be used as distance learning instruments. The agents, that don't have mobility, are: Contents Managers, Exercises, Examples, Interactions, Student Model and Communication (Silveira & Vicari, 2002);
- The AdaptWeb (Adaptive Web) project that studies adaptive hypermedia systems for distance learning via web, mainly adaptive interfaces (Musa & Oliveira, 2004);
- BAGHERA is a distance learning platform that has an interface for solving geometry demonstration problems. In the development a multi-agent system has been used made of non-humane agents that interact among themselves according to their competences, cooperating and collectively performing educative tasks. In the environment, each learner has three kinds of agents: Learning Agent Companion, Mediator and Tutor. Similarly, the teacher has two kinds of agents: Teaching Companion and Assistant (Pesty & Webber, 2004);
- ALLEGRO is an intelligent environment made of an intelligent tutoring system that offers individualized apprenticeship and a CSCL (Computer-Supported Collaborative Learning) that enables collaborative learning. The environment has been modeled as a MAS (Multi-agent System) that offers: autonomy, flexibility and adaptability (Vicari et al, 2007);
- MACES (Multi-agent Architecture for a Collaborative Educational System) is a multi-agent collaborative learning system for distance learning. Its architecture is made of human agents (Learners and Tutors) and by five types of artificial agents, namely: Diagnostic, Mediator, Collaborative, Social and Semiotic (Kown et al, 2007);
- AMPLIA (Intelligent Probabilistic Multi-Agent Learning Environment) is an environment that has been designed as an additional resource for medical students formation. Its users (learners, teachers and applications) are represented by autonomous agents that belong to a social network based on objectives that communicate, cooperate and negotiate. It has the following artificial agents: Learners, Domain and Mediator (Vicari et al, 2008);
- Content Adaptation in Mobile Multimedia Systems for M-Learning of the Bucharest Academy of Economic Studies in Romania (Revieu et al., 2008).

- TIDIA Ae (*Tecnologia da Informação no Desenvolvimento da Internet Avançada – Aprendizado Eletrônico*; Information Technology in the Development of the Advanced Internet - Electronic Learning) helps in learning activities, offering support to presential teaching and makes it possible to the user to keep a personal profile, a shared calendar, interact with teachers and students, perform tests, make available and share instructional resources (Tidia Ae, 2009);

3. Fundamental Concepts

The conceptual map, illustrated in Figure 1, presents the several concepts related to Adaptive M-Learning (Tavares & Luna, 2003).
In the map, the concepts are represented according to scheme described in Table 1.

Color scheme	Concept
	focus concept, i. e., Adaptive M-Learning
	driving and motivating concepts of the research about Adaptive M-Learning
	fundamental concepts. These subjects are the necessary knowledge for the Adaptive M-Learning elaboration
	relevant concepts, but not fundamental. These concepts will surely be used as a foundation or basis of other concept and to provide examples in practical situations
	conceptually important, but not relevant for the focus

Table 1. Conceptual map scheme.

According to the conceptual map, me may list as fundamental concepts: mobile technologies, learning objects, learning styles, student's pre-acquired knowledge and student's performance.
The knowledge of these concepts if of paramount importance so that the adaptive M-Learning architecture can be designed.

3.1 Mobile Technologies

Mobile technologies comprehend devices as the cellular phone, PDA and smartphone, that are used in the teaching and learning process to access instructional content anytime and anywhere, profiting by free time while waiting in a line or during displacement on a means of transport.
Notwithstanding, despite of the advantages of mobility it is necessary to point out the limitations of these devices as far as hardware and software resources are concerned, as: processing power, screen size, quantity of memory, typing difficulty, user expectation and functional limitations of the operating system of each device (Oliveira & Medina, 2007).

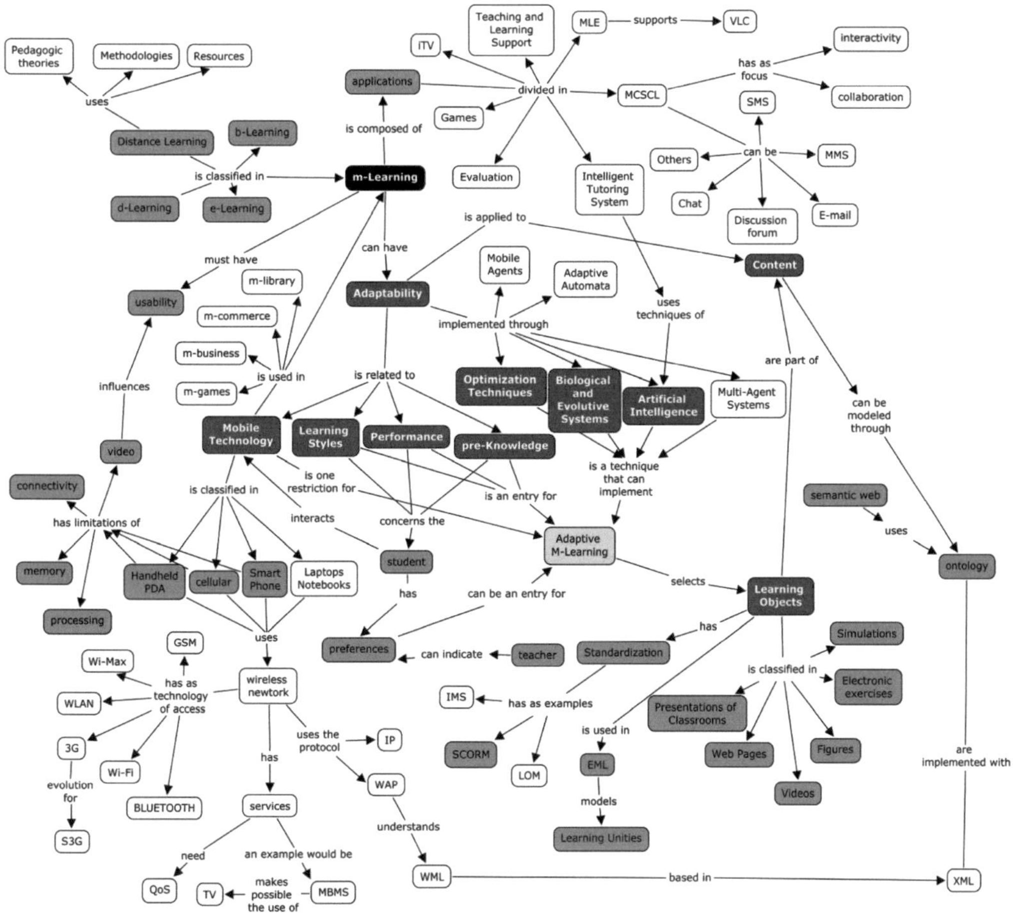

Fig. 1. Concepts related to Adaptive M-Learning.

3.2 Learning Objects

The term learning objects refers to any resource, digital or not digital, that can be used and reused for supporting the apprenticeship (Oliveira et al., 2003).

Some examples of learning objects are: web pages, images, audio resources, Flash animations, Powerpoint presentations, a game, a pdf text, a self-correcting electronic evaluation, etc.

To make the interoperability easier, or even possible, the learning objects must be standardized. Among the possible standards, in this chapter the learning objects descriptions are based on SCORM (Shareable Content Object Reference Model) (Scorm, 2004).

The SCORM is an unified set of specifications to make available e-learning contents and services. This set of specifications defines a model of content aggregation, a model of sequencing and an execution environment for learning objects (Scorm, 2004). It is important to emphasize that despite of having been planned for e-learning the SCORM fits to be used in M-Learning.

In SCORM, an object/resource is associated to metadata that allow to catalogue it and, then, look for and find it in online repositories.
One differential concerning the use of SCORM for the content development for distance learning courses is its focus on reusability, interoperability, accessibility and durability.

3.3 Learning Styles

Learning styles are defined, according to (Felder & Silverman, 1988), as a characteristic and prevailing preference concerning the way people receive and process information, considering the styles also as skills that may be developed.
There are several models that deal with this subject and among them we may cite:

- The Myers-Briggs Type Indicator (MBTI) (Myers & McCaulley, 1985);
- Kolb's Learning Style Model (Kolb, 1983);
- Herrmann Brain Dominance Instrument (HBDI) (Hermann, 1990);
- Felder-Silverman Learning Style Model (FSLSM) (Felder & Silverman, 1988).

We adopted the FSLSM model because it has already been used in the development of adaptive applications (Peña et at., 2002).
According to the FSLSM model the learning process has the following dimensions: processing (active/reflexive), perception (sensorial/intuitive), input (visual/verbal) and understanding (sequential/global).
The learning styles initial data may be obtained by means of a diagnostic tool, named ILS (Index of Learning Styles), that has a questionnaire with 44 items.
Some examples of the ILS' questions are illustrated in Table 2.

Question	Alternatives
I understand better after	experimenting.
	thinking about.
As entertainment, I prefer to	watch TV.
	read a book.
The idea of working in groups, with a grade for the whole group,	appeals me.
	does not appeal me.

Table 2. Examples of ILS' questions.

After carrying out the ILS test, the initial learning style is presented as shown in Figure 2.
According to Figure 2, if the student is between:

- 1-3 he/she is relatively well balanced on both scale dimensions;
- 5-7 he/she has a moderate preference for one scale dimension and will learn more easily if the educational environment favors this dimension;
- 9-11 he/she has a strong preference for one scale dimension, indicating that he/she may have real difficulties learning in an environment that does not support this preference.

3.4 Pre-acquired Knowledge

The pre-acquired knowledge of a subject or course refers to the contents that are mastered by the student. They can be obtained by applying a questionnaire with the objective of identifying what is already known by the student.

ACTIVE REFLEXIVE

11 9 7 5 3 1 1 3 5 7 9 11

<-- -->

SENSORIAL INTUITIVE

11 9 7 5 3 1 1 3 5 7 9 11

<-- -->

VISUAL VERBAL

11 9 7 5 3 1 1 3 5 7 9 11

<-- -->

SEQUENTIAL GLOBAL

11 9 7 5 3 1 1 3 5 7 9 11

<-- -->

Fig. 2. Obtained result by applying the ILS diagnostic tool.

3.5 Student's Performance

The term performance is related to the result achieved by the students in a given subject when they are evaluated or by the time they stay on a given topic under study. From these measurements, it is possible to estimate the student's performance and identify if it is necessary to reinforce any topic that has not been well learned yet (Amazonas, 2005).

4. Adaptive M-Learning: proposal of an archictecture

The adaptive M-Learning architecture, presented in Figure 3, has the following elements:

- Learner´s Side: represented by the mobile technology and by the student interaction with the content and interface;
- Content Server´s Side: made of modules that manipulate the mobile device's, the student's and the course's characteristics aiming at providing adaptability of the learning objects;
- Teacher´s Side: is in charge of manipulating the learning objects, the information that describe them, and the adaptation rules provided by the teacher.

It is important to emphasize that the architecture shown in Figure 3 presents the elements that manipulate the data which are necessary to provide the content adaptability. However, a complete educational system should include other elements, as for example: users and courses administration; synchronous and asynchronous collaboration tools; and system configuration tools.

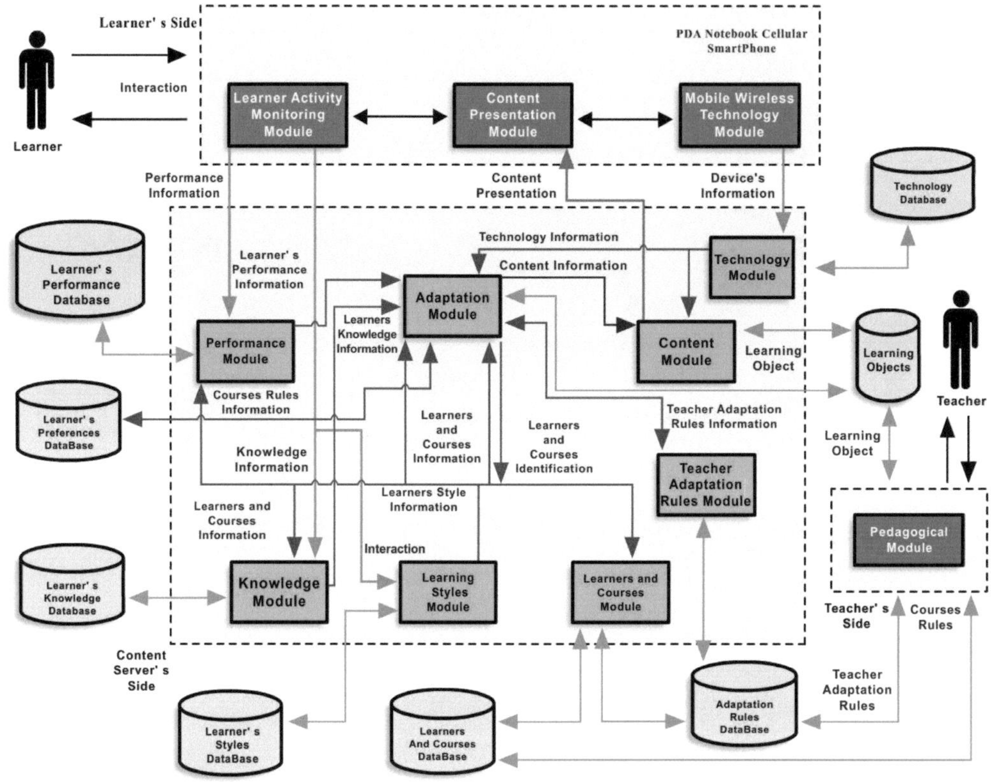

Fig. 3. Adaptive M-Learning architecture.

4.1 Learner's Side

The Learner's Side is represented by the mobile device, the content's presentation interface and by the interaction of the student with both the device and the content as well.

The Learner's Side modules are:

- Mobile Wireless Technology: this model gets information about the mobile devices as type of device (PDA, smartphone, etc.) and device's model;
- Learner Activity Monitoring: this model is in charge of monitoring the student's interaction with the content and the mobile device getting information about the interactions performed with the device, the interface and the learning object; the interaction time with the learning object; the idle time, i. e., the time interval the student has not performed any investigative action while staying at a given interface; the student's performance with the proposed activities;
- Content Presentation: interface presented to the student on the mobile device containing the learning object that has been selected according to the following parameters: learning styles, information about the mobile device, data about the

student's performance, interactions performed by the student both on the interface and device, and pre-acquired knowledge.

The initial students' preferences for types of specific objects, their initial learning style and pre-acquired knowledge, can also be obtained by means of the mobile device. However, it is worth to point out that a device with a screen that can show a larger quantity of content may be more adequate to get these initial values.

4.2 Teacher's Side

The Teacher's Side is made of the Pedagogical Module. This module is used to insert the learning objects and their respective information in a repository of objects and contents.

The information concerning the learning objects are coded according to the SCORM standard. Briefly, some of these information are: general data that describe the object; the characteristics related to the object's historic; its current state and all elements involved in its evolution; the object's requirements and technical characteristics; the object's educational and pedagogical characteristics.

These information and objects are obtained from teachers in the content and/or from developers of the learning objects.

In addition to these information, this module allows to insert and to obtain the adaptation rules that the teacher wants to apply to his/her course and to provide them to the adaptation module.

The data obtained from this module are essential to the adequate selection of the learning object, according to the adaptation parameters.

4.3 Content Server's Side

The Content Server's Side is responsible for:

- receiving information about the students' current knowledge, learning style and the mobile device's characteristics;
- storing the acquired knowledge, performance, interactions and learning styles in specific databases;
- manipulating the received information to enable the adaptation of the objects to the student's preferences and the device's characteristics, according to the course's adaptation rules provided by the teacher;
- send the adapted content to the client student.

The Content Server's Side is made of several modules that are described in the following sub-sections.

4.3.1 Techology Module

The Technology Module is the module that is in charge of receiving some data about the mobile device, as type and model, that make it possible to retrieve information about the device from the Technology Database, as illustrated in Figure 4. Using this information, it is possible to perform the device-based adaptation.

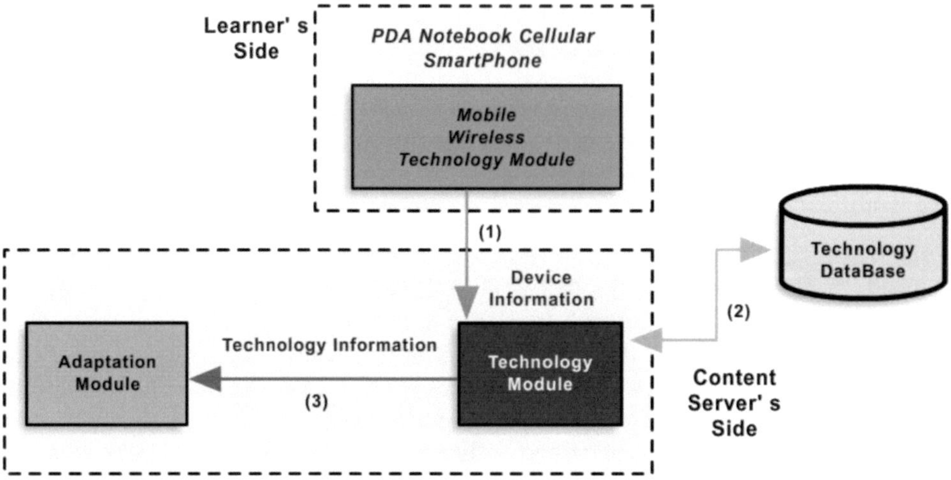

Fig. 4. Technology Module.

From Figure 4, we can verify that the message **Device Information (1)** is received by the Technology Module, that, by its turn, receives the message **Technology Information (2)** from the Technology Database and forwards it to the Adaptation Module **(3)**. The Adaptation Module is in charge of performing the adaptation to the device. The format of these messages is as follows:

- **Device Information** comprised of d = [d1, d2], where:
  d1: Device type: PDA, notebook, cellular, smartPhone;
  d2: Device model: LG Shine SLIM ME770d, Sansung Light CAM, among others.
- **Technology Information** comprised of t = [t1, t2, t3, t4, t5, t6, t7], where:
  t1: Transmission rate: number of bytes/second;
  t2: Keyboard type: numerical, alphanumerical;
  t3: Screen size: y bytes horizontal x z bytes vertical;
  t4: Type of access/technology: Bluetooth, GSM, WAP;
  t5: Operating system;
  t6: Quantity of memory: number of bytes;
  t7: Extra functions.

4.3.2 Performance Module

The Performance Module manipulates the data concerning the students' performance in the proposed activities and contents, as shown in Figure 5.

The performance data, named **Performance Information (1)**, are obtained by means of the achieved results in the activities performed by the student and/or by the time he/she has taken to complete a given content or activity of each course in which he/she is enrolled.

The Performance Module receives the message **Performance Information (1)**; gets the list of objects/performance manipulated by the student related to his/her course and content from the Learner's Performance Database **(3)**; requests and receives the rules of the programmatic content under study, named **Courses Rules Information (2)**; and mounts the message about the student's performance, named **Learner Performance Information (4)** and forwards it to the Adaptation Module.

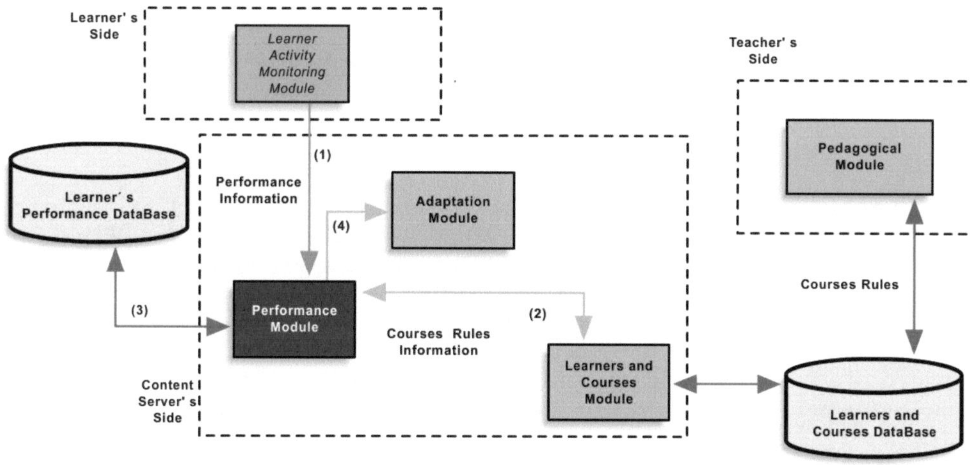

Fig. 5. Performance Module.

The format of the messages exchanged by the Performance Module are:

- **Performance Information** comprised of p = [p1, p2, p3, p4, p5, p6], where:
  p1: learner identification;
  p2: course identification;
  p3: content identification;
  p4: type of content, learning object as element of study (e) or as activity/evaluation (a) or collaborative tool (Forum, chat,...) (fc);
  p5: if p4 is equal to (e), p5 represents the time spent in the activity in seconds; if p4 is equal to (a), p5 represents the result achieved in the activity; if p4 is equal to (fc), p5 represents an account of the student participation in a collaborative activity that is not a learning object;
  p6: current object identification;
- **Courses Rules Information** comprised of c = [c1, c2], where:
  c1: course identification;
  c2: course's programmatic content containing an ordered list locp = (locp1, ..., locpn), where each locpi is comprised by the set [content identification, content type, keywords, performance or timing or participation]. It is important to observe that keywords = [k1, k2, ..., km], where m is the number of words that identify the subject.
- **Learner Performance Information** comprised of lp = [lp1, lp2, lp3, lp4, lp5 , lp6, lp7], where:
  lp1: learner identification;
  lp2: course identification;
  lp3: content identification;
  lp4: type of content identification to be selected, that can be: collaborative activity (Forum, chat, ...) (fc), learning object as element of study (e), or activity/evaluation (a);

lp5: list of object identification and type, related to the content identification, already selected/performed lpoi = [lpoi1, ..., lpoin];
lp6: if lp4 is equal to (e), lp6 represents the time spent in the activity in seconds; if lp4 is equal to (a), lp6 represents the result achieved in the activity; if lp4 is equal to (fc), lp6 represents an account of the student participation in a collaborative activity that is not a learning object;
lp7: current object identification;

4.3.3 Knowledge Module

The Knowledge Module performs the manipulation of the student's pre-acquired knowledge and of the knowledge acquired by his/her interaction with the contents/activities of an on-going course. This module is illustrated in Figure 6.

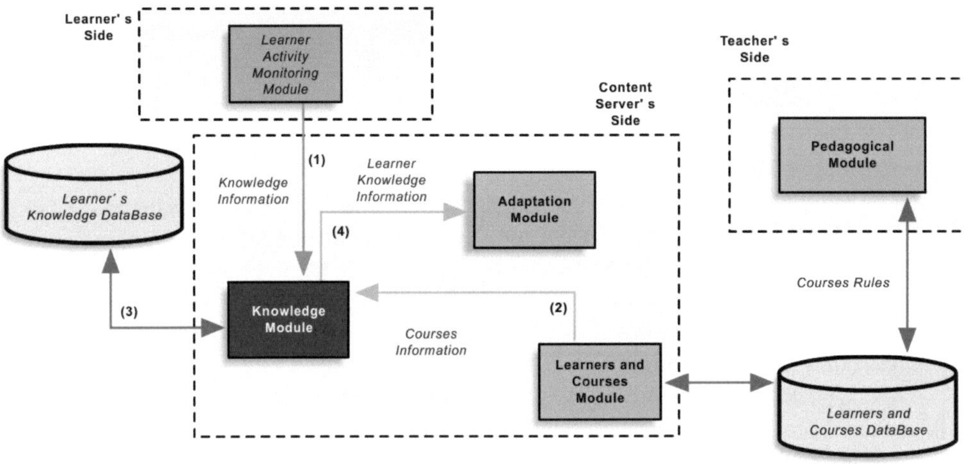

Fig. 6. Knowledge Module.

With the obtained by this module it is possible to identify what a student knows.
It is important to realize that depending on the pre-acquired knowledge it is possible that a student progresses along the course's content in a non-sequential way.
The data about the content manipulated by the student by his/her interaction with the learning object (message **Interaction Knowledge (1)**) is received by the Knowledge Module that gets information about the course (message **Courses Information (2)**) and about the subjects the student knows, from the Learner´s Knowledge DataBase **(3)**. The Knowledge Module prepares the **Learner Knowledge Information (4)** and forwards it to the Adaptation Module.
From Figure 6, we identify:

- **Interaction Knowledge** comprised of ik = [ik1, ik2, ik3, ik4], where:
  ik1: learner identification;
  ik2: course identification;
  ik3: content identification;
  ik4: interaction information.
- **Courses Information** comprised of ci = [ci1, ci2], where:
  ci1: course identification;

ci2: course's programmatic content containing an ordered list locp = (locp1, ..., locpn), where each locpi is comprised by the set [content identification, content type, keywords, performance or timing or participation]. It is important to observe that keywords = [k1, k2, ..., km], where m is the number of words that identify the subject.

- **Learner Knowledge Information,** based on the information about pre-known items of content, the course's programmatic content and the interaction with the current content, lki = [lki1, lki2, lki3, lki4] is generated, where:
  lki1: learner identification;
  lki2: course identification;
  lki3: next content identification to be selected;
  lki4: next type of content identification that can be a learning object as element of study (e), or activity/evaluation to be selected (a), or collaborative activity (fc) to be performed.

4.3.4 Learning Styles Module

The Learning Styles Module, illustrated in Figure 7, manipulates the data concerning the students' learning styles, independently from the course they are enrolled in.
The initial learning styles data are obtained by means of the ILS (Index of Learning Styles) and are stored in the Learner´s Styles DataBase (Felder & Silverman, 1988).

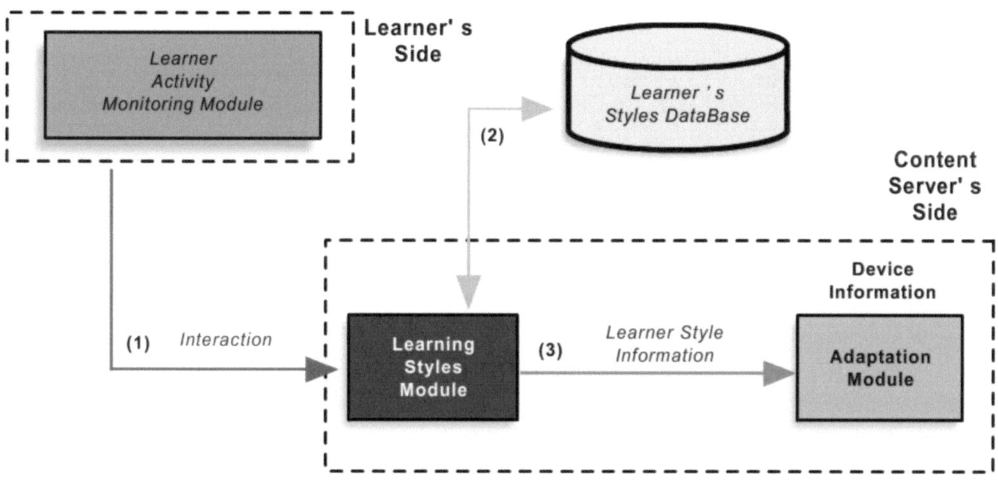

Fig. 7. Learning Styles Module.

The Learning Styles Module receives the information about the student's interactions with the learning object, message **Interaction (1)**, get the current data about the learning style from the Learner's Styles DataBase **(2)**, manipulates these data, modifying, if it is necessary, the student's learning style. Then, it stores the learning style in the Learner's Styles DataBase and sends the message **Learner Style Information (3)** to the Adaptation Module.
It is important to observe that by querying the Learner's Style DataBase about the object manipulation and current learning style, it is possible to track the style modifications.
From Figure 7, we observe:

- **Interaction** is comprised of i = [i1, i2, i3], where:
  i1: learner identification;
  i2: object identification.
  i3: interaction information.
- **Leaner Style Information** is comprised of lsi = [lsi1, lsi2, lsi3, lsi4, lsi5], where:
  lsi1: learner identification;
  lsi2: value in the input dimension: 0 - visual, 1 - oral/verbal, 2 - don't care;
  lsi3: value in the perception dimension: 0 - sensorial, 1 - intuitive, 2 - don't care;
  lsi4: value in the understanding dimension: 0 - sequential, 1 - global, 2 - don't care;
  lsi5: value in the organization dimension: 0 - inductive, 1 - deductive, 2 - don't care.

4.3.5 Learners and Courses Module

This module is responsible for obtaining the data related to a course's programmatic content, the rules of expected performance in the subjects, the items of content and the activities.

It is by means of these data that it is possible to verify what are the next contents to be studied by a student. This module is illustrated in Figure 8.

It is important to point out that the storage and organization of data in the Learners and Courses DataBase is done by a courses and students management module that is not part of this architecture.

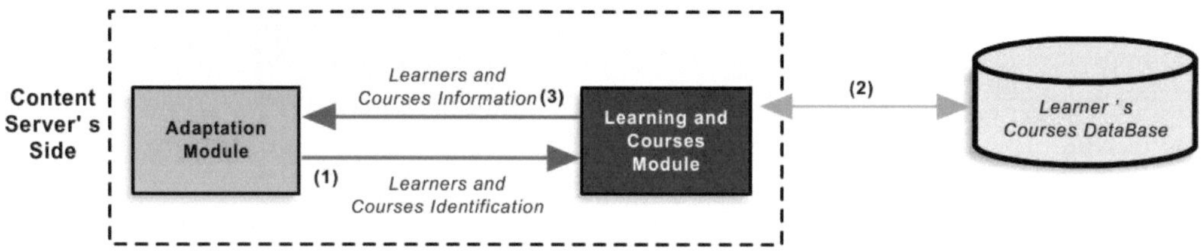

Fig. 8. Learners and Courses Module.

The Adaptation Module requests to the Learners and Courses Module the programmatic content of an on-going course by means of the message **Learners and Courses Identification (1)**. The Learners and Courses Module retrieves the data from the Learners and Courses DataBase **(2)** and send them to the Adaptation Module in a return **Learners and Courses Information (3)** message.

The formats of the messages are:

- **Leaner and Courses Identification** comprised of lci = [lci1, lci2], where:
  i1: learner identification;
  i2: course identification.
- **Leaner and Courses Information** comprised of lcinf = [lcinf1, lcinf2], where:
  lcinfi1: course identification;
  lcinfi2: course's programmatic content containing an ordered list locp = (locp1, ..., locpn), where each locpi is comprised by the set [content identification, content type, keywords, performance or timing or participation]. It is important to observe

that keywords = [k1, k2, ..., km], where m is the number of words that identify the subject.

4.3.6 Content Module

The Content Module, illustrated in Figure 9, is in charge of:

- retrieving the learning object that has its characteristics best adapted to the student and to the device;
- mounting an interface to be displayed on the device;
- forwarding the interface to the device.

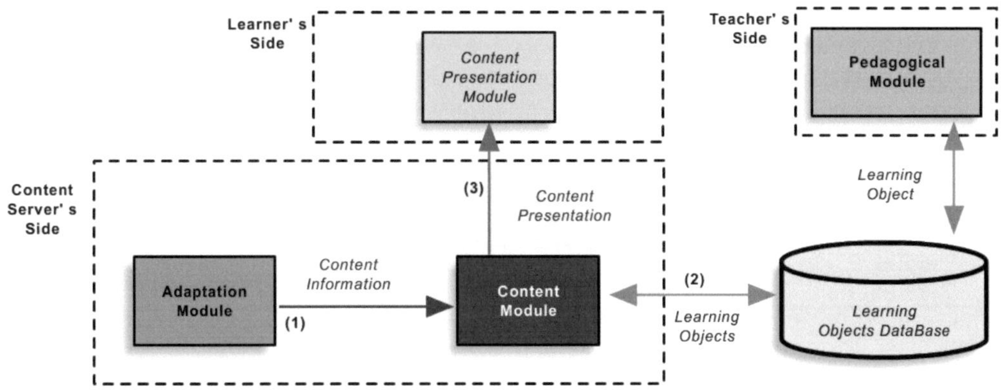

Fig. 9. Content Module.

The Content Module receives the message **Content Information (1)** from the Adaptation Module. This message carries: the course's, student's identification; the candidate learning objects; data about the mobile device. The Content Module selects one of the candidates learning objects **(2)**, stores the identification of the selected object, gets characteristics of the mobile device's interface, mounts the message **Content Presentation (3)** and sends it to the Content Presentation Module running on the mobile device.

From Figure 9, we have:

- **Content Information** comprised of ic = [ic1, ic2, iclo, icd1, icd2], where:
  ic1: learner identification;
  ic2: course identification;
  iclo: candidate learning objects in the form of a list (lo1, ..., lon). All these objects comply with the student's and the device's adaptation rules;
  icd1: device type: PDA, notebook, cellular, smartPhone;
  icd2: device model: LG Shine SLIM ME770d, Sansung Light CAM, among others.
- **Content Presentation** is the message with the interface that contains the learning object to be displayed on the mobile device.

4.3.7 Teacher Adaptation Rules Module

This module gets the adaptation rules from the Adaptation Rules DataBase **(2)**, inserted by teacher in his/her course, in response to the Adaptation Module request and sends them as the message **Teacher Adaptation Rules Information (1) (3)**.

The message **Teacher Adaptation Rules Information** allows the teacher to indicate what are the media that can be presented to the student and enables the configuration of the types of adaptation as well.
This module is illustrated in Figure 10.
From Figure 10 we have:

- **Teacher Adaptation Rules Information** comprised of tari = [tari1, tari2, tari3, tari4, tari5, tari6], where:
  tari1: course identification;
  tari2: list of media to be displayed, as for example: video, text/hypertext/hypermidia, audio, simulation, animation;
  tari3: performance adaptation, 0 - present, 1- missing;
  tari4: knowledge adaptation, 0 - present, 1- missing;
  tari5: learning styles adaptation, 0 - present, 1- missing;
  tari6: technology adaptation, 0 - present, 1- missing;

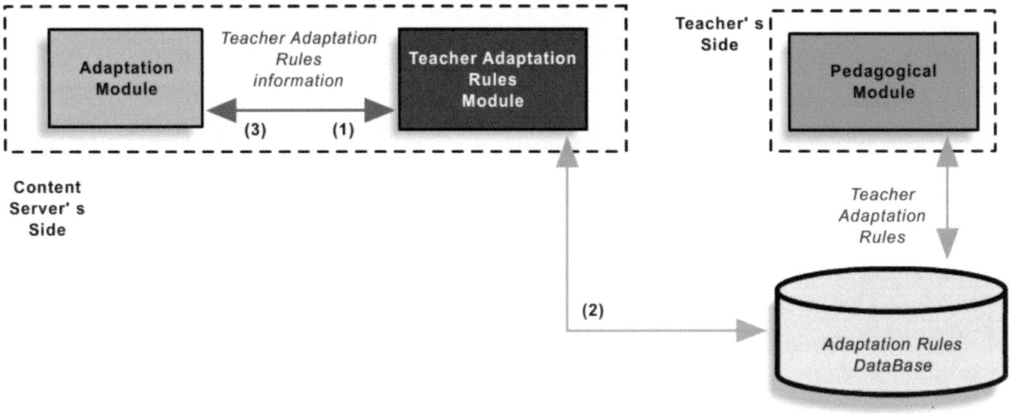

Fig. 10. Teacher Adaptation Rules Module.

4.3.8 Adaptation Module

The Adaptation Module is the central module of the adaptive M-Learning architecture. It receives the messages from the other modules **(1)**, gets the list of learning objects **(2)**, process them to find out which learning objects are adequate and adaptive to the student's and the mobile device's characteristics. Then, it prepares the message with the selected learning objects (**Content Information (3)**) and sends it to the Content Module.
The messages received and generated by the Adaptation Module have already been described in the previous sub-sections.
In Figure 11 we observe that, besides the messages received from the other modules, there is the **Teacher Adaptation Rules Information** containing the adaptation rules provided by the teacher and the types of media preferences informed by the student, in the case he has indicated any, obtained from the Learner Preference DataBase.

5. Adaptation Algorithm: Possible Techniques

In this section we will briefly explain some optimization and computing intelligence techniques to evaluate and verify the possibility of using them in the development of an algorithm responsible for the adaptation implementation.

The algorithm works inside the Adaptation Module, as illustrated in Figure 11. An algorithm's description, without taking into consideration any specific technique to solve the adaptation, is presented in Figure 12.

On line (d) of the algorithm shown in Figure 12, takes place the manipulation of the messages and input data. To do so, one or more techniques of optimization and/or computing intelligence may be used.

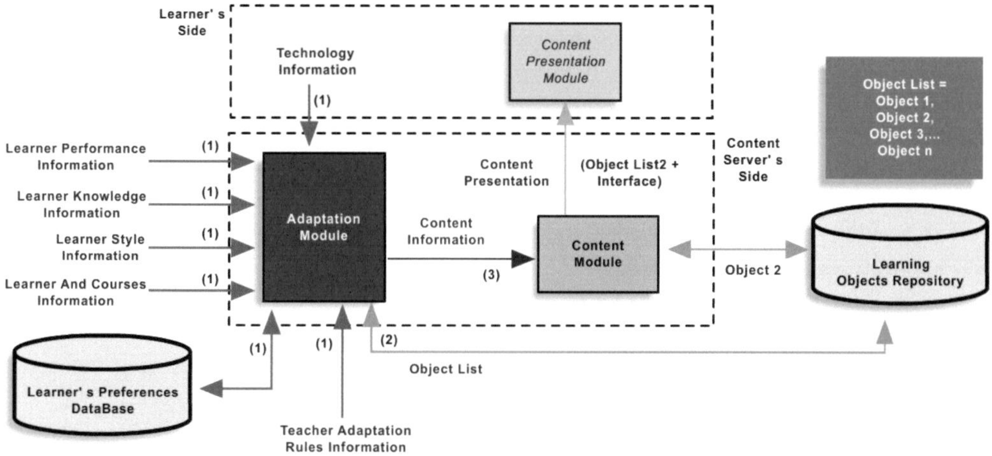

Fig. 11. Adaptation Module.

```
Adaptation Algorithm
Begin
    a) Receive the messages: Technology Information,
       Learner
       Performance Information, Learner Knowledge
       Information, Learner Style Information, Learner and
       Courses Information, Teacher Adaptation Rules
       Information;
    b) Gets the students' preferences;
    c) Gets the list of learning objects according to the
       SCORM standard;
    d) Processes all messages and data evaluating and
       selecting the most adequate objects;
    e) Mounts the message Content Information;
    f) Sends Content Information to the Content Module;
End.
```

Fig. 12. Description of the Adaptation Algorithm.

In the following sub-sections some of the studied techniques will be cescribed, namely:
1. fuzzy logic;
2. genetic algorithms;
3. ants colony optimization; and
4. graphs theory, more specifically the paths algebra proposed in (Herman, 2008).

5.1 Fuzzy Logic

Fuzzy logic is a non-standard logic elaborated by Lofti A. Zadeh in 1965 with which it is possible to capture imprecise information, described in natural language, and convert them to a numerical format that represent expressions that usually cannot be treated by the classical logic systems (Bittencourt & Osório, 2002; Zadeh, 1965).
The systems that implement fuzzy logic use a set of IF-THEN rules that are based on linguistics variables. Theses variables represent a fuzzy set that vary continuously in a range, named transition, between 0 (totally non-member) and 1 (totally member). The transition is represented by a membership function that outputs a number in the (0, 1) interval.
Shortly, according to (Bittencourt & Osório, 2002), the fuzzy systems should be able to:
1. define fuzzy variables and sets;
2. define IF-THEN rules and logical operators that manipulate fuzzy variables;
3. make inferences using the rules;
4. offer different methods to convert the fuzzy data to numerical values.

In the Adaptive M-Learning, it is possible to visualize some fuzzy variables, as for example:
a)performance: that represents the student's performance related to a learning object of a given activity. It could be defined as A [8.5 , 10] = best, B [7, 8.5] = good, C [5, 7] = regular, D [3, 5] = bad, E [0, 3] = worst. The membership function for variable is illustrated in Figure 13.

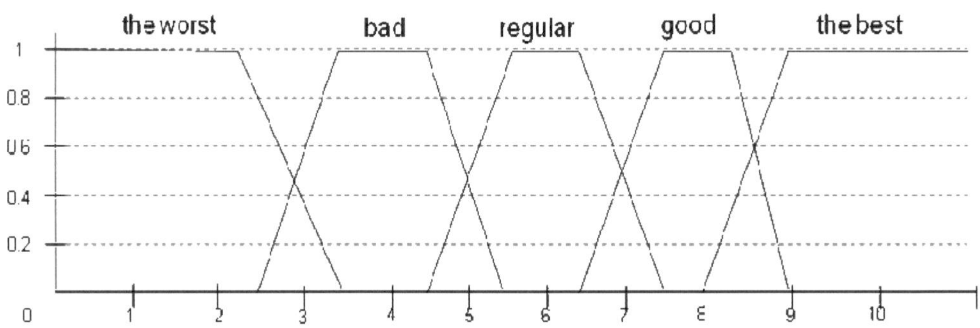

Fig. 13. Membership function for the performance variable.

b) timing: represents the time a student stays studying a learning object of the content type. We may define, for example, short time as a time interval between 0 and 3 minutes, an intermediate time from 3 thru 7 minutes and long time above 7 minutes. The membership function for this situation is illustrated in Figure 14.

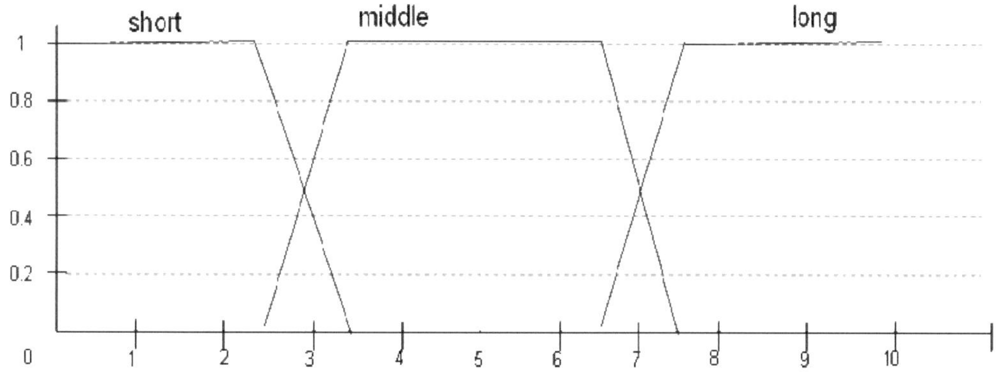

Fig. 14. Membership function for the timing variable.

5.2 Genetic algorithms

The genetic algorithms are a technique of search and optimization based on the Darwinian principle of reproduction and survival of the most apt individuals (Gwiazda, 2006).

These principles are emulated in the construction of computing algorithms that look for the best solution of a given problem, by means of the evolution of population of individuals, coded in artificial chromosomes.

In genetic algorithms, the chromosome is a data structure that represents one of the possible solutions in the problem's search space. The chromosomes are submitted to an evolutionary process made of: inheritance, mutation, selection, and crossover (also called recombination). After several cycles of evolution the population should be comprised of the most apt individuals. One of the possible stop criteria is the number of generations, represented by the number of evolution cycles.

A basic pseudocode for genetic algorithms is provided in Figure 15.

```
t ← 0; // indicates the first generation
initialize the population of individuals;
evaluate the fitness of each individual in the population
while a stopping criterium is not satisfied
begin
      Select best-ranking individuals to reproduce
      Breed new generation through crossover and/or mutation (genetic operations) and
give birth to offspring
      Evaluate the individual fitnesses of the offspring
      Replace worst ranked part of population with offspring
      t ← t + 1; // indicates the next evolved population
end.
```

Fig. 15. Basic pseudocode for Genetic Algorithms.

The Adaptive M-Learning may use this technique to look for the learning objects best adapted to the student's and to the mobile device's characteristics. However, the initialization of the population and the choice of a stopping criterium are complicating elements.

5.3 Ants Colony Optimization

Dorigo and his colleagues (Dorigo & Stützle, 2004) proposed a new multi-agent heuristic approach, named Ant Algorithm, in the beginning of the years 90. They showed that the ants behavior of following a pheromone track deposited by them could be used to solve optimization problems.

The Ant algorithm, that has been originally applied to the travel salesman problem, has been extended and modified by several researchers and then applied to other optimization and search problems.

The Ant Algorithm modifications resulted in the Ant Colony Optimization meta-heuristic.

The basic idea of the Ant Colony Optimization is that a large number of simple and artificial agents are able to build good solutions for hard combinatorial optimization problems by means of low level communications.

If an ant has to choose among different paths, those that were previously the most chosen by other ants, therefore with a high level of pheromone deposited on them, have a higher probability of being chosen again.

The artificial ants are implemented as parallel processes with the objective of building a problem's solution using an algorithm guided by a combination of: artificial pheromone; data of the problem; a heuristic function to decide between its continuation or ending.

The Adaptive M-Learning has to implement a search process with a high degree of complexity, as the learning objects' repository has dynamic characteristics that periodically modify the quantity of objects. However, the Ants Colony Optimization employs simple and artificial elements, the artificial ants, that working together can find good solutions for different kinds of problems (Dorigo & Stützle, 2004).

This technique is highly ranked to be used in the adaptation algorithm, but the determination of what will be used as pheromone is a difficult task.

5.4 Graphs Theory: a New Paths Algebra

In (Herman, 2008) a new paths algebra over directed and weighted graphs has been proposed. It has been used to solve the problems of finding the best path between a pair of source and destination nodes and the convergence of hop-by-hop mono and multi-constraint routing algorithms.

This new algebra defines a mathematical structure $(M, F, S, \leq_{ML})$, where:

- M is a set of routing metrics that, according to an optimization strategy, can represent any attribute or characteristic to be analyzed to choose the best path in a network;
- F is a set of metrics combination functions;
- S is a set of binary operations, i. e., an operation between two elements, that are applied to the value of the combined metrics along a path; and
- $\leq_{ML}$ is a multi-dimensional lexical ordering relation used to order the different existing paths between two nodes in a network.

The new paths algebra can be applied to solve some important problems, as for example, the problem of finding the best path as function of the physical impairments in a DWDM (Dense Wavelength Division Multiplexing) optical network, with automatic configuration of wavelengths and power adjustment, in which the power adjustment is limited by the specifications of the network's transmitters and receivers.

The implementation of the adaptation algorithm for the Adaptive M-Learning can be described as a problem of search of learning objects that are most adequate to the student's and to mobile device's characteristics. It is possible to model the problem as a directed weighted graph in which we want to find the best paths. According to this approach, the new paths algebra may be an interesting alternative.

6. Example of a Typical Situation

Assume that a Computer Science student traveling by bus during two hours decided to study the subject "Stack", related to the "Data Structures" course. To do so, he/she will use his/her cellular phone, model "LG Shine SLIM ME770d", that has the flash liteTM 2.0 installed, has 110 MB of memory available and can visualize documents in PDF and PPT. In addition to that, also assume that there are three objects in the Learning Objetcs Repository concerning the subject "Stack", stored according to the SCORM 1.2 standard (Scorm, 2004) and that can be accessed by this cellular phone model, as illustrated in Table 3.

ADL SCORM 1.2		Objects		
Number	**Name**	**Object 1**	**Object 2**	**Object 3**
1.0	General			
1.2	Title	Stack	Stack	Stack
1.6	Keywords	Stack, Push, Pop	Stack, Push, Pop	Stack, Push, Pop
4.0	Technical			
4.1	Format	ppt	flash lite	pdf
4.2	Size	102400	97280	51200
4.4	Requirement			
4.4.1	Type	Operating System	Browser	Operating System
4.4.2	Name	MS-Windows	Internet Explorer	Multi-OS
4.4.6	Other Platform Requirements	Powerpoint viewer, min 100MB memory	Player Flash Lite^{TM} 2, min 100MB memory	Acrobat reader, min 50MB memory
4.4.7	Duration	PT	PT 0h:30m	PT
5.0	Educational			
5.1	Interactivity Type	Mixed	Active	Expositive
5.2	Learning Resource Type	Slide	Simulation	Lecture
5.3	Interactivity Level	Medium	Very high	Very low
5.5	Intended End User Role	Learner	Learner	Learner
5.8	Difficulty	Easy	Very easy	Medium
5.9	Typical Learning Time	PT1h:55m	PT1h:20m	PT2h:40m
5.11	Language	PT	PT	PT

Table 3. Part of the ADL SCORM 1.2 metadata for three examples of learning objects about the subject "Stack".

Consider that the following data have been sent to the Adaptation Module:

- Technology Module's **Technology Information**: t = [100, alphanumerical, 176x220, WAP GPRS USB Bluetooth, Windows Mobile 5.0, 112640, Flash Java Vídeo MMS SMS];
- Performance Module's **Learner Performance Information**: lp = [ST_01, CCP_DS, Stack, e, [ ], e, 0];
- Knowledge Module's **Learner Knowledge Information**: lki = [ST_01, CCP_DS, Stack, e];
- Learning Styles Module's **Learner Style Information**: lsi = [ST_01, 0, 2, 1, 1];
- Learner and Courses Module's **Learner and Courses Information**: lcinf = [CCP_DS, (..., [Stack, e, [Stack, Push, Pop, Data Structure], PT3h:00m], ...)];
- Teacher Adaptation Rules Module's **Teacher Adaptation Rules Information**: tari = [CCP_DS, ANY, 1, 1, 1, 1].

Considering that the teacher has allowed access to the content by means of any type of media (informed by the Teacher Adaptation Rules Information), due to the characteristics of the mobile device (informed by the Technology Information) and, according to Fig. 11, given the availability of n objects (Object List = object 1, object 2,... , object n) in the repository, the Technology Adaptation would select the (object 1, object 2 and object 3) objects of Table 3.
If we consider the student's learning style/knowledge/performance (**Learner Performance Information**, **Learner Knowledge Information**, **Learner Style Information** and **Learner and Courses Information**) and the adaptation rules provided by the teacher (**Teacher Adaptation Rules Information**), and that the student has not any specific preference as midia and format are concerned, the object 2 would be selected (**Content Information**), because it is the only one that meets all requirements..

7. Discussion and Conclusions

In this chapter, it has been presented a proposal of a M-Learning environment where it is possible to identify three blocks in its architecture, namely: the student's and mobile device's; the server that is responsible for the learning objects adaptation; the teacher's.
This architecture comprises several modules and deals with aspects as mobile device technology, pre-acquired knowledge, learning style and student's performance. It also allows the teacher to influence the adaptation rules. All modules have been described along the variables manipulated by each of them.
In addition, it has been reported a comparison between alternatives concerning optimization techniques and computing intelligence that can be employed in the implementation of the Adaptation Module's algorithm. To illustrate how the Adaptive M-Learning works, an example of a typical situation has been described.
In summary, this architecture allows to build:

- a flexible environment, that enables the customization of learning objects mounting and obtention for a given course, and comprising several aspects of adaptation;
- an environment with "intelligence" to infer the need and suggest to the student a reinforcement of some topic of study.

At the time of writing this chapter the Adaptive M-Learning environment was an on-going research project. In order to have a complete environment, it was necessary to implement an algorithm using the reported optimization techniques and evaluate their complexities. It was also necessary to develop a simulator to illustrate how this environment works.

8. References

Amazonas, J. R. A. (2005). Alpha-elements generation modeling in Web learning environments. In: Global Congress on Engineering and Technology Education, Proceedings of GCETE'2005, v. 1, pp. 100-103, ISBN 85-89549-18-6, Santos, 2005, COPEC, Santos.

Bittencourt, J. R. & Osório, F. S. (2002). FuzzyF - Fuzzy Logic Framework: Uma Solução Software Livre para o Desenvolvimento, Ensino e Pesquisa de Aplicações de Inteligência Artificial Multiplataforma. In: III Workshop sobre Software Livre, Porto Alegre, 2002, Anais do III Workshop sobre Software Livre, Porto Alegre.

Dorigo, M. & Stützle, T. (2004). Ant Colony Optimization, MIT Press, ISBN 0-262-04219-3 Cambridge, MA.

Felder, M. R. & Silverman, L. (1988). Learning and Teaching Styles in Engineering Education. In: Engineering Education, 78, 7, pp. 674-681.

Gwiazda, T. D. (2006). Genetic Algorithms Reference Vol.1 Crossover for single-objective numerical optimization problems, Tomasz Gwiazda, ISBN 83-923958-3-2, Lomianki, Poland.

Herman, W. P. (2008). Formulação algébrica para a modelagem de algoritmos de roteamento multi-restritivo hop-by-hop, Ph.D. dissertation, Polytechnic School of São Paulo University, 2008, 206p.

Herrmann, N. (1990). The Creative Brain, Brain Books, Lake Lure, North Carolina.

Kolb, D.A. (1984). Experiential Learning: Experience as the Source of Learning and Development, Prentice-Hall, ISBN 0-13-29561-0, New Jersey, USA.

Kwon, O.; Im, G. P. & Lee, K. C. (2007). MACE-SCM: A multi-agent and case-based reasoning collaboration mechanism for supply chain management under supply and demand uncertainties, Expert Systems with Applications: An International Journal, v. 33, 3, October, 2007, pp. 690 - 705. ISSN 0957-4174.

Mcalister, M. J. & Xie, P. H. (2005). Using a PDA for Mobile Learning, Proceedings of the IEEE International Workshop on Wireless and Mobile Technologies in Education (WMTE´05), 3pp, ISBN 0-7695-2385-4, Japan, November, 2005, IEEE Computer Society.

Mermelsein, B. & Tal, E. (2005). Using Cellular Phones in Higher Education: Mobile Access to Online Course Materials, Proceedings of the IEEE International Workshop on Wireless and Mobile Technologies in Education (WMTE´05), 3pp, ISBN 0-7695-2385-4, Japan, November, 2005, IEEE Computer Society.

Musa, D. L. & Oliveira, J. P. M. (2004). Sharing Learner Information through a Web Services-based Learning Architecture WISM 2004, Riga, Latvia, June.

Myers, I. B. & McCaulley, M. H. (1985). Manual: A Guide to the Development and Use of the Myers-Briggs Type Indicator (2nd ed.), Consulting Psychologists Press, ISBN 0-89106-027-8, Palo Alto, CA.

Oliveira, I. C. A. (2003). A Construção de um Protótipo de Ambiente de Aprendizagem Utilizando Servlets e JSP, Dissertation, IPT-SP, March, 2003, 92p.

Oliveira, I. C. A.; Araújo JR. C. F. & Ledón, M. F. P. (2003). Objetos de Aprendizagem pra o Ensino de Programação em Engenharia e Computação, In: III International Conference on Engineering and Computer Education (ICECE 2003), Santos, March, v. 1.

Oliveira, L. R. & Medina, R. D. (2007). Desenvolvimento de Objetos de Aprendizagem para Dispositivos Móveis: uma nova abordagem que contribui para a educação, RENOTE - Revista Novas Tecnologias na Educação, v. 5, n. 1, Julho, 2007, Porto Alegre, CINTED/UFRGS

Peña, C. I.; Marzo, J. L.; Rosa, J.L. & Fabregat, R. (2002). Un sistema de tutoría inteligente adaptativo considerando estilos de aprendizaje. 6o Congreso iberoamericano de Informática educativa IE-2002, Vigo, España.

Pesty, S. & Webber, C. (2004) The Baghera multiagent learning environment: an educational community of artificial and human agents, Journal of CEPIS (Council of European Professional Informatics Societies), v. 5, n.4, August, 2004, p.40-44. ISSN 1684-5285.

Revieu, A.; Smeureanu, I. & Dardala, M. (2008). Content Adaptation in Mobile Multimedia System for M-Learning, In: 7th International Conference on Mobile Business - ICMB'08, Spain, v. 1, pp. 305-313.

Sampson, D.; Karagiannidis, C. & Cardinali, F. (2002). An Architecture for Web-Based e-Learning Promoting Re-usable Adaptive Educational e-Content, Educational Technology & Society Journal of International Forum of Educational Technology & Society and IEEE Computer Society Learning Technology Task Force, v. 5, n.4, October, 2002, pp. 27-37, ISSN 1436-4522, Special Issue on Innovations in Learning Technologies.

Scorm. (2004). Shareable Content Object Reference Model 2004 3rd Edition, ADL (Advanced Distributed Learning). Note http://www.adlnet.org/scorm.

Silveira, R. A. & Vicari, R. M. (2002). Developing Distributed Intelligent Learning Environment with JADE - Java Agents for Distance Education Framework, In: Intelligent Tutoring Systems 2002, Springer-Verlag, pp. 105–118, ISBN 3-540-43750-9.

Tavares, R., Luna, G. (2003). Mapas Conceituais: Uma ferramenta pedagógica na consecução de currículo. I Colóquio Internacional de Políticas Curriculares, November, Brazil.

Tidia Ae. (2009). Tecnologia da Informação no Desenvolvimento da Internet Avançada - Aprendizado Eletrônico. Note http://tidia-ae.usp.br/portal.

Trifonova, A. & Ronchetti, M. (2006). Mobile Learning: Is Anytime + Anywhere = Always Online?, Proceedings of the Sixth International Conference on Advanced Learning Technologies (ICALT ´06), ISBN 0-7695-2632-2, Kerkrade, July, 2006, 5pp, IEEE Computer Society.

Vicari, R. M.; Ovalle, D. A. & Jiménez, J. A. (2007). ALLEGRO: Teaching/Learning Multi-Agent Environment using Instructional Planning and Cases-Based Reasoning (CBR), CLEI Eletronic Journal, v. 10, n. 1, p. 4, June, 2007, ISSN 0717- 5000.

Vicari, R. M.; Flores, C. D.; Seixas, L.; Gluz, J. C. & Coelho, H. (2008). AMPLIA: A Probabilistic Learning Environment, International Journal of Artificial Intelligence in Education, IOS Press, v. 18. n. 4, pp 347-373, 2008, ISSN 1560-4292.

Zadeh, L. A. (1965). Fuzzy Sets, Information and Control, No. 8, pp. 338-353.

5

Dynamic Mathematical Learning Tools: Does It Work For Malaysian Classroom Learners?

Rohani Ahmad Tarmizi,
Ahmad Fauzi Mohd Ayub and Kamariah Abu Bakar
Institute for Mathematical Research,
University Putra Malaysia
Malaysia

1. Introduction

This is a very exciting time in the development of the educational tool because of recent breakthroughs in technology which are making mobile computing devices ever smaller, powerful, robust, affordable and practicable. In Malaysian schools, we have already seen considerable developments in the educational use of Information and Communication and Technology (ICT) to support classroom teaching of mathematics with nearly all teachers having access to laptops, data projectors and the Internet, and also accessible to mathematical softwares as well as the use of handheld graphing calculators. Currently, Malaysia is in full gear to steer its economy towards a knowledge-based society which also calls for sustained, productivity-driven growth and technologically literate workforce prepared to participate fully in the global economy of the 21st century. In line with this vision, Malaysia's National Philosophy of Education calls for „developing the potentials of individuals in a holistic and integrated manner, so as to produce individuals who are intellectually, spiritually, emotionally, and physically balanced and harmonious."
Much transformation has taken place, from the Smart School project to providing computer laboratories to thousands of schools in both rural and urban areas of the country. In tandem, other ICT-related projects which involved the training of teachers, school administrators and other school staff and innovative projects like the use of electronic books, e-learning, online learning and introduction of mathematical softwares and graphing calculators were rolled out to schools in the country.

2. Role of ICT in Mathematics Teaching and Learning

The role of ICT in mathematics education faces multiple challenges with the influx of new technologies introduced in the education system. Hence, computer-based technologies are now common in mathematics classrooms and the integration of these technologies into teaching and learning mathematics is supported by government policy in most countries. In Malaysia, the use of technology in teaching and learning of mathematics has consistently been one of the major emphases in Malaysian Integrated Curriculum for Secondary School

Mathematics. The concept of ICT in Malaysian Educaton System includes systems that enable information gathering, management, manipulation, access and communication in various forms. This means that ICT is used as an enabler to reduce the digital gap between the schools.

Teachers are encouraged to use the latest technology to help students understand mathematical concepts in depth and to enable them to explore mathematical ideas (Curriculum Development Centre, Ministry of Education, Malaysia, 2005). This emphasis is congruent with the NCTM's Technological Principle which states that, "Technology is essential in teaching and learning mathematics, it influences the mathematics that is taught and enhances students' learning" (NCTM, 2000, p. 24). The emphasis on integrating technology in the teaching and learning of mathematics is parallel with the aim of the mathematics curriculum: to develop individuals that are able to face challenges in everyday life that arise due to the advancement of science and technology (Curriculum Development Centre, Ministry of Education, Malaysia, 2005). However, technology does not replace the need for all students to learn and master the basic mathematical skills. Without the use of technologies such as the calculators or other electronic tools, students should still be able to add, subtract, multiply and divide efficiently. The mathematic curriculum therefore requires the use of technology to focus on the acquisition of mathematical concepts and knowledge rather than merely doing calculation.

There are many kinds of technology that are considered relevant to school mathematics which range from very powerful computer software such as Mathematica, Maple, and MathLab to much powerless technologies. For example, based on the Mathematics Curriculum Specification of Integrated Curriculum for Secondary School, the use of technology such as calculators, computers, educational software, websites in the Internet and relevant learning packages was highlighted as tools that can help to upgrade the pedagogical approach and thus promote the understanding of mathematical concepts in teaching and learning (Curriculum Development Centre, Ministry of Education, Malaysia, 2005). In addition, the application of these teaching resources will also help students absorb ideas, be creative, feel confident and be able to work independently or in group. School books are supplemented and complemented with CDs to enhance and enrich students understanding and make mathematics a fun-to-learn subject. The books were also organised with systematic features including exposes students to use of scientific and graphing calculators to obtain or check answer as well as introducing simple computer programming. Supplementary learning materials such as multimedia galleries, interactive activities, E-Tests and E-Maths Glossary were also provided to enrich and reinforce learning. Furthermore, the net-links materials were also attached at the end of each topic to encourage students to explore and gather more information as well as do research and to use ICT.

Prepelita-Raileanu (2008) suggested that teachers are to be educated concurrently with the increase use of information, communication technology (ICT). The role of teachers as organizers and distributor of the teaching have to be developed concurrently with the integration of ICT in any educational programmes. However much has to be explored and ICT, as any other tools in teaching and learning must be utilized and adapted to serve educational goals. Technology indeed has changed the way classrooms operate, integrating multimedia during learning, online accessibility thus making teaching and learning more interactive and participatory (Butler, 2008).

The rapid progress of technology has influenced the teaching and learning of mathematics. Many efforts are being made to enhance the learning experiences for students in learning mathematics. In the traditional teaching of mathematics, students are passive recipients when teacher passes complete information to them. Meanwhile, with the integration of technology such as computers and calculators, students are encouraged to get deeper understanding of concepts. Furthermore, technology can also develop a better understanding of abstract mathematical concepts by their visualization or graphic representation where it shows the relationships between objects and their properties. By having deeper understanding of concepts, this will increase the ability of the students when working with mathematics knowledge. Findings from Abu Bakar, Tarmizi, Ayub, Yunus (2008), also confirmed that students learning mathematics with the integration of technology were found more enthused and were enjoying their lessons more than students who had undergone the traditional approach. Consistently on students' level of avoidance, the mean of the group using technology was lower than that those perceived by the traditional group. This indicated that the technology group would not avoid using the software during mathematical learning activity.

Technological tools have been proven to be a very important aspect of the teaching learning process. Numerous studies show that the quality can be significantly enhanced when the tools are integrated with teaching. Research conducted showed that technological tools can enhance critical thinking, the level of conceptualization, and problem solving capacity. This novel technology is supposed to add value to education and to support more effective pedagogy by providing knowledge for learners and by enhancing communication that promotes learning.

The issue now being addressed is that does providing hands-on access for students to ICT in their normal mathematics lessons improved learning among these secondary students. These include the use computer softwares to provide mathematical modeling with 2D geometry and algebra; the use of 3D geometry software to develop visualization and modeling in space; and the use of hand-held devices with data-loggers in capturing and analyzing for experimental data. This paper sets out to exemplify the importance of educational use of ICT which can be to stimulate students' excitement and interest in dry and difficult subject like mathematics.

3. Use of Graphing Calculators

The use of technological props in mathematics teaching and learning namely the graphing calculators may benefit students and hence could materialise the Malaysian national agenda of introducing technology in the classroom. However, many teachers and parents believe that using technology may deprive students from employing their brains to perform computations and algebraic manipulations.

In Malaysia, calculators were strictly prohibited at both the primary and lower secondary levels before the year 2002. However, in 2002, usage of calculator was introduced for Form Two and Three students in lower secondary mathematics curriculum (Curriculum Development Centre, Ministry of Education, Malaysia, 2005). Currently, the usage of calculators is still prohibited in the primary grades while the usage of scientific calculators is prohibited in Form One. The latest reform in the Malaysian Secondary School Integrated Mathematics Curriculum calls for the need to integrate information technology in teaching and learning of mathematics. In response to this call, mathematics teachers and students are now encouraged to use scientific and graphing calculators in the upper secondary mathematics classroom. Moreover, currently, scientific calculators are already allowed to be used at the Malaysian Certificate of Education examination level (Curriculum Development Centre, Ministry of Education, Malaysia, 2005).

The use of graphing calculators in teaching and learning enable various kinds of guided explorations to be undertaken. For example, students can investigate the effects of changing parameters of a function on the shape of its graph. They can also explore the relationships between gradients of pairs of lines and the lines themselves. These activities would have been too difficult to attempt without technology. Exploratory activity in mathematics may facilitate an active approach to learning as opposed to a passive approach where students just sit back passively listening to the teacher. This creates an enthusiastic learning environment. This clearly shows the application of constructivist learning environment.

Graphing calculators also offer a method of performing computations and algebraic manipulations that is more efficient and precise than paper-and-pencil method alone (Waits & Demana, 2000). Examples include finding the solutions of simultaneous equations or determine the equation of a straight line that is passing through two points. The mathematical concepts underpinning those procedures are rich and important for understanding. However, students often seem to put more effort in calculation and correspondingly less to making sense of the problems. Both attention to concepts and skill would be desirable in mathematics learning.

Rather than just the development of mechanical and computational skills, graphing calculators also allow for cultivation of analytical adeptness and proficiency in complex thought process (Pomerantz, 1997). Problems representing real-world situation and data with complicated numbers can also be addressed. This would offer new opportunities for students to encounter mathematical ideas not in the curriculum at present. With appropriate use of graphing calculator, students can avoid time-consuming, tedious procedures and devote a great deal of time concentrating on understanding concepts, developing higher order thinking skills, and learning relevant applications.

Jones (2000) argued that when students work with graphing calculator, they have potential to form an intelligent partnership, as graphing calculator can undertake significant cognitive processing on behalf of the user. This argument is in line with the distributed cognition and cognitive load theories. Distribution of cognition such that the larger part of cognitive process is taken over by the graphing calculator thus allowing learners to focus more on problem solving. From the cognitive load perspective, the focus of learning is to acquire problem solving schema rather than to acquire automation of mental arithmetic per se that distracts the real aim of problem solving. The distracting activities might exhaust learners' mental resources such that these activities will impose extraneous cognitive load and hence will be detrimental for learning. Therefore, instructional strategy that integrates the use of graphing calculator seems logical to reduce extraneous and increase germane cognitive load. This is because, as a result of distribution of cognition, graphing calculator offloads part of the cognitive process that reduces extraneous cognitive load, and this allows the learners to focus on more processing tool relevant for learning. The tool will help free the mental resources to enable them to acquire the necessary schemas and automation, or in other words the strategy simultaneously increases the germane cognitive load.

The formation of an intelligent partnership between the user and the graphing calculator also provides a crucial aspect of constant monitoring and checking of information (Jones, 2000). This is to make sure that the solution produced by the tool is consistent with the user's knowledge and understanding of the problem at hand. Indeed, with intelligent technology like the graphing calculator, the potential exists for the partnership to be far more intelligent than human alone (Salomon et al., 1991). The fact that learners work intelligently with the tool can be considered as helping learners to reflect upon their cognitive processing activities during learning which improve their metacognitive awareness levels and hence reduces cognitive load of the learning activities.

4. Use of Autograph Softwares

Autograph is another technology which is a dynamic software for teaching calculus, algebra and coordinate geometry. Its environment has 2D and 3D graphing capabilities for topics such as transformations, conic sections, vectors, slope, and derivatives. In real-time, users can observe how functions, graphs, equations, and calculations. Autograph can be used for drawing statistical graph, functions, and vector and for transforming shapes. It also enables users to change and animate graphs, shapes or vectors already plotted to encourage understanding of concept. In mathematics class the use of mathematical software enable students to visualize and further understand mathematical phenomenon in real life.

Teaching by integrating Autograph in schools might increase the effectiveness and the quality of teaching. As mathematics class needs lots of interaction, reasoning, observation the above view clearly indicates that interactive software like Autograph can be useful in teaching and learning mathematics effectively. Use of Autograph help teachers in making students attentive towards the interactive whiteboard and acts as a medium of interaction among students or between teacher and the students with rapid responses. Teacher can attract the whole class to the interactive whiteboard just by using the mouse and keyboard, save the work and can be viewed later on. These facts clearly indicates that Autograph is an extremely useful educational tool for both mathematics teachers and students which help teachers to present the content for the whole class easily and students understand better due to its visual demonstration.

The use of Autograph allows learners to acquire skills and knowledge in using the computers whilst concurrently explore the potentials of the software (Nordin, Zakaria, Embi & Mohd Yassin, 2008; Ayub, Tarmizi, Abu Bakar & Yunus, 2008). Their findings indicated that integration of GSP in teaching mathematics can be aided by the module developed and that learning of graphs and functions through utilization of technology simplified learning and increase students understanding. Specifically, Stacey (2007) contended that the use of software in mathematical learning enhanced the understanding of mathematical concepts related to variables and functions as well as provides motivation for the learning of Algebra.

5. Use of Geometer's Sketchpad

The teaching and learning of geometry utilizing dynamic geometry softwares have been explicitly indicated in the new Malaysian secondary school syllabus implemented in 2003. In the mathematics syllabus, teachers were recommended to utilize the Geometer's Sketchpad (GSP) software licensed to be used in the Malaysian schools. It was developed partly under the Geometry Visual Project conducted in Pennsylvania and sponsored by the National Science Foundation. Geometer's Sketchpad (GSP) is a software programme that revolutionized the teaching and studying of mathematics especially in geometry. It is a computer software system for creating, exploring, and analyzing a wide range of mathematics concepts in the field of algebra, geometry, trigonometry, calculus, and other areas (Geometer's Sketchpad, Reference Manual, 2001). It is a dynamic geometry construction and exploration tool, which can make an enormous difference in the students' learning of Mathematics. It is easy to use and encourages a process of discovery in which students first visualize and analyze a problem and then make conjectures before attempting a proof. It is versatile enough to be used from primary six onwards through university undergraduates studies. Subject of mathematics that are relevant to be used with GSP are algebra, geometry, pre-calculus and calculus.

The GSP lets the user explore simple, as well as highly complex, theorems and relations in geometry (Giamatti, 1995) and has the ability to record students' constructions as scripts. The most useful aspect of scripting ones' constructions is that students can test whether their constructions work in general or whether they have discovered a special case. In addition, the GSP software provides the process of learning and teaching in a more creative way (Finzer and Bennett, 1995).

The purpose of this study is to investigate the instructional efficiency index of using graphing calculator (TI-84 Plus) and Autograph Software in teaching and learning of mathematics on Form Four secondary school students' in learning Quadratic Functions. Specifically, the objective of this study mainly is to compare the effects of utilizing the three technologies i.e. the graphing calculator, Autograph software and Geometer's Sketchpad on various performance measures in learning of Quadratic Functions topic.

6. Methodology

Experimental design was used for this study with students selected at random and assigned to four groups. The experimental group underwent learning using GSP, Autograph and graphing calculator technology while the control group underwent learning using conventional instructional strategy. Four phases were conducted, firstly the introduction to the software to be used by each particular group, followed by induction to the Quadratic Functions topic. Thirdly, students undergo the teaching and learning phase with the integration of the technology and Learning Activity Module. (see example of lesson activity using graphing calculator in Appendix 1) Finally sudents undergo the testing phase to examine the effects of the intervention provided during the learning sessions. An Achievement Test, the Paas Mental Effort Rating Scale and questionnaire were administered to the students. The data were analyzed using ANOVA and post-hoc analyses.

6.1 Population and Sample of Study

The target population of this study was Form Four students in National Secondary School in Malaysia. The samples selected for this study were Form Four students from two schools. The students were brought to the university to participate in the learning sessions. They were assigned to either of the four groups whereby group one were following the graphing calculator mode of learning, group two followed the Autograph learning mode, group three utilize the GSP and the fourth group was the conventional learning group.

6.2 Procedures

Four phases were conducted. In the first phase, the treatment groups were first introduced to the software. Each student in GC group was provided with one graphing calculator each. Students in Autograph group were provided with one computer installed with Autograph software whilst the third group was provided with GSP during the learning phase. In this phase, the students were required to explore and get familiar with the graphing calculator buttons and its functions and same also for the Autograph and GSP groups.
Then in second phase, students were introduced to the basic concept of the Quadratic Functions topic. In the teaching and learning using software phase, students were thought with constructivist approach where they were required to use exploratory and discovery learning on the topic. During the teaching and learning phase, students were given assessment questions to evaluate extent of short term learning. At the end of the learning or treatment session, students were given an achievement test. Teaching and learning phase for the GSP and Autograph group were same with the GC group. The control group's students were also guided by the same instructional format with one exception where the method used will not incorporate the use of TI-84 Plus graphing calculator, GSP and Autograph software. To assess mental load, students were required to state their mental effort expended or used for each question they answered in assessment and achievement test based on Paas Mental Effort Rating Scale.

6.3 Instruments

6.3.1 Mental Effort Rating Scale

Mental effort refers to the total amount of controlled cognitive processing in which a subject is engaged (Paas and Tuovinen, 2004). Mental effort is measured by a nine-point symmetrical category scale where the perceived mental effort is translated into a numerical value. Mental effort indicated the perceived amount of mental effort a student expended when solving mathematics problems given in the learning assessments during the acquisition phase and the posttest. It has 9- point symmetrical Likert scale measurement on which subject rates their mental effort used in performing a particular learning task.This is indicated by circled responses to the nine point symmetrical scale shown by students on the Paas Mental Effort Rating Scale (PMERS) given at the end of each question on acquisition as well as test phase.

6.3.2 Instructional Efficiency Index

This is a term which shows the relationship between learning and test (mental) effort and performance. In the study by Paas and Tuovinen (2004), mental effort (E) was measured on a scale of 1 (very, very, low mental effort) to 9 (very, very, high mental effort) whereas performance (P) was measured as the percentage of correct answers. The relative condition efficiency (E) is then calculated as

$$E = \frac{P - E_L - E_T}{\sqrt{3}}$$

Where E_L is the learning effort and E_T, the test effort (Paas & Tuovinen, 2004).

6.3.3 Mathematical Knowledge/Performance

Currently, there is more interest in how students acquire knowledge, how procedural and conceptual knowledge are linked and the mutual benefits of this linkage. Conceptual knowledge is defined by Hiebert and Lefevre as knowledge that is rich in relationship. It can be thought of as a connected web of knowledge, a network in which students are able to apply and link mathematical relationships to a variety of problems. Conceptual knowledge is characterised by links and a unit of conceptual knowledge cannot be an isolated piece of information. Furthermore, they emphasised that a piece of information is part of conceptual knowledge only if the holder recognises its relationship to other pieces of information. Hiebert and Lefevre note the following example of conceptual knowledge such as the construction of a relationship between the algorithm for multi-digit subtraction and knowledge of the positional values of digits (place value).

It is also assumed that conceptual knowledge is stored in some form of relational representation, like schemas, semantic networks or hierarchies (Byrnes & Wasik, 1991). It can be largely verbalized and flexibly transformed through processes of inference and reflection due to its' abstract nature and the fact that it can be consciously accessed. Therefore, it is not only bound up with specific problems but also can be generalised for a variety of problem types in a domain (Baroody, 2003).

On the other hand, as defined by Hiebert and Lefevre (1986), procedural knowledge in mathematics is composed of two parts namely the formal language or symbol representational, of mathematics and the algorithms, or rules, for completing mathematical tasks. It means that procedural knowledge can be classified as structural knowledge and algorithmic knowledge. The former is knowledge related to the meaning and appropriate use of mathematical symbols. It implies only an awareness of superficial features, but not knowledge of meaning or underlying structure. For example, we can write the string $x+2=3$ for some integer x, however the notation $2+=x3$ doesn't give an appropriate mathematical statement that falls under the first type of procedural knowledge. The algorithmic knowledge refers to step-by-step instructions that define precisely how to complete mathematical tasks or exercises in a predetermined linear sequence. For example, students who are able to do the algorithm for determining the value of x in $x+2=3$ is said to have the second type of procedural knowledge.

Procedural knowledge can also be described as the knowledge of operators and the conditions under which these can be used to reach certain goals (Byrnes & Wasik, 1991). This type of knowledge to some degree is said to be automated as it enables people to solve problems quickly and efficiently (Sweller, 2004; Tarmizi & Sweller, 1988; Schneider & Stern, 2005; Hiebert & Carpenter, 1992). According to Johnson (2003), automatization is accomplished through practice and allows for a quick activation and execution of procedural knowledge. In addition, as compared to the application of conceptual knowledge, its application involves minimal conscious attention and few cognitive resources. The automated nature of procedural knowledge implies that it is not or only partly open to conscious inspection and hence can be hardly verbalised or transformed by higher mental processes.

7. Effects of Graphing Calculator, Autograph, GSP and Conventional Strategy on Overall Performance

The means, standard deviations of the performance variable are provided in Table 1. For all statistical analysis, the 5% level of significant was used throughout the paper. The mean overall test performance for the graphing calculator group was 15.54 (SD = 3.14) meanwhile the mean overall test performance for Autograph group was 10.72 (SD = 3.47), whilst the GSP group was 11.78 (SD = 4.10) and the mean overall test performance for conventional group was 13.03 (SD = 3.65).

The one way ANOVA test results showed that there was a significant difference in mean test performance between GC group, Autograph group and conventional group, [$F(2,125) = 19.97$, $p<0.05$]. Further, planned comparison test showed that mean overall test performance of GC group was significantly higher from those two groups followed by conventional group and Autograph group have lowest mean. This finding indicated that the GC strategy group had performed better in test phase than the conventional group and Autograph.

Group	N	M	SD	SE
GC	42	15.54	3.14	.48
Autograph	39	10.72	3.47	.59
GSP	45	11.78	4.10	.54
Control	47	13.03	3.65	.53

Table 1. Comparison of overall performance

8. Effects of Graphing calculator, Autograph, GSP and Conventional strategy on Mental Effort

Means and standard deviations of the mental load expended during problem solving of each of the test question were obtained and as stated in Table 2. The mean mental effort during test phase of the GSP group was 5.61 and was the highest compared to mean mental effort of the Autograph group (M=4.95, SD = 1.88), followed by GC group (M=4.79, SD = 1.48) meanwhile the mean mental effort during test phase for conventional group was 4.46 (SD = 1.48). The one way ANOVA test results showed that there was no significant difference in mean mental effort during test phase between GC group and conventional group, ($F(2,98)= .709$, $p>0.05$). Further, comparison test showed that mean mental effort during test phase of GC group was lower than those of the Autograph group. This findings indicated that the GC strategy group had benefited from the learning sessions hence their mental effort was lower compared to the Autograph group.

Variables	Group	N	M	SD	SE
Mental effort (Test phase)	GC	38	4.79	1.48	.24
	GSP	45	5.61	2.03	.54
	Autograph	35	4.95	1.88	.32
	Control	28	4.46	1.48	.28

Table 2. Comparison of mental effort

9. Comparison of 2-D Instructional Efficiency Index of Utilization of Graphing Calculator, GSP, Autograph and Conventional Strategy

Table 3 shows results for evaluating the hypotheses 'There is significant difference in instructional efficiency index on groups using graphing calculator technology, Autograph and GSP technology and the conventional method in learning mathematics. The mean 2-D instructional efficiency for the GC group was .45 (SD = .84) and the mean 2-D instructional efficiency for control group was .22 (SD = .97) meanwhile the mean 2-D instructional efficiency for Autograph group was negative .51 (SD = 1.22) and the GSP group was negative .52 (SD = 1.26).

The results of a one way ANOVA test showed that there was significant difference on mean 2-D instructional efficiency index ($F(2, 98) = 7.047$, $p<0.05$) between the GC group, Autograph group and the conventional group. The planned comparison test on mean 2-D instructional condition efficiency index showed that the mean for GC group was significantly higher than conventional group followed by Autograph group. This suggests that learning mathematics by integrating the use of GC was more efficient than using conventional strategy and Autograph mode of learning.

Variables	Group	N	M	SD	SE
2-D instructional efficiency	GC	38	.45	.88	.1428
	Autograph	35	-.51	1.23	.2072
	GSP	45	-.52	1.26	.2213
	Control	28	.16	1.02	.1930

Table 3. Comparison on instructional efficiency

10. Effects of Graphing calculator, Autograph, GSP and Conventional strategy on Other Performance Variables

As can be seen from Table 4, the GC group (M=6.98, SD=.154) has a highest mean for the number of problem solved followed by Autograph group (M=6.64, SD=1.203) and the conventional group (M=6.28, SD=1.077). The one way ANOVA test showed significant differences, $[F(2,125) = 6.223, p<0.05]$. This implies that both groups solved more problems compared to the conventional group during solving the test problems.

The GC group (M=10.12, SD=3.06) has a highest mean for the total score of the conceptual knowledge followed by the conventional group (M=7.28, SD=3.63) and Autograph group (M=4.97, SD=3.24). Similar results were obtained from the total score of the conceptual knowledge, $[F(2,125) = 24.275, p < 0.05]$. This indicated that the GC, Autograph and the conventional groups were scoring differently based on the conceptual knowledge during the test phase. However, results obtained for the total score of the procedural knowledge showed no significant differences $[F(2,125) = 3.034, p> 0.05]$.

In learning mathematics, the relationship between concepts and procedures has been studied in order to gain better understanding in learners tendencies to learn algorithms by rote without developing any understanding of what they are doing (Hiebert, 1986). According to Hiebert and Lefevre (1986), the students' development of conceptual and procedural knowledge varies throughout their school years. In elementary school, the algorithm that students learn may not necessarily be connected to conceptual knowledge. They might develop the conceptual understanding of addition and subtraction through a story problem. However, this understanding may not be linked with the symbols used in arithmetic to describe the relationship between the numbers in the story. As students progress in schools, they are expected to learn more rules for manipulating symbols. Hence findings from this analysis indicated that both conceptual and procedural knowledge provide insights into learners understanding or performance. Since the GC group performed better than the other two groups, these findings may suggest that use of GC have impact on learning of algebra. Data analyses also indicated that there is significant difference in the total score of the test and number of error committed between GC and conventional group.

Variables	Group	N	M	SD	SE
No. of problems solved	GC	42	6.98	.154	.024
	Autograph	39	6.64	1.20	.193
	GSP	45	5.98	1.29	.233
	Control	47	6.28	1.08	.157
Total score of the conceptual knowledge	GC	42	10.12	3.06	.47
	Autograph	39	4.97	3.24	.52
	GSP	45	5.99	4.67	.65
	Control	47	7.28	3.63	.53
Total score of the procedural knowledge	GC	42	18.36	2.72	.42
	Autograph	39	16.92	3.86	.62
	GSP	45	18.40	1.39	.32
	Control	47	18.06	1.36	.19
Number of errors committed	GC	42	.79	.09	.09
	Autograph	39	2.29	2.87	.46
	GSP	45	1.95	1.54	.24
	Control	47	1.52	.90	.13

Table 4. Comparisons of selected variables

11. Conclusion

In this study, based on the 2-D instructional efficiency index calculation, utilizing graphing calculator was instructionally more efficient compared to conventional method and Autograph software. Use of GC had enhanced learning conditions with minimal extraneous cognitive load hence creating optimal learning condition.

Graphing calculators require students to apply their understanding of a concept so that it can be used effectively. There are many benefits using a handheld devices for instruction such as graphic calculator as reported by Ellington (2003). It was reported based on teachers' opinion that using handheld graphing calculator for instruction could increased time using technology, increased technology proficiency, student's motivation, collaboration and communication and individualized instruction.

Saurino et al. (1999) found that the use of graphing calculator technology provide students enjoyment to the use of technology, ease of portability and complete higher-level work with understanding. Meanwhile a study by Thiel and Alagic (2004) in three pre-calculus classes showed that students increased understanding of key concepts and ability to solve difficult problems when using graphing calculator. As they gain a deeper understanding of the material, students acquire the critical thinking and problem-solving skills they need to attain greater academic success.

A research conducted by Quesada and Maxwell (1994) found that students taught using the graphing calculator had significantly higher scores than those taught by traditional method. While Gage (2000) found that using graphics calculators had a significant effect on performance with functions and graphs for algebra students.

These findings suggested that in utilizing any technological tools, a comprehensive measures addressing issues of instructional efficiency is crucial especially when involving large scale and formal implementation of technology integration in teaching and learning. With systematic planning of instructions and good learning package, learning mathematics using graphing calculator and Autograph will give new view in mathematics teaching and learning. Therefore, this shows that dynamic software, particularly graphing calculator provide positive impact upon learners thus becoming potential tools in teaching mathematics at Malaysian secondary school level.

12. References

Abu Bakar, K, Tarmizi, R., Ayub, A. & Yunus, A. (2008). Exploring effect of utilizing Geometer Sketchpad on performance and mathematical thinking of secondary mathematics learners. Proceeding of the 7th WSEAS International Conference on Education and Educational Technology. Venice, Nov 21-23, 2008.

Ayub, A., Tarmizi, R., Abu Bakar, K, & Yunus, A. (2008). Perceived ease of use and usefulness of dynamic mathematical software: Experiences of Malaysian secondary students.Proceeding of the 7th WSEAS International Conference on Education and Educational Technology. Venice, Nov 21-23, 2008.

Alagic, M. (2003). Technology in the mathematic classroom : Conceptual orientation. The Journal of Computer In Mathematics and Science Teaching. 22(4). 381 - 399.

Bannert, M. (2002). Managing cognitive load - recent trends in cognitive load theory. *Learning and Instruction*. 12: 139 -146.

Baroody, A. J. (2003). The development of adaptive expertise and flexibility: The integration of conceptual knowledge and procedural knowledge. In A. J. Baroody & A. Dowker. *The Development of Arithmetic Concepts and Skills: Constructing Adaptive Expertise* (pp.1-33). Mahwah, NJ: Erlbaum.

Burill, G., Allison, J., Breaux, G., Kastberg, S., Leatham, K. & Sanchez, W. (2002). *Handheld Graphing Technology in Secondary Mathematics: Research Findings and Implications for Classroom Practice*. Dallas, TX: Texas Instruments Corp.

Butler, M. (2008). Professional Development for teachers using technology. Proceeding of the 7th WSEAS International Conference on Education and Educational Technology. Venice, Nov 21-23,2008.

Brynes, J. P., & Wasik, B.A.(1991). Role of conceptual knowledge in mathematical procedural learning. *Development psychology*, 27(5),777-786.

Camp, G., Paas, F., Rikers, R. & Van Merrienboer, J. J. G. (2001). Dynamic problem selection in air traffic control training: A comparison between performance, mental effort and mental efficiency. *Computers in Human Behavior*. 17: 575-595.

Chan, F. M. (2002). ICT in Malaysian schools: Policy and strategies. Paper presented at a *Workshop on the Promotion of ICT in Education to Narrow the Digital Divide*, 15-22 October. Tokyo Japan.

Curriculum Development Centre, Ministry of Education, Malaysia (2005). *Integrated Curriculum for Secondary School. Curriculum Specification, Mathematics Form 4.*

Ellington, A. J. (2003). A meta-analysis of the effects of calculators on students' achievement and attitude levels in precollege mathematics classes. *Journal for Research in Mathematics Education*. 34(5): 433

Finzer, W. F. & Bennett, D. S. (1995). From drawing to construction with the Geometer's Sketchpad.

Gage, J. (2002). Using the graphic calculator to form a learning environment for the early teaching of algebra. *The International Journal of Computer Algebra in Mathematics Education*. 9(1): 3-28.

Geometer's Sketchpad Reference Manual. (Fall 2001). Carlifornia: Key Curriculum Press.

Giamatti, C.(1995). Conjectures in Geometry and the Geometer's Sketchpad. Mathematics Teacher, Vol. 88,No. 6, p. 456-458.

Graham, A. T. & Thomas, M. O. J. (2000). Building a versatile understanding of algebraic variables with a graphic calculator. *Educational Studies in Mathematics*. 41(3): 265-282.

Hennessy, S. (2000). Graphing investigations using portable (palmtop) technology. *Journal of Computer Assisted Learning*, 17, 243- 258.

Heibert, J. (1986). *Conceptual and procedural knowledge: The case of mathematics.* Hillsdale, NJ: Lawrence Erlbaum.

Hiebert, J. & Carpenter, J.(1986). *Conceptual and Procedural Knowledge: The Case of Mathematics*. Hillsdale, NJ: Lawrence Erlbaum.

Heibert, J. & Leferve, p.(1986). Conceptual Procedural Knowledge in Mathematics: An Introductory Analysis. In Hiebert, J. (ed.), Conceptual and procedural Knowledge: the case of mathematics. New Jersey: Erlbaum.

Johnson, A. (2003). Procedural memory and skill acquisition. In I.B Weiner(Ed.), *Handbook of Psychology* (pp.449-523). Hoboken, NJ: Wiley.

Johnson, B. & Christensen, L. (2000). *Educational Research: Quantitative and Qualitative Approaches*. Boston: Allyn and Bacon.

Jones, P. (2000). Realizing the educational potential of the graphic calculator. In Edward. D. Laughbaum. *Hand-Held Technology in Mathematics and Science Education: A Collection of Papers*. Columbus, OH: The Ohio State University.

Kastberg, S. & Leatheam, K. (2005.) Research on graphing calculators at the secondary level: Implications for mathematics teacher education. *Contemporary Issues in Technology and Teacher Education*. 5(1): 25-37.

Merriweather, M. & Tharp, M. L. (1999). The effect of instruction with graphing calculators on how general mathematics students naturalistically solve algebraic problems. *Journal of Computers in Mathematics and Science Teaching.* 19(1), 7-22.

National Council of Teachers of Mathematics(2000). *Principles and Standards for School Mathematics*: Reston, VA: NCTM.

Nordin,N., Zakaria, E., Embi, M.A. & Mohd Yassin, R. (2008). Pedagogical usability of the Geometer Sketchpad Digital Module in the Mathematics teaching. Proceeding of the 7th WSEAS International Conference on Education and Educational Technology. Venice, Nov 21-23,2008.

Paas, F., Renkl, A., & Sweller, J. (2004). Cognitive load theory: Instructional implications of the interaction between information structures and cognitive architecture. *Instructional Science*.32: 1-8.

Prepelita-Raileanu, B. (2008). Learning and teaching in the digital age. Proceeding of the 7th WSEAS International Conference on Education and Educational Technology. Venice, Nov 21-23,2008.

Pomerantz, H. (1997). *The role of calculators in math education.* Dallas, Texas.Quesada, A.R. & Maxwell, M.E. (1994). The Effects of Using Graphing Calculators to Enhance College Students' performance in Pre Calculus. Educational Studies in Mathematics 27; 205-215, Kluwer Academic Publishers.

Saurino, D., Bouma, A., & Gunnoe, B. (1999). Sience Classroom management Techniques using graphing Calculator technology. A Collaborative teaching action research approach. Paper presented at the Annual meeting of the national association for research in Science Teaching. Boston, MA.

Quesada, A.R. & Maxwell, M.E. (1994). The Effects of Using Graphing Calculators to Enhance College Students' performance in Pre Calculus. Educational Studies in Mathematics 27; 205-215, Kluwer Academic Publishers.

Stacey, K. (2007). Using dynamic geometry software to motivate and assist problem solving in Algebra. Proceedings East Asia Regional Conference in Mathematics Education 4. Pulau Pinang, 18-22 Jun, 2007.

Thiel, R. & Alagic, M. (2004). Developing conceptual Understandings: Function and function related Concepts in Graphing Calculator Based Environment.

Salomon, G., D.N. Perkins & Globerson, T. (1991). Partners in cognition: Extending human intelligence with intelligent technologies. *Educational Reseacher* 20(3):2-9.

Schneider, M. & Stern, E. (2005). *Conceptual and Procedural Knowledge of a Mathematics Problem: Their Measurements and Their Causal Interrelations.* Retrieved 11 January 2006 from http://www.psych. unito.it/csc/cogsci/05/frame/talk/f610-schneider. pdf

Sweller, J. (2004). Instructional design consequences of an analogy between evolution by natural selection and human cognitive architecture. *Instructional Science.* 32: 9-31.

Tarmizi, R. A. & Sweller, J. (1988). Guidance during mathematical problem solving. *Journal of Educational Psychology.* 80(4): 424-436.

Paas, F. & Tuovinen, J. E. (2004). Exploring multidimensional approaches to the efficiency of instructional conditions. *Instructional Science.* 32: 133-152.

Waits, B.K., & Demana, F. (2000). Calculators in mathematics teaching and learning: past, present and future. *In Learning mathematics for a New Century: 2000 Yearbook,* ed.

M.J. Burke and F.R Curcio,p. 51-66. Reston, VA:National Council of Teachers Mathematics.

Appendix 1: Example of lesson activity using graphing calculator

Plotting graph of quadratic function f(x) = x^2

STEPS	INSTRUCTION	DISPLAY NOTES
1 To key in the function.	1. Press **Y=**	Y =
	2. Insert the function by pressing x^2	X,T,Θ,*n* ; x^2
3 To plot points on the graph.	3. Set the windows setting to ZDecimal. ♦ Press **ZOOM** ♦ Press **4**	ZOOM→ 4 : ZDecimal
4 To view the graph	4. To view overall of the graph ♦ Press WINDOW ♦ At Xmin , press -2 then press ▼ ♦ At Xmax , press 2 then press ▼▼ ♦ At Ymin, press -4 then press ▼ ♦ At Ymax, press 8 ♦ Press TRACE	WINDOW → Xmin = -2 Xmax = 2 Ymin = -4 Ymax = 8 → TRACE

On the return to Geometry in lecturing Technology

Francisco Mesa, Luis M. Marin and Antonio Gámez
University of Cádiz
Spain

1. Introduction

The traditional way of teaching mainly spreads the information out of the textbook and poses the solution of problems through memorization of formulas and facts. A change to more dynamic and hands-on methods has been adopted by many teachers and new innovative techniques are being applied in education. Technology can be a powerful strategy for change in education. The use of technology in the classroom can give all students a learning environment that allows and enhances discovery and creativity through the use of computer and educational software. The technological impulse in education is especially useful for the improvement of the teaching and learning process in Science and Technology.

In recent years, it is observed a generalized trend to create continuously even more sophisticated educational software. The approach for this is to design virtual environments plenty of details and options, in order to emulate real world, as close as posible. All the members of university community appreciate much these type of programs, because it allows students the acquisition of skills that will be probably required in their professional career. Nowadays, simulation programs are often used as a supplementary mean for the teaching of science and technology, especially when learning of a particular subject can not be accomplish through experiments and practice due to practical difficulties, and/or dangerous or expensive testing.

This can lead to a methodological dichotomy related to educational technology. On one hand, it can be found a huge development of computing resources, an increase on application issues for practice and experimentation. In contrast, there are few tools and limited perfomance of software applications for the understanding and reinforcement of theoretical concepts. In addition, there exists more active participation of students in practical applications, designed with a much more attractive and interesting presentation for students, increasing their motivation. On the contrary, passivity and lack of student motivation are usually proportional to the amplitude and complexity of the theory.

Consequently, the higher education may tend to enhance practical and rewarding usefulness and relegate the theoretical background to a lower level of enphasis. Hence, students may become professionals with excelent skills in the practical aspects of work, though with less solid understanding and knowledge of theory.

2. Geometry for lecturing Science and Technology

Fortunately, it is now a commonplace to remark the benefits of the ICT for education. In practice, all the members of teaching staff use, to a greater or lesser extent, some sort of technological resources to improve features of their teaching. The present educative reforms in some countries promote the use of the technologies as a support of the learning and teaching process and students are demanded to acquire skills related to personal computer and significant ICT tools.

There are several tendencies in the usage of technology for education. These trends are related to the hardware and software technologies. The first one is about the design of hardware devices. They are increasingly sophisticated and tend to integrate all types of multimedia resources. An example of this trend is the creation of the digital or electronic blackboard as a tool for teaching.

The second trend is the use of communication in support of teaching and learning, primarily using the online campus. It is used even if teaching and learning of subject matters is performed in a classroom. This trend enables the introduction of various materials, such as text, video, audio and others, with many formats and applications to widen the class issues.

Finally, there is a trend towards the creation of educational software. In the courses, computers support practical experimentation with computer simulations and other multimedia components, such as animations, video and audio clips, graphics and so on.

The main objective of an educational software project in science and technology is to integrate different ICT tools in teaching and learning. Most software programs claim to be very efficient for the teaching of knowledge in the theme and practical application of specific techniques.

There is a great number of applications of educational software and scholars have published a huge amount of didactic experiences. Despite the diversity in computer based learning environments, the software programs can be classified into three main categories based on their pedagogical approaches: Dynamic Learning Systems, Computer Systems, and Intelligent Tutoring Systems. Dynamic Learning Systems promote learning by discovery. Computer Systems aim improving the cognitive abilities of learners through the shift of focus from procedure to thinking. Intelligent Tutoring Systems try to integrate artificial intelligence principles into education.

Two features of education in science and technology have been emphasised by software programs: a) Calculus and mathematical operations, for instance, the Excel spreadsheet that embeds mathematical functions and diagrams. b) Simulation of laws, machines, systems, processes, structures, and so on. The most relevant applications of simulation in education are the remote laboratory and virtual laboratory. The remote laboratory exercises in real laboratory with the aid of hardware devices and appropriate software computer, data acquisition, control system and ICT tools. Virtual laboratory activities, based on computer simulations, artificially reproduce various science phenomena and complicated, expensive or inaccessible devices. They are the most promising though time consuming tecniques in educational software.

Much attention has been paid to computer environment in order to help students to understand the practical features and the enhancement of practical skills, However, few of software programs are dedicated to harness the theoretical knowledge of the subject matter. Therefore, it can be advisable to use computer programsm to help students in working Geometry and handling the geometric transformations implicitly found out through mathematical formulas in textbooks. With this modus operandi, it is reinforced the knowledge of theory, which is more difficult to understand and retain.

2.1 Advantages of Geometry-based software

In general, the teaching of the theory of subject matter is based on the oral explanation in class, with the aid of textbooks. Animated graphics, simulations and multimedia resources prepared to this effect can help for explanations, and there are many software tools in the market to help the teacher or educational support services in preparing such tools.

Depending on the level of the technological evolution of the institution and teachers, a student may face to an heightened number of different programs, each one with their own objectives, operational procedures and distinguished features. The benefits of these programs do not always overpass their disadvantages. The cost of the acquisition and maintenance of software can be substantiated by the use made of such programs. Changes in licensing policy of the owner firms may generate uncertainty in the acquisition of such programs, and technological changes also encourage the development of new educational software, so that the previously acquired software becomes rapidly obsolete. Many prefer the free software as a means to overcome these disadvantages, though it does not usually reach the performance of commercial programs.

In the teaching of technological matters, much of the theoretical explanations use concepts and formulas with evident geometric meanings. The full list of examples would be uncountable. A quick glance at a textbook in technology and engineering would probably find many hints of support for the theory based on geometric concepts, such as the sum of vectors, second-order equations, equilibrium points, linear equations, and similar.

It is not intended to state that the mathematical foundations of textbooks in science and technology are simple. The university must provide a substantial mathematical preparation during the undergraduate courses to successfully cope with especialized subjects in the field. Here, it is intended to stress that formulas, which are normally used in both the simplified theoretical model and practical applications, are not of special difficulty, unlike the problem under consideration, which may be of great complexity. The development of high-tech silicon industries and powerful algorithms empower the solution using computers of intractable problems to human capacity. In recent times, there are even competitions among supercomputers for solving problems of more than 100 million variables. Also, the aim is to remark that little attention is devoted to improve the teaching of theory through educational software. It is noted that many of the theoretical concepts are expressed with geometric formulas (Cederberg, 2004). Hence, the knowledge of the theoretical basis is deepened with simulations based on the geometry. A return to Geometry and the use of geometry-based programs are proposed. One of the advantages of working with Geometry is the student's familiarity with the concepts discussed in their pre-university period. In addition, it can be used the same computer programs at the secondary school, without the need to adapt them to the university environment, only the specific examples that are need to be designed. The adoption of simple software in Geometry also allows teachers to explore the creativity of students as they can design their own examples, which allows the design of teaching the course with a collaborative approach.

There are different strategies to incorporate Geometry in teaching technology:

a) The simpler strategy is to depict the geometrical concepts and formulas in textbooks, which is the most frequent one in secondary school.

b) Other strategy is to find out the geometrical representation of formulas. In this work, the analysis of symmetrical component in electrical power system is presented as an example of teaching theory using this strategy.
c) A refined strategy is to transform the mathematical formulas to achieve the analoguous geometric formulation. The analysis of the response of an automatic control system is focused on this strategy in this work and provides a fine example of helping research using Geometry.
d) A complementary strategy may be the preparation of animated textbooks. A brief discussion is made to present some packages that may perform this strategy and produce stand-alone textbooks.

2.2 CABRI description

As a result of Dynamic Learning approach, Interactive Geometry Software are computer programs which allow the creation and manipulation of geometric constructions, primarily in plane geometry. Cabri, GeoGebra and similar IGS programs try to work with simple concepts, without operational difficulty (Dreyfus et al., 1998). The quality of simulations one can build with these software programs in physics, engineering, astronomy, technical drawing or art, widens its use far beyond mathematics and helping much the student to reinforce and to deepen in the theoretical knowledge of the technological matters. In this work, Cabri examples have been chosen to illustrate the exposition.
Cabri Geometry is a commercial IGS produced by Cabrilog for teaching and learning geometry and trigonometry. Cabri handles all the constructions students have traditionally done with personal instruments. Lines, circles, points, triangles, vectors, conics, etc are easily created, manipulated and measured with toolbars and drop-down menus. Using powerful functions Cabri empowers geometrical exploration from simple figures to the most complicated for use and research in university. Students can see patterns, make conjectures, draw their own conclusions, and create alternative examples of the construction. Characteristics of figures are retained throughout transformation. An additional and interesting feature of Cabri is that plots curves of similar functions dependent on one or more parameters, which are modifiable by varying or animating the parameters.
It is preferred Cabri to others because it is easy to use and there are numerous Cabri examples that have been created during last years. In addition, applets for publishing the examples in internet can be prepared using CabriWeb. These applets may be available to anyone who has a computer connected to the Internet that can run Java.
There is, also, the benefit of having the students an easy-to-use and familiar tool at the start of activity in undergraduate studies. The focus and content of those activities can be on the behavior or properties of the phenomena being modeled by this tool, rather than on the mathematics of the modeling execution. Students can work at a higher level of mathematical sophistication without requiring analogously higher level of technical or conceptual sophistication with the software, since Cabri encapsulates both basic and sophisticated mathematical construction.

3. Geometry in Power Systems. The case of symmetrical components.

Although there are some industrial applications of electric power systems in direct current DC, the textbooks usually deal only with those based on the alternating current AC. The mathematical analysis of AC systems operates with complex numbers and variables, which have a geometric representation as vectors in a plane.
An extended version of vectors including changes in module and/or direction over time are phasors. The main electric magnitudes, such as currents and voltages, are presented as functions of time t and angular velocity ω. The phasors in a given electrical system are vectors that change their direction and amplitude depending on the factor ωt, though they have constant relative positions between them. Normally they are studied in a rotating reference frame, which makes them stationary.
Performance of an electrical device or system may be fully described by its phasorial diagram. This is important to establish the functional relations and mutual influences among the different components of an electrical system. The elements of a power system are the machines, transformers, transmission lines and loads connected to the system. In a 3-phase power system, phasors of current and voltages are balanced in normal operation. The 3-phase electric magnitudes, current or voltage, are formed by three phasors with the same amplitude and a phase lag of 120° between two of them. In Figure 1, on the left, it is drawn the sinusoidal ωt-dependent function of a generic balanced 3-phase system M, defined by:

$$M_R = 5\sin\omega t\,;\; M_S = 5\sin(\omega t - 2\pi/3)\,;\; M_T = 5\sin(\omega t - 4\pi/3)$$

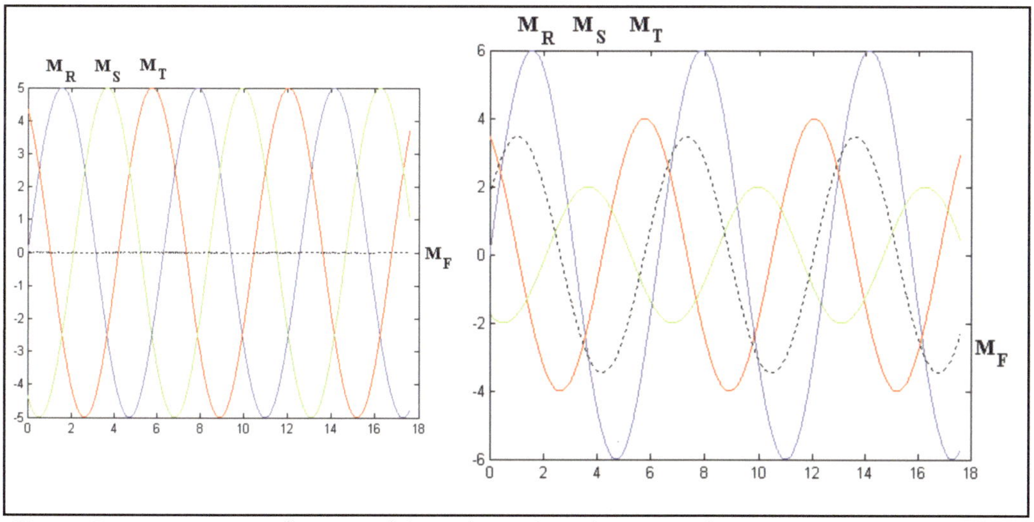

Fig. 1. Representation of sinusoidal ωt-dependent function of a balanced 3-phase system (left) and unbalanced 3-phase system (right).

The Figure 1, on the right, draws the sinusoidal ωt-dependent function of an unbalanced 3-phase system defined by:

$$M_R = 6\sin(\omega t - 0.5\pi/3)\,;\; M_S = 4\sin(\omega t - 1.8\pi/3)\,;\; M_T = 2\sin(\omega t - 5.4\pi/3)\,.$$

M_S is the vectorial sum of M_R, M_S, M_T phasors. The phasorial diagrams of these systems are depicted in Figure 2.

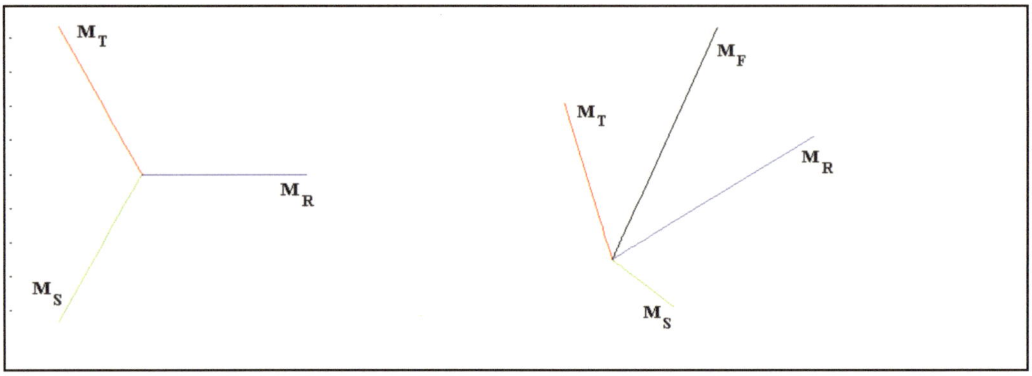

Fig. 2. Phasorial diagram of a balanced 3-phase system (left) and unbalanced 3-phase system (right)

One of the most important issues in the study and analysis of power systems refers to system failures, especially in the electrical transport system. A fault causes a failure on the system and, as a result, currents and voltages and other electric magnitudes usually become unbalanced. The failure analysis of power systems under faults uses the notion of symmetrical components, which helps to calculate the mathematical relationships between the values of phasors of unbalanced system .

The method is applied to the analysis of unbalanced systems to determine the symmetrical components of currents in the fault, and then find the currents and voltages at various points in the system. The most important application of symmetrical components theory is in 3-phase power systems, when it is necessary to simulate the dynamic response of the system due to faults, such as phase to ground, phase to phase, 3-phase short-circuit, and others. Besides, the symmetrical components theory gives clearer explanatios than others about many electrical phenomena, such as rotor heating in machines, neutral current and so on. The symmetrical components were introduced by Fortescue (Fortescue, 1918) to ease the calculations for unbalanced 3-phase systems. It uses the decomposition of the electrical variables, i.e. voltage and load current, into symmetrical components. The basic concept of this theory is to convert a set of three phasors into another set of three phasors with some desirable properties.

Acording to the symmetrical components theory, each one of unbalanced phasors can be decomposed into three balanced systems, known as the positive phase sequence (PPS), negative phase sequence (NPS) and zero phase sequence (ZPS), formed by:

- A balanced set of symmetrical components of positive sequence (direct sequence) that consists of three phasors of equal magnitude or module, displaced from each other by an equal phase of 120° and by a rotation as the original unbalanced set, i.e. RST, STR and TRS.
- A balanced set of symmetrical components of negative sequence (reverse sequence) that consists of three phasors of equal magnitude or module, displaced from each other by an equal phase of 120° and by a rotation, opposite to the original unbalanced set, i.e. RTS, TSR and SRT.

▪A balanced set of zero sequence of 3- coincident phasors. The three ZPS phasors are equal in magnitude or module and are all in phase with each other.

There is a compact mathematical formula to write out the Fortescue theorem. Let suppose a balanced 3-phase system of phasors M_R, M_S, M_T. The letter ***a*** is to be used to denote the operator that creates a 120° anti-clockwise rotation. This operator is a complex number defined by the following terms:

$$a = 1\angle 120^{\circ} = -0.5 + j\frac{\sqrt{3}}{2} \tag{1}$$

Suitable operations with operador ***a*** gives the following operators:

$$a^2 = 1\angle 240^{\circ} = -0.5 - j\frac{\sqrt{3}}{2};\ a^3 = 1\angle 360^{\circ} = 1\angle 0^{\circ} = 1;\ a^4 = 1\angle 480^{\circ} = a;\ ....$$

Having in mind these operators, the phasors of a balanced three-phase system of positive sequence can be expressed by means of:

$$(M_{1R}, M_{1S}, M_{1T}) = (M_{1R}, a^2M_{1R}, aM_{1R}) = (1, a^2, a)M_{1R} \tag{2}$$

That is, the phasor M_{1R} denotes the set of phasors of a balanced 3-phase system associated to the positive sequence $(1, a^2, a)$. The phasors of a balanced 3-phase of negative sequence can be also expressed as follows

$$(M_{2R}, M_{2S}, M_{2T}) = (M_{2R}, aM_{2R}, a^2M_{2R}) = (1, a, a^2)M_{2R} \tag{3}$$

That is, the phasor M_{2R} denotes the set of phasors of a balanced 3-phase system associated to the negative sequence $(1, a, a^2)$. Finally, the sum of vectors of the three 3-phase systems of symmetrical components (zero, positive and negative) gives the original unbalanced 3-phase system. This can be mathematically expressed as

$$\begin{bmatrix} M_R \\ M_S \\ M_T \end{bmatrix} = \begin{bmatrix} 1 & 1 & 1 \\ 1 & a^2 & a \\ 1 & a & a^2 \end{bmatrix} \begin{bmatrix} M_{0R} \\ M_{1R} \\ M_{2R} \end{bmatrix} \tag{4}$$

A simple matrix operation gives that the symmetrical component may be obtained from the original unbalanced vectors with the following equation:

$$\begin{bmatrix} M_{0R} \\ M_{1R} \\ M_{2R} \end{bmatrix} = \frac{1}{3} \begin{bmatrix} 1 & 1 & 1 \\ 1 & a & a^2 \\ 1 & a^2 & a \end{bmatrix} \begin{bmatrix} M_R \\ M_S \\ M_T \end{bmatrix} \tag{5}$$

The Figure 3 depicts a Cabri-based applet prepared for the geometrical demonstration of Fortescue theorem. This geometric application made in Cabri allows the analysis of failures in electric power systems using the symmetrical components.

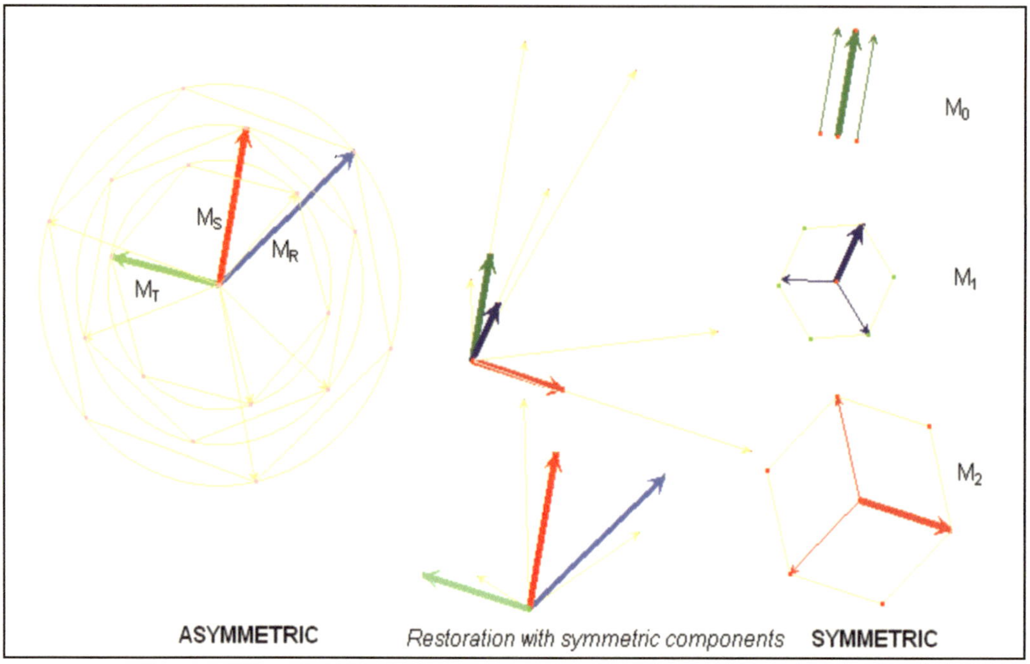

Fig. 3. Geometric analysis of symmetrical components of unbalanced 3-phase systems

On the left of the Figure 3, a phasorial representation of an unbalanced 3-phase system is drawn. The module of the phasors may be modified by changing the radius of the circle passing through the end of each vector and the direction of the vectors may be modified by moving the extreme point of each vector. The chart includes a procedure for obtaining the (1, a, a^2) sequence out of each vector. To this, it is drawn a regular hexagon inscribed in the circle that passes through the end of each vector.

With a simple geometrical procedure using the basic options in Cabri, sum of vectors and homotetic operation, it can be obtained the denoting phasors of the symmetrical components with zero, positive and negative sequence, respectively. The top center of the Figure 3 contains the geometrical design for the obtention of these vectors. With a translation of denoting phasors the equivalent 3-phase systems are drawn following similar procedure as in unbalanced system. The construction is depicted on the right of the Figure 3. At the bottom center of the figure is reconstructed the three-phase unbalanced system. The aim of the reconstruction is to check the validity of the formulas and that the procedure for the geometrical construction of symmetrical components has been correctly elaborated.

A particular case of unbalanced 3-phase system is generated by the phase to phase fault, which is one of the faults generally analyzed in textbooks. It is defined by the following condition: $M_S = M_T$. In this case, M refers to the voltage at the point of failure. A simple modification of the unbalanced 3-phase system in the Cabri applet is enough to check that $M_{1R} = M_{2R}$, the result that is also obtained by the mathematical analysis.

The Cabri applet gives more information, since it calculates the values of the modulus and direction of all the phasors, as well. It easily find solutions to all fault conditions and the analysis of system failures does not require a great amount of time.

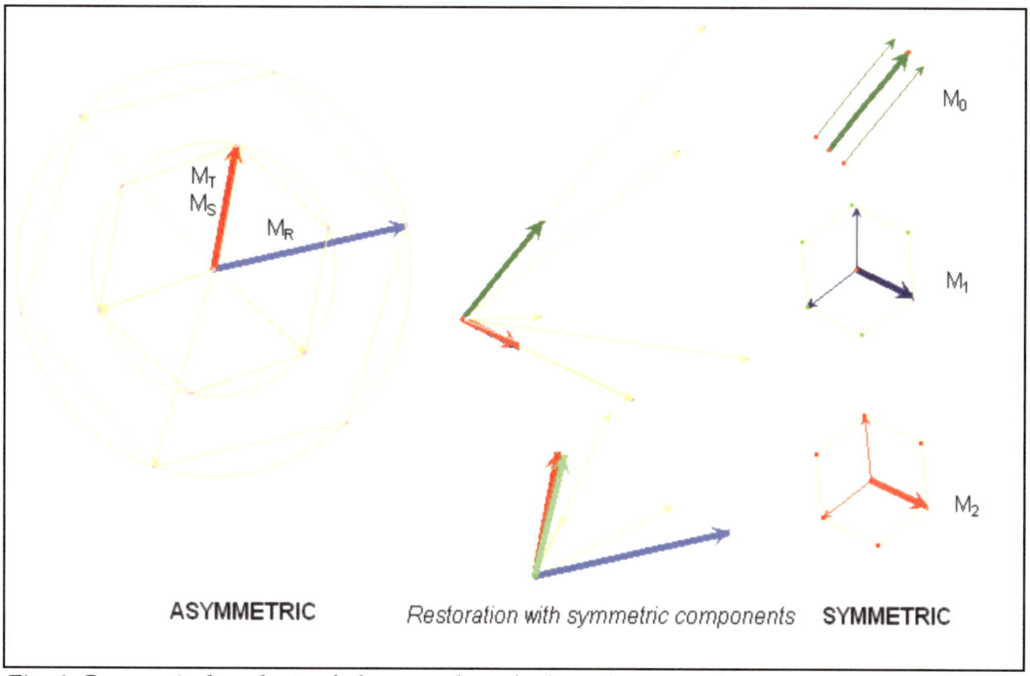

Fig. 4. Geometrical analysis of phase to phase fault in electric 3-phase systems.

4. Geometry in Automatic Control. A case

Control theory is usually divided in two parts: frequency domain and time domain. The study of controlled systems is often focused on the frequency domain for examining performance, stability and robustness of systems. Frequency domain techniques have been traditionally used to meet frequency domain specifications, such as gain and phase margins, which are traditional indicators of stability and robustness. Other authors have proposed techniques in the time-domain to meet damping factor and overshoot, which are alternate indicators. Undergraduate students learn much about some of these techniques for processes without time delay. However, processes with dead time are rarely considered in textbooks, since the equations related to them are highly nonlinear and analytical methods of analysis or design are not yet available (Ästrom & Hägglund, 2001).

In the frequency domain, many techniques take into account the Nyquist diagram to analyze properties of controlled systems. The drawback of working with the Nyquist diagram is that, besides the information about the stability of the system, it only provides information about the properties in the frequency domain. The system properties in the time domain are usually related to some points in the Nyquist diagram, which are obtained from heuristic procedures. This implies a high degree of inaccuracy and uncertainty. On other hand, the temporal properties of the system when time $t \rightarrow 0$ are related to higher frequencies, obtaining the value of the response when $\omega \rightarrow \infty$.

However, the Nyquist diagram delineates only the representation for the initial frequencies, which provide information about the behavior of the system in the time limit, to say, the stationary behavior of the system $t \rightarrow \infty$ is obtained for $\omega \rightarrow 0$.

It may be of great interest to find a diagram that can provide full information about behavior and properties of a system. This section offers a geometrical procedure to represent any response in a plane using the inverse modulus of open- and close-loop transfer functions. This representation can be related to second-order responses of specific overshoot, which is determined by the damping factor ξ. This representation correlates properties both in the frequency and time domains.

4.1 Damping factor curves and inverse of modulus representation

Model-based approaches are frequently used to simplify controller design process. They work under the assumption of a desired response closed-loop transfer function from input to output. The response of controlled plant may be modelled by a second-order plus time delay (SOPTD) in many industrial applications. The transfer function of system of a desired SOPTD response is:

$$H(s) = \frac{\omega_n^2 e^{-t_d s}}{s^2 + 2\xi\omega_n s + \omega_n^2} = \frac{e^{-t_d s}}{\alpha s^2 + \beta s + 1} \tag{6}$$

where s is the Laplace operator, $\alpha = 1/\omega_n^2$; $\beta = 2\xi/\omega_n^2$ and $\xi = \beta^2/4\alpha$.

The open-loop frequency response of model (6) is

$$L(j\omega) = \frac{e^{-j\Theta}}{1 - \alpha\omega^2 + j\beta\omega - e^{-j\Theta}} \tag{7}$$

where $\Theta = \omega t_d$. The modulus of $L(j\omega)$ is

$$\left|L(j\omega)\right|^2 = \left[\left(1 - \alpha\omega^2 - \cos\Theta\right)^2 + \left(\beta\omega + \sin\Theta\right)^2\right]^{-1} \tag{8}$$

Applying the following definitions

$$x = \beta\omega \;;\; y = 1-\alpha\omega^2 \tag{9}$$

the equation (8) can be transformed into

$$\left(x + \sin\Theta\right)^2 + \left(y - \cos\Theta\right)^2 = \frac{1}{\left|L(j\omega)\right|^2} \tag{10}$$

Equation (10) is a conic formula which describes a circle with radius $1/|L(j\omega)|$ centered at point (-sin Θ, cos Θ). It can be also demonstrated that the inverse of closed-loop transfer function $|H(j\omega)|$ is equal to the distance of point (x,y) from (0,0). and is equivalent to the value $|D|/|L|$, where D es the distance to the critic point (-1,0) in the Nyquist diagram. Rearranging equation (9), it is obtained that

$$y = 1 - \frac{x2}{4\xi^2} \tag{11}$$

It may be depicted the curves of equation (11) in a plane for different values of relative damping ξ ranging from zero to ∞, as shown in Figure 5, on the left . In the same plane, it can be depicted the circle described by different values of Θ, as in the center of Figure 5, and a joint representation of equations (10) and (11) may be as in Figure 5, on the right. It is easy to find that a point (x,y) in this curve is related to the triangle [unity radio, inverse of modulus of the open-loop (1/L leg), inverse of modulus of closed-loop (D/L leg)] defined by a specific value of Θ. The unit leg of this triangle makes an anti-clockwise rotation linked to the value of Θ.

The Figure 5 , on the right, shows the diagram obtained forf a SOPTD response when ξ=0.7. It is also shown the curve of a first-order plus time delay (FOPTD) response as a limit of SOPTD ξ=∞.

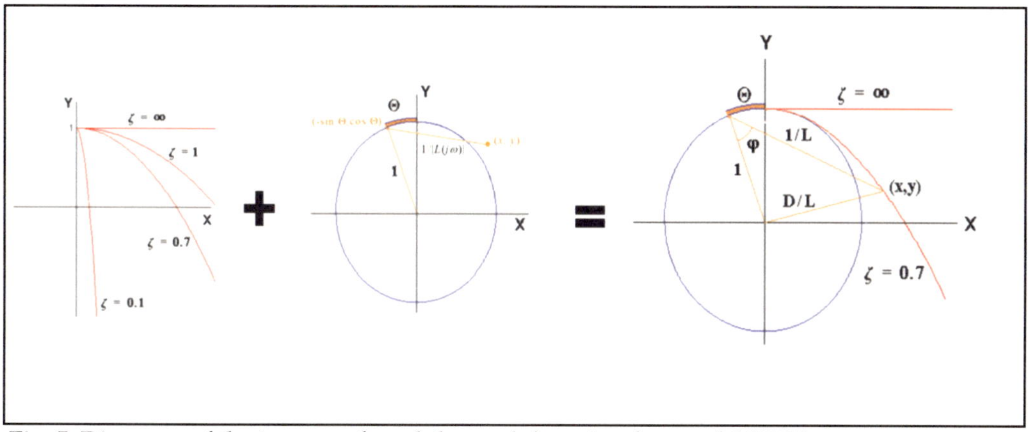

Fig. 5. Diagram of the inverse of modulus and damping factor of SOPTD responses

Notice that the argument of the open-loop response is measured by the angle between the unit and open-loop legs. The argument of the closed-loop response is measured on the central point (0,0) by the angle of the triangle formed with vertical axis and the closed-loop leg D/L.

4.2 Generalization to controlled systems

Consider a plant described by the transfer function G(s) and controlled by a controller C(s)

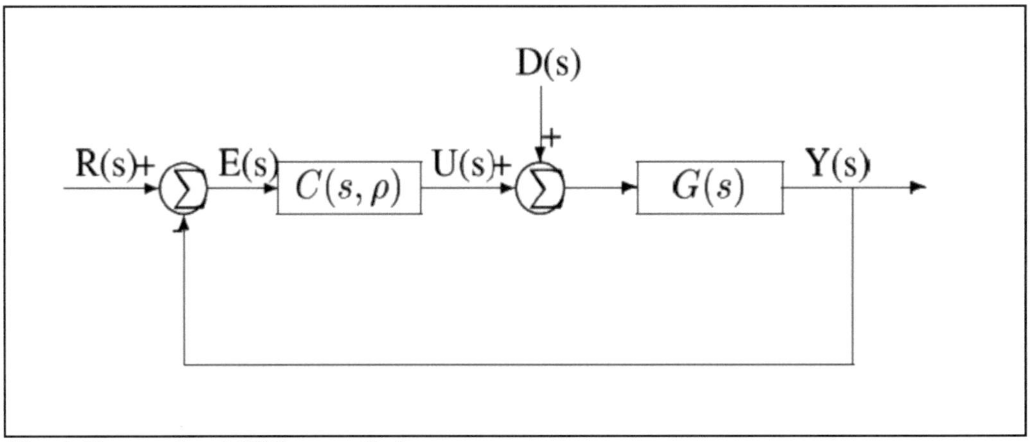

Fig. 6. Conventional SISO controlled structure

For the system in Figure 6, the closed-loop response upon set-point change is

$$H(s)=\frac{C(s)G(s)}{1+C(s)G(s)}=\frac{C(s)G_r(s)e^{-t_d s}}{1+C(s)G(s)}=\frac{e^{-t_d s}}{1+\dfrac{e^{-t_d s}}{C(s)G_r(s)}} \tag{12}$$

The equation (12) is similar to equation (6) if $e^{-t_d s}\,[C(s)\,G_r(s)\,]^{-1} = \beta_\Theta s + \alpha_\Theta s^2$. This is generally possible in the frequency domain provided that $t_d \neq 0$. Let define ξ^2_Θ as

$$\xi^2_\Theta = \frac{\beta^2_\Theta}{4\alpha_\Theta} \tag{13}$$

Applying the following definitions

$$X_\Theta = \beta_\Theta \;; \qquad Y_\Theta = 1 - \alpha_\Theta \omega^2 \tag{14}$$

and operating with equations (12), it is obtained the general equation

$$Y_\Theta = 1 - \frac{X^2_\Theta}{4\xi^2_\Theta} \tag{15}$$

The formula of this equation is similar to (11). Though its representation in a plane may be a complex curve, the formulation may be functionally considered as a ξ-curve. For each value of ω , that is Θ, there is a ξ-curve that coincides with the complex curve. This complex curve of equation (15) may be characterized by the dominant ξ-curve, which is generally denoted by the lower value of ξ_Θ. Therefore, any controlled system may be analyzed under the point of view of its dominant SOPTD ξ-curve. Innovation of this diagram is that combines time and frequency domains and that depicts main properties of open- and close-loop transfer functions. The main features of dynamic behavior for any transfer function may be also obtained with this diagram.

4.3 Geometrical analysis of main properties of SOPTD responses

Phase margin (Φ_m). From the basic definition of phase margin, the following equation is obtained.

$$\left| L(j\omega_g) \right| = 1$$
$$\Phi_m = \varphi_p = \arg\left(L(j\omega_g) \right) + \pi \qquad (16)$$

where ω_g is known as gain crossover frequency. For a given value of ξ, each point of ξ-curve fixes a value of Θ_g at a distance of one unit length. Given a choice of Θ_g and solving the system (10) and (11) for particular values of (x_p, y_p), it is obtained the relations between phase margin, the relative damping ξ and the feasible values of Θ_g. Figure 7, on the left, shows the construction of the phase margin in the proposed diagram.

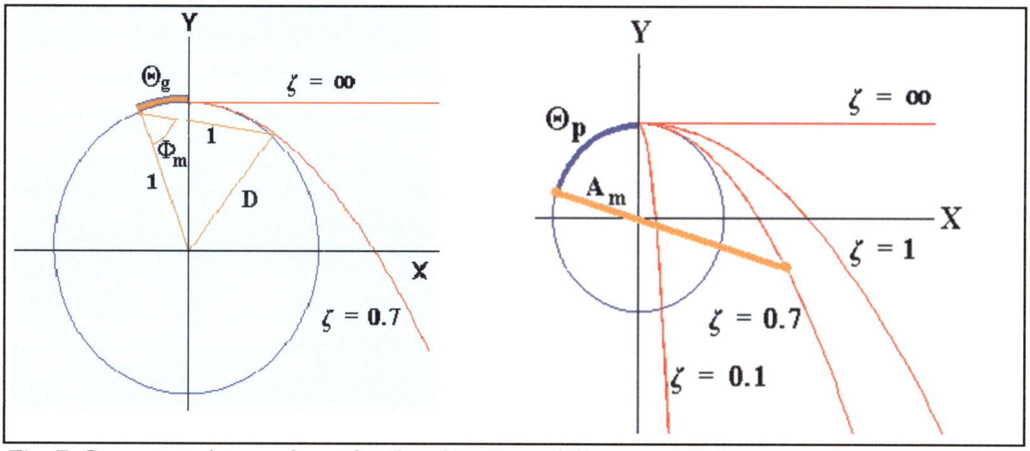

Fig. 7. Geometrical procedures for the obtention of Phase and Gain margins

Gain margin (A_m). The definition of gain margin gives

$$A_m = \left| L(j\omega_p) \right|^{-1}$$
$$\varphi_g = \arg\left(L(j\omega_p) \right) + \pi = 0 \qquad (17)$$

where ωp is known as the phase crossover frequency. The gain margin point at the ξ-curve is (xg, yg). The stability conditions of the SOPDT response only are satisfied when

$$x_g = \rho \sin \Theta_p$$
$$y_g = \rho \cos \Theta_p \tag{18}$$

where ρ= A_m-1 is the radius of the circle which meets the ξ-curve at the point (x_g, y_g).

Robustness. The point (0,1) in the proposed diagram has significant properties. This point indicates the ideal performance of response, because α= 0 and β = 0. The point (0,1) denotes the convergence point of all SOPTD and FOPTD responses. Then, the objective of controlled systems might be to achieve this ideal point, or a close point, for the frequency of phase margin. However, it also can be observed that there is no change of phase margin limit (60°) modifying ξ and that solutions of (x_p, y_p) around (0,1) have no robustness, since minor changes in the system parameters will carry it to instability.

In a practical situation, it is necessary to decrease the value of phase crossover frequency Θ_g to achieve acceptable performance robustness. It is of common sense to place Θ_g far from π/3 at least at a point which matches the minimum time delay margin. Then, the response becomes slower and robust. To avoid problems of robustness and achieve the quickest response, it must be selected the point of phase margin in the specified ξ out of the limits of a circle r centered at point (0,1). Hence, a coefficient of robustness may be defined as

$$r = \text{distance to point } (0,1) \tag{19}$$

In Figure 8, the point (x_r, y_r) may provide sufficient robustness against expected changes in time delay and parameter values of a controlled process.

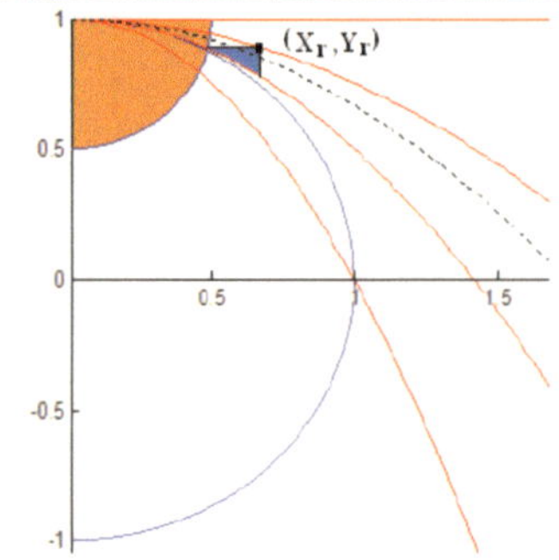

Fig. 8. Robustness against changes in time delay and parameters of a controlled process.

Overshoot. The overshoot OS for a desired closed-loop response can be obtained with

$$\ln OS = -\frac{\beta \pi}{2\alpha\omega_d} \tag{20}$$

Generally, a limit of the achievable maximum overshoot is specified in industrial applications. It is well known that the maximum percent overshoot will increase with decreasing ξ. For a second-order response, the relative damping ξ formula results from equation (11) and (12)

$$\xi^2 = \frac{\beta^2}{4\alpha} = \frac{\ln^2 OS}{\ln^2 OS + \pi^2} \tag{21}$$

This formula relates the OS and ξ . The curve ξ denotes points of equal overshoot. The lower of ξ, the greater overshoot.

4.4 CABRI-based representation of SOPTD responses

A Cabri graphical procedure is prepared to obtain the solution for a SOPTD that matches requirements. The construction of the geometrical procedure is shown in Figure 9.

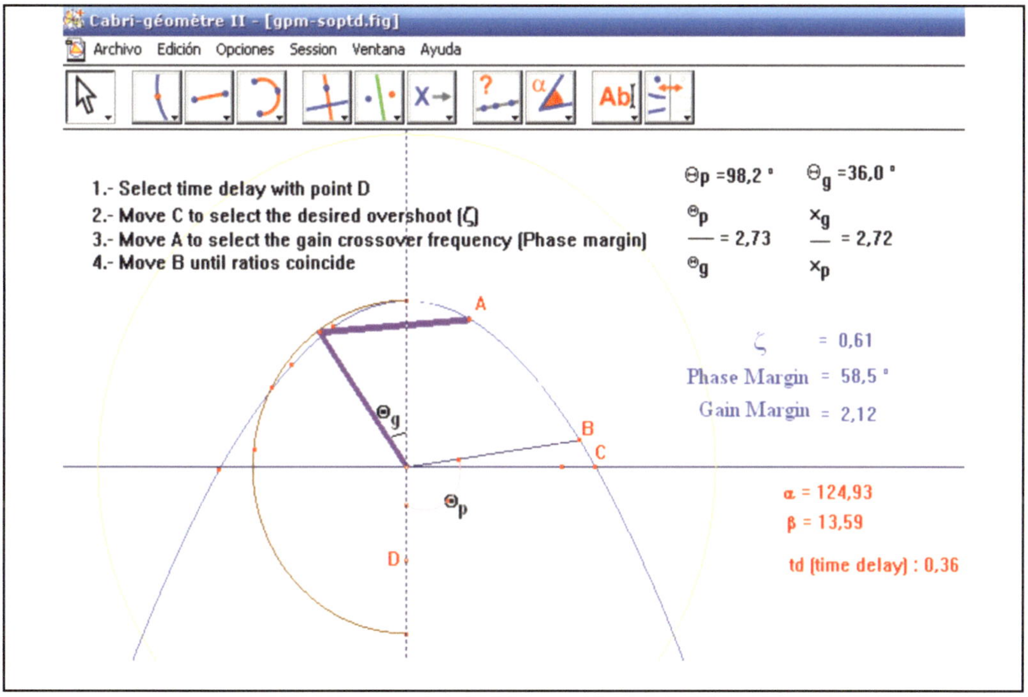

Fig. 9. Dynamic representation of ξ curves and inverse modulus with Cabri

The procedure is handled in four steps: Moving the point D is selected the time delay of response. Move C to select the desired overshoot, that is ξ . Move A to select the gain crossover frequency. Move B until ratios Θ_p/Θ_g and x_g/x_p coincide (condition of gain margin). With this condition, the solution of gain margin is obtained for a selected Θg. The exact values of gain and phase margins are displayed. Generally, the recommended range of gain margin is between 2-5 and the recommendation for the phase margins range is between 30-60°.

The use of a combined chart of frequency- and time-domain properties for a response can help designers to select adequate specifications of response. In a practical situation, the goal of design is to achieve acceptable performance while assuring stability. The goal of controller design might be to achieve the quicker and robust response without oscillations. Since performance depends on the type of controller and its tuning, controller design starts

from performance specifications. However, the criteria for setting specifications are normally based on empirical considerations. The application of CABRI-geometry may help to set adequately specifications.
The use of a combined chart of frequency- and time-domain properties for a SOPTD response can help designers to select adequate specifications. Usually, these specifications are set from empirical considerations. The Cabri diagram can be used in order to foresee the behavior of a controlled system. It also provides clearful explanations about some rules-of-thumb of controller design. The CABRI applet may be seen as a simple and easy pedagogical tool to analyze real systems.
From the graphical representation comes up the importance of an adequate selection of phase crossover frequency. The rest of performance properties in both domains hold on that choice. Working with the CABRI applet, it is illustrated the interdependency between different specifications. It has been also shown how many specifications are set without consistency, more often than not. Thus, students and operator can learn to discriminate good or bad design rules.

5. Animation in Textbooks

In the multimedia era, there has been a renovation in publication. This has occurred in many areas, such as newspapers, the academic world and in education. In this, contents such as animations, videos, and interactive demonstrations, are provided to students on CD-ROMs, DVDs, Blue-ray disks as part of textbook packages. This way, it is pointed out that students would be able to learn and memorize the concept much faster.
The animated textbooks will have motion in pictures of various concepts that have been traditionally explained by diagrams. The concept of the symmetrical components, for example, would be explained by an animation of the phasors rotating with ωt. In electrical power systems, animations would also be provided for various topics related to phasors (phase, amplitude and initial phase). Similar animations would be prepared for various concepts in science themes and for those in technology
The pages of the animated textbooks will also contain links to web sites related to the subject matter being explained in them to encourage students to explore the subject outside of their textbooks.
To date, these enhanced media have not been fully integrated into a self-contained textbook format. Instead, student are required to operate leaving the text to read a CD-ROM, DVD, download movie, open a Web link, and so on. These activities would all seem to distract from the continuity of an integrated educational experience—an actual enhanced, interactive textbook.
The Portable Document Format (PDF), developed by Adobe Systems Incorporated has become a de facto standard for digital publication. One of the main advantages of PDF is that documents are easily transferable between different operating systems, PDF files may be produced from a range of publishing packages in personal computers, along with free applications like LaTeX. Adobe Acrobat 3D Version 8 enables the inclusion of interactive figures within PDF documents, that other free packages have previously resolved for LATEX.
The LATEX *movie15* package (Grahn, 2009b) provides an interface to embed movies, sounds and 3D objects into PDF documents for use with LaTeX as well as pdfLaTeX. The

specification allows media file data to be completely incorporated into the PDF output, thus producing self-contained PDF documents. The LATEX *animate* package (Grahn, 2009a) provides an interface to create PDFs with animated content from sets of graphics or image files, from inline graphics, such as LATEX-picture PSTricks or just from typeset text. Unlike standard movie/video formats, package *animate* allows for animating vector graphics. The result is roughly similar to the SWF format. Thus, geometric animations may be included in textbooks.

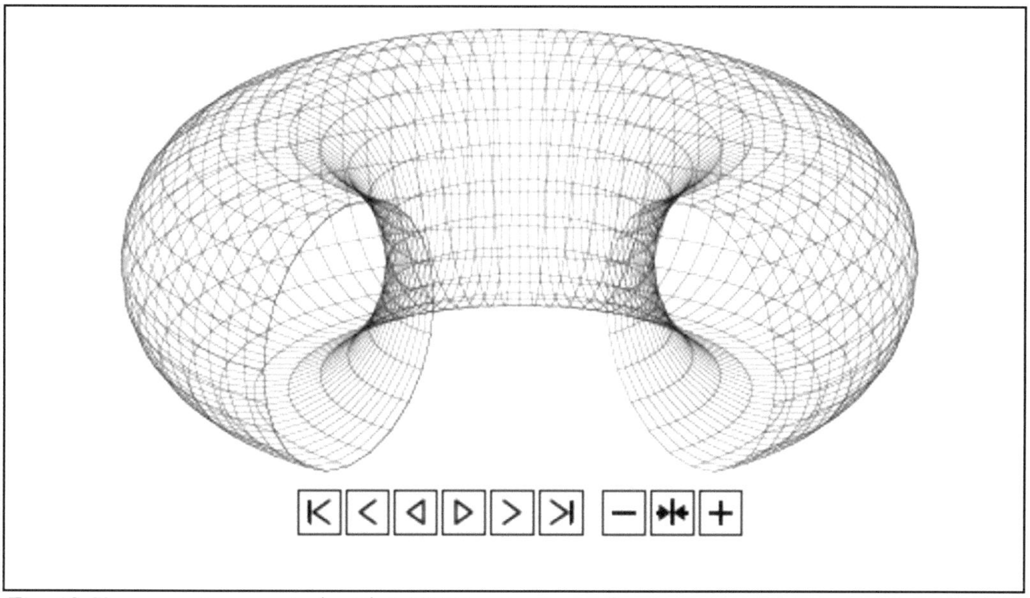

Fig. 10. Torus section created with LATEX animate package

The introduction of Geometry means that the theoretical explanations can be simple and affordable for both the teacher and the students, and proves the advantages of simplicity, continuity, understandability and extensibility in learning and teaching. Students explore dynamic illustrations, they develop ideas and find their own solutions for a given problem. This way of working supports autonomous and cooperative learning of technology at university. It encourages an active discovering approach to technological thinking. Students are more deeply involved in the process of finding and solving technological problems. This leads the students to increased activity and better understanding of new technological situations. The animation in textbooks also emphasizes the integration of interactive multimedia technology into the process of learning and teaching.

6. Conclusion

The practice of mathematics in the world outside education has changed considerably as a result of the development of powerful software tools. In general, however, little attention has been paid to Geometry. It has been demonstrated the convenience of Geometry for learning and teaching of tecnological matters in high level courses. The theoretical background of subject matters includes copious formulas that have a strong geometric

understanding. Two representative examples have been provided to exemplify the use of Geometry in teaching Tecnology with different strategies. In both cases, the use of geometrical models makes easy the apprehension, understanding and learning and avoids some of drawbacks encountered in most of sophisticatedl educational software.
Through accessible examples we have tried to give a concise view of just how IGS software tools could impact on an up-skilling technology by making more stimulating lectures and animated textbooks. A wider range of examples of such strategies is needed, besides an encouragement for more people to be involved in developing them.

7. References

Äström, K. J. & Hägglund, T. (2001) *The future of PID control*, Control Engineering Practice, vol. 9, 1163-1175.

Cederberg, J. N. (2004), *A Course in Modern Geometry*, Springer

Dreyfus, T. & Hillel, J. & Sierpinska, A (1998) *Cabri based linear algebra: transformations* European Research in Mathematics Education Conference

Fortescue, C. (1918), *Method of Symmetrical Co-Ordinates Applied to the Solution of Polyphase Networks*. AIEE Transactions, vol. 37, part II, 1027-1140.

Grahn, A. (2009) *The Animate Package*. URL: http://www.ctan.org/tex-archive/macros /latex/ contrib / animate

Grahn, A. (2009) *The Movie15 Package*. URL: http://www.ctan.org/tex-archive/macros/ latex/ contrib/ movie15

7

Delivering Synchronous and Asynchronous Educational Material in Conservation Science Using Various Communication Channels

Ioannis A. Kozaris and Evangelia A. Varella
Aristotle University of Thessaloniki
Greece

1. Introduction

Through existing information and communication technologies, learners and teachers can not only interact synchronously, but also have an efficient cooperation or collaboration over distance. Computer-supported collaboration learning is one of the most promising innovations to improve teaching and learning, since it achieves combination of communication technology with psychological and pedagogical aspects, along the lines of a constructivist approach (Silverman, 1995). Computer-supported collaboration learning can be a powerful tool in creating learning communities, where students have a chance to be present by developing explanations on the subject studied, and analysing knowledge in a collaborative way (Scardamalia & Bereiter, 1994). The importance of interacting and the influence it exercises on the learning process in distance education was described by Moore (1993) in a model called "transactional distance", *i.e.* the distance created between lecturer and learners, which potentially increases in distance education. The term "transaction" refers to a mutual action between environment, individuals and behaviour patterns in a particular situation. The distance education transaction is "the mutual action between teachers and students, in environments whose uniqueness is their separation from each other, and as a result exhibit unique behaviour patterns of distance education" (Moore & Kearsley, 1996). The transactional distance is affected by two variables, the dialogue or verbal interaction and its adaptation to distance learning. The transaction distance will decrease as the level of dialogue increases, and this will lead to an increase in the effectiveness of learning (Offir et al., 2008). There are essentially two kinds of interaction with regard to learning. One deals with a student individually interacting with content, and the other implies social activity: a student interacting with others about the content.

Two different types of computer-supported collaboration learning environments, that is two methods for implementing distance learning are used, according to the moment when student-teacher interaction takes place: asynchronous and asynchronous systems (Bafestou & Mentzas, 2002). Ellis et al. (1991) categorised group interactions according to time and space. Collaboration could be enhanced within a real-time or a non-real time interaction. A

distinction is made between same time (synchronous) and different times (asynchronous), and between same place (face-to-face) and different places (distributed).
Asynchronous communication allows students to exchange data and views in their own time and space, hence it is insensitive to time and geography. Asynchronous communication tools remove both geographical and temporal barriers. This type of collaboration offers some advantages. Firstly, students are not pressed to react in a short unit of time and secondly, they may organise their messages by “branching” them around themes (Veerman et al., 2000). Problems arise for asynchronous communication, when it is expected from two or more group members to work on a common task electronically, although they are coming from different countries, they have different background knowledge, and/or did not work together previously (Jaervelae et al., 2004). Additionally, isolation feelings are usually common among students participating in asynchronous communication, a fact causing diminished motivation for learning. On the other hand, in computer-supported collaboration learning synchronous environments students share data and views through the Internet in real-time like a face-to-face interaction without feeling isolated (Marjanovic, 1999). Example for synchronous communication tool is the live chat room, web-conferencing and other systems, which allow users to immediately exchange information. One of the challenges to communication technology is how to make distributed interactions as effective as face-to-face interactions, as human interaction, since mutual understanding or shared values and goals are hard to be created in a distant-environment. A remote interaction supported by appropriate technology, which will allow students to access further relevant information without interrupting the flow interaction, should be the solution. In most third-cycle education classes asynchronous and synchronous communication work hand-in-hand. They are symbiotic. In fact, a number of research studies, beginning in the late 1970s, concluded that "instructor use of nonverbal and verbal immediacy" fostered all kinds of benefits in the conventional classroom: more learning, more student motivation, more empowerment (Freitas, 1998, pp. 366-67).
Learning management systems such as Moodle or Blackboard, and real-time applications, such as videoconferencing, are used in order to create Virtual Learning Environments able to support Collaborative Learning. Their mediator role is essential to improve the educational experience in the scientific concepts. Especially, these mediators are largely useful in the field of science education, where lecturing material derives from predetermined texts, giving students little incentive to attend and participate in class. Learning management systems are server-based platforms that control access and delivery of on-line learning resources through a standard web browser. They are designed to support teachers in the management of computer supported educational courses. These systems consist of:

- "Communication tools", such as e-mail and a discussion board,
- Tools for organising the administration of a course, and
- Tools for student testing, through quizzes, and for disseminating the information.

A major opportunity provided through the use of new information and communication technologies in education is the use of multimedia material at the presentation of cognitive contents to the students. Multimedia computer-based training and learning including hypermedia technology has been an area of research for the educational experts. Experience in evaluating the quality of learning from hypermedia documents has been highly positive, and it has been established that a part of the positive attitude is due to the novelty of the medium (Brown, 1995). Relan and Gillani (1997) generally accepted from a pedagogical perspective that multimedia technologies have the potential to reshape and add a new dimension to learning. By incorporating multimedia technology in a dynamic system with good-quality educational material, it is now possible to develop effective new teaching and learning strategies. Multimedia technology plays an important role in education and training because of its ability to provide a virtual environment permitting learners to effectively acquire knowledge. With sound and visual effects, multimedia enhances computer simulation of the real life events. It has the potential to transform the classroom from a physical world to an unlimited imaginary virtual environment. Multimedia simulations can instantly put the learners in an environment, where they can discover, explore further knowledge actively. It has also facilitated several types of training, such as fire fighting, driving and flight simulations. Visual and audio can powerfully affect the learners' processing of information. In addition, Selwyn and Gordard (2003) emphasize that the use of multimedia technologies in educational institutions is seen as a necessity for maintaining an education relevant to the 21st century. The optimal use of multimedia technology in education and its full potential will only be realised if it is to be adopted not only as a vehicle for knowledge "delivery", but most importantly as an instructional tool.

Forming the world's largest network of networks, Internet now serves as a significant channel for delivering education, There are four ways of connecting a client computer to the Internet:

- Dial-up connection using a telephone line or an Integrated Services Digital Network (ISDN),
- Digital Subscriber Line (DSL),
- Cable TV connection,
- Satellite connection and
- T-Carrier systems.

The general rule about Internet connection is the faster, the better. The bandwidth and transfer rate determine how rapidly pictures, sounds, animation and video clips will be downloaded. Since multimedia and interactivity make the Internet such an exciting tool for information sharing, speed is the key. Dial-up access provides an easy and inexpensive way for users to connect to the Internet, however, it is a slow-speed technology and most users are no longer satisfied with dial-up or ISDN connections. The broadband access is now possible with TV cable, DSL and satellite links, and T-carrier systems. Broadband forms of connection are largely gaining popularity with the general public and with business, governmental, and educational organizations. Broadband systems divide the cable capacity into multiple independent bandwidth channels allowing several data transmissions to occur simultaneously over a single cable. Each transmission system is allocated a part of the total bandwidth

The Digital Subscriber Line (DSL) is a high-speed data service that works over Plain Old Telephone Service (POTS). It is a family of technologies that provide a digital connection over the copper wires of the local telephone network. Older ADSL standards could deliver 8 Mbps over about 2 km of copper wire. The latest standard ADSL2+ can deliver over 24 Mbps per user over similar distances. Many copper lines, however, are longer than 2 km, reducing thus the amount of bandwidth that can be transmitted.

Cable Internet access refers to the delivery of Internet service over the unused bandwidth on a cable television network. Users in a neighbourhood share the available bandwidth provided by a single coaxial cable line. Therefore, connection speed can vary depending on how many people are using the service at the same time. Speeds offered range from 3 Mbps to 30+Mbps. Often the idea of a shared line is seen as a weak point of cable Internet access. From a technical point of view, all networks, including DSL services, are sharing a fixed amount of bandwidth among a multitude of users - however, since because cable networks tend to be spread over larger areas than DSL services, more care must be taken to ensure good network performance.

Satellite Internet services are used in places, where other possibilities for Internet access are not available and infrequently moving locations. Internet access *via* satellite is available globally, including vessels at sea.

One-way multicast is used for IP multicast-based data, audio and video distribution. Most Internet protocols will not work correctly over one-way access, since they require a return channel.

Two-way satellite service sends data from remote sites *via* satellite to a hub, which then sends the data to the Internet. The satellite dish at each location must be precisely positioned to avoid interference with other satellites. Uplink speeds rarely exceed 1 Mbps and latency can be up to one second.

The T1 line is a common dedicated leased line used by many organizations. The T-carrier system was designed to combine multiple telephone conversations over one wire. Most T1 lines are dedicated fibre lines, but some may be copper connections.

A T1 line has 24 channels with speeds of 64 Kbps and can carry 24 concurrent conversations by converting each one into digital format and placing it on a channel. Fractional T-services are available, which enable an organization to lease only part of the T-service. T1 supports 24 channels at 1.544 Mbps total bandwidth. There are also greater capacity T-carrier lines such as T2, T3, etc. lines available for larger organizations.

Highly pronounced interdisciplinarity in both staff and course contents is a core feature and main characteristic in conservation science studies. History and archaeology; chemistry, physics and biology; geology and survey engineering; statistics and documentation; conservation and restoration - are fundamental topics, closely interconnected through the main goal of safeguarding the cultural legacy of the past. Being thus at the boundary of natural sciences and humanities, material heritage preservation is difficult to be covered in all its aspects in one institution, even a large university. Furthermore, it is crucial to offer non-systematic distant adult learners in-depth instruction on specific themes in an interactive manner, and this can only be achieved with the assistance of specialized scientists and tutors recruited in more than one area. An efficient reply to the problem is the formation of flexible hybrid schemes, characterized by extended use of a multidimensional e-learning system using both synchronous and asynchronous techniques.

e-Learning is at present widely recognized as a valuable and legitimate vehicle for the delivery of flexible learning, a scheme focusing on how students will engage in educational activities both meeting their needs and considering the options available to them(Pond et al., 1995), and on the ways analogous initiatives may be supported(Taylor and Joughin, 1997).

2. Connecting Geographically Isolated Areas Using Very Small Aperture Terminals Technology

The project is based on the concept of the interactive unified virtual classroom in both lecturing and practicing laboratory work; and is relying upon former experience in designing and setting up a multi-dimensional e-learning system using both synchronous and asynchronous techniques.

The current generation of equipment, easily providing portable and wireless apparatus, and the low-cost connection enable at present most universities teachers to utilise the richness of videoconferencing for achieving a more learner-centred teaching. Broadband technology allows ameliorating three to eight times the quality in picture and sound, so that these may approximate the images seen on television screens. Dual transmission of live action, enhanced with simultaneous transmission of video, PowerPoint slides, and audio tracks, is easily achieved.

Very small aperture terminals (VSAT) are proposed as a reliable architecture for putting into operation interactive unified virtual classrooms in isolated areas, and establishing learning activities in both lecturing and practicing laboratory work using synchronous techniques. The implementation of a network using very small aperture terminals is a secure and reliable medium to connect geographically dispersed locations in a situation where other connectivity options are not feasible. Transmission of live video to and from the hardware videoconference systems or PC is performed bi-directional over the satellite network.

The implementation of a network using very small aperture terminals (VSATs) is a secure and reliable medium to connect geographically dispersed locations. In a situation where other connectivity options are not feasible, VSATs offer two distant advantages, namely reduced deployment time and straightforward manageability (Cheah, 2001). VSAT networks provide low-cost access to communication services *via* satellite. A VSAT station is a micro-earth station using the latest innovations in the field, and proposing services comparable to those of large gateways and terrestrial networks. A typical terminal consists of the indoor (IDU) and the outdoor unit (ODU).

(a) (b)

Fig. 1. Indoor unit (a) and outdoor unit (b)

The latter is the VSAT interface to the satellite, since it contains the antenna and the electronics package, *e.g.* transmitting amplifier, low noise receiver, up-down converters, and frequency synthesizer. The indoor unit is the interface to the terminals or to a local area connection (LAN). The equipment requires minimal installation - up to a couple of hours - and simple trouble repair, and is easy to operate, while power necessities are low, and

eventually supplied by means of solar cells, given that fly-away VSATs are constantly transported, assembled and disassembled.
As seen in Figure 2, VSAT terminals are generally part of a network, with a larger earth station serving as master/hub. Hubs contain the intelligence to control the network operation, configuration and traffic; and are usually located in places, where the bulk of the network traffic originates and/or terminates. VSATs use a star network bearing satellite earth stations that rely on a large central hub. The two way connectivity between terminals is achieved by double hop link, with a first hop from VSAT to hub (inbound link) followed by a second using the hub as a relay to the destination VSAT (outbound link). Both inbound and outbound consists of two links, uplink and downlink. Alternatively the network may be hubless, the relevant mesh topology permitting all terminals to intercommunicate directly, and ensure by themselves network management and traffic control. Mesh topology is recommended for voice applications, where extended delay cannot be tolerated.

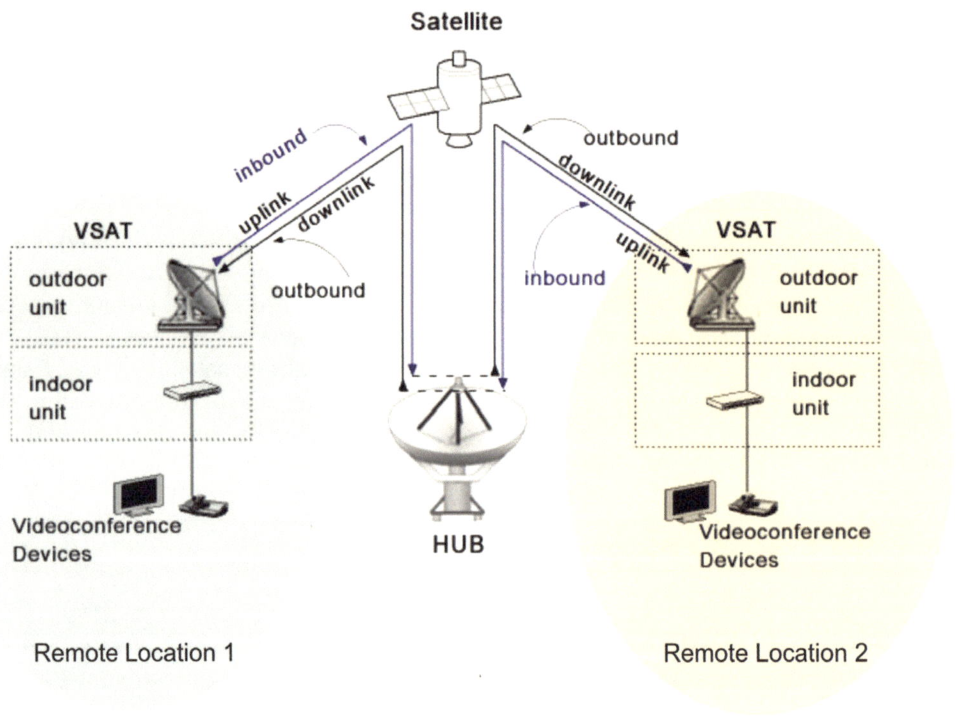

Fig. 2. Two-way star shaped VSAT network

Since they offer a wide span of solutions for most telecommunication needs, VSAT networks are suited for domestic and/or international applications, broadly falling into two categories, *e.g.* one-way applications or broadcasting, and two-way or interactive applications, which cover data, voice, video and high-speed point-to-point services. Current compression techniques enable video conferencing at data rates as low as 64 kbit/s. However, a 384 kbit/s rate is the best trade off between quality and cost. The chosen satellite service offers a bandwidth of 256 Kpbs outbound and 1024 Kbps inbound.

In each partner institution a videoconference classroom is set up as a remote node. Each virtual classroom has the minimum facilities required for videoconferencing:

- Coder-Decoder (CODEC) system (H.323 compliant),
- Video: camera and monitor,
- Audio: microphone and speaker,
- Connections to the IP (H.323).

These basic components must be present in every system, from desktop to room-based. Desktop systems are likely to utilise the monitor, microphone and speakers, supplied as part of the PC. All that is required to complete such a system is a CODEC and a camera, which may be integrated into a single compact unit. For roll-about and small room-based systems the speakers may be integrated with the monitor, and the camera and microphone may be integrated with the CODEC.

As a result of the limited power of VSATs on uplink, video transmission is feasible at low rate, using video coding and compression. Videoconferencing takes place via the IP (Internet Protocol) network, using the H.323 Standard. The H.323 standard (ITU, 2000) encompasses audio, video and data communications across packet-based networks - LAN, Intranet, Extranet and Internet. It is a set of standards developed to allow interoperation of multimedia products and applications coming from multiple vendors. It is addressing issues such as call and session control, multimedia and bandwidth management for point-to-point and multipoint conferences. A H.323 based videoconferencing system (VCON HD 3000) is used for the remote communication. The advantage of hardware-based codices is their capability to support high bit and frame rates in acceptable size large picture formats CIF (352x288). The videoconference system will give learners the feeling of a common study, benefiting of guest lecturers or collaborative teaching.

Fig. 3. Set-top videoconference unit (VCON HD 3000)

From an educational standpoint, most important issue in a virtual classroom is the establishment of communication and interaction among the participants (Greenberg, 2004) . This target can be enhanced by using oral communication between the remote classrooms, and text chat for the individual participants, in order to pool questions and facilitate discussing them. Text discussion groups will permit continuous interaction during and after any seminar. At a later phase, interest may focus on the development of a distributed infrastructure media on demand server, which will further contain information on future educational activities, *e.g.* time plan delivered courses and pre-instructional material, creating thus an e-learning grid on the topic.

The case studies considered are representative for several virtual mobility types, *e.g.* unified theoretical or practical classes, and vocational seminars; as well as "first aid line" meetings, usually founded on the shared concern about problems or the simple need for argumentation, and adopted to the requests presented by the persons involved. Laboratory training is simultaneously followed at all nodes, and is primarily focused on reviewing ambivalent results and adopting best practice examples. Live participation ensures interacting more or less the same way as when physically sharing the same site.

Evaluation is mainly consisting in the valorisation of a constant feedback in questionnaires, observation sheets and semi structured interviews for teachers and students. The overall axes used in organizing these procedures are based on generally acknowledged guidelines (Quality Assurance Agency for Higher Education, 2003), and are taking constantly into account the need for assessing both the learning material and outcomes *per se*, as well as the strategies employed for efficiently working in a virtual environment, while enhancing autonomy and involvement. Crucial parameters include didactic concepts, degrees of flexibility, quality of information, audiovisual receptiveness and friendliness of the equipment, interaction possibilities, and added value of participating in a model unified multi-component classroom.

A series of six vocational seminars comprising theoretical classes, problem-solving sessions and a pilot laboratory course, and dealing with conservation science issues, were delivered at the Aristotle University of Thessaloniki. The remote learners were encountered at their working places, namely two museums and four excavation sites located in Northern Greece and the adjacent Western Balkan countries.

Evaluation data permit an initial qualification of the system as used during the abovementioned exemplary situations. Questionnaires were distributed among thirteen professional conservators/restorers and twenty-two vocational trainees. As a crosscheck, lecturers and laboratory tutors were asked to complete observation sheets, while semi-structured interviews provided insight to specific issues, as well as to general impressions on the methodology used.

Course contents were in all cases judged very positively, since *viva voce* lecturing could constantly be combined with all types of multimedia support. Questioned on audiovisual receptiveness, lecturers were not always at ease with localising participants in the audience; in the same framework laboratory audiences markedly confirmed the preference for clearly focused-on persons or objects. There were no problems concerning sound and image quality, even where spectroscopic data, artwork visual aspects or text fragments were displayed. Interaction possibilities and friendliness of the equipment were positively evaluated, although vocational trainees were rather reluctant to use opportunities for interactive communication preferring to address the tutor present. Finally, the added value of participating in a satellite-delivered virtual learning environment was universally recognised.

The abovementioned virtual track of communication has been developed as an equivalent to further analogous applied distance learning initiatives (Suzuki et al., 2003). Characterized by flexibility, friendliness to the user and low cost, it is entirely meeting the difficulty of instructing isolated partners on issues not satisfactorily covered by individual study. The initiative is offering a clear enhancement in the quality of both organized seminars and *ad hoc* interventions, and may be considered as an excellent tool for integrating cut-off vocational professionals to the latest methodologies of their discipline.

3. Using Learning Management Systems for e-Learning in Conservation Science

The case study considered is the result of an ongoing project funded by the European Commission, Lifelong Learning Programme, Erasmus, Multilateral Projects, Virtual Campuses; titled: Systematization, Valorisation and Dissemination of e-Learning Courses in Conservation Science; and dealing with the implementation of teaching modules in cultural heritage preservation with the support of ICT technologies. Four European - Greece, Italy, France, and Spain - and one Arab Mediterranean - Morocco - countries are participating, represented by Aristotle University of Thessaloniki, Cà Foscari University of Venice, University of Avignon and the Vaucluse, Rey Juan Carlos University at Madrid, and Sidi Mohammed ben Abdellah University at Fez. aStyle Linguistic Competence, Vienna (Austria), is responsible for linguistic issues.

The virtual campus under discussion is encompassing specialized theoretical and practical modules on conservation science, as well as an open line dealing with concrete issues of immediate interest. The integration of the distance education network is using services of asynchronous techniques, in order to enhance the capability of material deriving from synchronous training to be archived and used. As a result, all curricula offered attain superior quality; while non-systematic remote adult learners are also presented with interactive in-depth instruction on specific themes treated by experts recruited in more than one institution. Real-time oral communication possibilities and simultaneous laboratory training of all attendees are ensuring a global feeling of unity among participants (Baecker, 2003). The virtual community thus constructed is responding to a factual need for creating a trans-national and intercultural shared language in relevant problem solving; and is meeting the urgent necessity for expanding pertinent encyclopaedic schemes, for creating scientific co-operations, and for permitting all contributors develop close multilevel contacts (Sedgers et al., 2005).

Fig. 4. Videoconferencing among remote sides

The educational environment is designed on the basis of a three-fold pattern - before, during and after each course unit or module. In the first phase learners are prepared for the course by having available all didactic material needed. During the frontal hours they are using videoconferencing, and webcasting/archiving; and afterwards they may benefit from study material, self-assessment opportunities and a meeting point with the instructor. Linguistic issues are attended to at all instances.

The first phase of the three-fold pattern, namely the period before entering the course, has been met in a multifaceted approach, encompassing archived preparatory material of various types, from text files and power point presentations to video presentations and multimedia modules; as well as selected bibliographical references and websites, and self-assessment tests at various levels. Thus, prerequisites are fully covered and the relevant private evaluation is perfectly controlled.

The courses are delivered in a synchronous manner *via* a videoconferencing and webcasting scheme. It is obeying the logic of a hybrid environment, *i.e.* a structured distance-learning setting with definite timetables, fixed audiences and locally organized examination schedules, in which videoconferencing is addressing the need for a multidisciplinary trans-national covering, and archived material is serving private study (Dede, 1996). The post-course phase is mainly based on the parallel activities of study - since the user can connect to the server at a later date and view the archived version of the videoconferences -, self-assessment, and direct questioning of the lecturer. Adult learners may use both the direct open line to the teaching staff, and the distributed infrastructure media on demand server.

Linguistic issues are answered by offering to all types of users the possibility of following on-line courses on language and terminology connected to conservation science issues, and of being consequently assessed, in order to permit them acquire the necessary minimum of linguistic and translation competences in terminology for entering the trans-national scientific community. A specialized on-line course, titled English for Specific Purposes: Conservation Science, is being created by the partners on the basis of the successfully completed Leonardo project English for Specific Purposes: Chemistry [http://moodle.esp-c.org], and is offered to students as a self-assessment and assessment tool. A further analogous instrument in several significant topics is the EChemTest, a computer-based multilingual test of European standard, developed by the European Chemistry Thematic Network and managed by the relevant Association [http://www.cpe.fr/ectn-assoc/echemtest/index.htm]. It is permitting evaluation of knowledge and skills in chemistry at four different levels, corresponding to the end of compulsory education; the beginning of university studies; the completion of the core chemistry syllabus in analytical, biological, inorganic, organic and physical chemistry; and the closing stages of master's curricula in synthetic and computational chemistry, and chemistry applied in conservation science. The English version is serving as an overall linguistic training and self-assessment possibility. Any other European language considered necessary for mastering specialized information on concrete issues may as well be approached by the abovementioned on-line courses.

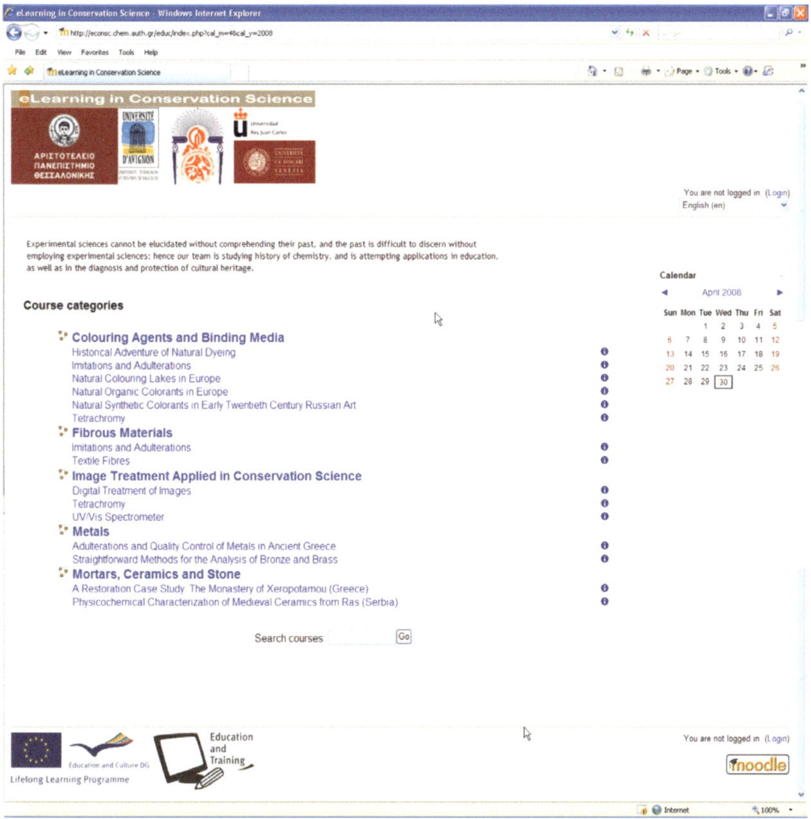

Fig. 5. e-learning portal layout using Moodle

The learning platform utilized consists of an open-source Course Management System (CMS), Moodle (http://moodle.org), and serving the learner-content interaction. The contents are divided in five major course categories, corresponding to the general topics: metals; mortars, ceramics and stone; colouring agents and binding media; fibrous materials; and image treatment applied in conservation science. Moodle permits having each course category managed by a team of experts belonging to all partner institutions.

The courses in Moodle are implemented in duplicated topic format. The first copy contains the didactic preparatory material, and the second is hidden. After the lecture, and while the first copy disappears, the second is revealed: it contains extra material in form of video archived lectures, and a virtual meeting place with learners. For later learner-teacher interactions in the created meeting place, Moodle is combined to a direct dialogue tool, actually a Web2 audio and video web conference system (DIMDIM browser-based web 2.0 service) (http://www.dimdim.com), giving the instructor the possibility to show over the Internet presentations, applications and the desktop, as well as to converse, and use the webcam. Since the tool is a presenter, only a browser plug-in is needed, attendees not having to install anything.

A video learning system, implemented through the ePresence platform (http://epresence.tv/products) for capturing, archiving and webcasting lectures, is sustaining both adult learners and any type of extended self-study. The ePresence system is developed at the Knowledge Media Design Institute, University of Toronto, is scalable, interactive, and able to support live and on-demand broadcasting.

Fig. 6. Dimdim plugin for Moodle

In each partner institution a videoconference classroom is set up as a remote node. Each virtual classroom has one or more cameras, microphones, loudspeakers, and monitors. A H.323 based hardware videoconferencing system is used for remote communication (VCON, 1998).

The pedagogical background to the overall structure is based on the theory of reasoned action, proposing that beliefs influence attitudes, which in turn may lead to intention and then generate behaviours (Turgeon, 1997).

The IT friendliness is checked according to the Research Model, an adapted version of the Technology Acceptance Model (TAM). Goal of TAM is to explain the determinants capturing the attitude and behaviour of a broad range of users towards IT, in the framework of two posited beliefs, namely perceived usefulness and perceived ease of use (Davis, 1993). Within the present context, perceived usefulness is defined as the students' prospective subjective probability that the course is at the required standard for ameliorating his knowledge and skills within the educational community and the job market; while perceived ease of use refers to the degree to which prospective users expect the three phases of the courses to be free from cognitive effort in what regards the IT environment (Johanssen et al., 1995).

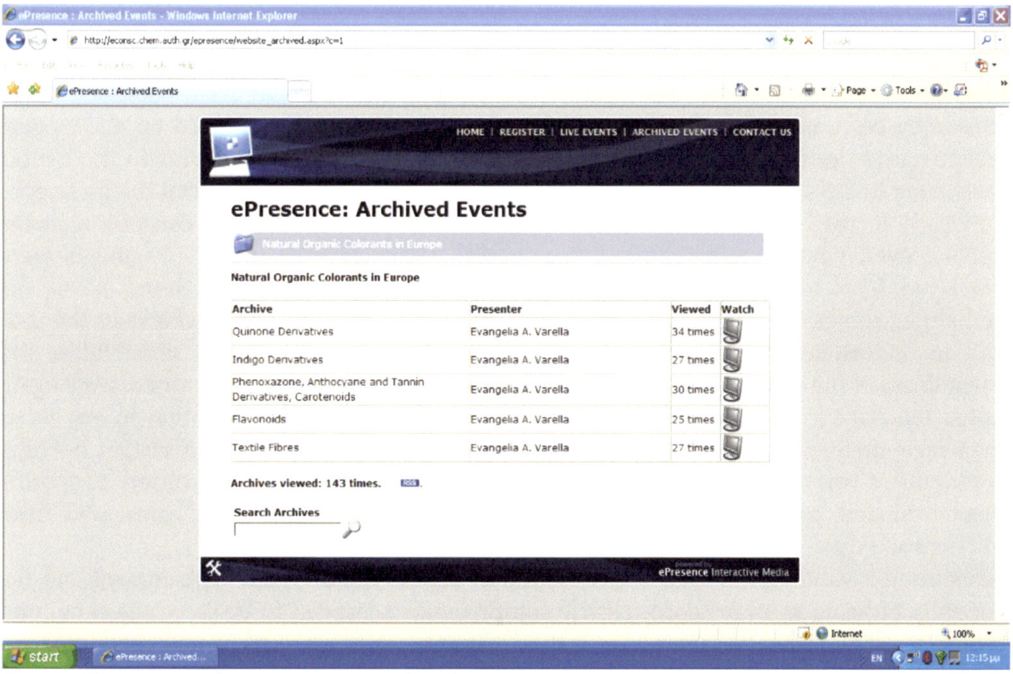

Fig. 7. ePresence video streaming and archiving

Offering a flexible e-learning environment, the case study under consideration permits activities to focus on the deployment of a suitable infrastructure and on the implementation of contents, while the user may easily adapt the learning path to his timely and geographical constraints. It is encompassing third cycle theoretical or practical classes, as well as *ad hoc* meetings, founded on the shared concern about problems or the simple need for argumentation, and adapted to the requests presented by the students involved. Laboratory training is simultaneously followed at all nodes, and is primarily reviewing ambivalent results and adopting best practice examples in both physicochemical and safeguarding issues. Evaluation is mainly consisting in the valorisation of a constant feedback in questionnaires, observation sheets and semi structured interviews for teachers and students. The overall parameters used in organizing these procedures are based on generally acknowledged guidelines, and are taking constantly into account the need for assessing both the learning material and outcomes *per se*, as well as the strategies employed for efficiently working in a virtual environment, while enhancing autonomy and involvement (American Distance Education Consortium.,2003). Decisive parameters include didactic concepts, degrees of flexibility, quality of information, audiovisual receptiveness and friendliness of the equipment, interaction possibilities, linguistic issues, and added value of participating in a model unified multi-component classroom (Pituch and Lee, 2004).

Evaluation data permit an initial qualitative characterization of the scheme, in the way it is used during the abovementioned first phase of the project. Sets of questionnaires were distributed among thirty-eight postgraduate students originating from all participating countries, for both lecture and laboratory attendance. As a crosscheck, teachers and tutors were asked to complete observation sheets, while semi-structured interviews provided insight to specific issues, as well as to general impressions on the methodology used. As already mentioned, the approach is based on the Research Model, an adapted version of the Technology Acceptance Model (TAM).

Course contents were in all cases judged very positively, since *viva voce* lecturing could constantly be combined with all types of multimedia support. Questioned on audiovisual receptiveness, lecturers were not always at ease with localising participants in the remote classroom; in the same framework laboratory audiences markedly confirmed the preference for clearly focused-on persons or objects. There were no critical problems concerning image quality, even where spectroscopic data, artwork visual aspects or text fragments were displayed. Main relevant difficulty appeared to be the multilingual background of teachers and students, since a dramatically higher sound quality was requested whenever the user had to understand notions uttered in a foreign language. Interaction possibilities and friendliness of the equipment were positively evaluated, although often learners were again rather reluctant to benefit from opportunities for interactive communication in any other than their mother tongue. Finally, the added value of participating in a virtual learning environment was universally recognised, with the argument that a great variety of specific theoretical and practical topics could both be discussed in depth and presented from different standpoints.

Structuring a valid equilibrium between respect for the multilingual environment and the necessity of being at all instances clearly comprehended, proved to be the greatest cultural challenge within the trans-national virtual campus. Although all contributors had an acceptable passive knowledge of English, nevertheless they insisted in having courses as well offered in other major European languages involved. Fluently French-speaking Moroccan participants and non-European Spanish native speakers were pronouncedly negative in the introduction of English as a generally operative language, while Middle East Arabs studying in Italy and Greece insisted on its overall application. To address the problem, and in addition to the specialized online training and assessment tools offered, partners introduced a consistent language policy by implementing a combined system in the frame of *viva voce* lecturing and multimedia support. Thus, talking in another language is mingled to an extensive English multimedia presentation and *vice versa*, while interactive communication is largely managed by the tutor present in each classroom. Being at least bilingual, the tutor is encouraging participation, and is *ad hoc* translating difficult notions, obeying at the sole criterion of permitting everyone to be largely understood.

Future work on the subject will address evaluation by external experts. Firstly the collaborating institutions, mentioned in the next paragraph, and then international panels - such as the Working Group on Chemistry and Cultural Heritage, European Chemistry Thematic Network Association - will be asked to be involved in validating the project's outcomes. Crucial axes for building up this stage include didactic concepts; degrees of flexibility; quality of information; audiovisual receptiveness and friendliness of the equipment; interaction possibilities; linguistic issues; and added value of the model unified multi-component classroom.

The project is structured at two interconnected levels, the partner universities and a number of collaborating institutions prepared to participate in the courses and evaluate the results. Further dissemination of the course will primarily focus on a most global covering of Europe and the Arab world, before taking into account other regions. Target groups will largely belong to postgraduate students in conservation science at the institutions involved. A second important target group are non-systematic distant adult learners confronted with specific problems or willing to keep their knowledge updated with the aid of the archiving system.

Characterized by flexibility, friendliness to the user and low cost, the virtual track of learning and communication presented is entirely meeting both the difficulty of covering all topics dealing with cultural heritage preservation in one place, and the urge to instruct isolated partners on urgent issues. The project is offering a clear enhancement in the quality of both organized courses and *ad hoc* interventions, and may be considered as an excellent initiative for creating a trans-national and intercultural virtual community using common approaches and sharing knowledge and skills in a highly interdisciplinary subject.

4. References

American Distance Education Consortium, Guiding principles for distance teaching and learning (2003), http://www.adec.edu/admin/papers/distance-teaching_principles.html.

Baecker, R. (2003). A principled design for scalable Internet visual communications with rich media, interactivity and structured archives. Proc. Centre for Advanced Studies on Collaborative Research.

Bafestou, G. & Mentzas G. (2002). Review and functional classification of collaborative systems. International Journal of Information Management, 22(4), 281-305.

Brown, P. J. (1995). Creating educational hyperdocuments: Can it be economic? Innovations in Education and Training International, 32(3), August, 202-208

Cheah J.Y.C., Very small aperture terminal satellite earth station, in: Encyclopaedia of Physical Science and Technology, R.A. Meyers (Ed.), N York 2001, 607-620 (9780122274 107); http://www.sciencedirect.com/science/article/B782V-4CKG1K4-YG/2/ffcff4e74244fa668 6aa29d3c3f9aa9f

Davis, F.D. (1993), "User acceptance of information technology: system characteristics, user perceptions and behavioral impacts", International Journal of Man-Machine Studies, Vol. 38 No. 3, pp. 475-87.

Dede, D. The evolution of distance education - emerging technologies and distributed learning, The American Journal of Distance Education, 10/2 (1996) 4-36.

Ellis, C. A.; Gibbs, S. J. & Rein, G. (1991). Groupware: Some issues and experiences. Communications of the ACM, 34(1), 39–58.

Freitas, F., Myers, S., & Avtgis, T. (1998). Student Perceptions of Instructor Immediacy in Conventional and Distributed Learning Classrooms. Communication Education 47(4), 366-72.

Johanssen,D., Davidson, M., Collins, M.,. Campbell, J and Hagg, B.B. Constructivism and computer-mediated communication, The American Journal of Distance Education, 9/2 (1995) 7-26.

Greenberg, A., Navigating the sea of research on videoconferencing-based distance education: a platform for understanding research into the technology's effectiveness and value (February 2004), http://www.wainhouse.com/ files/ papers/wr-navseadistedu.pdf.

ITU, Packet-based multimedia communication systems - ITU-T H.323, International Telecommunications Union, Geneva, November 2000.

Jaervelae, S.; Haekkinen, P.; Arvaja, M. & Leinonen, P. (2004). Instructional Support in CSCL. What we know about CSCL and implementation it in Higher Education, Kluwer Academic Publishers, Boston ISBN: 1-4020-7779-3, pp. 115-139.

Marjanovic, O. (1999). Learning and teaching in a synchronous collaborative environment. Journal of Computer Assisted Learning, 15(2), 129–138.

Moore, M. (1993). Theory for transactional distance. In D. Keegan (Ed.), Theoretical principles of distance education (pp. 22–38). London, New York: Routledge.

Moore, M., & Kearsley, G. (1996). Distance education: A system view. New York: Wadsworth.

Offir, B. Lev, Y. & Bezalel, R. (2008). Surface and deep learning processes in distance education: Synchronous versus asynchronous systems. Computers & Education, 51(3), 1172-1183.

Pituch, K. A. and Lee, Yao-Kuci. (2004). The influence of system characteristics on elearning use, Computer and Education.

Pond,K., Ul Hao,R.,and Wade,W., Peer review - A precursor to peer assessment, Innovations in Education and Training International 32/4 (1995) 314–23.

Quality Assurance Agency for Higher Education, Guidelines on the quality assurance of distance learning, London 1999; The American Distance Education Consortium, Guiding principles for distance teaching and learning (2003), http://www. adec.edu/admin/papers/ distance-teaching_principles.html.

Relan, A. & Gillani,B. B. (1997). Web-based instruction and the traditional classroom: Similarities and differences. In B. H. Khan (Ed.) Web-based instruction. (pp. 41-46). Englewood Cliffs, New Jersey: Educational Technology Publications.

Scardamalia, M. & Bereiter, C. (1994). Computer support for knowledge building communities. The Journal of the Learning Sciences, 3(3), 265-283.

Sedgers, J., Johnson, J., Smyth D., and Waite, V., Interactive distance learning, International Journal of Instructional Technology and Distance Learning 2/10 (2005) 85-91, http://www.itdl.org/Journal/Oct_05/Oct_05.pdf.

Selwyn, N. & Gorard, S. (2003). Reality bytes: Examining the rhetoric of widening educational participation via ICT. British Journal of Educational Technology, 34(2), 169.

Silverman, B. G. (1995). Computer Supported Collaborative Learning (CSCL), Computers & Education, 25 (3), 81-91.

Suzuki,I.,Yamada,K.,Yamakawa,T.,Hashiba,M., and Akazawa,K., Delivery of medical multimedia contents through the tcp/ip network using RealSystem, Computer Methods and Programs in Biomedicine 70 (2003) 253-258;.

Taylor,P., and Joughin,G., What is flexible learning? in: Teaching through flexible learning resources, Griffith Institute for Higher Education, Queensland 1997.

Turgeon, A., Implication of web-based technology for engaging students in a learning society, Journal of Public Service and Outreach, 2/2 (1997), 32-37.

VCON Videoconferencing, White paper on the H.323 standard (January 1998), http://www.vcon.com/pdfdoc/eng/wp/010429.eng.wp.h323_standard.pdf

Veerman, A.L.; Andriessen, J.E.B. & Kanselaar, G. (2000). Learning through synchronous electronic discussion. Computers & Educations, 34 (3-4), 269-290.

8

Impact of the New Economy on Business Informatics Education

Pere Tumbas, Otilija Sedlak and Predrag Matković
University of Novi Sad, Faculty of Economics Subotica
Serbia

1. Introduction

The "New Economy" of the 21st century is driven in large measure by advances in computing, information, and communications technologies (ICT). To be competitive and also developed country is to satisfy the needs such as the greater use of science and new technologies by average citizens; more interdisciplinary/multidisciplinary work; greater understanding of highly complex and interacting systems; new and renewed efforts at building community and solving local challenges in the face of globalization; and a substantial rethinking of business in general (Moore, 2007).

The changed view of reality in this way causes the need of defining completely changed needs in education. Many authors state that success in the global economy mostly depends on the new system of education. ICT has been applied in many new fields or the existing fields have been significantly broadened. The education system needs to be transformed and new components, which will adapt it to the requirements of globalization and the "New Economy", should be built. New and changed requirements for higher education have contributed to the development of initiatives to radically change the curricula especially in the field of Economy, Management and Business Informatics at many universities.

This Chapter shows components of the new education system, caused by globalization and the "New Economy". Also, the influence of developing ICT and their application to higher education is shown. Bases which should be obligatorily considered in developing new curricula in the field of Economy, Management and Business Informatics are described in detail. Requirements of the Bologna processes, requirements and standards defined during realizing the European projects, as well as requirements of the global economy are described before all.

In order to satisfy the identified requirements, the new Curricula of the Faculty of Economics in Subotica has been developed using innovated process which is significantly different from the previous ones. The Chapter also presents the realized results, as well as experience and attained effects of the newly-developed Curricula, especially in the field of Business Informatics.

2. Globalization, "New Economy" and Education

Globalization is a very real phenomenon that is transforming the world economic system including all business processes. With the emergence of a new development model, knowledge and information take on increasing importance. Thus, the era of globalisation has implications for knowledge, education and learning. One implication of this transformation is that a new system of knowledge, education and learning will include many components that do not exist in current educational system. This new system should include the following components (Cogburn, 1998):

- A focus on abstract concepts and uncertain situations - The academic environment is still preparing students to be capable to solve known problems, although reality very rarely or does not deal with clearly defined problems. Therefore, students should be prepared to recognize the problem first, collect necessary information, and then make decision in the complex and uncertain environment.
- Uses of holistic, interdisciplinary approach - Education and learning environment today is divided into very rigid academic disciplines. However, the e-society and the global economy need the holistic approach to the system. The interdisciplinary approach to researches is considered as critical in understanding the complex reality. This component is specially expressed with curricula in the fields of Economy, Management and Business Informatics.
- Enhances the student's ability to manipulate symbols and to acquire and utilise knowledge - Manipulating the symbols, which represent abstractions of the highest levels of some concrete forms of reality, is one of the most important requirements of today's economy. Also, globalization of the economy requires education increasing students' capability to access, assess, adopt and apply knowledge, to think independently to exercise appropriate judgment and to collaborate with others. The objective of education is no longer simply to convey a body of knowledge, but to teach how to learn, problem-solve and synthesize the old with the new.
- Produces an increased quantity of scientifically and technically trained students - Research and development become the key and critical components of the global development. The requirement that the staff is well trained in the field of science and technology is of special importance. Academic institutions come into contacts with research enterprises within the public and private sectors. Universities must quickly adapt to these needs and become a key component of new national systems of research and development.
- Encourages students to work in teams or virtual teams around the world - the need for capable students to work in teams is very expressed, therefore, they must possess developed capabilities for group dinamics, compromise, debate, persuasion, organisation, leadership and management skills. This is a very important component of the new system because academic institutions until recently developed just the opposite capabilities of students, where students' individuality was developed with a very limited size of the group work. Forming virtual teams for work in the global network is a speciality in international organizations dealing with research and development.
- Agile and flexible system - Academic institutions must be more flexible in attempts to satisfy different and very changeable needs of students in the global economy. It

means variety in time, place, approach and curriculum offerings. Academic course offerings should be adapted to reflect these new knowledge, education and learning requirements. It is necessary to emphasize the remove of borders existing between professors and students. New systems understand synchronic and asynchronous activities. Thus, in synchonic appear real time lectures, quizzes and group discussions, where students and professors can be in the same or different locations. With asynchronous activities appear archived lectures (in audio and video) that can be accessed at nearly anytime, anyplace.

Besides briefly described requirements of globalization according to the higher education, it is important to emphasize impact of "New Economy" on business informatics and information system education. The growing importance of ICT and innovation in the market place brings with it a need for the better management of professional knowledge for knowledge workers in the "New Economy". The educational system in these changed circumstances must satisfy requirements of Knowledge Economy and E-Business Management. Multidisciplinarity or interdisciplinarity of curricula is the key element of these requirements (Handzic, 2002).

2.1 Interdisciplinary - multidisciplinary Approach in Curricula Development

Historical experience on university teaching process indicates that computer programming disciplines contents evolutes from syntax and logical structures to solve practical cases, problems, or even immediate tasks, towards modeling complex tasks. The contribution from Information Technologies courses added to the Business Economics, Management and Quantitative Methods and Techniques courses, promotes a welcome synthesis approach, in terms of innovative curriculum proposals.

The multidisciplinary curricular structure tendency is a kind of horizontal aggregation. It is direct related with increasing complexity projects toward interdisciplinary times. Interdisciplinary orientation and inverted curriculum can be considered synonymous because under complexity parameters, claimed from interdisciplinary abstraction models, there is an indissoluble interdependence of the categories of knowledge. Interdisciplinary curricular trend is more recent and it has been practiced also, under isolated disciplines context. But, of course, its potentiality increase a lot, if it is supported by a global curricular proposal, putting all together, under a course inverted curriculum. It is inverted the direction, yet from generic - complex categories of knowledge, on those carries courses, to part categories of knowledge.

Business informatics is interdisciplinary and can be summarised as a socio-technological and business oriented subject with engineering penetration (Helfert & Duncan, 2006). The need for interdisciplinary, i.e. multidisciplinary approach in curricula development is confirmed by numerous developed fields of applied informatics, illustrated in Figure 1, where Business Informatics can be seen. Core subjects of the information age are illustrated in the same Figure.

The final curriculum as outlined comprises a balanced and interdisciplinary structure, which centered on ICT principles and focuses on transformation, models and methods. The ICT penetration throughout the programme is seen as an important characteristic, which differentiates this programme from management oriented information system degrees. Therefore the business informatics approach appears to us not only to be innovative with regard to its interdisciplinary character, but moreover the ICT perspective and the integration of cultural studies and practical experiences in an international setting equip graduates with required capabilities.

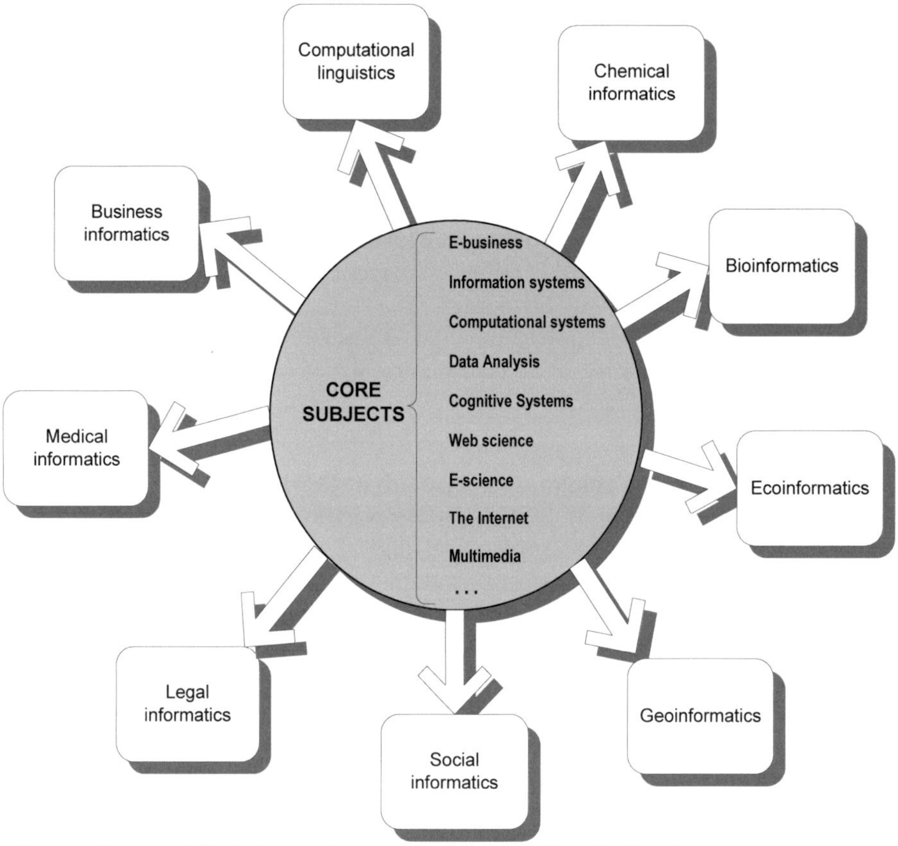

Fig. 1. Core subjects of the information age and fields of applied informatics

3. Fundamentals of Developing the Curriculum

Impacts of globalization and the "New Economy" on higher education have caused the development of new and significant changes of the current curricula at universities, especially in the fields of Economy, Management and Business Informatics. Except satisfying the cited requirements of globalization and the "New Economy", curricula have been completely harmonized with the requirements of the Bologna process and the need of creating the European Higher Education Area (EHEA). Results of some projects in the field of higher education (Tempus, Socrates, WUS), gave important contribution to their quality, where already implemented curricula and positive experience were analyzed in detail and used for developing new curricula.

After passing the Law on higher education, the missing legal framework for realizing new curricula was also provided in the Republic of Serbia in 2005. Faculties in the country have

approached to very intensive changes of their curricula. The Faculty of Economics in Subotica, as the leader in these processes, has changed its curricula at all three study levels. The Curriculum of the Faculty was developed in accordance with the established concepts of the Bologna process, attained results of the JEP Tempus projects, as well as the Euro-Inf Framework Standards of the Socrates project. Therefore, during developing the new Curriculum, requirements of globalization and the "New Economy" in the field of higher education expressed in the form of competences were especially taken into consideration.
Theoretical approaches gave us bases for research, but what we needed, in addition, were practical, simple approaches to curriculum development. For that, we turned to curriculum, instruction and assessment specialists such as Dee Fink and Grant Wiggins. Fink developed integrated course design (ICD) model, that includes the triad of learning goals, teaching and learning activities and feedback/assessment (Fink, 2003). Learning goals identify what we want students to learn, learning activities identify how students will learn what it is we want them to learn, and the feedback/assessment identifies how we will know students have achieved the intended goals. These components are all influenced by "situational factors", such as course context, professional expectations, and the nature of the subject, the students, and the teacher (Howard, 2007). Using ICD model, we desinged the coherent curriculum of the Faculty.

3.1 Concepts of the Bologna Process

Concepts of the Bologna Process represented the basis for developing the new Curriculum. The most important objectives of this process are (ECTS, 2007):

- Determining the joint qualifications framework for an easier diploma recognition and comparison,
- Implementation of a three-level cycle of university education system,
- Introduction of the common European Credit Transfer and Accumulation System (ECTS),
- Mobility of students and teaching staff,
- Promotion of the European cooperation in providing quality, and
- Promotion of European contents.

Following trends and international standards in the field of higher education, the Faculty of Economics developed new Curriculum making an important move to the complete new education system. Except the Bachelor studies lasting three years, the Faculty organizes Master studies lasting two years and the Doctoral studies taking three years to complete. This model of Curriculum "3+2+3" is the most often used in the European countries in the field of Economy, Management and Business Informatics. It is illustrated in Figure 2.
The presentation of the model in the form of a sandglass points to the inverted logic of learning, and gaining knowledge and skills. In the first two years, students gain mostly basic scientific and technological knowledge and theoretical methodological knowledge. The third year emphasizes major knowledge. The fourth year emphasizes them even more, while the fifth year turns the process to the applied methodological knowledge. The next three years understand the advancement of knowledge by the original scientific research work.

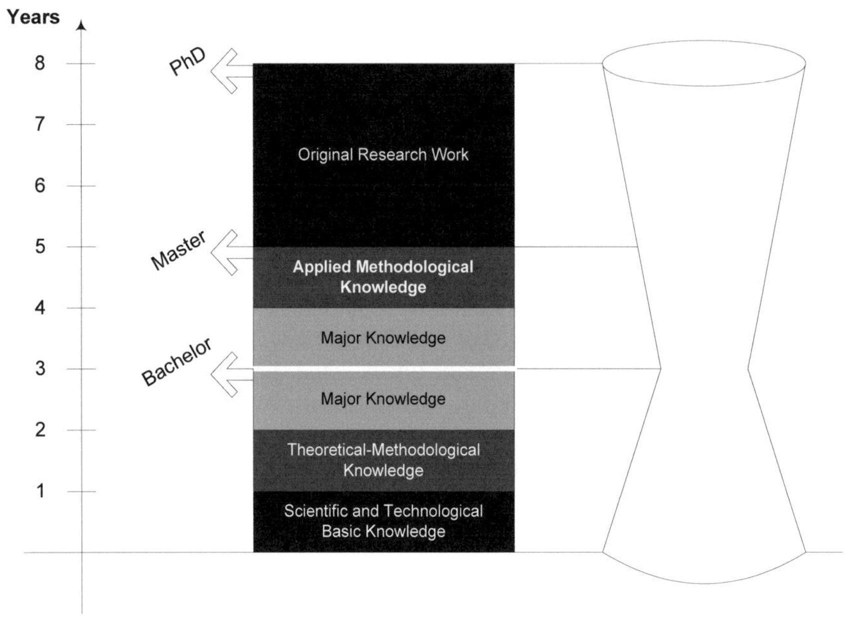

Fig. 2. The Model of Curriculum

The basic characteristics of the Curriculum are (Plančak, 2006):

- European Credit Transfer System - ECTS, that provides suppositions for including the Faculty into the European Higher Education Area. ECTS is a student-centered system based on the student workload, or notional learning time required to achieve the objectives of a programme. These objectives should preferably be specified in terms of the learning outcomes and competences to be acquired.
- 60 ECTS measure the student workload during one academic year. To calculate the equivalence between ECTS and the student workload of a study programme, it is necessary to emphasize that it is supposed that the student works 8 hours a day, 5 days a week and that there are average of 40 to 45 weeks in an academic year. It means that the student workload amounts to 1800 hours per year and in this case one credit stands for 30 working hours.
- The number of credits (X) belonging to one course is proportionate to the number of hours (Y) the student spends at all learning activities of the course. The proportion for defining ECTS points to the courses is: X: 60 credits = Y: 1800 hours.
- Workload is not linked with the level of the course (a core course may require less workload than an elective course).
- One-semester courses, classified into four categories: obligatory core courses, elective core courses, obligatory major courses and elective major courses. Depending on the level of studies, elective courses make 15% at the Bachelor studies, 20% at the Master studies and 50% at the Doctoral studies. This broad choice of majors and elective courses enable students a very narrow specialization.

- The Faculty used top-down method to allocate credits, where the programme is divided into course units or modules, to which are allocated a limited and reasonable number of credits in more or less standard multiples. Also, the Faculty, implemented the non-modularized system, where each course unit have a different number of credits.
- The Faculty implemented the even number system in credit allocation so the courses got 4, 6 or 8 ECTS. Therefore, the courses with 8 ECTS credits allows around 240 hours of work of a typical student, the courses with 6 ECTS credits allows 180 hours and the courses with 4 ECTS credits allows 120 hours.
- Credits in ECTS can be obtained after successful completion of the work required and appropriate assessment of the learning outcomes achieved.
- Learning activities include: lectures, seminars, practical works, homework, projects, placements, fieldwork, and preparation of exams, exams, and so forth.
- Mobility of the teaching staff, students and administrative personnel.
- Specially created diploma supplement, giving possibilities to emphasize characteristics of the student, his basic and specialist knowledge and skillfulness, successes and rewards awarded during his study at the Faculty.
- A number of small groups of students in both lectures and exercises, especially in the lectures where practical knowledge and skills are gained.
- Programs of courses are simply and transparently formulated, according to the basic requirements of the Bologna standards. They are the aim of the course, competences, short contents of the course, year and semester of the course, number of lectures and exercises, way and form of knowledge test, literature, teaching language, week schedules of classes with the date of tests and midterms, date of accepting the program, as well as the date of its last change.
- The assessment methods proposed by ECTS should provide the distribution of grades 10%-25%-30%-25%-10%, respectively for the grades 6-7-8-9-10 and meet the Gauss schedule. Therefore, 10% of students should pass the exam obtaining the grade six and ten, 25% of students should pass the exam obtaining the grade seven and nine, and 30% of students should pass obtaining the grade eight. From the total number of students, 90% should pass the exam obtaining one of passing grades.

Taking the accepted model into consideration, the distal aim of the Curriculum Business Informatics Major at the Faculty of Economics can be expressed in the following way:

- During the first three years of the Bachelor study, Faculty educates experts in the field of Business Informatics for efficient application of information technologies and contemporary software products in business in order to attain an increasing business effectiveness and efficiency;
- During the next two years of the Master study, students of the above average performance are enabled to choose narrow specialist fields and acquire new specialist knowledge, broaden theoretical and methodological knowledge in their narrow educational fields, and train for development and research projects;
- Further develop, in the course of the last three years of the doctoral study, research capabilities and the capabilities of the best students for educational

work, providing gradually in this way the teaching base of the faculties, scientific institutes and universities.
- Business Informatics can complement the managed-oriented stream of an information systems discipline, which often focuses on the business and management aspects.
- Business Informatics curriculum should include many related subjects ranging from business and information system strategy, to management and marketing, organizational concepts, modeling and information system architecture, programming, mathematics, statistics and operations research as well as computing, networking and communication technologies.

3.2 Results of the JEP Tempus Projects

The Faculty took part very successfully in realizing two JEP Tempus projects, whose primary objectives were to develop new curricula.

Tempus JEP-16067-2001: "Teaching Business Information Systems"' was realized in cooperation with:
- University of Brighton, School of Computing, Mathematical and Information Sciences, U.K.;
- University of Belgrade, Faculty of Organizational Sciences, Belgrade, Serbia;
- Centre for Research and Technology Thessaloniki, Greece;
- University of Vienna, Department of Computer Science and Business Informatics, Austria;
- University of Novi Sad, Faculty of Science, Novi Sad, Serbia.

Bachelor and Master Curricula contents of the project partners, in the field of Business Informatics and Business Information Systems, were analyzed in order to take over positive experiences and to innovate current courses. Aims and learning outcomes were defined at the level of curriculum, as well as necessary contents at the level of some courses. Special importance was paid to studying skills and knowledge in the field of Informatics in educating economists and managers. The conclusion was that it was necessary to introduce courses, both on Bachelor and Master level, in all majors in the fields of Economy and Management, which would enable broader application of ICT.

Tempus JEP-17027-2002: "Upgrading Business Information Studies in FRY" (Federal Republic of Yugoslavia), was realized in cooperation with:
- Universita Degni Studi di Udine, Italy;
- Faculte Universitaire Des Sciences Agronomiques de Gembloux, Belgium;
- Universita Degni Studi di Foggia, Italy;
- Wirtschatssuniversitat Wien, Austria, and
- University of Podgorica, Faculty of Economics Podgorica, Montenegro.

The result in this project was the first versions of Curricula of the Bachelor studies at the Faculty in the fields of Economy, Management and Business Informatics. The groups of obligatory and elective courses were indentified at the Faculty for the first time, as well as the groups of core-educational, theoretical-methodological, scientific-professional and

professional-applicative courses. Experiences of the European partners in the project of curricula development were taken over and build in.
The project identified application domains in Business Informatics Curriculum, created the distinction between general and specialised application domains and defined the amount of application domain that may need to be incorporated into a curriculum (Cowling, 2007).

3.3 Results of the Socrates Euro-Inf Project

The Faculty took part as partner in the project: Euro-Inf – Informatics Education in Europe and built on established framework standards in its Curriculum during the final design of the Curriculum of Bachelor and Master studies in the field of Business Informatics. The partners of Euro-Inf Project were:

- ASIIN (Accreditation Agency for Degree Programmes in Engineering, Informatics, the Natural Sciences and Mathematics), Germany,
- CEPIS (Council of European Professional Informatics Societies - 37 informatics societies from 32 countries),
- University of Applied Sciences Hamburg, Germany, and
- University of Paderborn, Germany.

The ultimate goal of the Euro-Inf Project is to facilitate European-wide professional recognition by the competent national authorities of informatics degrees. These recognitions are awarded by study programmes accredited on the basis of the programme outcomes and accreditation criteria defined in the Euro-Inf Framework Standards. The Euro-Inf, based on standards and accreditation systems, created a set of framework standards which were tested and refined through trial accreditations.
The Euro-Inf Project aims to create a framework for setting up a European system of Standards for assessing informatics education at the First Cycle and Second Cycle level. Based on the establishment and approval of this set of standards, the main objectives of the Euro-Inf Project are (Aszalos, 2008):

- to improve the quality of educational programmes in informatics;
- to provide an appropriate "European label" for accredited educational programmes in informatics;
- to provide a basis for comparing educational qualifications in informatics in the EHEA;
- to facilitate mutual transnational recognition by programme validation and certification;
- to facilitate recognition of accredited degrees in informatics higher education in accordance with the EU directives and other agreements;
- together with other field-specific standards and criteria, to contribute to the harmonisation of the EHEA;
- to support the mobility of informatics graduates;
- to contribute to international transparency - as one of the objectives of the Bologna Declaration, and
- to support improvements to the quality of informatics programmes in general.

The project defined: Learning Outcomes for First Cycle Degree Programmes and Second Cycle Degree Programmes. The programme outcomes are described in project as quality standards for competences, skills and knowledge a graduate of an accredited course would be expected to have achieved as the education base for practising their profession or for graduate studies.

Programme outcomes vary in extent and intensity in accordance with the differing objectives of the First and Second Cycle degree programmes. In the Euro-Inf project, they have been ranged in the following four categories (Euro-Inf, 2007):

- Underlying Conceptual Basis for Informatics,
- Analysis, Design and Implementation,
- Technological, Methodological and Transferable Skills and
- Other Professional Skills.

For each of the mentioned category expected learning outcomes for informatics programmes have been formulated. The first category "Underlying Conceptual Basis for Informatics" identifies capabilities that are essential to satisfying the other learning outcomes. Furthermore, it provides help for defining which knowledge and understanding graduates should demonstrate of their informatics specialisation as well as of the wider context of informatics.

Subsuming the aspects "Analysis, Design and Implementation" in a single category appears worthwhile because they describe the basic steps of a work cycle. The category "Technological, Methodological and Transferable Competences" refers to the expected ability of a graduate to work to combine and abstract his technical skills to solve problems involving aspects of a wider, technological context. Thus he is able to use appropriate methods and material to achieve an industrial objective.

Social or soft competences, listed under the category "Other Professional Skills" are crucial to communicate information, ideas, problems and solutions. Besides the so-called soft skills, the category refers to project management skills and the knowledge of disciplines and those ancillary principles that are relevant to the working environment of the graduates' specialisation.

4. New Solutions in the Curricula

The new Curriculum of the Faculty of Economics, realized in accordance with all defined and in advance described fundamentals, at three study levels has 9 Bachelor, 10 Master and 3 doctoral study programmes. Curricula are accredited at the national level.

Special attention in developing curricula is paid to the interdisciplinary of its contents; therefore, it is represented at all the study levels. Knowledge structure in the model of curriculum, illustrated in Figure 3, includes: basic knowledge (knowledge of economics, knowledge of business economics, knowledge of quantitative methods and techniques, knowledge of management and social science, knowledge of information technologies) and major knowledge. Major knowledge includes the group of core courses and the group of elective courses.

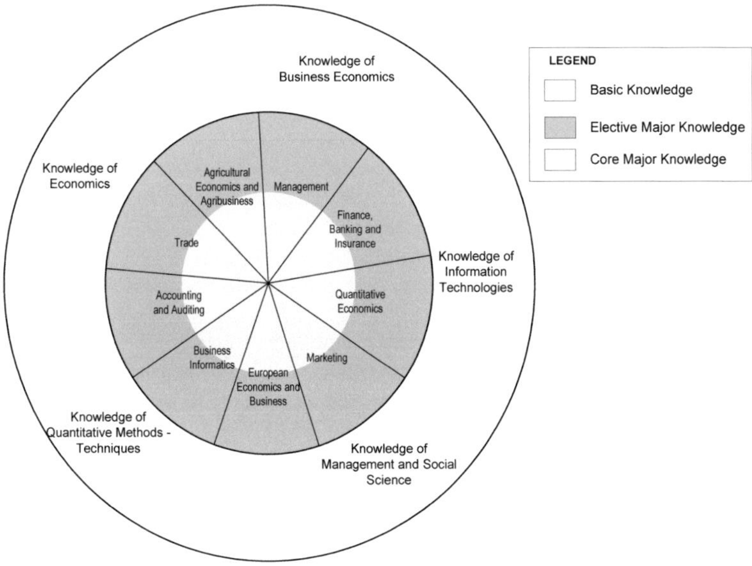

Fig. 3. Structure of Knowledge in the Model of the Curriculum

Major knowledge is in accordance with different majors in the curriculum model:

- Agricultural Economics and Agribusiness
- European Economics and Business
- Finance, Banking and Insurance
- Quantitative Economics
- Marketing
- Management
- Business Informatics
- Accounting and Auditing
- Trade

The central focus of the curriculum for Business Informatics is to educate individuals to plan and lead information system related projects. The core aim is enabling students to apply technological solutions and develop information system architectures to solve business problems of organizations. A major goal of this program is to prepare students for their future carrier in business informatics, either in academia or in practice. In addition to the strong knowledge in business informatics, the programme aims to enhance key transferable skills. This will enable the students to take on a variety of jobs in various types of organizations.

The fundation for the curriculum design is the learning process of a student, which is supported by learning situations that promote student activity and learning. Curriculum design is thus based on both the targeted learning outcomes and students entrance level, illustrated in Table 1. The learning process is being constructed in between these two from the various learning and teaching situations, assignments, counselling and assesment.

Subject specific competences	Description of the competence
Information Systems Competences	‣ Understands information system as a whole ‣ Understands the production, acquisition and deployment process of an information system ‣ Understands the principles of data management ‣ Is able to specify, design and implement secure software systems, databases, and user interface ‣ Is able to program ‣ Is able to document and decode documentation of an information system ‣ Is able to plan and implement training
Project Work Competence	‣ Understands the differences between various kind of ICT projects and the role of projects as a part of an organizational structure ‣ Understands the purpose of a systematic way of action in project work and is able to work in a responsible manner in ICT projects ‣ Is able to use and apply various ICT project planning and management methods ‣ Is able to identify and provide for possible risks related to ICT projects
Business Competence	‣ Understands essential business processes and functions ‣ Understands the role of ICT within an organization and its supportive role in business processes and their development ‣ Is able to develop business processes using ICT ‣ Understands the purpose of contracts, offers, licences and immaterial rights in their work ‣ Is able to serve costumers
Specialized ICT Field Competence	‣ Is able to apply their knowledge and skills in a specialized ICT field ‣ Is able to analyse, evaluate and develop operations in this field

Table 1. Subject specific competences for Business Informatics Curriculum (Adam, 2006)

The competence-based curriculum is outlined by learning outcomes, core competeces, to which the education aims at. The aims are:

- all our students with a set of general skills that require them to think analytically, express themselves clearly, work independently, meet deadlines, and encourage initiative;
- all our students with a set of subject-specific skills, appropriate to the level of their programme, that enable them to access, analyse, present and sustain coherent and logical argument, and implement and complete independent research in IT;
- all our students the opportunity to participate in processes of course review and evaluation.

Students who have successfully completed the programmes of study will have acquired:

- the analytical skills to understand and construct cogent arguments in the basic principles of ICT and apply these;
- an appreciation of the strengths and limits of their discipline through following complementary interdisciplinary or multidisciplinary programmes of study;
- literacy skills enabling them to assemble and structure material, and write concisely and coherently with reference to scholarly sources;

- quantitative skills to interpret, understand, and evaluate informatic data and appreciate both the limitations of the evaluation methods and the data used;
- the skills to produce a dissertation that is structured, well written, presents analysis and conclusions in a logical, coherent and transparent fashion and makes adequate reference to scholarly sources;
- a range of general transferable skills including decision-making skills inherent in the study of the discipline, computer literacy skills, the organisation and management of time, and the meeting of deadlines;
- an awareness of their own strengths and weaknesses through feedback on their work;
- opportunities to participate in course review and evaluation.

4.1 Curriculum in the Major of Business Informatics

The big change was the move to competency-based curricula. Identified learning outcomes were the basis to design the Curricula in the Major of Business Informatics (Baross, 2007). Studying the major obligatory and major elective courses, students of the Major of Business Informatics will acquire fundamental knowledge of the narrow specialized area. They will be trained to differentiate the kinds and resources of information systems, as well as ethical and social aspects of ICT and their impact on modern organizing and functioning business systems.

The choice of majors and gaining theoretical, domain and practical knowledge are special distal aims in the Major of Business Informatics, and, of course, every student. In this way, concrete aims of the educational system are attained: "know-what", "know-how" and "know-who". Students are directed to some narrow specialist fields, in the first and second year of the master study to meet their preferences, democratic education and satisfy their interest and learning need.

<u>BSc</u>

Features of the course/year	Name of the course	ECTS credit points
Core Obligatory/1	Information technologies	6
Major Obligatory/1	Programming	6
Major Obligatory/2	Databases	6
Major Obligatory/2	Information System Development	6
Core Obligatory/3	Business Information Systems	6
Major Obligatory/3	Intelligent Systems	6
Major Elective/3 (two of four)	• Development of Web Applications • Business Software Applications • Knowledge Management Systems • Structural Analysis and Design	2x6

Table 2. Courses in the field of Informatics according to the Curriculum of B.Sc degrees, Business Informatics Major

MSc

The Major of Business Informatics, Master degree is structured into two modules:

a) Module Information Engineering
b) Module Business Intelligence and Electronic Business

Module INFORMATION ENGINEERING		
Features of the course / year	**Name of the course**	**ECTS credit points**
Major Obligatory/1	Object Software Engineering	6
Major Obligatory/1	Business Process Modeling	6
Major Obligatory/1	Management of IS Project	6
Major Obligatory/1	Database Design	6
Major Elective/1	Two elective courses from Group 1	2x6
Major Obligatory/2	Methods of Software Development	6
Major Obligatory/2	Implementation of Information Systems	6
Major Elective/2	Two elective courses from Group 1	2x6
	Master diploma work	30

Major Elective Courses / Group 1	
1.	Database Administration Systems
2.	Supply Chain Management
3.	Customer Relationship Management
4.	Methods and Techniques of Data Analyzing
5.	Business Inteligence Systems
6.	Internet Applications Development

Module ELECTRONIC BUSINESS and BUSINESS INTELLIGENCE		
Features of the course /year	**Name of the course**	**ECTS credit points**
Major Obligatory/1	Object Software Engineering	6
Major Obligatory/1	Business Process Modeling	6
Major Obligatory/1	Business Inteligence Systems	6
Major Obligatory/1	Methods and Techniques of Data Analyzing	6
Major Elective/1	Two elective courses from Group 2	2x6
Major Obligatory/2	Customer Relationship Management	6
Major Obligatory/2	Web Portals	6
Major Elective/2	Two elective courses from Group 2	2x6
	Master diploma work	30

Major Elective Courses / Group 2	
1.	Database Administration Systems
2.	Database Design
3.	Software Agents and Soft Computing
4.	Performance Management
5.	Management of IS Project
6.	Internet Applications Development

Table 3. Courses in the field of Informatics in the Curriculum of Master degree, Business Informatics Major, illustrated according to the modules

PhD

Primary aim of the Curriculum of doctoral studies at the Faculty of Economics is to train the Ph.D candidates for their independent research work. The most significant part of the Curriculum is to prepare the themes of doctoral dissertations, carrying out researches, writing and defense of dissertations. Students are independent in choosing narrow scientific fields for their doctoral dissertations. They select the program they are interested in, the theme being relevant and current being in accordance with contemporary scientific trends in the field.

Candidates must specially concentrate on the methodology and scientific method in the field. An important aim of the curriculum is including the Ph.D candidate into the educational and scientific-research work at the Faculty. In this way, a systematic and serious training and recruiting the best students for the future work at the University will be attained.

When defining the research and educational structure of the doctoral studies, a great care is taken to select the themes, subjects and research projects connected to the scientific fields being in the focus of interest and which represent the basis for solving the current problems of contemporary business.

The Curriculum of the doctoral studies determines the aims and learning outcomes of the Curriculum, academic, i.e. scientific title, entrance requirements, list of obligatory and elective study fields, i.e. courses with general contents. It also determines the way and time for conducting studies, credits for each course in accordance with the ECTS, credits of the doctoral dissertation. It points to prerequisites for enrollment of some courses or groups of courses, elective way of courses from other study programs, requirements for passing from other study programs with the framework of the same or related study fields, and so on.

Three fields form the structure of the Curriculum:

- Lectures and consultations of core and major scientific fields with the obligatory and elective courses (A).
- Work in the scientific-research process (B),
- Doctoral dissertation (C).

The curriculum of doctoral studies is based and valorized in the following way:

Activity	ECTS
A - Lectures and consultations	**60**
A1 - Course of the major scientific field - Modul Management or Modul Economics (elective course)	10
A2 - Course of the major scientific field - Modul Business Informatics (obligatory course)	12
A3 - Course of the major scientific field - Modul Business Informatics (elective course) 1	10
A3 - Course of the major scientific field - Modul Business Informatics (elective course) 2	10
A3 - Course of the major scientific field - Modul Business Informatics (elective course) 3	10
A3 - Course of the major scientific field - Modul Business Informatics (elective course) 4	8
B - Work in the scientific-research process	**60**
C - Doctoral dissertation	**60**
	180

The doctoral studies last three years, i.e. six semesters. Lectures and consultations last two semesters, where elective courses cover 50% ECTS credits at least. Six courses make the major scientific field. The major scientific fields are Economy, Management and Business Informatics. Each of them is established from one obligatory (A2) and 8 elective major courses (A3), of which the Ph.D candidate enrolled in some major freely chooses four; the selected doctoral dissertation is done in accordance and agreement with the mentor.

The student suggests the subject, problems, objectives and the way of researching in accordance with the potential mentor. The doctoral dissertation is an original scientific research, contribution to science and an important contribution to solving practical problems. The doctoral thesis is registered and worked in selected scientific field.

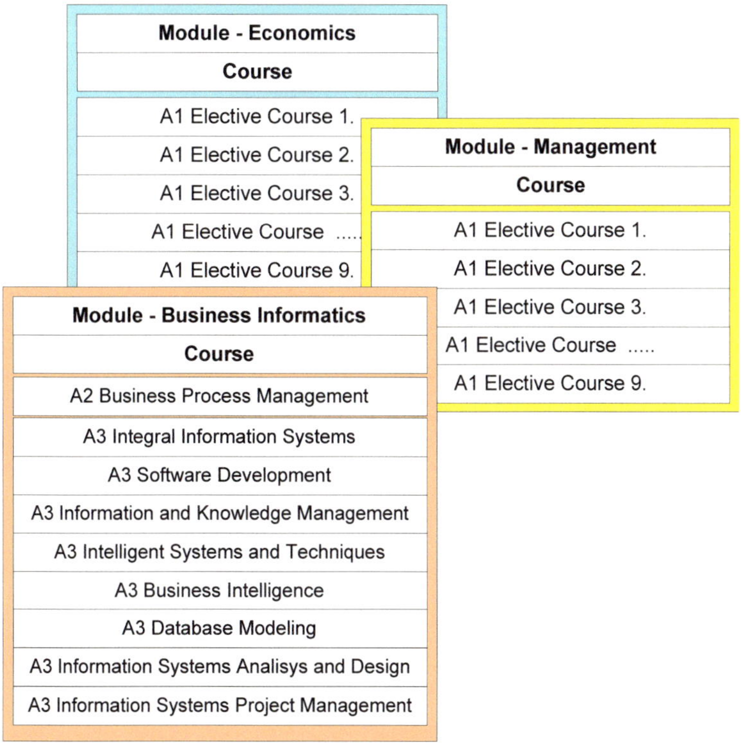

Fig. 4. Courses in the field of Informatics according to the Curriculum of Ph.D degrees, Business Informatics Major

5. Experiences and Effects of the New Curricula

The ECTS grading system is oriented to the study. The study process is in the focus of university education, contrary to the previous higher education system, where the emphasis was on the teacher and his transfer of knowledge. The basis of this system are competences that the student should acquire at the end of the selected curriculum, and the selected university degree. The curricula should clearly defines the study process and approximate the way and direction of professional development through defined learning outcomes and competences.

The basic principle of the ECTS grading system is obtaining credits according to the student workload. The analysis of the student workload, together with the analysis of contents is necessary for a successful curriculum defining. Workload measuring starts with time allocation needed to realize the study results defined in the curriculum and to finish some educational degree. After that, time is allocated according to different modules, courses, subjects, teaching units. Time allocation cannot be done according to the social prestige of the teacher and the course or any other irrelevant factor but rationally, to the needs of competences, study results, as well as the importance to apply it.

The analysis of the previous almost three years in applying the Bologna process at the Faculty points to the noticed and expressed direct proportional connection between preliminary exam obligations and study results. Namely, preliminary exam obligations have been gradually introduced in courses of the Curriculum in the forms of tests, midterms, projects, essays, case studies, and so on. At the final exam, oral or written, the student takes only part which has not been passed in the preliminary examination, as a midterm. The students are not obliged to pass preliminary exam obligations, but they have to take preliminary obligations and realize the established minimum to verify the course attendance and so acquire the right, on the basis of activity, to take the final exam. At the beginning, when preliminary exam obligations were less according to the kinds and volume, exam success was significantly lower. Also, the minimum level increase of credits for preliminary obligations make students more active during the whole term and they continually work in order to take the final exam with more knowledge and realize increased exam passing and higher grades, especially those who have not passed the segments of the Curriculum. The analysis of study results points to the fact in courses where these rules and standards are not satisfied, exam passing is significantly lower than where they are satisfied.

Of course, the number of attempts to pass exams influences efficiency of the study according to the Bologna processes. The increase of allowed number of attempts decreases efficiency and we can state that it is lower with us than in neighboring countries regarding to the legally defined three or four attempts, especially in those countries where the number of attempts is twice at the most. At the same time, the lack of the legal limit in relation to the possibility of repeated enrollment of the course during the study significantly influences efficiency. Therefore, students are usually allowed to enroll three times the same course at most. After that, the study of the selected curriculum is finished.

At the end, we should emphasize that the new methodology, which pays attention to the student and concerns what the student will learn, not what the teacher will teach, significantly determines the study efficiency. The change of proportion between the number of lectures and exercises in the Curriculum in favor of exercises and giving bigger importance to the contents which are taught, enable students to acquire empirical knowledge through practice and apply it in concrete situations instead of acquiring historical knowledge and knowledge to reproduce theoretical contents.

Effects of the new Curricula are also the following learning outcomes (Smith, 2005):

A: Knowledge and understanding

- Have demonstrated knowledge of the core principles;
- Have demonstrated an understanding of those core principles as they relate to other problems and issues;
- Have demonstrated a more detailed knowledge and understanding of an appropriate number of specialised fields of ICT;
- Have demonstrated a knowledge of quantitative techniques appropriate to the study of ICT;

B: Intellectual Skills

- Be able to use the power of abstraction to focus upon the essential features of an economic problem and to provide a framework for the evaluation of the effects of policy or other exogenous events;
- Be able to analyse an economic problem or issue using an appropriate theoretical framework;

C: Practical Skills

- Have displayed a knowledge of sources and content of economic information and data;
- Have demonstrated a knowledge of how to conduct and evaluate empirical work;
- Have demonstrated an ability to carry out empirical work using appropriate techniques;
- Have demonstrated the ability to carry out self-directed study and research;

D: Transferable skills

- Have an understanding of appropriate concepts in economics that may be of wider use in a decision-making context (e.g. opportunity cost);
- Have learnt to communicate economic ideas, concepts and information using means of communication appropriate to the audience and the problem at issue;
- Have learned to appreciate the importance of, and be able to construct, rigorous argument to help evaluate ideas;
- Have demonstrated a facility in numeracy and other quantitative techniques, such as correctly interpreting graphs;
- Have demonstrated competence in the use of a wide range of appropriate computer software.

5.1 Place and Importance of Informatics Courses in the Curriculum Model

Regarding to the wish to analyze the place of Informatics courses in the Curriculum, we shall analyze separately the Curriculum and the Major of Business Informatics, on one side and separately other majors on the other side. Namely, the model of the Curriculum is built so that Informatics and the courses in the field of Informatics in other majors are identical.

The Major Business Informatics combines informatics (the study of creating, applying and communicating information, mainly by computer systems) and management techniques. Its success is based on the powerful synergistic benefits that are released when business and administration concepts are integrated with computer science technology.

When the Curriculum is considered from the standpoint of Informatics and especially the Major of Business Informatics, it is important to emphasize its mission and aims: forming experts with knowledge in the field of analysis; designing; developing and implementing integral information systems and operative system management and its further development; then software product development; developing and implementing business intelligence systems, and e-business systems.

The curriculum courses in the field of informatics are studied as obligatory core courses, major obligatory courses and major elective courses. Obligatory core courses in the Curriculum are Information Technologies and Management Information Systems with special characteristics in some majors. They enable students of all the majors to acquire necessary theoretical and practical knowledge on contemporary information technologies and their implications on business.

In addition, they give the possibility to master basic skills in working on the computer with a view of creating the basis for achieving specific competences needed for data and information management, and business knowledge. In this way, students, besides the capability for information management, develop the capability to collect and select relevant data and information from various sources, as well as the capabilities for their qualitative analyses.

Studying the obligatory core courses in the field of informatics, students will acquire knowledge of informatics terms, realize all the suppositions for better cooperation with experts in the field of information technologies, and understand the significance of cooperation between the users and experts. Students will be able to learn independently, to choose and apply specific information technologies in some functional fields of economics and business, as marketing, finance, accounting, or in some branches of economics, as agriculture, trade, banking, insurance, and so on.

Studying the major obligatory and major elective courses, students of the Major of Business Informatics will acquire fundamental knowledge of the narrow specialized areas (Information Engineering, Electronic Business and Business Intelligence). They will be trained to differentiate the kinds and resources of information systems, as well as ethical and social aspects of information technologies and their impact on modern organizing and functioning business systems. The major obligatory courses enable the development of capabilities, self-confidence and knowledge of an independent learning and work. Students acquire methodological and practical knowledge on the application of different software development tools. They become skilled in the principles of development, methods, techniques and methodologies of developing software and business information systems.

Analyzing the place and importance of Informatics and courses of Informatics at some majors of the first two education level at the Faculty of Economics, the following statements can be quoted. First, at the Bachelor level studies, Major of Business Informatics, from the total 27 courses, students have eight courses in the field of informatics or 29.62%, illustrated in Figure 5. Considered proportionately, it may be too much. However, regarding to the need for creating the basis for two modules at the Master studies, to kinds and contents of the courses, it may be insufficient. Students acquire fragmentary knowledge in some fields that cannot be connected into the harmonious entirety to be applied in practice. Therefore, at this level of the study, the Curriculum should be segmented from the beginning to some modules, or rebuilt with the supplementary courses in the field of informatics.

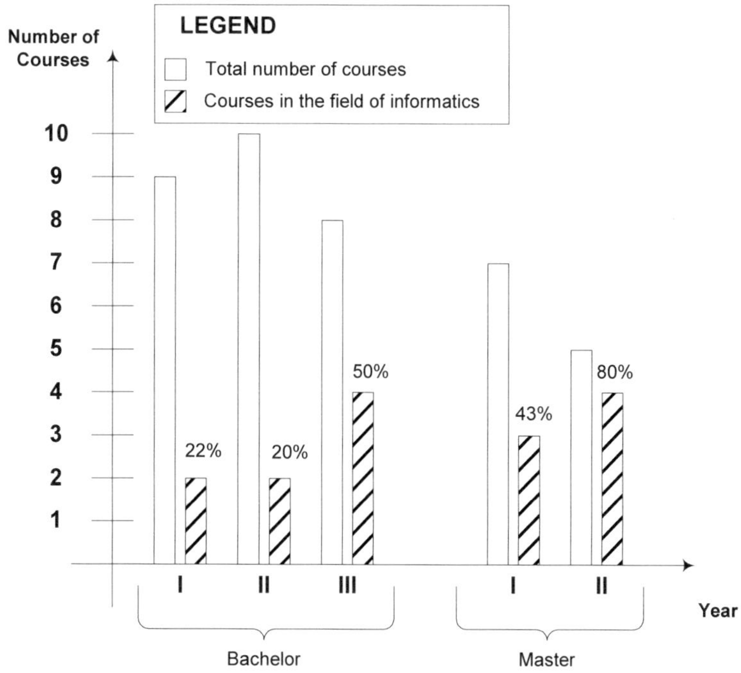

Fig. 5. Overview of the correlation between the total number of courses and informatics courses in the Major of Business Informatics

As for the other majors at the Bachelor three-year studies, from the 27 courses, students have only two courses in the field of informatics, or 7.40%, illustrated in Figure 6. It means an insufficient representation of courses in the field of informatics. This fact makes worse the contents of the other courses where the representation of informatics is insignificant. We cannot assert that our students are illiterate in informatics after three years of the study, but they are not quite ready to the challenges in practice. Their future employers do not expect traditional accountants with their sleeves rolled up any more, but the economists who use the world network and the newest software solutions in order to do qualitative analyses.

The analysis of the two-year Master study, the Major of Business Informatics, shows that there are even seven courses, from 12 in total, in the field of informatics, or 58.33%, illustrated in Figure 5. This percent completely satisfies every module. The weak choice of the courses at this level of the study is compensated by the possibility of choosing the modules. The number of major elective courses is satisfactory and it gives students the possibility to specialize narrowly.

If we analyze the two-year Master curriculum of the other majors, the situation is also very bad, the same as at the Bachelor studies. Only one from 12 courses is in the field of informatics, or 8.33%, illustrated in Figure 6.

Such a situation imposes the need of introducing new elective courses in the field of Informatics or, alternatively, to analyze the contents of existing courses, and, where it is possible, to build on the contents from the fields of Informatics.

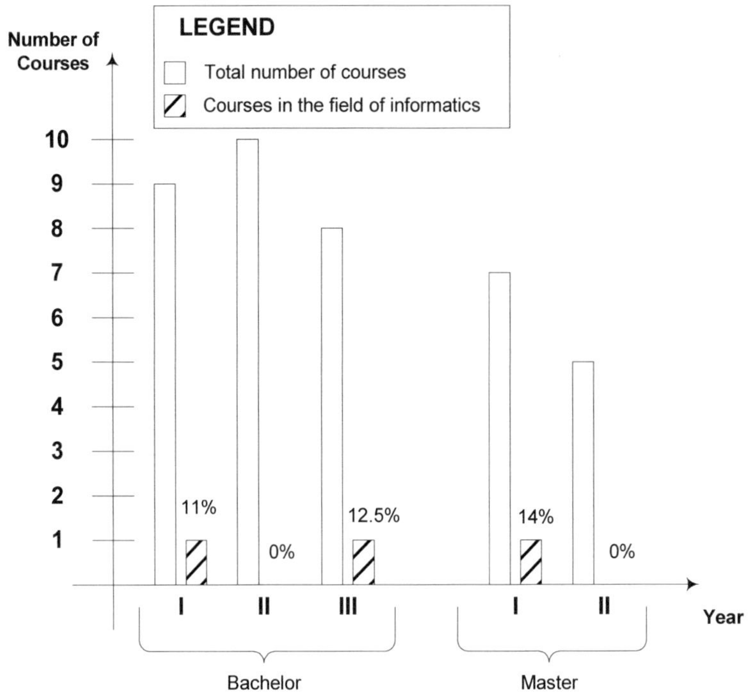

Fig. 6. Overview of the correlation between the total number of courses and informatics courses in other majors

6. Conclusion

The new Curriculum satisfies the set requirements. It is completely harmonized with the requirements of the Bologna process. Partner experiences from different European projects are built in it. At the same time, standards for curricula accreditation in the field of Business Informatics are accepted. Courses have up to date contents and they are completely in accordance with the expected and precisely defined learning outcomes. Also, set components of the new educational system established on requirements of the global economy were maximally respected. The Curriculum, regarding to its harmonization with other curricula in the environment, enables the mobility of students and teaching staff.

In general, the developed Curriculum is significantly better than the previous ones. Besides, it satisfies all the cited requirements and it is important to emphasize that the contents of all courses are up-to-date and in accordance with contemporary practical and scientific outcomes. Students perform their obligation efficiently and effectively because their activities are in accordance with students' workload. It is also important to say that easily applicative had replaced theoretical contents in the field of Business Informatics.

The study programme offers the students a professional oriented skill-set, enabling them to analyze business problems and develop information system solutions. In particular, following objectives for the course were set:

- The course will equip students to analyze business problems from both technological opportunities and business requirements.
- The course will equip students to develop solutions to business problems using ICT to its full potencial.
- Students will learn methologies that enable a clear understanding of business problems and the function of ICT in business.
- Students will understand constraints, both organisational and technological in designing information system solutions.
- Students will be provided experience in working in an inter-cultural work environment.

Besides the cited positive effects of the new Curriculum, it is necessary to say that some shortages have been noticed which should be eliminated in the next period. Before all, it is the need for Informatics courses in the majors of Economy and Management or, at least, including specific contents of some information technology fields in the current courses. In this way, informatics contents could get their appropriate importance, adequate to the role that ICT have in the contemporary world. Also, in Business Informatics Major, courses of Economy and Management should have contemporary contents important for implementing e-business and knowledge management.

The Curriculum, although built on the basis of determined learning outcomes, must respect, above all, learning outcomes relevant for labor markets. The learning outcomes are one of the basic elements of the study program, but their formulation is often a mere satisfaction of the form. They represent the potential for the substantial change of education process originating from, before all, the new philosophy of education that means the change of the focus of education from the process of lecturing to the process of studying.

In eliminating shortages, especially important contribution is expected from the processes and outcomes of internal evaluation of curricula, carrying out permanently and by means of which the feedback information is expected from all stakeholders about the quality of curricula, appropriate contents, missing contents, about what should be changed, and so on. Evaluation of this Curriculum is also expected by students when they graduate and begin to work. After all these evaluations, it will be clear how good the curriculum is.

Besides the concern for high-quality contents, introducing the new Curriculum needs time and resources in terms of marketing and promotion. All graduates can found roles as information system analyst or developer, business analyst, or IT consultant in various sectors, such as financial service industry, software industry, and the public sector. The excellent career opportunities of the graduates will make the program more attractive for students.

7. References

Adam, S. (2006) An introduction to learning outcomes. A consideration of the nature function and position of learning outcomes in the creation of the EHEA, Ed. Froment, E. et al., EAU Bologna Handbook, Raabe, Berlin.

Aszalos, L. (2008) Comparision of the Hungarian and Euro-Inf accreditation systems, Proceedings of the Informatics Education Europe III Conference, pp. 30-36, Venice Italy, December 2008, South-East European Research Centre.

Barros, J.P. & Garcia, L. (2007) The Bologna Process as a Motivator for Change, Proceedings of the Informatics Education Europe II Conference, pp. 146-154, Thessaloniki Greece, November 2007, South-East European Research Centre.

Cogburn, D. (1998) Globalization, Knowledge, Education and Traning in the Information Age, http://www.unesco.org/webworld/infoethics_2/eng/papers/paper_23.htm

Cowling, T. (2007) The Role of Application Domains in Informatics Curricula, Proceedings of the Informatics Education Europe II Conference, pp. 166-175, Thessaloniki Greece, November 2007, South-East European Research Centre.

Fink, L.D. (2003) Creating Significant Learning Experiences: An Integrated Approach to Designing College Courses, John Wiley and Sons, ISBN 0787960551, San Francisco.

Handzic, M. & Sciefleet, P. (2002) Impact of New Economy on IS Education: A Case of UNSW, Proceedings of the 17th International Conference on Informatics Education Research (ICIER 2002), pp. 9-19, Barcelona Spain, December 2002, International Academy for Information Management.

Helfert, M. & Duncan, H. (2006) Aspects on Information System Curriculum: A Study Program in Business Informatics, The Transfer and Diffusion of Information Technology for Organisational Resilience, Ed. Donnellan, B. et al., pp. 229-238, IFIP Vol. 206, Springer, ISBN 9780387344096, Boston.

Howard, J. (2007) Curriculum Development, Elon University organizational Web Sites, July 2007, Elon University.

Moore, A.H. (2007) The New Economy, Technology and Learning Outcomes Assessment, EDUCAUSE Quarterly, Vol. 30, No. 3 2007, pp. 6-8, ISSN 1528-5324.

Plančak, M. (2006) The European Credit Transfer System at the Universities, Alternative Academic Educational Network, ISBN 8670550644, Belgrade.

Smith, M.K. (2005), Competence and competency // http://www.infed.org./biblio/b-comp.htm (refered on 2009/04/10.)

ECTS European Credit Transfer and Accumulation System// http://ec.europa.eu/education/programmes/socrates/ects/index_en.html (refered on 2007/09/20.)

Euro-Inf Frameword Standards and Accreditation Criteria for Informatics Programmes // http://www.eqanie.eu/modules/download_gallery/dlc.php?file=12m (refered on 2009/04/05.)

Applying New Educational Methodologies in Overcrowded Groups: Experiences in Basic Mechanics

Marta C. Mora-Aguilar, J. L. Sancho-Bru and J.L. Iserte-Vilar
Universitat Jaume I
Spain

1. Introduction

By 2010-2011, European universities will have adapted their degrees to the new directives required by the Bologna process in the creation of the European Higher Education Area. The proposed educational model is based on the student workload required to achieve the objectives of a programme - objectives specified in terms of learning outcomes and competences to be acquired. The role of students becomes more important in the learning process. Active student participation is promoted, along with formative and continuous assessment.

However, the application of these directives entails a reorientation of most engineering studies in Spain, which is difficult to carry out in practice because of the particular features of Spanish higher education (Tovar&Cardeñosa, 2003). Different pilot experiments have been set up to achieve the adaptation of studies and methodologies, and a common conclusion has been drawn: these changes demand a considerable effort from lecturers due to the current student/lecturer ratio in Spanish universities and the fact that the amount of work is directly related to the number of students. In fact, the large number of students attending university classes in Spain often prevents the lecturer from providing education in an innovative way. This is the current situation on most Spanish engineering degree courses.

In this context, this chapter analyses the benefits and drawbacks that arise when changing teaching methodologies for overcrowded groups and describes possible strategies in order to accomplish the objectives set by the European harmonization. These strategies have been tested in the Mechanics major in several academic years, as explained in (Mora-Aguilar et al., 2008; Mora-Aguilar et al., 2009). Among them, e-learning methods appear as key elements able to compensate for the lack of resources necessary to make the changes required by the harmonization. In particular, e-assessment has been introduced in the Mechanics subject as an evaluation tool useful for conducting continuous assessment in large groups without increasing the lecturer workload.

The modifications have been gradually introduced in the subject with the aim of comparing results and drawing general conclusions that are discussed at the end of the chapter. These conclusions can be extrapolated to other engineering disciplines with similar problems.

2. The European Higher Education Area (EHEA)

The European Higher Education Area (EHEA) can be regarded as a higher education convergence process parallel to the economic and political agreements reached in the European Union. EHEA sprang from the Magna Charta Universitatum (Rectors, 1988), signed by European university rectors in 1988. After this first step, a series of institutional declarations (European Ministers Responsible for Higher Education, 1999, 2001, 2003a, 2003b, 2005) have settled the directions for the creation of this common higher education scenario in Europe.

One of the basic objectives, explicitly stated in those declarations, is achieving the mobility of professionals between the different countries, known as *cross-border employability*. The aim is to take up a system of easily readable and comparable degrees. This calls for a degree standardization process through the imposition of common structures (Clausen, 2005). One of the instruments for achieving this is the well-known European Credit Transfer System (ECTS), which establishes a unique *pattern* when it comes to *measuring* teaching contents. The significant formal reorganization of university studies implied by convergence, especially in countries like Spain whose starting point - its current higher education system- is quite a long way from the reference model (which is not very far from the present British system), also entails a redrawing of degree course contents themselves.

But the scope of the changes is not only formal and structural. The programme is even more ambitious because it is also aimed at transforming teaching methodology by focusing on the student learning process. It is a change in methodology. According to the Spanish government law defining the ECTS (Spanish Government, 2003), the new academic measures imply a new educational model to guide teaching programmes and methodologies. The proposed educational model is based on the student workload required to achieve the objectives of a programme, specified in terms of learning outcomes and competences to be acquired. The role of students gains significance in the learning process. Active student participation is promoted, along with a formative and continuous assessment.

3. Higher education in Spain: The case of the Mechanics major

The Spanish university system dates back to the Middle Ages. The oldest Spanish university is Salamanca, founded in 1218. The present system, however, is actually a descendant of the nineteenth century liberal university, inspired by the centralized French model. In the last few years, it has undergone the greatest growth in its history while, at the same time advancing towards a self-governing, and decentralized system.

As already mentioned, the higher education system is quite a long way from the model established by the EHEA. Nowadays, higher education is provided by both public and private institutions. Universities organize the studies grouping the subjects into curricula. The student obtains a university degree once a curriculum has been completed. The credit is the assessment unit and corresponds to ten hours of theoretical or practical teaching. Credits are obtained by the appropriate verification of the acquired knowledge. This assessment is generally in the form of written, or occasionally oral, examinations, established by each university. The subjects included in a curriculum are grouped into two educational cycles and may be classified as:

1. *Majors*: Compulsory material present in all curricula leading to an official degree. These represent 30% of the subject load during the first cycle and 25% in the second cycle.
2. *Compulsory Subjects*: These are designated by the university as compulsory for the student within the corresponding curriculum.
3. *Optional Subjects*: The University establishes these subjects for students to choose from.
4. *Free-choice Credits*: All curricula must devote at least 10% of all credits to free-choice activities, which may be standard subjects, seminars or other activities that can be freely chosen from those offered by the university or by another university, if permitted by the corresponding joint agreement.

Most universities in Spain have tried, at different levels, to adapt their teaching methodologies to move closer to the EHEA. A common feature of all these new methodologies tested is that they are based on individual support for students to be performed by lecturers, turning their classical role of *transmitters of knowledge* into a new one of *personal supervisors*, guiding students in constructing their own knowledge. The main changes needed in order to achieve the European harmonization objectives are very difficult to carry out when dealing with overcrowded groups, as occurs in most majors taught in the first years at Spanish universities. This is especially true in the most difficult disciplines that have a high failure rate and, as a consequence, have a large number of students enrolled every year. In this case, personalized monitoring of students is unfeasible. This is still an unsolved problem and a challenge in the field of educational innovation.

3.1 The case of the Mechanics major

The Mechanical Engineering degree is offered by 51 centres in Spain. The Mechanics major is taught in the first year of the degree. At the Universitat Jaume I, it consists of 60 hours of classroom education, of which 30 are lectures, 15 are problem-solving sessions and 15 are laboratory sessions. It is preceded by core subjects of physics and mathematics, essential for tackling the subject successfully. In addition, Mechanics is a fundamental discipline and is the basis of other majors taught in the following years of the degree.

The students regard Mechanics as a difficult discipline. The difficulty of the subject taught requires constant work from students. But students are not in the habit of studying every day and many of them begin to study only when the final exam date approaches. They are not able to assimilate the subject properly in such a short time and, as a consequence, they either give up studying the subject or focus only on the first part - Statics. In the latter case, the student can pass the exam if he/she has studied properly but lacks the skills and procedures taught in the Dynamics part, which are fundamental for subsequent years. Thus, there are many students who do not sit the examination as well as a high failure rate.

As a result, traditionally, a large number of students enrol in the subject every year. A total of 236 students enrolled in the academic year 2006/2007. Only 90 of them were enrolling for the first time, but no more than 57 of the remaining 146 students had previously sat any examination the major. This large number of students greatly hinders the development of educational innovation in the subject.

3.2 The role of students and lecturers in overcrowded groups

As will be explained below, the new initiatives clash with the reservations of lecturers and also with the attitude of students who, in many cases, prefer to maintain the classical evaluation scheme rather than undergoing continuous assessment, which requires constant and continuous effort throughout the entire course.

Lecturers

In overcrowded groups, the high student/lecturer ratio prevents the lecturer from achieving educational innovation. As a result, teachers usually employ classical teaching methodology based on lectures and assessment in the form of a single final exam. This methodology does not encourage the students to study the subject continuously and results in a high failure rate, mainly due to the number of students who do not sit the examination. Besides, lecturers are usually more reticent than students about changes.

Many public administrations and universities are attempting to make the transition to the new European model without any cost. This means lecturers are feeling that their workload has considerably increased while their remuneration remains unchanged. Furthermore, lecturers are asked to apply many methodologies that require small groups of students, but this is not feasible because it is impossible to increase the number of groups without extra funding for studies. In addition to the financial issue, teachers are having problems with the calculation of ECTS credits, because of students' reticence in providing information about their weekly workload. Last, but not least, an increase in the time spent on teaching tasks means a considerable reduction in time spent on research. This matter is especially worrying for lecturers who have not yet obtained a permanent position at the university and who consequently need to obtain research results in order to improve their curricula vitae.

Students

The overall number of universities in Spain has increased considerably, approximately doubling over the last 15 years (Ministry of Education and Science, 2007). For that reason, nowadays, most Spanish students attend the nearest university to their home and consider university as an extension of school, particularly in large cities where accommodation is expensive. In this way, they do not experience living away from home (for instance, learning to cook, washing dishes and other skills that are useful in order to live independently). Faced with the choice of either living with their parents or in a university residence or cheap room, most choose to live at home.

University students in Spain have good information technology skills but often lack autonomy and maturity and, therefore, require personalized attention. They are used to working in the short term, but not to dealing with long-lasting tasks that require constant daily effort. Students are not in the habit of studying every day and prefer to study only during the last few days before the final exam. Consequently, many students do not sit the examination and there is a high failure rate. Moreover, their strategy for preparing for the assessment often consists of selecting the easier parts of the subject, avoiding studying the rest, which leads to an incomplete training for successfully tackling future subjects and following a professional career. In addition, they students are very demanding and aware of their rights. This is not necessarily a negative feature, but it could be very beneficial if the students used this feeling to ask for better ways of learning, encouraging university lecturers to improve their teaching. However, such consciousness and attitude are not usually accompanied by the assumption of duties and obligations, and students do not impose such high standards on their own work.

3.3 Pilot experiments

For several years, some pilot experiments have been set up to harmonize studies at Spanish universities, with varying results. These pilot experiments have tried to assimilate all formal, structural and methodological changes. But many problems have been encountered. One of the main problems has been the lack of legislation, or rather the existence of non-updated legislation, because it was not until 26th October 2007 that the Spanish government approved the law to organize official University Studies (Spanish Government, 2007) that alters the higher education classification system. This legislative gap is even worse in the case of degrees qualifying students to exercise regulated professions, like Mechanical Engineering, because conditions to be met in those degrees were not established until 18th-20th February 2009 (Spanish Government, 2009a, 2009b).

For this reason, most pilot experiments have been aimed at exploring methodological changes and measuring students' workloads. But even in this field there are difficulties because of the situation explained above.

4. New Trends in Education: e-Learning

It is a fact that the new generation of students is very interested in information technologies. Besides, electronic learning is now a reality that has been made possible due to the recent advances in technology. Both circumstances establish the possibility of accomplishing the changes in education we have mentioned using the e-learning paradigm. Web-based tools, if properly used, can be of great help for academics, especially when dealing with overcrowded groups. As will be explained in the following paragraphs, they can complement traditional methods, giving the learner a more effective experience.

4.1 Internet-based learning environments development

In some way it can be said that *distance learning* began with the invention of writing. But it is much nearer in time, during the last decades of the twentieth century, when the history of technology-based education began, stimulated by the rapid evolution of electronic technologies. Almost every step in this evolution of technology-based education was first taken by big corporations that needed to train their large number of employees located around the world (Bersin, 2004). The first stage in the evolution of this technology-based education arrived with mainframe and mini-computers during the sixties and seventies. The next step came with the use of video networks capable of providing live instruction. Later, the CD-ROM technology was vastly extended and applied to distance training. But it was not until the last few years that the development of the Information and Communication Technology (ICT) associated with the Internet has allowed the creation of new web tools which can be directly applied to the teaching/learning process at all levels. These new tools are being adopted in higher education, and are even changing the concept of education itself.

A degree of specification in the use of certain terms must be made due to the appearance of a new and relatively broad vocabulary related to this kind of learning. Nowadays, different definitions of the term e-learning (electronic learning) can be found in the specialized literature. In a broad sense, the term e-learning applies to any learning method that uses electronic technologies such as computers, multimedia systems, etc. But this expression

commonly implies distance education (as opposed to face-to-face education) and, more precisely, learning-teaching methods that use web-based services via the Internet.
It is easy to find a close relationship between the enormous increase in distance learning courses that have appeared during the last few years and the popularization of the Internet. Along these lines, even the name of these courses has turned into *on-line courses*. But the relationship between e-learning and the Internet goes far beyond this. If the term *Web 2.0*, (O'Reilly, 2005), also known as the *social web*, has emerged to describe the new web-based technologies that allow much more user interactivity (social networks, wikis, blogs, folksonomy), the expression *e-Learning 2.0* has arisen to refer to educational techniques that involve these newer Internet technologies. Some of these recently developed technologies are specially designed for educational purposes. Among them, it is possible to distinguish between Learning Management Systems (LMS) and Learning Content Management Systems (LCMS) (Rengarajan, 2001). The difference between the two kinds of platform lies in the fact that LCMS is more focused on learning-content management, while the aim of LMS is closer to learning-activity management. However, there are several software platforms that offer both types of tools, closely integrated. Some of these platforms are restrictive software, the most popular among them being WebCT, eCollege, Desire2Learn and Blackboard. But it is also possible to find high quality open-source platforms like Moodle, Sakai, Claroline, ATutor. One of the criticisms levelled at these platforms is the common lack of pedagogical control (Govindasamy, 2002), as the majority of these platforms are focused on technical considerations, ignoring a true pedagogic analysis. In this way, the whole load of this analysis has to be done by the teacher responsible during the implementation of these web-based tools.

4.2 Blended learning

It is well known that nowadays most higher education institutions have adopted the above-mentioned platforms in order to manage their range of e-learning courses. This situation is affecting not only their on-line courses but also many face-to-face courses that are progressively trying to integrate those e-learning technologies as very helpful tools.
This kind of educational system, which combines face-to-face and e-learning methodologies, is called *blended learning* (also b-learning). The same kind of concepts is behind hybrid learning or mixed mode learning (Ginns & Ellis, 2002). The extent to which these new technologies are introduced and applied in face-to-face courses can vary enormously from one course to another. In some cases the use of b-learning may be very slight; it may simply consist of the publication of some documents on the web or on-line tutorials. But, in other cases, the importance of the on-line learning can be much greater than the face-to-face part of the course. In some of those courses, the face-to-face part may be reduced to mere guidance, advice, or explanation of the web-based tools.
Obviously, the best way to use these e-learning tools will depend on the particular features of the subject taught and also on the characteristics of the students studying the subject (number, age, technological skills…). This integration process is being studied nowadays and a deep methodological and pedagogical analysis is still necessary (Kelly et al., 2007; Barnard et al., 2009). But what seems clear is that many campus-based higher education institutions are adopting blended learning approaches to a significant degree, and, more importantly, this process can be carried out maintaining consistency with the values of traditional higher education institutions (Garrison, 2004).

4.3 E-assessment

In its broadest sense, e-assessment is the use of information technology for any assessment-related activity. The term e-assessment is becoming widely used as a generic term to describe the use of computers as part of the assessment process. E-assessment can be used to assess cognitive and practical abilities. Cognitive abilities are assessed using e-testing software; practical abilities are assessed using e-portfolios or simulation software.

An e-testing system basically includes two components: (1) an assessment engine; and (2) an item bank. The assessment engine comprises the hardware and software required to create and deliver a test. Most e-testing engines run on standard hardware so the main feature is the software's functionality. There is a wide range of software packages. The software does not include the questions themselves, these are provided by an item bank. Once created, the engine uses the item bank to generate a test. The creation of the item bank is more costly and time consuming than the installation and configuration of the assessment engine.

E-assessment has many advantages over traditional (paper-based) assessment. The advantages include lower long-term costs, instant feedback to students, greater flexibility concerning location and timing, improved reliability (machine marking is much more reliable than human marking) and enhanced question styles incorporating interactivity and multimedia material. But there are also disadvantages: e-assessment systems are expensive to establish and not suitable for every type of assessment (such as extended response questions). The main expense is not technical; it is the cost of producing high-quality assessment items.

Focusing on large groups, e-assessment can make the teacher's work easier. For subjects with a considerable number of students, standard exam correction can take an enormous amount of time. As a helpful tool for this purpose, most of the software platforms for e-learning, as presented in the previous section, include modules allowing different kinds of on-line assessment. They commonly provide tools that allow the conduction of multiple-choice questions, matching questions and short-answer questions. Depending on the kind of e-assessment chosen, it is possible to get automatic correction, allowing a huge time saving and immediate feedback for the students.

5. A Methodological Proposal for Overcrowded Groups

The difficulties mentioned in section 3 have been considered in order to propose a gradual adaptation to the new requirements in higher education deriving from the harmonization process. This proposal has been carried out in two consecutive stages (two academic years) which are detailed in the following sections. The first one deals with the adaptation of the learning program and the partial modification of the assessment system. The second one takes a further step towards the modification of the assessment system, introducing e-assessment in the Mechanics subject.

This scheme has been tested in the Mechanics major, already presented above, but the initial situation and problems found there do not differ from those arising in other engineering disciplines.

5.1 First stage: Adapting Content and Assessment

The first step in order to adapt the subject to the Bologna directives consisted of establishing the teaching objectives for the 2006/2007 academic year, which were the following:

1. To draw up the academic program in terms of skill and learning outcomes. This implied defining the different tasks that can be performed by a mechanical engineer and reviewing the subject program in order to adjust it to the new requirements and the allotted time.
2. To plan content classes in detail so that the lecturer could check whether the time management was realistic.
3. To adapt the assessment system with the aim of encouraging the students to study the subject every day and increasing their motivation by making the subject achievable and close to them.
4. To study the strategies and methodologies that best suited the subject, with regard to the constraints mentioned above.

In order to accomplish these objectives, different tasks were performed and the results are detailed below.

Before amending the program, an effort was made to contextualize the subject in the degree. In this sense, an analysis of the professional background related to the degree was conducted. As a result, a list of general and specific objectives (learning outcomes) was produced and those related to the Mechanics subject were extracted.

Besides setting goals related to content, we examined the skills and attitudes essential for any engineering work, realising that the subject should stress their development. Some of the basic skills developed were problem-solving ability, abstraction capacity, autonomy in learning and adaptation to new situations. Responsible attitudes also had to be promoted, as well as critical thinking and respect for the rules of use and maintenance of equipment and working tools.

Once the goals were clearly established, we analysed the existing subject program and methodology as well as the agendas and methodologies of the previous and related subjects. In particular, we reviewed the curriculum of subjects such as Physical Foundations of Engineering and Mathematical Foundations of Engineering and noted that, traditionally, some concepts already contained in the Physics subject were being taught again in Mechanics. As a result, some modifications of the subject were made. Specifically, we grouped some items, changed some laboratory sessions and removed several sections which dealt with issues already studied in previous subjects or considered to be less important for the future professional development of the students. These reductions allowed us to go into greater depth in the most important aspects of the subject.

Adaptation of evaluation and assessment

Teaching does not consist in simply following a set of rules or applying a particular technique, but requires thinking about how to engage the students in the learning process, and this is only possible through renewing teaching methodologies.

In this sense, the assessment process occupies a central role in teaching because it helps to ensure and verify the quantity and particularly the quality of the learning process. The process should be clear and known by the students and the weight given to each assessment element should provide the student with an idea of which objectives and contents are most important.

The assessment system was partially modified in order to encourage students to study the subject every day and increase their motivation by making the subject achievable and close to them.

The modification of the assessment therefore had a threefold purpose:

1. To spur the students on to greater efforts, bringing the subject closer to them and linking its contents to the knowledge they already had.
2. To encourage pupils to lose their fear of the subject and to sit the examination.
3. To adapt the assessment to the new program established.

Three types of assessment were used in order to achieve the above goals. The first one - **diagnostic assessment** or pre-assessment - provides the instructor with information about students' prior knowledge and misconceptions before beginning the subject. The second one, the **formative assessment,** takes place during the learning activity and provides the instructor with information on how well the learning objectives of a given activity are being met. The last one, the **final or summative assessment**, summarizes learners' development at the end of the course.

Two evaluation itineraries were considered and both are detailed in Table 1. The first one (A1) is aimed at students who regularly attend classes. The second one (B1) is designed for students who do not regularly attend classes because they have attended them in previous years, or who prefer to be assessed through a summative assessment. Itinerary B is the one previously followed in the subject, except for the initial test, and itinerary A includes the modifications carried out. In order to pass the subject the student had to obtain at least a 50% of the total score, for both itineraries.

Assessment type	ITINERARY A1		ITINERARY B1	
Diagnostic assessment	Initial Test (mandatory)	0%		
Formative assessment	Suggested Problems (Self-evaluation)	0%	Suggested Problems (Self-evaluation)	0%
	Laboratory Sessions (reports)	10%	Laboratory Sessions (reports)	10%
Summative assessment	Partial Examination	45%	Final Examination	90%
	Final Examination	45%		
	Final mark	100%	**Final mark**	100%

Table 1. 1st stage: Assessment itineraries in the Mechanics subject.

Firstly, the **diagnostic assessment** is a simple test, which takes place on the **first day of classes** and is not considered in the final mark. The test is marked quickly and its results are shown in blocks of content, so students realise the items they have mastered and the items they must review. It is a kind of motivating element as it requires only very basic knowledge of physics and mathematics. Secondly, the basic laboratory sessions review basic concepts in physics.

In order to encourage the students to study continuously and to achieve a change in their conception of the subject, there is a collection of **suggested problems**, a **partial examination** and **laboratory sessions** distributed throughout the course.

The collection of suggested problems has been designed to help the students in the self-assessment of their knowledge at the end of each content unit. These problems have the numerical solution included, but it is the student who must reach the result by their own means. The lecturer encourages the students to solve them on their own and to attend tutorial sessions in order to resolve any questions they may have. Due to the large number of students enrolled in the subject, it is not feasible for the teacher to set individual problems and to correct them one by one. For this reason, the numerical solutions of the problems are included and individual doubts are resolved in the tutorial sessions.

The **partial examination** is an optional test allowing the students to assess their knowledge of the first part of the subject and leave the second part for the final exam. If the mark in the partial exam is greater than or equal to 40%, the student will be assessed in the final examination only on the second part of the program.

The **laboratory sessions** are optional but part of the final mark. They are evaluated by means of a report reflecting the practical work done, while there is an analytical verification of the measurements taken in the lab.

Results from the first stage. Discussion

The results obtained from this stage were encouraging, with 33.47% of the enrolled students having passed, while the percentage had never exceeded 15% in previous years. The main reason was the increase in the number of students sitting the examination (53.39% of the enrolled students compared to 36.32% the preceding academic year), which confirmed the initial approach that one of the main reasons for the high failure rate observed in the subject is that students do not sit the examinations. It is important to point out that 89.87% of the students who sat the partial examination finally passed the Mechanics subject. That means students who studied more continuously achieved good results. Furthermore, the mean score for Dynamics was 42%. Another benefit observed was an increase in the use of the tutorial sessions for asking questions related to the subject, which proved that the changes introduced had motivated the students to study more continuously.

However, some important limitations were observed:

1. Little guidance was still given by the lecturer and should be increased, taking into account the student's profile.
2. One of the facts observed over the last few years in the tutorial sessions was that many students were trying to solve problems without having properly studied the theoretical foundation of the subject, and this problem had not been solved.
3. The time spent by lecturers increased considerably with the partial examination.

5.2 Second stage: Introducing e-learning tools

Due to the changes introduced, the number of students enrolled in the Mechanics subject fell by 17% in the academic year 2007/2008 (from 236 to 196 students enrolled). This was a good result considering that, every year, 90 new students begin their studies on this degree course.

The changes carried out were reviewed, with some being retained and others, such as the assessment, modified and improved, taking into account the limitations observed in the first stage.

The new proposal for the 2007/2008 academic year involved conducting educational developments in various fields in order to fulfil the objectives established above. In this sense, continuous assessment was proposed, not only to verify the degree of fulfilment of the objectives, but also to guide the students in their learning process. In fact, if the assessment is problem-centred, a theoretical comprehension of the foundations of the subject is being assumed, and this may not be the case. Moreover, if the students are able to continuously self-assess, they will also be able to correct their deficiencies over time. This requires giving not only their marks, but also a list of the concepts or techniques in which they do not reach the objectives established for the major.

Alternatives considered, advantages and disadvantages

On the one hand, the implementation of continuous assessment in large groups, with more than fifty students enrolled, is really difficult to carry out by the lecturer because of the amount of time involved in correction tasks. For that reason, although this is a good methodology in order to encourage the students to study the subject continuously, face-to-face continuous assessment was ruled out in the Mechanics subject.

On the other hand, as the Universitat Jaume I is considered a face-to-face university, the faculty must teach a minimum number of classes, and it made no sense to develop an entirely virtual subject.

All these reasons lead inevitably to the development of a blended learning methodology. However, it must be remembered that there are a variety of activities that can be done within the framework of the b-learning methodology. Among these, e-assessment was considered as the most appropriate for the goals established above, i.e., to achieve the study of the theoretical foundations of the subject without a huge increase in the lecturer's work.

For the introduction of e-assessment in the Mechanics subject, the Moodle software (Moodle, 2007) has been used. Moodle is the acronym for Modular Object-Oriented Dynamic Learning Environment. It is a free software package for producing Internet-based courses and web sites. It can also be referred as a Course Management System (CMS), a Learning Management System (LMS) or a Virtual Learning Environment (VLE), although it also contains tools from a LCMS system. It is a modular system that offers considerable flexibility with the possibility of adding or removing functions at many levels.

Moodle platform is widely used in the Universitat Jaume I. One of its main advantages is that is easy to maintain and update. Except for the installation process, it requires virtually no maintenance by the administrator. Its interface allows the easy creation, management and usage of the course by the lecturer and also by the students. The registration and authentication of the participants is quite simple and secure and there is a large community continuously improving the software, based on documents and troubleshooting. It is based on constructivist pedagogical principles: learning is particularly effective when achieved through sharing with others.

Diagnostic and formative e-assessment

We have implemented the e-assessment for the diagnostic and formative assessments while the summative assessment has remained the same (paper-based). On the Moodle platform there are very different tools, but we have used two of them: Questionnaire and Task.

Two itineraries have been considered, as in the first stage. The first one (A2) consists of continuous assessment and is aimed at students who regularly attend classes. The second one (B2) is designed for those who prefer to be assessed through summative evaluation. Both itineraries are described in Table 2. Once again, the student had to obtain at least a 50% of the total score of the selected itinerary in order to pass the subject.

Assessment type	ITINERARY A2		ITINERARY B2	
Diagnostic assessment	Initial e-test (mandatory)	**0%**	Initial e-test (optional)	**0%**
Formative assessment	e-tests	**20%**	Suggested Problems (Self-evaluation)	**0%**
	Suggested Problems (Self-evaluation)	**0%**		
	Laboratory Sessions (e-reports)	**10%**	Laboratory Sessions (e-reports)	**10%**
Summative assessment	Partial Examinations	**38%**	Final Examination	**90%**
	Final Examination	**32%**		
	Final mark	**100%**	**Final mark**	**100%**

Table 2. 2nd stage: Assessment itineraries in the Mechanics subject.

Itinerary A is made up of four kinds of activities:

1. **Initial e-test**: This is a mandatory e-test for students who want to participate in the continuous assessment itinerary. This test was created on Moodle with the Questionnaire tool. The aim of this test is to determine the student's prior knowledge of the mathematics and physics required in order to tackle the subject properly.
2. **E-tests.** These are electronic tests carried out during the course for the various units of the major. They are composed of theoretical and practical questions and were also created on Moodle. The aim was to ensure that the students learn or, at least, read and understand the theoretical foundations of each subject unit before tackling the practical problems. These tests provide indirect guidance for students, because they allow them to check their knowledge in every unit of the subject and perform feedback.
3. **Suggested problems**: This activity remained the same as the previous year.
4. **Laboratory sessions**. The laboratory sessions are considered optional, but contribute to the final grade. They are assessed through an e-report on the practical work done and with theoretical calculus verifying the measurements obtained in the laboratory. The handing in of these documents was performed on Moodle using the Task tool, where the student is allowed to upload the e-report during a specific period of time.
5. **Partial Examinations (paper-based).** During the course there were two partial exams allowing the students to assess their knowledge of the first part of the subject and leaving the second part for the final exam. Only if the mark in each partial examination was greater than or equal to 40% would the student be allowed to be assessed only on the second part of the program in the final examination.

Questionnaires in Moodle

The Questionnaire is a powerful and flexible tool that allows the lecturer to design consistent tests and establish assessment strategies that would be impossible to carry out on paper. In fact, there is a wide variety of questions (multiple choice, true/false, short answers, gap-filling...) organized by categories within a bank of questions (for re-use in other courses). Questions can be created in HTML, with multimedia elements and can be imported from external text files. It is also possible to generate random questionnaires from

multiple choice questions stored in the bank. It has the great advantage that the time spent by the students can be limited and correction is immediate.
In the Mechanics subject, questionnaires have been used in the initial assessment and in the e-tests. Every questionnaire has an access page shown in Fig. 1 but the access button is only active the selected day and during the time permitted for doing the test, i. e., about an hour.

Fig. 1. Questionnaire access page.

Examples of theoretical and practical questions are displayed in the Figures 2, 3 and 4.

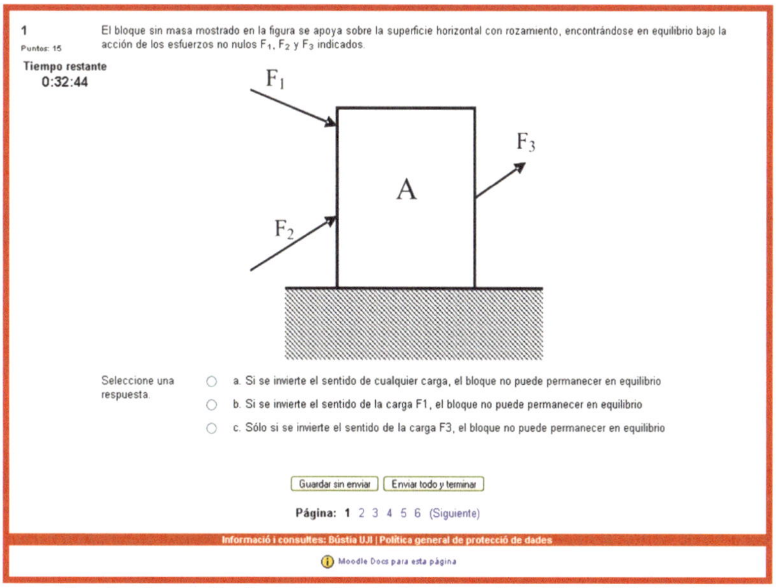

Fig. 2. An example of a theoretical multiple-choice question (Unit: Friction).

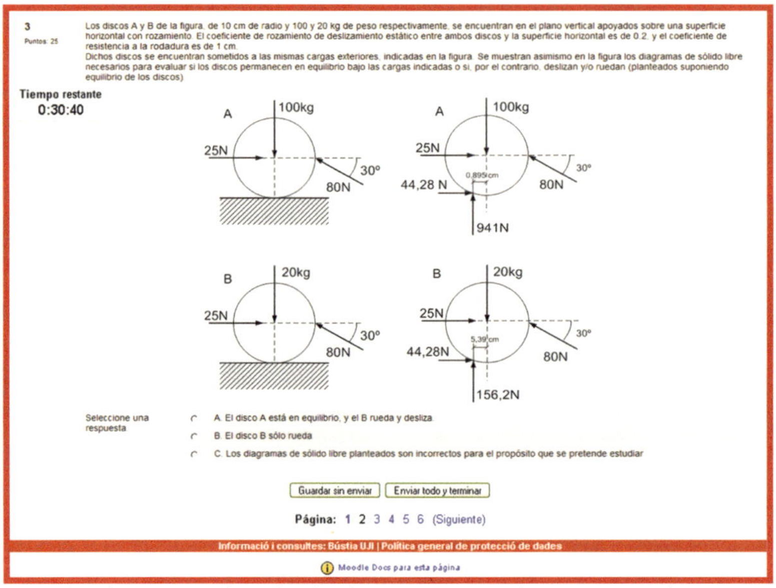

Fig. 3. An example of a practical multiple-choice question (Unit: Friction).

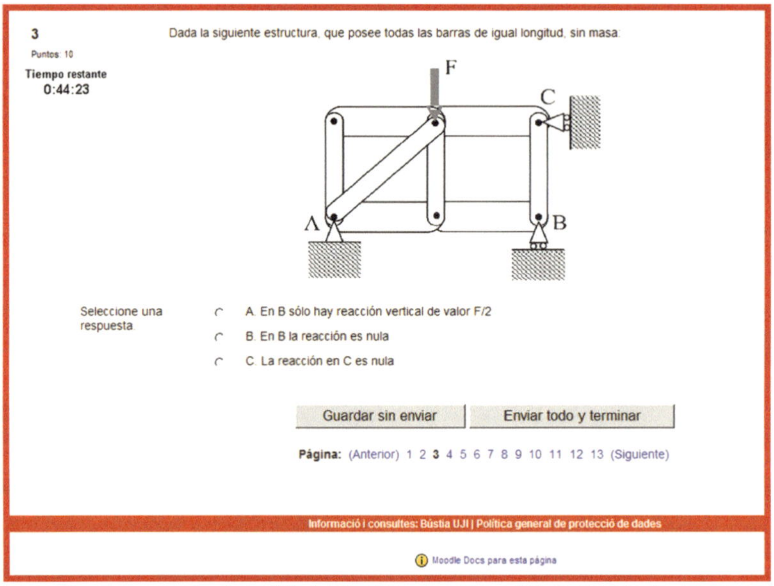

Fig. 4. An example of a practical multiple-choice question (Unit: Statics).

Tasks in Moodle

A Task is a Moodle tool that allows lecturers to assign work, which will be prepared in an electronic format and uploaded to the server. The documents are stored for later assessment, with the possibility of adding a review that will be sent to the student by e-mail.

For every task it is possible to specify the delivery deadline, which appears in the course schedule, as well as the highest mark that can be assigned to the task. The students can upload their work (in any file format) to the server and it records the date they have uploaded it.

A global view of the different tasks, groups and lecturers has been developed in order to simplify the uploading of e-reports. The various tasks can be accessed from this page, shown in Figure 5.

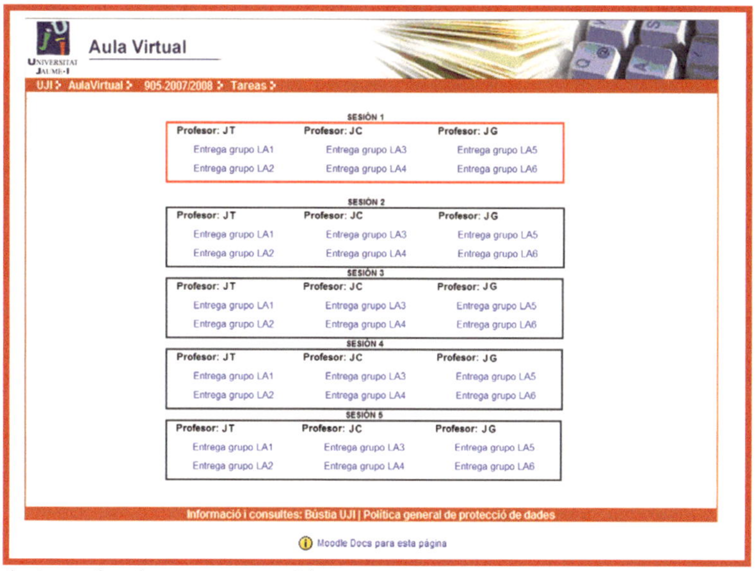

Fig. 5. Global view of tasks, groups and lecturers.

The lecturer can also check how many tasks have been scheduled, which are their deadlines and how many reports have been uploaded (Figure 6).

Fig. 6. List of tasks in the subject, with deadlines and uploaded reports.

From the main page shown in Figure 5 students can access their corresponding tasks in order to upload their e-reports. The task access page is also displayed in Figure 7.
The conditions for accessing the task are similar to those explained for the Questionnaire tool. In fact, a task can only be accessed during the period of time scheduled for it. This period usually lasts a week. During this week students can deliver their work and amend it as many times as they want, until the deadline of the task. Subsequently, lecturers will score the uploaded e-reports and students will view their grades on the same web-page.

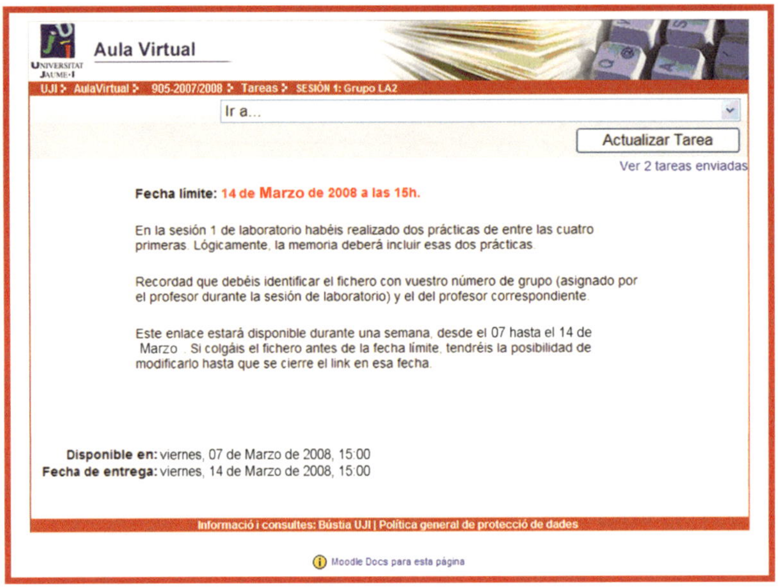

Fig. 7. Task access page.

Results deriving from the second stage

The results obtained from the second stage are better than those obtained from the first stage of the gradual adaptation:

1. More continuous study has been ensured, according to the percentage of students that sat the e-tests and partial examinations. The percentage of students that sat the partial examination was 59.4% compared to 52.54% the previous academic year. The percentage of students that sat the e-tests was 68.2%.
2. The percentage of students sitting the examination has significantly increased, from 36% in the academic year 2005/2006 to 53.39% in the academic year 2006/2007, under the proposal presented in the previous section, and to 63% the last academic year (2007/2008) with the new proposal presented here.
3. 89% of the students who sat the partial examination did finally pass the Mechanics subject.
4. An increase in the use of the tutorial sessions for asking questions related to the subject has been identified, with a mean of 3 students per tutoring session. However, this is a very small number.
5. The percentage of enrolled students who passed the subject has also increased from 33.47% in the academic year 2006/2007 to 36% the last year. It must be pointed out that this percentage never exceeded 15% in previous academic years.

6. When asked, the students assess the initiative positively, but they complain about the workload.
7. No correlation has been found between the marks from the e-tests and the marks from the partial examinations.
8. The new proposal has slightly increased the lecturer's workload, which was already high with the previous proposal.

7. Conclusions and Future Work

The changes introduced at the second stage allowed students to study more continuously, improving the percentage of enrolled students sitting the examinations and the percentage of students passing the subject.
The task of guidance carried out by the lecturer has indirectly increased, by means of the feedback given to the students in the e-test results. The e-tests have also helped ensure a proper and continuous study of the theoretical foundation of the subject, which was not achieved in the first stage of the proposal. In this way, the students have been able to make a better use of their attendance in class.
But the lecturer's workload has increased, largely because of the introduction of the second partial examination, and also because of the e-tests. As no correlation between the marks in the e-tests and the marks in the partial examinations has been found, a more in-depth study should be carried out in order to ensure that the partial examinations could be replaced by e-tests, with a smaller workload for the lecturer.

8. References

Barnard, L.; Lan, W. Y.; To, Y. M., Paton, V. O. & Lai, S.L. (2009). Measuring self-regulation in online and blended learning environments. *Internet and Higher Education,* Vol. 12, No. 1, January 2009, pp. 1-6, ISSN 1096-7516.

Bersin, K. (2004). *The Blended Learning Book,* Pfeifer (John Wiley and Sons), ISBN 0787972967, San Francisco, USA.

Clausen, T. (2005). Undergraduate engineering education challenged by the bologna declaration. *IEEE Transactions on Education,* vol. 48, nº 2, May, pp. 213-215, ISSN: 0018-9359.

European Ministers Responsible for Higher Education. (1999). The European Higher Education Area, *Bologna Declaration,* June, Bologna, Italy.

European Ministers Responsible for Higher Education. (2001). Towards the European Higher Education Area, *Prague Declaration,* May, Prague, Czech Republic.

European Ministers Responsible for Higher Education. (2003a). Realising the European Higher Education Area, *Berlin Declaration,* September, Berlin, Germany.

European Ministers Responsible for Higher Education. (2003b). Forward from Berlin: The Role of the Universities, *Graz Declaration,* September, Graz, Austria.

European Ministers Responsible for Higher Education. (2005). The European Higher Education Area. Achieving the Goals, *Bergen Declaration,* May, Bergen, Netherlands.

Garrison, R. & Kanuka, H. (2004). Blended learning: Uncovering its transformative potential in higher education. *Internet and Higher Education,* vol. 7, nº 2, pp. 95-105, ISSN: 1096-7516.
Govindasamy,T.(2002).Successful implementation of e-Learning: Pedagogical considerations. *Internet and Higher Education,* vol. 4, February, pp. 287-299, ISSN: 1096-7516.
Ginns, P. & Ellis, R. (2007). Quality in blended learning: Exploring the relationships between on-line and face-to-face teaching and learning. *Internet and Higher Education,* Vol. 10 No. 1, January 20027, pp. 53-64, ISSN: 1096-7516
Kelly, H. F.; Ponton, M. K. & A. P. Rovai, A.P. (2007). A comparison of student evaluations of teaching between online and face-to-face courses. *Internet and Higher Education,* Vol. 10 No. 1, January 20027, pp. 89-101, ISSN: 1096-7516
Ministry of Education and Science. (2007). The Spanish Educational System, Retrieved: http://www.sispain.org/english/educatio/enlargem.html.
Mora-Aguilar, M. C.; Sancho-Brú, J. L.; Rodríguez-Cervantes, P.J. & Iserte-Vilar, J. L. (2008). The challenge of improving teaching methodologies in overcrowded groups: experiences in basic Mechanics. *Proceedings of the International Technology, Education and Development Conference,* ISBN: 978-84-612-0190-7, Valencia, Spain, IATED eds.
Mora-Aguilar, M. C.; Sancho-Brú, J. L. & Iserte-Vilar, J. L. (2009). Alternatives for evaluation in overcrowded groups: the e-assessment. *Proc. of the Int. Technology, Education and Development Conference,* ISBN: 978-84-612-7578-6, Valencia, Spain, IATED editors.
Moodle, version 1.9. (2007) http://www.moodle.org
O'Reilly, T. (2005), *What's the Web 2.0?* September 2005. http://www.oreillynet.com
Rectors of the European Universities. (1988). *Magna Charta Universitatum,* September, Bologna, Italy.
Rengarajan, R. (2001). LCMS and LMS: *LCMS and LMS: Taking advantage of tight integration.* Click2Learn Inc. August 2001. http://www.e-learn.cz/soubory/lcms_and_lms.pdf
Spanish Government. (2003). REAL DECRETO 1125/2003 de 5 de septiembre, por el que se establece el sistema europeo de créditos y el sistema de calificaciones en las titulaciones universitarias de carácter oficial y validez en todo el territorio nacional (in Spanish), *BOE* (http://www.boe.es), September, Madrid, (www.boe.es).
Spanish Government. (2007). REAL DECRETO 1393/2007 de 29 de octubre, por el que se establece la ordenación de las enseñanzas universitarias oficiales (in Spanish), *BOE* (http://www.boe.es), October, Madrid.
Spanish Government. (2009a). Orden CIN/311/2009, de 9 de febrero, por la que se establecen los requisitos para la verificación de los títulos universitarios oficiales que habiliten para el ejercicio de la profesión de Ingeniero Industrial (in Spanish), *BOE* (http://www.boe.es), February, Madrid.
Spanish Government. (2009b). Orden CIN/351/2009, de 9 de febrero, por la que se establecen los requisitos para la verificación de los títulos universitarios oficiales que habiliten para el ejercicio de la profesión de Ingeniero Técnico Industrial (in Spanish), *BOE* (http://www.boe.es), February, Madrid.
Tovar, E. & Cardeñosa, J. (2003). Convergence in higher education: effects and risks. *International Conference on the Convergence of Knowledge, Culture, Language and Information Technologies,* pp. 1-5.

10

The use of SCORM in a community based Learning Management System

Luigi Colazzo, Andrea Molinari and Nicola Villa
University of Trento, Department of Computer and Management Sciences - Laboratory of Maieutics
Trento, Italy

1. Introduction

The paper illustrates our experience as designers, developers, experimenters and administrators of a virtual communities system (VCS) used by the Faculty of Economics of our University. The idea to equip the faculty with such a platform goes back to the end of the 90s and the platform itself has in the meantime undergone at least total and several partial restructuring processes, starting from being an e-learning system and evolving into the idea of managing and supporting virtual communities. In the years that followed, considerations based on our double role of administrators of a real service and developers of software have convinced us of the need for a radical change of the platform. The main reasons for this decision can be summed up as follows:

An e-Learning system used in a real teaching context cannot act as an isolated system but must be considered as one of the components of the whole information system of a teaching institution (Colazzo & Molinari, 2002).

The metaphor of 'course' used in that first creation was adequate for covering the needs of communication and cooperation that take place in the daily work of a teaching institute.

The daily interaction of subjects within the community of people that gravitates around a course needs to have a higher level of flexibility in defining roles, rights, duties, permissions, etc. within the environment of that same "community".

Following this conviction the system has been completely rewritten and the new version is at present in use at our university as a technological platform for projects of blended learning at our and other faculties. The system is called On Line Communities and will briefly be described under point one of this paper. Recently On Line Communities has been adopted as a model by the Autonomous Province of Trento (Italy) for developing their own technological platform for Life-Long Learning (LLL) projects. As a consequence, we are at present rewriting the software in order to adapt it to the requirements of our customer. On Line Communities is a multi-standard system, that is to say a system purposefully neutral compared to the nature of objects in use. There are various reasons for this decision taken many years ago and which has proved itself most productive. To sum it up:

A Learning Object (LO) by definition can be a very simple or complicated object, from a text to a very complex software: to put a constraint on LOs accessible through the VCS does not seem to be indicated.
A VCS aimed at university teaching has a high variability in the nature and format of the LO, for example, an LO containing a textual demonstration of a theorem will almost certainly be written in Latex, while the text "De bello gallico" could be made accessible in Html rather than in PDF file.
University lecturers like to change their courses from one year to the next and often prefer to use their own LO rather that those available on the market or on the web. Furthermore, a lecturer would hardly use the LO of another lecturer unless s/he wanted to make a point. This, therefore, eliminates the need for a Repository and also a great deal of the meta-data.
Basically, On Line Communities considers LO to be any kind of electronic document that can be used /exchanged through the net: from a text to a hardware. This choice will remain substantially unvaried but among the requirements of the new application, that aim at training courses of the Trentino provincial administration, there is the need to consent the use of didactic material consistent with the Shareable Content Object Reference Model (SCORM) standard of ADL (Advanced Distribuited Learning, 2004). The authors of the SCORM-compliant material have to respect the specifications of re-usability, duration, portability, inter-operational function and accessibility. The specifications of the structure of the didactic material of a SCORM package is based on the use of meta-data through which it is possible to represent: a) the navigation method and the sequencing in the structure; b) the meta-data of the learning objects (LOM) of a specific course, that is the aggregation model (CAM). The LOM are not very effective in as much as their aim is that of defining a conceptual scheme for the representation of the internal structure of a learning object, but they do not define the contents of a learning object itself.
The representation of the learning objects covers an aspect of primary importance, especially if these are interactive (Díaz et al., 2007). One of the requirements imposed by the need of our customers is indeed that of allowing the use of didactic material consistent with the SCORM standard; a method which, as we shall see, differs from our own approach. This is how the motivation emerges to study solutions compatible with our platform, in such a way as to maintain it independent. The work is organized in the following way: in section one we will suggest a more detailed vision of our e-learning system, called On Line Communities, introducing also the new life-long learning project called L3. In section two we will describe the approach used to integrate into our system packages of SCORM type and the problems that a standard can create within a pre-existing e-learning applicative. In particular we want to concentrate on the enclosure of the standard to training experiences different from those initially foreseen by its authors, such as for example the use of interactive didactic forms on behalf of the course teacher. Finally, in part three, we will tackle a most delicate question that concerns the accessibility of didactic material adhering to the standard. As we shall see, in fact, this latter is a delicate point in the architecture of most SCORM-compliant tools that are in contrast with, for instance, Italian law.

2. E-learning and Lifelong learning: On Line Communities

In this section we will recap the characteristics of *Comunità On Line* portal (*OnLine Communities* - COMOL) (Colazzo et al., 2007), the VCS used in an example for our argumentation. The project started in 1998 under the name *Corsi On Line* (*Online Courses*) and in 2002 it evolved from a traditional e-learning system to a new platform based on the metaphor of virtual learning communities. On Line Courses was a system based on the initial idea of *Course*: all its functionalities were contained in the services within every course. The active services were divided in:

- Synchronous communication systems (chat, remote application control, video-conference);
- Asynchronous communication systems (course management, forum, mail group);
- Presentation systems (information about the lecturer, the program and the organization of the courses and the exams, timetables, books, course syllabus);
- Upload/download services (for the learning objects and the connected documents).

The project continued its activity up to the academic year 2005/2006, with 670 active courses, 17.000 users and 1.300.000 total accesses. In the final part, the project has supported the transition to the new On Line Communities project, started in 2002 with a total re-engineering process of the system. The object of the new *On Line Communities* was to create a space in the web, where it could be possible to widen the universe of relations between the actors of the didactic processes. The core of the application is composed of some abstract entities, Virtual Communities, People (Students, Professors, Administrative Staff) and Communication Services. In detail, a virtual community is a space on the web dedicated to a collaboration objective, populated by people who communicate among each other, using a series of communication systems. These are general instruments that allow to maintain the relationship between people.

The portal is able to include one community into another, or to aggregate the communities into a transversal super-community. With these types of mechanisms it could be possible to model many types of collaborative structures, even of a high complexity. For example, hierarchical structures like Faculties, Didactic Paths, Courses, Work Groups related to a course. *On Line Communities* was released outside the test areas in 2005, but had been experimented since 2003. As from 2005 it was being used by the entire faculty of Economics of our University and others faculties are still experimenting the system in many types of courses. At present the system has more than 1600 active communities, 9000 users and more or less 1,500,000 real accesses since May 2009 (see Figure 1).

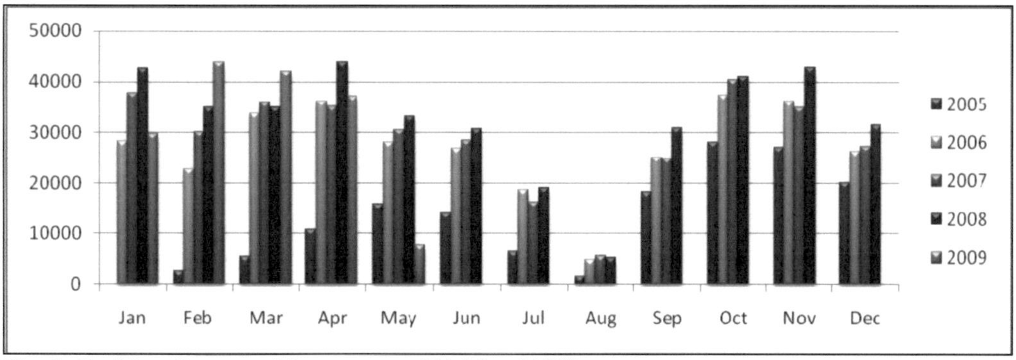

Fig. 1. On Line Communities accesses [8th May 2009]

L3 (LifeLong Learning) is a project to be implemented by our university, commissioned by the Autonomous Province of Trento (PAT) as a collaboration platform aimed at becoming a technological environment for training projects within the PAT itself and connected entities. In the specific case our intervention has a special valence in as far as it supports the starting up and the fruition of an e-procurement at the service of all the Public Administration of the Trentino Province. The aim of our work is mainly technological. That is to say that our task is to supply the Autonomous Province of Trento with an instrument enabling it to implement internal training processes. The system we are developing has, however, two specific characteristics:

- The system will operate on a territorial basis characterised by solid co-operation among citizens.
- The system should be able to guarantee temporal continuity of the training experience which goes beyond the single case of training and ideally will extended to many years.

These circumstances and previous experiences in creating e-learning platforms within the university have induced us to use as a basic metaphor for our system that of "virtual learning community". At the same time, however, this context of application has brought up a number of questions, crucial in a life-long learning environment. Indeed, while in an academic institution the learning communities for the bigger part coincide with the training experience (one course, one study line, etc.) in the case of life-long learning the communities are more permanent. In a certain sense they pre-exist virtual communities and survive the training experience itself.

One of the limitations of the system that the provincial body has imposed, concerns the possibility to use within its structure material consistent with the SCORM/AICC standard. Such requirement necessitates the re-planning of some of the services of the original system for the university, since the metaphor of community contrasts with that of a traditional course contained within the SCORM packages.

3. Integrating SCORM into a virtual community system

The integration of the SCORM standard is an element of primary importance in many of the projects in the field of e-learning. The integration within our system of the functionality and the advantages offered by the standard requires major focus on the definition of which method should be adopted so that the standard adapts itself to the metaphor of the virtual learning communities. The functional integration of the world of SCORM into an VCS concerns mainly four different functional areas:

- Tools for Authoring of SCORM compliant material;
- Up-Load of SCORM compliant material into the VCS,
- Download of SCORM material through the platform (SCORM packages and single SCO or ASSET)
- fruition of the SCORM material directly from within the VCS.

From a practical point of view we have identified three types of possible approaches to make our VCS compatible with the standard (Buendia Garcia & Hervas Jorge, 2006), that obviously require different efforts. A first level of adaptation (figure 2) allows the up- and download of the entire SCORM package, to display its structure and download the single resources (Asset o SCO) contained within it. This approach seems easy to be created and, furthermore, it offers minimal functionalities to users compared to the real complexity and potentiality of the standard.

Fig. 2. Structure and contents of a SCORM package as presented in On Line Communities

One relevant problem indeed, especially for a traditional LMS with high user loads as our *On Line Communities*, concerns not so much the access and creation of a tree-view of the material, as the decompression of the contained material in case of download of chunks of the material itself. Indeed, for the first function the SCORM package contains an XML file that represents its content in a hierarchical form. The real problem is an architectural one: the SCORM package that represents the course (or the module, or lesson) especially with videos or html pages, can contain high numbers of files and can be of noteworthy dimensions. Having to compress them in order to permit partial download, problems of architectural choices occur:

- to load a SCORM package and then during the download phase carry out the "on-demand" decompression for the index file (IMSMANIFEST.XML) and for the various components of the package
- as above, but with immediate decompression after the upload of the index file, in such a way as to facilitate the browsing phase of the same to seek the desired chunk
- to load a SCORM package and at the same time carry out the decompression in a second repository of the whole SCORM package.

The advantages and disadvantages of the various alternatives are quite clear: within On Line Communities the third hypothesis has been chosen in function of the high work load and the users present in the system. The adopted solution sees as main drawback the doubling (at the least) of the storage occupation which, however, enables to avoid having to decompress "on the fly" upon request by the user very heavy SCORM packages, perhaps for several users at the same time. We have observed, for example, that when the teaches sends a note of availability of new didactic material, especially during the period of lessons, On Line Communities has a clash of accesses and requests for downloading material within few minutes. It is clear that, further to not being able to avoid these peaks, finding the SCORM package both in its hierarchic form *and* in its already available component, makes the task easier.

The second level of more complex implementation concerns the development of a player of SCORM that enables the execution within the system of SCORM courses (Bamidis et al., 2007), that is the guided navigation through the lessons of a course, the carrying out of a test, the taking up of the same at a later moment, etc. The implementation of an internal player presents two critical aspect:

- storing the current state of the fruition and, therefore, memorizing the various states in which the SCORM module can be used. In the case of off-line player, meaning not connected to the platform, everything is much simpler. In case of a platform of the size and user number like ours, and in particular in view of its heavy interactive use and in real time on behalf particularly of students, this solution appears to be architecturally complex.
- the flexibility on the player within the platform and/or the client: indeed, within the SCORM package we can find potentially anything and, from what we have observed in our experiments, the knowledge of and the adherence to the SCORM standard of various authoring software is decidedly to be improved upon. Naturally, if the user does not succeed in using the package because of a non adherence to the standard, the fault inevitably and undeservedly goes to the platform and not to the creator of the LO.

It must, however, be added that this hypothesis has a decidedly appealing aspect, concerning the management of bandwidth usage: in this case, from our early experiments, the direct fruition appears to be a more attractive solution than the download on one's own PC of a SCORM package in order to use it "off-line", because the waiting time and the fruition might consent a decidedly better load-balancing of net and platform resources than (perhaps at the same time) downloading of the whole package.

The last and final integration level identified contemplates the creation of an authoring system (Celentano & Bochicchio, 2006) so that in future authors can create complete and certified SCORM packages in a guided way (Parmar et al., 2007).

This option appears for now to be of low priority for a series of reasons both technical and tactical:

- Further to customizing opensource software for our platform, this operation is certainly not painless
- Sophisticated SCORM authoring environment already exist outside our platform and so there is the risk of "reinventing the wheel"
- We are, above all, not convinced that people who create didactic material are ready to abandon their own authoring environment in order to learn a new one, especially with a conceptual meta-structure (SCORM standard) which, however hidden in the software of SCORM authoring, makes the workload heavier. We well know, also from personal experience, that who is used to creating didactic material with PowerPoint™ is unlikely to change opinion and who produces didactic material with Latex™ will have difficulty in changing such a powerful and flexible environment which had taken him/her so long to learn.

Our choice has been to proceed in a first phase leaving the tutors the possibility to publish materials created outside On Line Communities, and other users the navigation within them. It seemed to us an interesting solution to integrate the use of SCORM packages into the download service of didactic material of a course in that specific service. The motivation that determined this choice was dictated by the wish to maintain the user service of didactic material "transparent" compared to the format of the materials themselves. Thinking, for instance, of the notes of a lecture taken with a normal word processing software, in such a case there is no service called "textual material" because it is contained within the download of the didactic material (figure 4). In the same way, a lesson too, created previously through SCORM standard, can be downloaded from the material section just like the notes of the lessons (figure 3).

Fig. 3. Material service that also integrates the download of SCORM packages

Among the functionalities to create, there is the fruition of SCORM courses; this is possible through a nesting structure of the frame, since a SCORM course is basically composed of a set of pages that have to be reproduced "as they are". The interaction as far as navigation and evaluation of user input is concerned, will take place through the appeal of the primitives defined by ADL, inserted into the SCO, that is, the fundamental resources of the SCORM package. The structure, and even its tree representation, is however in contrast with the guidelines of accessibility that we adopt, as will be described in section three, in as much as problems are introduced both from a point of view of accessibility as well as incompatibility with some browsers.

Even the aspect concerning authoring of SCORM packages is of no simple implementation: the obligations defined in the Content Aggregation Model (CAM) of the third version of SCORM 2004, in the IEEE specifications upon which it is based (IEEE 1484.12.1) (IEEE, 2002) and in the application profile of CNIPA (Italian National Center for the Computer Science in the Public Administration) indicate the possibility to take into consideration a sub-total of meta-data in order to simplify the creation of compatible courses. This may enable us to create a service less invasive than it might be, so that the authors of the system may be helped in writing lessons.

One open question that we have been asking ourselves concerns the applicability of a web 2.0 approaches to the definition of SCORM didactic contents. This is an important question since the solutions adopted in the web are those in which the author is no longer classifiable with informatics; on the contrary, each web user - according to this approach - can be author of contents. In this context, collaborative and interactive applications, within which users are free to publish information on whatever topic, have become more and more popular. Part of this category can be considered services like wiki (Leuf & Cunningham, 2001) or blog (Kline & Burstein, 2005) that offer collaborative environments in which users can exchange information. Even On Line Communities and its evolutions in the projects of life-long learning for training courses of employees of the provincial administration, integrates services of this type but with the important addition of combining these services with the concept and architecture of "community" that, as we have seen, completely conditions and warps any e-learning service. Each user can create within the system a personal blog in which to interact with his/her colleagues establishing a social network on a community level in the widest sense, from the secretariats to courses, from recreational to research groups. This kind of collaborative and cooperative approach in which all members of the community can take part to reach a final aim, unhinges the classical concept of static lesson in which only the teacher could generate knowledge. In this case all users who take part in the learning process are able to help each other (taking part in forum, chat, wiki, etc.) improving social relations that are being established in order to favor learning.

In such ideal context of web 2.0, we unfortunately notice how the use of SCORM type packages could be a critical element, because it is not suitable to this type of solution. A lesson created according to standard is in fact static, consisting only of the information that the author had decided to offer to those following the course, the list of the lessons (even if up-datable at a later date by the author) will be adopted by the student in "as is" mode, without the possibility for interaction with the contents. This creates a relevant limitation because it transforms what could be an interactive path into a "cul-de-sac" where only the teacher controls the learning modality of the student. The possibility to include, always on behalf of the author, interactive contents within the lessons (for example, Flash™ videos of objects that can help users to understand concepts) is not excluded but it is in function of what the teacher decides to insert and not of what the user would really like.

For this reason our choice has been to integrate SCORM into our system, yet avoiding to link On Line Communities indissolubly to the standard; this is a decision we have been following up ever since the birth of the system in such a was a to make it "transparent". Hence, the integration into the system does not mean the complete adoption of the standard but rather to offer users the possibility to use their own material quite freely.

4. Accessibility of SCORM tools and packages

Among the various characteristics of an e-learning application aimed at studying and working population there is certainly the accessibility of the system for disabled people. The difficulty to access the contents within the SCORM packages is a question not widely dealt with so far but certainly of primary importance, given its diffusion (hoped for) and the enormous potential that it contains. We would like to introduce the topic of accessibility of

SCORM-compliant materials, that is, the whole range of solutions and strategies suitable to make web information usable also by both physically or mentally disabled people. Part of this category are all those problems that a disabled person can meet when s/he accesses and uses information in web pages incompatible with assistive tools, because of an interface developed without the simplest usability principles. In our opinion, there is another serious problem regarding the accessibility of SCORM material: most of the statements we found in literature, citing the words "accessibility" and "SCORM", are intended in a totally different way from what they mean to unpaired people, with a general sense like "accessibility means more people can access to electronic materials". Unfortunately, the term "accessibility" is used in SCORM documentation as "The ability to locate learning content in multiple locations and to deliver it to multiple locations." Accessibility to unpaired persons is not addressed in the SCORM specifications (Craddock, 2003).

Up to now various international as well as national directives have been issued on the subject; we have already mentioned this question in other works, underlining for instance the incompatibility between national law (in Italy, for instance, law of 9th January 2004 (Italian Parliament, 2004) and local norms concerning the territory in which our research group is active. Having amply treated this topic in a previous work, here we just want to remind of the guidelines issued by WAI (internal organism of W3C), called Web Content Accessibility Guidelines in the version 1.0 issued in 1999 (Chisholm et al., 1999)and the version 2.0 (Caldwell, 2007) at present under revision.

On the basis of these guidelines, but also of the technical requirements foreseen by Italian law, we wish to concentrate on the analysis of a possible level of accessibility of courses offered according to SCORM standard; going back to what we said in the previous section, it is necessary to distinguish two different cases:

- the accessibility of the applications in order to offer courses
- the contents good and proper, codified according to meta-data indicated in the standard.

As far as the contents are concerned, created directly by the user and loaded within a SCORM package, the accessibility level does not depend on the standard employed but, rather, on the modality through which the user has created the didactic contents. We are thinking of the notes of a lesson codified through a text document, in case they are accessible in the same way, they will also be after having been imported into the package itself. In the same way, in case the created information and documents are already inaccessible because of their incompatibility with the above mentioned standard, the same will apply also for the lessons presented in the package. After all, the standard does not degrade the accessibility of the contents presented, but simply tries to offer its original state.

The question concerning the accessibility of the interface of an application for offering SCORM material is quite different; from our point of view this question is particularly important since we do not want to degrade the level of accessibility of our portal after the integration with the service for the use of SCORM packages. One of the pre-requisites of the player is the use of Javascript language; this is in clear contrast with the WAI recommendation, particularly 6.0 present in the first version of the WCAG, while the Italian legislation does not advise to use scripts in requisites 15 and 16 of the Italian law.

The interface of a SCORM package player is normally structured using a frame, separating graphically the contents of the lessons from navigation. This characteristic is in strong contrast not only with the WAI guidelines and requisite 2 of the Italian law but actually with the best practices followed by web developers. The use of frames indeed has been abandoned by the majority of programmers who prefer the implementation of different structures, more efficient and also more accessible. This is why the choice of CNIPA, an Italian public body, in setting up the regulations for the development of e-learning sites allows the use of SCORM player based on frames, appears strange to us. The directive for e-learning specifically affirms that "*the use of frame is allowed only in e-learning platforms that rely on SCORM is allowed, and exclusively for including the imported contents and for tracing activity*" (CNIPA, 2007).This choice is probably dictated by the need to make already developed e-learning applicative like ours, compatible with material previously created according to standard.

For these reasons our work group is oriented towards the development of a different solution that will guarantee the accessibility of the importation and visualization of SCORM material within the Online Community. The necessity to guarantee the use of SCORM learning objects from our e-learning portal can be a risk factor concerning the general accessibility of the system, which is configured as a fundamental requirement. The intermediary solution that has been adopted, that is, the visualization of the contents presented in LO SCORM and the possibility to download material contained it (text documents, html, images, etc.) has been thought to be completely fully accessible. In contrast with the classical tools available, we do indeed not use a frame for the implementation of this service. The list of lessons appears through javascript language but it has been implemented by a mechanism so as to be usable also in case fruition through a browser that does not support the language. As already mentioned, the user will be able to access the various contents present in the documents, but for obvious reasons we cannot guarantee the full accessibility of the downloadable material. Indeed, we are not able to control the conformity of the standard of the contents of the single files created and loaded in the packages on behalf of the users; classical examples are HTML pages, created autonomously outside our portal, that risk to be inaccessible if the author does not respect the various requirements.

5. Conclusion

This paper presents a necessarily synthetic view of the problem created, within already existing e-learning platforms, of two very important topics for such systems and in general for didactics assisted by ICTs, that is, the use of SCORM standard with its architectural implications on the platform itself, and the problems created by these adoptions in terms of accessibility. We have presented the solutions applied to these questions within our On Line Communities platform, in which the basic philosophy of the platform, that is to say, the idea of virtual community, offers advantages of implementation and possibility for superior development in contrast with the closure created by the simple concept of "course" as a container of SCORM material. The solution we have described in this section reflects this philosophy; we have not created SCORM-compatible communities but we have foreseen the possibility to create, insert and visualize lessons of this time within the space we are offering our users. The aspect of accessibility of SCORM material is, however, a complex problem, especially because of some incongruences in the finality of the standard, in its formulation and its legislative aspects, that make its implementation obligatory. A solution to these questions or, even possible structural intervention on the standard, on the technologies available to diversely able people and on the legislation would be most welcome.

6. References

Advanced Distribuited Learning (2004). *SCORM 2004 3rd edition - Content Aggregation Model,* retrieved from http://www.adlnet.gov/downloads/AuthNotReqd.aspx?FileName=SCORM.2004.3ED.DocSuite.zip&ID=237

Bamidis, Panagiotis D.; Nikolaidou, Maria M.; Konstantinidis, Stathis Th. & Pappas, Costas (2007). *A Proposed Framework for Accreditation of Online Continuing Medical Education,* Computer-Based Medical Systems, 2007. CBMS apos;07. Twentieth IEEE International Symposium on Volume , Issue , 20-22 June 2007 Page(s):693 - 700

Buendia Garcia, F. & Hervas Jorge, A. (2006). *Evaluating e-learning platforms through SCORM specifications.* In: Proceedings of IADIS Virtual Multi Conference on Computer Science and Information Systems (MCCSIS 2006) (15 - 19 May 2006). www.iadis.org/Multi2006/Papers/15/S020_EL.pdf

Caldwell, B.; Cooper, M.; Guarino Reid, L. & Vanderheiden, G. (2007). *Web Content Accessibility Guidelines 2.0,* W3C working draft

Celentano, M. & Bochicchio, M. (2006). *A Real-Time Authoring Tools For Scorm-Compliant Learning Objects.* In E. Pearson & P. Bohman (Eds.), Proceedings of World Conference on Educational Multimedia, Hypermedia and Telecommunications 2006 (pp. 2061-2068). Chesapeake, VA: AACE.

Chisholm, W.; Venderheiden, G. & Jacobs I. (1999). *Web Content Accessibility Guidelines 1.0,* W3C Recommendation

CNIPA (2007). *Vademecum per la realizzazione di progetti formativi in modalità e-learning nelle pubbliche amministrazioni,* second edition. In: I Quaderni n. 32, april 2007, Rome

Colazzo, L. & Molinari A. (2002). *From Learning Management Systems To Learning Information Systems: One Possible Evolution Of E-Learning.* In: Proc. Communications, Internet and Information Technology (CIIT) Conference, St. Thomas, USA - November 18-20, 2002

Colazzo, L.; Haller, H. & Molinari A. (2007). *WAYS – What Are You Studying? A community tool for learners on the move.* In: Proc. of ED-MEDIA 2007, edit by Craig Montgomerie & Jane Seale,June 25- June 29, 2007; Vancouver BC, Canada

Craddock, G. (2003), *Assistive Technology - Shaping the Future,* ISBN 1586033735, IOS Press

Díaz, F.; Osorio, M.; Amadeo, A. & Schiavoni, A. (2006). *Standardizing Educative Content with SCORM: A Case Study.* In C. Crawford et al. (Eds.), Proceedings of Society for Information Technology and Teacher Education International Conference 2006 (pp. 318-323). Chesapeake, VA: AACE.

IEEE (2002) *Draft Standard for Learning Object Metadata* – IEEE 1484.12.1. Retrieved from http://ltsc.ieee.org/wg12/files/LOM_1484_12_1_v1_Final_Draft.pdf.

Italian Parliament (2004). *Disposizioni per favorire l'accesso dei soggetti disabili agli strumenti informatici, Legge 9 gennaio 2004, n. 4*

Kline D. & Burstein D. (2005). *Blog!: How the Newest Media Revolution is Changing Politics.* In: Business, and Culture, Squibnocket Partners, L.L.C.

Leuf B. & Cunningham W. (2001). *The Wiki way: quick collaboration on the Web.* In: Addison-Wesley Longman Publishing Co., Inc. Boston, MA, USA

Parmar, K.; Anane, R.; Hendley, R. J. (2007). *Architecture of a SCORM-Compliant Assessment Authoring Tool*, 2007. ICCSA 2007. International Conference on Computational Science and its Applications, 26-29 Aug. 2007 Kuala Lampur, Malaysia, Page(s):110 - 117

11

Product design teaching processes worldwide analysis and comparison for a future on line design studio

Serena Selva
Politecnico di Milano
Italy

1. Introduction

The author thinks that the education about product design discipline is a fertile field of research and innovation, in particular concerning the debate on the project educational approach that today is openness to new issues.
The chapter purposes to identify the base information to reach an on line design teaching process to adopt within the Design Studios around the world.
The first step done is based primarily on a collection of data to structure an objective view on what is happening and has occurred in a number of countries and higher education institutions concerning product design. The original data will enable the researcher to understand what constitutes a valid sample of countries that have an interest in product design education. In particular this kind of analysis is connected with socio-economic and industrial contexts to understand especially how technology and geographic borders are driving change in the workplace. The data is particularly relevant in order to understand the economic development of a country and its relation to an educational context. The research is also posited on a geographic and cultural/historical analysis .
The following part of the research is the analysis of practice. The majority of work has been completed within design studios and through carefully structured interviews with both lecturers and students. This study will draw comparisons between context and curriculum, and consequently highlight coherences and incongruities.

2. Research field

Prior to analysing both the context and the product design curriculum, the researcher furthermore established a set of clearly defined criteria to determine which continents and subsequently which countries, were appropriate for the study in addition of the previous description. The criteria are two: Economic trends and higher education and product design courses.
These two criteria are closely related to ensure an effective balance between Industrial production to education and the result of their application is illustrated in figure 1 which

represent graphically the interesting Countries for the identification of a number of institutions to use as case studies.

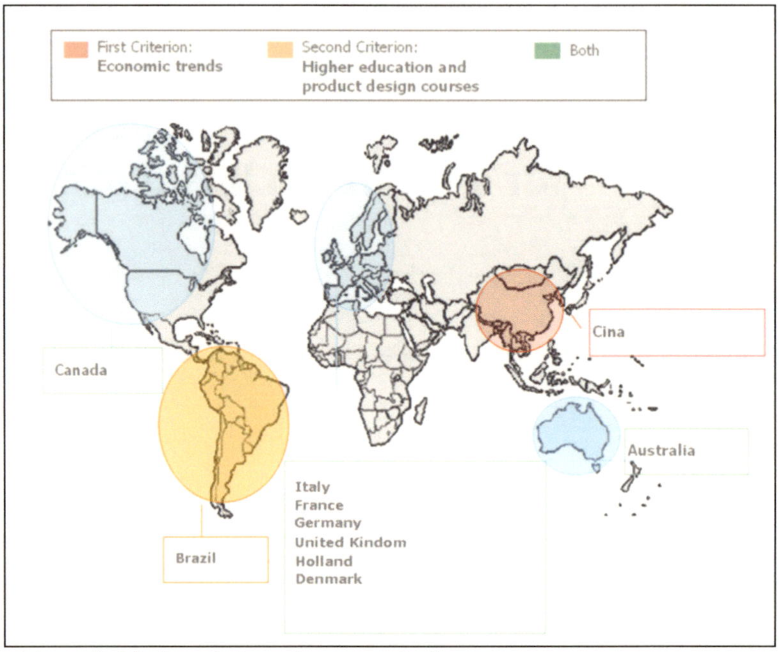

Fig. 1. Countries suitable for a interesting case study

It was fundamental to analyse the historical context where the different contemporary industrialised world school models were developed in order to understand the current ones and, according to Steve Brint's (Steve Brint, 1998) declarations, also to realise how the differences in the school structure directly weigh on the working opportunities in students' lives. This research part examined the scholar structure, in particular the didactic system, to identify key differences between nationality, experiences, attitudes and opportunities for students: in synthesis the relation between society and the school.
The industrialized world students participate within a global culture: blue jeans, rock music, the same age company and a higher and higher independence are common characteristics more or less everywhere, alternatively, there are important national differences behind these known common styles and these differences are strictly related to the school system in the different countries. The result is that there are different national student stereotypes: the cultural distinction of the British sixth former; the impenetrable Japanese juku student; the outwardly breezy American one. Brint (Steve Brint, 1998) suggests that these national types have to be thought as a product of a specific national character, or of peculiar historic experiences. But these national characteristics are indeed linked to the differences in education's organization itself. The differences in the school structures are connected to the young students differences in the way of thinking and acting: to differences which they have in perception of the existing borderlines among social classes, to differences in their readiness in concentrating and committing themselves, to the different importance that the

consciousness of opportunities existence compared to social class consciousness assumes and even the degree of confidence they have in the future.
Parallel to this historical context analysis, the author analysed the national context, industrial and economic contexts, and historical and cultural context.
In detail

- the analysis of the national contexts (main aspects for the product design in each individual Country identified) comprised a review of industrial, economic, historical and cultural contexts;
- the industrial context is analysed on a country basis to ascertain the type of industrial system (ratio of small and medium enterprises to multinationals), the industrial sector by size (%) and the import-export (volume);
- the economic context was examined as a macro-area (or on a continental basis) because countries within a continent have comparable economies and can be analysed to ascertain economic trends, economic dynamics and the value of imports-exports;
- the historical and cultural contexts were analysed on a country basis to ascertain the existence of a history or culture of design.

After the previously discussed analysis, it was necessary to ascertain whether universities or schools of art and design in general, have developed curricula to meet the changing market demand, or whether they have been developed to push ideas of design into the market. Furthermore, it is of interest to assess whether classroom work is effective in relation to industry, as this impacts on the extent to which industry will then employ product designers.
In addition, the number of students that enrol on courses will help the author to understand the relation with the marketplace, the political context and the level of economic demand within a country. Therefore, the author terms a University with a large number of students a 'mass university/school', because students are educated to become designers who are able to satisfy mass needs. Within this distinction, the student has to become aware of a lot of concepts, but not with any deep knowledge. The student, on graduation, must be ready to work in a market that requires a product designer with abilities to approach a variety of projects. In contrast, an 'elite university/school' has a small group of students per classroom and, frequently, disciplines are concentrated in practical modules, often the result of a historical tradition. These institutions were typically conceived and monopolised by the landowner and commercial social classes, who wished to preserve the culture of the old aristocratic class.
Ideally, the education that these two different schools offer should be the same. In addition, the author wishes to understand if the number of students are determined by the opportunity offered by the institution (in terms of space, number of lecturers, fees, etc) or by the market. Henceforth, the researcher has investigated product design curriculum throughout a number of institutions and has focused in particular on the disciplines that the students learn. This examination is made to understand which approach the school utilises, and whether it is mainly practical or theoretical.
This division is designed to compare (in % terms) the disciplines adopted in schools/universities, as it is considered unlikely that two or more institutions will share the same module content, even where they share comparable titles. This allows the author to

identify the approach utilised by the institution and, in particular, which knowledge it offers to future product designers.
The above described analysis allowed the author to understand which "modules" could be identified as 'Design Studio' relating to the contents and the results that the school section scheduled.
The Design Studio identification was determined by the analysis of the thematic area that the module had to treat. This part was developed by the author in order to be able to compare the process used within different institutions (placed in different countries).
The Design Studio process identification appropriate to become a case study, has highlighted the language difference used at a global level: the result is a problem that includes most education (both university and non) at a worldwide level, but often also at a continental one and sometimes even at a national one. For this reason, identifying case studies has been the result of in-depth interviews held with Master or Bachelor Degree Courses Project leaders, with teachers and students, after analyzing the Program Handbooks.
Identifying the examples was not an easy task for the author due to the schools' curriculum description and the paucity of detail surrounding module content. The recognition of the "right" Design Studio to analyse was determined by the previous description and also by the availability and the interest of teachers and students in the research who helped the author with personal interviews and answering e-mails.
It could be surmised that there is not a single definitive criteria for the identification of the Design Studio therefore the author adopted a varied and pluralistic methodological approach in identifying appropriate studios for investigation.
In synthesis the author analysed the 'Design Studio' because it is the module that integrates together all disciplines acquired by the students.
In order to study the module and to be able to compare it with the others, it was necessary to establish a format with the main characteristics of some phases of a teaching process. In this way the author had the basis to compare the processes by similarities and implementations.
After the analysis of three case studies in different countries, the author determined a number of phases that were the bases for the next case studies. This determination was fundamental because in every school the same phases were called with a different name, so it was necessary to find a name and the content (teacher request and outputs) of every phase to have an unique language at the end of the analysis.

3. Results

3.1 About design education and the context

"Based on the understanding that every design object is a cultural sign and belongs to historical, social, environmental, economic and political contexts, design can't be generalized and reduced to an hermetic and pre-deterministic issue. On the contrary, the consciousness of the complexity and cultural diversity of the world in design studies and practices is fundamental. In this sense, it is necessary to adopt holistic and interdisciplinary approaches, taking into account the various factors involved within the product development process and consider the ambiguous nature of design, which is both linked to development

processes and to products that emerge from them, comprising a confluence of objective and subjective aspects"(Ono & Loschiavo dos Santos, 2003)
The design area has historically sheltered various movements and discourses, some of them more and some others less directed to universal and particularistic approaches, which have, in turn, influenced design both in theory and practice.
Design education plays an important role in the development of design knowledge, research and practice and it is essential to adopt an interpretive and holistic approach, taking into account the complexity that characterizes life within a world where cultural diversity as well as social, economical, industrial, political and environmental contexts, amongst others, must be focused on the fulfilling of people's requirements for artifacts from a perspective of cultural and social responsibility and commitment (Ono, 2005).
Based on research on industrial design and cultural diversity conducted by Ono (Ono, 2005), the research developed demonstrated some fundamental interrelations that could be helpful for orientating design education and practice. It is based on respect to cultural identities and focused on the catering for people's requirements for products, and on the development of their autonomy, identity and wisdom, as well as on the sustainable, social and economical development. Figure 2 illustrates the Ono idea (Ono, 2005) about design that the author used as basis to identify the factors that could influence the teaching process with the product design studios.

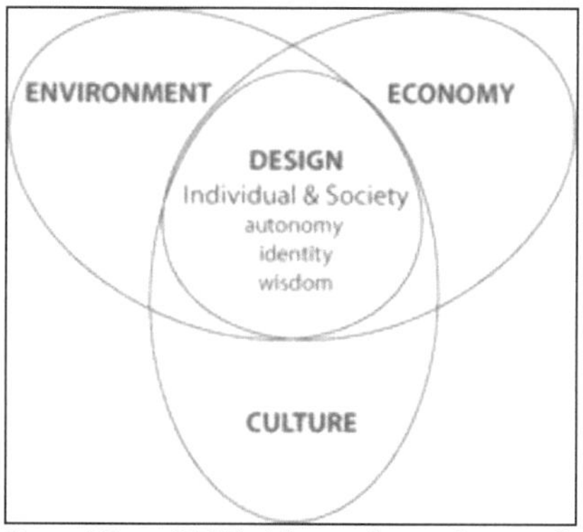

Fig. 2. A representation of Ono (Ono,2005) ideas about interrelations that could be helpful for orientating design education and practice

These factors analyzed in every case study, to understand how and how much the design studio process is influenced, are:

- the link with the context (economical and industrial in a hand, and cultural and historical in the other hand)
- the design culture consolidated inside the school/institute;
- the presence of different Design Courses within the schools and, as a consequence, the sharing among the various approaches to the discipline;
- the design research conducted inside the institutions related.

All these factors together allow developing a multidisciplinary sensibility towards the limits of the discipline itself.

3.2 About the curriculum and the school approaches

Before the design studio analysis the author studied the curriculum of schools to understand witch trend between practical and theoretical, and artistic and technical approach is more adopted within the design institution.

Through the examination of the modules, to understand the approach adopted in every school, it is shown that in thirteen schools analyzed (Figure 3) only three cases present equilibrium between "artistic and technical approach", with a low inclination for the theoretical subjects. The other schools present a clear inclination to the technical approach with a relevant for the theoretical subjects, but the differences between theoretical and practical are significant. Indeed these differences were the reason of interest for the analysis of the Design Studio.

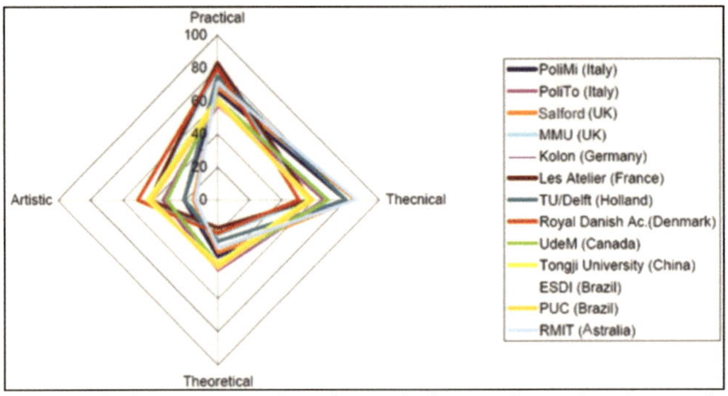

Fig. 3. Representation of the approach adopted from the schools analyzed through the curriculum

It was interesting to identify the disciplinary orientation of every institution through the modules analysis and their value in ECTS (European Credit Transfer System). Figure 4 underlines the project work importance and the trend of every school to teach disciplines in a very different way (Scientific and Humanistic).

The author categorized all the modules in this way because it is important to know the general school inclination towards some disciplines to understand the reasons of an option about teaching design process within the design studio instead of another one.

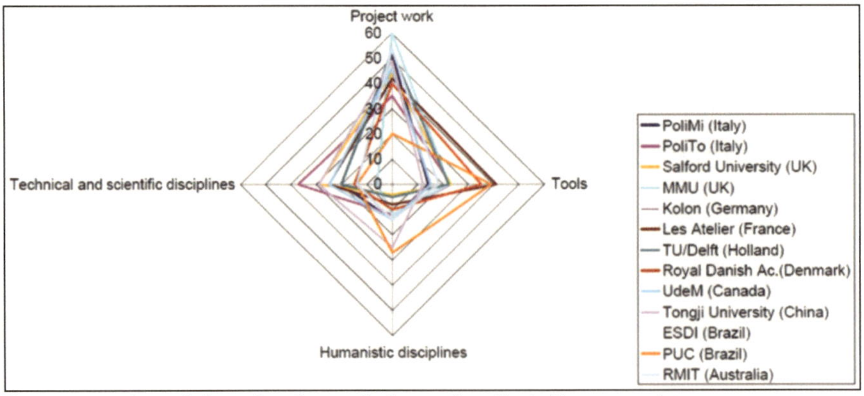

Fig. 4. Representation of the school trend about the disciplines taught

Before analyzing the design studio, the author analyzed the relation of it with all the modules to understand if there are differences between the institutions. The results are illustrated in Figure 5 where it is possible to recognize that:

- in the first case the design studio is supported by a series of optional seminars;
- in the second case the design studio is supported by a number of compulsory modules both theoretical then practical that are present in the curriculum
- in the third case the design studio is supported by some compulsory theoretical modules taught before starting the design studio, and other modules that are developed during the design studio semester with a strong link and information exchange with the design studio subject.

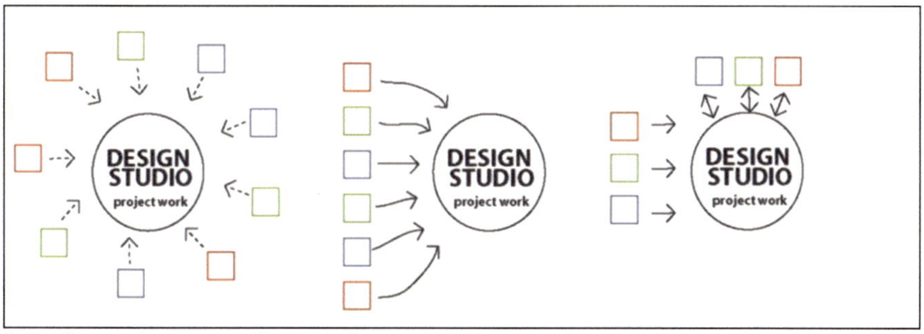

Fig. 5. Correlation between all modules and design studios

3.3 About design studios

The analysis of Design Studios provides the author with tools to identify 3 macro-phases present in every case study.
In detail the macro-phases are: Primary analysis, Design Goals and Project development.
Each of them was analysed with the identification and integration of twenty-two phases. This procedure was essential to have the same parameters of comparison between all the case studies.
At the end of the analysis, the comparison shows (Figure 6) that the Primary analyses are very similar between schools with the same approach. In particular the institutions which have an artistic approach apply for that phase only for some aspects and, on the other hand, the institutions with a technical approach make a deep and extended primary analysis.
For the Design Goals macro-phase all the institutions present a similar process and phase sequence, the only difference is the way to manage the brief: in some cases it is given to the students at the beginning of the Design Studio, in other cases it is developed by the students at the end of the first phase (primary analysis).
The Project development macro-phase is equal, in process terms, into all the Design Studios analysed, with only some differences in temporal conditions and in management of the experimental model.

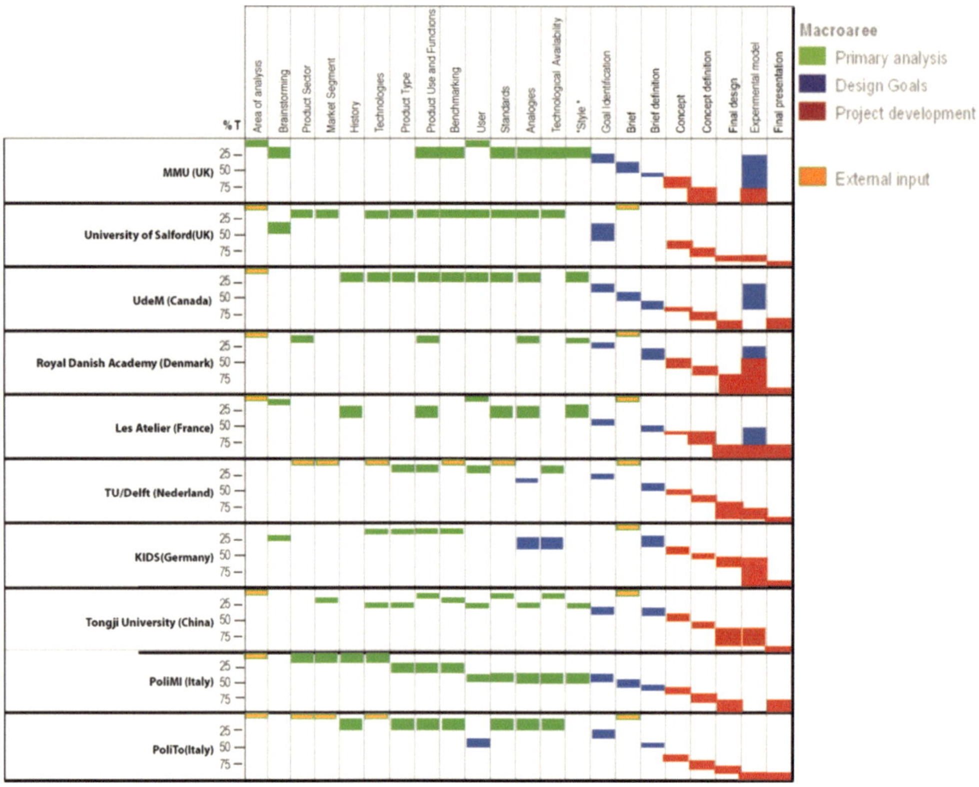

Fig. 6. Comparison between all the design studio analysed

The research has been developed in order to reach the definition of a teaching process useful for Design Studio development within an international context.

From the analysis of the Design Studio teaching processes the most advisable solution appears to be the statistic classification of all the design steps. This solution, however, is not acceptable if one considers the aspects analyzed in each case study. Particularly, two evaluation terms appear to be highly relevant:

- the time factor: the time dedicated at each design studio;
- the curriculum: disciplines taught and their relationship with the design studio.

Moreover, the differences amongst the various schools related to the time factor along with the relationship between the design studio and the other subjects, suggest a solution of implementation of the Design Studio with short devoted Design Studios. These dedicated short periods of the Design Studio could allow an official recognition of the contents and the steps that are developed in other schools without messing up the didactic structure.

These two hypotheses do not look like being the ideal solution: for this reason the author compares the factors that influence and have influenced the phases and the steps within every Design Studio teaching process (Figure 7).

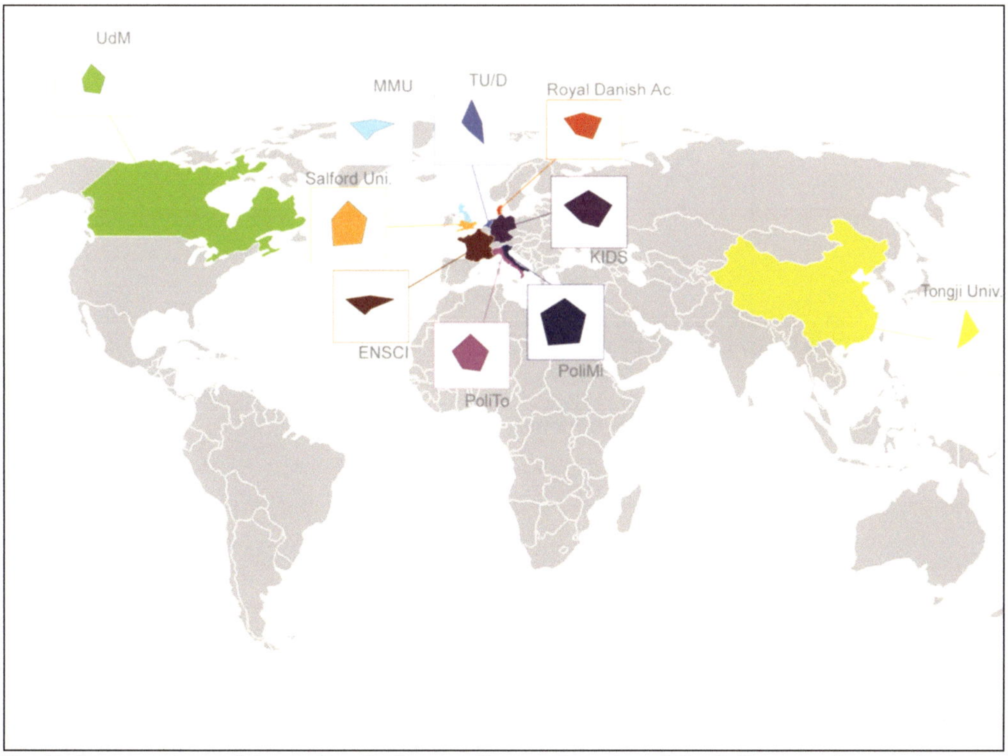

Fig. 7. An overview of the entire design studios analyzed and the influence of every factor

4. Conclusion: possible future developments

The images below illustrate how every factor influenced the process within the design studio analysed.

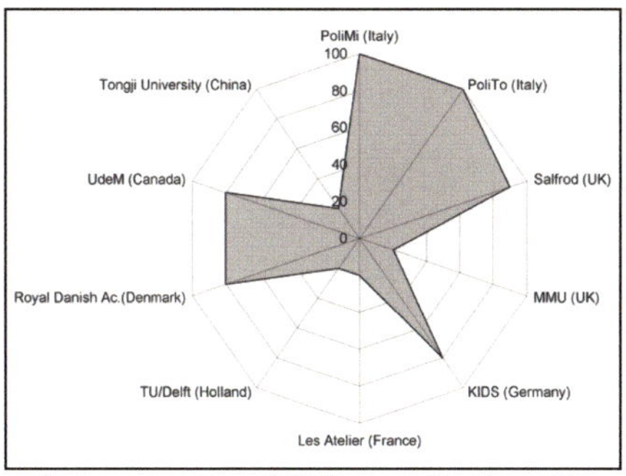

Fig. 8. Comparison between the presence of different Design Courses within the school.

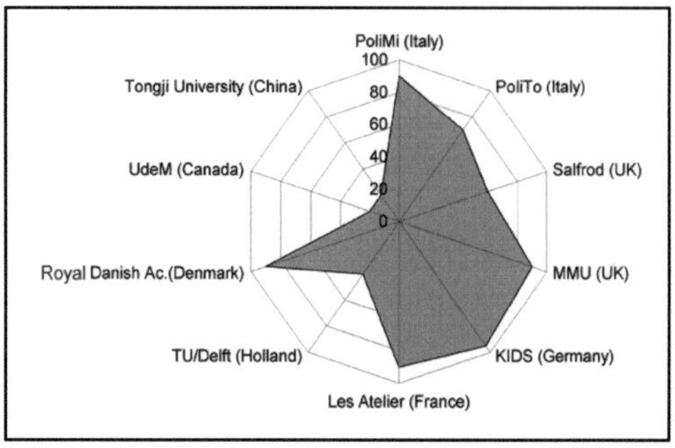

Fig. 9. Comparison between the influence of the cultural and historical context within design studios.

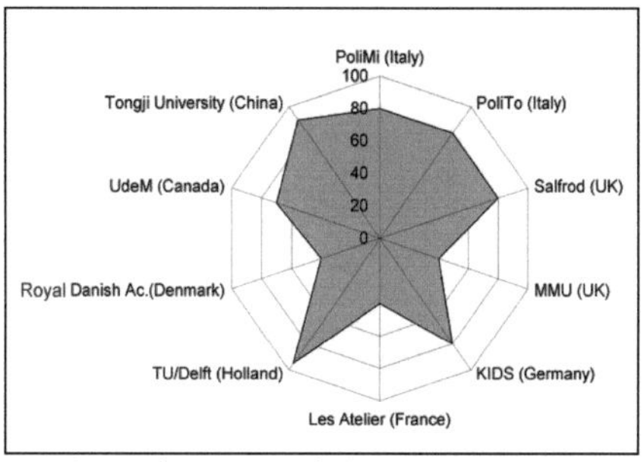

Fig. 10. Comparison between the influence of the economical and industrial context within design studios

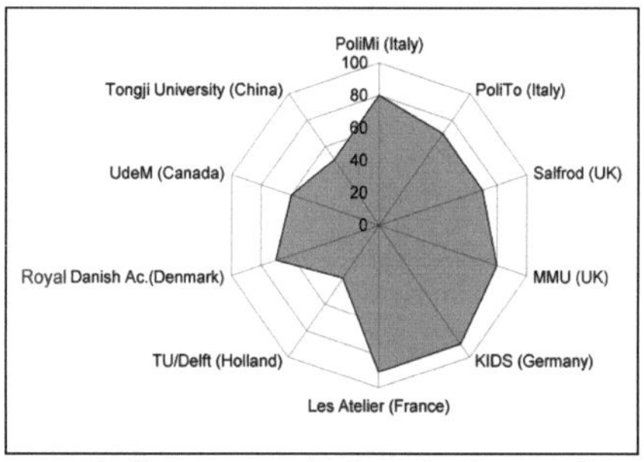

Fig. 11. Comparison between influences of the design culture consolidated inside the institute in relation with the process within the design studio.

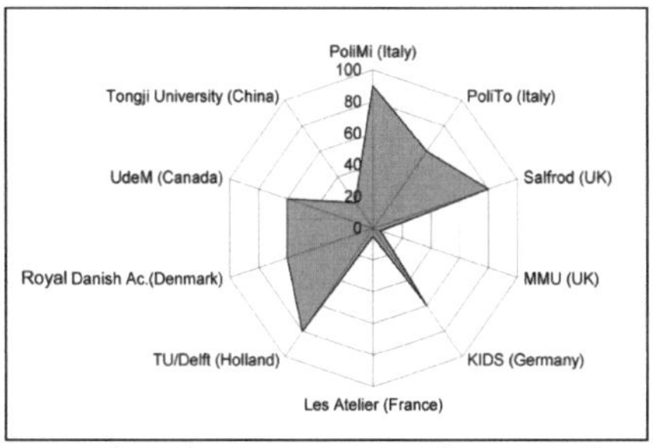

Fig. 12. Comparison between the designs researches conducted inside the institutions related with the process within the design studio.

Throughout the comparison between every singular factor that has influenced the design process within the product design studios analysed, the author thinks that it will be possible to create an on line design studio where every institution can see what is not developed in its own teaching process. In this way there is the possibility to understand where the own process is more or less lacking, and to try to implement its own process adopting a phase (or more) from other institution which have developed the phase process in another way.
This proposal intends to contribute to facilitate Countries cooperation in the field of Product design Higher Education and to help in improving Industry-University relations concerning to new product and market development, in the context of globalisation and localisation. The idea has the purpose to improve the integration at an international level between the factors that influenced the teaching process within design studios and the needs of the Institution to remain competitive about product design education and the global requests that are in constant change.
The specific objective is to reach an improved integration at an international level between product design teaching practices and local country needs (in particular market and industry needs) through the development of new phases inside the design studios if necessary.
The expected results are the delivering of a on line design studio on validated and integrated teaching content and methods, oriented to the industry and market needs of each country.
The on line design studio strives also to create a common field for teaching-staff exchange by its on line environment and the reached awareness of project's aims.
The on line design studio will be intended as a single project module which can be seen both as a self-standing specialization course and as a part of a design studio, depending on each University academic system.
Educational goals of the on line design studio could be:

- To improve design skills dealing with product innovation issues
- To improve the capability of blending and/or shifting to different cultural contexts
- To learn process for managing the complexity of the product systems
- To experiment co-design dynamics by a constant interaction with several disciplines and approaches to the product setting activity

Indeed nowadays in the countries with advanced or developing economies there is a constant and fast growth in industrial and economical fields. This corresponds to a growth of the contacts, ventures and agreements between the companies. Thus, economical and manufacturing know-how has being shared and tuned to be efficient on a global market. But both design policies and strategic planning are still reliant on local situations, which have to be analysed and understood. HE institutions can offer initiatives, like this project, to become a more active partner of the integration process and to improve their capabilities to interact with industries and actors of the global economical development.

5. References

Aldrich, R., (1996). *Education for the Nation*, London, Cassell

Biggs, M.A.R., (2006). *Editorial: the role of context in art and design research*, Working Papers in Art and Design 4

Brit's, S. (1998). *School and Societies,* Pine Forge Press, Thousands Oaks, California

Bürdek, B. E. , (2008). *Design. Storia, teoria e pratica del design del prodotto*, Gangemi Editore

Micklethwaite, P., (2005). *Discussing Art and Design Education: Themes from terviews with UK Design Stakeholders*, International Journal of Art & Design Education, N 24.1 NSEAD pagg 84-92

Ono, M. M., Loschiavo dos Santos, M. C., (2003). Design wisdom: beyond the frontiers of reductionist discourses, Proceedings of *5th European Academy Of Design Conference*, Barcelona, 28-30 April 2003

Ono, M. (2005). Cultural approach in design education, Design Education; Proceedings of *Tradition & Modernity (DETM2005) conference,* NID (INDIA), 2 - 4 March 2005

Perks, H., Cooper, R., Jones,C., (2005). Characterising the Role of Design in New Product Development: An empirically-derived Taxonomy, in: *Journal of Product Innovation Management*,Volume 22 Issue 6

Popovic, V., (2004) Expertise development in product design – strategic and domain-specific knowledge connections, in: *Design Studies*, Vol. 25, N 5, September 2004, pagg 527-545

Richardson, V., Hermann, F., McNeil, D., Lohmann, J., Waterfall, S., Ramchandani, N., Wigglesworth, S., Lovegrove, R., and Grange, K., (2005). *The seven ages of design*. Blueprint

Stokes, A., (2005). *Education for masses and masses…*, in newdesign , issue 31, pagg 16

12

Longitudinal Analysis of Students' Readiness for b-Learning Courses: Implications for the European Higher Education Area

José Manuel Ortega Egea, María Victoria Román González,
Pedro Eugenio and Gracia Vitoria
University of Almería
Spain

1. Introduction

Information and Communication Technologies (ICTs) are fostering great changes in diverse social and economic settings (Alba et al. 1997; Hoffman & Novak, 1996; Parasuraman & Colby, 2001). Researchers from different academic fields are analyzing the effects of Internet technologies in several areas: commercial transactions (e-Commerce), contacts with the public administration (e-Government), provision of health services (e-Health), and education processes (e-Learning) (Bitner et al., 2000; Gefen & Straub, 2003; Yarbrough & Smith, 2007).

For learning and training purposes, the implications of new information technologies are evident in students' learning processes, teaching methodologies, and the interactions between lecturers, students, and pedagogical materials. New digital services offer great possibilities for educational purposes, in terms of the management and supply of contents to students, as well as a higher potential to continually monitor students' progress. Two main applications of Internet technologies should be highlighted in higher education settings (Tiffin & Ragasingham, 1997):

a) Mixed systems (*b-Learning* or "blended learning"), which combine more traditional presence-based teaching with *online* learning methodologies;

b) Complete systems (*e-Learning*), in which distance education relies solely on the use of Internet technologies, both for student tutoring and delivery of contents.

A review of digital technologies' main characteristics for educational purposes suggests the existence of a significant overlap between certain requirements of the European Higher Education Area, such as the ECTS credit system, and the potential of e- and b-learning services: remote management of students; time flexibility in students' work; reduction in the volume of contents; higher emphasis on continuous evaluation; combining classical (presence-based) education with auto-study and practicals; and the possibility of real-time "student-lecturer" contacts (presence-based, videoconferences, chats, or IP phone calls), and delayed contacts (debate forums and e-mail). In this context, new information technologies are expected to play a pivotal role in aiding students to accomplish more autonomous learning activities.

Thus, the application of e- and b-learning approaches is increasingly being promoted by European, national, and regional public authorities. The European Parliament and Council, in the Decision Number 2318/2003/CE of 5th of December 2003 (European Commission, 2003), paid considerable attention to the development of virtual higher education campuses, which should contribute to the effective integration of new information and communications technologies into Europe's education and training systems (e-Learning Programme).

The document "*La Integración del Sistema Universitario Español en el Espacio Europeo de Enseñanza Superior*" -The Integration of the Spanish University System into the European Higher Education Area- (Ministerio de Educación, Cultura y Deporte, 2003) acknowledges that substantial institutional and structural modifications are needed for the adaptation to the European Higher Education Area. Such changes should, within an information and knowledge society, "help universities face the challenges derived from innovation in the creation and dissemination of knowledge" (Ministerio de Educación, Cultura y Deporte, 2003).

Proper attention should also be given to the personal traits of certain individuals, specially students and lecturers, because of their key role in the adaptation process to the European Higher Education Area. Adequate levels of readiness, perceptions, and attitudes towards online learning (Featherman & Pavlou, 2003; Taylor & Todd, 1995), among students and lecturers, are needed to ensure a successful application of Internet-based services into courses currently being adapted to the European Higher Education Area. This paper will focus on the analysis of students' perceptions and readiness for online learning. Future studies should also examine lecturers' readiness for e- and b-Learning.

In particular, this paper contributes to the analysis of students' readiness for online education (in this study, *b-Learning* or "blended learning"), by presenting the results of a longitudinal analysis carried out among students of the following b-learning courses, offered at the University of Almería (Spain) between the years 2006 and 2008: "International Trade" (Business Administration Studies), "Public Relations and Protocol" (Tourism Studies), and "Tourism Marketing Research" (Tourism Studies).

2. Research Purposes and Methods

In this section, the authors describe the main purposes and methods selected for data collection among students of the b-learning courses "International Trade", "Public Relations and Protocol", and "Tourism Marketing Research". All three courses were taught online, using the WebCT 4.0 e-Learning platform. 75% of theoretical and practical credits were virtualized, which represents the maximum degree of virtualization allowed at the University of Almería for b-learning courses.

2.1 Students' Workload

Excessive workload has been identified as a common barrier for student learning and success, both in online courses (e- and b-Learning), and in those currently being adapted to the requirements of the European Higher Education Area (Ministerio de Educación, Cultura y Deporte, 2003). In fact, an excessive amount of coursework has been identified as a key

factor leading to student withdrawal in e-learning courses (Packham et al., 2004). Therefore, lecturers and designers of e- and b-leaning courses should adequately analyze and adapt the levels of difficulty and workload for students. Due to current processes of convergence to the European Higher Education Area, students' working time requirements should adhere to the usual recommendations of 25 to 30 student working hours per ECTS credit.
To analyze the amount of students' coursework, students were asked to estimate the time dedicated to the different course activities, in the courses "International Trade", "Public Relations and Protocol" (academic years 2005/2006, 2006/2007, and 2007/2008), and "Tourism Marketing Research" (academic year 2007/2008). In this regard, students were asked to provide the following information along with each course activity:
- Amount of time dedicated to study.
- Time dedicated to prepare the activity (e.g., searching for information and additional resources)
- Time dedicated to writing.
- Time needed for presentation / sending.
- Brief comment on the contribution of the activity to students' learning.

2.2 Attitudes, Readiness, and Perceived Barriers for Students

A review of previous literature confirms the complexity of individuals' acceptance (resistance) and adoption (rejection) processes of information systems (Burton-Jones & Gallivan, 2007; Lapointe & Rivard, 2005). In this regard, the integration of *online* learning systems into higher education requires a proper understanding of diverse factors potentially influencing students' and lecturers' acceptance of e- and b-learning systems.
Particularly, further research is needed into students' attitudes, readiness, and perceived difficulties in b-learning environments. In this sense, factors related to students' perceived difficulties, lack of adequate training (Taylor & Todd 1995; Venkatesh 2000), or the level of learning actually acquired in online courses, compared to traditional presence-based ones, have been linked to student failure in e-learning courses (Packham et al. 2004).
During the second semester of the academic years 2006/2007 and 2007/2008, a brief questionnaire was used to obtain information about the attitudes, readiness, and potential barriers for students taking part in the b-learning courses "International Trade" and "Public Relations and Protocol". To facilitate the data collection process, this questionnaire was included in a "control test" that students had to pass at the middle of the semester. The following issues were addressed in this brief survey:
- Availability of computer at the usual study place.
- Availability of Internet access at the usual study place.
- Ease of access to computers at the college campus.
- Difficulty of b-learning courses, compared to traditional ones.
- Needed dedication to b-learning courses, compared to traditional ones.
- Understanding of b-learning courses, compared to traditional ones.
- Learning acquired in b-learning courses, compared to traditional ones.

3. Results

This section describes the results obtained in the longitudinal analysis of students' coursework perceptions, as well as their attitudes, readiness levels, and perceived barriers for success in b-learning environments.

3.1 Analysis of Students' Workload

As shown in Table 1, during the academic year 2005-2006, the estimated working time that each student had to dedicate to the "Public Relations and Protocol" and "International Trade" courses represented 107 and 127 hours, respectively. Several modifications to the structure of both courses contributed to reduce the estimated working hours during the year 2006-2007: 87 working hours in "Public Relations and Protocol" and 114 hours in "International Trade".

Course	**Total Hours**		
Public Relations and Protocol	**2005/2006**	**2006/2007**	**2007/2008**
Estimated Working Time	107	87	80-90
International Trade			
Estimated Working Time	127	114	100-110
Tourism Marketing Research			
Estimated Working Time	-	-	95-105

Table 1. Longitudinal comparison of students' coursework

In the academic year 2007/2008, the course "Tourism Marketing Research" (Tourism Studies) was added to the analysis of students' workload. Data corresponding to this b-learning course, as well as "Public Relations and Protocol" (Tourism Studies) and "International Trade" (Business Administration Studies), evidence the existence of rather stable and reasonable estimations of students' required work over time.

Taking into account that these are 6-credit courses, it is evident that none of the estimations of students' working time surpass the usual recommendations of 25 to 30 student working hours per ECTS credit (González & Wagenaar, 2005; Lavigne, 2003). According to these recommendations, the total student workload should lie between 150 and 180 working hours in the analyzed courses. In fact, the estimations shown in Table 1 may suggest the need for increasing the work requirements in these three b-learning courses.

This would nevertheless be inconsistent with common student opinions and complaints about having to make too many activities during the semester. In this sense, a limited number of students in the courses "International Trade" and "Public Relations and Protocol" provided spontaneous comments or "complaints" pointing to the inclusion of an excessive number of practical activities throughout the semester.

3.2 Analysis of Attitudes, Readiness, and Perceived Barriers for Students

Next, this paper examines the attitudes, levels of readiness, and perceived barriers by students taking part in the courses "Public Relations and Protocol" and "International Trade", during the second semester of the academic years 2006-2007 and 2007/2008.

3.2.1 Availability of computer at the usual study place

First, students were asked about the availability of personal computers (PCs or laptops) at their most usual study place. Considering that personal computers represent the most-widely used device to access the Internet, and computer usage is a prerequisite for participation in e- and b-learning courses, this variable should be still regarded as a key potential barrier for success in the b-learning courses analyzed in this study (see Table 2 and Figures 1 and 2).

	International Trade		Public Relations and Protocol		Total	
	2006/2007	2007/2008	2006/2007	2007/2008	2006/2007	2007/2008
Always	57 (68.7%)	45 (68.2%)	48 (70.6%)	50 (69.4%)	105 (69.5%)	95 (68.8%)
Sometimes	23 (27.7%)	15 (22.7%)	16 (23.5%)	16 (22.2%)	39 (25.8%)	31 (22.5%)
Never	3 (3.6%)	6 (9.1%)	4 (5.9%)	6 (8.3%)	7 (4.64%)	12 (8.7%)
Total	83	66	68	72	151	138

Table 2. Availability of computer at the usual study place

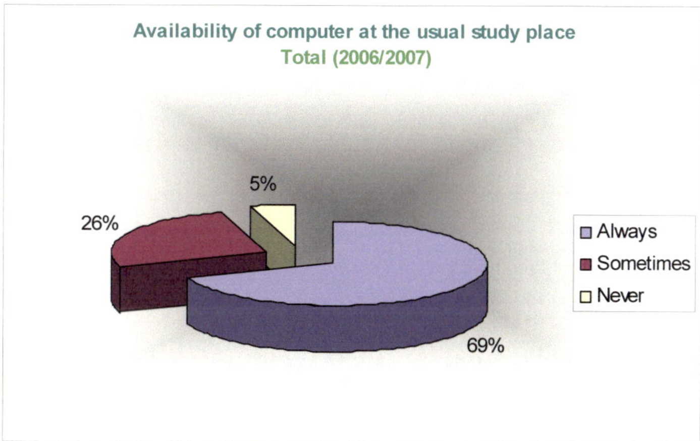

Fig. 1. Availability of computer at the usual study place (2006/2007)

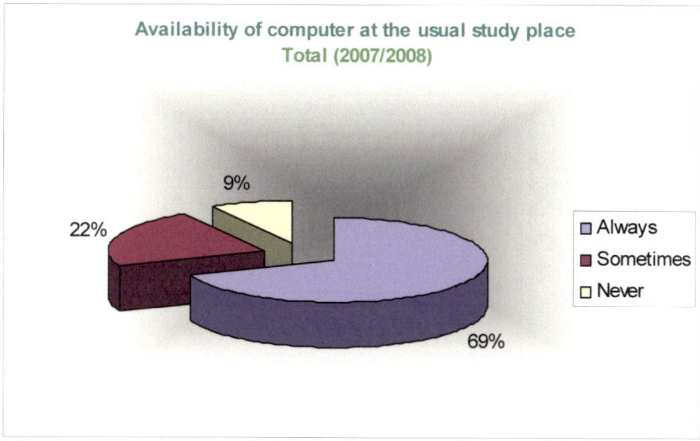

Fig. 2. Availability of computer at the usual study place (2007/2008)

The results reflect a very similar situation for students of both courses, which belong to different study programs (Business Administration and Tourism Studies). In the academic years 2006/2007 and 2007/2008, a majority of students (approx. 70%) states that they "always" have a personal computer available at their usual study place. Nevertheless, the total accessibility of personal computers at the place of study did not seem to be guaranteed for all students in the year 2006/2007, as evidenced by the fact that 25% of students could only access a computer "sometimes", and 5% could "never" access one.

Interestingly, despite continued policies and efforts of public authorities and private entities (especially of the University of Almería), aimed at ensuring and increasing student access to computers and the Internet, the situation does not seem to have improved in the year 2007/2008. Again, the percentage of students indicating that they can "never" or just "sometimes" access computers stays stable at 31%.

Considering that previous data refer to students currently taking part in b-Learning courses, with 75% of virtual credits, such students should experiment much more difficulties during the learning process.

3.2.2 Availability of Internet access at the usual study place

Next, student were asked with regard to the availability of Internet access at their usual study place. As with personal computers, problems to access to Internet, whether at home, university campus, or other places, would represent a very significant barrier for successful participation in e- or b-learning courses (see Table 3 and Figures 3 and 4).

	International Trade		Public Relations and Protocol		Total	
	2006/2007	2007/2008	2006/2007	2007/2008	2006/2007	2007/2008
Modem	14 (16.9%)	14 (21.2%)	13 (19.4%)	15 (20.8%)	27 (18.0%)	29 (21.0%)
ADSL	53 (63.9%)	33 (50.0%)	41 (61.2%)	39 (54.2%)	94 (62.7%)	72 (52.2%)
No	16 (19.3%)	19 (28.8%)	13 (19.4%)	18 (25.0%)	29 (19.3%)	37 (26.8%)
Total	83	66	67	72	150	138

Table 3. Availability of Internet access at the usual study place

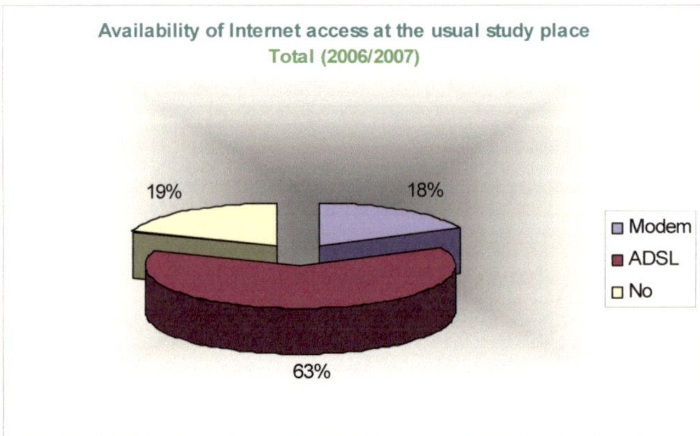

Fig. 3. Availability of Internet access at the usual study place (2006/2007)

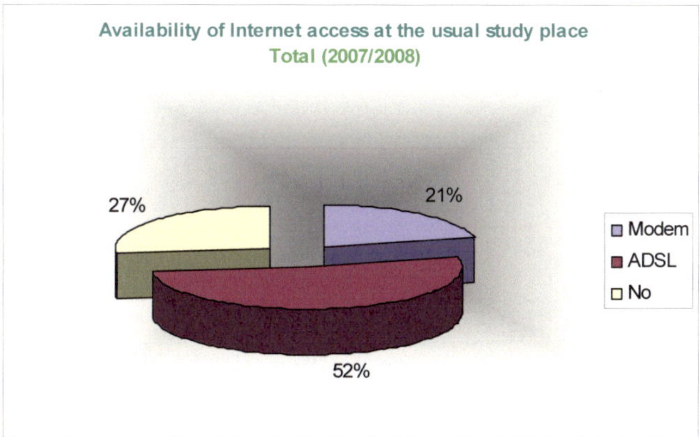

Fig. 4. Availability of Internet access at the usual study place (2007/2008)

The analysis of data of the "International Trade" and "Public Relations and Protocol" courses, reveals a practically identical situation with regard to the availability of Internet access at students' usual place of study. Nevertheless, a negative evolution of the available types of Internet access can be observed over time. In the academic year 2006/2007, a significant share of students (19%) could not access the Internet at their usual study place. This percentage was even higher (27%) during the following academic year.

As previously noted, this represents an important barrier to students' content access, usage of communications tools, and performing of programmed activities on the WebCT e-learning platform. Careful attention should be paid to data related to student access to computers and the Internet, as b-learning courses include diverse practical activities throughout the semester, which must be properly made and delivered within designated times.

3.2.3 Ease of access to computers at the college campus

It is also interesting to examine how easy it is for students to access computers (PCs or laptops) at the university campus. This variable could be regarded as a partial measure of success obtained by policies and efforts, aimed at ensuring computer access in public universities (see Table 4 and Figures 5 and 6):

	International Trade		Public Relations and Protocol		Total	
	2006/2007	2007/2008	2006/2007	2007/2008	2006/2007	2007/2008
Always	46 (55.4%)	30 (46.2%)	21 (30.9%)	27 (37.5%)	67 (44.4%)	57 (41.6%)
Sometimes	36 (43.4%)	34 (52.3%)	43 (63.2%)	42 (58.3%)	79 (52.3%)	76 (55.5%)
Never	1 (1.2%)	1 (1.5%)	4 (5.9%)	3 (4.2%)	5 (3.3%)	4 (2.9%)
Total	83	65	68	72	151	137

Table 4. Ease of access to computers at the college campus

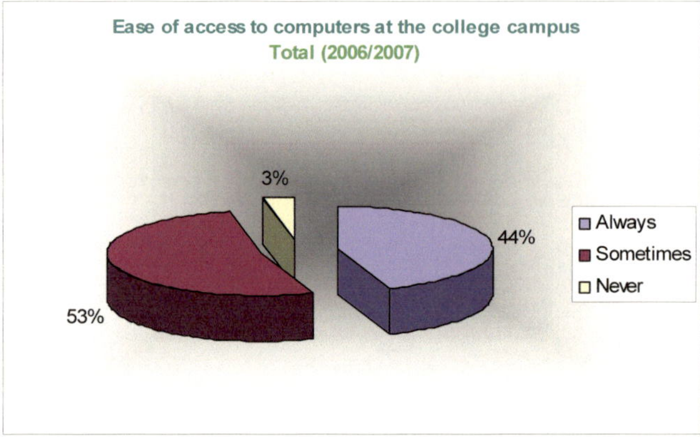

Fig. 5. Ease of access to computers at the college campus (2006/2007)

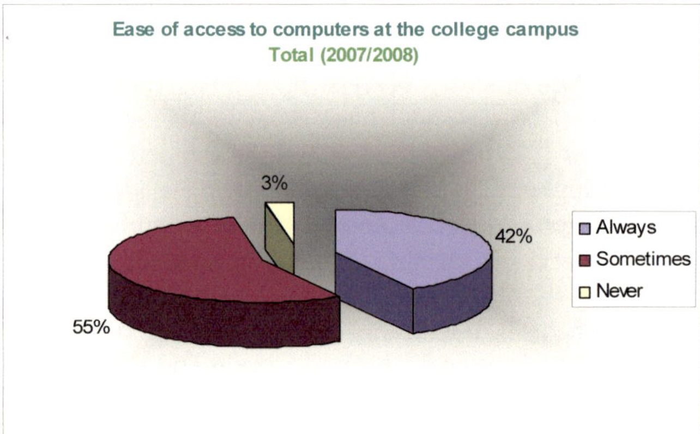

Fig. 6. Ease of access to computers at the college campus (2007/2008)

With regard to the ease of access to personal computers at the college campus, certain differences were observed during the year 2006/2007 between students of the analyzed b-learning courses. While 56% of students in the "International Trade" course indicated that they could "always" easily access personal computers at the campus, this percentage was only 31% for students of "Public Relations and Protocol". These differences between courses were attenuated, according to the 2007/2008 survey, with 46% (International Trade) and 38% (Public Relations and Protocol) saying that they could "always" access with ease to computers at the university campus.

The comparison of total results, across the analyzed academic years, reveals similar response patterns over time. In global terms, the results suggest the existence of improvement potential, with regard to the policies put forward by the university, aimed at improving the availability of computer equipment for students. In this sense, over 50% of surveyed students in both courses, indicates that they can only access "sometimes" personal computers with ease at the college campus.

3.2.4 Difficulty of b-Learning courses, compared to traditional ones

A relevant aspect for the adequate planning of online or b-learning courses relates to the correct distribution of students' workload in each course. This is of paramount importance within the new teaching-learning framework of the European Higher Education Area, which regards students' work and learning as a central concern. In this context, students' opinions are examined with regard to the perceived relative difficulty of b-learning courses, compared to those using traditional teaching methodologies (see Table 5 and Figures 7 and 8):

	International Trade		Public Relations and Protocol		Total	
	2006/2007	2007/2008	2006/2007	2007/2008	2006/2007	2007/2008
Higher	37 (45.7%)	31 (47.0%)	37 (55.2%)	30 (41.7%)	74 (50.0%)	61 (44.2%)
Equal	38 (46.9%)	31 (47.0%)	25 (37.3%)	38 (52.8%)	63 (42.6%)	69 (50.0%)
Lower	6 (7.4%)	4 (6.1%)	5 (7.5%)	4 (5.6%)	11 (7.4%)	8 (5.8%)
Total	81	66	67	72	148	138

Table 5. Difficulty of b-Learning courses, compared to traditional ones

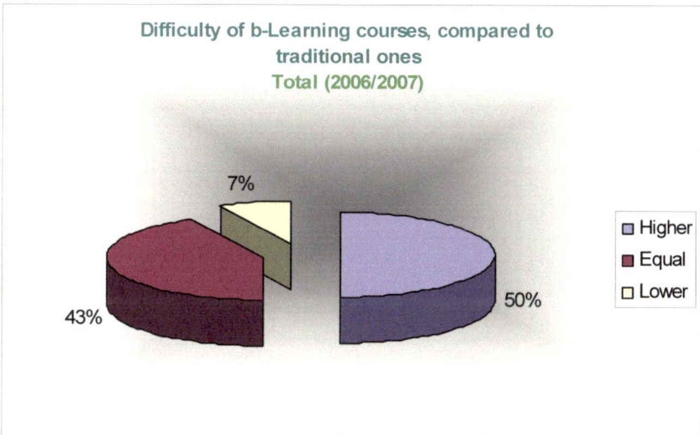

Fig. 7. Difficulty of b-Learning courses, compared to traditional ones (2006/2007)

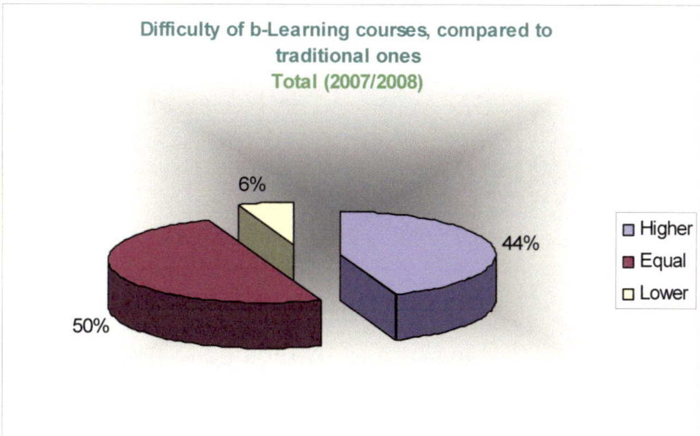

Fig. 8. Difficulty of b-Learning courses, compared to traditional ones (2007/2008)

The results of the 2006/2007 survey showed that most students perceive that the structure and methodology used in b-Learning courses involves a higher difficulty, compared to traditional courses. This perception was especially significant (56% of respondents) among Tourism students taking part in the "Public Relations and Protocol" course. The survey conducted during the year 2007/2008, reveals a slight improvement of students' perceptions in both courses, with most students (approx. 50%) estimating an "equal" difficulty in b-learning and traditional courses.

During the year 2006/2007, an excessive load of activities seemed to be the main cause of students' negative opinions, in particular among students of the "Public Relations and Protocol" course. Almost all additional comments spontaneously provided by students explicitly pointed to an excessive load of activities. The changes performed to the structure of this course may have contributed to more positive student opinions.

3.2.5 Needed dedication to b-Learning courses, compared to traditional ones

Considering students' repeated opinions about an excessive amount of activities, an alternative method is used to estimate students' workload in the "International Trade" and "Public Relations and Protocol" b-learning courses. In this regard, students' were directly asked to estimate the necessary dedication to b-Learning courses, in comparison with traditional ones (see Table 6 and Figures 9 and 10):

	International Trade		Public Relations and Protocol		Total	
	2006/2007	2007/2008	2006/2007	2007/2008	2006/2007	2007/2008
Higher	59 (71.1%)	28 (43.8%)	42 (61.8%)	36 (50.7%)	101 (66.9%)	64 (47.4%)
Equal	19 (22.9%)	28 (43.8%)	19 (27.9%)	29 (40.8%)	38 (25.2%)	57 (42.2%)
Lower	5 (6.0%)	8 (12.5%)	7 (10.3%)	6 (8.5%)	12 (7.9%)	14 (10.4%)
Total	83	64	68	71	151	135

Table 6. Needed dedication to b-Learning courses, compared to traditional ones

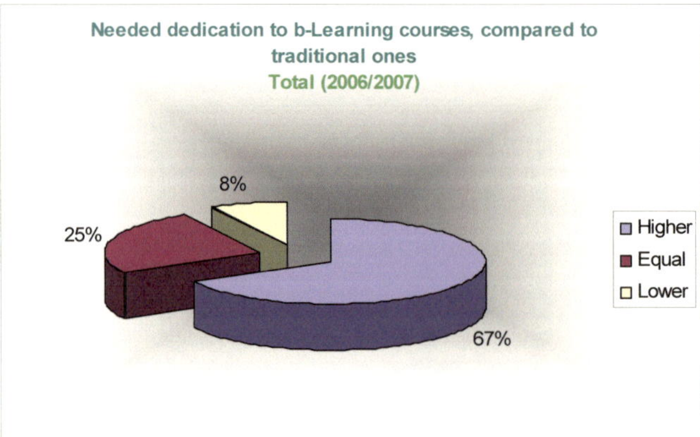

Fig. 9. Needed dedication to b-Learning courses, compared to traditional ones (2006/2007)

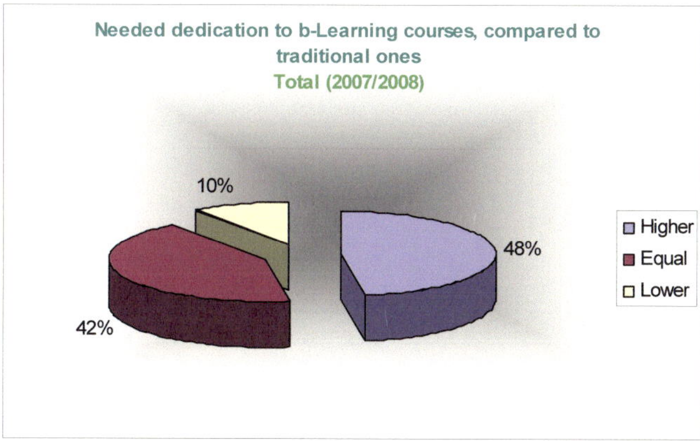

Fig. 10. Needed dedication to b-Learning courses, compared to traditional ones (2007/2008)

Consistent with the estimations of students' workload, discussed in section 3.1, the results of the 2007/2008 survey evidence a relevant improvement of students' opinions of the necessary dedication to pass b-learning courses, compared to traditional ones. In this sense, the percentage of students indicating the need for "higher" dedication and effort to b-learning courses, decreased from 67% to 48% between 2006 and 2008. This improvement was especially significant among students of the "International Trade" course, as a result of performed modifications. Again, these results emphasize the importance of a careful analysis and planning of the necessary student work in e- and b-Learning courses.

3.2.6 Understanding of b-Learning courses, compared to traditional ones

The sixth question of the survey analyzed students' self-reported understanding of b-learning courses, compared to those using traditional teaching methods. The analysis of this indicator provides useful information on issues related to adequacy of contents or content structure, clarity of presentation, or design features of the analyzed courses (see Table 7 and Figures 11 and 12):

	International Trade		Public Relations and Protocol		Total	
	2006/2007	2007/2008	2006/2007	2007/2008	2006/2007	2007/2008
Higher	23 (27.7%)	8 (12.5%)	18 (26.5%)	14 (19.7%)	41 (27.2%)	22 (16.3%)
Equal	28 (33.7%)	24 (37.5%)	16 (23.5%)	31 (43.7%)	44 (29.1%)	55 (40.7%)
Lower	32 (38.6%)	32 (50.0%)	34 (50.0%)	26 (36.6%)	66 (43.7%)	58 (43.0%)
Total	83	64	68	71	151	135

Table 7. Understanding of b-Learning courses, compared to traditional ones

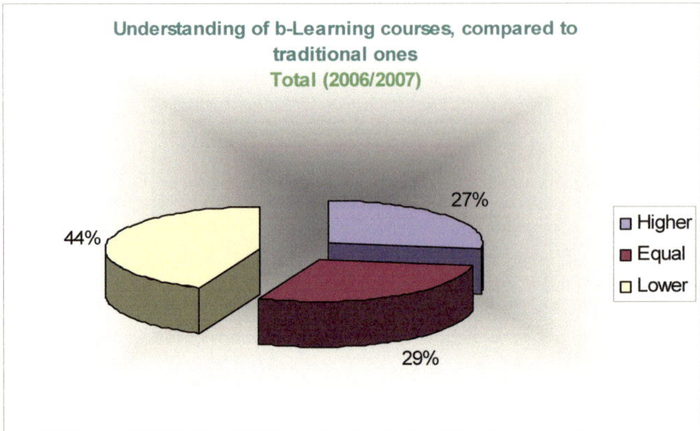

Fig. 11. Understanding of b-Learning courses, compared to traditional ones (2006/2007)

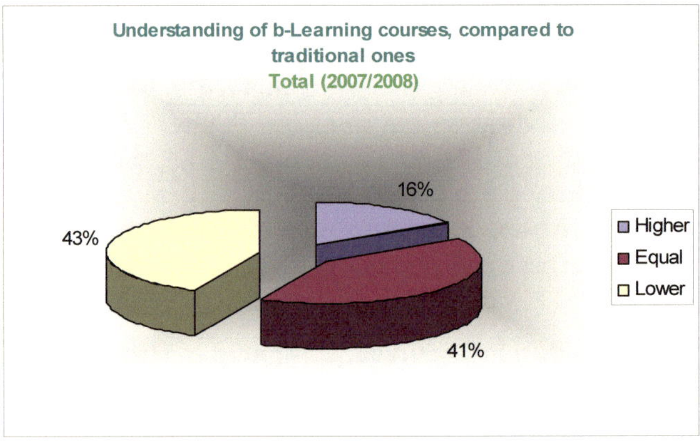

Fig. 12. Understanding of b-Learning courses, compared to traditional ones (2007/2008)

The 2006/2007 data showed the existence of student groups with different readiness or skills to successfully get through b-learning courses. In both courses, there was a similar share of students (around 27%) showing a better understanding of contents provided in b-learning courses, compared to traditional ones. Nevertheless, there was also a significant percentage of students (38% in "International Trade"; 50% in "Public Relations and Protocol") showing a lower understanding of contents in online courses. In "Public Relations and Protocol", the results especially pointed to the need for a careful review of the contents and formal structure of this course.

The results of the 2007/2008 survey reveal significant changes, compared to the 2006/2007 study. A lower share of students (16%, compared to 27%), state that their understanding of b-learning courses is "higher", than in traditional ones. In this sense, there seems to be a shift towards the "equal understanding" response category. In contrast to the academic year 2006/2007, more negative responses were obtained among students of the "International Trade" course.

3.2.7 Learning acquired in b-Learning courses, compared to traditional ones

Finally, students were asked about their perceived levels of learning acquired in b-learning courses, compared to traditional presence-based ones (see Table 8 and Figures 13 and 14).

	International Trade		Public Relations and Protocol		Total	
	2006/2007	2007/2008	2006/2007	2007/2008	2006/2007	2007/2008
Higher	26 (31.3%)	15 (23.4%)	22 (32.4%)	18 (25.4%)	48 (31.8%)	33 (24.4%)
Equal	38 (45.8%)	37 (57.8%)	34 (50.0%)	37 (52.1%)	72 (47.7%)	74 (54.8%)
Lower	19 (22.9%)	12 (18.8%)	12 (17.6%)	16 (22.5%)	31 (20.5%)	28 (20.7%)
Total	83	64	68	71	151	135

Table 8. Learning acquired in b-Learning courses, compared to traditional ones

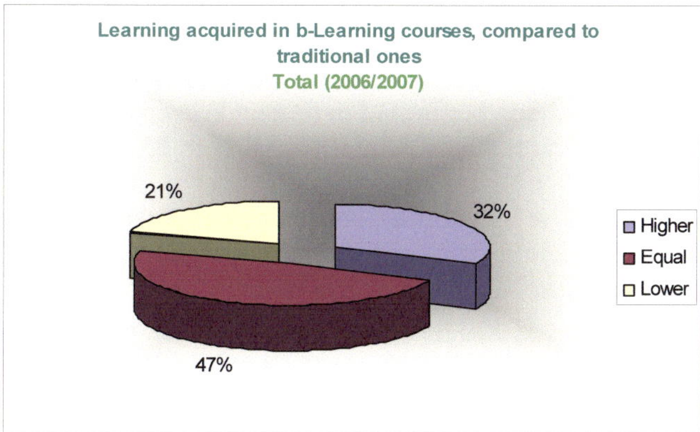

Fig. 13. Learning acquired in b-Learning courses, compared to traditional ones (2006/2007)

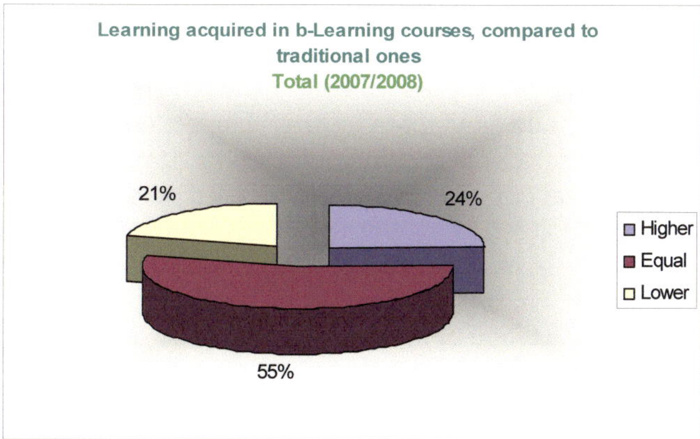

Fig. 14. Learning acquired in b-Learning courses, compared to traditional ones (2007/2008)

Similar results were obtained in both courses, with most students indicating that online and traditional teaching methods contributed to "equal" learning levels. The comparison of 2006/2007 and 2007/2008 data, reveals a shift of responses from the "higher" learning acquired in b-learning courses, to the "equal" response option. Students showing a negative readiness or deficient skills to succeed in e- or b-learning courses, account for 21% of respondents in both academic years.

4. Conclusions

The results obtained in this study emphasize the importance of a correct adaptation of difficulty and workload levels for students of b-learning courses, in order to properly reflect the requirements of the European Higher Education Area. Likewise, the formal structure of contents in e- and b-learning courses should also be properly designed, so that several detected problems can be avoided, such as a deficient understanding of contents and, as a result, lower student learning. Such modifications should lead to higher rates of student success, and minimize the probability of student withdrawal in online courses.

The analysis of student responses revealed several complaints about the inclusion of an excessive number of practical activities in two of the analyzed courses, "International Trade" and "Public Relations and Protocol". However, such student opinions do not match up with the workload estimations performed in three b-learning courses, which evidence a proper adequacy to the common recommendations of 25 to 30 student working hours per ECTS credit.

Next, this chapter provided a longitudinal analysis of additional factors, related to the attitudes, levels of readiness, and perceived barriers by students taking part in b-learning courses, which may help to explain student acceptance or resistance to online learning and systems and methodologies. A significant group of students experienced problems in accessing to computers and the Internet at the usual place of study (including the college campus). Considering that using personal computers and the Internet are prerequisites for participation in e- and b-learning courses, access to Internet-enabling devices and the Web itself should be granted to all students.

Student opinions of needed dedication and effort to pass online courses (b-learning courses in this case) seem to be improving, according to data from the academic years 2006/2007 and 2007/2008. A trend toward more positive views of online learning is evident in certain student comments, pointing to "higher student involvement", and "easier and more frequent 'student-to-student' and 'student-to-lecturer' interactions" in online courses. Based on students' responses, the relative difficulty and learning acquired in b-Learning courses seems to be comparable to that of traditional presence-based ones.

Nevertheless, there is still potential for improvement in students' readiness for e- and b-learning courses. The analysis of spontaneous comments and observations, provided by students of the b-learning courses "International Trade" and "Public Relations and Protocol", enabled the identification of additional relevant barriers and aspects for student learning in b- and e-learning courses:

- Need for continuous student work and participation in online courses.
- Students' desired periodic feedback on actual performance made in each course activity.
- Complaints about the structure and depth of contents delivered through the online learning platform.
- Traditional dependence of students' work on direct lecturer supervision.
- Requests for a higher share of presence-based classes in b-learning courses.
- General preference for traditional presence-based learning among certain students.

5. References

Alba, J.; Lynch, J.; Weitz, B.; Janiszewski, C.; Lutz, R.; Sawyer, A. & Wood, S. (1997). Interactive Home Shopping: Consumer, Retailer, and Manufacturer Incentives to Participate in Electronic Marketplaces. *Journal of Marketing*. Vol. 61, No. 3, (July 1997) pp. 38-53, ISSN 1547-7185

Bitner, M.J.; Brown, S.W. & Meuter, M.L. (2000). Technology Infusion in Service Encounters. *Journal of the Academy of Marketing Science*. Vol. 28, No. 1, (January 2000) pp. 138-149, ISSN 1552-7824

Burton-Jones, A. & Gallivan, M.J. (2007). Toward a Deeper Understanding of System Usage in Organizations: A Multilevel Perspective. *MIS Quarterly*. Vol. 31, No. 4, (December 2007) pp. 657-679, ISSN 0276-7783

European Commission (2003). Decision No 2318/2003/EC of the European Parliament and of the Council of 5 December 2003 Adopting a Multiannual Programme (2004 To 2006) for the Effective Integration of Information and Communication Technologies (ICT) in Education and Training Systems in Europe (elearning Programme). *Official Journal of the European Union*. Vol. 345, (5 December 2003) pp. 9-16

Featherman, M.S. & Pavlou, P.A. (2003). Predicting e-Services Adoption: A Perceived Risk Facets Perspective. *International Journal of Human-Computer Studies*. Vol. 59, No. 4, (October 2003) pp. 451-474, ISSN 1071-5819

Gefen, D. & Straub, D. (2003). Managing User Trust in B2C e-Services. *e-Service Journal*. Vol. 2, No. 2, (Winter 2003) pp. 7-24, ISSN 1528-8234

González, J. & Wagenaar, R. (2005). *Tuning Educational Structures in Europe: Universities' Contribution to the Bologna Process*, Publicaciones de la Universidad de Deusto, ISBN 978-84-9830-132-8, Spain

Hoffman, D.L. & Novak, T.P. (1996). Marketing in Hypermedia Computer-Mediated Environments: Conceptual Foundations. *Journal of Marketing*. Vol. 60, No. 3, (July 1996) pp. 50-68, ISSN 1547-7185

Lapointe, L. & Rivard, S. (2005). A Multilevel Model of Resistance to Information Technology Implementation. *MIS Quarterly*. Vol. 29, No. 3, (September 2005) pp. 461-491, ISSN 0276-7783

Lavigne, R.d. (2003). *ECTS Credits and Methods of Credit Allocation*, http://www.unican.es/NR/rdonlyres/7105C0EE-73E1-4865-8AD3-62F812337AB2/4785/Doc23.pdf

Ministerio de Educación, Cultura y Deporte (2003). *La Integración del Sistema Universitario Español en el Espacio Europeo de Enseñanza Superior*, http://www.um.es/vic-convergencia/eees/documentos/ponencias/intedracion-eees.pdf

Packham, G; Jones, P.; Miller, C. & Thomas, B. (2004). E-Learning and Retention: Key Factors Influencing Student Withdrawal. *Education + Training*. Vol. 46, No. 6/7, pp. 335-342, ISSN 0040-0912

Parasuraman, A. & Colby, C.L. (2001). *Techno-Ready Marketing: How and Why Your Customers Adopt Technology*, The Free Press, ISBN 978-0684864945, New York, NY

Taylor, S. & Todd, P.A. (1995). Understanding Information Technology Usage: A Test of Competing Models. *Information Systems Research*. Vol. 6, No. 2, (June 1995) pp. 144-176, ISSN 1526-5536

Tiffin, J. & Ragasingham, L. (1997). *En Busca de la Clase Virtual: La Educación en la Sociedad de la Información*, Paidos, ISBN 978-8449304026, Barcelona, Spain

Venkatesh, V. (2000). Determinants of Perceived Ease of Use: Integrating Control, Intrinsic Motivation, and Emotion into the Technology Acceptance Model. *Information Systems Research*. Vol. 11, No. 4, (December 2000) pp. 342-365, ISSN 1526-5536

Yarbrough, A.K. & Smith, T.B. (2007). Technology Acceptance among Physicians: A New Take on TAM. *Medical Care Research and Review*. Vol. 64, No. 6, (December 2007) pp. 650-672, ISSN 1552-6801

13

Learning and teaching strategic management: a continuous improvement

César Camisón-Zornoza, Montserrat Boronat-Navarro
and Ana Villar-López
Jaume I University
Spain

1. Introduction

In the context of Bologna Process, Spanish Universities has been adapting in the last years their degrees, methodologies, and teaching and evaluating methods to converge to the European Higher Education Area. In this chapter we describe the evolution in the methodology we apply to the subject Strategic Management that pertains to the fourth course of the Degree in Business Administration and Management at the Jaume I University in Spain, in order to adapt it to the new challenges this new context offers.

Management students had to face a more complex business context with international economies, diverse workforces and rapidly changing technologies (Billimoria, 2000). Moreover, teachers must be also prepared to these changes and to new teaching approaches more centred on the improvement of student's competences.

One of the points the Bologna Process stresses is encouraging the use of a teaching-learning process more focused on students. To this end, we pretend to promote the role of the lecturer as a guide in the learning process and not only as an individual who transfers knowledge. Moreover, the Bologna Process emphasizes the development of student's competences. Among others competences, students of management, as future professionals, need to develop skills in team working, in analyzing, interpreting and giving solutions and recommendations to different management situations.

To these aims, during the last academic courses, we have used tutorial sessions with a reduced number of students that form a group with 5 or 6 students maximum. The tutorial sessions are used weekly and the aim of these sessions is to guide to the students to develop a project related with the design and selection of the strategy in a real firm of the socio-economic surrounding of the Jaume I University. In the tutorial sessions the lecturers of the subject manage the groups with the elaboration of the project, and they help the students with the doubts they may have. It is aimed that these sessions help to a better understanding of the theoretical concepts applied to the concrete case of each selected firm by the groups. Thus, this methodology is consolidated with the experience of the previous courses, but it needs to be improved continuously, considering the new demands and necessities of the new students. The aim of the project we analyze in this chapter is to consolidate the use of tutorial sessions as a method of learning-teaching, to improve with this methodology the competences developed by students, and to obtain more satisfied students with the learning process and with a greater motivation and interest for the subject. After the third year of application, we explain in this chapter results about the consolidation of the methodological changes.

In the next section we provide a theoretical base of the project developed. The third section presents the overview of the course, where methodology of the course and phases of the project we develop to apply this methodology are explained. Then, we present and analyze results of the project, and we finish with the section where conclusions are explained.

2. Background

Teaching Strategic Management requires being able to offer to the students a wide range of capabilities that allow them to perform a manager job. Learning Strategic Management requires a considerable amount of time and effort. To address a greater emphasis on teamwork and development of student competencies, practice-centred techniques are used in the practical sessions of the subject Strategic Management. Practice-centred approaches emphasize knowledge acquisition through the individuals´ social or cultural surroundings, which are central to how concepts are understood and how learning occurs (Sargent et al., 2009). From a constructionist perspective, knowledge is created when new information is available and it is developed through social interactions that develop the own reality of individuals implied (Daft & Weick, 1984). Knowledge is attached in time and space to particular situations and cultures, and therefore practical knowledge applies to the subjective experience of the individual (Raelin, 2007). Therefore, teaching strategic management requires the creation of a learning environment that facilitates this kind of knowledge construction.

Furthermore, this fact implies also that the role of the teacher must change, from a simple transmitter of knowledge to a facilitator of learning. Students must be encouraged to be more autonomous and more reliable in the development of their own competences (Raelin, 2007). It is appropriate that students work in groups because this structure provide a safer environment in which experiment with others to get different learning goals than working individually (Michaelsen et al., 2002). Teachers must maintain a close contact with students, provide feedback of the work done and reinforce their contributions (Raelin, 2007). Therefore, the use of tutorial sessions with small groups of students should be very suitable for the accomplishment of this task.

This mode of learning-teaching process entail several advantages, and two of the more evident are that learning occurs willingly when it is closer to real activities and with the own culture of individuals, and moreover, learning is acquired through discursive interactions between students and between them and the teacher (McLellan, 1995; Raelin, 2007). The teacher must propose a task and guide an assist to the students in the development of the proposed task. The task proposed is the solution or analysis of real-world problems, since this kind of contextualized approach generates learning from a human interaction in the analysis of this problem (Raelin, 2000). The literature but also several programs in worldwide universities show how there is a growing appreciation of the need to integrate theory and practice through approaches that introduce requirements of the real business environment (Raelin, 2007).

The introduction of methodologies more centred in the application of real situations and on the learning process of the students are also in accordance with the aim of the European Higher Education Area objectives. Therefore, as a teachers of strategic management we develop a project to introduce and reinforce this kind of methodology.

3. Overview of the course

In this chapter, we describe a classroom structure in which a combination of traditional masters classes with a practice-centred approaches took place, and then we analyze results of the methodology applied. With regards to the theoretical part of the subject, it is based on the master classes, in which the participation of the lecturer and the individual work of the student are combined. We propose also to improve this part of the sessions by suggesting to the students some situations of firms in which they must analyze the appropriate strategy or do a strategic analysis of the situation, and also by reading and analyzing some real news from the economic newspapers about change in firms or in markets. In the practical part of the subject, tutorial sessions are used weekly and the aim of these sessions is to guide to the students to develop a project related with the design and selection of the strategy in a real firm of the socio-economic surrounding of the Jaume I University. In the tutorial sessions the lecturers of the subject manage the groups with the elaboration of the project, and they help the students with the doubts they may have.

The development of the project that teachers follow to improve the subject has followed the three last academic courses the same structure. The first phase consists on the planning of the project, the second phase deals with implementation and the last one relates to control and evaluation of the project. These phases are explained with more detail next:

A. Planning

The planning of the project includes all the activities to detect the need of improvement of the subject, the justifications of these activities and the development of the actions that will be carried out. In this stage are also included the meetings that will be held among the different lecturers of the subject to define the planning of the course and to analyze the student results of the previous year in order to detect strengths and weaknesses.

B. Implementation

We include here the performance of the tutorial sessions with the students that we use in the practical part of the subject. The tutorial sessions are used weekly. The aim of these sessions is to guide to the students to develop a project related with the design and selection of the strategy in a real firm of the socio-economic surrounding of the Jaume I University. In the tutorial sessions the lecturers of the subject manage the groups with the elaboration of the project, and they help the students with the doubts they may have. It is aimed that these sessions help to a better understanding of the theoretical concepts applied to the concrete case of each selected firm by the work groups. Therefore, during tutorial sessions, students discuss the practical dilemmas but also the application or not of concepts ant theories to these actions.

C. Control and evaluation

To carry out a correct control of the achievement of the purposes of this project, we obtained feedback from the students through a survey every academic course. Since the students are the main beneficiary of the changes introduced, it is relevant to know their satisfaction with the process. In this sense, the student could be seen as the customer of the service, and he evaluates the quality perceived as their global opinion of the excellence of the service (Zeithaml, 1988). On the first stage of application of this kind of methodologies, students must react again this practice-based method, since it not give students universal answers. Nevertheless, as students perceive that this learning method enhance their knowledge and competences, their perception should improve. Therefore, we consider the evaluation of the methodology by students as a relevant approach to measure the development of our objectives. Moreover, the evaluation of the projects can be carried out also through the qualitative observation of the lecturers about the evolvement of the subject and the learning-teaching process, which we include in the assessment of the different results that we will analyze.

4. Results and analysis of the project

As we have explained in the previous section, to carry out a correct control of the achievement of the purposes of the project, was obtained feedback from the students through a survey.

First, to consolidate the use of the tutorial sessions, we asked the students to evaluate the experience of working in groups through the tutorial sessions. As we can observe in Table 1, the students are highly satisfied with this experience. Considering that the measurement scale has the value 1 as the minimum and the 5 as the maximum, we can observe over the three courses a high punctuation for all the items. It should be remarked that in the three analysed courses the results show a high predisposition of the students to work in group. This fact can be due to the benefits they achieve through this methodology (interaction with other students, more proximity to the lecturer, a more attractive learning process).

In general, the high punctuation that the students give to the evaluation of the tutorial sessions allows us to consider that students evaluate positively this methodology as a tool of learning-teaching process.

Questions	Course 2006/2007			Course 2007/2008			Course 2008/2009		
	N	Average*	Standard deviation	N	Average*	Standard deviation	N	Average*	Standard deviation
This experience has allowed me to apply the theoretical knowledge to real situations	68	**3.79**	0.68	129	**3.87**	0.79	131	**3.63**	0.96
This activity will be useful in my professional future	68	**3.47**	0.87	129	**3.59**	0.93	131	**3.32**	0.93

My predisposition to work in teams is high	68	**4.07**	0.86	129	**3.96**	0.82	131	**3.95**	0.96
My predisposition to work in teams is higher now than at the beginning of the course	68	**3.31**	1.17	129	**3.52**	1.05	131	**3.16**	1.21
This activity has helped me to know better to the rest of the partners	68	**3.72**	0.92	129	**4.10**	0.97	131	**3.87**	1.15
* The evaluation of the answers was done through Likert scales 1-5 points, were 1 is TOTALLY IN DISAGREEMENT and 5 TOTALLY IN AGREEMENT.									

Table 1. Evaluation of the tutorial sessions

Secondly, in order to evaluate the consolidation of the tutorial sessions as a method of learning-teaching in the practical part of the subject, we asked to the students about the contribution of the tutorial sessions to the understanding of the subject. In the three courses, we can observe that the results of the survey show that through this methodology is achieved a higher and better understanding of the theoretical concepts, as it is shown in Table 2. Because the scale has the value 1 as the minimum and the 5 as the maximum and all the items overcome the average value of 3. It is worth note that in two academic courses the most valued characteristic of the tutorial sessions has been that through this methodology is achieved a more progressive and continuous of the concepts of the subject. In the course 2007/2008 this item obtained also a high punctuation but the students valued better the fact that through this methodology is achieved a higher and better assimilation of the theoretical concepts.

Questions	**Course 2006/2007**			**Course 2007/2008**			**Course 2008/2009**		
	N	Average*	Standard deviation	N	Average*	Standard deviation	N	Average*	Standard deviation
Through this methodology is achieved a higher and better assimilation of the theoretical concepts	68	**3.79**	0.68	129	**3.86**	0.86	131	**3.59**	0.97

Through this methodology is achieved a more progressive and continuous of the concepts of the subject	68	**4.07**	0.86	129	**3.82**	0.77	131	**3.62**	0.92
The development of the tutorial sessions has facilitated the learning process	68	**3.31**	1.17	129	**3.69**	1.00	131	**3.50**	0.96
* The evaluation of the answers was done through Likert scales 1-5 points, were 1 is TOTALLY IN DISAGREEMENT and 5 TOTALLY IN AGREEMENT.									

Table 2. Contribution of the tutorial sessions to the understanding of the subject

We also asked the students to evaluate the contribution of the tutorial sessions to the interaction with the lecturers. As we can observe in Table 3, in the three analysed courses the results show that the use of tutorial sessions actually favours in a great measure the interaction between student-lecturer. It also favours the change in the role of the lecturer and promotes a learning process more active and participative. Over the three years, the students coincide pointing that the most important contribution of tutorial sessions is the fact that they favour the exchange of ideas with the lecturers.

Questions	**Course 2006/2007**			**Course 2007/2008**			**Course 2008/2009**		
	N	Average*	Standard deviation	N	Average*	Standard deviation	N	Average*	Standard deviation
The tutorial sessions favour the exchange of ideas with the lecturers	68	**3.97**	0.75	129	**3.80**	1.03	131	**3.95**	0.89
This methodology has helped me to know better the lecturers	68	**3.84**	0.85	129	**3.61**	1.08	131	**3.69**	1.09

I have perceived a change in the role of the lecturer in the learning-teaching process thanks to these sessions	68	**3.75**	0.83	129	**3.51**	0.99	131	**3.41**	0.90
The role of the lecturers in these sessions is the that of guiding to the student in the learning process	68	**3.93**	0.69	129	**3.70**	0.93	131	**3.51**	0.91
The role of the lecturer in these sessions is that of transmitter of knowledge	68	**3.53**	0.83	129	**3.32**	1.02	131	**3.26**	1.04
* The evaluation of the answers was done through Likert scales 1-5 points, were 1 is TOTALLY IN DISAGREEMENT and 5 TOTALLY IN AGREEMENT.									

Table 3. Contribution of the tutorial sessions to the interaction with the lecturers

Also with regards to the development of the methodology, but in this case to their contribution to the development of students competences, we asked also to the students about the role of tutorial sessions to develop a set of capabilities that we consider crucial for its training as a future managers. In table 4 are presented the results of the student's evaluation of the contribution of the tutorial sessions to develop the mentioned capabilities in the academic courses analysed. As we can observe, the use of tutorial sessions helps to the students to develop capabilities so important such as to make a critic reasoning, recognize and manage diversity, take joint decisions and/or defend their own ideas, among others. It is remarkably the fact that the students of two courses (2006/2007 and 2008/2009) coincide in the fact that the most important contribution of the tutorial sessions have been to help them to learn to respect others opinion.

Questions	**Course 2006/2007**			**Course 2007/2008**			**Course 2008/2009**		
	N	Average*	Standard deviation	N	Average*	Standard deviation	N	Average*	Standard deviation
Capability to make diagnosis	68	**3.49**	0.58	129	**3.66**	0.76	131	**3.26**	0.96
Positive attitude for the change and innovation	68	**3.68**	0.76	129	**3.70**	0.76	131	**3.37**	0.84

Capability of analysis and synthesize	68	**3.78**	0.74	129	**3.83**	0.80	131	**3.55**	0.77
Capability to organize and plan	68	**3.99**	0.80	129	**3.64**	0.83	131	**3.58**	0.78
Written communication and realization of projects	68	**3.94**	0.80	129	**3.45**	0.94	131	**3.84**	0.79
Computing knowledge applied to the business study	68	**3.26**	0.96	129	**3.64**	0.77	131	**3.74**	0.85
Information management	68	**3.55**	0.89	129	**3.42**	0.91	131	**3.32**	1.02
Ability to talk in public	68	**3.49**	1.09	129	**3.51**	0.84	131	**3.47**	0.85
Problems resolutions	68	**3.46**	0.91	129	**3.81**	0.81	131	**3.34**	0.90
Joint decision take	68	**3.96**	0.70	129	**3.80**	0.79	131	**3.82**	0.80
To identify and search information	68	**3.97**	0.79	129	**3.62**	0.77	131	**3.88**	0.85
Conflicts resolution	68	**3.54**	0.86	129	**3.78**	0.91	131	**3.45**	0.81
Development of interpersonal abilities	68	**3.68**	0.93	129	**3.46**	0.94	131	**3.58**	0.95
To recognize the diversity and multiculturalism	68	**3.35**	0.98	129	**3.85**	0.86	131	**3.40**	1.01
Respect others opinion	68	**4.03**	0.82	129	**3.68**	0.81	131	**4.03**	0.95
Critic reasoning	68	**3.93**	0.67	129	**3.94**	0.80	131	**3.76**	0.90
To expose and defend the own ideas	68	**3.93**	0.83	129	**3.72**	0.83	131	**3.89**	0.81
To detect the own strengths and weaknesses	68	**3.79**	0.93	129	**3.54**	0.82	131	**3.77**	0.80
Autonomous learning	68	**3.49**	1.02	129	**3.51**	0.84	131	**3.58**	0.94
Leadership	68	**3.54**	0.90	129	**3.46**	0.94	131	**3.63**	0.82
* The evaluation of the answers was done through Likert scales 1-5 points, were 1 is TOTALLY IN DISAGREEMENT and 5 TOTALLY IN AGREEMENT.									

Table 4. Contribution of the practical part of the subject to the development of the next capabilities

Therefore, we have observed that the use of these sessions makes that the students get a better understanding of the subject and a nearer relationship with the lecturers and it also favours the development of important managerial capabilities that will be crucial for its professional future.
Finally, to check if the use of tutorial sessions enables us to obtain more satisfied students and students more motivated and interested in the subject we have obtained also their general opinion over the three academic courses through a yes/no question.
With regard to the satisfaction of the students with the use of tutorial sessions, as it can we observed in the Figure 1, students are highly satisfied with the use of this methodology. Figure 2 shows the percentage of satisfied and dissatisfied students. It is worrying the fact that the percentage of students dissatisfied with the use of tutorial sessions has increased in the second year. Nevertheless, the percentage of students with satisfied increases in the last year, but it not reaches the level of the first year of application. Although the percentage of students not satisfied with the tutorial sessions is marginal, it should be considered in future years and it is necessary to think about the possible problems that these students may have had.

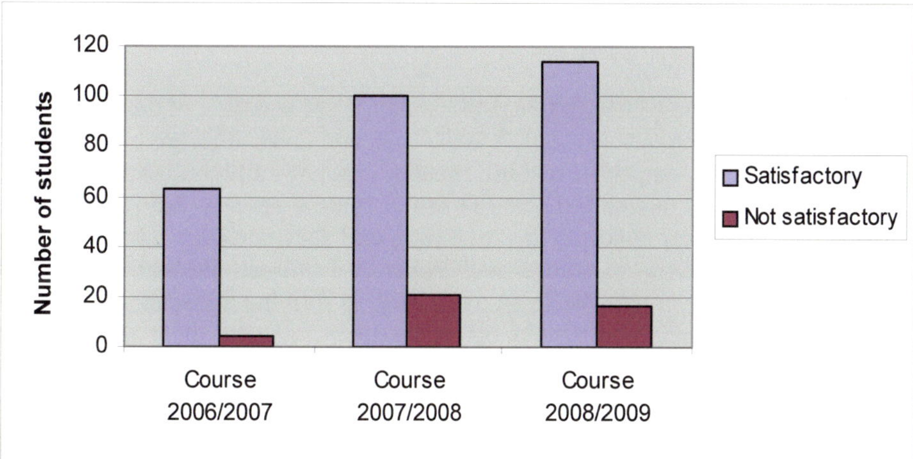

Fig. 1. General evaluation of the student's satisfaction with the tutorial sessions

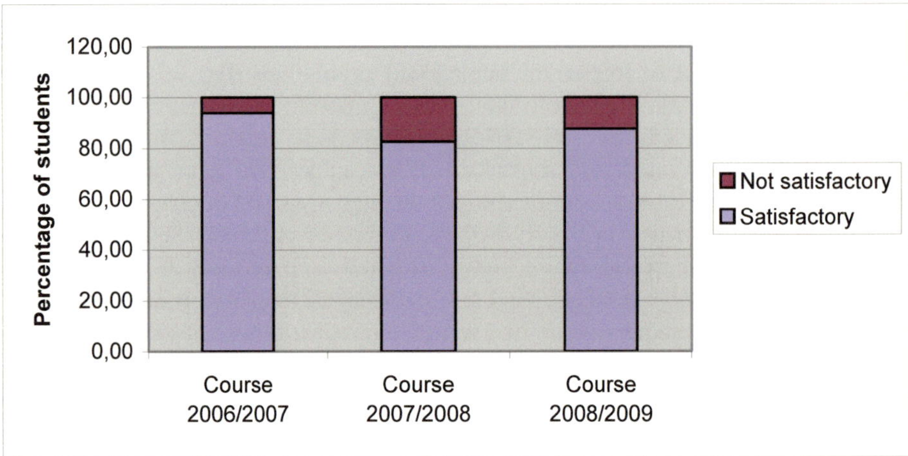

Fig. 2. Percentage of students in each academic year with their evaluation of their satisfaction with the tutorial sessions

5. Conclusion

The analysis of the data presented in this paper shows that the results of the projects carried out over the academic courses 2006/2007, 2007/2008 and 2008/2009 are highly satisfying. We have overcome all the expected results. The students have a high degree of satisfaction with the development of the subject and the use of tutorial sessions has allowed them to apply better the theoretical concepts to a real case, and they consider also that the use of tutorial sessions help them to understand better the subject. Furthermore, the close interaction among students and lecturers necessary to develop satisfactorily the tutorial sessions favours the creation of a valuable relationship between them that favours the exchange of ideas and has a positive effect in the learning process. The use of tutorial sessions also favours the development of some capabilities extremely valuable for its professional future such as the ability to have a critic point of view and to understand and cope with different points of view. All these facts put together have had as a result students interested in the subject and satisfied with the tutorial sessions. In general terms, the main result of these projects after three years applying them has been to obtain a more satisfied students with the learning process, students with a greater motivation and interest for the subject and with a stronger knowledge in strategic management. This practice-oriented methodology allows the creation of an environment of learning where students develop they learning through a social and constructivist approach, since through the interaction with their partners and with the teacher allow them to a develop their learning process.

As challenge for futures years, we should mention the necessity to reflect on the use of tutorial sessions given the fact of a decreasing rate in the level of satisfaction with them. Although the percentage of dissatisfied students is marginal and the rate of satisfied students surrounds all the years the 90%, we consider important to think about the reasons that have lead to dissatisfy a few students. Furthermore, we pretend to introduce other activities to bring nearer the necessary competencies to perform their future professional activity as well as new activities that provide to the students a better understanding of the business literature.

6. Acknowledgment

This research was supported by various educational programs financed by the *Unitat de Suport Educatiu* at the Jaume I University.

7. References

Billimoria, D. (2000). Teachers and learners: Whither our own development?. *Journal of Management Education*, Vol. 24, No. 3, 302-303, ISSN 1052-5629.

Daft, R.L. & Weick, K.E. (1984). Toward a model of organizatons as interpretation systems. *Academy of Management Review*, Vol. 9, 284-295, ISSN 0363-7425

McLellan, H. (1995). *Situated learning perspectives*, Education Technology Publications, ISBN 978-0877782896, Englewood Cliffs, NJ.

Michaelsen, L.K.; Knight, A.B. & Fink, L.D. (2002, Eds.). *Team-based learning: A transformative use of small groups*, Praeger, ISBN 157922086X, New York.

Raelin, J.A. (2000). *Work-based learning: The new frontier of management development*, Prentice-Hall, ISBN 0201433885, Upper Saddle River, NJ.

Raelin, J.A. (2007). Toward an epistemology of practice. *Academy of Management Learning & Education*, Vol. 6, No. 4, 495-519, ISSN 1537-260X

Sargent, L.D.; Allen, B. C.; Frahm, J.A. & Morris, G. (2009). Enhancing the experience of student teams in large class. Training teaching assistants to be coaches. *Journal of Management Education*, published online on March 25, 2009 as doi: 10.1177/ 1052562909334092

Zeithaml, V.A. (1988). Consumer perceptions of price, quality and value: a Mean-End Model and synthesis of evidence. *Journal of Marketing*, Vol. 52, 2-22, ISSN 0022-2429

14

A Multidisciplinary Experience in the European Context

María Amalia Trillo Holgado, Roberto Espejo Mohedano and Cristina María Gámez-Fernández
University of Cordoba
Spain

1. Introduction

The design and implementation of a transverse activity is explained in this chapter. It has been developed and still is at the University of Cordoba (UCO) in Spain, undertaken in the degree of Technical Engineering in Computer Science in the branch of Management, taught at the High Polytechnic School. Three teachers are involved in such experience, very much in line with European Higher Education Area (EHEA), since self-learning, the use of new Technologies, a close relation with the labour market, interdisciplinary learning and the development of competences are especially focused in this activity.

Besides, as recommended and defined by some authors, a deep approach to learning is also carried out in this experience (versus a superficial approach). Through this, students perform an emotionally satisfactory and integrating learning which contributes to their personal growth.

2. The multidisciplinary experience

2.1 Context

Technical Engineering in Computer Science, Management branch is currently developed in three academic years.[1] As it is officially described, a Computer Management Engineering Technician is an applications analyst. The education curriculum for this degree is based upon the interrelation of many branches of the scientific field, such as Maths, Logic, Engineering, Linguistics, Physics, Electronics, Statistics, Economy, etc. Together with these disciplines, specific matters related to Computer Science and applications are also taught. Therefore, Computer Management Engineering Technicians develop their work by bearing always in mind the final user of computer equipments. Thus, a technician studies such needs, create and adapt software to them.

---

[1] http://www.uco.es/organiza/centros/eps/en/index.php

This experience is developed by three teachers who are responsible for seven different subjects during the three academic years. The amount of subjects involved can be found in Table 1.

PLAN OF STUDY	SUBJECTS	TYPE	ECTS CREDITS
First year	Business Economics	Core	5,5
Second year	Statistics	Core	10,0
Second year	English applied to Computer Science II	Core	4,0
Third year	English applied to Computer Science III	Elective	3,5
Third year	Data analysis	Elective	3,5
Third year	Business Management	Elective	5,5
Fourth year	Degree Final Project	Core	5,5

Table 1. Distribution of the subjects in the plan of study

The aim of this experience is mainly to provide students with a global and meaningful learning which integrates different disciplines within their plan of study. Two factors tremendously help in this experience. First, the fact that these subjects can very easily be interrelated, and second, the fact that these subjects are disseminated along the plan of study in a very convenient way for carrying out the activity. Students are more and more required by the European knowledge society to be enabled by Higher Education Area to have a critical and analytical capacity and a more practical education based on realistic and practical information.

In addition, the frame of this experience is theoretically tied with the aim of achieving the principal aspects characterising the deep approach to learning (Entwistle, 1988; Ramsden, 1992; Biggs, 1999). A list of the prevalent features which define a student undergoing a deep approach to learning is displayed (Hernandez & cols, 2001; Yan & Kember, 2004):

- Learning becomes an emotionally satisfactory act.
- A qualitative notion of learning is maintained so that students transform, modify their ways of regarding the world, become creators, foster their self-learning, promote their personal development.
- Motivation is founded upon students' interest in their matters, basically in understanding them as well as in being able that their learning bears a personal meaning.
- Performing a task is understood as a means for personal enrichment.
- Students become able to plan their work and carry it out. So they are enabled to long-term program as well as positively welcome suggestions about it.
- The strategies employed by students are based on their interest in their subjects, as they use it to maximise their understanding of them and to satisfy their curiosity.
- Different components of a given matter are related to each other and integrated as a whole.
- Inherent meaning of a matter is always inquired about.

- By examining logical arguments and relating evidences with conclusions students interact in a critical and active manner with a given matter.

Finally, through the tendencies marked by the EHEA (European Association for Quality Assurance in Higher Education, 2005) in the definitions of the new grade, master and doctorate titles have a strong emphasis on the acquisition of competences, understood as "knowledge in context". In this sense, Higher Education has to foster a life project which includes professional development, and therefore, this experience must be understood as such.

2.2 Description of the Activity

The description of the experience is explained below on a yearly basis.

First year in the plan of study

During the first year students must enrol in *Business Economics*, subject where they must become familiar with the basic aspects which configure a given business reality. Students are provided with basic general concepts of business, paying special attention to the key variables influencing the normal progress of each of the departments belonging to such company. This subject covers a very wide and practical knowledge which is being more and more difficult to teach every year, due to a main reason: students show gaps in their previous knowledge as well as in learning techniques. Therefore, some methodological dynamics are developed together with the use of a software tool helping students to partially solve these problems. In this sense, such technological support has been possible thanks to the work of senior students. Specifically the preparation of their final projects have allowed the creation of a series of applets (see Fig. 1) which have been incorporated in a virtual platform supporting the work in the subject. It is important to highlight at this point that several statistical tools that students will have to use next year have been incorporated in some of the internal calculus provided to students in this software. Thus, this platform allows students with simulation practices related to each of the four main parts in which the subject is distributed (Fig. 1).

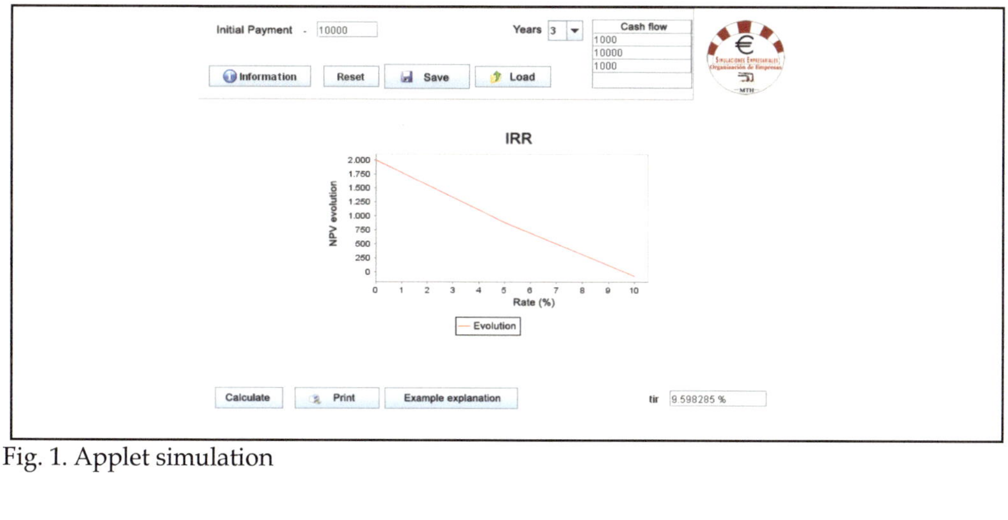

Fig. 1. Applet simulation

Once students have acquired the fundamentals of the subject, students are required to undertake a project about setting up a business where all the previously acquired concepts must be put into practice. Such project is accomplished in groups of up to five members. When this work is finished, all the information can be introduced in other softwares also being worked out by senior students' final projects (Fig. 2).

Fig. 2. Business creation software

This software works by allowing a constant competitive comparative score between the multiple results obtained by the different groups of students, similar to other software programs marketed through some consultants or specialized companies in simulation software.[2] As a final task, students have to write an abstract in English in which they briefly explain and assess their experience.

Second year in the plan of study

During the second year, students may enrol in the subjects *Statistics* and *English applied to Computer Science II*, although it is also possible that students do not accomplish first year and only choose some subjects from second year.

The subject *Statistics* is divided into three main parts: linear programming, descriptive statistics (taught during the first semester) and statistical inference (taught during the second semester). Among other tasks, in each of these parts, students must undertake teamwork where they use the acquired knowledge by applying them to real situations. This work must be handed in by following format guidelines, including an abstract in English. This work must also be presented in class.

In this way, students of *Statistics* are asked to carry out several projects. They necessarily need to use their theoretical knowledge previously acquired in *Business Economics* in the

[2] www.arkhe.com; www.bsg-online.com; www.cesim.com.

previous year. Therefore, during the first semester students have to continue improving some aspects related to the business they created last academic year, mainly focused in predicting sales, transport costs optimization, marketing costs optimization, management, product choice or data gathering and market samples.

Statistics is focused on the development, analysis and interpretation of surveys during the second semester. For this end, students are asked to create a survey first and to analyse their results secondly about the competition affecting their merging businesses. For such end, students have to create a questionnaire, select a significant sample, analyse the obtained results and, lastly, extract and learn to properly interpret the data so as to be able to conclude the study using the tools available for this.

The subject entitled *English applied to Computer Science II*, constituting the second part of *English applied to Computer Science I* taught in first year, also develops a series of activities related to the aforementioned subjects. Students enrolled in *English applied to Computer Science II* are already intensely familiarised with reading technical, scientific and academic texts belonging to their field of study. However, it is during second year when students are systematically instructed in writing this type of documents. In order to establish a meaningful relation between the previously coursed matters, students are shown the abstracts they prepared for the subject *Business Economics*. Before abstracts are taken to the class, the English teacher provides them with other real published articles taken from prestigious publications of the field as a way to offer models to imitate in the future. Once they are prepared to assess their own abstracts' linguistic structure and content, they are asked to analyse the way of improving them as a previous exercise before creating new versions of their abstracts. Apart from this activity, students are also linguistically trained in preparing a correct survey in English, as they need to create them for the subject *Statistics* also taught during the first semester.

Third year in the plan of study

During third year, *English applied to Computer Science III*, *Data Analysis* and *Business Management* are the three subjects involved in the experience.

English applied to Computer Science III is taught during the first semester. As this is an optional subject, not many students enrol and the activities undertaken in the subject are more related to their immediate future as active members of the labour force. Therefore, preparing their *curriculum vitae* (CVs) is one of the core activities. Another activity that they have to do is to prepare a job interview in English. In this sense, instructions and the right tools are provided to them so that they not only properly adequate to the situation but also become able to participate in the allotment of workers according to their more developed competences. It is interesting that all these activities are usually framed within a list of businesses they created in first year provided by the teacher of *Business Economics*. It is unavoidable to find students who coursed that subject a long time ago and that did not have to do this activity. In these cases a list of businesses is available to all so that they only have to choose the ones they like most and pretend that this is their own creation.

Also coursed during the first semester is the subject *Data Analysis*. The aim of it is the use of computer tools so as to practice more efficiently the contents acquired in the subject *Statistics*. One of the activities proposed during the first part of the semester is the elaboration of a detailed final report which summarises the results provided by the statistic software, by way of a first research work dealing with the results and conclusions obtained the previous year. Such report must be written both in Spanish and in English.

During the second semester, many of the concepts developed in *English* are taken up again in *Business Management*. This subject is mainly focused on the importance of managerial decisions as guaranteeing the success of a given business. For this subject, students have to analyse the sector to which the businesses they created belong from the perspective of their specialty, i.e. Computer Science for Management. The aim of the activity is that students can finally provide a solution to any aspect where they have detected a weakness and a possible improvement. As an option to this project, students can undertake another activity consisting in properly managing workers' competences in their business.

Fourth year in the plan of study

It is essential at this point to mention the cooperation and help obtained from students who decide to develop the computer tools used in this experience. These students have normally coursed these subjects and been in this experience themselves, which provides them with a general perspective of the needs.

Therefore, such students have developed some of the aforementioned computer tools as their degree final project (Fig. 3).

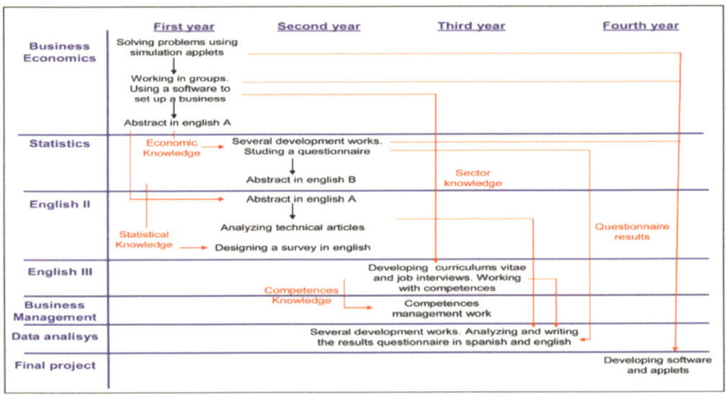

Fig. 3. Relations between subjects

The aim of this kind of activities is that students work and acquire many of the generic competences: teamwork, problem solving, organization and planning capacities, communication abilities both in their mother tongue as well as a foreign language.

3. Materials used in the experience

In order to carry out this experience, several materials have been necessary. First of all, the intense cooperation of the three teachers who participate in these subjects; second, several computer tools have also been of great help. Specifically, a server and some computers having access to Internet are necessary for the implementation of the experience.

4. Evaluation process

Evaluation is going to be considered here in two different senses:

- On the one hand, evaluation understood as the way of assessing if a student properly acquired the contents of a given subject. In this context, this type of activities allows teachers to do a continuous evaluation, as it is also proposed from the European Higher Education Space philosophy.
- On the other hand, the evaluation of students' opinion about this experience, but also about the performance of their own classmates.

In order to obtain information from the previous issues, students were asked their views about the following items concerning other students' essays:

- Originality of the problem/case proposed.
- Difficulty of the problem/case proposed.
- Clarity in the oral presentation.
- Ability in the oral presentation.
- Clarity of the resources used (.ppt files presentations mainly).
- Technicality used.
- Specific real problem/case.
- Clear definition of objectives.
- Results shown.
- Conclusions drawn.

The assessment of the different activities carried out in the subjects belonging to the experience have necessarily to be independently marked by each teacher, since assessment is always done about what students have acquired in each subject. Besides, it would be extremely difficult and inappropriate to ask another teacher to assess a project carried out in a subject completely alien to their own field. In spite of this fact, a joint assessment was done in the past with negative results since it proved unadvisable from the point of view of the students' learning.

Evaluation percentages are always provided to students so that they know well in advance how their work will be continuously assesed and how their final marks are obtained. These are described below.

Business Economics:

Final examination (include contents from theoretical and practical sessions): 70%.

Activities autonomously developed: 20%.
Attendance and participation: 10%.

Business Management:
Final examination: 80%.
Activities autonomously developed: 20%.

Statistics:
Final examination: 40%.
Teamwork: 35%.
Attendance and participation: 10%.
Activities proposed in class: 15%.

Data analysis:
Teamwork: 60%.
Attendance and participation: 20%.
Activities proposed in class: 20%.

English applied to Computer Science II:
Final examination (include contents from theoretical and practical sessions): 70 %.
Activities: 30 %.

English applied to Computer Science II:
Without exam, just essays and other activities (100%):
· Oral presentation (one or two students) and summary: 30 %.
· Reports handed in once a month: 20%.
· Reading form (one book minimum): 20%.
· CV and cover letter: 10%.
· Attendance: 10%.
· Activities proposed through moodle: 10%.

In the subject *English applied to Computer Science II*, the activity related to the writing of an abstract is only one of the many text types that students have to learn to properly write. Therefore, it has a direct influence of their final marks for the subject but it is just one of the many written exercises they have to do for the subject.

In relation to *English applied to Computer Science III* students are also asked to carry out a series of speaking, listening and writing activities among which are the ones related to this experience. Thus, there actually is an influence in their final marks but it is very imprecise to establish a percentage.

Students were asked if they considered the experience interesting, according to the following specific questions:

- The method used is in accordance with the ECTS philosophy.
- Students conceive as a good way to learn the fact that they should write essays and expose them afterwards.

- o Students would like to modify this working system in order to return to traditional system.
- o They believe that through these activities they understand better the subjects in a real context.
- o They think the results obtained by the rest of the working groups were interesting.
- o They would like to change this system for the next period.

5. Problems Detected and Solutions

In each stage of the experience different problems emerge. In first year, students frequently lack the necessary knowledge to understand and pass many of their subjects. This may be due to the qualitative change between Secondary education and Higher Education. Moreover, students do not present homogeneity in their education, since Secondary Educative system allows them to have chosen subjects related to Humanities or other areas not appropriate for this degree. Thus, this means that students enrolled in first year subjects frequently show very high variability in their individual choices and education, which makes teaching very difficult.

Another problem found in the implementation of this experience lies in the fact that the subjects involved in it are taught during very different time spans. Thus, these subjects are distributed along the whole plan of study and can either be taught during the first or the second semester. Apart from this, in the case that subjects are not core, students can freely choose to enrol in them, which makes extremely difficult to control if the same students have already taken part in the project. The fact that these subjects are scattered in semesters can actually make students lose a global perspective in the connection between them.

Finally, it is particularly difficult to assess students simultaneously in all the subjects or in a given set of subjects. As a consequence, a joint evaluation has been discarded. A similar experience was unsuccessfully carried out in a more modest scope between the subjects *English applied to Computer Science III* and *Business Administration* due mainly to the evaluation system. It proved to be really difficult to make evaluation for each subject depend on each other as first, each teacher has his/her own personal criteria; second, different contents are evaluated in each subject and making marks depend on other subjects can become counterproductive for students' personal abilities and competences. Thus, teachers have independently established the percentage of each activity for their own subjects but a common concept is always actively remembered to students in class: the fact that this is part of a broader experience in which they are taking part and which will allow them to be able to improve a project from very different perspectives and fields.

Several other problems are explained specific to each to each subject involved in the experience. In relation to *Business Economics*, it is very difficult to delimit the variables that students have to handle in their projects about setting up a business. This problem has been solved by the software previously referred to (see Fig. 2). *Business Management* has also faced a problem regarding students' choices, that is to say, when students do not wish to continue their project in the same market sector either because they have lost interest in it or because they feel it as worn-out. In these cases, the teacher provides them with projects carried out by other students in previous years so that they can choose among a wide variety. A similar procedure is followed for the subjects *Statistics, Data Analysis* and *English applied to Computer Science II* and *III* as they share the same kind of problem: as students do not normally pass their subjects yearly it is probable to find that groups are completely broken when they reach last years and therefore it is not possible for most of them to continue the work they started in the first years. In these cases, teachers usually allot previous works to their newly created groups with students who are following the plan of study with difficulties.

6. Conclusion

This experience is adapted to the philosophy of the new European Higher Education Area as it requires a very high dose of transverse work between subjects, which provides students with an overview of their studies from a more immediate, lively and practical perspective. This is possible through the close cooperation of teachers in charge of a group of subjects in this degree. Moreover, it contributes to the acquisition of some basic competences that are very important to student's future successful immersion in the labour market.

Besides, students are asked to evaluate the activities put in practice. There has been so far a very positive answer. Our results suggest that students think that they learn more easily and that the knowledge they acquire is more practical. On the other hand, it allows to link different subjects, providing them with a wider perspective of their degree.

Teachers believe that the experience is interesting since it allows them to implement creativity as well as a deeper knowledge of the contents taught.

More specifically, the figures that the student survey provides are the following (they evaluated the questions in a scale ranging from 1 to 5):

- 100% think that the method used is agreed to ECTS philosophy. The punctuation is 4.11.
- 92.7% of students conceive as a good way to learn the preparation of some written works firstly and its public explanation afterwards. The punctuation is 4.01.
- 97% of students would not like to change this system of work to return to the traditional system.
- 97.6% think that through these activities they understand better the subjects in a real context.
- For the 98% of the students the results obtained by the rest of the working groups were interesting.
- 92.7% do not want to change this system for the next period.

A more than interesting data appears when students are asked evaluate their classmates: more often than not they mark each other with lower punctuation than teachers do. Specifically, 20.4% of students marked fellows with lower grades than teachers. One example of it is an average score of 6.8 from students and 8.6 from teachers.

7. References

Biggs, J. (1999). *Teaching for Quality Learning at University*, Open University Press and the Society for Research into Higher Education, ISBN 0-335-20171-7, Buckingham.

Entwistle, N. (1988). *Styles of Learning and Teaching*, David Fulton, ISBN: 1-853-46104-0, London.

European Association for Quality Assurance in Higher Education (2005). Standards and guidelines for Quality Assurance in the European Higher Education Area, 11f.

Hernández, F & cols. (2001). Los enfoques de aprendizaje en estudiantes universitarios españoles. *Revista de Investigación Educativa,* Vol. 19, No. 2, 2001, 465-489 ISSN 0212-4068.

Ramsden, P. (1992). *Learning to Teach in Higher Education*, Routledge, ISBN 0-415-30345-1, London.

Yan, L & Kember, D. (2004). Avoider and engager approaches by out-of-class groups: the group equivalent to individual to individual learning approaches. *Learning and Instructions*, No. 14, 27-49, ISSN 0959-4752.

15

ECTS: Teaching Innovation Experience in Business Administration at the Escuela Superior de Ingeniería (College of Engineering) in Cádiz

Ángel Cervera Paz, Víctor Pérez Fernández and Francisco Rubio Cuenca
Universidad de Cádiz
España

1. Introduction

The European Credit Transfer System means, as well as specific measures for the convergence of European university degrees, the need to raise new ways of teaching and learning. This is a change-oriented education to put in the student activity and develop their skills and abilities. This new approach to education focuses on students and their ability to learn and it requires more prominence and higher shares of compromise, while the teacher becomes a companion in the process of learning that helps the student to achieve certain tasks.

In this context, we have been working in the introduction of ECTS, as a pilot project at the College of Engineering (ESI) in Cádiz (hereafter with orthographic stress) . We are trying to involve our pupils in different methods of active learning and continuous assessment.

In this paper we offer the results of our three years experience concerning our adaptation to the European Credit Transfer System (ECTS). The introduction of the ECTS model experience at the Escuela Superior de Ingeniería (College of Engineering) in Cádiz and specifically in the Bachelor of Science in Mechanical Engineering degree and in the second cycle of Engineering Management, led us to adapt some of our subjects -Business Administration and Production Management, Problem Solving Techniques in Industrial Organizations and Competitiveness and Innovation- in Business to this new way of teaching.

We intend to analyse the results of our findings and compare them with those obtained in these subjects over a period of time which will allow us to compare traditional teaching with the ECTS model.

Our approach has been carried out on the following aspects: the contextualization of these subjects, the methodology used, criteria and method of assessment, valuation of results, conclusions and proposals for improvement.

Moreover, we will contrast the students' opinions about the teaching-innovation experience carried out in one of the subjects studied, "Competitividad e Innovación en la Empresa" (Competitiveness and Innovation in Business).

2. Teaching previous to the introduction of ECTS

Higher education is generated and developed within a social context, thus becoming a basic component of every society's cultural development. As every cultural and scientific device, it is constantly evolving in the same way as the society from which it takes its elements and to which it yields its achievements. However, evolutionary changes require a careful process of thinking, critical analysis and political sensibleness. Hence, we need to tackle changes within the university system without missing the right path towards progress as encouraged by the cultural and scientific knowledge provided by universities (CIDUA, 2005).

Within this context, we will make an outline of the previous situation before showing where we are heading for by describing our present teaching experiences within the Business Administration department at the Escuela Superior de Ingeniería (College of Engineering) in Cádiz.

2.1 The European Higher Education Space (EHES)

The outstanding changes in our environment have had two important consequences for institutions (Lowendahl & Revang, 1998): 1.- Market orientation is viewed in a different way as clients are not anonymous any more but full-name persons, and 2.- The need for knowledge workers is gradually growing, leading us towards the economy of knowledge on the threshold of the 21st century.

The university is not unaware of this changing situation as these transformations of its environment have important consequences for the university itself. Basically there have been four relevant changes for universities (Keller, 1998): the excessive number of students due to the demand for higher-level knowledge; the changes in university funding due to restrictions and limitations of public expenditure; the new information technologies, which facilitate new ways of searching for and accessing information; and the growing demand for permanent training as a consequence of a greater social demand for skilled workers.

Three other relevant changes (Vilalta, 1998) should be added to the ones already mentioned: An increasing international competitiveness for funding, higher social requirements regarding the quality of university services and actions together with the controversy over the traditional assumptions for university recognition.

As an indisputable agent in the task of creating and spreading knowledge, the university should not obviate the above-mentioned changes. Apart from taking specific actions towards the convergence of European university degrees, the EHES will thus involve the need of proposing new ways of teaching and learning so as to meet the threefold purpose of creating and spreading knowledge, adequate professional training as required by the production system, and educating citizens for their whole commitment with social, political and cultural life together with the making of a more democratic society based on the ideals and principles of equality, solidarity and justice.

Within the guidelines put forward by the European Higher Education Space, special attention is devoted to the student-as-learner as the main objective of the teaching processes. The university system will thus provide the material, professional, human, organizational and educational resources required by students in order to improve the quality of their learning process. The training of competent professionals and citizens should include the

knowledge, attitudes and abilities required from them to get fully and efficiently involved in their personal, social and professional life.
Therefore, the redefinition of higher education goals assumed by the European convergence process involves a deep change in the teaching approach carried out so far by universities, as shown in Table 1 below (Benito & Cruz, 2005).

Traditional Teaching	ECTS Teaching
teaching contents	teaching to learn
content-centered	student-centered
technical training	comprehensive training

Table 1. Traditional vs ECTS Teaching.

This is a new life-long learning approach. As stated by Delors (1996), "each individual's accumulation of knowledge reserves from an early age as a supply of unlimited resources at a later stage is not enough. Moreover, she should be prepared for cashing in on every chance she may have in her life for updating, deepening and enriching her early knowledge and for being able to adapt to a constantly changing world".

2.2 Our subjects

As previously stated in the introduction to this chapter, we will analyse three of our subjects: two of them belong to the second-cycle degree on Industrial Organization Engineering: Problem-Solving Strategies in Industrial Organizations and Competitiveness and Innovation in Business. The other subject belongs to the Industrial Technical Engineering branch of Mechanical Engineering: Business Administration and Production Management. Our approach will include the following aspects: contextualization of each subject, teaching methodology and assessment.

2.2.1 Business Administration and Production Management

Business Administration and Production Management is a course included within the Industrial Technical Engineering branch of Mechanical Engineering offered by the Department of Business Management to first year students during the second four-month term in our College. It is a main 6-LRU-credit (or 4.5 ECTS credits) subject. Credits are distributed evenly between theory and practice.
Our aim is that, taking into account the integrating approach of business management, students should acquire the ability to assess and analyse tactical and strategic aspects directly related to production management from a theoretico-practical perspective.
It is the only subject within this degree with an economy-oriented content, although centred upon production. It is therefore a stand-alone subject whose skills and knowledge are not linked to any of the other subjects.
During the 04-05 year, we followed a traditional teaching method: formal lectures together with problem solving and theoretical explanations. At the beginning of the course, the students had access to the learning materials necessary to follow the lessons: a handbook with the different units corresponding to the course syllabus, including the formulation of the problems to be solved. Lessons had a theoretico-practical orientation. In spite of being

formal lectures, we invited students to take an active part in their learning process, by making the lessons as dynamic as possible.
During the 04-05 course, the assessment of this subject was carried out by means of a final exam divided into two parts: theory and practice. The final overall qualification was the result of the arithmetic mean between both parts as far as at least 40% of the score was reached in each part. This qualification could be increased regarding participation as well as the works done and presented and handed in in class.

2.2.2 Problem-Solving Strategies in Industrial Organizations

Problem-Solving Strategies in Industrial Organizations is a second-year, first-term subject within the Industrial Organization Engineering degree. It is a main 6-LRU (4.5-ECTS) credit subject. Credits are distributed evenly between theory and practice.
Theory contents centre upon problem resolution as 'quantitative methods' are essential in this subject. The main purpose of this subject is not only problem solving itself, but also to get to know the adequate approach for each one of the situations we might come across when dealing with service and industry business management. Within this context, our goal is to introduce a set of strategies to help managers cope with decisions. Up to the academic year 04-05, a traditional teaching method was carried out: formal lectures together with the explanation and resolution of set problems.
The assessment of this subject was carried out by means of a final exam consisting of a number of exercises about the contents specified on the subject's syllabus (100%).

2.2.3 Competitiveness and Innovation in Business

Competitiveness and Innovation in Business is a first-term subject also taught in the second year of the Industrial Organization Engineering degree. It is a main 3-LRU (3-ECTS) credit subject. Credits are distributed evenly between theory and practice.
Its goal is for students to reach a satisfactory level of knowledge regarding the role of innovation and its implications with organizational competitiveness. (Universidades Andaluzas, 2004).
The subject is divided into two parts: part one has five topics while part two has only one. These topics supplement and expand those acquired in the previous year's subjects Business Strategies and Policies I and II, though this time clearly oriented to innovation processes.
A teaching methodology closer to the traditional approach was followed up to the 06-07 academic year: Formal lectures and guided outlines for case analysis as well as in-class individual and/or collective tutorials (Universidad de Cádiz, 2007).
This subject was assessed by applying a 30% weight to class activities (essays and oral presentations, case debates, etc.) results and a 70% to a compulsory final exam result. This exam should be passed with a minimum score of 4/10 to be added to class activities results.

3. ECTS Experience

We need to face the process of convergence with Europe as an effort to improve the quality of the public services offered by the university by innovating the traditional ways of teaching and learning (Pérez Fernández & Cervera, 2008).

It basically consists in changing the traditional model -oral transmission of knowledge, note-taking and reproduction of transmitted knowledge through tests and exams- into a new approach which would strengthen the tutorial nature of the university's educational role, paying attention to each student's specific professional and academic learning needs (CIDUA, 2005).

Taking these basic principles as a starting point, in this chapter we will show the teaching experiences affecting three of our subjects -Business Administration and Production Management, Problem-Solving Strategies in Industrial Organizations and Competitiveness and Innovation in Business. What used to be a model experience will be compulsory in the coming years for all the subjects at the Escuela Superior de Ingeniería de Cádiz and the acquired knowledge will encourage the transmission of knowledge. Our approach will include the following aspects: contextualization of each subject, teaching methodology and assessment.

3.1 Competences and Abilities

Once the subjects have been contextualized in section 2.2, in this section we will deal with the consequences of changing the traditional model with this new approach. This involves a different way of learning based not only on each course's specific knowledge, but also on a number of abilities and skills corresponding to a variety of competences making a complete description of each subject and, in turn, of each degree.

Table 2 schematically shows the competences to be applied and developed by students doing any of the three subjects analysed in this chapter.

	Business Administration and Production Management	Problem-Solving Strategies in Industrial Organizations	Competitiveness and Innovation in Business
Cognitive Competences (To know)	Estimate and planning of work and design techniques.	Knowledge of basic concepts of design and systems administration.	Innovation. Management systems. Business administration. Processes and systems. Business policies and strategies. Accountancy and finance.
Procedural/Instrumental Competences (To know how)	Assessment and treatment of expenses. Planning.	Modelling complex situations. Computer-aided problem solving. Decision-making. Interpretation of results. Improvement in management.	Technological innovation management. Quality management. Planning and development of new processes and products. Strategic Planning. Administration Systems Design. Legislation.

Generic transversal competences	.	Ability for analysis and synthesis. Ability for solving problems. Autonomous learning. Ability for applying knowledge to practice. Ability for team working. Appropriate handling of bibliography.	1.Instrumental: Ability for analysis and synthesis. Ability for planning and management. Oral and written communication in mother tongue. Ability for information management. Ability for solving problems. Ability for making decisions. 2.Personal: Team work. Interpersonal relations skills. Scientific reasoning. Ethical commitment. 3.Systemic: Autonomous learning. Ability to face new situations. Creativity. Initiative and enterprising spirit. Concern for improvement.
Attitudinal Competences	Leadership, decision-making and teamwork.	Quantitative reasoning. Critical awareness and responsibility. Appreciation of autonomous learning. Show interest in the widening of knowledge and information search.	Critical awareness and responsibility. Ability for deep thinking. Appreciation of autonomous learning. Appreciation of the relevance of teamwork. Show interest in the widening of knowledge Flexibility. Result orientation. Initiative. Ability for connecting with the surrounding evironment.

Table 2. Competences to be developed by students.

3.2 Methodology: lessons and assignments

3.2.1 Business Administration and Production Management.

As a consequence of the introduction of the ECTS model experience in the Bachelor of Science in Mechanical Engineering degree at the Escuela Superior de Ingeniería (College of Engineering) in Cádiz during the academic year 2005-06, we intended to adapt our subject

Business Administration and Production Management to this new way of teaching by reducing the weight of formal magisterial lectures in favour of encouraging the participation of students.

In the same way as during the 04-05 year, since the very beginning students had access to the handbook which included the main topics and a list of problems. As an innovation, in order to make the work and participation of students easier, a book with a full collection of solved and explained problems was edited by midterm.

However, a new, completely different approach to the one we had had on the previous course was made clear right from start. Hence, some of the set only-theory units of the course should be prepared by the students themselves being aided by the teacher in tutoring sessions.

As for assessment, the students made up work groups. Both group (power-point presentation) and individual (answers to individual questions) work were assessed. It was a success as 64.81% of students registered chose this option from start. The groups were to make two oral presentations on the theory topics. They should defend their presentations individually by answering set questions.

In class, we started with the first theoretico-practical unit from the syllabus by explaining both the theory and its associated problems. Regarding the practical part of each unit, we should point out that they were reluctant to take the floor and publicly show their work.

The main problem with introducing the new methodology was overcrowded classrooms, which hindered the beginning of the "pilot experience".

During the 06-07 year, we used an approach similar to the one in the preceding course. Oral presentations and lesson planning were organized in the same way, although our experience was used for providing more accurate instructions and organizing the role of students in oral presentations in a better way.

Concerning resources, bibliographical references were available from the beginning of the term. A major innovation was the implementation of the course within the UCA's Virtual Campus platform (http://www2.uca.es/escuela/ingenieria), which allowed us to introduce new aspects and improvements, namely, the course chronogram, teacher's slide shows, activities and handouts counting for the students' assessment, interesting links (videos, pictures of manufacturing plants, specialized papers, etc.); communications tools, such as a chat line where students could posit and solve their doubts amongst themselves, or by making queries to the teacher, and, last but not least, practice tests from previous courses together with solved tests so that they could check them before revisions.

3.2.2 Problem-Solving Strategies in Industrial Organizations

Although this subject was not involved in pilot experiences during the 05-06 course, we started to work in this line from that year. Thus, a few innovations were introduced, including the implementation of this course in the Virtual Campus Moodle platform. Materials were available to students prior to class presentation and they were asked to hand in the practices corresponding to presented topics in order to assess daily work.

Practice sessions were carried out by organizing students into small groups (up to three students). This way of working did not seem adequate as most of them preferred to work individually.

During the 06-07 academic year, as we tried to adapt to this new teaching approach, a number of innovations added to the ones already going on: practice tests, assessment of attendance, implementation of 24-hr communications tools allowing students to make interesting questions or queries about the subject to be replied by either the teacher or peer students.

3.2.3 Competitiviness and Innovation in Business

In the same line as the case above, the methodology was radically changed from the 06-07 year, although by then this subject was not involved in a pilot experience.

Due to the good results of the 06-07 course, the 07-08 syllabus featured the same methodology. However, after a few years teaching this subject we have verified that students having decided to attend lessons rarely gave up, as it is a second-cycle subject, with only a few students, most of them with their own jobs, and therefore committed to the specific subjects they took up. Based on this experience, during the second lesson we asked students if they were willing to get more involved, taking part in oral presentations and making weekly assignments to be shared by the rest of the group, etc. so that they could skip the exam. They were all for this option. This proposal was based on our experience of previous years regarding the high level of class attendance and students' participation. Hence, the methodology would be basically the same, except for the demand of a greater commitment to "daily work" (De Miguel, 2004).

The proposal consisted in changing the criteria of assessment by altering percentages: 70% would be for set activities and 30%for the exam, which would thus be optional. To benefit from this alternative, students should regularly attend lessons -which could be easily controlled as there were 14-16 attending students.

In addition, they should keep a log book (Universidad de Cádiz, 2007, b-c) where they should outline daily work. This outline would consist of both theoretical contents and cases analysed in the class. They should also keep a record of all individual, group and class set activities.

3.3 New resources and in-class introduction of ICTs

The introduction of ICTs (Information and Communication Technologies) has greatly contributed to the change in methodology. Things have been gradually changing as our university has dedicated large sums to equip the various campuses with appropriate hardware/software technology.

Funding for hardware could be divided into two groups: general and class-specific fundings, which include new and more powerful network servers, full campus wiring, the introduction of a wifi network throughout university premises, videoconference rooms in all colleges and faculties, new computing rooms and the option for students to borrow laptops from the libraries.

Regarding classrooms, teachers' desks are all equipped with fixed computer systems and video projectors. These equipments have access to the Internet, providing the class with online teaching resources and applications (e.g. access to virtual classroom) together with other complementary resources from the Internet or from the university intranet.

Regarding software, the virtual classroom plays an outstanding role, allowing teachers to expand their teaching activity beyond classroom periods and being increasingly used by staff. It is a permanent aid for teachers as they can include contents in a variety of formats, namely .pdf and powerpoint presentations, videos, weblinks, and so on. Moreover, the virtual classroom forums are used not only for online discussions but also as a task submission and assessment site. All in all, innovations galore. To cash in on these resources, the teacher should change her way of thinking and her traditional methods. She should acquire the appropriate training and be keen to learn so as to adequately use these tools with students, with the trade-off that most students are more used to interacting with these platforms than the teachers themselves.

In this line, the three subjects in this analysis have been implemented in the virtual classroom. They have been gradually provided with a greater amount of contents and forums where students may interact with the teacher and/or other students, as well as assessable assignment forums. Teachers have thus made a great amount of effort to get the appropriate training in the new applications and to adapt materials to them. However, this should be viewed as a current investment to yield better results in coming years. As a result, the contents of the subject Business Administration and Production Management have been hooked up to the university's OCW platform, making them available for everyone (*http://ocw.uca.es/organizacion-de-empresas/administracion-de-empresas-y-organizacion-de-la*).

New technologies have allowed us to introduce other innovations in the Competitiveness and Innovation in Business lessons, where Internet access has been used by the teacher to illustrate class examples with a variety of business websites and videos. As we first introduced these resources during the 2007-08 academic year, by the end of term students were asked their opinions about ICT usage. More precisely, they were asked whether accessing business websites, online applications, videos and blogs during lessons were novel activities as compared to other subjects of their degree. The results are pictured (Cervera & Beira, 2008) in the pie chart below (fig.1), where values range between 0 (utterly disagree) and 5 (fully agree or fully adequate).

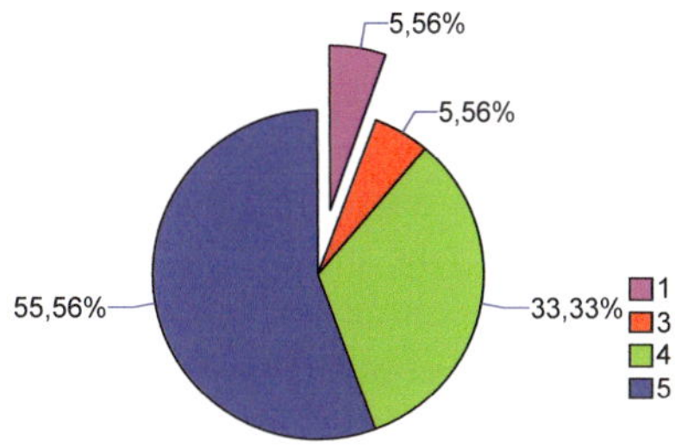

Fig. 1. Use of ICTs has been innovative.

They were also asked whether the subject would improve with the inclusion of links to all virtual classroom resources.

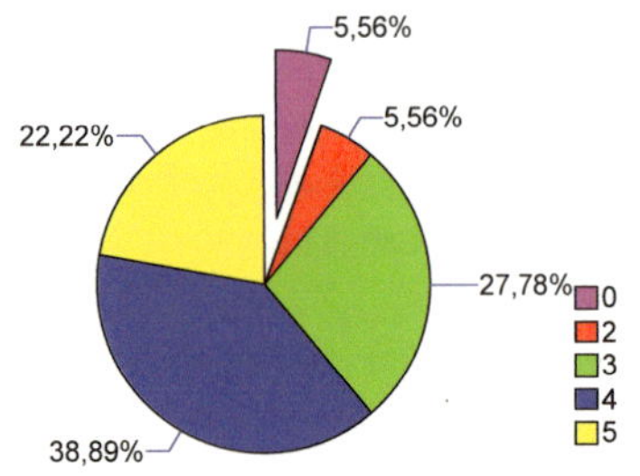

Fig. 2. The inclusion of virtual classroom contents improves virtual classroom.

As a result of students' suggestions during the 2008-09 academic year, the virtual classroom has been increasingly adding all the online resources used in the lessons. Furthermore, we have been trying to apply this approach to the other subjects. The virtual classroom has been a valuable aid for the student's training, monitoring and assessment.

3.4 Assessment of academic results

In this section we will analyse the academic results for all those subjects included within the pilot experience, as compared to results from previous years when assessment relied only on written theory and practice tests.

3.4.1 Business Administration and Production Management.

As stated above (section 2.2.1.), during the 04-05 course, the assessment of this subject was carried out by means of a final exam divided into two parts: theory and practice. The final overall qualification was the result of the arithmetic mean between both parts as far as at least 40% of the score was reached in each part. This qualification could be increased regarding participation as well as the works done, presented and handed in in class.

During the 05-06 year, assessment was considerably changed. Two theory tests were performed consisting in oral presentations of main topics. Each student was assessed individually through a set of questions about the topics. If the result was over 2 out of 5, the results of both tests would be added making an arithmetic mean with the results of the objective test done in class on the rest of units. The final exam was structured into two tests, a practice test -consisting in solving problems similar to the ones solved in class- and a theory test -on units 5, 8, 9, 10, 11, 12 and 13. In order to calculate the theory-practice mean a minimum score of 4 out of 10 was required in each part.

During the 06-07 course, the criteria of assessment were similar to those of 05-06. However, a better monitoring of the students' work has been carried out on the virtual classroom. The following aspects were particularly assessed: 5% for problems solved by students in class (two problems were required during the course), 5% for submission of enlarged summaries of topics introduced in lectures. The other 90% was assessed by theory and practice exams, with the same marking. To be able to apply the mean between theory and practice they should score at least 35% (out of the 90% corresponding to both tests within the overall results of the course). The theory exam was divided in turn into two parts: An oral presentation exam (50% of overall theory results) and an objective test for the rest of the units (remaining 50%). In the same way, the practice exam consisted of a number of problems scoring half the overall qualification.

We must make it clear that these criteria were applied only to those students who regularly attended lessons. Those students who did not attend lessons regularly were offered both a theory and a practice exam based on the syllabus contents.

Table 3 shows the number of registered students as well as the number of submitted and passed tests for three official exam calls. Table 4 shows rates for academic results by means of success and performance rates for the different calls. The success rate is measured as the quotient between passed and submitted tests; on the other hand, the performance rate is measured as the quotient between passed and registered students. On the other hand, figures 3 and 4 show the data collected from tables 3 and 4.

EXAM CALLS	REGISTERED	SUBMITTED	PASSED
JUNE 04/05	128	98	51
JUNE 05/06	108	71	8
JUNE 06/07	136	88	39

Table 3. Academic results.

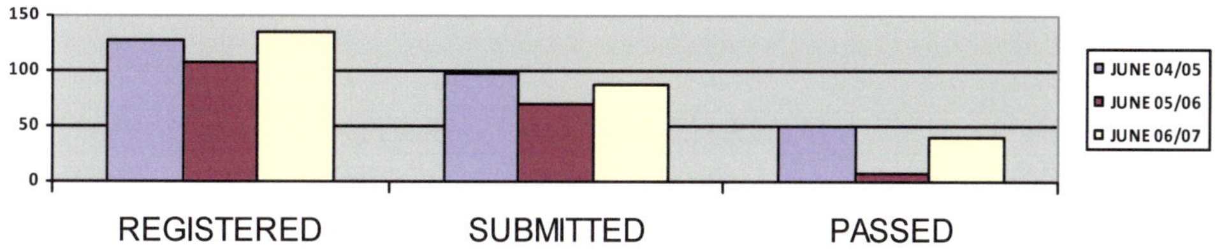

Fig. 3. Registered students, submitted and passed tests in the different calls.

EXAM CALLS	SUCCESS RATE	PERFORMANCE RATE
JUNE 04/05	52,04%	39,84%
JUNE 05/06	11,27%	7,41%
JUNE 06/07	44,31%	28,68%

Table 4. Academic results rates.

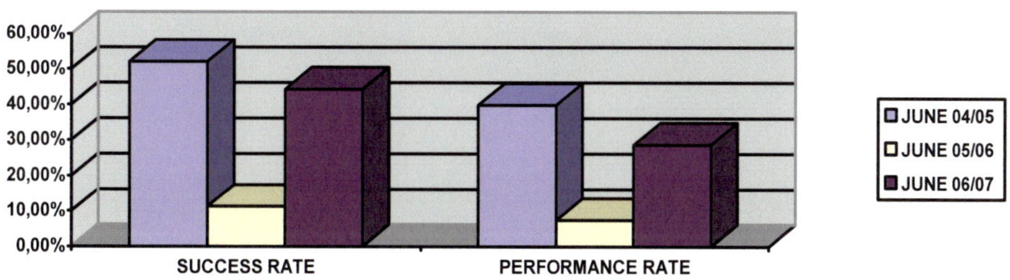

Fig. 4. Success and performance rates for the different calls.

3.4.2 Problem-Solving Strategies in Industrial Organizations

During the 04-05 year, the assessment of this subject was carried out by means of a final exam consisting of a number of exercises about the contents specified on the subject's syllabus (100%).

In the 05-06 year, assessment was the same as for the previous year, except for a 5% coming from the results of submitted practices.

Since the 2006-07 academic year there have been major changes in the assessment system. Two options were suggested: The first option features the student not willing to carry out the activities set out throughout the year. In this case, the student is assessed by a final exam consisting in solving a variety of exercises on the contents specified on the subject's syllabus (100%). Class attendance is assessed (5%) from at least 70% attendance to complete sessions. The second option features the student willing to carry out the activities set out throughout the year, in which case assessment will be carried out in the following way: hand-in tests for units 1 to 4 (10%), hand-in tests for units 5 to 8 (10%), final exam (80%).

To be able to access the hand-in test the student is required to have submitted all set exercises in due course. Finally, class attendance will be assessed (5%) from at least 70% attendance to complete sessions.

Table 5 shows registered students as well as submitted and passed exams for the different calls. Table 6 shows academic results rates by means of success rate and performance rate for the different calls. On the other hand, figures 5 and 6 show the data collected from tables 5 and 6.

EXAM CALLS	REGISTERED	SUBMITTED	PASSED
FEBRUARY 04/05	40	20	10
FEBRUARY 05/06	48	26	18
FEBRUARY 06/07	39	17	15
FEBRUARY 07/08	38	21	18

Table 5. Academic results.

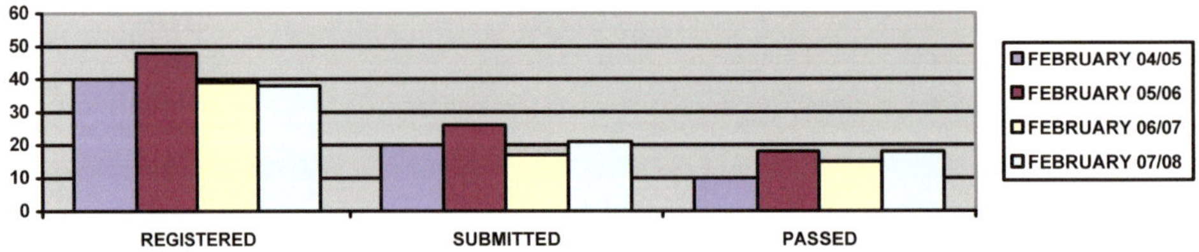

Fig. 5. Registered students, submitted and passed tests in the different calls.

EXAM CALLS	SUCCESS RATE	PERFORMANCE RATE
FEBRUARY 04/05	50%	25%
FEBRUARY 05/06	69,23%	37,5%
FEBRUARY 06/07	88,24%	38,46%
FEBRUARY 07/08	85,71%	47,37%

Table 6. Academic results rates

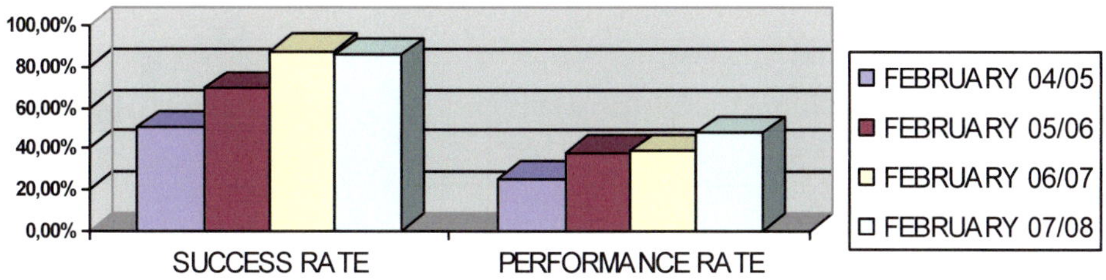

Fig. 6. Success and performance rates for the different calls.

3.4.3 Competitiveness and Innovation in Business

During the 06-07 academic year, this subject was assessed by applying a 30% weight to class activities (essays and oral presentations, case debates, etc.) results and a 70% to a compulsory final exam's results. This exam should be passed with a minimum score of 4/10 to be added to class activities results, as shown above in section 3.2.3.

As explained above, in the 07-08 second class there was a change in the way of working, which brought about a new way of assessment which basically consisted in changing percentages: 70% for daily work and 30% for an optional exam. Therefore, those who kept daily set activities up to date and passed them could reach a remarkable (up to B+) result.

The work carried out consisted in two novel individual activities; critical and extensive reading of six papers which were also to be summarised; working on a topic related to the concept of organization leading to the submission of an organization chart thereof; making a summary of all theory units; making oral presentations in groups on the additional references about innovation. We finally assessed extra, optional activities related to innovating experiences in different areas. These activities were all registered on a logbook students should keep updated and finally submit for assessment (70%).

Table 7 shows the number of registered, submitted and passed students for the different calls. Table 8 shows the academic results rates by means of the success rate and the performance rate in the different calls. On the other hand, figures 7 and 8 show the data yielded from tables 7 and 8.

CALLS	REGISTERED	SUBMITTED	PASSED
FEBRUARY 06/07	36	21	20
FEBRUARY 07/08	30	22	22

Table 7. Academic results

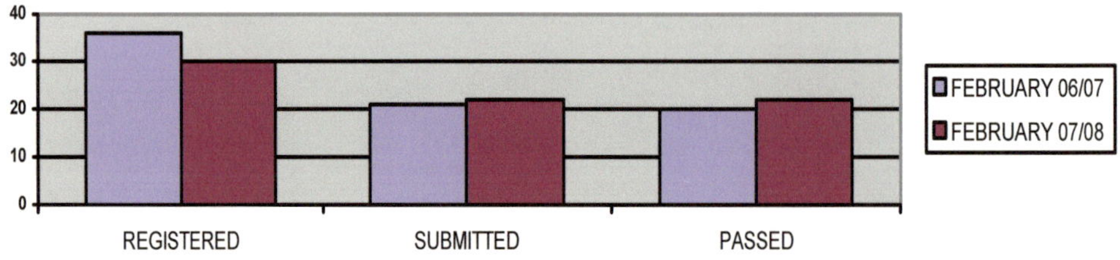

Fig. 7. Registered students, submitted and passed tests in the different calls.

EXAM CALLS	SUCCESS RATE	PERFORMANCE RATE
FEBRUARY 06/07	95,24%	55,55%
FEBRUARY 07/08	100%	73,33%

Table 8. Academic results rates.

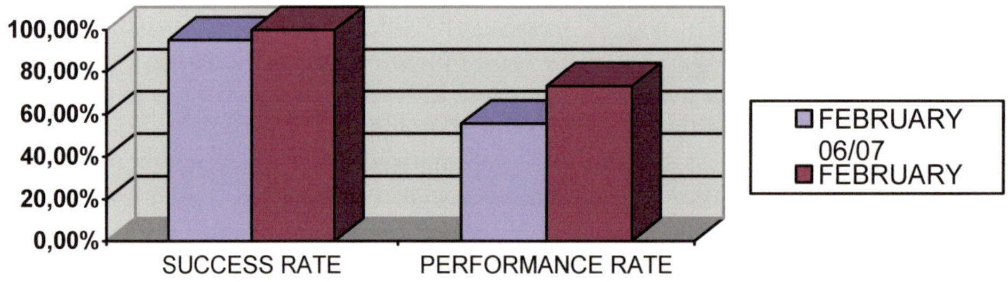

Fig. 8. Success and performance rates for the different calls.

Students taking this subject during the 07-08 academic year were given the following end-of-term questionnaire:

1º) Why have you taken up the Industrial Organization Engineering degree? Tick one or several of the following options:

a) Personal interest. b) Professional interest (as it is/will be demanded by my employers). c) both.

2º) Regarding the two types of assessment of this subject, namely traditional (i.e. exam + assignments) and alternative (i.e. logbook + assignments + participation), which of them has made a greater contribution to your learning?

a) Traditional. b) Alternative.

3º) The teaching methodology used is suitable for the "alternative" system of assessment. 0-1-2-3-4-5

4º) This assessment method encourages your work. 0-1-2-3-4-5

5º) This assessment method encourages group work. 0-1-2-3-4-5

6º) Group work improves your perception of the subject's contents. 0-1-2-3-4-5

7º) Group work encourages the debate on subject-related topics. 0-1-2-3-4-5

8º) The resources used by the teacher have been innovative as compared to other subjects. 0-1-2-3-4-5
9º) Using the virtual campus resources for teaching this subject would be a boost. 0-1-2-3-4-5
Grading: 0 (utterly disagrees, completely inadequate) up to 5 (fully agrees, fully adequate).
Figures 9 to 17 below show the questionnaire results by means of pie charts.

1º) Most students took up the IOE degree driven by both personal and professional interests, personal interest predominating over professional interest (fig. 9).

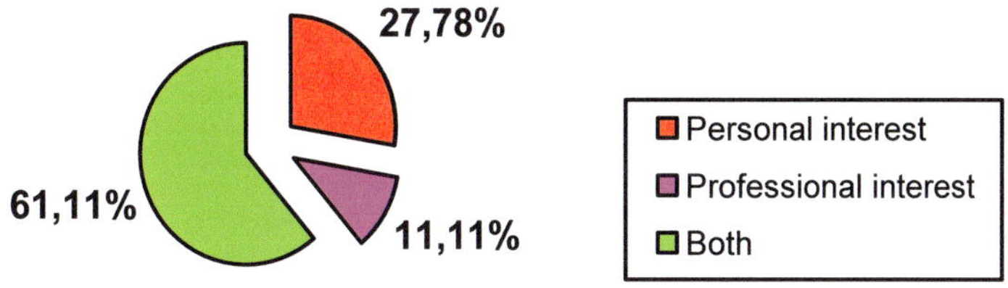

2º) 100% of students prefer the alternative way of assessment as opposed to the traditional one (fig.10).

3º) The adequacy of the teaching methodology used yields the following percentages (fig. 11).

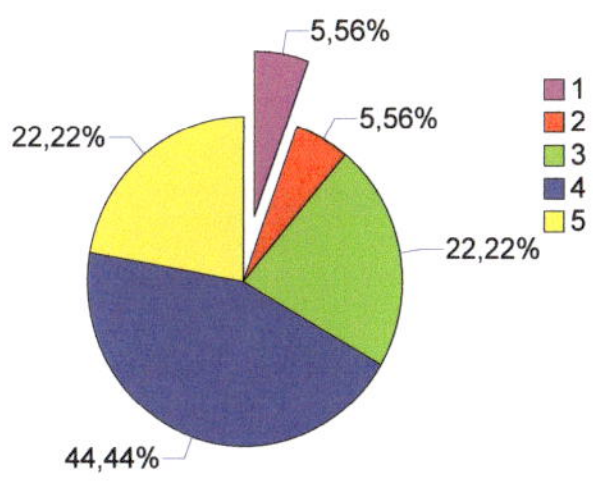

4º) The adequacy of the assessment method used yields the following percentages (fig. 12).

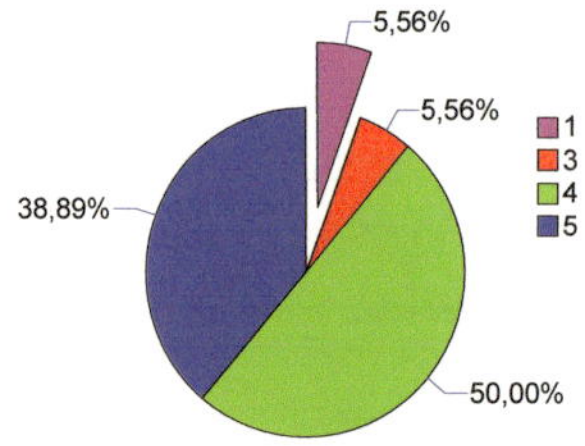

5º) "This assessment method encourages group work" yields the following percentages (fig. 13).

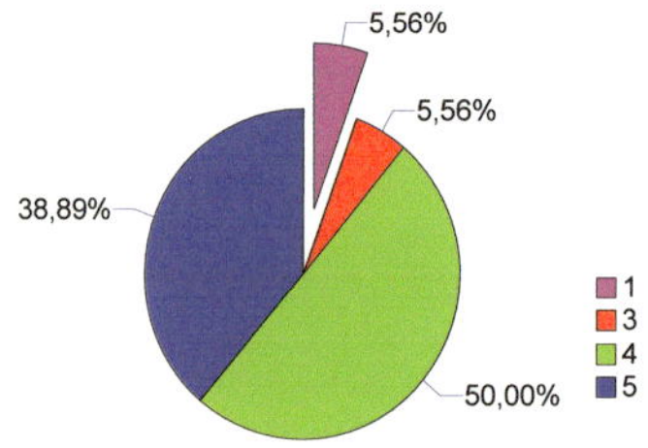

6º) "Group work improves your perception of the subject's contents" yields the following percentages (fig. 14).

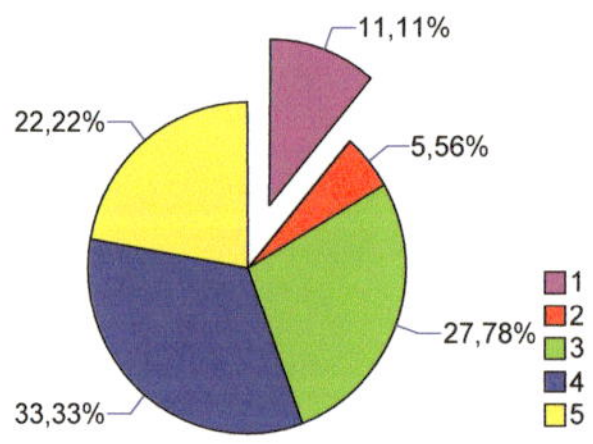

7º) "Group work encourages the debate on subject-related topics" yields the following percentages (fig. 15).

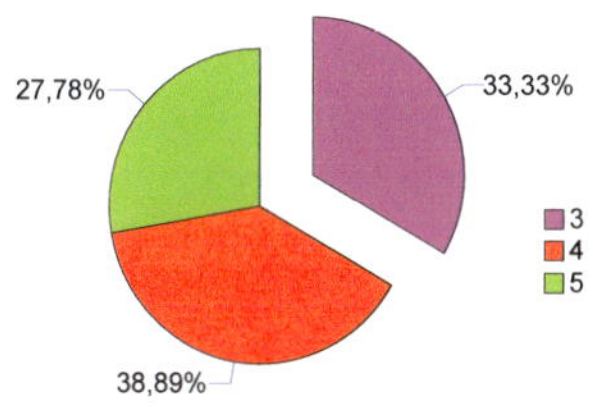

8º) "The resources used by the teacher have been innovative as compared to other subjects" yields the following percentages (fig. 16).

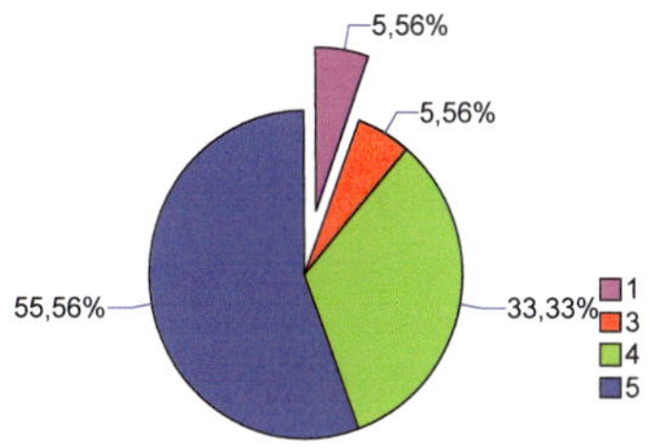

9º) "Using the virtual campus resources for teaching this subject would be a boost" yields the following percentages. (fig. 17).

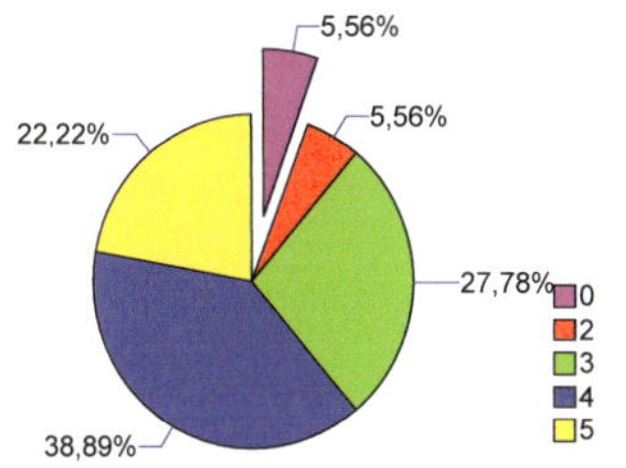

4. Conclusions

First of all, we should point out that we have always used the traditional method of assessment for the September calls, that is, practice/theory exams assessing the whole subject. That's why we have not included the data thereof when analysing the results of the different subjects.

In general, the changes made to the assessment system of the different subjects have been quite positive, particularly those affecting second-cycle subjects. The virtual classroom featured as a powerful tool from which we can still make the most of as it greatly helped monitoring students' work.

As stated above, we have particularly dwelt on the 07-08 academic results of Competitiveness an Innovation in Business reaching the following conclusions based on the questionnaire results:

- Most students study for professional and personal reasons.
- All students prefer the alternative method of assessment.
- The methodology followed satisfied students and the assessment carried out has encouraged both individual and group work.
- The resources we used are quite innovative as compared to other subjects and students suggest that the subject's content should be included in the virtual campus.
- The degree of satisfaction of the students polled has been medium-high regarding the teaching methodology followed.
- From the pilot experience being carried out, the assessment method followed has been quite satisfactory both from the academic results' and the students' perspectives, taking for granted that the number of students should be kept low.
- Some of the advantages of the teaching methodology followed are the student's positive attitude towards assignments, the student's personal commitment to developing her own "handbook" for the subject, her critical attitude and thought to meet set cases, her initiative to propose new cases, examples and additional bibliography on each topic.

Regarding the trade-offs of this experience, we must point out the need for a more active participation in the lessons and a comprehensive monitoring thereof, as well as the fact that assignments should be submitted in due course.

5. References

Benito, A.; Cruz, A. (2005). Nuevas claves para la docencia universitaria en el Espacio Europeo de Educación Superior, Narcea, ISBN: 8427715013,

Cervera Paz A.; Beira Jiménez, J.L (2008). *Perspectiva del alumnado en la innovación docente en Competitividad e innovación en la empresa en Ingeniería de Organización Industrial*, 16° Congreso Universitario de Innovación Educativa en las Enseñazas Técnicas, de Septiembre de 2008 Cádiz .

Delors, J. (1996). *La educación encierra un tesoro*: Unesco-Santillana, Madrid

De Miguel, M., *Modalidades de enseñanza centradas en el desarrollo de competencias*, Universidad de Oviedo, (2004). *Experiencia Piloto de Créditos Europeos*. Universidades Andaluzas. Guía Docente Común de Ingeniería en Ingeniería en Organización Industrial. 2004. *Formación básica para la adaptación al EEES*, septiembre de 2006/ enero de 2007, Universidad de Cádiz, 2007 (b). http://www2.uca.es/escuela/ingenieria *Informe sobre Innovación de la Docencia en las Universidades Andaluzas*. Comisión para la Innovación de la Docencia de las Universidades Andaluzas. CIDUA. 2005.

Keller, G. (1998). *The new importance of strategic management at universities*, Seminario Universidad : estrategias para avanzar, 19-21 enero, Barcelona. *Jornada de intercambios sobre Experiencias Piloto de Crédito Europeo*. Universidad de Cádiz, 2007. *Jornada sobre enseñanza virtual*, febrero de 2007, Universidad de Cádiz, 2007 (c).

Lowendahl, B.; Revang, O. (1998). Challenges to Existing Strategy Theory in a Postindustrial Society. Strategic Management Journal, Vol., 19, 1998.

Pérez Fernández, V.; Cervera Paz, A. (2008). *Análisis de Experiencias Docentes Aplicadas en Asignaturas de Organización de Empresas en Distintos Cursos y Titulaciones en la Escuela Superior de Ingeniería de Cádiz,* 16º Congreso Universitario de Innovación Educativa en las Enseñazas Técnicas, Septiembre de 2008, Cádiz.

Vilalta I Verdú, J.M. (1998). *Dirección y planificación estratégica en la universitat politécnica de catalunya,* Seminario Universidad : estrategias para avanzar, 19-21 enero, Barcelona.

16

Adapting to the EHEA: A case study

Miguel Arevalillo-Herráez, José Manuel Claver
and Alfredo Rosado-Muñoz
School of Engineering, University of Valencia
Spain

1. Introduction

Launched in 1999 by the Ministers of Education and university leaders of 29 countries, the so-called Bologna Process aims to create a European Higher Education Area (EHEA) by 2010; it has further developed into a major reform encompassing 46 countries. Taking part in the Bologna Process is a voluntary decision made by each country and its higher education community to endorse the principles underlined in the European Higher Education Area.

One major objective of the Bologna Process is to facilitate and encourage mobility of students and workers in the EHEA. As current educational models differ considerably between countries, this requires the establishment of a set of common guidelines so that study programs delivered across Europe can be easily compared. To this end, a common credit system has been designed. The ECTS (an important tool used for credit transfer and student work measure) plays now an important part in curriculum design and in validating a range of learning achievements. In this system, credits reflect the total workload required to achieve the objectives of a programme, which are specified in terms of the learning outcomes and competences that should be acquired.

Using a common credit system makes study programmes easier to compare, and therefore facilitates mobility and academic recognition. However, there are other important implications to the use of ECTS. In particular, the ECTS system requires a new educational model which must guide the programmes and the methodologies used for teaching. These should be focused on learning outcomes and student-centred learning (SCL), and not exclusively on the number of teaching hours.

In some countries, the set of common guidelines can be easily accommodated into their current educational models. In others, more extensive changes are needed. In the particular case of Spain, the implementation of the ECTS requires a change of mentality, and a transformation of the underlying educational model. On the one hand, the structure and duration of the degrees will be significantly altered and this requires that the process be carefully managed. The reform will mean the end of a long standing Spanish tradition of centralised definition of degrees, both in their names and in a large part of their contents. Universities will have a very large autonomy to define their programmes and the name of their degrees, and will have to account for the results by means of an evaluation and accreditation process not present before. On the other hand, undergraduate education is currently centred on teaching, with credits measured in terms of the number of hours delivered. However, the new educational model places a special emphasis on learning and student effort; and on the use of the most adequate educational strategies to achieve the objectives, competences and transferrable skills that the module pursues.

Besides, the new educational model implies other important changes in teaching and learning methodologies, with a significant reduction of student contact (in favour of other self-learning strategies). From this perspective, a transition period is required so that both lecturers and students familiarize with it. Students need to improve their interpersonal skills, communication abilities, work organization, time restrictions, etc. and lecturers must prepare new more appropriate working materials (for lecture hours, lab hours and home study) with these objectives in mind. The preparation of such materials is a challenging task for lecturers because they have to face not only technical aspects of the subject but also the development of a teaching plan (adapted to the new methodologies) to achieve an optimum learning process.

The objective of this chapter is twofold. In the one hand, it attempts to provide a set of general guidelines and good practices which can be useful to other national and international universities currently involved in a process of change of the underlying educational model. This section explains how the School of Engineering started the process of adapting to the EHEA. In the other, it shares the results of a number of experiences and suggests a series of teaching methods to increase student involvement in the learning process. In the first part we describe the action plan in detail, with a special emphasis on educational issues. In particular, we describe the actions performed to facilitate the process of change, and how these have been monitored and controlled. The second part of the chapter focuses on the description of some techniques which have been adopted in different modules to improve the existing teaching and learning process.

2. PART I: Activities at the School of Engineering to promote the EHEA integration.

The University of Valencia is one of the oldest and largest universities in Spain. Located in the city of Valencia, it was founded in 1499, and currently has around 50,000 students from which 2,000 belong to the School of Engineering. As part of a plan for a continuous adaptation to society changes, the University is committed to provide a smooth transition to the new educational paradigm. To this end, at an institutional level, the University of Valencia has encouraged Faculties to start a series of Educational Innovation Programs, and a number of activities have been organized to share the experiences and provide the teachers with new materials, helping them to adapt or incorporate new teaching models. At a Faculty level, since 2005, the School of Engineering has developed its own action plan, composed of a set of activities which can be classified into five major categories:

2.1 Analysis

The first activity before proposing specific actions was to perform a series of studies in order to check the current knowledge of the teaching staff in different areas such as the EHEA, teaching competences to students, level of innovation in courses and teachers´ attitude to use new teaching techniques. All this information was obtained by a quiz done in early 2006 completed by 85 percent of the teaching staff. Some of the most interesting results are shown in Table 1. (complete results can be accessed at http://www.uv.es/eees).

What is the amount of information existing about the EHEA?					
None	A few	Enough	Too much	NA (not answered)	
0%	55%	39%	1%	4%	
What is your knowledge about the EHEA?					
None	I know only some aspects	An intensive knowledge	NA		
8%	80%	9%	3%		
Do you think that teachers are ready to start the transition process to the new paradigm?					
Yes	No	NA			
45%	49%	7%			
In your opinion, what actions are needed for a successful adaptation?					
Training	Information	Time	Material Resources	Nothing	Others
66%	45%	67%	76%	0%	8%
How much do you think that the EHEA will change your daily teaching work?					
Nothing	A Little bit	Moderately	Significantly	A lot	NA
0%	4%	17%	54%	22%	3%

Table 1. Some of the results obtained from a quiz fulfilled by the teaching staff at the UV-School of Engineering.

As it can be appreciated, most of the teachers were not very familiar with the EHEA adaptation process. However, they were worried about its impact in their teaching activity and demanded information and actions aiming at providing them with better capabilities to design an appropriate teaching plan.

2.2 Informational process

Once the main needs were detected, it was clear that an action plan should be started in order to provide more information about the EHEA and all its details about the formal aspects of the educational change, but not only that; a strong focus should be given in the teaching techniques to improve the so-called transversal competences: collaborative work, project based learning, learning through writing, etc; and moreover, several techniques to address a better organization of the courses allowing different types of evaluation and proposing several self-learning activities to assure that the autonomous work hours are really busy and fruitful for the student.

During this process, a periodicity in the activities must be followed, i.e. it is important to measure the regularity of them, not being too wide neither too narrow in time to avoid the staff to forget or get tired. In any case, several actions were done:

1. Invite some relevant persons at the University level in order to clearly explain how the institution is facing the changes, the demanded tasks to the faculties, and the support offered. In this case, some conferences from the European Convergence vice Rector and the Rectors' delegate for the EHEA were done.

2. Receive information about the process carried out in other national and European universities. It was very important for us to know how other institutions were adapting to the EHEA, how they apply different techniques, how they promote the participation of the staff, how they arrange the tuition, etc.
3. Inform about the level of work done by other faculties inside the University of Valencia. This was a surprising activity because we could find that some close faculties and teachers were making an important effort to adapt the EHEA. Several lecturers from different faculties described their experiences and the activities they employed in daily classes. It was a very interesting serving to encourage other colleagues to start with some innovative activities in class.

2.3 Training

In parallel with informational activities, other training seminars, workshops and conferences were also proposed. The main aim of these activities was focused in guiding the teachers when addressing important changes in his tuition, moving from a traditional teaching model (passive students) to a more dynamic approach. These activities were carried out by relevant persons in the field of teaching for engineers, describing the common problems addressed when moving to a new teaching system, the organization of such systems, the cautions that must be taken, and so on. In general, the aim was to guide the teacher and allow him to be "fearless" in taking the challenge of modifying the structure of courses.

2.4 Pilot Projects

After the second year of promoting all the aforementioned activities, the full coordination of the first year of Bachelor Engineering in Telecommunications was attempted. The EHEA system was not yet active at that time, however, it was of common thought that some steps toward that direction could be done in order to explore possibilities. Specifically, the main aim was to explore the possibility of establishing a better coordination among teachers of the same group so that the same rules were adopted for all courses and check if some competences could be worked-out among different courses.

Of course, it should never be adopted a strategy where many new concepts are included, this can be opposed to the desired effect and some students, or even teachers could feel deceived. Thus, in a three year horizon, new coordination concepts were introduced every year. First, simple activities were hold, such as a teacher coordination meeting every month and a schedule plan for proposing tasks to the students in order for them to follow a regular work load along the academic year. Second, internal activities in the courses were introduced by most of the teachers (some tutorial sessions were held, more problem oriented classes done and project-based learning was used in some courses). Third, an attempt to incorporate some important competences was also made. In this case, oral expression, written abilities and autonomous problem solving were chosen.

The experience obtained in this project evidenced a number of pitfalls concerning the new organization. Regarding the coordination among teachers, it is common to have different points of view. In this sense, the presence of a coordinator proposing and verifying the

course plan becomes necessary. Besides, the teacher's work load significantly increases the teachers who participate require full involvement; otherwise, the students will not feel that the system works as a single block and this fact might decrease the success rate.
On the contrary, many advantages are obtained. Students can follow a teaching system able to develop their skills, learning theoretical contents but also improving different aspects concerning the integral education of an engineer in ethical aspects, decision-making, group work, project development and self- organization. Moreover, these activities have led to an increment in the online materials available to students, helping them with the homework.

2.5 Additional activities

In order to complete the activities at the School of Engineering, other side aspects apart from teaching are proposed. As an example, a continuous collaboration with companies exists so that students can spend some periods at the companies and some courses and conferences from important company professionals are proposed to students. Of course, traditional exchange programs are promoted; they are very popular among students, allowing them to experience different teaching methods used in other universities and broaden their social view.

Finally, with the objective to increase teacher's involvement, some other activities were funded by the School. For instance, the attendance to some conferences outside the University, the financial support required to start some innovative action in class, or small expenses which might help teachers start new and interesting learning systems.

3. PART II: Teaching Techniques Adopted

This part describes some of the teaching techniques which have been taken into practice in an attempt to improve the teaching and learning process. These have been incorporated into existing modules, some as pilot experiences. First, we present a method to encourage an even participation of group members, when cooperative strategies are used. Then, we describe the benefits of using competitive strategies, explaining how the introduction of an assessed competition into one of the modules has helped motivate students. Next, we present a technique to increase student support by introducing the role of a "support student". Last, we describe how coursework based learning has been used in two more modules.

3.1 Encouraging an Even Participation of Group Members

Team work gives the student an opportunity to engage in discussion, take responsibility for their own learning, and thus become critical thinkers (Totten et al., 1991). When working in small groups, students can share their strengths at the same time as they develop other weaker skills, and they tend to learn more and retain contents longer than when these are presented in other instructional formats (Davis, 1993). Apart from a greater enjoyment and motivation (Beckman, 1990; Slavin, 1983), students also develop a number of transferrable skills and values. They learn to deal with conflict, acquire problem solving abilities and improve their interpersonal, social and communications skills.

A major problem when using group based teaching strategies is maintaining an even collaboration of the team members. When most of the work in performed outside the classroom, some students may try to hide behind the rest of the members and avoid part (or all) of their responsibilities. Several strategies have been proposed to handle this problem (Davis, 1993). Some examples are keeping the groups small, allowing teams to dismiss members when they do not contribute adequately, or performing anonymous assessments at the end of each task, in which each student has to state the contribution of each member (Walboord, 1986).

In this section we describe two techniques which use cooperative learning to encourage student interaction and improve their learning experience.

A First Attempt

A first attempt in this direction was made during the academic year 2007/08, in a third year compulsory module called "Programming languages", studied as part of the Computing degree.

The method was supported by Aula Virtual, an LMS (Learning Management System) that the University makes available to students and faculty members. During the lecturer sessions (or using the LMS), activities related to the subject taught are proposed. Examples of these activities are developing a software application or giving a presentation on a related topic. Only one group of students may voluntarily take responsibility for each activity, and each activity is assigned a deadline and a value which determines the maximum score that the group may attain. At the end of the semester, students are ranked by the course points achieved and mark guarantees are given to the first few ranked students. If a student who has achieved a mark guarantee obtains a lower mark in the semester examination, the former replaces the latter. To encourage team work, the activity may be performed in groups of up to five members, and the individual scores achieved are independent of the number of students who performed the activity. With this strategy, active learners who prefer learning by doing can find an additional motivation, at the same time as other more reflective learners are not jeopardized.

To achieve an even contribution of all members and avoid shirkers, the presence of passive students is strongly penalized and has an effect on the entire group. After the activity deadline students have to publish their solution in a forum created for this purpose in the LMS, and present their work during a lecture session. All group members should be present at this event and they have to offer a question time in which the lecturer and/or other students in the classroom may address questions about the activity to any particular member of the group. If that student does not answer it correctly, the entire group loses the entire score. Because of the competitive component in the scheme, other students are encouraged to study the solution provided by the group and ask related questions to those students that they believe are the weakest in the group.

In some occasions, friendship and respect for others force a student who lacks interest in the subject do her share of the work to avoid that others get penalized. For this reason, once a group of students has taken responsibility for an activity, no member may drop from the

team. However, there is not commitment from any of the students to stay in the same group for future activities. This causes that shirkers be rejected and that students with a common learning preferences group together in other activities.
As side effects, this scheme motivates activists to attend the lecturers so that they can pick up the activities they like most. At the same time, the solutions provided by the groups are revised and provided as learning materials for the entire class.
Some interesting responses are detailed below:

a) The groups were dynamic, in the sense that their members were constantly changing. In many cases, the group started with the maximum number of members allowed, but its size reduced to three or four members in the next activity.
b) There were a few activities that were performed by a single person. In many cases, this was due to competition (an attempt to obtain a higher score than other members who have commonly worked together). However, there were two students who preferred to perform all tasks in an individual basis. In this case, we convinced these two students to form a group, in an attempt to motivate the development of their team work skills.
c) After the first four classes, only 15 of the 25 students attending the lectures had participated in some activity. After ten lectures, only 7 students continued in the scheme. Some students were highly discouraged when they realized that other students were far ahead in the ranking, and this caused that some other students decreased their performance levels once they had achieved a score which ensured them a passing grade.
d) Some students who achieved a good mark guarantee did not attend the semester exam. They preferred to dedicate more time to prepare other modules rather than to study for a module which they had already passed.

Although some of these are positive aspects, the student behaviour described below in c) and d) made us re-consider the strategy and propose a more robust method to achieve the same objective.

Refined Strategy
During the academic year 2008/09 we used a different strategy to palliate the effect of uneven participation of group members. While still penalizing the presence of passive students on the entire group, the competitive component is eliminated.

In this occasion, students have to attend four examinations during the course, and the final grade is obtained as the average of the scores achieved at each examination. However, each of these scores is influenced by the geometric average of those obtained by each member of the team. In particular, the individual score for each examination is averaged with the geometric average of the marks obtained by all team members.

Each examination has an associated course work load that students must perform outside the classroom. This work has to be performed in teams, and it is closely related to the contents of each examination. Although students are given freedom to group themselves as desired, they are advised about the risks of having too many members. Although the amount of work is independent from the size of the team, the geometric average strongly penalizes low marks, and these are more likely as the number of members increases.

With this scheme, the final grade is composed of an individual and a team component. The objective we pursue is to encourage students to help each other, hence promoting collaborative learning.

The results of using this methodology are summarized below:

a) Although groups were dynamic, there were not as many changes in the group members as in the previous case. With a few exceptions, the groups formed at the beginning of the semester were maintained throughout the entire course.
b) Although initially there were some large groups (up to 6 members), these soon divided into two. The students realized that the probability that one person fails to do their share increases with the number of members.
c) In general, the marks obtained by all team members were homogeneous. Although there were a few cases in which one member failed to meet his/her objectives, it was not common that other student in the same group performed extraordinary well.
d) In many cases, some questions in the examination were variations of some which appeared in the course works. This caused that, although some teams decided to divide the work between their members, they usually organised post-discussion sessions to explain the results to each other. In fact, most groups organised study session on the previous days to an examination, with an obvious benefit to the learning process.
e) Some weak student s became forced to make an effort so that the marks of other team members did not get affected negatively. Besides, the felt supported by the rest of the team members who also were interested in pulling their grades up.
f) Student participation was noticeably increased. While in previous years, attendance was about 50% (measure on registered students), this year rates close to 80% were achieved.
g) No significant negative effects were observed. A questionnaire processed at the end of the course revealed that most students enjoyed the experience, preferred this collaborative way of learning and considered that they learn better than by using traditional teaching methods.

Although both techniques aimed at encouraging an even participation of group members, only the second one really obliges all students to participate. While the competitive component of the first strategy finally discouraged some students, the second approach established a common goal for the team and enabled student collaboration, resulting in a significant educational benefit.

A side effect to both approaches is that it forces teams to adopt a stronger position against shirkers. In many cases, members of a team do an extra amount of work to compensate for the presence of a shirker. However, with the strategies presented in this section, the grade of the rest of the members is significantly affected. This causes that shirkers be rejected by other team members.

3.2 Use of Competitive Strategies

Competitive learning has been criticized because they may have destructive outcomes, such as promoting selfishness or increasing anxiety levels. Besides, using competition as an extrinsic reward may turn the genuine intrinsic interest in increasing competence into an interest for demonstrating they are better at a specific task (Butler, 1989). In this section we show how making an appropriate use of this type of techniques can also help the learning process, increasing student motivation and making them aware of their knowledge with respect to other students in the same group.

The technique described in this section is currently used in a programming module that introduces the C and C++ programming languages to first year students. In this module, a competitive learning strategy has been incorporated into the teaching plan with a twofold purpose: a) as a form of extrinsic reward to motivate students and b) to complement the support for the cooperative and individualistic learning styles.

In particular, two of the traditional lab sessions have been replaced by competitive assessments. At the start of the tests, students are given a specification of a simple computer game they have to implement, together with an executable file of the game already implemented. The specification contains some basic requirements and some possible extensions, each with an associated score which indicates the score that students achieve by implementing it correctly. Students have to produce a source code that implements the features in the specification. The duration of the assessment session is planned so that it lasts the same as a single laboratory and thus no submission is allowed after that time.

All solutions submitted are ranked by score. The first implementation in the ranking is assigned the maximum mark, and the last which achieves at least the basic requirements the minimum passing mark. Other results in between are scaled linearly between these two marks according to their ranking positions. To avoid that students lose motivation, sessions are carefully designed so that a basic solution is easily achievable. The marks obtained in the competitions have an important impact on the mark for the laboratory sessions.
In this case, there are several benefits associated with the use of the technique:

a) The competitions constitute a milestone for the learning process. The two competitions are scheduled away from the exam period so that students have the time to review the contents, and little hints are provided so that they can train for the event.
b) It develops a sense of a team. Although students are already working in pairs during the laboratory sessions, there are no time limits or other constraints that make coordination necessary. In the competition, students need to develop a strategy and really work together with a common aim.
c) All students acquire a global perspective of their own learning in comparison to the rest of the class. Their position in the ranking is a good indication of their progress and allows them to judge their knowledge in relation to that of the rest of the class.
d) The competitive environment imposed by the set-up avoids any type of plagiarism.

As part of a subjective analysis, students are asked on an individual basis about the competition. Most students enjoy the experience and remark on the positive effects of working in pairs under a competitive environment. As an interesting issue (and more objective evaluation) it is also worthwhile to remark that an observable correlation exists between the marks obtained in the practical sessions and those obtained in the competition.

3.3 Increasing Student Support

One major problem in many university modules is offering an adequate support for the set of activities that a student must perform to fulfil its objectives. In the particular case of the programming module described above, special difficulties are found to provide support to certain academic activities. On the one hand, a series of exercises are proposed during the lecture sessions. These are usually more complex than programming examples provided in class and allow supervising student progress. On the other hand, supervised laboratory sessions are provided other than those scheduled for the module. These are specially addressed to students having difficulties with the subject.

The first of these activities implies grading exercises, and providing adequate feedback to make students aware of their level of knowledge. The second, an effort so that the lecturer is available for an additional time. To provide continuous feedback to both lectures and students, the figure of the so called "Support Student" has been introduced. These are students in the last courses of the Computer Engineering degree who assist lecturers in the teaching. To this end, it has been agreed with the Computing Department that support students can earn credits for such an activity.

Support students mark exercises and hand them back to the student in a week time, reporting the main difficulties and student mistakes to the lectures. Besides, they replace the lecturer in the additional laboratory sessions mentioned above. In particular, 60 minute weekly sessions supervised by support students complement the usual 90 minute sessions at key stages of the course (such as dates close to the examination period).

In this context, support students have allowed us to increase student support significantly. Furthermore, they facilitate monitoring the group and detecting potential problems in advance.

3.4 Coursework Based Learning

Deliverables can be a useful complement to promote learning outside class sessions. However, they require that the lecturer (or its assistants) provide appropriate feedback to the students. This is a time consuming activity for lecturers and the feedback which is usually offered is generally scarce.

Meanwhile, class sessions are usually boring for students, and they tend to adopt a passive attitude. In order to solve this problem, some teachers promote a previous reading of contents. Nevertheless, this reading activity is not as effective if it is does not focus on key aspects of the contents.

In order to maintain the pace of the class, combining explanation and student participation, we have developed a methodology that combines previous readings with deliverables, so that it becomes a guided activity. The deliverables include a series of questions that the student must solve before attending class. Then, the class session is fully dedicated to solving the deliverable. By using this methodology, the lecturer can combine explanations of contents with the student's participation, and provide him/her with an adequate feedback. At the same time as the lecturer explains the correct solutions to the exercises, student questions are answered and their results are discussed.

After each class session, the teacher collects the deliverables (which may be individual or in teams), checking that they have been completed. The number of deliverables handed is reported to each student by using the university's learning management system. The empty cell effect is an important incentive to encourage students to submit their deliverables on time. As the deliverables are solved and commented during the class, the revision task reduces to testing that the deliverable has been completed, becoming less time consuming for the lecturer.

The use of deliverables based on a previous reading has also been adopted for laboratory sessions. In this context, laboratory classes are evaluated according to two major criteria: The first one is associated with a deliverable about the contents of the lab session, which must be handed in at the start of the laboratory session. The second one is related to the work developed by students during the lab session and the outcomes achieved.

This methodology is currently used in two modules of the Computer Science degree. These modules are called "Introduction to Computer" (IC), a first year compulsory module, and "Microprocessor Based Systems" (MBS), a third year elective module.

In these cases, the strategy also makes use of basic knowledge examinations, mainly based on questions that are contained in deliverables or closely related to them. To pass these exams, a student must answer most questions correctly, permitting a single mistake.

Another group activity aims to develop writing skills. To this end, each work group must write a report describing the activities which they have performed during the week. This group report is revised by the lecturer, who provides adequate feedback on its contents and the correctness of their writing.

The first effect of this methodology has been a significant increase in student attendance to lecture sessions (from 20% to 80%). No such an effect has been noticed on laboratory sessions, as it is usual that all students attend. At the same time, a noticeable increase in the number of student passing the module has been achieved (from 25% to 60% in the IC module, and from 25% to 80% in MBS module).

3.5 Remote laboratories

It is very important to provide students with tools they can use to support their learning outside teaching hours. For courses where the usage of hardware or special equipment is essential for a proper learning of the subject, it is common that laboratory hours are not enough to fully practice all the topics which should be covered. This argument is also valid for the equipment. Because of high prices only a reduced number of units are available, causing restrictions on student access.

The proposal for these cases was to develop a remote laboratory web system where the students can access the hardware located at the University premises, being able to use the system as if they were physically in the laboratory (controlling the system via activation of web controls and receiving information via web pages or a camera placed close to the equipment). At the School of Engineering, such a web system has been developed. Figure 1 shows its main structure. The main parts of the system are the web server including the user management and the web controls for the equipment interface; and the hardware communication system with the target equipment for downloading control program and activating/reading digital and analogue signals from the equipment.

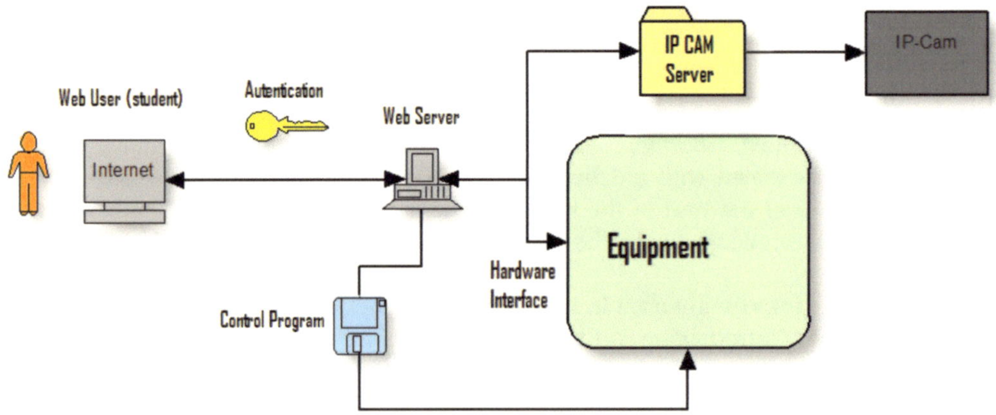

Fig. 1. General diagram of the proposed remote laboratories access system.

The use of this approach provides many different benefits. First, any user can access hardware system at any time 365 days, 24 hours a day; this fact makes it possible to access hardware systems which are usually restricted to research or advanced courses. Second, the lecturer can easily evaluate the student (according to the teacher needs, the web server might be programmed to track the students' actions). Last, the student can use dangerous systems in a safe way (e.g. chemical instruments, radioactive measurements, etc.); if some restrictions are included in the hardware control, the student could only handle the desired controls, opposite to the physical presence where the user can control any action whether it is necessary for the task or not.

At the moment, a general platform has been built and used for some courses related to ABB® industrial robot programming, FPGA programming, microprocessor programming and power electronics. The platform uses a modular structure so that most of the modules can be re-used and only the specific hardware interface with the target equipment needs to be customized. The web page http://labserver.uv.es is the web address where the user can access the system.

The results showed that users feel very comfortable with the system, and consider its best value the possibility to work with it at any time and from any place. The statistics showed that most of the users take advantage of the maximum time offered by the system (time is limited to 30 minutes because no concurrent users can access the hardware at the same time), with an average usage time of 24 minutes per user. In case of the Industrial Robot system, a self-evaluation tool was incorporated, indicating the correctness of the proposed movement programming activity. The tracking system included in the web server showed that users feel involved with the system, downloading different programs until the right one was achieved. Although we have not found important problems with concurrent accesses to the system, a queuing system has been included to allow users to make reservations for time slots in case the system is being used.

4. Conclusion

This chapter has dealt with the experience of the School of Engineering at the University of Valencia in adapting to the EHEA. In particular, the most important actions have been described. These have focused on encouraging teaching staff to adapt their teaching methods, so that transferrable skills and competences are included as part of the objectives of the modules that they deliver. Although there were faculty members who rejected the new proposals, these were a minority. In general, once the actions were completed, the teaching staff were more involved and informed about the EHEA. This caused a higher interest in modifying teaching procedures and gave rise to other educational initiatives. After some years from the start of the action plan the School of Engineering is more involved in the EHEA; effectively applies its guidelines; and offers more educational activities to students.

The EHEA implies a new educational model (with important changes in teaching and learning methodologies), and some in-class actions are also required. In this direction, some specific experiences have been presented. In particular, a method to encourage an even participation of group members in collaborative tasks; the use competitive strategies as an extrinsic reward to motivate students; a technique to increase student support, by introducing "support students" to assist lecturers; the use of coursework based learning to promote certain transferrable skills; and the use of remote laboratories to provide full access to restricted resources.

All these techniques have been introduced in the context of the new EHEA, in an attempt to improve particular aspects of the existing teaching and learning methods. Although a significant progress has been made, improvement of teaching methodologies is still in process. Indeed this should be an on-going process which should never end. This fact has been recognised by the University of Valencia and its School of Engineering, by providing support to the teaching staff in different ways. As an example, the school is financing the attendance of lecturers to educational events and some training programs have been started (including a series of courses, workshops and conferences).

5. References

Beckman, M., Collaborative Learning: Preparation for the workplace and democracy, College Teaching, 38(4), 128-133, 1990

Butler, R., Interest in the task and interest in peer's work in competitive and non-competitive conditions; a developmental study, Child development 60(3), pp. 562-570, 1989

Davis, B.G. Tools for Teaching, Jossey-Bass Publishers: San Francisco, 1993

Slavin, R.F., When does Cooperative Learning Increase Student Achievement?, Psychological Bulleting, 94(3), 429-445, 1983

Totten, S. ; Sills, T. ; Digby, A., & Russ, P. Cooperative learning: A guide to research. New York: Garland, 1991

Walvoord, B. F Helping Students Write Well: A Guide for Teachers in All Disciplines. (2nd ed.) New York: Modern Language Association, 1986.

The Importance of Cooperative Work in the Faculty and in the Classroom

M. G. Montoya, R. Herrada, C. Gil,
F. G. Montoya and A. Alías
University of Almeria
Spain

1. Introduction

The present work highlights the interest in improving teaching in the University by understanding the changes which arise when lecturers work cooperatively and extend this educational practice to their classrooms. However, it would seem equally appropriate to refer to the teaching team as a collective agent in the students' education and also as a model. On the other hand, we should bear in mind the whole educational centre (Faculty and University) both as the field educational development and as the field of more informal learning.

In a society which seems to be dominated by individualism and competitiveness, why is it that in the educational field more value has been given recently to cooperative work? The answer surely lies in the economic factor and our obsession with efficiency, in particular the widespread belief that tomorrow's society will demand and place a high value on work teams based on cooperation. Duran Gisbert considers that the capacity to cooperate is one of the main interpersonal competences of a "knowledge workers", (Gisbert, 2001). In the new economic framework, work is organized in interdisciplinary and multicultural teams which are capable of working in contexts which are subject to rapid change. In such teams participation and a cooperative style of work are highly valued.

Given this scenario for the future, it will be necessary for both students and lecturers to develop cooperation in the classroom in order to be prepared for the society of tomorrow. When lecturers cooperate in their teaching work they are supporting and promoting a climate of cooperation in their classrooms, their universities and in society as a whole.

Society needs its future citizens to learn cooperatively as opposed to the individualism in which social and work relationships are so steeped. We should combat the desire to convert learning into a competitive scenario which sets goals reserved for a few "excellent" students. Individualism in the classroom gives rise to anachronic situations such as the students considering it an obstacle "to have to wait for the group to develop a piece of work in which all those involved learn and reach a common goal".

Interaction among teaching staff is not promoted either, since lecturers are mainly required to master the subject they teach. The more they specialize, the further they go from shared knowledge with other areas, and in particular from the common core of the students learning process which is shared by all those involved in the teaching task. Moreover, specialization usually leads us to consider content as the main concern, "teaching everything or what is relevant", as opposed to encouraging students to acquire the tools which will give them access to knowledge.

The idea is still held that working separately the students will be able to put the pieces of the puzzle together and give them some coherence. In so doing the students will become citizens who are capable of facing up to life. It would be a mistake to believe that everyone has the same chance of solving the puzzle, or that they will do so at more or less the same time. Likewise, we would be mistaken to think that if the pieces of the puzzle are designed separately they will fit together exactly.

On the other hand, the creation of the European Higher Education Space has resulted in the definition of a new educational paradigm in university studies, as has been made clear in the different international and national forums related to this context (EHES, 2005), (Tunning, 2002). The typical features of this new educational model require the development of a professional profile in which the roles and activities of students and lecturers are no longer the traditional ones. Modifications must therefore be made to both the content of the subjects and especially the way in which they are taught, affecting lecturers and students equally.

The principal features of the intended educational model which make it a more effective tool for the challenges which have to be confronted are (Fernández, 2006):

- A learning-centred educational model, requiring a shift from teaching to learning, and particularly teaching to learn to learn, and to learn for life.
- An educational model centred on autonomous learning of the student under tutorship of the lecturers.
- An educational model focussing on the results of learning, expressed in terms of generic and specific competences.
- An educational model that focusses on the learning process - education as cooperative work between lecturers and students.
- An educational model that demands a new definition of the learning-teaching activities.
- An educational model which proposes a new organization of learning: modularity, multidisciplinary and cross-disciplinary curricular spaces, as part of the global educational project (Curriculum).
- An educational model that makes strategic use of evaluation, making it an integral part of the learning-teaching activities. There should be a revaluation of the formative or continuous evaluation and a review of the final or qualificative evaluation.
- An educational model that measures the work of the student, using the ECTS as a tool to construct the curriculum, taking the competences or results of learning as a basis. This model will also act as tool to guarantee the transparency of the different systems of higher education.
- An educational model which places greater importance on technologies of the information and the communication and their possibilities to develop new ways of learning.

In this sense, one of the basic recommendations for the Implantation of the European Higher Education Space is that the work of educational innovation should be carried out by a coordinated educational team and not in an individual way in each of the subjects.

Nevertheless, it is well known that the most university lecturers work individually, which has led students to regard subjects as isolated entities without any links between them. It goes without saying that the students´ workload at any given time is not known.
Given this situation and bearing in mind the new educational paradigm, one of the challenges is to get lectures from the same degree and the same year to work together in teaching teams, responsible for organizing and scheduling all those activities which affect the same group of students.
Moreover, lecturers who cooperate with their colleagues in a team also tend to practise this activity in their classes, as cooperative work is not a technical process, but rather an attitude which impregnates all aspects of the educational centre's life and shapes the culture of cooperation, which extends to all times and situations.
On the other hand, in the specialist literature, (Aronson & Patnoe, 1997; Johnson et al., 1991; Johnson et al., 2006), there is sufficient support for cooperative learning as a strategy which improves both the quantity and the quality of the work of a group of students.
The present chapter, based on the experiences of our teaching group, named *COMPING,* (Montoya et al., 2007; Montoya et al., 2008), aims to show that coordinated action can achieve both educational and social aims which would otherwise not be attained. It also shows that as a result of collective action we obtain benefits which are both sought after and shared by all: holistic education of the student and the professional development of the lecturer.
Although most of the studies carried out on teamwork among teachers have focussed on Primary and Secondary Education (López, 2007), the majority of their considerations can also be applied to the university. In our specific case, the fact of belonging to a teaching group has allowed us to work in conjunction as a team, enhancing our teaching skills with a constant process of reflection, training and innovation, through a meeting point and a strategy of permanent communication using taking advantage of a virtual learning platform.

The rest of this work, will attempt to answer some of the following questions: Do lecturers work as a team?, Do lecturers need to develop the competence of teamwork of cooperative work in teaching teams?, What problems arise from teamwork?, What is the basis for cooperative work?, Why is teamwork important?, Which competences does it develop?.

2. Do Lecturers work as a team? Do we need to develop this competence? Why is individualism the prevalent attitude among lecturers?

Despite consensus on the need to work as a team and to collaborate, lecturers very seldom do so. Individual work, and all too often individualism, are present in the daily work of numerous lecturers who work independently of their colleagues and who do not encourage cooperative work in their classes.
One of the major difficulties facing cooperative work, as has been explained earlier, is the competitiveness and individualism which characterizes our teaching faculties and our society as a whole. Many writers on this topic agree that individualism, secretism and isolation are constantly to be found in our educational system: most lecturers continue to teach alone, in the isolated atmosphere of their classrooms.

One of the fundamental causes of individualism on the part of lecturers is the conditions in which they work, and more generally, the regulations which impose on them the structure of their post. The fact that the initial training of lecturers, and the whole of their university education, tends to give teamwork a minor or secondary role, reinforces in future lecturers the idea prevalent in our society that this way of working is only useful for tasks of little importance, as relevant activities tend to be based on competitiveness and efficiency.

Competitive societies establish a more or less open struggle between the people or groups they comprise. In such a context the interdependence of aims or resources is impossible, since there are relationships of negative reciprocity in which the projects of others are felt to interfere with one's own. Competitiveness complicates and can even prevent interaction between lecturers (Gitlin, 1987).

Competition creates a social environment which is contrary to cooperation, but on occasions lecturers do not work together on teaching tasks due to a lack of stimuli, since, on the whole, teaching work is not valued as highly as research tasks.

Another disadvantage which arises from cooperation is the so-called balkanization (Day, 1999). This refers to a type of cooperation which divides and separates lecturers into isolated, and often confronted, sub-groups within the same department or faculty. Balkanization can be said to occur when lecturers work together more closely than in an individualistic society, but in groups, remaining loyal and linking themselves to a given collective of colleagues. A radical proposal would be to suppress departmental organizations in favor of course/degree-level ones (teaching teams on both a horizontal and a vertical plane). This would approach the mobile mosaic in which universities would have more permeable departmental limits, lecturers could belong to more than one department, their category would not be so important, and this type of organization and its leadership would be expected to change in time. Once differences in prestige and power within the departments are eliminated or at least reduced, leadership and its rewards would also be reduced, and the third step would be to debate conflicts and solve them in a continual process of sincere, democratic and ethical procedures. In this way, power struggles would not lead to new hierarchies or balkanization processes.

As a rule, lecturers find it difficult to work as a team even when they want to. They have no tradition of working in this way, and neither have they been prepared to do so. Book states that even though teachers might like to work cooperatively and share their ideas with their colleagues, they do not know how to do so, (Book, 1996).

Educational institutions demand that they collaborate with their colleagues in certain unalterable conditions. Cooperation can be encouraged, but it cannot be required of lecturer, as that would contradict the very principles on which it is based.

3. Why is cooperative work important? On what is it based?

Most lecturers agree on the need for cooperation in their teaching work in order to innovate, to change and in general to develop the educational system. Cooperating and collaborating is not easy in our social and cultural context, but our experience as a teaching group has allowed us to confirm that teams of lecturers working in conjunction support one another in order to reach shared goals. It is true that this activity goes against the grain of the neoliberal globalised view which tries to create a single pedagogic belief based on values such as individualism, competitiveness, obsession with efficiency and separating the means from

the end. However, it is also true that the work of these groups of lecturers is creating an alternative horizon. Guided by a utopian aim which implies the practice of solidarity and social justice, they also contribute towards a truly democratic society. In short, by cooperating we are part of the necessary cultural battle to combat neoliberalism and create a culture of cooperation.
From the perspective that these thoughts provide we can understand the reasons why collaborating is not an easy task, but also why it is indispensable one.

3.1 Requirements for cooperative work

Cooperative work does not merely imply that several people work together. Those people must be working towards common goals in such a way that individual team members are not able to achieve their aims unless their fellow team members achieve theirs. In cooperative work nobody succeeds at the expense of others, and individual triumph is incompatible with collective failure. A set of objectives which unite the team, the common goal, is of paramount importance in teamwork. These shared goals must motivate team members to carry out a common task. According to (Johnson et al., 1991) cooperation consists of *"working together to achieve common goals"*. These authors also outline the conditions which cooperative teamwork should fulfill:

1. There should exist positive interdependence of aims, resources and roles, so that individual success and group success are interrelated. In a cooperative scenario individuals strive to obtain results which are beneficial both for themselves and for the rest of the group.
2. There should exist both individual and group responsibility regarding the attainment of aims.
3. The group as a whole must accept responsibility for achieving the proposed aims, while at the same time individual members are responsible for successfully carrying out their corresponding part of the task. Nobody can oppose the work of other group members and responsibilities cannot be diluted within the group.
4. Group members should possess the skills of interpersonal and group exchange.
5. There should be an awareness of collective functioning which allows the group as a whole to asses to what extent the aims are being achieved and efficient working relationships are being maintained. The group must decide whether their members' actions have positive or negative repercussions, and consequently they should either encourage or modify said actions.
6. There should exist face to face interaction, in such a way that proximity and dialogue allow the creation of dynamics of help, support and reinforcement among team members. In this way they acquire a personal commitment to one another and to their common goals.

The interdependent structure of aims intrinsic to cooperative work contrasts sharply with the independent objectives of individual work and the opposing goals which are characteristic of competitive tasks. In individual work each participant works in isolation, and in competitive tasks each individual competes with the others, and the achievement of one individual's aims is detrimental to those of the others. In the opinion of Little in (Little, 1996), the above-described interdependence of aims also constitutes the defining characteristic of cooperation and it is manifested in the fact that each member of the group promotes the growth of the others.

Sharing educational aims constitutes, especially for Rosenholtz, one of the conditions which influence the depth with which lecturers collaborate and offer one another advice and support. For this author, whether or not there is concensus regarding educational aims is most important. She considers that when there is a moderate or low degree of concensus regarding aims, lecturers tend to stress their students' mistakes rather than their achievements. However, when there is a high degree of concensus and shared aims, desires and values, the teaching staff give priority to educational principles and the students' interests, thus creating a wave of opinion which affects even new arrivals and leads to a positive line of work, (Rosenholtz, 1989).

Not only does cooperative work offer a way to improve the completion of tasks, it also constitutes a different approach to teaching, providing a novel response to habitual teaching problems.

Cooperative activities must not be promoted by external compensation or maintained as compulsory tasks. As such, the basic requirement for carrying out cooperative activities is the existence of shared objectives. Going back to the idea that the existence of common goals is the basic characteristic which allows us to define teamwork, we could say that sharing teaching goals constitutes a fundamental and nonnegotiable requirement on which teamwork among teachers must be based.

Democracy and equality of opportunities are essential elements for producing the communication which forms the basis of cooperative work. Arnaus develops this idea when explaining that only horizontal exchange favors dialogue, since self-sufficiency and the feeling that one is in a superior hierarchical position have quite the opposite effect, (Arnaus, 1999).

One of the most interesting and valuable cooperative strategies is investigation-action, which considers that education is made up of structures whose change cannot be brought about by any one individual, but rather by a process of combined reflection in which the participants develop their own solutions to the problems they face. The cooperative nature of investigation-action is stressed, claiming that this activity is the missing link towards collaboration among teachers in which cooperative work acquires a central role.

a) We can identify the teaching teams that have carried out cooperative work by the activities the lecturers employ.

b) When the lecturers get involved frequently and progressively in dialogues regarding teaching.

c) When they observe one another frequently and provide constructive criticism on each other's teaching.

d) When they propose, design, research, evaluate and prepare teaching materials as a group.

e) When they learn from others while teaching.

3.2 Conditioners for the practice of cooperation

Cooperation is considered to be impossible if there are not equal conditions to express one's opinion, decide and act. Several authors stress that hierarchy puts a brake on the possibility of dialogue and prevents collaboration; besides citing (Freire, 1984), we could also refer to (Habermas, 1997), for whom any collaborative work must be carried out in an ideal situation in which all those affected should have equal right of speech. Hierarchy is contradictory to equal opportunities and therefore makes it impossible for true collaboration to take place.
However, our own experience leads us to agree completely with (Hargreaves, 1995) in that the practice of true cooperation reduces the workload, as responsibilities and pressure are shared.
In short we can say that in the course of our work we have seen that true collaboration cannot be imposed, as making it compulsory produces maladjusted cooperative practices, namely artificial collegiality and balkanization. The results of our experience allow us to state, to use a botanical simile, that collaboration is like a wild plant which will grow wherever it finds a favourable habitat, but which is ill-adapted to life in captivity. It cannot be cultivated in a nursery, but if we wish to maintain and promote it in its natural environment, we must provide it with suitable conditions in which to evolve.
We have already remarked that the prevalent values in our society prevent cooperation from flourishing. The individualism and competitiveness promoted by neoliberalism imply a division of labour based on considerations of efficiency. This means that cooperation is often relegated to minor roles or adopts maladjusted forms which limit it to the allocation of tasks, not really intending that it should work towards a common goal. Nevertheless, though cooperation is not always considered a value, it is necessary to create a culture of collaboration in which it practised and promoted. This is the opinion of (Fullan, 2001), who states that without the capabilities of collaboration and relating it is not possible to learn enough to become an agent of social improvement:
"Our ability to learn is limited if we remain isolated. The ability to collaborate, on a small or large scale, is becoming one of the basic requirements of postmodern society. Personal strength, providing it is open (i.e. directed toward research), and efficient collaboration go hand in hand - indeed, without personal strength collaboration would have more form than content. Personal skills and group skills feed off one another in learning organisations. People need one another to learn and carry out projects", (Fullan, 2001).

4. Why have we decided to work as a team? What are the benefits for students, lecturers and the faculty as a whole?

On the whole it is fair to say that education is considered a difficult task and a challenge to teachers. Even the most experienced teachers require assistance, and if they ask for help their professional value is by no means questioned. In a cooperative working environment help is given and offered in order to attain common goals, and this undermines the self-esteem of nobody, rather it is considered necessary and recommendable (Rosenholtz, 1989). Cooperative thinking regards education as a collective task and offers the necessary conditions to improve it via analysis, experimentation and peer-evaluation. Along these lines, Clemente Linuesa explains some of the advantages of cooperative work: "The collaborative culture leads to processes of enrichment which are fomented by dialogue, debate and even confrontation and arguments. This may well be a source of difficulties, but these will undoubtedly be offset by the benefits obtained. Moreover, these processes allow all uncertainties and doubts about the educational process to be shared. Sharing common problems is a way of learning to solve them, whereas the fear of failure often arises from the feeling of isolation. Cooperation foments an atmosphere of trust, of being open to the experiences of others, and this provides the teacher with greater confidence", (Clemente Linuesa, 1999).

Another aspect to bear in mind is the desprofessionalization in the integral education of specific people which arises from the division of education into multiple disciplines, each of which has a group of specialised teachers. According to (Martínez Bonafé, 1998), this division of work separates the concept of education from putting it into practice, and the teacher becomes a technician carrying out what is prescribed. This in turn demands a concerted effort of cooperation within the teaching team (Gimeno Sacristán, 1988). Cooperative work, then, makes very clear sense in our society, in our educational system in general and in the University in particular, and there is obviously a need for it, even though it does not correspond to predominant values. This need demands that we work towards a culture in which cooperation is not only possible, but becomes habitual practice. *"Dewey states that education is carried out in social interaction by means of communication. Cooperation is one the principles which must guide teachers to develop their teaching activity with students and to work with their colleagues/peers. Rather than facilitating education, processes of cooperation actually constitute the very essence of education"* (Angulo Rasco, 2000).

4.1 Benefits of Cooperative Work among Lecturers

Cooperative work among lecturers is not easy, demanding as it does numerous requirements which are not always fomented by the teaching environment. Nevertheless it is a worthwhile task. Numerous authors have outlined the benefits of cooperative work among teachers (Little, 1996; Hargreaves, 1995):

1. It offers moral support and assurance to group members, increasing the possibility to carry out research tasks and to put innovative ideas into practice.
2. It increases coordination between teachers, encouraging their involvement, to the benefit of the degree course and the centre.
3. It reduces excess work, since responsibilities and pressure are shared.
4. It increases teachers' capacity for reflection and facilitates access to new ideas and creativity.
5. It provides more opportunities to learn and foments continual improvement.
6. It supports social transformation and a change of values.

As we have seen, cooperative work provides many advantages, but the most important one is the moral support and assurance that it provides to group members. Our experience as a teaching group has shown us that working together as a team we feel more confident, since our teaching work is backed up by our fellow team members. According to (Hargreaves, 1995), this support constitutes one of the principles which facilitate perfectionning and improvement of teaching. Through cooperative work the most vulnerable aspects of teaching are shared, thus reducing uncertainty, strengthening personal resolve and overcoming failure and frustration which might otherwise stand in the way of improvement. This personal betterment promotes the professional development of the lecturers who practise it. Among the principles which Hargreaves claims can be achieved through cooperative work, two are directly related to the above-mentioned development as professionals: opportunities for learning and the stimulus for continual improvement. Cooperative teamwork increases lecturers' opportunities to learn from one another, as in cooperating they seek solutions to the problems which arise, and in this way they perfect their methodology. Learning and improvement are based on cooperative relationships.

Improving teaching performance implies evolving in thought and behaviour in the most integrated way possible. The person, their knowledge and know-how must all advance. We cannot talk of teacher development without talking of training. The two concepts are closely linked. Professional development occurs when teachers exercise their capacity to reflect on the educational decisions taken and to reason through those decisions bearing in mind the social and political context. According to (Helsby, 2000), the two most important ways in which cooperation foments professional development are the access it provides to new ideas and the increase in lecturers' self-confidence to adopt innovation. Once again it is clear that a lesser degree of uncertainty constitutes a positive element for innovation and professional development.

Johnson states that in cooperative work lecturers seek to satisfy their needs by sharing and cooperative exchange. When they offer and obtain security and psychological support, they are attending their personal needs; if they give and receive pedagogic advice they are satisfying instructional needs; and finally, when they organise the coordination of their students' learning they are attending organisational needs. The latter appear with the convenience of coordinating the students' learning and of achieving greater coherence among classes. This has several consequences, (Johnson, 1999):

1. It multiplies lecturers' efficiency, as they all share the same aims, attitudes and ideas.
2. It allows us to identify what is important and to discard what is not, without incurring in contradictions and incoherent attitudes.
3. It helps to avoid the omission of key aspects or unnecessary repetition.
4. It increases the coherence of the teaching team as they are all acting along the same lines of cooperative work for the benefit of the students.
5. It allows attitudes to be developed which would not be attained by the individual work of isolated lecturers.

One of the basic recommendations for the Implantation of the European Higher Education Space is that innovative educational work should be carried out in the framework of a coordinated teaching team, and not in an individual manner in each subject. Some specific examples in which lecturers will have to coordinate to fulfil these goals are (Montoya, 2008):

1. Analysing as a whole the students' workload and schedule (total number of hours or the effort required both inside and outside the classroom according to the ECTS), in such a way that the total work demanded of the student is suitable and is distributed reasonably each week.
2. Drawing up a chronogram of evaluations and work to be handed in, with optimum distribution from the students' point of view, without overlapping of different subjects.

3. Revision of the work to be covered in order to avoid overlapping, incoherence or omission (horizontal and vertical coordination).
4. Establishing connections between subjects by means of integrated sub-projects of varying size, so that the contents of different subjects are integrated and sequential continuity is established.
5. Designing the itinerary or the competences which will certify what has been learnt from the cross-curricular competences selected.
6. Supporting the use of common active methodologies such as cooperative learning, case studies, problem/project-based learning, etc., which allow us to develop the itinerary of competences.
7. Assigning tutors for each student, accompanied by a tutoring schedule and a rational timetable (tutorials, seminars, free mornings or afternoons).
8. Proposal of internal or external activities and shared supplementary material.
9. Carrying out surveys as a means of feedback on the process, group reflection and proposals for improvement.

Teamwork, therefore, increases the coordination between lecturers both horizontally and vertically, involves them more in the structure of the degree course, and leads to improved performance of the students, since it facilitates the allocation of responsibilities among lecturers, risk taking and the adoption of different new teaching strategies. In these circumstances the efficiency of the faculty and the course's capacity to respond to the needs of the current environment are greatly enhanced.

4.2 Benefits of Cooperative Work for the students: the development of competences

Cooperative work developed through students' cooperative learning guarantees the acquisition of basic social skills which are important for carrying out work and which also require that students are committed to their own learning process, as experience with our students has taught us (Gil et al., 2007; Gil et al., 2008; Montoya et al., 2008). In summary, it promotes the following:

1. Development of interpersonal skills.
2. Development of high level intellectual skills.
3. Responsibility, flexibility and self-esteem.
4. Work of all: each individual bears part of the responsibility towards his/her colleagues.
5. Generation of support networks for students at risk.
6. Generation of a greater degree of enthusiasm and motivation (in both lecturers and students).
7. Promotion of in-depth as opposed to superficial or memory learning.

This relationship also favours the efficient completion of the task and the personal and social relationships of those involved in the cooperation due to the motivation it provides and the superior reasoning it encourages. The personal relationships between participants also become more positive, that is more committed and team-oriented, and the mental health, self-esteem and social development of all participants improve. These benefits of cooperative activity can be grouped in three large categories: better performance, more positive relationships and improved mental health. The better performance is due to the greater level of reasoning and motivation which the group foments. As regards the capacity to reason, constructivism provides students with the chance to mediate and learn from one another. This interaction leads them to socio-cognitive conflict and provides them with the opportunity to help themselves in the zone of close development (Duran Gisbert, 2001). Cooperation also constitutes a social strategy and a chance for personal betterment. Belonging to a group implies forming part of a collective which offers security and friendship, but also the communication established between group members cements a relationship which satisfies their needs, desires, motivations and interests. It also leads to the growth of their personal identity, as they appropriate beliefs, emotions and motivations which are present in the collective. The individual and social development of group members is therefore promoted.

The collective process involved in cooperation also favours the participants' social development by increasing their degree of social maturity and their socialisation resources.

4.3 Our Teaching Group and the use of the Virtual Platform

In the field of education, new information and communication technologies are giving rise to a wide variety of tools which greatly facilitate not only the students' learning process, but also the coordination between lecturers.

Our teaching group (COMPING), was created both as a training project and to foment a coordinated and united teaching team with a common approach and aims (Montoya et al., 2007; Montoya et al., 2008). Our way to work and communicate has been via the WebCt platform (Fig. 1). This has allowed us to develop our own knowledge of the above-mentioned topics on the one hand, and to practise the coordination of a course as if we were a teaching team on the other. Working in this way has also allowed us to reduce the number of meetings to be attended while at the same time maintaining daily communication with each other.

In this way the course created for the platform fulfils three fundamental tasks:

- First of all, as commented previously, it constitutes a forum and meeting point for all the lecturers in the team.
- Secondly, all updated general information generated by a given group is available to students at any time throughout the course.
- Finally, the university community as a whole can find all the actions developed in the framework of the project and take an active part active in its progress.

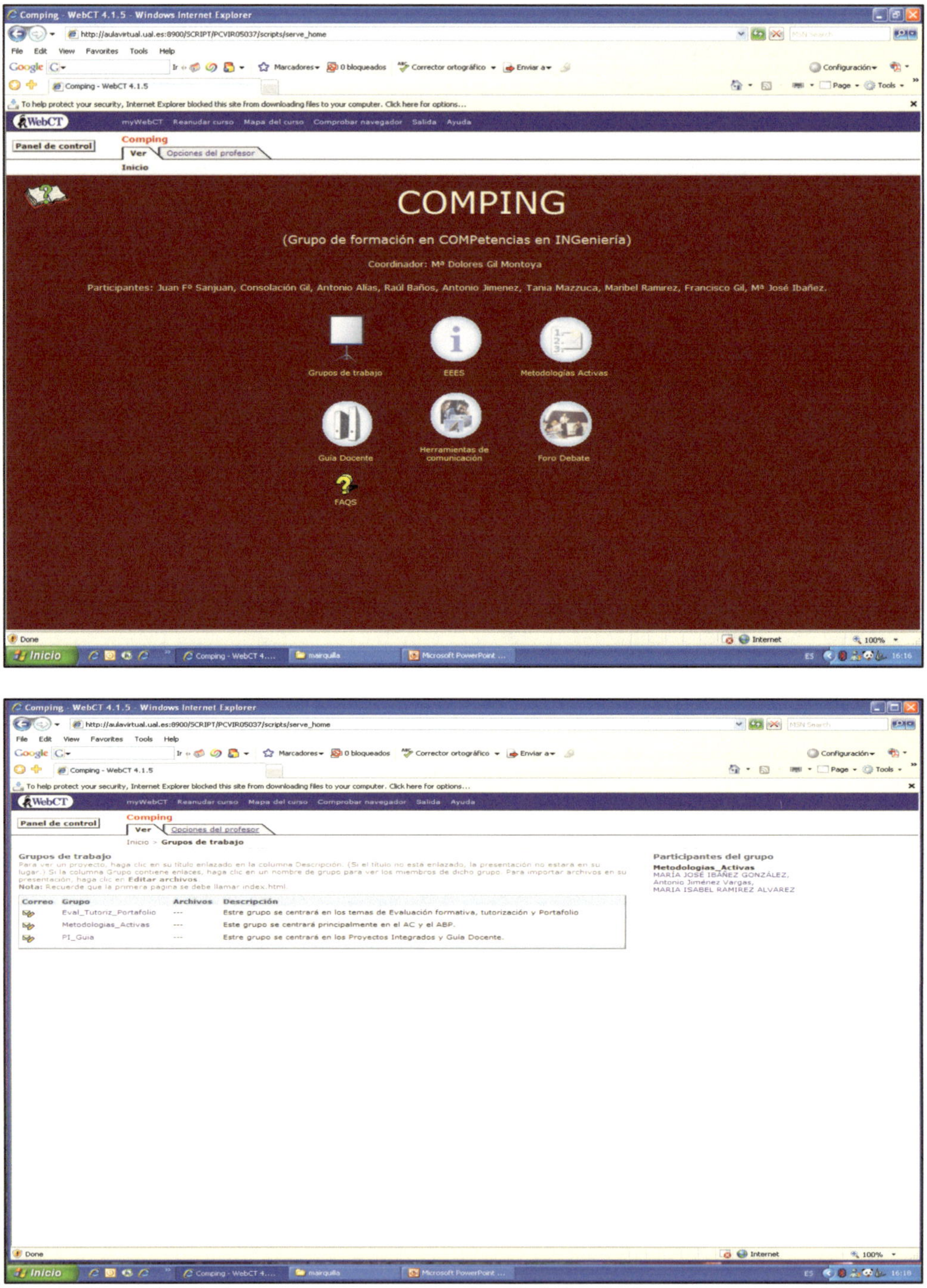

Fig. 1. Example of the course created on the WebCt platform for our teaching group "Comping" (Work on engineering competences) with three cooperative work groups.

5. Proposals to promote Cooperative Work among teaching staff

In our experience, cooperation has many advantages: it provides the chance to carry out difficult tasks thanks to the support of the group; it increases coordination among teaching staff and involves them in the improvement of the degrees and centres/faculties; but most importantly, the members of the group give each other moral support and confidence. Most of the teachers involved feel that they carry out their professional duties with a greater feeling of confidence and with the backing of their colleagues.

Through cooperation, according to (Johnson, 1991), lecturers satisfy personal needs, obtaining security and psychological support; they satisfy teaching needs, as they receive pedagogic advice; and they satisfy organisational needs on coordinating their students' learning. Though all three types of needs are important, the personal ones are particularly so, since our experience as a teaching group has shown us that confidence and psychological support are indispensable for professional innovation and development. Lecturers usually conceptualise this development as personal enrichment, they continually refer to it as one of the most important advantages of cooperative work.

One of the ways cooperation contributes to improving teaching is its capacity to foment innovations in degrees.

If we want practical innovation to be encouraged in our classes, therefore, we should turn to cooperation with other lecturers. As we can see in the following quote, is of the same opinion, basing the capacity to implement reforms on the learning of behaviour, skills and beliefs which are produced through interaction:

"The theory of change which I have been expounding clearly points to the importance of the relationships between colleagues in the same centre. Changing implies learning to do something new, and interaction is the cornerstone of social learning. The new sense, new behaviours, skills, abilities and beliefs depend to a significant degree on whether the teaching staff work in isolation or exchanging ideas, support and positive feelings on their work. The quality of work relations among staff is linked closely to its implementation." (Fullan, 1999).

If we wish to promote cooperative work we will have to implement measures which help to encourage this type of activity. These measures should be established from all areas or institutions which have something to say on the matter: educational authorities, universities, centres and faculties and their management teams, departments, teaching staff and other groups such as teacher training units.

Going back to the first point, the existence of common goals, brings us to the final aim of this chapter: how to develop cooperative work in the centre/faculty and in the classroom.

1. To develop initiatives of cooperative work and teamwork it is necessary to promote interest in carrying out common projects.
2. Teaching groups must have the autonomy to decide the contents of their teaching activity and the time needed to carry it out. Only in this way can true cooperation be achieved.
3. It would be convenient to analyse the type of cooperative work adopted by a group, to evaluate and take advantage of the possibilities it offers, and to continue progressing toward a greater degree of interaction.
4. To improve the teaching-learning process and to enhance teaching professionality, teaching staff should work in teams. This practice provides numerous advantages such as

offering moral support for innovation and reform, improving the capacity for analysis, and supporting the change in values.

5. Cooperative work improves self-esteem and gives rise to the establishment of shared norms, bonds of affection and social relationships. By recognising others as people we can relate to and work with, we participate in an experience of personal development and social solidarity.

6. Cooperative work should be promoted to improve the training of lecturers and their professional development.

7. To facilitate cooperative work we should try to ensure that the group members possess certain characteristics such as compatible educational beliefs, willingness to debate and democratic attitudes. We should also try to minimise the effects of competitiveness and the lack of cooperative tradition in education and the existence of universities and centres/faculties whose organisational structures make cooperation difficult.

8. To combat the individualism which usually characterises teaching and prevents access to new ideas, we should promote, within a cooperative framework, that individuality which encourages the teachers' initiative and creative strength.

9. We should ensure that the cooperative work is authentic, not simply a process of artificial collaboration masquerading as joint work but not providing any of its benefits.

10. Centres/faculties should do their best to avoid situations of collaboration in isolated groups, such as departments or areas, which prevent the development of the centre or faculty as a whole.

11. When evaluating the performance of teaching staff, we should take into account the merits achieved through cooperative activities and teaching coordination.

12. New organisational structures should be created which include several departments or which are transversal to several of them. This would alleviate the balkanization effect which the current structures produce.

13. We should design and promote organisational structures which complement the different areas and departments in centres and faculties. These structures would group the teaching staff according to alternative criteria which each centre should establish (projects to be developed, priorities, activities, etc.). In this way collaboration would be encouraged by working within structures which the centre would establish according to its own goals.

14. We should create mechanisms by which the teaching staff can cooperate in voluntary groups which deal with topics of personal and common interest.

15. The times at which the teaching staff are not directly occupied with students should coincide.

16. Areas and departments should be managed truly democratically in order to avoid them becoming politicised groups in which the struggle for power and status leads to an organisation of work segmented into balkanized groups.

17. The management team should organise the distribution of teaching work in such a way as to make cooperation necessary.

18. Centres and faculties should assess the evolution of their collaborative processes, bearing in mind the processes themselves rather than the ends achieved.

19. We should foment and reinforce the evolution of teaching organisations that are structured horizontally and vertically, in which cooperative work is the basis for achieving common aims.

20. The initial training of teaching staff should be substantially modified, including in the curricula contents which encourage reflection on cooperative activities and their advantages, using methodologies aimed at practising cooperation in all subjects, while also promoting collaboration among the teaching staff in charge of training.
21. Permanent training of teaching staff should pay special attention to cooperation, on the one hand as an element of the working methodology in the classroom, and on the other as a topic for study and consideration in the methodology of the centre.
22. Permanent training activities should also be modified substantially, preferably basing methodology on cooperation among lecturers, given the great potential of this activity for professional development.
23. Both initial and permanent training should encourage skills of interpersonal exchange and awareness of group functions.
24. All parties involved in the educational process should ensure that suitable conditions are created and maintained for cooperation among lecturers to be both necessary and possible, thus contributing towards the development of a culture of cooperation.

The development of collaborative cultures in educational centres carries multiple pedagogic, social and political implications. As authors such as (Tonucci, 1981) or (Freire, 1984) have long expounded, collaborating and cooperating with colleagues in teaching tasks implies committing oneself to a society based on different values; now we also know that cooperation brings us many benefits, such as stimulating our professional evolution and creating emotional bonds which enrich us and allow us to recognise ourselves by recognising our colleagues as people with whom we wish to share. The intuition which guided us in our first years of teaching has with time become a conviction: more than ever we consider it necessary to build a society in which cooperation is considered positively, while at the same time rejecting competitiveness and the hierarchy that goes with it. In short, we wish to foment a society in which a culture of cooperation can be developed; one which recognises the priority of ethics and justice over the market, and which is based on collective values of solidarity.

6. Conclusions, Cooperative Work: The Great Challenge

This cooperative culture is not characterised by the number of meetings called or by how long they last, but rather by the depth of the relationships created and the way in which cooperation extends to all areas, enabling it to improve continually. Moreover, the importance of cooperative work goes much further, as it implies committing to an educational system and a society based on values which are opposed to individualism and competition. This is, in fact, the true challenge facing cooperative work.
The results obtained with cooperative work surpass the individual capabilities of the group members, as the group is the sum of its parts. Indeed, cooperative work has allowed us to carry out a whole process of reflection, training and innovation in our own teaching practice. In short, the numerous positive consequences that cooperative work offers both students and lecturers are: it reduces uncertainty, facilitates access to new ideas, improves efficiency and efficacy, reduces overload of work, increases the capacity for reflection, makes needs of different types common elements, achieves better performance, establishes more positive personal relationships, enhances mental health, stimulates creativity, allows

us to understand better how others think, defends professional interests and demands, adapts the curriculum to the context and to the students' needs, and above all creates the bases for new theoretical constructions, increases opportunities to learn, to improve continuously and to advance in one's professional career. Cooperation, moreover, constitutes the basis for any innovation, whether among lecturers or students. Sharing common aims in educational programming, taking them into the classroom and assessing them as a team allows lecturers to learn and improve continually. Teacher training should foment the skills of teamwork.

Another of the facts which underline the current need for teamwork among lecturers is the importance that cooperative work takes on in teaching teams. The compartmentalization which characterizes education today, and the resulting desprofessionalization in the competence of relating knowledge, requires a reprofessionalization in the new competence of cooperating in the framework of a teaching team. Cooperative work, therefore, is more necessary today than ever before. However, the importance of cooperation goes further still, as it implies a move towards a society based on different values.

Generally speaking, those lecturers who work in a team with their colleagues tend to practice this activity in the classroom with their students, because cooperative work is not a technical process, but rather an attitude which suffuses all aspects of the educational centre and conforms the culture of collaboration which spreads to all moments and situations, providing the assurance that we can abandon teaching based on control. This culture is not characterized by the meetings which are held, but rather by the relationships maintained, with a predominant atmosphere of help, confidence and mutual sincerity. What remains uppermost in our minds from our experiences of cooperative work is not the results obtained, but rather the very process of joint work.

Cooperation and teamwork are necessary and can make a decisive contribution to improving the educational system. Despite the difficulties this type of work entails, it constitutes one of the most urgent needs of current education. It also supposes a real challenge: that of achieving a new education for a better society.

Cooperative work among lecturers implies a definitive change in values, opting for a different, more equalitarian society in which we all seek and learn: a move from "I think " to "we believe".

7. References

Angulo Rasco J. F. et al. (2000). *Pedagogías del siglo XX*. Barcelona. Cisspraxis. Spain.

Arnaus, R. (1999). *"La formación del profesorado: Un encuentro comprometido con la complejidad educativa"* In Pérez Gómez, A.; Barquín Ruiz, J., Angulo Rasco, J. F (Eds.) Desarrollo profesional del docente política, investigación y práctica. Madrid. Akal. 1999. Spain.

Aronson, E., & Patnoe, S. (1997). *The jigsaw classroom: Building cooperation in the classroom* (2nd ed.). New York: Addison Wesley Longman.

Book, C. L. (1996). *Professional development schools.* In SIKULA, J. (Ed.). Handbook of research on teacher education, pp. 194-212. USA. McMillan Library. 1996.

Clemente Linuesa, M. (1999). ¿Es posible una cultura de colaboración entre el profesorado?. *Revista de Educación,* nº. 320, , pp. 205-221. 1999.

Day, C. (1999). Developing teachers. The challenges of lifelong learning. London and Philadelphia. Falmer Press. 1999.

Duran Gisbert, D. (2001). Cooperar para triunfar. *Cuadernos de Pedagogía* nº. 298, enero, pp. 73-75. Barcelona. Cisspraxis. Spain.

EHES, (2005). The European Higher Education Area- Achieving the Goals. Communiqué of the Conference of Ministers responsible for Higher Education in Bergen on 19 May 2005 (http://www.blogna-bergen2005.no).

Fernández, A. (2006). Nuevas Metodologías docentes. *Apuntes del taller organizado por la Unidad de Formación del profesorado de la Universidad de Almería.* Spain

Freire, P. (1984). *Pedagogía del oprimido.* Madrid. Siglo XXI.

Fullan, M. (2001). *Leading in a culture of change.* San Francisco.Jossey-Bass.

Gil, C.; Montoya, M. G.; Alías, A.; Baños, R. (2007). Comparative Study Between Individual and Group Activities. *International Technology, Education and Development Conference.* ISBN:978.84-611-4516-4.Valencia, Marzo. 2007.Spain

Gil, C.; Montoya, F. G.; Baños, R.; Alías, A.; Montoya, M. G. (2008). Competencies Development in Engineering via Active Methodologies. *International Technology, Education and Development Conference,* ISBN: 978-84-612-0192-1.Valencia, Marzo. 2008. Spain.

Gimeno Sacristán, J. *(1988). El currículum: una reflexión sobre la práctica.* Morata. 1988

Gitlin, A. (1987). *Common school structures and teacher behaviour.* In SMYTH, J. (Ed.). Educating teachers. Changing the nature of pedagogical knowledge pp. 107-119. Lewes. The Falmer Press. 1987.

Habermas, J. (1997). *Teoría de la acción comunicativa.* Complementos y estudios previos. Madrid. Cátedra. Spain

Hargreaves, A. (1995). La modificación de las culturas de trabajo de la enseñanza. *Kikirikí Cooperación Educativa,* nº. 35, diciembre 94-febrero 95,pp. 49-61. 1995.

Helsby, G. (2000). *Multiple truths and contested realities. The changing faces of teacher professionalism in England. In DAY, C.; FERNÁNDEZ, A., HAUGE, T. E. y MOLLER, J. (Eds.)* The life and work of teachers. International perspectives in changing times, *pp. 93-108. Nueva York. Falmer Press.*

Johnson D. W.; Johnson R. T. & Smith K. A (1991). *Cooperative Learning: Increasing Collage Faculty Instructional Productivity,* Vol. 20, No. 4.

Johnson, D. W.; Johnson, R. T. & Holubec, E. J. (1999). *El aprendizaje cooperativo en el aula.* Barcelona. Paidós.

Johnson D. W.; Johnson R. T. & Smith K. A. (2006). *Active Learning: Cooperation in the College Classroom.* Edina, MN., Interaction Book Company. Third Edition.

Little, J. W. (1996). *Teachers as Colleagues.* In LIEBERMAN, A. (Ed.): Schools as collaborative cultures: creating the future now, pp.165 -193. London. Falmer Press.

López, A. (2007). *El trabajo en equipo del profesorado.* Editorial GRAÓ. 2007.

Martínez Bonafé, J. (1998). *Trabajar en la escuela.* Madrid. Miño y Dávila. Spain

Montoya, M. G.; Gil, C.; Alías, A. & Montoya, F. G. (2007). The Importance of Teaching Teams as a Formative and Innovation Strategy. *International Technology, Education and Development Conference.* ISBN:978.84-611-4516-4. INTED. Valencia, Marzo 2007. Spain.

Montoya, M. G.; Gil, C.; Baños, R.; Montoya, F. G. & Alías, A. (2008). Cooperative work in the faculty and in the classroom: a key to coordination of the teaching staff and development of students' competences. *International Technology, Education and*

Development Conference. 1. ISBN: 978-84-612-0192-1. INTED. Valencia, Marzo 2008. Spain.

Rosenholtz, S. J. (1989). *Teacher´s workplace. The social organization of schools.* Columbia. Teachers College Press. 1989

Tonucci, F. (1981). Viaje alrededor de "El Mundo". *Diario de Mario Lodi y sus amigos.* Laia. Barcelona. Spain.

Tunning, (2002). Tuning Educational Strucrtures in Europe. Informe Final Proyecto Piloto Fase I. 2002 (http://www.relint.deusto.es/TUNINGProject/index.htm).

18

The Evaluation Carrousel: an Assessment Tool for Interdisciplinary Science Innovation Education

Adri Proveniers and Jan Westra
Eindhoven University of Technology / Department of Architecture, Building and Planning
Eindhoven, the Netherlands

1. Introduction

The majority of new technological developments and derived products are results of interdisciplinary science and interdisciplinary science application. From a viewpoint of the more 'classical' research methodology and education methodology the interdisciplinary science scholarship is regarded as a mythical and misty activity. Also in university ranking systems and in university research programs interdisciplinary science education is treated in a stepmotherly way.

On the other hand: the European Union (EU) Treaty of Lisbon and the Bologna Declaration lay emphasis on - especially - interdisciplinary science education. Architecture - as an 'interdisciplinary discipline' balancing on the edge of Arts and Sciences - deals from head on with this kind of problems. So the authors of this chapter argue that some recent advances in architecture education can offer 'lessons to be learned'.

Almost by definition, innovative technologies and derived services and products have to be developed in an interdisciplinary way: all kinds of bits and parts from less sustainable products, services, production and realization processes have to be reshuffled in new innovative, sustainable and peaceful ways. This important role of interdisciplinary science invention contrasts sharply with the poor image of it in traditional academic science education. One of the backgrounds of this scientific misunderstanding of interdisciplinary technological science might be the multi-paradigm character of it.

In architecture science education, similar interdisciplinary innovative problems are handled on a daily basis already for already more than 2000 years. The functioning of the Design Studio as a particular education format for this type of education will be briefly mentioned. The main subject of this chapter will be the educational role of the accompanying forms of assessment, especially the Evaluation Assessment Carrousel, which is developed at the Department of Architecture, Building and Planning, Eindhoven University of Technology.

The characteristics of the Evaluation Assessment Carrousel are discussed, among that the high important methodological feature of dealing with two different assessment levels:

- The clash of different conceptual ideas.

- The further technical detailing of these ideas.

The functioning of the Evaluation Assessment Carrousel will be illustrated true a real event: The Evaluation Assessment Carrousel of the festal closing of the autumn semester 2008-2009. Finally, conclusions will be drawn regarding the benefits of the Evaluation Assessment Carrousel for mono-disciplinary as for multidisciplinary education as well.

2. Urgent Necessity for European 'Interdisciplinary Science Innovation Education' and some dimensions of it

To encounter the intensifying competition of the Global Economy, the Lisbon Treaty of 2000 and the new start of this Lisbon Treaty in 2005 want to secure our European standards of living by increased emphasis on high developed products and services. An important role is foreseen for university education, especially technology and innovation (EU, 2005). The nowadays Financial Crisis lays still more emphasis on stimulation of economic growth true education, research and innovation, although National Government economic rescue plans tend to fall back on their more traditional economies.

In addition - as we all know - 'Global Climate Change' also covers world wide all our artificial processes and assets: agriculture, mining, industry, infrastructure, transport, services, energy, buildings and houses. The IPCC report 'Climate Change 2007; Mitigation' (IPCC, 2007) examples the vast dimensions of the problem. It discusses a large number of possible measurements against Climate Change, divided in different economical sectors: energy supply, transport, buildings, industry, agriculture, forestry and waste management. All mitigation measurements are expressed in Equivalents Giga Ton CO2. All in a global perspective and also for every measurement the rate of certainty and uncertainty is given. It is only an interim report and only covers the problem of CO2 emission and reduction, but it already needs more than 800 pages! Regarding the nowadays oppressive, upsetting, interrelated and global problems, a necessary 'Green Innovation' also needs a new inspiring, dynamic innovation mechanism what appreciates the interwoven, economy driven - but also moral driven (to provide serious world wide conflicts) - aspects of it.

So traditional educational programs, which already break adrift of their traditional technology-driven course, due to the Bologna Declaration (EU, 1999) introducing the Bachelors - Masters System, again and again will have to re-orientate themselves towards more market-driven interdisciplinary innovative directions.

3. In Contrast: the Poor Image of Interdisciplinary Technological Science Education

The relatively poor image of interdisciplinary technological science education is in sharp contrast to the new European Union (EU) emphasis on technological innovation.

By tradition, Universities of Technology are gathered around the leading mono-disciplines mathematics, physics and chemistry. These are the most important departments of the Universities of Technology. They 'own' the bulk of the hardware of the university: the main frame computers, the laboratories, libraries, prototype plants, and so on. Also a large part of the different educational programs are taken by these main departments. So the gather the main part of the annual budgets and it seems that these departments also deliver automatically the Rector Magnific of the Universities of Technology as well.

In governance research funding there is also hardly any place for multi-disciplinary science research. In the boards, which have to assess future research programs for possible future funding, the mono-disciplines are in the majority. Sometimes it is even not possible to get a multidisciplinary research proposal through the first assessment round.
Also in the governance educational quality assessment cycles multidisciplinary departments always have to explain their most basic principles of their education programs and research activities to the mono-disciple assessors from the rivaling mono-discipline departments. So it seems hardly impossible to gain a real recognized position. In coherence with this, interdisciplinary departments are very vulnerable for reorganizations. When universities have to cut their budgets, the traditional mono-discipline departments always seem to be in favour, while multi-disciplinary departments have to be totally reshuffled most of the times: their staff, their faculties, their educational programs, their research programs.

4. An overall Methodological Aspect of Interdisciplinary Science Application: a Rivalry of Theories and a Rivalry of Conceptual Ideas

One of the backgrounds of this scientific misunderstanding of interdisciplinary technological science might be the multi-paradigm character of it. The more classical relationship between the academic theoretic development of science and the technological utilization of science leads to an almost algorithmic relationship. Basic scientific research is beneficial to the academic theoretic development of science and is addressed to falsification of parts of new theory accordingly to the empirical cycle. The technological development usually takes place at universities of technology and uses all kind of theory as application. These applications have far most an algorithmic form with standardized formulas and well known rules of application. These standardized formulas and well known rules of application form steady guidelines for academic educational assessment.
In interdisciplinary science application - where architecture is gathered - there are several fields of science and several – usually not compatible – theories. Instead of the almost algorithmic relationship between theory and utilized technology, there is in interdisciplinary science a rivalry between theories and in the innovative application of these theories: a rivalry of conceptual ideas. Kuhn – the 'founding father' of scientific paradigms – states that in classical theoretic science the paradigms can only exist one after one other (1rst paradigm - clash of paradigms - 2nd paradigm – et cetera) (Kuhn, 1962). Kuhn him self states that architecture is an exception to this rule: in architecture more than one paradigm can be valid at the same time (Kuhn, 1970). After all, in architecture every rival conceptual idea has through its own expressed specific style, comfort, structural system, materialisation, detailing, specific architectural history, specific architectural theory, etcetera its own technical and scientific setting.

5. Architecture as outstanding example for Interdisciplinary Innovation Education

Architecture can be an outstanding example for interdisciplinary technological development, as it is an 'interdisciplinary discipline' balancing on the edge of Arts and Sciences – what deals from head on with interdisciplinary design and development problems. Already the Roman Architect Vitruvius, who has written the first known

professional book series about Architecture: his well known Ten Books on Architecture (Vitruvius, De Architectura/On Architecture), lays emphasis on the interdisciplinary character of Architecture. The architect has to have knowledge of almost all the existing sciences of those days: writing of treatises, drawing, sketching, geometry, optics, arithmetic, architectural history, philosophy, music, acoustics, medicine and metrology, astronomy, law, economics, and earth sciences.
Vitruvius in Book I chapter 1: The Education of the Architect
Verse 1: 'The Architect should be equipped with knowledge of many branches of study and varied kinds of learning, for it is by his judgement that all work done by the other arts is put to test. This knowledge is the child of practice and theory. Practice is the continuous and regular exercise of employment where manual work is done with any necessary material according to the design of a drawing. Theory, on the other hand, is the ability to demonstrate and explain the productions of dexterity on the principles of proportion.'
Verse 2: 'It follows, therefore, that architects who have aimed at acquiring manual skill without scholarship have never been able to reach a position of authority to correspond to their pains, while those who relies only upon theories and scholarship were obviously hunting the shadow, not the substance. But those who have a thorough knowledge of both, like men armed at all points, have the sooner attained their object and carried authority with them.'
Regarding to Pytheos, who said that the architect should be leading top-class on all those different Arts and Sciences (Vitruvius, Book 1, prologue, verse 12) Vitruvius comments that that is virtual impossible. Vitruvius points out to Pytheos that all Arts and Sciences are composed of two things: the actual craft work and the theory of it (ibid, verse 15): 'The actual undertaking of works which are brought to perfection by the hand and its manipulation is the function of those who have been specially trained to deal with a single art' (ibid, verse 16). 'The theory is shared with other scholars' (ibid, verse 15), because 'in all sciences many points, perhaps all, are common so far as the discussion of them is concerned' (ibid, verse 16) (logic and methodology). It appears, therefore, that he has done enough and to spare who in each subject possesses a fairly good knowledge of those parts, with their principles, which are indispensable for architecture that he is capable to pass judgement and to express approval in the case of those things or arts (ibid verse 16).
The Ten Books of Vitruvius are well known for their strong technical theoretical fundamentals and for his introduction of the human proportions as a frame to the whole: the famous Icon of men standing in the centre of both square and outer circle. Some parts of the ten Books also handle fresh water systems, sewerage systems, fortification of cities and also big weaponry construction to besiege fortified cities, so he was a Civil Engineer and Mechanical Engineer as well. And in a certain way of speaking: an 'unsuspected technician'. But, to point out some origin, perception and cultural meaning to architecture, he also uses a kind of literary prose with partly historicized, partly theological, partly mythical origins. For example the mythical origin of society, living together and building (book 2, chapter 1) and the origins of the 'classic orders' in warriors, gods and goddesses (book 4, chapter 1). So he also knows how to market his architectural products and give these cultural, religious, esthetical and literary 'brands', what makes him in the eyes of nowadays 'hard core technicians' an holistic, non-rational suspect again .

The discussion between Vitruvius and Pytheos refers to the key issues of multidisciplinary innovation education: how to educate such a broad scale of disciplines and how to assess the results of this education ?

6. Design Studio and Design Studio Assessment

From times in immemorial student focused learning in so called Architectural Design Studio's takes up an important part of the educational programme of architectural education (on university level: 30 to 70 percent of the programme, dependent of the year of study). The Design Studio can be described as a kind of Master Class Education and consists of some 12 to 15 students and - in most cases a professional – Master. In the Design Studio's students work on so called 'open-ended' and 'ill-structured' design assignments. Students present their work continuously and the Master responds to it out of his academic and professional habitat.

Important parts of the Design Studio Education are the assessments: the so called 'Critics'. Half way and at the end of the studio period (mostly a semester) the student has to defend his design 'in public' in front of the rest of the students, a committee of teachers and other professional and / or academic experts. These 'Critics' can be regarded as a 'notorious weak point' in today Design Studio Education. The 'Critics' cost a lot of – scarce – education time (a half to a whole day per Design Studio Group in the Masters), gave a lot of fear to the most of the students and are ineffective to give substantive feedback to:

- The design.
- The design reasoning.
- The oral and visual presentation techniques.

The basic principles of the Design Studio originate in the Master – Mate Relationship in the Middle Ages. Traditional production was the primary goal of this relationship, but there was also an educational aspect in it. The Middle Age Guild System had also the system of Masterpiece and a Jury System, which decided if the Made could become a Master.

The Jury decided behind closed doors and also in those days the Jury have some objective criteria but also a lot of subjective criteria. Notorious are the historic stories about all kinds of social and economic aspects what influenced the size of the Guilds and the number of Made who become Master.

Each country and language region has his own historical processes from Master – Made Building Guilds to today Architecture Education Institutes. In the Netherlands the first regular form of (very basic) Civil and Building Engineering Education started in the year 1756, when a Nobility Lady left a legacy for orphans to 'learn a decent job and be no longer be a burden for society'. They were educated in mathematics, building dikes and locks, shipbuilding and building (Schilt in Goldhoorn, 1996).

In the year 1817 the government founded a Royal Academy for Art and Architecture in Amsterdam and Antwerp, following the French Ecole des Beaux Arts (ibid). The Ecole des Baux Arts is gradually accepted as the start for modern architecture design education throughout the Western World. For the first time an important part of the architectural education took place through design assignments and design competitions (Grand Prix). They had Design Studio's and Design Studio Masters (both financed directly by the students themselves). Students have to deliver their designs in a fixed time and the designs were assessed through a Jury. Next to the design assignments they also had handbooks and

exams for building technology and structural design (the famous technical handbooks of Durand were both used at the Ecole des Baux Arts and the Ecole Polytechnique) (Kooijman 1995).
However, The Jury Assessment of the Ecole des Beaux Arts took place behind closed doors without any oral presentation from the students. This was also the case for all the following Schools of Architecture throughout the Western World. The closed jury system is gradually evolved since mid twentieth century into an open assessment, where the student presents his design for a Jury and fellow students. The Jury can have tricky questions and all types of unexpected and unwanted and psychological unpleasant comments. Students get undesirable high stress levels, have real black outs, get real burn outs and even worse (Anthony, 1991; Doidge, Sara & Parnell, 2000; Hall Jones, 1996; Wilkin, 1999).
In the USA this form of Jury Critics started in the fifties after the post war democratic wave after the second word war (ibid). In Europe it started after the student movements in the sixties: first in the northern countries, later in the south.

7. Educational 'Context' as a Factor

Assumedly due to the organisational context of the Anglo American School systems the Jury Critics systems have their most pure forms in UK and USA. The Critics can be very hard and with a big psychological impact on the students. A great deal of the specific literature about Critics is from Anglo American origin.
In UK and USA there is an extensive admittance exam and procedure before students can start their studies. When you passed the admittance exam of most American Schools you can never fail for an exam: you only get an A, B, C or D level. So critics CAN be hard, because only one bad Critic has no strong impact on the study carrier. And critics MUST be hard because students without any talent at all have to be convinced that is better for them to leave 'by their one's own free will' (when students pass their admittance exam only around 10 to 15 % leaves without successful ending).
The American Schools of Architecture also are strongly focused on only architecture. In the Netherlands the main stream architecture education takes place at Universities of Technology with a broader scope: our Department at Eindhoven University of Technology is named: Architecture, Building and Planning. So a more gradual selection process can take place during the Bachelors in the direction of pure architecture, or a direction with more structural design, or more building technology, or more urban design, etcetera, or: exit. Also students can fail for every exam and there are time-performance related restrictions. So students without any talent at all have the tendency to leave really by their one's own free will (from the first year students only around 50 % get their final degree).
The Jury Critics have such a tied bond with the organisational context of the Anglo American School systems, that the suggestions of change in the Anglo American literature about Jury Critics are all formulated 'inside the Box' and hardly any of the suggestions of change are 'thinking out of the Box':
Kathryn H. Anthony gives in her excellent research rapport more than 30 alternatives to the traditional Design Juries, with as common themes (Anthony, 1991, pages 132-135):
"Increased student participation

- Focus on the design process as well as the design product.
- Clarifying criteria and demystifying design.

- A higher level of learning.
- Not all students need to be present.
- Less tension and no public humiliation.
- Less time.
- Different physical environments and presentation media.
- Experiment and evaluate".

Other guidelines are (Anthony, 1991; Doidge, Sara & Parnell, 2000):

- Soften it up: give first year students and other Bachelors a more gentle kind of pre-critics.
- Give some training to the first year students for presentation, poster session, etcetera.
- Inform the Jury Members about their potential disastrous psychological impact.
- Try to establish some rules with the Jury Members.
- Give students a lot of tips as way of precaution:
    - Time management for the whole length of the Design Studio.
    - Try to get some sleep in week of the Presentation.
    - Try to eat healthy food in de week of the Presentation.
    - The well-known Presentation tips.
    - Suitable clothing and body language.
    - All kinds of Psychological tips.

Hall Jones and Wilkin go further and make the connection between the marking system of students as one of the functions of the Jury Critics and the poor learning potential of it: much to high stress levels, to incidental and not systematic, no real discussion because of 'damage control', etcetera. (Hall Jones, 1996; Wilkin, 1999).

Hall Jones suggested to remove the marking system out off the Jury Critics, so that it can take on a more educational role (Hall Jones 1996). Doidge, Sara & Parnell wonder what else will than fulfil the valid functions of the traditional Jury Critics. And: does the Jury Critics than just will be a kind of tutorial? (Doidge, Sara & Parnell, 2000, page 69).

8. Thinking Out of the Box

The Department of Architecture, Building and Planning of the Eindhoven University of Technology is much broader than only architecture and it is also focussed on more than one architectural main style. This broad approach has resulted in the development of Design Education Systems (Proveniers, 2005), Collaborative Design Systems (Schmid & Pa'l, 2002) and Design Assessment Systems which are specially focussed on interdisciplinary design and development and therefore methodological very suitable for interdisciplinary science innovation education.

The Design Assessment System: the Evaluation Assessment Carrousel, is addressed to an open assessment and further development of already conceptual developed designs by professional experts. The Evaluation Assessment Carrousel does not bear that burden of typical Anglo American organisational context, so it can focus on new innovative aspects of future architecture education and even beyond that: basic backgrounds of interdisciplinary science cooperation for innovation.

9. Basic Principle of the Evaluation Assessment Carrousel and 'Full Carrousel

The basic principle of the Evaluation Assessment Carrousel can be best explained with a very simple variant in which four innovators simultaneously present their innovative ideas in the four corners of a hall. There are also four assessors. At the end of the first session the assessors 'turn a quarter of a circle' and the second session of innovators presentations starts. After four sessions the assessors 'have made a full circle', but of course this still isn't a real carrousel!

It really gets beneficial - and also exciting - when you scale it up to 20 or more innovators with 10 or more parallel innovator presentations and you also make a random mix up of the Assessors. Several different types of scheduling are possible, so that all innovators present their work 2, 3 or 6 times and the assessors make a double number of 'Carrousel turns'. Each presentation takes some ten minutes. After one round each student has 'a time-out' of one round, to make a few notes regarding additional comments and ideas.

10. Benefits of the Evaluation Assessment Carrousel

The benefits of the Evaluation Assessment Carrousel are:

- It frees the so feared traditional Jury Critics from its 'darker side' and makes it a motivating and inspiring happening.
- It increases the developmental role: during several presentation rounds innovators learn to make their conceptual idea more complete.
- It gives all the participants the opportunity for a quick scan of quality of the other innovations.
- It creates more insight and involvement by the different academic and / or professional expert guest critics.
- It saves time (and so: also money) from innovators and academic and / or professional expert guest critics.
- It deals with an overall aspect of interdisciplinary science application: a rivalry of theories and a rivalry of conceptual ideas (see next section).

11. Assessment of Interdisciplinary Innovative Design: Two Levels

As already stated some sections before: in interdisciplinary science application - where architecture is gathered - there are several fields of science and several – usually not compatible – theories. Instead of the almost algorithmic relationship between theory and utilized technology, there is in interdisciplinary science a rivalry between theories and in the innovative application of these theories: a rivalry of conceptual ideas.

This rivalry of conceptual ideas - at which each single idea is based on and executed in different technologic scientific bodies of knowledge - demands a special form of educational assessment. This educational assessment needs to deal with two different levels:

- The first level of the clash of different conceptual ideas from different students.
- The second level of the quality of the further execution of each of those conceptual ideas and the technical detailing of it.

So the fear of Doidge, Sara & Parnell that Jury Critics without marking function has hardly any educational assessment function is groundless! The 'Evaluation Assessment Carrousel' addresses itself mainly to the level of competing conceptual ideas. During several presentation rounds students learn to make their conceptual idea more complete, as they learn from comments from the mix of different academic and / or professional specialists. Design Studio teachers use it as a quick scan of quality of the other Studio's and for the other guests it leads also to increasing commitment. Students can use this experience later on the day, when they present their design to their Design Studio teachers. The teachers also take in to account the second level of interdisciplinary innovative design: the execution of the idea and the technical detailing. After all the presentations, when the students have left the room, the teachers can study drawings, written presentations, etcetera and give the marks.

This two level assessment model corresponds also with scientific insight in educational assessment. Moerkerke and Dochy distinguish two basic forms for the educational assessment for complex academic competence:

- Holistic assessment methods what in this case can be used for the ranking of competing conceptual ideas.
- Rational (checklist) assessment methods what in this case can be used for ranking of the further execution of the conceptual idea and the technical detailing of it.

Moerkerke en Dochy conclude that for the educational assessment for complex academic competences a mix of both is used (Moerkerke & Dochy, 1997). The resemblance with the answer from Vitruvius to the remarks of Pytheos is remarkable: a distinction between conceptual ideas and refined technical detailing of these conceptual ideas!

12. The Carrousel in Full Action: the Festal Closing of the Autumn Semester 2008-2009

In the night preceding the Evaluation Assessment Carrousel students make their last preparations to their posters, models and oral presentations. The electronic lock system of the building is already activated and some of the students are too late and they wait inside the door till a 'lost' faculty with an electronic key leaves the building and they also can slip away.

An other student in architecture sits with his fellow housemates: students from other departments in their favourite student-pub. For the final time he tries to explain to them where his concept is all about. He draws it at the back site of a beer mat and this time he is so successful in image it in words and views, that he decides to take the beer mat with him to the next days Carrousel!

It is early morning of Friday 19th of December 2008. It is a dark and cloudy day and the lights of the Christmas tree's in the hall of the department building enlightens the first students to arrive to put their posters and models at the most eye-catching spots on the 4th floor. Later the dean arrives, who is in charge of the Carrousel and also the Design Studio teachers and the first guests critics who want to have a first preview to be better prepared. There is a light excitement in the 'Atelier': Four Pre-Master Design Studio's with students who finished a kind of Bachelor Degree else were and want to do their Masters in Architecture in Eindhoven. So for them it is a kind of admittance assessment for the Masters

(regular Eindhoven Bachelors have 'free access' to the Masters). For the Design Studio teachers there is also some excitement: it is more or less a kind of assessment for them to.
The four weeks project was about the rearrangement of a large square in one of the formal villages, what now form Eindhoven: an urban conglomeration of 15 km by 15 km. In the facades of the square and also in the neighbouring streets, are stores with more than local customer interest - although it is not the city centre of Eindhoven. That's why the square is used as parking place, but not at Saturday, when there is a well-known large food and merchandise market at the square, with opportunity to purchase nice deals, because it is nearly Sunday (in the Netherlands shops are closed on most of the Sundays). There are all kinds off multi-cultural fast food and to visit it, is a special kind of fun shopping. Students analysed the square and surroundings, developed conceptual ideas for the rearrangement of the square and bits of facade (first level of innovative assessment). They also made the further detailed design of one of the new buildings (second level of innovative assessment).
Beside academic and / or professional Guest Critics, the dean has arranged a film crew who -temporary - places an impression of the designs and the Evaluation Assessment Carrousel on a local neighbourhood internet page and also citizen are invited. There is a growing excitement when starting time is near...
To organise this all could be a hell of a job, but not when you use a smart open ended scheme!

Design Studio Assessment Carrousel Organisational Scheme

	1	2	*3*	*4*	*5*	*6*	*7*	.	*14*
1	A		G		D				
2	B		H		E				
3	C		I						
.									
33		A							
34		B							
35		C					et cetera		
36									

1 .. 14: ***Presentation rounds***
1 .. 36: Students
A, B, C ... Critics
X,Y,Z 'Mystery Guest Critics'

When a student arrives, his or hers name and number are put on a screen on the wall and he or she gets the Carrousel Scheme. He or she receives a big paper sheet with on it his or hers number of arrival (1...36). He or she puts his / hers paper sheet on top of his / hers Poster presentation.
When a Critic arrives, his or her name and character are put on an other screen on the wall and he or she gets the Carrousel Scheme as well. He or she receives a big paper sheet with on it a character (A ...Z).
The Carrousel Scheme is 'instant put together', so 'the Carrousel can 'turn and turn' even when students and Expert Critics are coming late or don't show up at all.

The dean sounds the gong and the first round starts. It is still not at ease and the paper sheets with numbers and characters function as a kind of 'meeting point device'. When the dean observes that a number of discussions are in a finishing stage, he sounds the gong for the second round. He may 'play' with the time to establish different educational and communicational goals. Students have one round off, so they have some time to write things down and adjust their presentation. Or later on: to listen to fellow students.
After two hours turning of the Carrousel, the Critics were invited to a lunch, also for an informal evaluation. In the afternoon the 'one to one' student - teacher assessments took place where marks and / or 'strong advices to leave' were given.
Afterwards, a drink for staff and students, a final emotional release and the end of the semester is near .
An Impression of this Design Studio Assessment Carrousel was for a couple of months available at: www.citytv.nl , so citizens, other professional experts and local politicians could also benefit of the expertises.

13. Conclusions and Discussion

This study examined the possibilities for the Evaluation Carrousel to function as an assessment tool for by the European Community stimulated interdisciplinary science innovation education. The particular position of interdisciplinary science innovation education is comparable with that of academic architecture education: a two millennia old discussion between Vitruvius and Pytheos refers to the key issues of multidisciplinary innovation education: how to educate such a broad scale of disciplines and how to assess the results of this education?
The functioning of the Design Studio as a particular education format for this type of education was only mentioned briefly. The problem of the assessment was placed in its educational context:

- In more single-paradigm, mono-discipline, rational approach Schools of Technology traditional assessment methods as 'Design Critics' will be used.
- In more multi-paradigm, interdisciplinary, mixed holistic and rational Schools of Technology the Evaluation Assessment Carrousel can be used.

The Evaluation Assessment Carrousel tackles a problem what occurs by interdisciplinary science innovation: the presence of two different assessment levels:

- The level of the clash of different conceptual ideas from different students.
- The level of the quality of the further execution of each of those conceptual ideas and the technical detailing of it.

Basically, this multi-paradigm issue and this two level assessment issue can be regarded as the modern version of the two millennia old discussion of Vitruvius and Pytheos again: the equilibrium between a single paradigm mono-disciple approach and a multi-paradigm multi-disciple approach.
The Carrousel is an excellent assessment tool for particularly the first level:

- It provides a quick scan for Design Studio Teachers for quality of interdisciplinary innovative competing conceptual ideas.
- It functions also as an additional educational tool: the 'on the job training' for students to complete their creative conceptual ideas.

So - in a wider scientific educational perspective - the Evaluation Assessment Carrousel can serve as a suitable educational assessment model for other innovative interdisciplinary science practise, if this practise leads to a rivalry of theories and a rivalry of conceptual ideas.
The Evaluation Assessment Carrousel already turns over more than 15 years at the Department of Architecture, Building and Planning at Eindhoven University of Technology. The educational aims are sharpened and organisational problems were tackled true the development of the flexible organisational scheme.
New 'out of the box thinking' applications are:

- The use as a kind of admittance assessment for the Masters, since the activation of the Bachelors Masters system from the Bologna Declaration, as described in a preceding section.
- The use as a 'bonding device' since the Faculty grows apart also since the start of the Bachelors Masters system
- The use as a 'start up' for scientific assessment of education and/or research of the department by governance committees.

The Evaluation Assessment Carrousel will enlighten the multi-paradigms and multi-concepts character of multidisciplinary technological education for all participants of the Carrousel. Even for mono-disciplinary scientists and mono-disciplinary assessors in governance educational quality reviews and governance research quality reviews as well! Especially when they are familiar to the problems, themes and subjects which are handled in that particular Evaluation Assessment Carrousel.
Referring to the differences between (most) American Schools of Architecture and the broad based Department of Architecture, Building and Planning at Eindhoven University of Technology, the Evaluation Assessment Carrousel can also bridge the gap between single paradigm, mono-discipline, pure rational approach Schools of Technology and multi-paradigm, interdisciplinary, mixed holistic and rational Schools of Technology. Annual or semester based, the Evaluation Assessment Carrousel gives students a glimpse in a multi-disciplinary environment, to give them a glimpse in their multidisciplinary future World ?

14. References

Anthony, K.H.,1991, Design Juries on Trial; the renaissance of the Design Studio, New York, Van Nostrand Reinhold.

Doidge, C. Sara, R. and Parnell, R. Parsons, M. (Cartoons), 2000, *The* Crit; an Architecture Student's Handbook, Oxford, Architectural Press.

EU, 1999-06, The Bologna Declaration

EU, 2005-04, Mobilizing the brainpower of Europe: enabling universities to make their full contribution to the Lisbon Strategy.

IPCC: Metz, B., Davidson, P.R., Bosch, P.R., Dave, R., L.A. Meyer(eds) (2007). Climate Change 2007: Mitigation; Contribution of Working Group III to the Fourth Assessment Report of the Intergovernmental Panel on Climate Chance, IPCC), Cambridge (UK) and New York, Cambridge University Press.

Goldhoorn, B., 1996, Architectuur als discipline, Rotterdam, Nai Uitgevers.

Hall Jones, S., 1996, Crits; an examination; In: Journal of Art and Design Education, 15 (2), 33-141.

Kooijman, D., 1995, Wortels van het Architectuuronderwijs, Delft, Delftse Universitaire Pers.

Kuhn, Thomas S., 1962, The Structure of Scientific Revolutions, Chicago, University of Chicago Press, 1970 (2nd edition).

Kuhn, Thomas S. 1970, Comment on the Relations of Science and Art; Comparitive Studies in Society and History, Chicago, University of Chicago Press.

Moerkerke, G. and Dochy, F.,1997 Het toetsen van complexe vaardigheden (pagina 232) In:ten Dam, G.,van Hout H.,

Terlouw,C. &Willems, J, 1997, Onderwijskunde Hoger Onderwijs; Handboek voor docenten,Assen, van Gorcum.

Proveniers, A.G.W.J., 2005, PhD thesis,'Leren-Creëren';een kernstrategie voor het eerstejaars atelierwerk in het universitair bouwkundig ontwerponderwijs. Bouwstenen 96, Department of Architecture, Building and Planning, Eindhoven University of Technology, the Netherlands.

Schmid, P. & Pa'l, G., 2002,An Attempt to Support Housing and Housing Science by the Method Holistic Participation (MHP) in the Light of Sustainable Development, in: The Proceedings of the XXX IAHS World Congres on Housing, 9-13 September 2002, Coimbra, Portugal, Pedro Bastista-Artes Gráficas, Portugal.

Wilkin, M., 1999, In: Doidge, C. Sara, R. & Parnell, R. Parsons, M. (Cartoons), 2000, The Crit; an Architecture Student's Handbook, Oxford, Architectural Press.

Vitruvius, The Ten Books on Architecture, Translated by Morris Hicky Morgan,1960,New York USA, Dover publications

Vitruvius, De Architectura / On Architecture Edited from the Harleian Manuscript 2767 and translated into English by Frank Granger, 1955, Cambridge Massachusetts USA, Harvard University Press.

19

Common Mistakes in the Application of Continuous Evaluation Methodologies in Spanish Universities

Juan M. Sanchez and Enriqueta Antico
University of Girona
Spain

1. Introduction

Since 1999, when the Bologna declaration was signed with the objective of creating a European Higher Education Area (EHEA) by 2010, a process was started to modify and adapt the teaching methodologies to this new set-up. Although this might be seen as only affecting European universities, it should be noted that America too has seen the need to modernise its teaching practices. For scientific studies, the standards of scientific education published by the *National Research Council* (NRC, 2000) have examined the contents and pedagogy of scientific learning and teaching, and new standards aimed at improving and modernizing scientific education are being developed.

It is interesting to observe how many teachers and specialists refer to alternatives to conventional lectures and tutorials as "new teaching methodologies" when most of these have in fact a long history of use behind them. For example, many lecturers call problem based learning (PBL) a "new teaching methodology" when the first written reference that we have found to its application in scientific studies dates from 1902 (Smith and Hall, 1902), more than 100 years ago.

Biggs and Tang (Biggs and Tang, 2007) write "in the days when university classes contained highly selected students, the lecture and tutorial seemed to work well enough. However, the increasingly drastic changes in the tertiary sector have redrawn the university scene -not entirely disadvantageously- for teaching quality." We are now seeing a greater diversity in the backgrounds of students presenting themselves in our classes, with non-traditional entrance qualifications, unequal prior knowledge and experience, and different learning styles (Brown et al., 1994). Bodner indicated that the traditional view of knowledge is "based on the hidden assumption that knowledge can be transferred intact from the mind of the teacher to the mind of the learner" (Bodner, 1986), and educators only have to focus on getting knowledge into the heads of their students. It is clear that "teaching and learning are not synonymous; we can teach, and teach well, without having the students learn" (Bodner, 1986).

There is no need to find better methodologies than lectures because there is no unique and optimum teaching methodology that works for every student. The lecture is perfectly adequate for a motivated student, but will always be insufficient for poorly motivated ones. So, the question that we have to ask as teachers is "How can we teach in a way that non-motivated students learn as motivated ones?" In this situation, it is necessary to move from passive teaching methodologies (e.g., the lecture) to active ones (e.g., PBL) as effective teaching should get the majority of students using high cognitive level processes that active students will use spontaneously (Biggs and Tang, 2007).

The main part of the methodologies that have been developed in recent years are based on the cognitive constructivism theory of Piaget, which breaks with traditional teaching models. Piaget suggests that learners cannot be given information that they immediately understand and use. Instead, people must build their own knowledge through experience, which enables them to create mental frameworks in their heads. These schemes are changed, enlarged, and made more sophisticated through two complimentary processes: assimilation and accommodation. Students should be able to build their own comprehension without repeating parrot fashion those concepts that have been explained to them or that they have read.

It is a characteristic of human nature that we try to find meaning, order and coherence in all the situations we face, including those where we do not have a part, or the whole, of the information required. Our goal as teachers is to achieve that students act in a similar way during their learning process. This is not an easy task, and it becomes more complex when we have to deal with poorly motivated students. To provide more meaningful learning for our students, we must use teaching methodologies that are both appropriate to the particular field of learning and which encourage the use of critical thinking. Those methodologies only requiring that student seats down to receive information passively must be avoided (McKeachie, 1986).

In the specific case of the Spanish university system, the almost complete lack of pedagogical formation of the university teachers has presented an important problem in this process. In Spain, university lecturers are not required to have any specific pedagogical formation before starting to teach at undergraduate level although primary and secondary school teachers do receive full training. It should be noted that during the last few years some Spanish universities, as is the case of the University of Girona, have been introducing different, non-mandatory, post-graduate courses devoted to university level teacher training.

Most teachers who have been working with different "alternative" methodologies since 1999 have been applying these methodologies without having received the necessary theoretical and practical background. This process of self-formation has gone largely unrecognized by the institutions.

2. Assessment Methodologies

The most complex, and least developed, issue regarding the application of alternative methodologies is how to asses students fairly. Continuous evaluation systems seem to be the most widely accepted by the university community in our country. This option seems to be, a priori, the fastest and simplest way to adapt traditional evaluation methodologies, which are based around a final written assessment, to the alternative methodologies. For most subjects, this apparently "simple" adaptation process has resulted in the "simple" application of different short written assignments during the term and a final assessment at the end. The mark of the students usually requires the use of a spreadsheet to calculate the final end-of-term mark giving each assessment a specific percentage value as part of the whole mark. The final exam is given a significantly greater weighting in the final calculations. Furthermore, students are normally required to pass this final exam in order to pass the term. Given this situation, it is not surprising that students wonder why they are required to perform so many assessments during the term when in the end, as with traditional evaluation, their success is dependent upon an end of term pass. This failure to provide a clearly distinct model is one of the main student criticism of the Bologna system as they see it as only increasing the level of dedication that they are required to make.

It is well known, as Boud writes, that "assessment methods and requirements probably have a greater influence on how and what students learn than any other single factor" and that "this influence may well be of greater importance that the impact of teaching materials" (Boud, 1988). Unfortunately, conventional evaluation methods are not usually adequate for alternative teaching methodologies. Therefore, our assessment strategies need a major overhaul to adapt to the changing conditions in higher education (Brown, 1999).

Brown and Knight have suggested a wide range of reasons why teachers assess students (Brown & Knight, 1994). The following might be emphasized:

- provide feedback to students so they can learn from mistakes and build achievements
- classify or grade student achievement
- enable students to correct errors and remedy deficiencies
- motivate students and focus their sense of achievement
- consolidate student learning
- help students to apply abstract principles to practical contexts
- estimate students' potential to progress to other levels or courses
- guide selection or option choice
- give teachers feedback on how effective we are being at promoting learning

An appropriate assessment method has to be able to *describe* (those aspects under discussion), *assess* and *repair* (learning mistakes and deficiencies). Traditional assessment methods are usually adequate for the second objective (assessment) but tend to forget the advice and support that students need to succeed in their studies (Brown, 1999). Another negative characteristic of traditional assessment methods is that evaluation usually takes place at times which are for the convenience of the academic programme or the teacher, rather that at the most appropriate moment for the development of the learning process of the student. Moreover, traditional methods based on a final assessment exam do not take into account the possibility of introducing feedback processes that allow students to be help to solve their mistakes and deficiencies.

A continuous evaluation system should be based on *formative* evaluation, or *process* evaluation, which is a method of judging the effectiveness of a programme whilst the programme activities are taking place (*formative* evaluation focuses on the *process*) (Bhola, 1990). *Summative* evaluation, or *product* evaluation, is not completely adequate as it is a method of judging the worth of the programme at the end of the programme activities by means of a grading system. Unfortunately, institutions always ask teachers to grade students, so requiring *summative* evaluation.

We have performed a systematic and statistical study into the efficiency of evaluation methodologies using different assessments during the term together with a final assessment exam to determine their effect as a continuous evaluation methodology.

3. Methodology

The results evaluated in this study have been obtained over five academic years (Table 1). The subject taught was "Advanced Analytical Chemistry", which is taken by students during the fifth of the eight terms that make up the Chemistry degree in the Science Faculty of the University of Girona (Spain).

Year	Students		Final Assessment	Pass Rate[b]	Marks	Pass Rate[b]
	Enrolled[a]	Sat exam	Mean (Min - Max)		Mean (Min - Max)	
2003/04	63 (23)	54	4.36 (1.67 - 7.87)	37%	**4.36** (1.67 - 7.87)	37%
2004/05	62 (16)	51	4.40 (1.88 - 7.43)	37%	**5.41** (2.48 - 8.16)	67%
2005/06	44 (13)	36	4.35 (1.97 - 6.88)	36%	**5.82** (3.47 - 8.36)	86%
2006/07	41 (9)	33	5.41 (2.28 - 8.22)	79%	**6.58** (3.76 - 9.07)	93%
2007/08	38 (2)	32	5.64 (3.67 - 7.47)	82%	**6.32** (3.59 - 8.22)	94%

Table 1. Results obtained by students in the final assessment and their marks for "Advanced Analytical Chemistry".

[a] The number of repeating students enrolled in the subject is given in brackets.

[b] Percentages are of the number of students sitting the final assessment exam.

Alternative methodologies were not in use during the first academic year (2003/04) evaluated: a single end of year final written exam was taken. The results obtained during this first year are taken as a reference to compare with the results in the final assessment exams of the other years, during which alternative evaluation methodologies have progressively been introduced.

A simple continuous evaluation methodology, based on different partial assessment exams during the term (at the end of each thematic block) and a final overall assessment exam at the end of the term, was used in 2004/05 and 2005/06. During this period, no feedback processes from the results obtained in the partial assessments were recorded. The final mark was determined by the simple summing up of the marks (each with its specific percentage

weighting). The homework of the students solving numerical problems and their oral presentation of practical cases were also introduced in the calculation of the final mark.
A self-correction process of the partial assessments, by the students themselves (individually and in small groups), to check the tests was introduced during 2006/07. Students have to discuss their answers with other members of the group to find the most appropriate one. They then have to propose their individual marks for the test to the teacher. Afterwards, tutorials of small groups are held to review the students' mistakes and misconceptions. This methodology allows to focus partial assessments exams as review exercises of the learning process of the students, rather than as just a simple exercise in grading. As a result, teachers obtain useful information about the knowledge and skills being acquired by students. The most important benefit of this methodology is that this feedback process allows teachers to detect the skills and knowledge that are not being adequately assimilated by students, and so solutions to correct them can be applied in time.
In order to compare and evaluate the effectiveness of the changes introduced in the learning process of the students, equivalent final assessments have been applied each year. These have been prepared following the same format as the one used during the first year of the study (2003/04). An effort has been made each year to prepare final assessment exams that have the same number of questions as well as a similar level of difficulty. Table 1 shows the results obtained by students in the final assessment exams, with the marks obtained each year.

4. Discussion

Statistical evaluation of the results presented in Table 1 show that there is a significant difference between the students results obtained each academic year in final assessment exams. Moreover, there is also a significant difference in the final qualifications of the subject when the percentages applied in the spreadsheet calculations are modified.

Source of Variation	**Sum of Squares**	**df**	**Mean Square**	**F**	**Sig.**
Between Groups	63.8	4	15.96	9.44	0.002
Within Groups	339.8	201	1.69		
Total	403.6	205			

Table 2. Results of the ANOVA test for the marks of the final assessments, grouped by academic years.

An *ANOVA* test has been applied to compare the results in the final assessment exams grouped by academic years and a significant difference (P=0.002) between the marks is observed (Table 2). The *Scheffé test*, applied to detect the source of differences, reveals that the marks fall into two groups (Table 3). The first group contains marks obtained in 2003/04, 2004/05 and 2005/06 (P=1.000). The second block has marks obtained during the last two academic years studied (P=0.959).
During the first academic year studied, 2003/04, sixty-three students were enrolled in the subject (23 were repeating the year, 36.5%). The students' mean mark in the assessment was 4.36 out of 10 (Table 1) and 37% of the students (20 students) passed the subject (percentage

calculated from the students who sat the test). All 40 new students sat the assessment exam and all the students that passed the exam, 20 students, were from this group. So, the pass rate of the group of student that sat the exam for the first time was 50%. Similar percentages were obtained in previous years for this subject: the inspection of academic records showed that in the previous 10 years the pass rate has ranged from 42 to 58%. A pass rate of around 50% must be considered very low when we take into account that this is a fifth term subject. At this level, students have taken all basic chemistry subjects and several advanced topics. The background of chemical knowledge of these students should be more than enough to obtain a much higher pass rate in this subject and so we are led to conclude, at least in the case of this subject, that an evaluation methodology based exclusively on final assessment is not appropriate. A further weakness is that any pedagogical conclusions which are drawn by the teacher on the bases of the results can only be applied in later years, the present students will obtain no benefit from this.

(I) Year	(J) Year	Mean Difference (I-J)	Sig.
2003/04	2004/05	-0.04325	1.000
	2005/06	0.01046	1.000
	2006/07	-1.04633	0.014
	2007/08	-1.28259	0.001
2004/05	2005/06	0.05371	1.000
	2006/07	-1.00308	0.023
	2007/08	-1.23935	0.002
2005/06	2006/07	-1.05679	0.029
	2007/08	-1.29306	0.003
2006/07	2007/08	-0.23626	0.971

	Year	n	Sub-Group for $\alpha = 0.05$	
Scheffé[(a,b)]	2005/06	36	4.3514	
	2003/04	54	4.3619	
	2004/05	51	4.4051	
	2006/07	33		5.4082
	2007/08	32		5.6444
	Sig.		1.000	0.959

[a] Sample size of the harmonic mean = 39,523.
[b] The harmonic mean is used.

Table 3. Scheffé test results for the multiple comparison of the studied variables.

During the next two academic years, 2004/05 and 2005/06, a new evaluation methodology was tested. As indicated in the methodology section, this was based on different assessment exams during the term and a final assessment exam at the end of the term. Skills and

abilities other than the level of knowledge acquired by the student were also taken into account and were included in the calculation of the final mark of the subject (e.g., the ability to solve numerical problems was evaluated from the presentation of different handouts, and communication skills were evaluated from oral presentations made in class). It was thought that this simple way of applying a continuous evaluation methodology would increase the dedication of the students to the subject, so improving their learning. However, the application of this methodology only helped students to obtain better marks without discernable improvements in the learning process being observed (Table 1 and 2). Results in the final assessment during these two years did not show any significant difference from those obtained in 2003/04 (P=1.000), and a similar percentage of students (37% in 2004/05 and 36% in 2005/06) were able to obtain pass marks in the final assessment.
The increase obtained in the final marks of the subject was the result of the assessment exams performed during the term and the other marking tasks. Participation in the continuous evaluation methodology was voluntary in 2004/05. All new students (n=46) and 2 repeaters decided to participate in this methodology. The other 3 students evaluated only sat the final assessment. It was decided that for the students accepting the continuous evaluation methodology the term work/final assessment weighting would be 60%/40%. Marks in the final assessment exam were not found to increase, and only 37% of the students passed this test. Nevertheless, 67% of the students passed the subject due to the greater weighting of the term time assessments.
The continuous evaluation methodology was also voluntary in 2005/06 but the weighting given to the tasks evaluated during the term was increased to 70%. The pass rate in the final assessment exam remained constant (36%), but the percentage of students who passed the whole subject increased to 86% due to the greater weight of the continuous evaluation elements.
These results demonstrate that the use of a continuous evaluation methodology based on different assessment tasks during the term without any feedback process significantly increases the academic marks of the students (i.e., mean final marks are more than 10% higher than the mean marks in the final assessment exam, Table 1) and yields "better" statistics for the performance of the subject. However, the learning of the students does not improve. The level of content comprehension remains unchanged (i.e., mean marks and pass rates in the final assessment exam did not change during the first three years of this study). The most remarkable and important conclusion is the fact that an increase in the weight of the evaluation tasks performed during the term results in higher marks in the final marks.
A feedback process allowing pedagogical improvements to be made was implemented in 2006/07. This feedback was based on self-evaluation and the revision of the assessment exams by the students themselves, followed by tutorials of small number of students (typically 3 or 4). This methodology allowed teachers to detect those concepts that were misunderstood by students. The feedback process gave teachers time to attempt to find solutions to these problems whilst the academic year was still in progress. The results of the self-evaluation and revision results were used to programme tutorials specifically devoted to helping students to review and correct those concepts, skills and abilities that were poorly misunderstood. The results obtained in the final assessment exam show a significant increase in the mean marks (5.41 in 2006/07 and 5.64 in 2007/08) and an 80% or higher pass

rate each year. The weighting of the tasks along the term was maintained in a 70%, which resulted in the final pass marks reaching up to 94%.

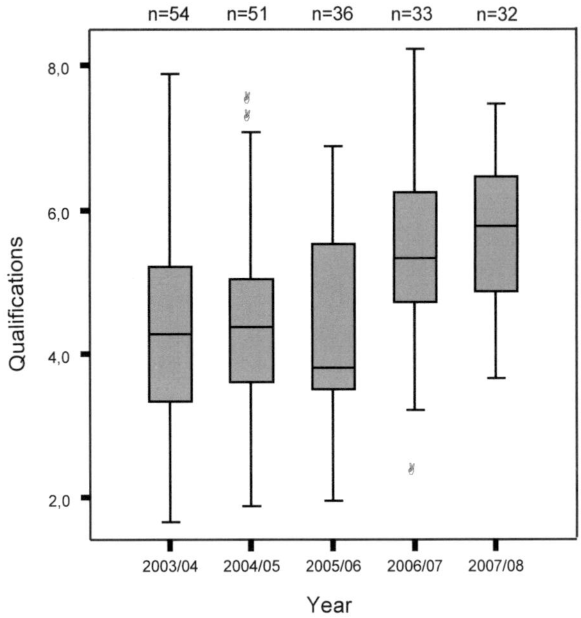

Fig. 1. Box-plot showing the distribution of the students' marks in the final assessment exams.

Figure 1 shows the box-plots with the distribution of the students' marks in the final assessment exams. The lowest mark in the 2006/07 exam was 2.28 but this should be considered an outlier. When this value is removed, the lowest mark was 3.22, almost two units above the lowest marks obtained in previous years. The lowest mark in 2007/08 was 3.67. These last two years were the only ones where the mean marks of all students were higher than 5 (as much as 10 points in the exam).

In 2006/07 and 2007/08, a survey was distributed among students at the end of the term (Table 4). This was prepared in order to obtain direct information as to the effect this continuous evaluation methodology was producing in their learning. The answers obtained from students were very positive and the following trends can be noted:

- An increase in student dedication to the subject was observed.
- Student performance was higher or equivalent to that obtained through conventional lectures.
- The presentation of assessment exams as homework exercises and the marking of them has helped teachers to check the level of knowledge assimilation and comprehension during the term.
- Students are strongly in favour of solving assessment tasks as group exercises as this gives them the opportunity to discuss and revise the subject matter. It is important to note that students are more demanding in their requirements for good and clear explanations than they are from teachers. This results in increased student dedication in the preparation of group meetings.

Question	Answers and Percentages
Hours of weekly dedication to the subject (excluding lectures).	• 1-3 hours (44%) • 3-6 hours (44%) • 6-10 hours (4%) • Only before an exam (8%)
Dedication compared with subjects with conventional evaluation methodologies.	• Lower dedication and better results (16%) • Higher dedication and better results (32%) • Equivalent dedication with better or equivalent result (48%)
Handing in of the assessments exams as group exercises.	• Adequate for reviewing and increasing learning (84%) • Not useful (12%) • Did not reply (4%)
Has it been useful to work in groups when preparing the assessment exams to be handed in?	• Yes (88%) • No, it would be better to work individually (4%)

Table 4. Answers obtained from the students in the survey about the evaluation methodology used in the subject "Advanced Analytical chemistry" in 2006/07 (n=25).

5. Conclusions

Results obtained in this study indicate that the simple application of continuous evaluation methodologies based exclusively on different assessment exams during the term and a final assessment exam at the end are not sufficient to improve the learning process of students. However, this process has been widely accepted by many lecturers in Spanish universities as a simple way of transforming traditional evaluation methodologies so that they meet the requirements of the Bologna declaration: what is achieve is greater success in the statistics for the subject. There is a close correlation between an increase weighting being given to term time assessment tasks and higher end of year marks. This result may be well looked upon by university administrators as at first sight it would seem to represent a real improvement, which may bring with it certain advantages from their perspective. However, there it is seen quite clearly that the learning of the students is not significantly improved.

In order to obtain an improvement in student learning, it is necessary to apply continuous evaluation methodologies that include feedback processes. Feedback received from assessment tasks performed during the term must be evaluated appropriately by teachers to apply corrective measures when needed. The advantage of partial assessment exams is that teachers still have time to find solutions to problems which are encountered. This is impossible when only a final exam is given.

There are two main trends from feedback processes that have to be taken into account by teachers when trying to apply these methodologies:

1. It is necessary to consider a profound revision of the contents of subjects. It is very important to select only those contents that are really essential to student learning at undergraduate level. The current system in Spanish universities is based on overloaded programs, which are set before the beginning of each term. Lecture schedules are very tight and no time is programmed to apply feedback methodologies. It is necessary to schedule tutorials with a small number of students to review and solve students' misconceptions. Moreover, this feedback process has to be fast (just a few days). When there is an excessive delay in the feedback, students will be focussed on other topics and will not give priority to learning lessons from it (Race, 1999). This problem was detected during our first feedback process. Tutorials were scheduled two weeks after the assessment in order to allow teachers enough time to review the tests. During tutorials, students communicate to us that they did not remember the answers they had given as too long a period had gone by.
2. The larger the assessment task programmed, the greater the time needed for the evaluation work of the lecturer and the greater the pressure on teachers to produce the feedback (Gibbs, 1992). Hence, teacher dedication to the subject increases considerably when continuous evaluation methodologies are applied. Spanish university institutions need to make an effort to reduce the number of subjects that teachers have to teach each term: this does not mean a reduction in the hours given over to teaching but rather a change in how this time is used. The changes proposed to teaching methodologies in the Bologna declaration actually require a significant increase in the workload both of teachers and students. If this is not taken into account by institutions, the changes proposed by the EHEA will be a failure and there will be no other option than to return to traditional lecture-based methodologies.

6. References

Biggs, J. & Tang, C. (2007). *Teaching for Quality Learning at University*, 3rd ed., Open University Press, ISBN: 9780335221264, Berkshire (UK)

Boud, D. (1988). *Developing Student Autonomy in Learning*, 2nd ed., Nichols Pub. Co., ISBN: 0893972916, New York (USA)

Bodner, G.M. (1986). Constructivism: A Theory of Knowledge. *Journal of Chemical Education*, Vol. 63, No. 10 (October, 1986), 873-878, ISSN: 00219584

Brown, S.; Rust, C. & Gibbs, G. (1994). *Strategies for Diversifying Assessment in Higher Education*, Oxford Centre for Staff Development, ISBN: 1873576234, Oxford (UK)

Brown, S. & Knight, P. (1994). *Assessing Learners in Higher Education*, Kogan Page, ISBN: 0749411139, London (UK)

Brown, S. (1999). Institutional Strategies for Assessment, In: *Assessment Matters in Higher Education: Choosing and Using Diverse Approaches*, Brown, S. & Glasner, A., (Ed.), 3-13, Open University Press, ISBN: 033520242X, Buckingham (UK)

Gibbs, G.; Jenkins, A. & Wisker, G. (1992). *Assessing More Students*, Oxford Brookes University, Oxford Centre for Staff Development, ISBN: 1873576102, Oxford (UK)

McKeachie, W.J.; Pintrich, P.R.; Lin, Y.G. & Smith, D.A.F. (1986). *Teaching and Learning in the College Classroom: A Review of the Research Literature*, National Center for Research to Improve Postsecondary Teaching and Learning (NCRIPTAL), The University of Michigan, ISBN: 9998463424, Ann Arbor (USA)

NRC (National Research Council), Committee on the Development of an Addendum to the National Science Education Standards on Scientific Inquiry, Steve Olson and Susan Loucks-Horsley (2000). *Inquiry and the National Science Education Standards: A Guide for Teaching and Learning*, National Academic Press, ISBN: 0309064767, Washington DC (USA)

Race, P. (1999). Why Assess Innovatively? In: *Assessment Matters in Higher Education: Choosing and Using Diverse Approaches*, Brown, S. & Glasner, A., (Ed.), 57-70, Open University Press, ISBN: 033520242X, Buckingham (UK)

Smith, A. & Hall, E.H. (1902). *The Teaching of Chemistry and Physics in the Secondary School*, Longmans, Green and Co., New York (USA)

20

Verbal and Pictorial Stimulus of Package Design in Right-to-left Languages According to Brain Laterality

Kambiz Heidarzadeh Hanzaee, Ph. D.
Tehran Science and Research Branch, Islamic Azad University (I.A.U.)
Iran
heidarzadeh@srbiau.ac.ir

1. Introduction

The form of the package itself can influence consumer perception. The components of the package can combine to communicate all sorts of informative and emotional messages. Informative messages include the brand logo, the product description, promotional messages, and usage directions. The emotional aspects offer a wide range of design possibilities, such as package colors, the style of logos, symbols, photographs and illustrations. Every word and every visual detail must be structured carefully in order to establish memorability for specific brands.

Enhancing brand equity, one of the objectives of marketing managers, is affected significantly by package design. Distinctive packaging ensures better recall of the product and especially of the brand name. Brand memorability is one of the most important factors in a brand name (Lee and Ang, 2003), because it reduces consumer search costs (Grace and O'Cass, 2005). Creating a high level of brand awareness and a positive brand image in consumer's memory maximizes brand equity (Dong and Helms, 2001). According to Lin, perceptual image plays an important role in forming consumer impressions (Lin, 2004). Brand image consist of brand cues such as name, logo, and packaging design. Research on recalling brands as memory target, gaining informed insight into familiar processes such as how we recognize visual cues, how we store or retrieve memories, and even why we forget, provides a useful foundation for brand psychology (Franzen and Bouwman, 2002).

But in this sense, the brand itself is not a memory target but a cue that might facilitate recall or inference of previously-learned brand associations (Warlop et al., 2005). To increase the recall of brand cues, we should consider the result of research on brain laterality which has shown that perception is not symmetrical. Although the two sides of the brain are similar in appearance, and every structure in each hemisphere is mirrored on the other, the functions of each cortical hemisphere are different. For our purpose, we can mention the differences between verbal and pictorial stimuli to the specialized functioning of the brain's left and right hemispheres (Holbrook and Moore, 1981). According to Janiszewski's research (1990), verbal ads are preferred when placed on the right, and the converse is true for pictorial ads. This stems from the fact that the human nervous system is designed for each cerebral hemisphere to receive information primarily from the opposite side of the body. The right hemisphere is the more efficient processor of pictorial information and the left is capable of analyzing verbal information (Janiszewski, 1990). According to this brain laterality the positioning of the elements in a pack design is related to perception of those elements, recall or missing the elements while looking at them walking in a mall.

Moreover, there is some evidence that language differences may affect consumer information processing (Schmitt et al., 1994) not only in terms of mental representation, but also in the way they are organized and retrieved from memory (Tavassoli, 1999).

In this article we describe specific elements of package design to investigate and evaluate the maximization of pack recall through the positioning and layout of the elements of a pack in right-to-left languages.

2. Package design

As the marketing of consumer products becomes increasingly competitive, more companies are treating the product package both as a point-of-purchase advertising vehicle (Schwartz, 1975) and as a component of marketing and advertising (media, promotion, packaging, copy) (Hodock, 1980). In this situation, the high cost of developing appropriate graphics, shapes, and logos dictates the need to evaluate the package's effectiveness (Schwartz, 1975) and consumers' ability to retrieve brands and identify products in busy perceptual fields such as grocery stores aisles (Keller, 1991).

In Kumar's research, cueing the product with the pictorial contexts at a point of recall improved when pictorial contexts were less similar; this is another proof of the role of distinctive package design. The role of pack design changed with the move to self-service (Danger and Brookfield, 1987) and the pack became an essential part both of the selling process (Rettie and Brewer, 2000) and of selling power. The design of the pack itself may be an incentive to buy.

In one analysis of senior marketing managers, design was mentioned as the most important performance of a new product by 60 percent of respondents (Bloch, 1995). While packaging attracts attention and communicates objective and emotional information about the contents (Schwartz, 1971) there is an underlying thesis that packaging decisions should be driven by marketing rather than by aesthetic or artistic considerations (Danger and Brookfield, 1987). Despite the importance of brand differentiation as a competitive advantage (Aggarwal, 2002), and of visual attention as a vital and often the only way to acquire information about brands in consumer choice contexts, it has been disregarded in marketing research. In perceptual analyses, consumers examine sensory features of the stimulus, such as shape, color, and size; they decipher the stimulus into categorical codes, such as brand name, pictorial and verbal information for a brand package, and they select certain elements of the stimulus over others (Pieters and Warlop, 1999). According to managerial issues, the main point is that investment in design can be better matched to the anticipated target market to avoid either under- or over spending. Sales forecasts also might become more accurate if the centrality of product aesthetics to a market can be assessed and considered in light of the design characteristics (Bloch et al., 2003).

Of course, some individual, social, and situational characteristics (such as different genders and handedness) should be considered in perceptual experience (Friedmann and Zimmer, 1988). This involvement of the user makes the packaging an essential element in both the communication of brand values and as an essential part of the brand (Connolly and Davidson, 1996). Whether consumers remember a brand name, a brand image, or a benefit conveyed in an ad depends on several factors that marketers need to consider (Schmitt et al., 1993). Personal factors, such as needs, values, and motives, modify the message communicated by the packaging or the advertisement and advertising campaigns should reduce psychological distance between the self and the product image (Horowitz and Kaye, 1975).

Considering package design as an ad, and that a positive effect is transferred from ad to brand, led to the conclusion that ad likeability results in brand likeability (Fam and Waller, 2004), and making a brand strongly in customers' minds with very positive and relevant association (Baker et al., 2005) leads to more sales. As Schmitt et al. (1993) have mentioned there are different researches on ad memorability that has focused on the relative impact of pictorial information versus verbal information. Also according to their research on print advertisements three components a) visual information b) verbal information and c) brand name may be related to one another and memory also depends on the existing interrelations among different elements in the ads apart from their layout. Base on Janiszewski (1988), (1990) and Rettie and Brewer (2000), the layout (right/ left) of different elements has also some effects on the preference of that advertisement in left-to-right languages.

Packaging has to work in a more crowded competitive context both in the retail environment and in the kitchen (Thompson, 1996). An estimated half of all grocery purchases are unplanned, and according to a survey by the Henley Center, 73 percent of purchase decisions were made at the point of sale (Rettie and Brewer, 2000); it therefore seems that time pressure is another factor in supermarket purchases, so pack design has a great effect on decision making.

According to Tsai (2005), there is conceptual brand purchase model (Figure 1), in which repurchase intention of the brand is designated as the outcome construct, and brand purchase value, with the three dimensionalities of symbolic value, affective value, and tradeoff value treated as mediators, preceded by the juxtaposing constructs of perceived image, emotional experience, perceived quality, and price acceptability of the brand.

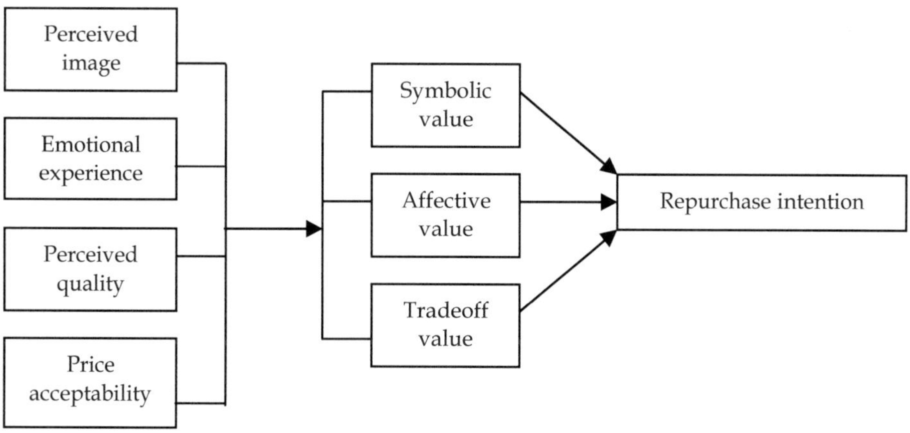

Fig. 1. Tsai's Brand Purchase Value Model

In detail, the conceptual definitions of all the constructs are:
Antecedents:
Perceived image is the consumer's perception of social approval and identifiableness with the brand image (brand cues including packaging design).
Emotional experience is the consumer's emotional reaction derived from direct experience with the branded product.
Perceived quality is the consumer's perception of the functional benefits and performance of the branded product.
Price acceptability is the consumer's judgment of the fairness of the branded product's price and his/ her ability to afford the price.
Mediators:
Symbolic value pertains to the way in which the consumer evaluates the product's brand name in terms of the valence assigned to the brand's reputation and its capability for self-expression.
Affective value refers to the consumer's overall feelings of the branded product.
Tradeoff value is related to how the consumer evaluates the branded product's value with economic and monetary considerations (Tsai, 2005).
Having a significant role in repeated purchasing, package design has become an important item; therefore manufacturers use vivid packaging design to make their brand more noticeable (Pieters and Warlop, 1999). So, some kind of novelty, unexpectedness, and incongruity leads to higher cognitive elaboration (Meyers-Levy and Tybout, 1989) and special displays draw attention to products and brands they prefer to sell (Allenby and Ginter, 1995). Such attempts assume that visual attention is a precondition to subsequent processes that eventually lead to choice, and that increased visual attention will increase the likelihood of choice. Despite the common assumption of a significant association, the attention–choice relationship never has been examined directly (Pieters and Warlop, 1999).
In order to assess the package, several types of tests help to make a good judgment about the design: the visibility test, evaluating the legibility of package graphics and lettering; the impact of different elements on a package, or the preference for one package over another. These tests use a tachistoscope (T-Scope), angle and blur meters, and eye movement tests (Rettie and Brewer, 2000).
There are several different types of tachistoscope (T-Scope) (Schwartz, 1975). Tachistoscopy has been used to assess pack visibility since the World War II, when it was used in training in the recognition of aircraft silhouettes (Rettie and Brewer, 2000). A T-Scope controls the length of time a stimulus package is exposed to the subject, down to fractions of a second (Schwartz, 1975). It has an electronic shutter, which allows one to control the exposure precisely. It has been used to measure the impact of the packaging, the legibility of the pack graphics, and the shelf standout of different packs (Rettie and Brewer, 2000). But now PCs, using software programs, are able to do the job of the tachistoscope.
Image tests, a second test to assess the packaging, evaluate underlying consumer attitudes toward the package and toward the product. Finally, usage tests uncover and measure functional attitudes and reactions toward the package (Schwartz, 1971). In this paper we did not go through the image and usage tests of package assessing.

3. Brain Laterality

Laterality is the preference that most humans show for one side of their body over the other. Brain laterality or hemispheric laterality refers to the asymmetry of the brain.

Although the left and right sides of the brain are physically symmetrical, they are not identical in their functions or organization. The left hemisphere processes language (Rettie and Brewer, 2000), and numerous studies have found that the right hemisphere plays a special role in processing the emotional properties of non-verbal stimuli. These studies support a model of right hemisphere specialization for emotional processing (right hemisphere model), possibly because of the greater involvement of the right hemisphere in mechanisms of automatic and behavioral arousal (Nagaea and Moscovitch, 2002).

As the two sides of the brain have different specializations, there is an inherent bias in the processing of stimuli, depending on which side of the body perceived them (Rettie & Brewer, 2000). This is the reason that perception is not symmetrical. A long history of reports of right-hand side visual field superiority for letter and digit stimuli (Madden and Nebes, 1980) has demonstrated the relationship between the concept of brain laterality and the positioning and recall of pack elements.

Visual mental images can be divided into perceptual and memory images. Perceptual images arise when an object, or its reproduction, is actually present. In contrast, memory images are those of the absent object and are therefore stored as remembered perceptual images, in the absence of the object itself (Groeppel-Klein, 2003). While the effect of memory images is weaker than that of perceptual images, they can to some extent produce the same effects as perceptual images; thus, the memory images are perceived as reality. The findings suggest that both the perception of an object and the retrieval of its memory image involve the same neural processes in the brain. By this reasoning, Groeppel-Klein pointed to the relation and influence that positively toned memory images of a mall have on shopping mall assessment outside the mall, which is the same as what the perceived mall environment does when consumers are in the mall.

So as Groeppel-Klein (2003) infers about shopping malls, and according to the similarity that exists in the effect of memory image, "picture in the head" and perception of the object, we can conclude that positive memory image can influence the retrieval of the object, especially for very vivid memory images. This vividness, according to Groeppel-Klein, refers to how colorful, detailed, and varied the memory image appears to the "mind's eye." So we can consider vividness as a factor that corresponds to the information rate and the amount of subconscious processing. It also can be attributed to specialized hemispheric analyses that depend on the complexity of the information being processed (Janiszewski, 1990).

Using a newspaper format, Janiszewski (1988) found that pictorial ads were liked better when placed to the left of a certain article, whereas verbal ads were liked more when placed to the right of the material. Material in the left visual field directly engages the right hemisphere, and material in the right visual field directly engages the left hemisphere (Janiszewski, 1990). Both eyes perceive the visual area, but information from the outer right visual field initially goes only to the left hemisphere, while information from the outer left visual field initially goes directly to the right hemisphere (Rettie and Brewer, 2000). Therefore, a pictorial ad placed in the left visual field directly engages the right hemisphere. The right hemisphere provides a more accessible subconscious trace of pictorial information when a conscious evaluation is performed. Similarly, the left hemisphere provides a more accessible subconscious trace of verbal information when a conscious evaluation is performed (Janiszewski, 1990).

In addition to the asymmetry that is in perception of different functions, there is some evidence of a gender difference. One consistent finding in the neuropsychological literature is that women are better at some verbal tasks, and that men are better at some spatial tasks. Also women tend to perform better on verbal learning and recall tasks, according to the logical memory subtest of the Wechsler Memory Scale, and list learning on the California Verbal Learning Test, and the Rey Auditory Verbal Learning Test (Ragland et al., 2000); this has been also supported by Halpern (1986).

In addition, there are some differences between right- and left-handed people. Language functions are left-hemisphere lateralized in approximately 76 percent of left-handers, 10 percent show right-hemisphere lateralization, and the remaining 14 percent show bilateral representation of language functions. There also have also been some observations that in 85–89 percent of right-handers (Welsh and Elliot, 2001), the left hemisphere contributes to the control of both hands, while the right hemisphere does not contribute to the control of the right hand. According to Welsh and Elliot (2001), 89 percent of the right-handed and 63 percent of the left-handed participants in a survey demonstrated a left hemisphere advantage in reaction time. In right-handers, the left hemisphere contributes to the reaction of both sides, while the right hemisphere does not contribute to reaction of the right side (Medland et al., 2002). It also is predicted that left-handed people would have a reversed brain division of labor.

4. Methodology

Applying the research in order to examine whether the layout of the pack elements has any effects on their memorability, we considered the factor of being on right- or left-hand side of the package. So the following hypotheses have been conducted.

H1: Pack copy will have a higher recall when it is on the right-hand side of the pack.

We know that the material in the right visual field directly engages the left hemisphere, and the left hemisphere processes language. So the left-hand side of the brain, which processes verbal stimuli, will directly receive verbal stimuli from the right-hand side of the pack. By this reasoning we want to assess whether being on right-hand side have any influence on better recall of the verbal stimuli on packages.

H2: Non-verbal material will have a higher recall when it is on the left-hand side of the pack.

This is related to pictorial or non-verbal elements of the pack. The right hemisphere plays a special role in processing the emotional properties of non-verbal stimuli. And the material in the left visual field directly engages the right hemisphere. So we can get result that the right-hand side of the brain, which processes non-verbal stimuli, will receive those stimuli directly from the left-hand side of packages and we want to examine whether being on left-hand side have any effect on better recall of the non-verbal stimuli of the packages.

This research was done randomly on 76 female and 76 male students of Azad University of Iran. The questionnaires were split equally between women and men because of brain laterality differences between genders, with women generally showing less (Rettie and Brewer, 2000). All of the participants selected were right-handed because left-handed people tend to have different brain lateralization than right-handed people (Rettie and Brewer, 2000).

The stimuli were the elements of two sets of packages of grocery products. One of the sets included an original packages and the other one contained the same packages in which the verbal and pictorial components were reversed by Photoshop software. As shown in plate 1 and 2, each set comprised of five packages which are obvious by the name of the products. The packs in reversed set were of a high standard and not distinguishable from the originals.

We selected packages with both simple and complicated designs for our sets. We tried to select the ones which had a lower reputation in the market in order to prevent the participants from filling in the questionnaires based on their previous information.

We used the visibility test to compare the legibility and recall of "element impact" on the package to that of the others. Using computer software with better precision and visibility than tachistoscope (each pack was exposed to participants for 500 milliseconds) we compared our results to those in previous research.

As the brand cues consist of a set of verbal and nonverbal components, we selected some of the elements of each pack. We showed the same elements in both the original set and the reversed set. Each respondent saw one set of five packs, the original version (A) or the mirror version with reversed verbal and visual elements (B). An equal number of respondents saw each of the two sets. It means thirty-eight of 76 men saw version A and the remaining 38 saw version B. The same was true for 76 women; thirty-eight of women saw original version and the remaining 38 saw the reversed.

Every five packs in each set were shown for a time of 500 milliseconds. Respondents were asked to examine the packs but just look straight at the center of the pack (Rettie and Brewer, 2000). After the participants were shown each pack of a set, they were asked to fill in a section of a simple questionnaire about that pack and we tested their ability to recall the verbal and visual elements of that pack and also they were asked about the visual appeal of the package.

Altogether, we considered 15 recall questions from the elements of all five packs of the sets, which consisted of 8 recall questions about the verbal stimuli to evaluate H1 and 7 recall questions about the pictorial stimuli to evaluate H2.

The questions, selected elements, and the number of them for each pack differed according to their complexity and design.

For assessing our hypotheses we considered the answer of any recall question as "Yes" if the participants have been name that stimulus correctly and completely. Then we calculated the Yes answers for different categories: 1- verbal stimuli which were on right-hand side of the pack 2- verbal stimuli which were on left-hand side of the pack 3- pictorial stimuli which were on the right-hand side of the pack and 4- pictorial stimuli which were on the left-hand side of the pack.

OROUEI

PARDISA

ESHTROUDEL

CHOCO
WAFER

SEFID MORGH

Plate 1. Five packages - Original set

OROUEI

PARDISA

CHOCO
WAFER

ESHTROUDEL

SEFID MORGH

Plate 2. Five packages - Reversed set

As both dependent and independent variables, Recall (Yes/ No), Stimuli (Verbal/ Pictorial) and Position (Right/Left), were categorical, we used Chi-Square test for analyzing the answers. For the first hypothesis we collect the answers into two column; correct answers to verbal stimuli which were on right-hand side and those which were on left-hand side even in original or reversed set. And for assessing the second hypothesis, we do the same for pictorial stimuli. The results are shown in next section.

5. Findings

H1

As it is observable in Table 1, we have collected the correct answers for verbal stimuli on right- and left-hand side of the packs. Then we did the chi-square test in order to analyze the results. The amount of calculated x^2 is 19.52, and $x^2_{0.05(7)}$ is equal to 14.07. Since the amount 19.52 is bigger than 14.07 we can conclude there is some dependency between the recall of verbal stimuli and their position.

With the aim of measuring the association, we used the contingency coefficient. C coefficient would be 0.18 which shows a week coefficiency. Also as we can see in the table 1, the ratio (P) of being on the right-hand side and being on the left- is very close to each other, with a small priority for copy on right. The amount of N is equal to the number of 76 participants who have seen 8 verbal elements.

Brand	Stimuli	Correct recall F_{oi} Copy on right	Copy on left	Total
OROUEI	اروئی	54	25	79
	میگو برگر	36	32	68
PARDISA	پردیسا	65	50	115
CHOCO WAFER	ویفر شکلاتی	49	59	108
	مغز فندق	33	31	64
ESHTROUDEL	اشترودل	20	26	46
SEFID MORGH	مجانی	33	22	55
	۱۵تایی	39	15	54
	Total	329	260	
	N	608	608	
	P	0.54	0.43	

Table 1. Verbal stimuli recall

H2

For evaluating the pictorial elements and getting result for the second hypothesis, we prepare a table same as to verbal elements as it is shown in Table 2. The amount of calculated x^2 for this table is 5.45 which is smaller than $x^2_{0.05(6)}$. So it shows that there is not any dependency between the recall of pictorial stimuli and their position.

Brand	Stimuli	Correct recall F_{oi} Picture on right	Picture on left	Total
OROUEI	Food in the plate	17	23	40
	Sandwich	21	20	41

PARDISA	Dates	33	43	76
CHOCO WAFER	Wafers	26	24	50
ESHTROUDEL	Food in the plate	36	25	61
SEFID MORGH	Man	53	46	99
	Egg	40	43	83
	Total	226	224	
	N	532	532	
	P	0.42	0.42	

Table 2. Pictorial Stimuli recall

6. Discussion

In this study we had eight recall questions related to verbal elements for examining H1, in which two of the stimuli, number 4 and 6, did not receive any preferences for being on right. Although 0.54 percent of the correct recalls have had the preference to be on right but the difference of this ratio with the ratio of being on left is not so much. We explain in previous section that the coefficiency of the position and the verbal stimuli is just 18 percent.

On the other hand from seven recall questions related to pictorial stimuli about H2, four of the elements, number 2, 4, 5 and 6, did not have any favorite for being on the left-hand side. This means that from the correct recalls on the left (224), 48 percent were more easily recalled than those on the right. So in total 532 observations, about 20 percent of answers have supported H2. These evidences show that we can not expand the outcomes to all the cases and the results of prior studies for left-to-right languages such as English might not be valid for right-to-left languages.

It is obvious that considering the only factor of position would not be enough. There are many factors such as the background color, font color, accompany with other elements, being on top, bottom or center and etc. which get involved in pack design and do influence the memorability of elements and the retrieval. Thus they should be taken into account in order to obtain proper conclusion.

One of the important items we met was the existence of an association of stimuli. Rettie and Brewer (2000) described this as a "flash". For instance we can consider a group of verbal and pictorial elements as well as a numerical element, altogether as one united stimulus. Can we select a part of whole pack and consider pictorial elements such as the man and egg with the verbal stimuli of "۱۵ تايي" in one set, as one element? This is a question that needs further studies to answer.

Plate 3. A flash stimulus

About numerical elements, we had one recall questions that examined best positioning of numbers; we categorized it as verbal stimuli and it supported our hypothesis of better retrieval on the right-hand side of the pack as H1 (Table 3). Of course one element is not enough to obtain the results. Should they be considered as verbal or pictorial stimuli? Or they might have their own characteristics.

Brand	Stimuli	Correct recall		Total
		F[illegible]		
		Copy on right	Copy on left	
SEFID MORGH	۱۵تایی	39	15	54

Table 3. Numerical stimuli recall

7. Limitations and further research

As we mentioned before, some limitations affected the result of this survey. One of them was related to packages; having a small numbers of packages to evaluate was a source of bias because it was difficult to find packages with the appropriate positioning of verbal and pictorial elements by which the reversed version could be strikingly different and suitable for assessing our hypotheses. Also we had to consider that the stimuli had to be of a nearly same size. Incidentally, for further research the need to consider more packages from other fields in addition to groceries, could bring more insights into this subject.

Another bias that we faced while collecting the data was that some participants already were familiar with the packages, so they completed the questionnaires on the basis of previous information. We tried to select packages that were not popular in the market. Although we did not have many of such respondents, this bias could be considered in future researches. Of course, for surveys with more packages and more participants, it would be a serious limitation that should be avoided.

The lack of packages with flash elements prevented us from being able to study more complicated positioning. Also the effects of other factors such as color, font size or the position of being on the center of a pack were not considered in this survey. And also because of having just one numerical element we were not able to study on these elements precisely.

For this reasons we suggest future researchers to use the artificial packages, designed by the research group, in order to control all of the factors precisely and so avoid these kind of limitation. They could control the positioning of the elements, flashes, their colors, and font size in order to measure the effects of different factors individually or in combination with each other. The familiarity of participants with packages then will cease to be a problem. In this way flashes also, as unique elements, can be studied more.

This promises valuable results as memory researchers have devised a large number of tasks in which subjects are presented with a cue and required to recall an item associated with it (Lockhart, 2000).

8. Managerial implications

Given that packaging is considered as a point-of-purchase advertising vehicle, so pack design is of a high value for marketers. One of the factors of pack effectiveness is the consumers' ability to retrieve brands and identify products in busy perceptual fields. In this situation the design of the pack itself may be an incentive to buy. Considering package design as an ad, and that a positive effect is transferred from ad to brand, led to the conclusion that ad likeability results in brand likeability. Making a brand strongly in customers' minds with very positive and relevant association leads to more sales as the perceived image of a brand name is one of the most effective factors that results in repurchase.

So one of the targets is making the brand name more self-expressive and according to the existence of brain laterality, we should remember the factors that affect this. The position of the elements is one of the factors that stem from this issue. There are many researches show that to recall some elements of the pack better, we should pay attention to the position of the elements as well as the aesthetic parameters of the pack. These researches which have done for left-to-right languages show verbal elements of pack are better recall on the right side and pictorial elements on the left side.

By these explanations the magnitude of pack design which is related to specific characteristics of target market is clear. The main point is that investment in design which is better matched to the anticipated target market will avoid either under- or over spending. Language differences are one of the factors which vary in different market and may affect consumer information processing. These effects are not only in terms of mental representation, but also in the way they are organized and retrieved from memory.

Since many of the world's countries mainly in Asia, Middle East and Africa have written languages with the right-to-left structure specially Arabic and Persian, this issue has a great importance. According to OIC (organization of the islamic conference) the population of Islamic countries is about 1.5 billion. Considering the 6.6 billion world's population, a market size of 22 percent has a worth of great marketing research. Some of these countries like Malaysia, Turkey, Indonesia, UAE, Saudi Arabia, Iran, Nigeria, Egypt, Algeria, Pakistan, Iraq, Morocco, Kazakhstan, Bangladesh, Tunisia and Kuwait are notable markets. According to ITC (international trade center) countries such as Turkey, Malaysia and United Arab Emirates have in order 138, 131 and 110 billion dollars import and the other above countries with a range of about 70 to 10 billion dollars import amount are judged as significant markets.

The results of our study in right-to-left languages showed the factor of position according to brain laterality should be taken into account for verbal elements. Elements such as brand name, some promotions or some benefits conveyed in an ad, which are important to retrieve, would be more advantageous if being on the right side in order to arouse higher recall.

But for pictorial elements we were not successful to prove the assumption that being on the left side leads to higher retrieval. So for positioning the pictorial materials of packs we have more choices in the layout, even as an association with other parts especially verbal elements.

9. References

Aggarwal, P. (2002), The effect of brand relationship norms on consumer attitudes and behavior, Dissertation, The University of Chicago.

Allenby, G.M. and Ginter, J.L. (1995), "The effects of in-store displays and feature advertising on consideration set", International Journal of Research in Marketing, Vol. 12, pp. 67-80.

Baker, C., Nancarrow, C. and Tinson, J. (2005), "The mind versus market share guide to brand equity", International Journal of Market Research, Vol. 47 No. 5, pp. 525-542.

Bloch, P.H. (1995), "Seeking the ideal form: Product design and consumer response", Journal of Marketing, Vol. 59, pp. 16-29.

Bloch, P.H., Brunel, F.F. and Arnold, T.J. (2003), "Individual Differences in the Centrality of Visual Product Aesthetics: Concept and Measurement", Journal of Consumer Research, Vol. 29, pp. 551-565.

Connolly, A. and Davidson, L. (1996), "How does design affect decisions at point of sale? Journal of Brand Management, Vol. 4 No. 2, pp. 100-107.

Danger, E.P. and Brookfield, V.T. (1987), Selecting colour for packaging. London: Gower Technical Press.

Davidson, H., Cave, K.R. and Sellner, D. (2000), "Differences in visual attention and task interference between males and females reflect differences in brain laterality", Neoropsychologia, Vol. 38, pp. 508-519.

Dong. L.C. and Helms, M.M. (2001), "Brand name translation model: A case analysis of US brands in China", Journal of Brand Management, Vol. 9 No. 2, pp. 99-115.

Fam, K.S. and Waller, D.S. (2004), "Ad likeability and brand recall in Asia: A cross-cultural study", Journal of Brand Management, Vol. 12 No. 2, pp. 93-104.

Franzen, G. and Bouwman, M. (2002), "The mental world of brands - Mind, memory and brand success", Journal of Brand Management, Vol. 9 No. 6, pp. 481-486.

Friedmann, R. and Zimmer, M.R. (1988), "The role of psychological meaning in advertising", Journal of Advertising, Vol. 17 No. 1, pp. 31-40.

Grace, D. and O'Cass, A. (2005), "Service branding: Consumer verdicts on service brands", Journal of Retailing and Consumer Services, Vol. 12, pp. 125-139.

Groeppel-Klein, A. (2003), "Minding the mall: Do we remember what we see? Advances in Consumer Research, Vol. 30, pp. 56-67.

Halpern D. (1986), Sex Differences in Cognitive Abilities, Hillsdale, NJ: Erlbaum.

Hodock, C.L. (1980), "Copy Testing and Strategic Positioning", Journal of Advertising Research, Vol. 20 No. 1, pp. 33-38.

Holbrook, M.B. and Moore, W.L. (1981), "Feature interactions in consumer judgments of verbal versus pictorial presentations", Journal of Consumer Research, Vol. 8, pp. 103-113.

Horowitz, I.A. and Kaye, R.S. (1975), "Perception and Advertising", Journal of Advertising Research, Vol. 15 No.3, pp. 15-21.

Janiszewski, C. (1988), "Preconscious processing effects: The independence of attitude formation and conscious thought", Journal of Consumer Research, Vol. 15, pp. 199-209.

Janiszewski, C. (1990), "The influence of print advertisement organization on affect toward a brand name", Journal of Consumer Research, Vol. 17, pp. 53-65.

Keller, K. L. (1991), "Memory and evaluations in competitive advertising environments", Journal of Consumer Research, Vol. 17 No. 4, pp. 463-476.

Lee, Y.H. and Ang, K.S. (2003), "Brand name suggestiveness: a Chinese language perspective", International Journal of Research in Marketing, Vol. 20, pp. 323-335.

Lin, I.Y. (2004), "Evaluating a servicescape: the effect of cognition and emotion", Hospitality Management, Vol. 23, pp. 163-178.

Lockhart, R.S. (2000), "Methods of memory research", in Tulving, E. and Craik, F.I.M. (Eds.), The Oxford Handbook of Memory, New York: Oxford University Press, Inc., pp. 45-57.

Madden, D.J. and Nebes, R.D. (1980), "Hemispheric differences in memory search", Neuropsychologia, Vol. 18, pp. 665-673.

Medland, S.E., Geffen, G. and McFarland, K. (2002), "Lateralization of speech production using verbal/manual dual tasks: meta-analysis of sex differences and practice effects", Neuropsychologia, Vol. 40, pp. 1233-1239.

Meyers-Levy, J. and Tybout, A. M. (1989), "Schema congruity as a basis for product evaluation", Journal of Consumer Research, Vol. 16, pp. 39-54.

Nagae, S. and Moscovitch, M. (2002) ,"Cerebral hemispheric differences in memory of emotional and non-emotional words in normal individuals", Neuropsychologia, Vol. 40, pp. 1601-1607.

Pieters, R. and Warlop, L. (1999), "Visual attention during brand choice: The impact of time pressure and task motivation", International Journal of Research in Marketing, Vol. 16, pp. 1-16.

Ragland, J. D., Coleman, A.R., Gur, R.C, Glahn, D.C., and Gur, R.E. (2000), "Sex differences in brain-behavior relationships between verbal episodic memory and resting regional cerebral blood flow", Neuropsychologia, Vol. 38, pp. 451-461.

Rettie, R. and Brewer, C. (2000), "The verbal and visual components of package design", Journal of Product & Brand Management, Vol. 9 No. 1, pp. 56-70.

Schmitt, B.H., Tavassoli, N.T., and Millard, R.T. (1993), "Memory for print ads: Understanding relations among brand name, copy, and picture", Journal of Consumer Psychology, Vol. 2 No. 1, pp. 55-81.

Schmitt, B.H., Pan, Y., and Tavassoli, N.T. (1994), "Language and consumer memory: The impact of linguistic differences between Chinese and English", Journal of Consumer Research, Vol. 21, pp. 419-431.

Schwartz, D. (1971), "Evaluating packaging", Journal of Advertising Research, Vol. 11 No. 5, pp. 29-32.

Schwartz, D. (1975), "T scope package test sample size", Journal of Advertising Research, Vol. 15 No. 3, pp. 45-57.

Tavassoli, N.T. (1999), "Temporal and associative memory in Chinese and English", Journal of Consumer Research, Vol. 26, pp. 170-181.

Thompson, L. (1996), "Lifting the lid on packaging research", Journal of Brand Management, Vol. 3 No. 5, pp. 289-295.

Tsai, S.P. (2005), "Utility, cultural symbolism and emotion: A comprehensive model of brand purchase", International Journal of Research in Marketing, Vol. 22, pp. 277-291.

Warlop, L., Ratneshwar, S., and van Osselaer, S.M.J. (2005), "Distinctive brand cues and memory for product consumption experiences", International Journal of Research in Marketing, Vol. 22, pp. 27–44.
Weems, S.A. and Zaidel, E. (2005), "The effect of response mode on lateralized lexical decision performance", Neuropsychologia, Vol. 43, pp. 386–395.
Welsh, T.N. and Elliot, D. (2001), "Gender differences in a dichotic listening and movement task: lateralization or strategy?", Neuropsychologia, Vol. 39, pp. 25–35.

21

Research, Development and Technology Transfer (R & D & TT) in the Field of Engineering Materials and Related Technologies

Jaroslav Jerz
Institute of Materials and Machine Mechanics, Slovak Academy of Sciences
Slovakia

1. Introduction

The proper choice of engineering material and manufacturing process appropriate for a specific industrial application is most often based on an engineer's experience and on the recommendation of product supplier. This is why the choice is mostly identical with the same material or process which has been used obviously before. But nowadays, this approach in modern life style works only rarely, because it has usually several serious drawbacks. Two engineers setting the same problem may not arrive to the same conclusion. The choices are therefore extremely dependent on individual`s knowledge and the producer can only hard show to customer the quantitative reasoning behind them. Moreover, these approaches considerably inhibit innovations - they do not systematically explore all possibilities that could deliver better results.

Real decisions on proper choice of engineering material and appropriate manufacturing process have much broader objectives, e.g. to minimize cost or the "cost per unit of function". But besides this so called "financial cost", the same principles for selection can be applied also to "environmental costs" such as energy or CO_2 footprint. This "eco-design" is another, at present increasingly significant, area in which only an integrated materials strategy provides benefits.

This novel approach to understanding of the world of engineering materials has been outlined recently. The method develops both an understanding of material properties and skills in selecting materials and process to meet design specifications. Nowadays this approach is strongly supported by extensive computer-based methods and tools in order to help engineering students much better understand the "world" of materials, because engineers obviously make things, and they make them of engineering materials. Materials property data are therefore essential to a wide range of people and functions in engineering enterprises - not only engineers and designers needing the right property data for engineering simulations, but also buyers aiming for optimal purchasing decisions and, of course, also managers concerned with regulatory compliance. Information on materials properties is also of fundamental interest to the materials engineers, quality assurance, testing personnel and others who generate, control and supply it (Marsden, Warde & Fairfull, 2007).

2. New approach to materials research and education

The research, development and education in the field of engineering materials is today still strongly affected by its more recent history, in which the physicist played a great role. The physicist's point of view leads us to concepts of atomic bonding, geometry of molecular and crystal structures, crystal defects, alloy theory and phase stability, kinetics of phase transformations, mechanisms of plasticity and fracture and so on, gradually moving up through the length-scales from the atomistic through the microstructure to the macroscopic.
This concept is the foundation on which the subject rests and for that reason there is an averseness to approach it in other ways. But it is a path that creates one serious difficulty: the most important information the engineer really needs to perform his or her role as a maker of things comes only at the end or not at all. Nevertheless, there are powerful arguments for the teaching of this scientific method, like the rigour, the ability to apply logical thought and reasoned experimentation to physical problems in the broadest sense. The subject of materials is, of course, very broad, drawing together understanding from physics, chemistry, mathematics, computer science, etc. That is why the material science is more or less an applied science, because development and applying of materials bridges these "pure" scientific disciplines.
There is an alternative approach developed over the last 20 years by Prof. Ashby and his colleagues from University of Cambridge (Ashby & Cebon, 2002). It is based on the other extreme: the satellite view of "Planet Materials" – its occupied continents and its empty oceans - giving, from the start, some ability to navigate in this new virtual world of engineering materials (Fig. 1). It is then possible to focus in progressively, exposing a gradually increasing level of detail. The main aim of this approach is by no means to reject the fundamentals underpinning of physics and chemistry, but these can be developed as the details requiring them come into focus. The essential motivation for this helpful concept is to give the engineering students tools that they can immediately start to use in their role as engineers or designers. This "thinking behind the approach" makes maximum use of computer-assisted methods that further stimulate engagement of student and support project work that can be set by the teacher or self-generated by the student.

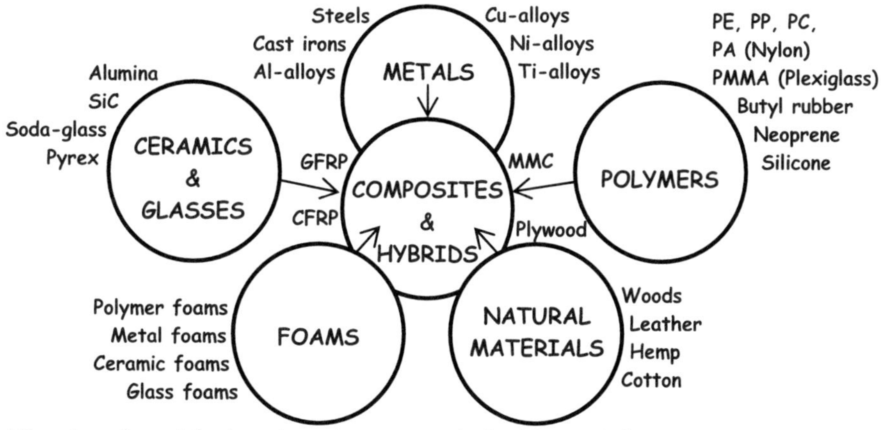

Fig. 1. The virtual world of engineering materials (Ashby & Cebon, 2002).

The "world" of engineering materials (Fig. 1) shows the "families", like: polymers, metals, ceramics, glasses, natural materials, and composites and hybrides that can be synthesised by combining these. Each family embraces classes, sub-classes and members. Every member is characterised by a set of attributes - its "property profile". This structure has the merit that it is easily understood and allows a helpful concept: that of the "material property chart", of which Figure 2 is a simple example. It is a map of one slice through material-property space. It plots stiffness, measured by Young's modulus, against weight, measured by density. It is one of a set, mapping the territory occupied by each family and the spaces in between. The bold balloons enclose the members of the families: metals, polymers, ceramics, foams and so on. Within each of them are the classes; if the resolution were sufficient, the members would come into focus.

Student interest is stimulated by encouragement to use these to explore the materials world. For engineering students it is very stimulating to use modern advisable software - so called Cambridge Engineering Selector (CES) to create charts with any desired combination of properties, giving the ability to zoom in on any selected part to increase resolution, and to access records for the attributes of individual materials.

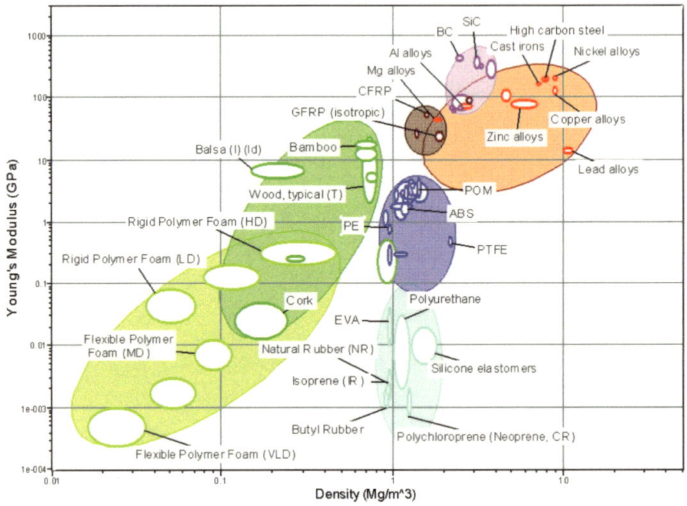

Fig. 2. The material property chart illustrated relationship between Young's modulus and Density for engineering materials created using the CES software with the Level 1 database (Ashby & Cebon, 2002).

The first level of CES software contains limited data for 80 of the most widely used engineering materials, selected from the six basic families described in Fig. 1. Each material record of CES starts with a brief description of the material illustrated with an image of a familiar product in which it is typically used, continuous by numeric data for the most basic mechanical, thermal, electrical and other physical properties and ends with a list of common material applications. Moreover, there are also manufacturing processes for shaping, joining and finishing treated in a similar, very simple way: a brief description is followed by a schematic illustrating how the process works and a brief list of attributes and industrial applications. The first level of CES allows engineering student to explore materials and processes without being overmastered by details, which are for him or her by that time fairly "non-essential". The further - second level retains this same format expanding the range of attributes for which data are listed and adding information on design, technical details and possible environmental concerns. This allows using more ambitious exercises and projects during education of expectant engineers, but still without smothering them with information. The final - third level develops this approach still further, providing a tool with which the sufficiently skilled engineers and designers are after graduation of both previous levels already familiar, but now they are capable of professional exercises and projects aimed to selection of proper engineering material and manufacturing process for real industrial application. It is possible to use at present roughly 3,700 engineering materials and 240 related processes for this purpose by means of this unique approach.

3. The engineering materials of nearest future

3.1 Developmental trends in the field of material science

The advanced technologies for utilizing energy sources with higher efficiency and for manufacturing of innovative industrial products with both higher functionality and environmentally friendly "eco-design", are based mainly on the research and development (R&D) of new engineering materials. The high-powered accumulation of results based on a long-term perspective and stable research environment is unavoidable for extensive development of material science. Thus, as one of the most important effort of each state with the ambition to be economically prosperous, it is extremely important to gain wide public understanding and achieve steady progress in this research field.

Material science, unlike culture or art, is the typical example of practical science. Its purpose is exclusively to be put to real use and therefore it has been used as a method, which is able to immobilize the framework of society based on the outworn ways of thinking. From global point of view the main mission of material science is efficient development of convenient materials desired by society in response to social needs. It has played a significant role in supplying products of steel, concrete, aluminium, polymers, semiconductors and various other engineering materials that society needs. However, there are many confirmations that besides this mission, the material science has a strong sense of being used to get a better understanding of the principles of natural phenomena.

The material science is at present steadily more or less the practical science, not to make the framework of society more rigid, but to appeal its existence to each other in various separated scientific fields. A lot of attention is being given nowadays to advanced material technologies with high potential to be applied soon in the industrial praxis and mainly to material science fields that have high productivity. The fact of this matter is that human being is always pushing ahead with R&D that is narrow, deep, separate and especially so short-termed as possible (Shinohara, 2008).

But unfortunately, it seems the time is coming when mankind becomes aware that present environmental and energy problems are inseparable part of the growth of material science. The approaches to practical material science should then be also revised. We need even now to return to basics - to pursuit the principles of natural phenomena, rebuild material science in an inter-connected manner, discover the best solutions of problems and establish a new kind of modern material science that is not captive to specific fields of materials or practical science.

Some of the most perspective fields of future material science are therefore shortly introduced in several next chapters.

3.2 Metallic glasses

Offering some of the highest specific strength and resilience values known among bulk materials, the amorphous metallic materials, more commonly termed metallic glasses, have the large potential to revolutionize the field of material science and engineering. The next decades will surely bring exciting advantages of this material class, as just now is the humankind on the threshold of exploiting new opportunities for their microstructural design, opening up much broader application of the fascinating materials formed from metallic glasses.

The term "glass" means in scientific terminology any material that can be cooled from a liquid to a solid without crystallizing. Most metals do crystallize as they cool, arranging their atoms into a highly regular spatial pattern called a lattice. But if crystallization does not occur and the atoms settle into a nearly random arrangement, the final form is a metallic glass. Through effectively probing the fundamental mechanism responsible for deformation in metallic glasses nanoindentation has the potential to provide the answers necessary for their industrial applications.

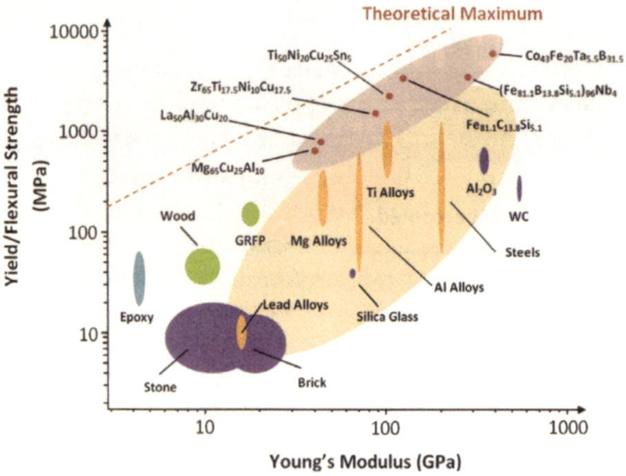

Fig. 3. The yield (metals, composites and polymers) or flexural strength (ceramics) as a function of Young`s modulus. Diagram shows strength of metallic glasses (light red) over conventional crystalline metals (light orange) (Ashby & Greer, 2006).

Metallic glasses exhibit mechanical and physical properties representative of a completely new paradigm in material science, because their structure lacks the dislocations and grain boundaries, which are inherent in crystalline materials. The elastic strain may regularly approach about 2% without of premature deformation of slip, thereby facilitating strength and hardness values which are far beyond those of crystalline metals (Fig. 3). In the work representing the highest strength, specific strength and specific Young`s modulus of any bulk metal, it has been found (Inoue et al., 2003) a fracture strength of 5 085 GPa and Young`s modulus of 268 GPa for $Co_{43}Fe_{20}Ta_{5.5}B_{31.5}$ alloy. Besides these extremely advisable mechanical properties, metallic glasses exhibit extremely high values of toughness, low mechanical damping, good corrosion resistance and high magnetic permeability coupled with low coercivity to give superior soft magnetic properties. However, recently discovered advances have allowed more amenable geometries needed for generating various novel metallic glass products. The particularly intriguing possibilities of relatively low temperature superplastic forming operations are up to now insufficiently exploited. Tensile specimens following superplastic forming in the supercooled liquid region are able to withstand the elongation of 1 600% at $Zr_{41.25}Ti_{13.75}Cu_{12.5}Ni_{10}Be_{22.5}$ alloy (Wang et al. 2005 - Fig. 4) and even over 20 000% at $La_{55}Al_{25}Ni_{20}$ one (Nieh et al., 2006). The high-quality golf club heads, baseball bats and tennis racquets have benefited from significantly enhanced elasticity, while high strength and hardness can be utilized for production of medical and aerospace coating applications. The absence of crystallization during casting process in conjunction with high melt density ensure low casting shape fidelity which is the not only advisable factor for any thermomechanical forming operation but in particular relevance in the production of various micro electromechanical systems.

Fig. 4. Tensile specimen made of Zr41.25Ti13.75Cu12.5Ni10Be22.5 alloy following superplastic forming in the supercooled liquid region (Wang et al., 2005).

Recent observations has emphasized that densest packing which is the typical for monatomic metallic glasses is a key factor governing their structure and properties. But dense packing, even when non-crystalline, is certainly not random. The chemical interactions between the elements in alloys are very important. Glass-forming ability is enhanced when the elements of an alloy have a negative heat of reaction (i.e. in a system such as nickel-boron, Ni-B bonds are preferred in comparison with Ni-Ni or B-B bonds). The relevance of such chemical effects emerged in many structural studies of metallic glasses such as $Ni_{81}B_{19}$ that there are no B-B nearest neighbours.

Fig. 5. Structure of $Ni_{81}B_{19}$ metallic glass showing quasi-equivalent solute-centered clusters (Greer, 2009).

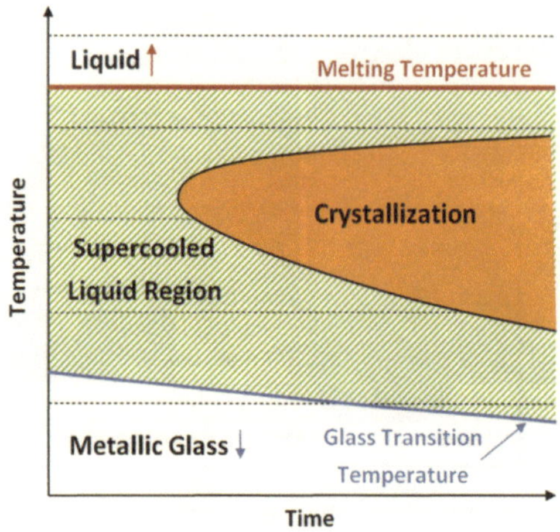

Fig. 6. Schematic time - temperature transformation diagram for metallic glasses. Crystallization rate is determined by the competing effects of undercooling and reaction kinetics. The supercooled liquid region exists between the melting and glass transition temperatures over time periods not exceeding that required for crystal nucleation. (Burgess & Ferry, 2009).

Many criteria have been proposed for selection of alloy compositions that would favour glass formation, but none of them shows universal advisability. The crystallization of melt during cooling becomes thermodynamically possible below the liquidus temperature T_l and is kinetically hindered below the glass-transition temperature T_g (Fig. 6). Glass formation is most likely when the gap between T_l and T_g is minimized and is indicated by a high value of the reduced glass-transition temperature $T_{rg}= T_g / T_l$. The higher values of T_{rg} are associated with lower critical cooling rates for glass formation. As T_g appears to be independent on composition, high values of T_{rg} are indicated by depressions of T_l and indeed glass-forming ability is particularly good at deep eutectics which are more likely to be found in multicomponent systems. As the critical cooling rate for glass formation is reduced, an amorphous structure can be made in thicker sections, commonly represented by the maximum diameter of cylinder that can be cast into a fully glassy form. The compositions for which the critical diameter exceeds 10 mm are considered to form so called bulk metallic glasses (BMGs). The history of their recent development is shown in the Table 1.

From technological point of view it is extremely important that metallic glasses show viscous flow at elevated temperatures. The ability to use various hot-forming processes obviously used for conventional glasses and for thermoplastic polymers is very advantageous, especially when combined with the high strengths obtained on cooling. Most BMGs are in liquid state too strong for good thermoplastic properties, but strategies are beginning to emerge to design alloys that can be easily cast into glasses, yet are comparatively fragile and therefore easily shaped (e.g. BMG with the composition $Zr_{35}Ti_{30}Cu_{8.25}Be_{26.75}$ thanks to a record large interval of 159 K between the glass-transition and the crystallization temperature shows exceptionally good thermoplastic workability).

The first demonstration that glass formation could be achieved for metallic liquid was made in 1959 in laboratory of California Institute of Technology (CalTech) by Prof. Pol Duwez and up to now, this institute is leading force in the research, development and

commercialization of metallic glasses. Their so called Liquidmetal® Technologies controls the intellectual property rights with more than 20 patents on the composition, processing and usage of technology related to these high performance materials and products revolutionizing the materials world.
The first material revolution occurred in the 1800's, when Sir Henry Bessemer of England invented a process to mass-produce steel inexpensively. Cheaper steel was crucial to the modern industrial revolution. Construction of factories, automobiles, railroads, bridges and high-rise buildings was made possible by the availability of steel. During the 1900's, chemists invented thermo-plastics, which dramatically reduced the cost of manufacturing by using one mold for thousands of parts and thereby revolutionized industrial production for the second time. In this 21st century, scientists at Caltech develop a unique Liquidmetal® Technologies described in this chapter. While the Bessemer Process and thermo-plastics technology dramatically improved the cost paradigm of their day, BMGs with the trademark Liquidmetal® are in the nearest feature able to redefine the cost and performance paradigm simultaneously. Their superior properties are obtained by recent revolutionary scientific and technological innovations.

Base metal	Composition (atomic %)	Critical diameter (mm)	Year
Pd	$Pd_{40}Ni_{40}P_{20}$	10	1984
	$Pd_{40}Cu_{30}Ni_{10}P_{20}$	72	1997
Zr	$Zr_{65}Al_{7.5}Ni_{10}Cu_{17.5}$	16	1993
	$Zr_{41.2}Ti_{13.8}Cu_{12.5}Ni_{10}Be_{22.5}$	25	1996
Cu	$Cu_{46}Zr_{42}Al_7Y_5$	10	2004
	$Cu_{49}Hf_{42}Al_9$	10	2006
rare earth	$Y_{36}Sc_{20}Al_{24}Co_{20}$	25	2003
	$La_{62}Al_{15.7}Cu_{11.15}Ni_{11.15}$	11	2003
Mg	$Mg_{54}Cu_{26.5}Ag_{8.5}Gd_{11}$	25	2005
	$Mg_{65}Cu_{7.5}Ni_{7.5}Zn_5Ag_5Y_5Gd_5$	14	2005
Fe	$Fe_{48}Cr_{15}Mo_{14}Er_2C_{15}B_6$	12	2004
	$(Fe_{44.3}Cr_5Co_5Mo_{12.8}Mn_{11.2}C_{15.8}B_{5.9})_{98.5}Y_{1.5}$	12	2004
	$Fe_{41}Co_7Cr_{15}Mo_{14}C_{15}B_6Y_2$	16	2005
Co	$Co_{48}Cr_{15}Mo_{14}Er_2C_{15}B_6$	10	2006
Ti	$Ti_{40}Zr_{25}Cu_{12}Ni_3Be_{20}$	14	2005
Ca	$Ca_{65}Mg_{15}Zn_{20}$	15	2004
Pt	$Pt_{42.5}Cu_{27}Ni_{9.5}P_{21}$	20	2004

Table 1. Representative bulk metallic glass composition with the critical largest diameter of cylinders that can be cast fully glassy and the year of first report (Greer, 2009).

3.3 Lightweight structural materials

The main role of structural materials is to have the ability to support a large load safety. The resistance to plastic deformation is the yield stress and the one to fracture is the tensile strength. As the yield stress and the tensile strength increase, a load that a material can support increases. Therefore, if materials show a constant yield stress, the weight of the structural components that support a given load can be decreased when the density of material is small. This index (yield stress/density) is referred as specific strength.

Metallic materials that have a lower density than steel, which is the most highly used structural material, are generally called light metals or lightweight structural materials.
Table 2 shows the physical properties of most frequently used structural metals. The density and the Young`s modulus are properties that depend only on the chemical composition. However, the yield stress and the tensile strength are the structural sensitive properties, which depend also on the metallic crystal microstructure.

Metal	**Density (1000 · kg/m³)**	**Young`s Modulus (GPa)**	**Melting point (°C)**
Iron (Fe)	7.87	210	1536
Titanium (Ti)	4.54	115	1666
Aluminium (Al)	2.69	70	660
Magnesium (Mg)	1.74	45	650

Table 2. Physical properties of structural metals (Tsuzaki, 2008).

The yield stress of steel can be increased by control of microstructure even up to over 800 MPa. Table 3 shows mechanical properties of structural metals, which includes steels with a yield stress over 1400 MPa and aluminium (A7075) over 500 MPa. These materials exceed the specific strength of 150 MNm/kg and they can be therefore both classified as a lightweight structural materials that are more than 10-times lighter than industrial pure iron with the specific strength of only 12 MNm/kg.

Material	**Yield stress (MPa)**	**Elongation (%)**
Iron – industrial pure	98	60
High tensile strength steel (HT80)	834	26
Ni-Cr-Mo steel (SNCM439)	1471	8
Ti – industrial pure	170	27
Ti-6Al-4V alloy	920	14
Al – industrial pure	15	30
Al-Cu-Mg alloy (Duralumin)	195	15
Al-Zn-Mg alloy (Extra Super Duralumin)	505	11
Cast Mg alloy	70	7
Wrought Mg alloy	160	6

Table 3. Mechanical properties of structural metals (Tsuzaki, 2008).

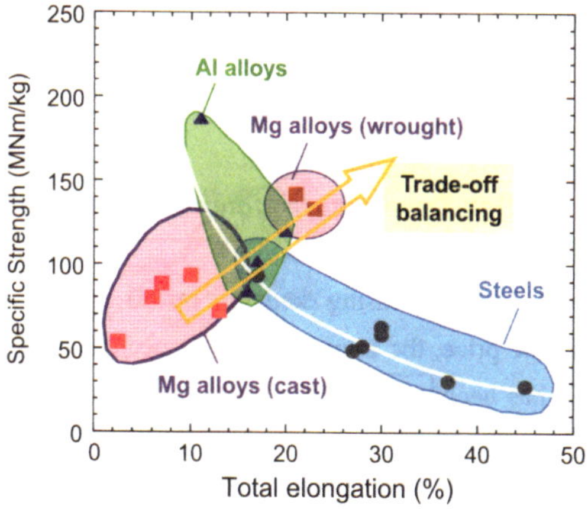

Fig. 7. Relationship between total elongation and specific strength (Tsuzaki, 2008).

The main application potential of lightweight structural materials is mainly in industries such as automotive, aircraft and space industries, shipbuilding, etc., where they are utilized with the aim to reduce the weight of vehicles. But numerous material related problems arise when we intend to save the weight by employing the lightweight materials with high specific strength. The first problem area is of course the cost. Titanium alloys are typical lightweight metals with superior characteristics, but seldom to be applied in vehicles because of their high cost. The expensive titanium alloys are even in the aircraft field employed mainly to military planes. The second problem is deterioration of formability. The elongation decreases as the yield stress or the specific strength increases. Various lightweight components are produced using a plastic deformation called press forming and therefore the increasing of elongation is being demanded despite their high strength. As shown in Fig. 7., this is a challenging issue to be overcome. The control of microstructure using nanotechnology is being carried out for this type of scientific encounter. Nevertheless, for the processing of lightweight high strength materials many other problems remain in such areas, e.g. machinability or weldability.

3.4 Nanostructural materials for energy and environment sectors

The current nanotechnology science investigates new materials and substances with a strong sense of scale, from the molecular and atomic level to sizes on the nanometer order. The search for various nanostructure-controlled materials is being conducted and many developments are being made in this scientific field. Various studies performed with the purpose of having new developments in material science made through nanotechnology play useful roles in solving essential problems in the fields of environment and energy such as saving energy, reducing negative impacts on the environment and finding alternatives for scarce natural resources.

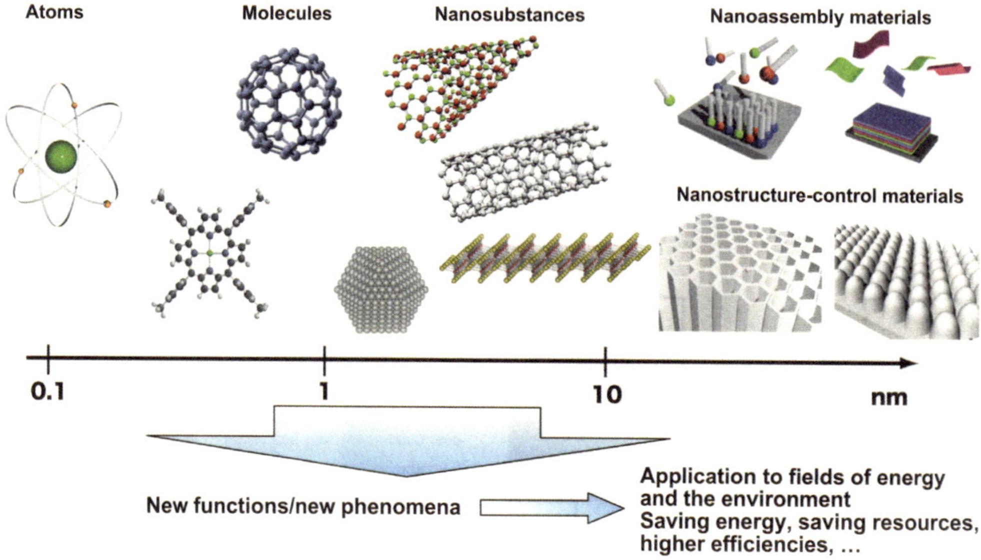

Fig. 8. Illustration of recent developments in material science through nanotechnology (Sasaki, 2008).

The development of nanotechnology-driven materials for the application in the fields of saving energy and reducing of environmental impacts is at present organized into four approaches:

a) *Investigation of new phenomena and functions on the atomic and molecular level*

Thanks to rapid progress in technologies that permits single electrons or molecules to be individually manipulated typified by the scanning probe microscope, it is now possible to approach phenomena and properties of materials that had been impossible up to now. Recent developments in this field are particularly proceeding on phase change memory, magneto-resistance memory, resistive random access memory, atomic switches and other modern devices that have reached the extremes of miniaturization. Each such nanometer-scaled switch is the non-volatile programmable solid-electrolyte device, so it has properties invisible in ordinary semiconductor devices. This atomic switch achieves the switched-on state by means of a metal filament, so it is characterized by having a smaller resistance in the switched-on state than the other devices. It is suitable for the application in low power consumption and high-speed signal transmission circuits. It is possible to shrink the surface area of a switching circuit to 1/30 of a conventional circuit when an atomic switch is used, what allows to incorporate many switches into a single chip. This makes possible to develop devices that can achieve many types of functions on a single chip. The operation of the atomic switch was initially confirmed using a sulphide system as the ion conductor, but recently its operation has also been confirmed in a metal oxide system that can be more easily embedded into semiconductor devices. However, as operation principle of atomic switches differs from that of semiconductor devices, it is even not known whether or not the same evaluation techniques can be used as in case of semiconductor devices.

b) *Development of new functions for nanoscale substances*

The discovery and synthesis of nanotubes, nanorods, nanosheets, nanoparticles and many other new substances that have various size and dimensionalities (Fig. 8) stimulate the investigation of new functions derived from the size effects and unique shapes. For example, high efficiency of electron emissions and hydrogen storage are possible using nanotubes, while superior electronic and magnetic functions are achieved with nanosheets. The exploration of wide range of applications is therefore unavoidable.

In the field of energy and environment, applied research is mainly focused to creation of nanoordered functional and structural materials with advanced physical properties for energy savings, which contribute to environmental improvement and conservation. There are many possibilities on the creation of functional nanostructural materials for high-energy savings and new environmentally friendly systems such as solar batteries, fuel cells, hydrogen storage nanotubes and self-cleaning TiO_2 nanocoatings. The recent developments in the field of self-assembled nanostructural materials are aimed to removing of hazardous chemical substances selectively, as well as to creation of new nanoporous materials which possess a selective catalytic function. In the field of oxide nanomaterials, recent progress in nanofabrication techniques has lead to the creation of advanced electronic materials and various interesting properties have been explored by control of nanostructures and nanospaces in glasses (amorphous semiconductors), cement constituents ($12CaO \cdot 7Al_2O_3$) and other commonplace materials.

c) *Fabrication of new materials by nanoassembly technologies*

Through the development of techniques for the integration and creation of arrays of organic-inorganic nanomodules, a wide variety of materials can now be designed in the sense of assembling them from parts and as a result, it is now possible to develop advanced functions that would be difficult to achieve with a single substance. Various industrial applications of highly efficient energy conversion elements are expected.

Typical examples of molecular assembly have included the manufacture of single-molecule films and molecular wires. For example, the development of organic electronics had previously been concerned with its applications to lightweight and thin devices, but more recently, there has been a focus on the environment and energy problems, and accordingly they have attracted attention as eco-materials and alternative materials as substitutes for rare materials. For example, while silicon is mainly used as the material for solar cells and thin-film transistors, demand for such is expected to increase in the future. The value of organic materials as an alternative material for silicon is at present also often reviewed. For example, the conventional amorphous silicon thin films are deposited by plasma CVD process which consumes large energy amounts, they may be replaced by organic thin films that could be produced by printing methods or other low-temperature, less energy-intensive processes (Wakayama, 2008).

d) *Fine control of nanostructures*

By achieving fine control of the types of atoms and their arrangement within inorganic crystal lattice, the control of materials and substances that take advantage of nanoscaled porous structures and the control of the degree of dispersion of nanoparticles and clusters dispersion becomes possible along with an extremely wide range of other new technologies.

Porous ceramics comprising nanopores connected to each other are widely used as catalyst carriers or filters. A wide-spread technique is the method of manufacture of porous glass that utilizes the phase-separation phenomena of borosilicate glass. Glass that was heat-treated and phase-separated in the phase-separation temperature range is subjected to acid etching treatment to elute the phase with boron oxide as the primary component, thereby obtaining porous silica glass with pores of several nanometers in diameter. When the phase-separation treatment and acid etching is performed after being spun into hollow glass fiber, a heat-resistant hollow-yarn membrane of an inorganic oxide is formed. This can be used in industrial applications, e.g. for water purification and various filters.

3.5 Nature-guided material processing

Natural materials are remarkably efficient, because they fulfill the complex requirements posed by the way plants and animals function and that they do so using as small amount of material as possible. Many of these requirements are mechanical in nature: the need to support static and dynamic loads created by the mass of the organism, by blood pressure, etc. The same is true for plants: they must support themselves, tolerate wind and snow loading. Some of them are thermal or electrical: the need to insulate, transpire, sense, and actuate. And most natural materials are sustainable, recyclable, and — when disposal is necessary — biodegradable.

Almost all natural materials are composites and consist of a relatively small number of polymeric and ceramic components or structural building blocks, which often are composites themselves. Wood, bamboo and palm consist of cellulose fibers in a lignin/hemicellulose matrix, shaped to hollow prismatic cells. Collagen is the basic structural element of soft tissues like tendon, ligament, skin, blood vessels, muscle and cartilage. Mineralized tissues - antler, bone, dentine and enamel for instance - are composed mainly of hydroxyapatite with varying degrees of residual collagen. Hair, hooves, horn, wool, and reptilian scales are made of keratin. Insect cuticle contains chitin in a matrix of protein. From a mechanical point of view, there is nothing very special about the structural building blocks. It is the structure and arrangement of the components that give rise to the striking efficiency of natural materials (Ashby, 2008).

A number of advanced bio-materials have been developed recently to allow repair or replacement of tissue. They are bio-compatible and, in some cases, even able to stimulate cell growth. They resist attack by body fluids or, if attacked, it must be in a way that allows the body to absorb the corrosion products benignly. All these bio-materials are also able to carry the cyclic loads imposed on them by the normal functioning of the body, and to do so for many years. Among polymers, polyolefins, consisting only of carbon and hydrogen, are the least toxic. They have properties that more closely match those of tissue than do the properties of metals. Principal among them is ultra-high molecular weight polyethylene, UHMWPE. Acrylics find use both as contact lenses and as cements for bone hip and other joint replacements. Silicone elastomers are used for cosmetic implants.

Learning from and attempting to come closer to duplicating the wonders of nature has continued to be an age old challenge for material scientists and engineers. With the widespread use of processing tools at present due to the advancements in nanotechnology, in many fields, it is becoming increasingly possible to make breakthroughs that come close to the truly complex mechanism of nature rather than simply simulate the pattern as in the past. A lot of research has come to recognize the importance of learning from nature and living organisms. Professor Hideki Ishida from Tohoku University (Japan) proposed a completely new approach to manufacturing and lifestyle by scientifically looking at "Nature`s Cycle" which is a product of the endless repetition of verification and selection throughout Earth`s history and by redesigning what are essential for the human ecosystem among them (Fig. 9). This approach is called "Nature Tech". Until now, the concept of "Learning from Nature and Living Things" has been associated with refined simplicity and beauty, or conversely, mind-boggling complexity and detail. However, we need to learn much more from nature in which moderation is used to obtain essential structures and functions, using only a minimum of non-hazardous natural elements to create objects with a minimum amount of energy. We need to have the sense and observation skills to re-design as well as techniques to imitate so that we can go beyond just admiring nature.

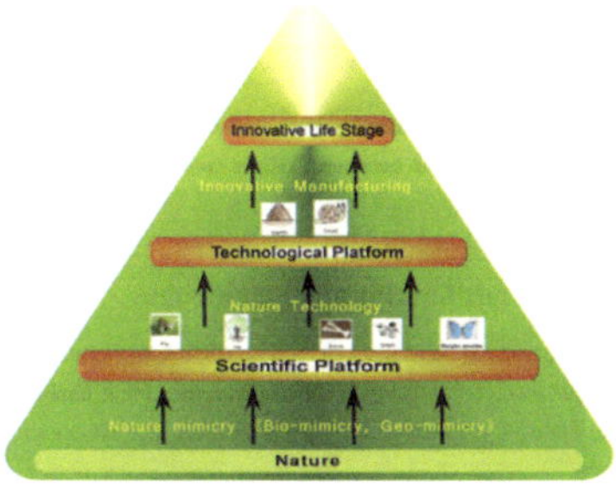

Fig. 9. Concept of "Nature Tech" (Kakisawa, 2008).

4. Networking of institutions fostering by R&D&TT of engineering materials

The experience from countries with high economic level shows at present the great necessity to create conditions for faster and more efficient transfer of knowledge on recently developed materials and technological processes into the industrial practice. Establishment of excellently equipped research centres for technological transfer, which serve mainly to the purposes of small and medium size enterprises, is an essential prerequisite to raise the level of manufacturing possibilities, and thereby these ones support the further technological progress.

The creation of the networks linking the institutions and experts working in the field of material research and development of related technologies is the reliable practice in many countries with advanced industrialized economy. There are many examples of similar virtual networks organizing these activities very successfully. One of the most advanced European network in this field is Materials Valley e.V. (www.materials-valley-rheinmain.de) established in 2002 in the German region of Rhein-Main, which links about 750 industrial companies and 120 high educational and research institutions. The similar network CORONET - Thermoplastic Composites Infrastructure Cooperation Network (www.coronet.eu.com) links 18 institutions from 9 European Union countries working in the field of thermoplastic composites.

The region of Central Europe is nowadays a region of materials science with tradition. Favourable tax laws, sustainable economic growth and directions accommodating investors ensure above-average growth of direct foreign investments in this region. Large industrial companies such as VW, Peugeot, KIA or Siemens already profit of the economic advantages of this region. The volume of procurement of eleven companies manufacturing products and components exclusively for automotive industry within the radius of 300 km around

Bratislava – the capital of Slovakia - increased to more than EUR 40 billion in the year 2008. That is why the professional research and education in connection with the state-of-the-art infrastructure is of the highest importance. The virtual network for R&D in the field of engineering materials and related technologies was recently established for this purpose in Slovakia and represents a valuable contribution from this point of view. The virtual network for technological innovations MatNet which links Slovak scientific, academic and industrial institutions dealing with research and development in the field of engineering materials and accompanying technologies has been created in order to enable more efficient transfer of knowledge on modern materials and advanced manufacturing processes of their production, pretreatment and joining from the academic community into the Slovak industrial companies. One of the network objectives is to establish the centre that organizes educational courses not only for developers and designers, but also for university teachers, scientific workers and doctoral students. The aim of these courses is the training in new complex principles of structural and functional components creation, on the basis of proper material selection with regard to functionality, type of operation loading and cost of product or construction and synchronized optimization of component outline and appropriate production process. During the courses, the participants have an opportunity to work on one's own with real databases containing properties of nearly all current engineering materials, as well as parameters of modern manufacturing processes and to learn the use of these databases in proposals of optimum design of components and structures for various industrial applications (Jerz & Košút, 2008).

The main communication platform of the network is the web portal MatNet - Slovakia (www.matnet.sav.sk), gathering and depositing useful information about materials and processes via various Slovak and international sources. The ambition of recently established Slovak network for innovations - MatNet is to enable developers from Slovak industrial companies (working e.g. in automotive, electrical, mechanical, building, aircraft, chemical, food and other industrial sectors) more effectively cooperate with scientists and experts from the academic community in order significantly to enhance the quality of their products.

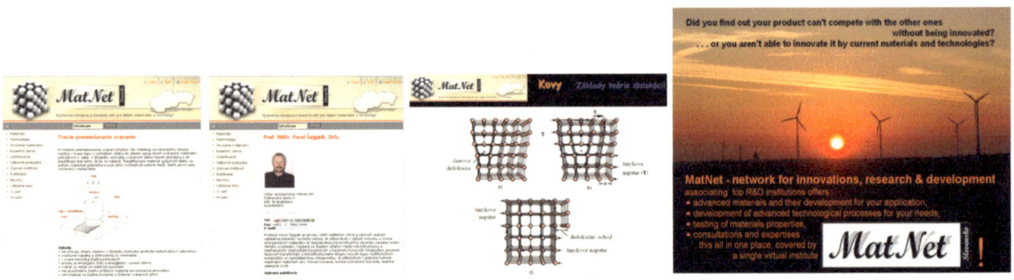

A B C D

Fig. 10. Records of the web portal MatNet - Slovakia (examples) describing: A - technology of friction stir welding, B - expert of the network MatNet., C - e-learning lesson: "Metals - Theory of Dislocations". D – Home page of web portal MatNet.

5. Conclusion

The activities supporting innovations in the field of engineering materials and accompanying technologies should enable a more efficient linking of scientists and experts from the academic community to the industry, effective transfer of knowledge and more rational purchase of equipment, realisation of complex projects, etc.
Further enlargement of networking activities is therefore essential. The process of involving local companies into the research activities for large industrial producers and suppliers will be speeded up through activities aimed to establishment of research driven clusters with participation of governmental institutions, both regional and local research stakeholders, local enterprises and large multinational producers. This is the main approach how to eliminate the consequences of ominous crease in economic grow. The importance of these activities is crucial because of enormous potential of huge capital investments as the consequence of future extensive industrial expansion.

6. Acknowledgment

The support of the Institute of Materials and Machine Mechanics of Slovak Academy of Sciences under the project Emergence of Research Driven Clusters in Central Europe (ERDC, Grant No. 202855, 7FP-REGIONS-2007-2) is gratefully acknowledged.

7. References

Ashby, M. F. (2008). The CES EduPack Database of Natural and Man-Made Materials, Granta Design, Cambridge, UK, www.grantadesign.com

Ashby, M. F. & Cebon, D. (2002). New Approaches to Materials Education, Granta Design, Cambridge, UK, www.grantadesign.com

Ashby, M. F. & Greer, A. L. (2006). Metallic glasses as structural materials, In: *Scripta Mater.*, Vol. 54, No. 3, pp. 321–326

Burgess, T. & Ferry M. (2009). Nanoindentation of metallic glasses, *Materials Today*, Vol. 12, No. 1-2, January-February 2009, pp. 24-32, ISSN 1369-7021

Greer, A. L. (2009). Metallic glasses . . . on the threshold., *Materials Today*, Vol. 12, No. 1-2, January-February 2009, pp. 14-22, ISSN 1369-7021

Inoue, A., et al. (2003). Cobalt-based bulk glassy alloy with ultrahigh strength and soft magnetic properties, In: *Nature Materials*, 10, p. 661

Jerz, J. & Košút, J. (2008). The importance of effective knowledge transfer of modern engineering materials and advanced technologies into the industrial praxis. *Proceedings of International Conference of Education, Research and Innovation ICERI 2008*, CD-Proceedings, ISBN: 978-84-612-5091-2, Madrid, November 2008, Publisher: International Asociation of Technology, Education and Development, IATED, Valencia

Kakisawa, H. (2008). Nature Tech Materials, In: *Materials Outlook for Energy and Environment*, pp. 78-79, NIMS, Sengen, Tsukuba, Ibaraki, Japan

Marsden, W.; Warde, S. & Fairfull, A. (2007) Meeting the Materials Data Management Needs of Engineering Enterprises, Granta technical paper, Granta Design, Cambridge, UK, www.grantadesign.com

Nieh, T. G. & Wadsworth, J. (2006). Homogeneous deformation of bulk metallic glasses, In: *J. Scripta Materialia,* Vol. 54, No. 3, pp. 387-392

Sasaki, T. (2008). Nano-driven Energy/Environmental Materials, In: *Materials Outlook for Energy and Environment,* p. 61, NIMS, Sengen, Tsukuba, Ibaraki, Japan

Shinohara, Y. (2008). Encouraging Material Science, In: *Materials Outlook for Energy and Environment,* pp. 1-2, NIMS, Sengen, Tsukuba, Ibaraki, Japan

Tsuzaki, K. (2008). Light structural materials, In: *Materials Outlook for Energy and Environment,* pp. 56-57, NIMS, Sengen, Tsukuba, Ibaraki, Japan.

Wang, G., et al. (2005). Superplasticity and superplastic forming ability of a Zr–Ti–Ni–Cu–Be bulk metallic glass in the supercooled liquid region, *J. Non-Cryst. Solids,* Vol. 351, No. 3, February 2005, pp. 209-217

Wakajama, Y. (2008). Nanoassembly Materials, In: *Materials Outlook for Energy and Environment,* pp. 66-67, NIMS, Sengen, Tsukuba, Ibaraki, Japan

How to develop a University educational guide? Some suggestions for its graphic design

Begoña Jorda-Albiñana, Olga Ampuero-Canellas,
Jimena González-del-Río and Jose Armijo
Universidad Politécnica de Valencia
Spain

1. Introduction

It is being a more common practice that universities edit and distribute a document called educational guide or study guide at the beginning of each academic course. This publication is principally for students and contains information and details referred to the institution. For example, study plan and subjects, management team and staff directory, history, services (library, secretary, laboratories), building plans, etc.

This study guide constitute a fundamental support for new students who need more information because they do not know the centre. Also is a useful tool for old students because it serves as reminder of the information they already know or as a referral of new data.

In addition, this educational guide can serve as an introduction letter for the institution for those who are interested in knowing some more about its academic aspects. The educational guide could be given to future students, parents, high school students, visitors, congress assistants, etc. In these cases it constitutes a superb instrument for showing and promoting the institution.

These two segments determine two basic functions of the educational guide. On one hand this publication has an informative purpose since it has been created to inform about main issues as subjects, schedules, telephones, etc. On the other hand it has a promotional function because it can become a kind of business card in order to introduce the center to the different audiences.

Besides, this second function reveals that both the contents and the form play a fundamental roll which is not only to inform but also to promote and to persuade by transmitting a suitable and attractive image of the university.

The following pages present some guidelines about how to design one of these Teacher Guides including suggestions about the use of typography, images, grid and components of the Visual Corporate Identity. One of the Guides made for the Engineering Design Upper Technical School of the Universidad Politécnica de Valencia (Spain) is presented as example at the end. The comment regarding to decisions made about the design to be used in this Teachers Guide may serve as an example for the suggestions that have been presented.

Fig. 1. Studies Guide 06-07

2. Color

Color is an important element in any graphical design since it not only heightens the presence of the poster, packaging, logo or brochure and distinguishes it from the competition but also because it can communicate certain values, concepts or meanings.
Color language is probably nowadays the most universal of all because it has a very significant presence in analogies and connotations within popular language. Although color was also created to distinguish itself from the others it was also thought as the purest and most millenary vehicle of communication. Color selection and use in design must follow certain guidelines (Ferrer, 1999).

2.1 Color in the design

Designers refer to three variables when using colors: tone, brightness and saturation.
Tone defines color thorough the wave long that dominate it's expectrum (Ferrer, 1999) and it's what we normally call color: green, blue, red, yellow...
Brightness refers to lightness or darkness contained in a tone (Ferrer, 1999; Carter, 1997) and can be also describe as the amount of white or black mixed with the tone (Chijiiwa, 1999). Value distinguish between light colors and dark colors: a color is lighter or brighter if white has been added and darker or less bright. (Carter, 1997).
Saturation is related to color intensity o pureness and goes from matte to bright or from an intense tone to a opac one depending on how much gray is in it (Ferrer, 1999).
It's also possible to distinguish between cool and warm colors. In general, red, orange and yellow transmit warmness and blue, green or purple transmit coolness (Carter, 1997).

2.2 Choosing and combining colors

Chijiiwa (1999) indicates some parameters about how to choose and use color for the design of a Teachers Guide. First of all, he considers necessary to know colors which includes to familiarize with their three characteristics (tone, brightness and saturation), the uses and

emotions associated with each color and the six great chromatic categories (warm, cold, light, dark, intense and dull).
This distiction seems to be more useful when combining two or more colors. According to Chijiiwa (1999), it's important to ensure that it exists a reasonable gap between those colors that will be mixed. So if colors have a similar tone, it should have different brightness and saturation; or if colors have similar brightness, saturation and tone may be differents.
Main goal of the design may be determined next. For achieving it, it becomes useful to answer the following questions:

- What type of effect you want to obtain?
- What colors will transmit better that effect?
- Are those colors topic or have been used too much? What other possibilities are available?
- Do those colors adjust to your potential public? Are they legible? Are they showy?
- Can you improve the effect by changing some colors?

Once the main goal has been determined, it's convenient to decide coulour (light or dark) brightness. Although people usually classify colors by their tone, luminosity is much more important when determining the general aspect of the design. In fact, all colors with the same brightness (for example, all light colors or all dark colors) are similar enough without considering shade. Nevertheless, colors with the same shade but with different values (for example, blue sky, turquoise and navy blue) can be surprisingly different and hard to combine.
So choosing brightness first the general design effect is chosen as well: Do you wish an intense and showy design? Or light and smooth? Or better dark and discreet? Or dull and grey?
Furthermore, it is important to consider that it is more important to vary brightness and clarifying or darkening colors than to vary tones when combining colors. If light and dark colors are contrasted, the scheme will be showy and three-dimensional. If only tonalities appear contrasted, the final scheme seems to be flat and poor.
Regarding to the number of colors to be used for the design, Chijiiwa (1999) considers it necessary to limit the number of coulours in order to increase chromatic armony. Two or three colors should be enough, five would be excessive. Besides, it is necessary to make sure that only one color exists and establishes the guideline for the rest of the chromatic scheme.

Fig. 2. Chromatic selection for the 04/05 CD Studies Guide version

Besides, intense colors must be used with moderation to avoid an annoying perception rather than spectacular effect. They have to be used in general for details (for example headline) and light or dull colors for background.

Lastly, Chijiiwa (1999) suggested to use an achromatic color (black, grey or white) to get a harmonious result. White or black have a simplicity and an elegance that is able enough to attract our attention as much as the most showy and intense colors. Apart of that, all colors combine with black or white.

2.3 Color Language

According it (1995), people experiment colors in three levels: phycological, cultural and asociative. The psichological answer is universal and involunteer and regarding to it, red color acelerates pulse while green decreases it.

Color is also related to traditions established in each culture. For example, black is the color of death in Occident while in some oriental countries it it white. Associative experience also reflects those expectations produced by colors as a result of marketing efforts along time that makes for example that the combination of white and red remembers people to Coca-Cola.

According to March (1989), associative characteristics of colors can be acquired (for example red that is related to danger) or symbolic (for example blue is associated to cleanliness and green to health and wellness).

Nevertheless, there is no unique code for the use of color because the meaning of each color depends on different factors: experiences, taste, fashion… ad the meaning it has today can become totally different tomorrow (Ferrer, 1999).

Several authors include in their works the most comon meanings related to every color from the symbolic, cultural or marketing associations that have been acquiring along time. The following table includes the most important meanings and uses colors have in Graphic Design sector.

Color	Associations	Use in Graphic Design
Black	Darkness, sadness, mourning, death, uglyness, night, deepness, hate, heavyness, fear, magic	Great backgorund color because other colors bring out over it. Perfect to transmit concepts as elegance, wealthy, high quality, selection.
White	Purenessm, peace, inocence, virtue, truth, goodness, lightness, elegance, cleaness, esterility, coolness, simplicity.	Creates distance and space. As background color takes away brightness and tone from the other colors. Used as secondary color in order to obtain visibility and impact.
Green	Nature, freshness, humidity, life, heakth, ecology, hope.	Cirjury and first aid equipments.
Red	Blood, fire, revolutionary pasion, comunism, emotions, movement, force, agresivity, intensity, rage.	Dominates the collection, bring out the profiles and atracts attention strongly.
Orange	Warmness, frienship, excitement, spontanity fall.	Cheap goods.
Blue	Constant, fidelitym trust, meditation, misticism, serenity.	Masculine products, cleaning products, transportation and financial sector.
Yellow	Joy, loud, sun, wealthy, inteligence, intuition.	Great impact.

Table 1. Color Meanings (Ferrer, 1999; Wills, 1999; Chijiiwa, 1999; Heller, 2004).

3. Typography

It is necessary to consider the election of the font as well as its location within the page when we talk about typography. Both purposes may consider two Basic functions of typography: linguistic and aesthetic (Martín Montesinos & Mas Hurtuna, 2001). On one side, text readability will be reached, on the other, transmitting a correct graphic image, attractive and consequent to those values that want to be transmitted.
Recommendations about the correct use of Typography are listed bellow.

3.1 Choosing Font

The more anodyne a letter is, the more legible it becomes. Therefore a familiar typesetter font will be chosen for the Teacher's Guide in order to transmit the information to the receiver as efficiently as possible considering the importance of this process.
Another aspect to be regarded is that well-proportioned and open characters that show the regularity of the classic typographical families (Helvetica, Times New Roman, Garamond, etc.) are easier to read than those types with edgings, decorations and irregularities (Carter, 1997). So typeface selected for the Teacher's Guide may be that kind.
Regarding to the number of typefaces to be used in the design, it turns out too annoying to read more than two different typographical families in the same page. For that reason, it is recommended to use only one typeface family and to vary its size and thickness (usindg typefaces) in case some part of the text has to be reinforced.
Scripts also brings out part of the text. Nevertheless, it may be used carefully because too many characters are inclined in a text it is more difficult to be read (Carter, 1997).

About Capital letters and lower-case letters, a text written in capital letters makes the reading slower (reading speed decreases 12%) and occupies more space (Carter, 1997). The difference in regard to legibility is because small letters add visual signals to the text (various shape letters, ascendants, descendants and word forms) that makes the reading easier whereas capital letters lack of this visual variety. It is better to use lower-case letters and leave Capital Letters for special cases (for example, titles, key words within the text, etc.).

Last, it is important to determine font size correctly because too big or too small letters tire readers easily when examining plain texts. When defining what size is more appropriate, we have to consider that the height of the "x" influences more in the legibility of the text than the size of the letter (10 or 12 points) (Bix et al., 2003).

3.2 Text Location in the page

Once typography has been chosen it's necessary to decide how to locate text all over the page. This decisions are related to aspect such line size, number of columns, space between lines, text direction, etc. There are some guidelines for this as well that make reading much easier.

Regarding to line size, if text lines are too long, it becomes tedious. On the other side, if text lines are too short its reading produce a discontinue movement of the eyes, that reader get tired as well. So it is essential to look for a coherent line length as well as to maintain the body of the text.

At the same time, a correct space between lines makes reading much easier. Reduced space between could make readers confuse a line with the following one. Oppositely, if space is too large finding the following line becomes more difficult.

Refearing to text direction, the disposition of our eyes makes horizontal vision more natural than vertical vision. Therefore, a text horizontally written is easier and quicker to be read than another vertically written.

Regarding to text alingment, It seems that left alignment is the most legible since space between words is homogenous and in case lines finish in different points readers can easily locate the beginning of the following line. That's why it's more convenient for long texts. Right alignment makes it difficult to locate the following line that is why it should be only used for short texts. Centred alignment gives text a very formal appearance and should not be considered long texts. Last, justified text is uniform and unsuitable hollows do not interrupt the fluency of the text its reading becomes easier and appropriate for long texts.

According to text color, it should be selected thinking about obtaining the best legibility. Legible color combinations present tone contrast (warm and cold), brightness contrast (light and dark) and/or saturation contrast (intense and dull) but brightness contrast is the most important of all. It is also important to know that texts are clearer when dark letters are over a light back (Carter, 1997).

3.3 Typography Language

Typography exist to be read and to be seen as well (Willberg & Forssman, 2003) so values beyong simple meanings can be transmited through written words.

Typefaces have character as people do and it can be expressed through it's global effect - through it's force and smoothness- and through it's individual ellements as well (March, 1989).
Written text is usually related to peronal, organic, unique and espontaneous while printed text is impersonal, neutral, objective, precise and universal (Ruder, 1992).
In the same way, each type family transmit different values. According to Blanchard (1988), gothic typographies remember ancient times, the past, middle age, religion or gastronomy; Garamond typography suggest elegance and tradition; typographies like Bodoni or similar las tipografías como Bodoni are associated to dignity, asuterity and coolness; Optima give the sensation of a modern clasisism; sans serif letters as Helvetica or Univers refer to modernism, industry and funcionalism; typographies like Antique Olive transmit an elegant modernism; and scripts suggest personal writting.
As written text creats kind of figure and its draw doesn't help at all if there are no connotations related to the sense that wants to be transmited, selection of typography may be directed by the idea (Moliné, 1999). This way, form and content may transmit the same meaning and communication may be much more effective.

4. Image

Images play an important role in all designs. Not only they transmit those information that can not be shown by text but also they add attractive to the graphic aspect of the page. Images are a more intensive stimulus than words. Therefore they are more perceptible and easier to remember. (Underwood & Klein, 2002).
Photos, illustrations, graphics, schemes or tables are kind of images that could be used for a Teacher's Guide depending of the information that would like to be transmitted.

Fig. 3. Images example

4.1 Use of Images

In some cases images used in a Teacher's Guide belong to other graphical products made previously but merely they are specifically created for their insertion in the guide. No matter their origin, they may have a homogeneous aspect in order to get a coordinated design and to transmit the same values.
It is much easier to get this homogeneity when images are specifically created for the Guide while they could be very different between each other when taken from previous works according to graphical aspect. Designers have different options to create homogeneity in this cases:
- Use the same color range for all.
- Unify font type, style and size used in graphic or tables.
- Insert image into the page in the same way: with or without margin, with or without border, etc.

4.2 Images

According to several criteria, we can classify two different types of images.
Regarding to fidelity towards represented object, images can be realistic or non realistic. Realistic images represent object with great fidelity and it can be easily identified. Non realistic images are abstract and their presentation is not clear enough (Underwood & Klein, 2002).
Images could be also classified according to the represented object (places, things, animals, people…), proximity to the object or vision angle.
According to the technique used for producing them we can distinguish between Illustration, which is an interpreting drawing of reality; and photography that is an image obtained from reality.
Illustration shows the individual and peculiar point of view of its creator in a more evident way and it is used most of the times as a contrast for photography or as support for a better communication and for understanding contests. On the other side, photography offers a depersonalized and objective image (Newark, 2002).

5. Grid

Every design need to be built over a grid that is the invisible structure that organizes graphical material in a surface guiding the position of the elements that compose the design. For designers it constitutes the minimum structure from which their work begins. The gride has a double function: to support designer by deciding how to place elements in each page and to unify the design on the other.
So when designing a Teacher's Guide it's necessary to create a grid that guides the localization of every single element in each page.
The interpretation of the graticule system must be as freely as necessary so that it works correctly. This freedom will be responsible of providing richness to the design that otherwise could be lifeless.
The distribution of elements in the design transmits different impressions. The symmetrical disposition of elements within the composition tends to communicate values related to strength, integrity, elegance and order but it can appear rigid, impersonal, predictable or tedious. On the other extreme, asymmetry insinuates movement and freedom.

6. Corporate Identity

The study guide constitutes one of the different communication elements of the university or school so it can be included in the corporate identity according to Melewar & Jenkins (2002) specially in the chapter "communication and visual identity".
In the actual university environment, corporate identity and specific theme "communication and visual identity" are considered as a powerful source of competitive advantage and a way of presenting the main characteristics of the organization in an effective and consistent way to all of the relevant stakeholders (Melewar & Akel, 2005).
Including Teacher's Guide in corporative identity means that the design of the guide may be in concordance the style and philosophy of the organization, it means with characteristics and values that represents it and ensure this way that no opposite or different image could be transmitted if other elements are used.
According to visual and graphic design aspects, this means that the Travel Guide may follow the established graphic parameters of the University or School. Each University should have a special regulation regarding to colors, typography, formats, grids, images, etc. that should be checked before starting the design of the Guide and guidelines should be followed as well.

7. Design of a Teacher's Guide

We will apply the guidelines above to view a description of the teaching guide published in 2007 by the Engineering Design Upper Thechnical School of the Universidad Politécnica de Valencia (Spain). The commentary of the design used in this guide will explain in a graphic way all the recommendations made.
First, regarding to corporate identity, the design of the guide follows the guidelines set in terms of corporate visual identity by University and School. In the first case, the instructions for submitting the mark of the Universidad Politécnica de Valencia have been followed. In the second case, the School corporate color (blue) has been chosen. Also, design tries to transmit the characteristic values of the School: innovation, technology and dynamism.
White color is chosen for the background because it will allow a better legibility of the texts. The color for the text is gray characteristic of an industrial and technological world. Furthermore, not using the traditional combination white-black for text, a more modern image will be provides and it will be present more attractive to young public. The corporate color of the School is used to highlight titles and other important information.
Typography only used throughout the guide is Univers family. This type family has the advantage of being in agreement with the values that will be transmited (industry, technology, functionality). To reach a good degree of legibility typography must be familiar to the public target.

Fig. 4. Type family (Univers)

The text on the page is presented in two columns to avoid an excessive line length. Text direction is horizontal and justified alignment.

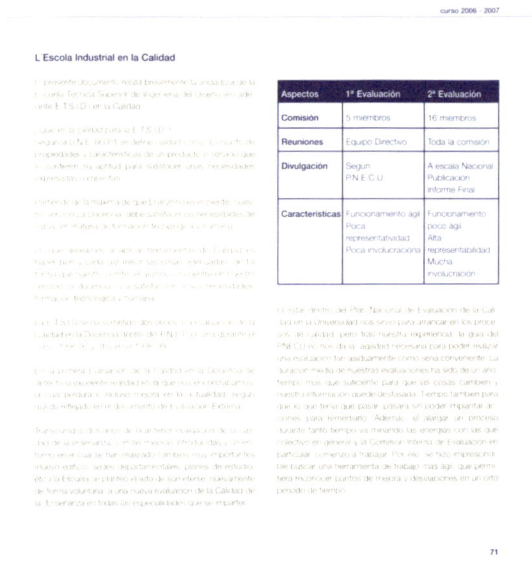

curso 2006 · 2007

L'Escola Industrial en la Calidad

Aspectos	1ª Evaluación	2ª Evaluación
Comisión	5 miembros	16 miembros
Reuniones	Equipo Directivo	Toda la comisión
Divulgación	Segun P.N.E.C.U.	A escala Nacional Publicacion informe Final
Caracteristicas	Funcionamiento ágil Poca representatividad Poca involucraciónа	Funcionamiento poco ágil Alta representabilidad Mucha involucración

71

Fig. 5. Double column texts

Images are chosen instead of illustration because they are in relation with the ideas of technology and relevance set out. Finally, to avoid excess of color on the page, black-withe images are used.

8. References

Bix, L.; Lockhart, H.; Selke, S.; Cardoso, F. & Olejnik, M. (2003). Is x-height a better indicator of legibility than type size for drug labels?. Packaging Technology and Science, Vol.16, 199-207, 0894-3214

Carter, R. (1996). Diseñando con tipografía 2: Logotipos, papelería de empresa, identidad corporativa, Index Book, 849211147X, Barcelona

Carter, R. (1997). Diseñando con tipografía 3: Color y tipografía, InterBooks, ISBN 968777603X, Mexico

Chijiiwa, H. (1999). Combinar el color: guía creativa para realizar 1.662 combinaciones cromáticas, Blume, 8480763191, Barcelona

Ferrer, E. (1999). Los lenguajes del color, Fondo de cultura económica, 9701813731, México

Heller, E. (2004). Psicología del color: cómo actúan los colores sobre los sentimientos y la razón, Gustavo Gili, 8425219779, Barcelona

Hine, T. (1995). The total package, Little, Brown, 9780316365468, Boston

March, M. (1989). Tipografía creativa, Gustavo Gili, 8425214076, Barcelona

Martín Montesinos, J.L. & Mas Hurtuna, M. (2001). Manual de tipografía. Del plomo a la era digital, Campgràfic, 8493167738, Valencia

Melewar, T.C. & Akel, S. (2005). The role of corporate identity in the higher education sector. Corporate Communications: An International Journal, Vol.10, No.1, 41-57, 1356-3289

Melewar, T.C. & Jenkins, E. (2002). Defining the corporate identity construct. Corporate Reputation Review, Vol.5, No.1, 76-91, 1363-3589

Moliné, M. (1999). La fuerza de la publicidad: saber hacer buena publicidad, saber administrar su fuerza, Cinco Días, 8480364998, Madrid

Newark, Q. (2002). ¿Qué es el diseño gráfico? Manual de diseño, Gustavo Gili, 9688874051, México

Ruder, E. (1992). Manual de diseño tipográfico, Gustavo Gili, 9688872008, Mexico

Underwood, R.L. & Klein, N.M. (2002). Packaging as brand communication: effects of pictures on consumer responses to the package and brand. Journal of Marketing Theory and Practice, Vol.10, No.4, 58-68, 1069-6679

Willberg, H.P. & Forssman, F. (2003). Primeros auxilios en tipografía. Consejos para diseñar con tipos de letra, Gustavo Gili, 8425218853, Barcelona

Wills, P. (1999). Todo lo que necesita saber sobre los colores, Ceac, 8432912360, Barcelona

Providing Quality Research Supervision in Contemporary Graduate Schools: Empowering Research Graduates to Perform in the Knowledge Economy

Dr. Janet Carton, Dr. Steve Jerrams and Dr. Anthony Betts
Directorate of Research and Enterprise
Dublin Institute of Technology
143-149 Lower Rathmines Road, Dublin 6.
Ireland

Background

In the current uncertain climate that exists in graduate research education, how does the university sector meet employer's demands for effective new starters holding research degrees? Increasingly, the focus is placed on the development of rounded education providing more than knowledge in a single discipline. This development is becoming embedded in the structural frameworks of Higher Education Institution's (HEI's) and requires delivery from a centrally co-ordinated platform. Models of graduate education platforms are prolific across Europe, allowing a 'buffet' selection approach to be made by new institutes who can select from existing functional programmes. However, when considering the demands for quantity and quality of research outputs, it is equally important to identify and address the needs of those supporting, creating and developing the research activity leading to a quality graduate education system. A serious deficit in the understanding of revised roles and responsibilities within research supervision currently exists. A central issue confronting supervisors is how to achieve quality, effectiveness and productivity of their work in this changed and challenging environment {1}.

This study focuses on the Dublin Institute of Technology (DIT), the largest third level institute in Ireland. DIT has recently created an umbrella style, virtual graduate school to deliver an industry relevant graduate education platform. This school encompasses numerous interdisciplinary research areas, as diverse as creative arts and media, nanotechnology, materials science, biomedical and elastomer engineering, radiation and environmental science and optometry. The school must be equipped to manage the delivery of all graduate support programmes including supervisor specific programmes.

DIT committed to support and develop a scheme to professionalise supervisory practice as supervisors frequently base their approach to supervision on their own, sometimes unexamined experiences as a research student {2}. As providers of the first *Research Supervisor Training Programme* in Ireland, the authors have now launched an industry and professions focussed *Development Programme* and a collaborative supervisory initiative with a number of Irish HEIs. This *Development Programme* supports adaptable, flexible supervisory practice which is seen as key in maintaining awareness of broader issues {2}. It is intended that this commitment to research supervisory standards will strengthen the institute's mission in delivering research graduates of calibre in their field, who possess an enviable skills base, leading to broader employment opportunities.

Analysis of DIT's supervisory support programmes which have been offered for seven years, has shown that supervisory capacity and development is key to providing quality research graduates to industry and the professions. This work examines the model adopted by DIT in realising this objective and discusses the complicated issues associated with advising and developing the capabilities of both inexperienced and experienced research supervisors.

Keywords
Research supervisor development programme, graduate research school, graduate education.

1. Introduction

Based on National HEI consensus {3} and on the outcomes of the Bologna Process seminar on *"Doctoral Programmes for the European Society'* {4} a number of guiding principles have been identified as key to the development and structuring of 4th level European education. Ireland as a knowledge economy has identified the need to double the number of its doctoral graduates by 2013 in line with the Strategy for Science Technology and Innovation (SSTI, {5}). In order to sustain a competitive position and contribute to economic and social development, graduates must now exhibit skills that demonstrate greater employability outside academia.

Accompanying the pressure for increased research outputs and more graduates with wider skills, is the requirement to identify and address the needs of those supporting, creating and developing the research activity that underpins a quality graduate education system. Research supervisors face an ever growing challenge in meeting academic quality assurance standards and supporting skills acquisition for their students. Each component of the equation must be in place to achieve this balance and establishing effective research supervisory practice which underpins a contemporary graduate programme framework is a key to success.

A pivotal aim of Graduate, 4th Level Ireland, is to equip graduates with the appropriate skills required to help secure Ireland's economic success in the 21st Century {6}. The SSTI proposed the development of graduate schools to lead the creation of *'structured, relevant generic and transferable professional skills training enabling PhD graduates to develop careers in diverse sectors of the economy'* {5}. The Irish Universities Quality Board agreed that, as well as provision of resources, development of these skills requires collaboration {7}.

The SSTI has indicated that the quality of research can be improved by increasing the number of research teams led by internationally renowned principal investigators and that up-grading of existing infrastructures and development of new and innovative facilities is required to support research. Under the recommendation of the HEA and Bologna, a key guiding principle for the development of doctoral research is defining and establishing *'the crucial role of supervision and assessment* {3,4}.

2. Aims and Objectives

The Dublin Institute of Technology (DIT) is addressing a central element of a successful graduate education platform leading to improved retention, completion rates, throughput and research output resulting from the development of a *Research Supervisor Support and Development Programme.* This initiative is in line with the additional principles {3,4} of effective development in doctoral research which require graduate education to be *'responsive to changing economic and societal needs'*, *'ensuring value for money'* and *'embedding graduate education in institutional strategies and policies'* and will enhance institutional supervisory capacity. The DIT proposes a management structure to implement a *Research Supervisor Support and Development Programme* which will meet these recommendations.

In the development of this programme, the Institute clearly identifies 1) Key issues surrounding traditional supervisory practice, including the development of supervision which supports the production of graduates fit for purpose in the modern employment arena. 2) The needs of industry and the professions to be met by today's graduates. 3) An effective graduate school model, to facilitate the management of supervisor programmes and graduate training.

3. Issues Surrounding Supervisory Practice

The EUA report on *'Doctoral Programmes in Europe's Universities: Achievements and Challenges'* {8} promotes the notion that stakeholders (universities and public authorities) must do more to widen participation, to improve mechanisms for supervision and assessment and to promote the international mobility of doctoral students. They must also take steps to ensure that professional skills development is an integral part of all doctoral training {8}. The report also shows that national funding policies for doctoral education are often too fragmented, with a lack of co-ordination between government ministries, research councils and other funding bodies. This leads to a lack of consistency, equitability and standardisation amongst the key objective deliverers.

In the UK, HEFCE's policy on *'improving standards in postgraduate research degree programmes'* has for a number of years required that all new supervisors undertake mandatory specified training {9}. The University of Caledonia Glasgow, for example, have approached the need for supervisor training in the context of i) improving PhD Students' experience, ii) improving completion rates and iii) satisfying external quality expectations, while University College London, University of Newcastle and Monash University amongst others, view the programme as an important career development mechanism for supervisory staff.

There are complicated issues for any institution in relation to managing, advising, supporting and developing inexperienced as well as more seasoned research supervisors. The *Research Supervisor Support and Development Programme* developed at DIT aims to advise, support and guide both new and inexperienced research supervisors in best practice and institutional regulations pertaining to supervision of research masters and PhD students. This programme was developed in the light of two clearly identified needs; (i) to address the lack of quality assurance and standardisation of practices in research supervision and (ii) a requirement to encourage staff to engage in research activity. Following each programme, a review leading to recommendations for overcoming these issues was carried out. In summary, the following areas were consistently raised as areas of concern in research supervisory practice;

i) How to positively influence completion rates and throughput
ii) Roles and responsibilities of students, supervisors and the host institute
iii) Duration of research and maintaining relevance
iv) Dealing with problematic students
v) Supervising part-time students
vi) Supervising international students (for whom English was not their primary language)
vii) Consistency in application of regulations for research
viii) Supervisory support on an institute basis
ix) Funding opportunities (seed funding, student scholarships)
x) Research student employment…a changing landscape
xi) Institute acknowledgement of supervisory practice - professional development and career progression.

It was clear from participant feedback that the traditional model of supervision, which was personality dependent and consistently followed the same process that supervisors themselves had been exposed to, was not ideal in managing the above areas. The context of supervisor training in modern higher education requires a focus that enables supervisors to become adaptable and an awareness that different understandings about what research actually is has consequences for supervisory practice {2}.

4. Graduate Employment Needs of Industry and the Professions

The challenges facing higher education in this domain are immense. The SSTI (2006-2013) has highlighted the need to strengthen measures increasing interaction between companies and higher education institutions nationally and regionally. Researchers trained in Europe should be confident that their qualifications will be pertinent to their careers {10,11}. In an effort to identify the needs of the Irish Industrial employment market, the Research Support Unit in DIT interviewed a number of key industrial stakeholders in Ireland (Iona Technologies, Lucent Technologies, Intel) with a view to identifying their needs from Irish graduates. An additional event, hosted by the Higher Education Authority of Ireland {3} gathered perspectives from academic, industrial and professional stakeholders nationwide. In essence, the core requirements of graduate employees were identified as follows;

- Depth in specific discipline
- Breadth in other areas of the graduate's own discipline and a broad knowledge of related disciplines
- Soft skills (eg. Team working)
- Context and vision (a viable understanding of the values and goals of the organisation and what is being undertaken)

Most agreed that understanding the context and having vision are the most difficult qualities to identify in potential postgraduate employees.

In playing a major role in an improved knowledge society, it is believed that structured graduate education will enhance personal development for graduate students, instead of perpetuating an outmoded academic research ethos. DIT developed a structured graduate programme which incorporated the key skills areas identified by the Irish Universities Association (IUA) Skills Statement {12}. This involved the incorporation of defined learning outcomes and skills set acquisition for graduate students.

An important benefit from the structuring of supervisory supports is increasing expertise and experience which will enhance co-supervisory practice and assist in the production of relevant, viable and timely research outputs.

5. Management of Graduate Education in the Dublin Institute of Technology

How do institutions with dynamic and evolving graduate education profiles manage this development? What operational and structural support mechanisms will optimise the graduate output and most importantly the student experience? With a view to addressing the supervisory issues highlighted in section 3 and with the aim of supporting and developing research activity among inexperienced research staff, DIT examined the graduate school model as an effective management structure.

Two main models of graduate school have emerged in Finland, which is regarded as an innovator in the graduate school education system. These are the inter-university, subject-focussed and the intra-university / interdisciplinary models {10,13}. The former, serves to bring students and academic staff together, working in a single discipline or field across the country and works at its best when focussing on established areas of research excellence. The latter model serves to bring together students and academics from different disciplines within a single institution. Intermediate models with common features also exist.

DIT, encompasses education programmes in trade apprenticeships, undergraduate degrees, postgraduate degrees, postdoctoral research, consultancy and numerous R & D activities with industry. From this perspective, models adopted by other HEIs in Ireland were also studied. In the seven Irish universities, a wide variety of structures are used to manage postgraduate provision. These range from Graduate Studies Offices, Research Offices, Graduate Schools, Faculty Research Committees, Research Institute's, Research Support Units, Centres and Groups {7}. Some institutions have adopted discipline specific Graduate Schools (eg. University College Dublin (UCD) and Trinity College Dublin (TCD)) where

PhD programmes are firmly embedded in a Graduate School infrastructure which is concurrently part of institution-wide management structures {14}. In UCD, the governance of its five graduate schools accommodates common structures for student entry and assessment. It is commonly recognised that Graduate Schools based within faculties or disciplines will normally only flourish in institutions with large postgraduate student numbers (UCD has the highest postgraduate cohort in Ireland {14}). In the UK, discipline based models are less popular than the institute-wide umbrella model {9}. In practice these institute-wide systems, facilitate standardisation of training, mentoring and assessment and avoid duplication of procedures. They also provide branding and an identity for the Institute's Graduate Programme externally. The management of finances is also standardised and centralised and thus more efficiently managed than when operational across multiple schools.

DIT set up a Graduate School Working Group which examined the implementation of an appropriate graduate programme model and associated management structures. In line with institute and national strategies, existing institute infrastructure and mindful of the advantages and disadvantages of existing models, DIT established its graduate programme based on the following framework:

- An umbrella Institute with overarching responsibility for provision of all postgraduate research (excluding taught programmes) irrespective of discipline.
- The Graduate Research School (GRS) will manage the monitoring, assessment and training of postgraduate research students under its Graduate Research Education Programme (GREP). All postgraduate students are registered with the GRS.
- The GRS will initially take a virtual structure and accommodate a Dean of the Graduate School and associated core staff. Upon relocation to the DIT's new single Campus (Grangegorman), the GRS structure will be revised to incorporate key facilities for research students and supervisors (eg. meeting rooms, writing facilities, IT support etc.).
- The GRS will operate the GREP through inter-disciplinary and inter-institutional collaboration. Promotion of student mobility and cross-disciplinary knowledge transfer are considered paramount.
- It is imperative that the GRS will have its own policy making and implementation powers, with properly articulated aims {9, 15].
- The success of the GRS will also be dependent on 'buy in' from all sectors of the institute and the school being part of DIT's operational plan, so maintaining and managing its own budget.
- Promotion of interdisciplinary and inter-institutional supervisory teams.
- Regulations for postgraduate study by research will be clearly identified and modified as appropriate within the Graduate School structure.
- There will be GRS support and development for all research supervisory associated activity.

Within this operational framework, research supervisors require institutional assurance of the following;

i. Support from senior management level

ii. Exposure to best practice
iii. Central support and guidance facilities (that prevail throughout the research process)
iv. Encouragement for and acknowledgement of, supervisory practice

The establishment of regulations regarding the supervision of research students vary widely between HEIs. However, issues regarding the effective supervision of students leading to the timely production of quality research theses, publications and enhancing the research activity of any discipline are ubiquitous.

6. Research Supervisor Support and Development Programmes

The trend in the UK towards supervisor support has been in the form of structured, often compulsory training, targeting new staff to the university. The authors developed and launched the first *Research Supervisor Training Programme* in Ireland in 2001. The programme had a specific aim, to support, guide and advise new and inexperienced research supervisors in the formal and informal processes surrounding the supervision of graduate research students.

Key Components of a Research Supervisor Training Programme

One of the key marketing points for these programmes is to remove any references to 'training' from the title. DIT re-launched their programme as the *Research Supervisor Support and Development Programme* which was met more positively by staff. The ethos of such a programme must encourage participation and therefore it was agreed that initially, the programme must be delivered on a non compulsory basis. Based on International best practice and on an experimental basis, the programme developers identified that the following were key elements in the structure and content of a successful research supervisor support programme. Programmes should ideally;

- *Contain small participant groups (10-15 max)*
- *Have mixed discipline representation*
- *Cover Institutional Regulations*
- *Include research student input*
- *Incorporate case study analysis*
- *Demonstrate roles & responsibilities (Supervisors, Students and Institute)*
- *Identify milestones in research process*
- *Demonstrate advantages of supervisory teams*
- *Vary delivery of programme through presentations, working groups, case studies, experience sharing*
- *Facilitate follow up sessions & ongoing support*

The next stage in developing such a support programme is accreditation. For supervisory staff who have acquired substantially more years of experience, a refresher course was developed in order to engage staff in ongoing best practice acquisition. Supervisory programmes structured in such a manner can be managed effectively within an institute-wide umbrella graduate school structure.

Collaborative Approach

As with the success of graduate skills programmes, collaboration on supervisor development is optimal. A collaborative initiative with a number of other Irish HEI has been established with a view to developing supervisor support nationally covering the core areas of research supervisory practice as highlighted above. Initiatives being driven include the following;

i) Development of a *Research Supervisor Network*, supporting the interaction of staff from across institutions to discuss supervisory issues.
ii) Creation of a *Research Supervisor Database* (demonstrating expertise and experience in research) thus facilitating development of *collaborative supervisory teams*.
iii) *Development of A Doctoral Supervision Handbook* with a standard code of best practice with National relevance (having implications for policy in the Irish HE context).
iv) *Programme Accreditation.* Development of a recognised qualification in *Postgraduate Research Supervision*

Each of these initiatives will provide access to expertise in supervisory practice, supporting mentoring and experience sharing.

7. Conclusion

Embedding of a dedicated management structure in line with any HE institution's strategic plan will facilitate the following:

i) Equity in research supervisor support and development across HEIs
ii) Supervisor support on issues related to roles, responsibilities, institute regulations, case studies, drawing from the experience of the consortium and international codes of best practice
iii) Enhanced collaboration and skills sharing of cross-institutional supervisory teams leading to effective use of public funds with broad access to expertises across institutes
iv) Enhancement of supervision quality
v) Increased institutional supervisory capacity
vi) Improved student experience and programme quality
vii) Enhancement of student skills base
viii) Improved throughput and completion rates
ix) Development of Institutional Research Profile

Structured *Research Supervisor Support and Development Programmes* will have national relevance, create a framework for equity in standards and assessment and deliver value for money in the management and development of graduate research education. A quality programme provides a framework in which all interested HEIs will benefit. It is anticipated that through the implementation of the management model and support programmes, research supervisors will be empowered to meet the demanding challenges that higher education faces in academic and professional employment arenas for postgraduate research students.

8. References

1. Research Training and Supervision Development. Margot Pearson and Angela Brew. Studies in Higher Education *Volume 27*, No. 2, 2002
2. Postgraduate Research Supervision: A Process of Knowledge Management. Fang Zhao. ultiBASE Articles, May 2001.
3. HEA Graduate Education Forum http://www.hea.ie/index.cfm/page/sub/id/1041. Dublin, Ireland, 28/2/06-1/3/06
4. Doctoral Programmes for the European Society. Bologna Seminar Salzburg, 2005.
5. Strategy for Science, Technology and Innovation (SSTI) 2006-2013. Department of Enterprise Trade and Employment, 2006. http://www.entemp.ie/science/technology/sciencestrategy.htm
6. Irish Universities Association, Reform of 3rd level and creation of 4th Level Ireland: Securing Competitive Advantage in the 21st Century, October 2005.
7. Good Practice in the Organisation of PhD Programmes in Irish Universities. National Guidelines. Irish Universities Quality Board, 2005.
8. Doctoral Programmes in Europe's Universities: Achievements and Challenges. European Universities Association, 2007.
9. A Review of Graduate Schools in the UK. Woodward D., Denicolo P., Hayward S., Long E.. UK, Council for Graduate Education (UKCGE), 2004.
10. Inventing Our Future Together. European Commission. The European Research Area: New Perspectives. Green Paper 4/4/2007
11. Transforming Ireland, A Better Quality of Life for All. National Development Plan 2007-2013. Executive Summary, 2007. http://www.ndp.ie/docs/NDP_Homepage/=1131.htm
12. Irish Universities' PhD Graduates' Skills Statement. Irish Universities Association, 2008. www.4thlevelireland.ie/publications/Graduate_Skills_Statement.pdf
13. PhD Training and the Knowledge-Based Society. An Evaluation of Doctoral Education in Finland. Dill D., Mitra S., Siggard Jensen H., Lehtinen E., Makela T., Parpala A., Pohjola H., Ritter M., Saari S. Publications of the Finnish Higher Education Council, 2006.
14. UCD Strategy for Graduate Education: UCD 4th Level. http://www.ucd.ie/registrar/educationstrategy/documents/Strategy_For_Graduate_Education.pdf
15. Providing for the Postgraduate Market, an Investigation into Exclusive Facilities for Postgraduates. Brown T. National Postgraduate Committee, Troon, Ayrshire, UK, 2003.

Knowledge in Technology Networks: A case study based institutional approach

Michael Steiner[+]*, Christian Hartmann* and Michael Ploder*
[+]*Department of Economics, University of Graz /*
**Institute of Technology and Regional Policy, JOANNEUM RESEARCH*
Forschungsgesellschaft, Graz
Austria

1. How networks think

"Do networks think and if so, how do we know?" can be used as an introductory question for this paper. It takes up the provocative issue of "how institutions think" (raised by Mary Douglas, 1984) and extends it to include the interpretation of clusters and networks as institutions. In this paper we attempt to analyse the extent to which networks can be regarded as institutions. We also try to ascertain the importance of learning and knowledge exchange in networks, both from a theoretical and empirical point of view, and tentatively measure the forms and content of knowledge exchange.

Since Porter's (1998, 2000) original definition of clusters as "geographic concentrations of interconnected companies, specialized suppliers, service providers, firms in related industries and associated institutions in a particular field that compete but also cooperate", emphases within cluster analysis have changed considerably. The recent debate has focussed more on how far and in what ways clusters foster knowledge creation and organizational learning, and has placed greater emphasis on the organic-evolutionary dimension of cluster-based industrial agglomerations.

In the following section we will give a short outline of the institutional aspects of networks and their knowledge-specific character (section 2), identify and outline different empirical approaches in identifying the form and content of knowledge exchange. This entails use of the concept of organizational learning, the methodological approach of social network analysis, and of intellectual capital reporting in measuring intangible assets (section 3). The final section contains our conclusions (section 4).

2. Knowledge – in need of institutionalized cooperation

A vast literature concentrating on the combination of clusters, innovation, and regional development now exists. It appears that the process of innovation is favoured by regionally concentrated interaction of (mostly) small firms, mutually exchanging information and creating knowledge in formal and informal ways. It has been emphasized that networking has to be regarded as an important form of innovative activity. This has not only been taken up by regional scientists but also by various strategic management and industrial dynamics approaches to inter-firm cooperation (Vonortas, 2000). It has also been extended to questions of identifying competences and capabilities in strategic management at different levels of economic interaction (Felin & Foss, 2005).

The question as to what extent these economic interactions are in need of specific guiding and coordinating institutions is a further new element in the cluster debate. Interactions need institutions (such as markets); yet if the focus is on learning and knowledge, markets alone will not suffice for such forms of interaction and additional institutions will be needed (Bünstorf, 2003). Clusters may be regarded as coordinating institutions for knowledge sharing, providing a cognitive framework for transforming information into useful knowledge (Audretsch & Lehmann ,2006, Steiner, 2006).

As clearly foreseen by Adam Smith, a central fact about the modern process of innovation is that it is based on a division of labour. He quickly recognized what is now called the social nature of the innovation process. The social process induced by division of labour produces efficiency gains, from both specialization and professionalization, but it also requires a supporting framework to help connect the component contributions of the different agents. As far as knowledge and skills are concerned, this aspect of connectivity, or technology transfer, cannot be effectively coordinated by conventional markets: we need specific institutional arrangements.

Yet - as has been outlined recently by Helmstädter (2003) - the idea of connectivity transcends the usual problems of the 'division of labour' - there are additional and non-trivial problems of 'knowledge sharing', which thus far, have not been properly appreciated by the New Institutional Economics.

- The pure transaction cost approach misses fundamentally the essence of knowledge as an economic resource. "The new institutional economics deals with institutions that govern the interactions taking place under the division of labour, but leaves aside the division of knowledge activities that go with it" (Helmstädter, 2003, 14). Once the object of interaction between participating actors is knowledge, the character of interaction changes - the institutional conditions for an efficient division of knowledge are different.
- The main differences reside in the form of interaction and in the impact of interaction. Under the division of labour the transaction of goods and services is paramount, and subject to the rules of competition and to exclusivity of use and consumption. Under knowledge sharing it is knowledge and skills that are paramount, and these are subject to co-operation and the increase of knowledge for all (inclusivity). Whereas the division of labour involves differentiation and separation of method, mode and product, knowledge sharing involves internalization and recontextualization.
- The most important 'institutional' consequence is that "cooperation is the basic institution of the process of the division of knowledge" (Helmstädter, 2003, 32). But the degree of cooperation depends again on the type of knowledge use: the area of application has stronger competitive elements whereas knowledge creation and transfer are dominated by non-economic competition (status, acceptance) and cooperation. The interest thus lies here in identifying those institutions that make knowledge sharing efficient.

This institutional approach emphasizes that the growth of knowledge depends on intended and unintended individual processing of experiences, i.e. 'learning', while the

interpretation, transfer and use of experiences is influenced by interaction between individuals and between organizations, i.e. 'organizational learning'.
This new understanding of networks as institutions for learning and knowledge exchange leads to further reflections concerning the forms, channels and mechanisms of knowledge exchange. This exchange occurs through interaction, and the structure of the interaction therefore influences the extent of knowledge diffusion (Gay & Dousset, 2005). Here, two explanatory approaches exist, but they tend to oppose each other (Giuliani, 2005, 4). The one attributes knowledge with a highly public nature, so that learning, knowledge sharing and innovation within clusters is externality-driven. The alternative approach points to the necessity to include specific features of the firms and of firm-level learning in order to understand the interaction of firm-level and cluster-level learning. The first approach (whereby Giuliani includes both the economists' perspective on 'localised knowledge spillovers' and the economic geographers' view of clusters and 'collective learning') emphasizes the strong relationship between spatial clustering, knowledge spillovers, and firms' innovative output - 'proximity' and 'territory' lead to a quasi-automatic diffusion of knowledge leading to innovation. The automatic nature of this mechanism is questioned by economic geographers, who regard geographical proximity per se as insufficient, and who emphasize the additional role of social and relational proximity in entailing an interactive and cumulative effort by co-localized firms, which nevertheless results in unstructured and diffuse local interactions. The second approach points to the heterogeneity of firm knowledge base, different firm capabilities, the existence of 'technological leaders' and 'gate keepers' in a local community. These differences have an effect on the mechanisms by which knowledge is transmitted and indicate that knowledge diffusion is not an accidental collective process but is rather structured by the relative distance of firms' knowledge bases (Giuliani & Bell, 2005).
In the following pages we will present summaries of several case studies - all undertaken within the province of Styria/Austria. These provide insight into, and allow comparison of different forms of learning and knowledge generation and diffusion in clusters and networks and in other institutions of knowledge sharing. Each of them represents a specific solution - in different institutional form - to the problem of efficient knowledge exchange and its measurement.

- The first study concentrates on forms of organizational learning. The clusters under scrutiny are regarded as organizations skilled at creating, acquiring and transferring knowledge in diverse but systematic ways. The focus here is on the specific systems and forms of learning at the cluster level.
- The second case uses the tool of social network analysis to differentiate between forms and content of interactions within a network. The main interest here lies in the relative importance and weight of knowledge intensity of the interactions of firms and the subsequent structure of the network.
- A change of perspective is then taken by looking at the specific position of two firms within the network. Both are part of it but - due to their different knowledge orientation and capabilities - have different positions in the network and participate in distinct forms.
- Finally, a further institutional level - a so-called "competence centre", an applied precompetitive sectoral research institution linked with industrial partners and thus forming an additional specific network - is analyzed by means of intellectual capital

reporting. Here the focus is on how different kinds of intellectual capital can be identified and how this capital can be used not only for measuring the knowledge intensity of the network of the competence centre but also for indicating - as relational capital - research driven links to external institutions.

3. How to measure knowledge in networks: summary results and interpretation of empirical approaches

3.1 Organizational learning between firms in specific clusters

3.1.1 Learning systems

Organizational learning - as the outcome of overlapping activities of individual, firm and interfirm learning - requires the presence of specific systems for the transformation and combination of these related spheres. In order to identify forms of learning in clusters and between firms we focussed on two learning systems: participative and informal learning (for a more extensive elaboration see Steiner & Hartmann, 2006).

Informal learning systems may be present at cluster level in the form of informal meetings at conferences or in bars, communities of practice, networks with fellow graduates (old boys' networks), or social networks. Informal meetings (Saxenian, 1996) take place in bars or in the lobby at conferences. Such meetings are mainly focused on the transfer of knowledge on a personal face-to-face basis. Communities of practice (Wenger, 1996) include informal teams which emerge spontaneously. They engage in problem solving, and comprise employees of different firms. Learning takes place in the discussion and fixing of technological problems. 'Old boys' networks' (Saxenian, 1996) are formed by graduates of particular universities. In such networks technological or organisational problems can be discussed freely on an informal basis. Learning arises through the exchange of alternative perspectives. Social networks (Hendry et al., 1995) arise in local sporting clubs and charity organizations (i.e. Rotary Club etc.). In such networks information and knowledge can be exchanged informally and learning takes place in the reflection of work-related problems. Facilitated exchange of experiences (Oess, 1991) takes place in semi-formal meetings which are held in order to discuss particular issues. The efficient exchange of knowledge is enabled through a facilitator, either external, or nominated by the group.

Participative learning systems may be present at cluster level in the form of formal R&D-teams at interfirm level, interfirm teams working on a joint project, participation in benchmarking clubs, or joint preparation of tenders in consortia. Interfirm R&D-teams (Dodgson, 1996) are formed by researchers of universities, R&D-institutions and firms. Within such teams a strong transmission of knowledge from the regional knowledge infrastructure to the participating firms takes place. Interfirm project teams (Pedler et al., 1997) are formed by members of several firms. Within such teams new production programs are launched or new software systems are implemented. Learning arises through the need for continuous problem solving in the course of the project. Benchmarking clubs (Pedler et al., 1997) have been formed by several firms in order to identify good practice for routines at firm level. Learning occurs through the active transfer of good practice between the club members. Consortia (Balling, 1997) collaborate on preparing bids for public or private tenders. Knowledge about particular markets and/or technological problems is exchanged among the firms in the course of the preparation process.

Learning system	Particular forms at cluster level
Informal learning system	- informal meetings in bars or at conferences etc. - communities of practice - „old boys networks" - social networks (clubs etc.) - facilitated exchange of experiences
Participative learning system	- interfirm R&D teams - interfirm project teams - benchmarking clubs - participation in consortia

Table 1. Particular forms within learning systems
Source: Steiner, M., Hartmann, Ch. (2006), Organizational Learning in Clusters: A Case Study on Material and Immaterial Dimensions of Cooperation, Regional Studies

3.1.2 Results for Styrian clusters

Based on 149 in-depth interviews in the leading firms of five main clusters in Styria the following results were obtained:

	Chemical	IT	Wood	Metal	Auto
Informal meetings in bars or at conferences	80%	90%	74%	46%	67%
Communities of practice	16%	25%	22%	18%	21%
Old boys networks	30%	50%	22%	23%	31%
Social networks	5%	10%	14%	5%	21%
Facilitated exchange of experience	42%	20%	53%	33%	26%
Informal learning systems: summary mean figure	35%	39%	37%	25%	33%

Table 2. Particular forms of informal learning systems in Styrian clusters
Source: Steiner, M., Hartmann, Ch. (2006), Organizational Learning in Clusters: A Case Study on Material and Immaterial Dimensions of Cooperation, Regional Studies

Table 2 shows the relative importance of informal learning systems. The data show the relative importance of each system as an important source of learning and knowledge acquisition outside the enterprise.

	Chemical	IT	Wood	Metal	Auto
Interfirm R&D-teams	50%	55%	41%	41%	50%
Interfirm project teams	21%	70%	50%	50%	67%
Participation in consortia	6%	35%	12%	21%	22%
Benchmarking clubs	17%	40%	54%	47%	53%
Participative learning systems: summary mean figure	23%	50%	39%	40%	48%

Table 3. Particular forms of participative learning systems in Styrian clusters
Source: Steiner, M., Hartmann, Ch., (2006), Organizational Learning in Clusters: A Case Study on Material and Immaterial Dimensions of Cooperation, Regional Studies

Table 3 presents the relative importance of the different forms of participative learning system for the five Styrian clusters examined. Also, for participative learning, the data of the four particular forms are aggregated through the generation of the corresponding mean value. The data presented reflect the percentage of firms in each cluster that engage in the respective type of learning system.

The results can be summarized as follows (for details see Steiner & Hartmann, 2006): The learning orientation in Styrian clusters depends as much on the corresponding working cultures within the relevant industries as it does on the existing value chains and the prevailing competitive structure. In the IT and automobile cluster a tradition of joint working and knowledge acquisition through formal and informal teams already exists. This is because the just-in-time production mode in the automobile sector and the necessity of large multidisciplinary interfirm teams in the IT-sector promote new collaborative working styles and attitudes among the corresponding workforce and management. In the chemical cluster such a team-oriented working style is - except with respect to the employment of R&D-teams - virtually unknown. Collaborative learning in interfirm project teams or benchmarking clubs does not fit the business style and culture of this cluster. On the other hand, informal means of knowledge acquisition are of relatively greater importance in this cluster. In the wood, machinery and metal clusters, a team approach towards learning is currently developing both at an organised formal level, and at a rather spontaneous informal level. The size of the clusters in terms of number of member firms seems to have no influence on learning orientation: The IT and the chemical clusters, are both small in terms of numbers of member firms, but still differ strongly in their learning orientation.

3.2 Social network analysis

3.2.1 Data and indicators

Social network analysis is a helpful tool in discussing the structure of networks and allows for the mapping and measuring of the relationships (communication and transaction) between different actors, i.e. the existence, context and portfolio of relations between actors in a regional network. It is a method for exposing the underlying relations between different actors, and for revealing those phenomena which cannot be reduced to the properties of individual actors or firms. Thus, relations have to be interpreted as properties of systems rather than of individual actors.

The analysis here focussed on the mechanical engineering, machinery, and automotive sector forming a well-known cluster in Styria (for a more extensive elaboration see Steiner / Ploder 2008). The starting point was a large system supplier in the automobile sector located in the region. Application of the snowball method led to the identification of firms belonging to different sub-sectors and cultivating related supply-chain and innovation-strategies. This produced a 32-actor-network comprising 18 industrial firms, 5 service firms and 9 R&D institutions.

The selected indicators of the relations cultivated by these agents cover three dimensions of interaction: direct delivery relations, R&D, and technological innovation in a competitive and a pre-competitive context. The following three dimensions of interaction were employed:

(DELIV): The firms were questioned concerning direct delivery relations (goods or services) to clients, suppliers or partners (in the case of synergetic product bundles). The direct delivery of goods and services is not reduced to its material dimensions but is extended to include innovation-related questions in the context of quality and information management or capacity extending investments.

In order to take account of different R&D capabilities and innovation strategies two dimensions of relations with respect to knowledge generating processes were distinguished.

(COMP): Competitive research and development and innovation processes are short and medium term oriented and mostly associated with direct expectations of return or with a direct tender or offer.

(PRE-COMP): The second R&D dimension surveyed concerned the level of interaction in the context of pre-competitive R&D. Pre-competitive research and development aims at extending the product spectrum, as well as at introducing new processes and alternative materials. Pre-competitive research includes fundamental research, which is an activity designed to broaden scientific and technical knowledge not yet linked to industrial or commercial objectives, and industrial research, which is research aimed at developing or improving new or existing products, processes or services.

Applying the basic concepts of social network analysis, the focus was placed on density and centrality. Density is indicated by the ratio of relations actually realized to the total number of maximum possible relations - it yields information on the general structure of the network as a whole.

Centrality is also a core feature identified in network analysis. The concept of centrality provides insight into the specific features of the interaction of the actors in the network and their specific position and/or embeddedness in the network.

3.2.2 Forms and contents of interactions

The focus here lay on identifying the most striking features of the network and the network dimensions as a whole, as well as considering the position of individual actors within the network.

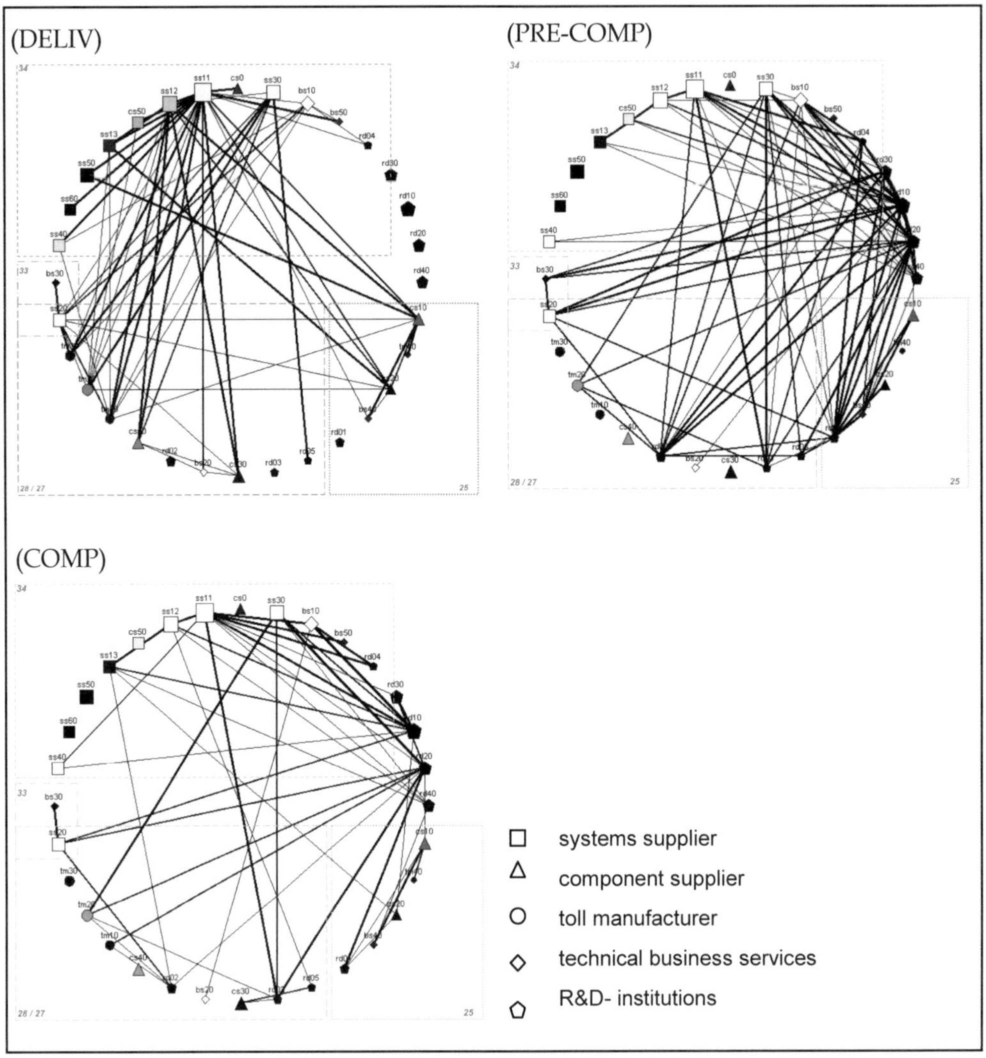

Fig. 1. Comparative presentation of the observed dimension of networking
Source: Steiner, M., Ploder, M. (2008), Structure and Strategy within Heterogeneity: Multiple Dimensions of Regional Networking, Regional Studies

Direct delivery relations have the weakest density. With respect to direct deliveries, most of the firms in the observed network are oriented towards international markets and regional input-output relations have been reduced. This is also reflected by average closeness centrality (even when indirect linkages are considered) which is higher among interactions in the context of competitive R&D and innovation processes than among direct delivery relations, although the densities and number of actors involved (nodes) are comparable. While competitive R&D and innovation processes, especially in the case of domestic system suppliers, are partially similar in density to direct delivery relations, the regional density of the network of pre-competitive R&D is much higher. While R&D institutions are of negligible significance with respect to direct delivery relations, the network is based to a considerable degree on relations with cooperative R&D institutions. Beyond the coverage of the total network of actors (including all international relations) the network analysis reveals another explanation for the high density of the network dimension of pre-competitive research and development, namely the permanent relations prevailing among the R&D institutions (e.g. semi-public cooperative research institutions and universities). The lower density of the network COMP in comparison to PRE-COMP may be explained by several factors. Competitive R&D and innovation are to a high degree in-house activities, partly owing to time-pressure, but also for reasons of confidentiality. Especially in the case of system suppliers, a considerable amount of competitive research and development and innovation processes involves clients and suppliers outside the region and internationally.

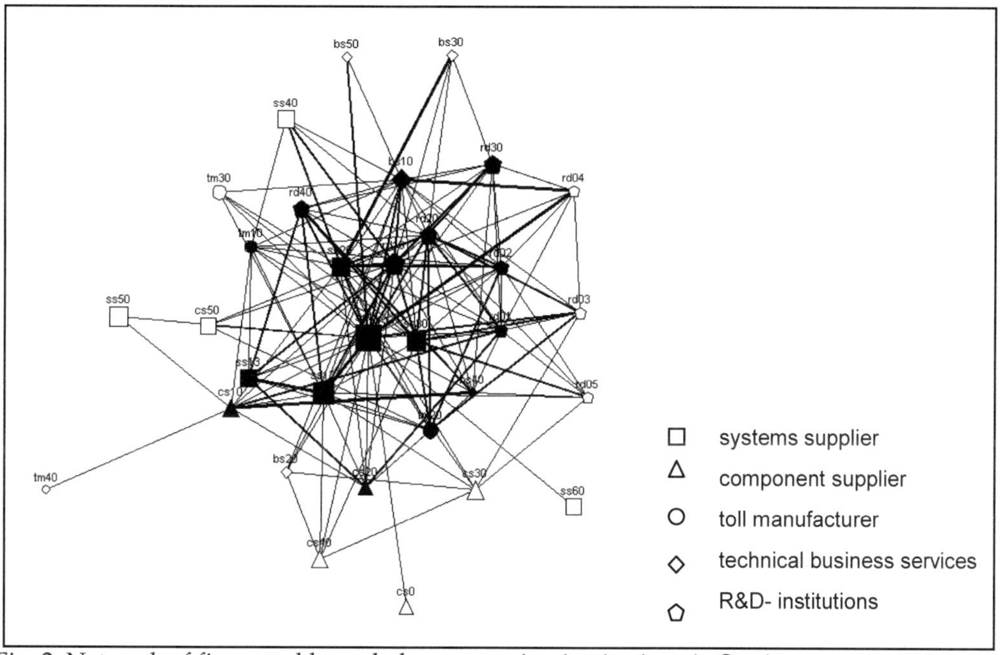

Fig. 2. Network of firms and knowledge generating institutions in Styria
Source: Steiner, M., Ploder, M. (2008), Structure and Strategy within Heterogeneity: Multiple Dimensions of Regional Networking, Regional Studies

Figure 2 gives an overview of all relations recorded and combines the three dimensions discussed above. Without going into the details concerning the different additional indicators of network analysis (for further discussion see Steiner & Ploder, 2008), the following important features can be outlined:

- In its regional dimension the network is strongly based on knowledge intensive relations. The graphical representation of the network relations, its decomposition, as well as the measured densities all reveal that the immaterial dimensions are stronger than the material ones: the highest density was obtained for pre-competitive R&D interactions. While the firms do have extensive supplier relations, these are relatively weak within the region and within the network. However, their knowledge oriented relations are to a large degree regionally concentrated.

- The interactions are strongly structured: there are distinct leading actors in the network as a whole, both receiving and emitting more flows than others. Position is mainly dependent on size, export orientation, but also on the respective position in the value chain.
- These positions differ according to the type of interaction. Especially in pre-competitive research, local universities and cooperative R&D institutions have an important role and assume gate keeper functions. But firms with higher R&D capacities also take up such a role, indicating the necessity of a well-developed, internal knowledge base.

3.3 Focussing on the microlevel – the relative position of firms in the network

The network reveals very different positions of the agents: Some are at the center, some are at the periphery. Some have very frequent interactions, some are rather isolated in the network. The following two examples - taken from the social network analysis above - provide empirical evidence for complementary linkages of firms in the network to different innovation carriers, both cooperative R&D-institutions and technical engineering services.

3.3.1 'High R&D capacity and intensive interaction with knowledge generating institutions' – case 1

The first firm (ss 20 in the total network) is an independent manufacturer of measuring and analysis devices for science and industry with considerable R&D-capacities. The firm is engaged directly in translating the findings of natural science so as to develop high quality measuring and analysis devices used in the foods and beverages sector, in pharmacy and in medicine.

The firm is vertically highly integrated and is embedded in smaller networks following niche strategies. The partners of the firm in direct delivery (component and toll-manufacturers) and partners in competitive and pre-competitive research and development (key clients, highly specialized business services, universities) are not identical. On the delivery side, the observed firm interacts with component suppliers in the field of die casting, spray casting, plastics processing, electronics, sheet metal forming, manufacturing of high performance glasses.

The firm has a relatively high in-degree centrality in respect of direct deliveries. The out-degree centrality of the firm in the region in the dimension of deliveries is considerably low owing to the high export intensity.

A high share of the turnover is reinvested in R&D -activities, 10% for intramural R&D and an additional 10% of the turnover for extramural R&D. While radical innovations and market novelties mostly emanate from R&D or client-partners, incremental improvements are promoted by internal R&D. R&D and production and marketing of new products are concentrated within the region.

The firm has a relatively high value for betweenness centrality, because it is not located in the core of vehicle manufacturing - the focus of the above analysis - but at the interface with other sectors such as manufacturing of plastic products or measurement techniques. The respective analysis of typical firm strengthens the thesis that the more firms act in market

niches demanding highly specialized cooperation partners, the more they tend to long-term cooperation.
A well established cooperation base includes university partners, and an independent research laboratory (firm bs 30 in the total network). The latter supplies firm ss 20 exclusively with science driven R&D activity and is an important source of innovation. The firm significantly gains from this long-term-partnership with firm bs 30 which is based on social trust and the long-term personal contact of both entrepreneurs. Although firm ss 20 directly and intensively cooperates with universities and other knowledge generating institutions it decided to participate in a cooperative research centre (Polymere Competence Center Leoben - PCCL - see below 3.4.2) in the field of polymers and plastics. The given framework allows intensive cooperation in terms of R&D-projects, but also provides a common framework for the targeted education of young academics and open exchange of information in the sense of communities of practice.

3.3.2 'Low R&D-capacity and weak interaction, yet attractive partner' – case 2

The second firm (cs 10 in the total network) is an affiliate of an international firm group. The firm is active in the field of plastics for the aerospace and automotive industry. The firm works on the basis of work drawings and detailed specifications for both automotive and aerospace clients.
The firm has a relatively low in-degree centrality in respect of direct deliveries because of international sourcing strategies. The out-degree centrality of the firm in the region, in the dimension of deliveries, is considerable low owing to the high export intensity. As a result of the relative immobility of the local labour-force and the small capacity of the regional labour-market most of these firms had the chance to retain key-personnel, competences, and thus the regionally integrative potential of the personnel.
Although the firm has relatively low R&D-capacities, limited absorptive capacities and rather weak contact to university research it has nevertheless been able to establish a contract-based (flexible) partnership to a technical business service firm, and a long-term (but low cost) partnership to the cooperative R&D-institution (PCCL - see below 3.4.2) already introduced in case 1. An technical engineering service (firm bs 40 in the total network) is the major carrier of innovation for firm cs 10 and supports the development and implementation of new products from scratch to market launch.
Firm cs 10 is an active partner of the competence center but no pro-active driver and carrier of new R&D-projects. Nonetheless the partnership is attractive.
The (outward) R&D-efforts are concentrated on the aerospace sector, where 90% of the R&D is carried out by a regional engineering service firm specialized in plastics and polymer technology and in a small part by the competence center already mentioned in the case of firm ss 20.
Both firms considered here (case 1 and case 2) do not cooperate directly in terms of pre-competitive R&D, show different innovation capacities and pursue different individual strategies in R&D-cooperation.
The relatively low current costs of membership, clear rules of interaction and the stable framework of the competence centre seem to be open enough for partners with significantly different innovation capabilities. The set-up provides a flexible framework not only for direct interaction but also for indirect knowledge transfer, in the sense of communities of practice.

Such an institutionalised competence centre - having its own specific network but being integrated in larger informal networks - is the focus of the fourth approach to identifying and measuring knowledge in and between firms.

3.4 Intellectual capital reporting as an approach to measuring intangible assets in networks

3.4.1 Components of intellectual capital

Intellectual capital reports are intended to complement conventional financial reporting. They analyse and assess the intangible assets of organisations in a structured way and thus help to gain additional insight into the internal value of organisations (RICARDA, 2007), as well as their potential for knowledge generation, and knowledge sharing both internally and externally.

While academic interest has to date mainly focussed on intellectual capital reporting in single organisations (i.e. firms, universities, applied research organisations), a recent systematic attempt at applying the concept to knowledge intensive networks and clusters has been made within the RICARDA project[1]. The case study presented below is based on the results of this project and provides some insight into the potential and limitations of this approach in dealing with clusters and networks.

Due to their specific character, networks entail certain challenges with respect to the preparation of intellectual capital reports. Since networks, in contrast to organisations, do not possess a clear boundary, categories of intangible assets need to be modified accordingly (RICARDA, 2007). Thus, using the three typical components of intellectual capital, and applying them to knowledge intensive networks, we have the following definitions (Edvinsson & Malone, 1997, adapted):

- Human capital is defined as the knowledge that employees bring and take with them when they join or leave the organisation (firm etc.) belonging to the network. It includes the knowledge, skills, experiences and abilities of people. Some of this knowledge is unique to the individual, some may be generic.
- Structural capital is defined as the pool of knowledge that stays in the network at the end of the working day. It comprises the organisational routines, procedures, systems, cultures, databases, etc. It allows knowledge to be codified to some extent, so that a certain degree of independence with respect to specific individuals results. Some routines may be legally protected and become intellectual property.
- Relational capital is defined as all resources linked to external relationships of the formal network management, such as external R&D-institutions, other clusters or networks, external stakeholders (e.g. regional policy) or non-member firms.

Table 4 provides an additional overview of examples of intangible assets in networks that fit into the three categories introduced above. The first column indicates the dimension of intellectual capital, the second column specifies the related categories of assets, and the last column provides working definitions for empirical work.

---

[1] RICARDA stands for "Regional Intellectual Capital Reporting - Development and Application of a Methodology for European Regions" and has been carried in the framework of Regions of Knowledge with funding of the European Commission under the 6th Framework Programme.

Dimension of Intellectual Capital	Asset	working definition
Human Capital	Knowledge base	profile of network's member organisations and its employees (in general and those involved in network activities)
	New capabilities and training opportunities	Institutionalised learning capacities for employees of network's member organisations provided by network management
Structural Capital	Interorganisational learning	Learning of network member organisation's employees in joint activities of network member organisations
	Interrelation and partnerships	Interrelations and partnerships between network member organisations
	Common ties, norms and mutual trust ("social capital")	Common ties, norms and mutual trust ("social capital") between network member organisations.
	Common infrastructure and services	Infrastructure and services available for network members only ("club goods")
	Management capacity and institutionalization	Network management's activities and procedures
	Innovation capacity	R&D and innovation activities of network member organisations
Relational Capital	Sound embedding into regional and national innovation system	Links to relevant innovation policy stakeholders outside the network
	Cooperation with other networks, clusters or single organisations	Links to relevant external stakeholders in the field of work of the network

Table 4. Examples for intellectual capital of networks
Source: RICARDA (2007)

3.4.2 Intellectual capital reporting in an Austrian knowledge intensive network

The network

The Polymer Competence Centre Leoben GmbH (PCCL) was founded as a cooperative research company within the framework of the Kplus programme of the Austrian Ministry of Transport, Innovation and Technology and as a competence centre in Polymer Engineering and Science. Since its founding in 2002 it has been based in Leoben (Styria) and operates offices in Graz (Styria) and Wels (Upper Austria) with a management team of 6 (full-time equivalents) and about 80 employees in all. By combining the scientific, engineering and methodological competence of leading polymer research institutions (12 scientific partners) with the technology, application and market-development expertise of the polymer industry and the service sector (40 company partners), the centre links the science-based approach of existing academic institutions with the applied research and product development approach of the polymer industry (Hartmann et al., 2007).

A main mission of PCCL - as part of the general mission of the competence centre programme in linking science and industry - is to carry out a joint research programme to generate new knowledge and know-how in specific areas of polymer engineering and science, thus enhancing its own R&D competencies and those of its scientific and industrial partners. The application of a science-based methodology to industrial problems and the transfer of research findings, new and available knowledge, promotes the competitiveness of the PCCL and its partners. PCCL also seeks to promote regional development by enhancing the attractiveness of the location for domestic and foreign investors, spin-offs, and start-up companies. The PCCL was a pilot network in the framework of the RICARDA project (Hartmann et al. 2007).

Examples of intangible assets within PCCL

In order to give concrete examples for stocks of intangibles at the level of a knowledge intensive network, selected indicators collected at the PCCL will be presented and discussed in the section below. The discussion follows the structure of human, structural and relational capital introduced above. In addition, the concrete categories are also in accordance with the assets presented in table 4.

Human capital: The measurement of human capital in knowledge intensive networks is usually associated with the existing knowledge base at the time of the assessment and/or with the acquisition of new capabilities and skills by the employees of the network partner organisations. Table 5 represents the scientific and technological knowledge base of the PCCL network for 2006 by taking the number of employees with a university degree.

	employees with university degree	
	full time equivalents	**head count**
PCCL	52.4%	64.1%
scientific partners	63.3%	68.2%
partner companies	11.9%	15.3%

Table 5. Share of employees with university degree in the network (2006)
Source: Hartmann et al. (2007)

As can be seen, the distribution of this knowledge base is rather asymmetric in the PCCL network. While scientific partners (i.e. universities) have the highest share of academic staff (almost two thirds of their total staff), directly followed by the competence centre itself, the partner companies show much lower rates of personnel with academic training.

Structural capital: Structural capital was measured in the PCCL along several dimensions, but in particular in terms of the innovation output of the whole network. Table 6 provide the results for PCCL's member firms for the years 2003-2005. In order to operationalise the innovation output, the categorisations of the EU community innovation survey were applied.

	In percent of PCCL company partners		
	2003	2004	2005
introduction of new or significantly improved goods	74%	68%	80%
introduction of new or significantly improved services	56%	69%	65%
introduction of new or significantly improved methods of manufacturing or producing goods or services	70%	74%	79%
introduction of new or significantly improved logistics, delivery or distribution methods for inputs, goods or services	33%	53%	42%
introduction of new or significantly improved supporting activities for your processes, such as maintenance systems or operations for purchasing, accounting, or computing	58%	72%	68%

Table 6. Key innovation indicators of PCCL company partners
Source: Hartmann et al. (2007)

Innovation output - as can be seen - fluctuated for the relevant times-span for all categories under scrutiny; the levels of intensity also differ between some of the categories. While patterns of product and process innovations are somehow alike at a high level innovations in logistics do not seem to play an important role for the member firms of the PCCL network.

Relational capital: The dimension of relational capital has been observed for the PCCL network with a particular focus on co-operations with other networks, clusters or single organisations. As a concrete operationalisation the number of collaborative R&D projects that did not receive funding of the Kplus programme has been under scrutiny (see table 7).

	R&D projects	
	total number	share
Non-K*plus* 2005	45	100%
Non-K*plus*-projects 2005 performed with partner companies of the (PCCL-) network	14	31.1%
Non-K*plus*-projects 2005 performed with external companies	31	68.9%

Table 7. Share of PCCL R&D projects involving external R&D institutions/networks in 2005
Source: Hartmann et al. (2007)

While the first row of table 7 presents the total number of collaborative R&D projects without Kplus funding for the year 2005, the second row shows the number and relative share of those projects carried out with partners in the PCCL network, while the third row contains the number and relative share of those projects undertaken conducted with external partners. As can be seen, the projects that have been performed with external companies account for more than two thirds of the total and can be considered as an indicator of knowledge spillover extending far beyond the original network.

4. Conclusions

The approaches and results presented here show that knowledge and learning in its organizational form is no longer a black box - different methods allow not only for the conceptual definition and the recognition of the importance of organisational learning, but also for its quantification at different levels and in different forms. It can also be shown that knowledge creation and knowledge sharing is in need of specific institutions with different degrees of openness, institutionalization, and exclusivity - extending from rather closed hierarchical forms to more open market-like exchanges.

- Clusters as learning organizations are among the non-market devices by which firms seek to coordinate their activities with other firms and other knowledge-generating institutions. Thus, clusters can be interpreted as subtle and differentiated institutions for co-operation and interactive learning and as such they can be of considerable strategic significance (Steiner & Hartmann, 2006, 504). Yet the results of this approach also show that the forms of learning - within specific clusters - differ according to the technology used, competitive position, and orientation to regional or international markets.
- Patterned coordination does not arise automatically as a result of individual human action, nor does policy automatically create the necessary institutions. The creation of new institutions such as competence centres can be interpreted as a manifestation of institutional alertness on the side of policy makers. They can generate - as the intellectual capital reporting has shown - more knowledge and knowledge diffusion than originally intended: relational capital as an indicator of knowledge spillover is rather strong. Competence centres are primarily a closed club serving their direct partners in industry. But they also extend their knowledge creation function to organizations outside the original institutionalized network.
- The social network analysis applied here reveals that networks are strongly based on knowledge intensive relations. But these relations are no mechanical result of routine-like networking: The firms pursue different sourcing strategies; their activities comprise a portfolio of interactions. The different dimensions of interaction coincide only to a small degree: supplier relations are more or less separated from knowledge intensive ones. There is no automatic parallelism of interactions. This does not exclude automatic spillovers of knowledge connected with supplier relations, but it does illustrate that the higher intensities of knowledge exchange as indicated by the revealed forms of interaction are consciously and selectively chosen, and are not a mere by-product.
- This also implies that knowledge management is a task to be fulfilled at different levels: Firms establish a variety of types of interactions and relationships each of them having different impacts on the knowledge generation and diffusion process. Mariotti and

Delbridge (2001) speak of the necessity for firms - in the face of knowledge ambiguity, of knowledge related barriers, of tacitness and complexity of knowledge - to engage in the management of a portfolio of ties. But individuals and firms alone are, from an economic point of view, not capable of delivering sufficient amounts and varieties of knowledge.

This leads to the final conclusion emphasising the differentiated need of institutionalization of knowledge generation and sharing - clusters, networks and related forms of interfirm cooperation are necessary preconditions for and reveal - as the empirical approaches have shown - different forms of 'thinking'.

5. References

Audretsch, D. B. & Lehmann, E. E. (2006). The role of clusters in knowledge creation and diffusion: an institutional perspective, In: *Clusters and Regional Development. Critical reflections and explorations,* Asheim, B., Cooke, Ph., Martin, R. (eds.) pp. 188-198, Routledge, Oxon

Balling, R. (1997). *Kooperation: Strategische Allianzen, Netzwerke, Joint Ventures und andere Organisationsformen zwischenbetrieblicher Zusammenarbeit in Theorie und Praxis,* Peter Lang, Frankfurt am Main.

Bünstorf, G. (2003). Processes of knowledge sharing: from cognitive psychology to economics, In: *The Economics of Knowledge Sharing,* Helmstädter, E. (ed.), Edward Elgar, Cheltenham, pp. 74-99.

Dodgson, M. (1996) Learning, Trust and Inter-firm Technological Linkages: Some Theoretical Associations, in COOMBS R., RICHARDS A., SAVIOTTI P.P. and WALSH V. (Eds) Technological Collaboration - The Dynamics of Cooperation in Industrial Innovation, pp. 54-75, Edward Elgar, Cheltenham

Douglas, M. (1986/1991). *Wie Institutionen denken,* Suhrkamp, Frankfurt.

Edvinsson, L. & Malone, M.S. (1997). *Intellectual Capital,* Harper, New York.

Felin, T. & Foss, N. J. (2005). Strategic Organization: a Field in Search of Microfoundations. *Strategic Organization* , 3, 441-55.

Gay, B. & Dousset, B. (2005). Innovation and network str*uctural dynamics: Study of the alliance network of a major sector of the biotechnology industry. Research Policy,* 34 (10), 1457-75.

Giuliani, E. (2005). *The structure of cluster. Knowledge and Networks: Uneven and Selective, not Pervasive and Collective.* DRUID Working Paper No. 05-11.

Giuliani, E. & Bell, M. (2005). The micro-determinants of meso-level learning and innovation: evidence from a Chilean wine cluster. *Research Policy,* 34 (1), 47-68.

Hartmann, C.; Niederl, A. & Breitfuss, M. (2007). *Pilot RICARDA Intellectual Capital Report for the Polymer Competence Center Leoben,* Mimeo, Graz.

Helmstädter, E. (ed) (2003). *The Economics of Knowledge Sharing, A New Institutional Approach,* Edward Elgar, Cheltenham, UK and Northampton, MA, USA.

Hendry, C.; Michael, A. & Jones, A. (1995). *Strategy Through People - Adaption and Learning in the Small-Medium Enterprise,* Routledge, London.

Mariotti, F. & Delbridge, R. (2001). *Managing Portfolios of Ties in Inter-firm Networks,* Paper to be presented at the Nelson and Winter Conference, Aalborg, Denmark.

Oess, A. (1991). *Total Quality Management: Die ganzheitliche Qualitätsstrategie,* Gabler, Wiesbaden.

Pedler, M.; Burgoyne, J. & Boydell, T. (1997). *The Learning Company*, McGraw-Hill, London.
Porter, M.E. (1998). *On Competition*, Boston, Harvard Business School.
Porter, M.E. (2000). 'Location, competition and economic development: local clusters in a world economy', *Economic Development Quarterly*, 14, 15-34.
RICARDA (2007). *Intellectual Capital Reporting for Regional Cluster and Network Initiatives*, Manual on the RICARDA Methodology, Berlin.
Saxenian, A.L. (1996). *Regional Advantage - Culture and Competition in Silicon Valley and Route 128*, Harvard University Press, Cambridge, MA.
Steiner, M. (2006). Do Clusters Think?: an institutional perspective on knowledge creation and diffusion in clusters, In: *Clusters and Regional Development. Critical reflections and explorations*, Asheim, B.; Cooke, Ph. & Martin, R. (eds.), pp. 199-217, Routledge, Oxon
Steiner, M. & Hartmann, Ch. (2006). Organizational Learning in Clusters. A Case Study on Material and Immaterial Dimensions of Cooperation, *Regional Studies*, Vol. 40.5, 2006, pp. 493-506
Steiner, M. & Ploder, M. (2008). Structure and Strategy within Heterogeneity: Multiple Dimensions of Regional Networking, *Regional Studies, 42:6, pp. 793-815*
Vonortas, N. S. (2000). Multimarket contact and interfirm cooperation in R&D, *Journal of Evolutionary Economics*, 10 (1-2), pp. 234-71
Wenger, E. (1996). Communities of Practice: The Social Fabric of a Learning Organization, *Healthcare Forum Journal*, 39, pp. 20-26

25

Higher Education Systems: Postsecondary Vocational & Technical Education Developments in Comparison

Peter A.J. Englert and Wolf Dieter Grossmann
University of Hawaii
USA

1. Introduction

Key parameters of modern change processes in many economies and societies are the growth of knowledge and global digital information potential, major drivers for the move towards innovation or knowledge society. The influence of these drivers on higher education is remarkable and will provide a challenging framework for development opportunities of higher education systems and institutions. A major element of change is the explicit or implicit mandate to regional and national higher education systems of social relevance and alignment with economic development. Higher, i.e. post-secondary vocational & technical education has teaching, learning and degree structures that are generally and intuitively well aligned with a polity's economy or economic development strategy. However, structure, depth and breadth of higher vocational & technical education are very different for different educational cultures based on the polities' historical social and economic development trajectory. In this chapter an analysis of knowledge and information growth and its effects on vocational & technical post-secondary education will evaluate current organizational characteristics as well as degree structures of different educational cultures, including New Zealand, the United States of America, China, and Germany. Qualitative comparative analysis will provide suggestions for future development opportunities of higher technical & vocational education as a key element for the construction and development of innovation or knowledge society. The role of post-secondary vocational & technical institutions in life-long learning, continuous human resource development, and workforce education will be briefly discussed. Opportunities of vocational & technical education as a major access portal to other forms of higher education for large parts of polities will also be considered.
Higher education, for many centuries and in may cultures a privilege of the few, has with the onset of the Industrial Revolution in the Western world and over time become a major factor in the development of nations and their economies, and therefore by necessity accessible to large fractions of populations around the globe. The history of vocational, technical, and professional education, for a long time separate and not part of higher

education, and its subsequent integration or not into the post-secondary higher education environment is a worthwhile subject for detailed analysis in different education cultures.
The knowledge and information content of almost all human activities, including social and economic activities has dramatically changed. In the higher education environment several trends are reflecting this change: The transformation, e.g. in the United States of America into pre-professional and professional degrees of what were previously liberal arts degrees or research based precursors of academic doctoral degrees manifest some of these changes. This trend is highlighted by the significant growth in abundance and number of pre-professional and professional degrees awarded, especially of professional master's degrees and, to a much lesser extent, professional doctorates. The drivers for these developments are also the drivers for the further advancement of vocational & technical education and hence, the progressive integration of vocational & technical education into post-secondary education systems in many education cultures is another change indicator.
The intent of this chapter therefore is, to evaluate through qualitative comparative analysis effects of these macroscopic drivers of change on the location and position of vocational & technical trajectories within frameworks of education, the associated scholarship and research & teaching content, and the development of degrees in vocational & technical institutions within post-secondary education systems.

2. Higher Vocational & technical Education in Postsecondary Systems

There are many different higher education cultures present in the major regions of the globe. Many of these cultures have developed as a result of the growing and changing needs of societies in line with their historical and economic development. Today, and as a result of growth in content and knowledge, higher vocational & technical education is firmly embedded in several higher education systems and cultures. The location of vocational & technical education within education systems, its position within systems of higher education, and its functions in economy and society shows a large variation of approaches between countries. A first attempt of understanding these different approaches would be to find the general location of vocational & technical education within education and its position within higher education systems.
There are many different ways of describing higher education systems. For the purpose of higher vocational & technical education we need measures of fit between the activities of higher education systems and areas of economic activity. Therefore geographically and politically defined areas, such as national economies, or local & regional state economies with some economic autonomy will provide a useful framework. Both public and private higher education providers contribute through their activities to a given national or regional economy, whether they are aggregated into statutory systems of higher education for reasons of convenient administration or not. The most common areas of study should be national economies and national higher education systems.
There are many different and sometimes very sophisticated classification systems for higher education and its institutional components (McCormick & Zhao, 2005). For the purpose of this chapter the general components of higher education systems can be classified by the type and content of education provided, such as general, professional or vocational & technical, and degrees granted.

This classification is simple as it needs to be applicable to almost any higher education system around the globe. Experience shows a large degree of variation across countries.

- Non-baccalaureate institutions
    - General
    - Professional
    - Vocational &Technical
- Baccalaureate institutions
    - General
    - Professional
    - Vocational &Technical
- Comprehensive Masters institutions
    - General
    - Professional, Vocational &Technical
- Comprehensive Doctoral institutions
    - General
    - Professional
- Specialized post-graduate institutions
    - General, Professional

Implicit in this characterization is that vocational & technical signifiers transform into those of professional education as degree level increases. At doctoral institutions professional degrees constitute only a minority of those awarded except in areas such as medicine and law. Furthermore, within the framework of national definitions, professional and vocational & technical education is frequently not considered to be part of higher education, especially at the non-baccalaureate level, but sometimes also at the baccalaureate level. On the other hand, general education providing units at the non-baccalaureate level are sometimes considered to be part of higher education systems. For the purpose of a comprehensive framework, professional and vocational & technical education needs to be included in the analysis of all higher education systems when its curricular structure clearly exceeds basic skill training, whether it is formally considered so or not.

3. Knowledge and Information Potential Growth

Of the major sources that influence the future development of higher education: knowledge and information potential growth was, is and will be a significant driving force (Duderstadt, 2000; Katz, 1999). In addition, the growth in information potential has emerged as a major driver of economies. One of the key results of knowledge growth is the history of the development of higher education itself, the creation of disciplines and the establishment of ever more disciplines over time as well as the differentiation of categories of higher education institutions.

3.1 Knowledge Growth

Knowledge growth is frequently characterized by the time it takes for valid and not redundant or obsolete knowledge of a field or society to double. The time constants provided for one doubling of human knowledge vary significantly with academic discipline or other knowledge field, and are generally assumed to be between 5 and 14 years. Aspects of knowledge growth were discussed almost twenty years ago. Key publications by Romer, Stern, and Castells give an early comprehensive description of the development of knowledge society (Romer, 1990; Stern et al., 2000; Castells, 2000a, 2000b, and 2004).

In higher education we see several effects of knowledge growth. More and more qualified workers are required in private and public enterprises, and polities encourage investment supporting the participation of larger fractions of their populations in higher education.

Knowledge does not only grow, also the knowledge about changes of knowledge evolves very rapidly. This directly affects education institutions of all types, as they have the creation and transmission of knowledge as one of their main elements. An example of knowledge about knowledge change is direct and fast access through the Internet to scientific journals, another is search through search engines, general ones such as Google as well as those for scientific papers, e.g. through Google Scholar. Whereas we can expect that this new development will accelerate, even present knowledge about knowledge changes does only slowly become effective. It is moderated by a multitude of factors, e.g. administrative, political, organizational, slow learning and human difficulties. For example, all scholars should be engaged in using such possibilities, but observation shows that this is not yet the case.

Knowledge also grows through combination of different types of knowledge. This has two effects, one, it further accelerates knowledge growth and the other is that it makes knowledge more complex. For example, a sophisticated combination of knowledge bodies has brought about Geographical Information Systems (GIS). The more advanced GIS have features which can only be used by highly trained, large and specialized groups - something which higher education institutions by their nature cannot easily provide. Particular examples of combinations of knowledge bodies include interdisciplinary fields such as the new genomics. As higher education institutions in general have difficulties in interdisciplinary synthesis they face the risk that they are increasingly left behind by external providers and their service and software packages.

A conceptual presentation may be useful in demonstrating a particular effect of the increasing volume and diversity of knowledge which will greatly influence the structure of education institutes and their relationship to each other. This phenomenon is outlined in Figure 1. It shows the increasing separation between originally related fields of knowledge.

In reality and from a holistic point of view, everything is connected with everything else, although not everything is closely connected with everything else. Thus, Figure 1 demonstrates an increasing necessity for co-operation between different fields of knowledge, to keep knowledge relevant. Accordingly, it becomes increasingly more necessary for higher education institutions to co-operate, even if their scope and mission seem to be very different. With further growth of knowledge, an individual education unit or country can cope ever less with the total amount of knowledge which further increases the necessity for co-operation at many different levels.

Other effects of knowledge growth on higher education areas arise in the field of business. As demand for knowledge workers increases and as knowledge acquisition and creation becomes more complex, higher levels of accomplishment and degrees are required for occupations and professions. More and higher levels of specialization have appeared, and new and mostly higher forms of qualifications emerge (Englert, 2007).

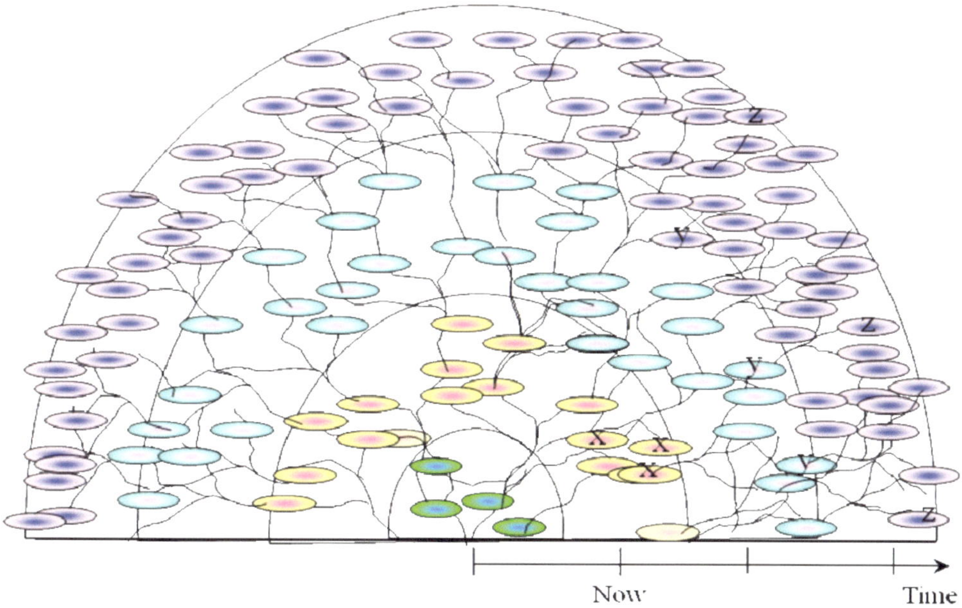

Fig. 1. Increase in number of knowledge fields over time and their resulting increasing separation. Here, x, y, z are knowledge fields that were initially related (x), but they evolve (y) differently and become increasingly disparate (z). This Figure, in principle, also indicates the relative growth of knowledge useful for the four economic macro sectors, with the innermost half sphere representing the 1st sector, the next half sphere the 2nd sector and so on.

Statistics on participation rates in higher education are published by national and international agencies. The growth in participation in higher education is evident in almost all polities of the globe, developed and developing countries. From 1991 to 2004, global participation in higher education grew from 68 Million to 132 Million, or almost by a factor of two (UNESCO Institute for Statistics, 2006).

Within higher education in many economies the bachelor's degree was and is the terminal preparatory degree for many occupations and participants. However, the growth of knowledge created and the knowledge required to fulfill professional functions in modern economies is leading to a growth in Master's degree development and enrollment. A further trend indicating knowledge growth and its reflection in the appearance of new advanced degrees is seen in professional doctorates (Englert, 2007).

3.2 Information Potential Growth

Information and digital communication are now globally prevalent and available. High-information-products, information-rich and communication intensive products and services, are currently developing fast (Ernst, 2005). As a result, information and information technology enters many established goods and services and changes their nature. Consequently, information content and knowledge requirements are growing in all economic sectors including goods production and service sectors, and that is where higher vocational & technical education plays a major role.

According to Dyson (Dyson et al., 1994), the large-scale availability of information is, in its effects on human societies and economy, comparable to the transition from the agricultural to the industrial age when, due to the steam engine, a big supply of energy could be accessed, i.e. fossil coal.

3.3 Knowledge and Information in Economic Sectors

Economic changes resulting from effects of knowledge and information potential growth drivers can be assessed by sketching their effect on economic macro sectors. The term "sector" is used with two meanings in economics: the first meaning is the multitude of well-established 'general sectors' such as retailing, wholesaling, computer manufacturing or telecommunications, and the second meaning concerns four "macro-sectors". The 1st sector is the primary products and resources sector and contains in particular agriculture, forestry, fisheries, and mining. The 2nd sector is classical goods production or manufacturing. The 3rd sector contains service products, including diverse services from health care to tourism. As large amounts of information are becoming a major resource it can be observed that within all classical sectors products and services are developed which are very high in information content and/or transportation of information and knowledge and could be defined as the 4th macro-sector. Examples are: multimedia products, Experience Economy (Pine & Gilmore 1999), the Internet, networks for cellular phones, or nanotechnology

In addition, the emergence of knowledge and information rich products and production modes sees the rise of a new workforce, called "highly qualified people" in many publications of the OECD (e.g. OECD Publishing, 2008), a phenomenon which was basically already described by Schumpeter in 1939 for the 1920s wave of basic innovations. Castells gave an early comprehensive description of the development of the knowledge society (Castells 2000a, 2000b, and 2004). Grossmann (Grossmann, 2001) describes strategies for regional development in the information society and provides systems models for their description with some real applications to planning and management.

The concept of information-rich and communication intensive products and services asks for workforce education that can adapt to this changing and increasingly more complex environment. The opportunity but also increasing responsibility of providing this workforce lies clearly in the area of higher education. This leads to conflicts with established education and requires a partial transformation of higher education.

3.4 Example: Textile Industry

In China and in many other countries of Asia the development of classical goods production was considered the most important driver in transforming primary production based agricultural societies into modern ones. In India as well as in China increases in knowledge based services including innovation also play a major role in the transition (Ernst, 2006). As discussed above, knowledge and information potential are transforming both goods production and services by enriching both macro-economic sectors through changing established products into information rich and communication intensive ones, through creating new ones, and through changing production and supply processes (Farrell, 2003).

For many developing countries the transfer of textile production from Europe and North America played a major role in building Gross Domestic Product and personal income. Basic drivers were initially production cost considerations and low-wage workforce availability for classical and labor intensive production establishments. This paradigm has changed under conditions of knowledge and information potential growth. Moazzem (Moazzem et al., 2007) argues that textile production in Bangladesh since its inception in the early 1980s has developed with support of different international policies, such as the Multi-Fiber Arrangement (MFA), a Generalized System of Preference (GSP), and various policies at the domestic level. With the membership of China in the World Trade Organization and the phase out of the MFA in 2005, a number of challenges are confronting the apparel sector of Bangladesh. In the changing scenario, it has been projected that without having product diversification by applying more advanced technologies, Bangladesh would be unable to retain its market share. Moazzem continues to argue, that 'in order to be competitive in the global market, apparel exporters of Bangladesh have to reduce lead time, ensure 'lean retailing', provide support of full supply chain, have the capacity for supplying bulk volume of orders, develop compliance standard and take measures for workers health and safety'.

While implicitly recognizing some elements of the potential impact of knowledge and information potential growth in this industry, the analysis is far from complete. To the contrary and in extension of major arguments of this chapter, De Raeve (De Raeve, 2007) sees the development of textile products in an urgent need for adequate knowledge circulation, and for faster and more effective translation of scientific results into innovative commercial products. Information potential adds the dimension of more flexible small batch oriented manufacturing processes that allow a better consumer orientation through 'mass customization'. This is a clear argument for the transformation of the industry from a resource base to knowledge and information influenced base. And while this analysis was undertaken from a European point of view it does have general validity.

These tensions are present in all aspects of goods production and service provision environments and require significant flexibility in educating and preparing a workforce that can embrace these and predicted future changes. Therein lays a challenge and opportunity for higher vocational & technical education.

The European textile industry viewpoint shows that in current circumstances economies with an interest in stability may need to consider regaining strength in advanced goods production and services. Given that wage differentials for an advanced workforce diminish in international comparison, the increasing presence of such a workforce is, among others, a key factor in determining location and establishment decisions for goods production and service sector companies. This provides an additional reason for giving serious consideration to strengthening or, in some circumstances, re-developing and almost re-inventing higher vocational & technical education.

4. Location and Position of Higher Vocational & Technical Education

The location of vocational & technical education within an education system and the position of higher vocational & technical teaching institutions and their present functions in frameworks of education systems are very much dependent on development histories and the societal purposes they were originally established for. In some educational cultures vocational & technical education is introduced in compulsory education before transition into specialized skills training or higher education. Vocational & technical secondary education trajectories are not always constructed to provide access to higher vocational & technical education or to higher education in general. This may be by design or for historical reasons. An analysis of position and location of vocational education may find reasons for this status or arguments for change.

A comparative analysis of different education cultures may be helpful in evaluating aspects of existing paradigms and future development trends.

TYPE OF EDUCATION	PR CHINA		USA		NEW ZEALAND		GERMANY		
	U	V&T	U	V&T	U	V&T	U	V&T	
Pre-school	3		4		2		(3)		
Compulsory Primary Education	6		6		6		4+2		4+2
Compulsory Junior Secondary School	3	3	3		2	2	6/7	5	4
Senior Secondary School (compulsory in some countries)	3	3	3		4/5	3		2/3	(3)
Higher Education First Degree	4	3/4	4	2	3	2/3	5	3/4	2/3/4
Higher Education Second Degree	3		1-3		1-3	1-3		2/1	2/1
Higher Education Highest Degree	3		4-6		4-6		1-5+	3	

Table 1. Location and position of vocational & technical education in different countries

Due to the complex nature of the subject only general trends can be considered, sometimes leading to simplified statements.

The first column of Table 1 indicates the levels of education provided in each of the countries, including compulsory education and higher education. The subsequent columns describe parts of the education system that are general and provide access to general higher education indicated by 'U' and those that can be considered vocational and technical indicated by 'V&T'. Although there seems to be a seamless transition between secondary and higher vocational & technical education, this is not consistently so. The complexities are alluded to in the following chapters.

It is also important to observe where decisions are made about educational systems and where oversight lies in broad terms. Table 2 provides a comparison of some indicators on accreditation and coordination of higher vocational & technical education (IAU, 2008). The oversight over education in general and over vocational & technical education is highly variable between countries. In the United States of America, the several States do have authority over all forms of education. Coordination and accreditation in general is therefore regional or even local. In New Zealand, all forms of higher education are centrally coordinated through the Tertiary Education Commission (TEC), while accreditation of programs for all non-university education, i.e. also for higher vocational & technical education is provided by the New Zealand Qualifications Authority (NZQA). In China, provincial Departments of Education or Municipal Commissions are responsible for the regionalized Vocational & Technical Colleges, while programmatic oversight still lies with

COUNTRY	INSTITUTIONS	ACCREDITING AGENCY	COORDINATIO N AGENCY
PR CHINA	VOCATIONAL/TECHNICAL COLLEGES (JUNIOR COLLEGES)	REGIONAL	CENTRAL
GERMANY	UNIVERSITIES OF APPLIED SCIENCE OTHER	REGIONAL CENTRAL	REGIONAL REGIONAL
UNITED STATES	ASSOCIATE COLLEGES COMPREHENSIVE UNIVERSITIES	REGIONAL	REGIONAL
NEW ZEALAND	INSTITUTES OF TECHNOLOGY POLYTECHNICS	CENTRAL	CENTRAL

Table 2. Vocational & technical education institutions, accreditation and coordination

the central Ministry of Education. The situation is more complex in the Federal Republic of Germany. There the several states have overall authority over almost all education including universities of applied sciences and their higher vocational and technical teaching. However, other forms of vocational & technical education are regulated (but not coordinated) by the German federal government. This applies to forms of higher vocational & technical education not associated with universities of applied science. In general, regionalization or centralization of accreditation or coordination of higher vocational & technical education can influence the effectiveness and flexibility of its delivery.

4.1 Location of Higher Vocational/Technical Education

Compulsory primary education is available in China, the United States, New Zealand and Germany for almost identical time frames and age groups (IAU 2008). The exception from the canonical starting at age six of compulsory primary schooling in the group of national economies compared is New Zealand. Here compulsory primary education begins at the age of five.

The length of compulsory primary education for all countries is six years. A specific commonality between them is that compulsory primary education is comprehensive, i.e. no occupation oriented curricular activities or directions are offered. The first major differentiation occurs therefore at the transition to junior middle school, i.e. to secondary education. China offers a special vocational & technical education track to students beginning at the age of twelve. The United States and New Zealand continue comprehensive, i.e. non-specialized schooling for all students until the end of senior middle

school, with a few specialization options through electives in vocational & technical education and other areas during the last years of schooling (Pucel, 2001).
The situation in Germany is more complex. Junior and senior middle schools leading directly to university and university of applied sciences admission can have a general humanistic or strong mathematics and science orientation, but not usually a technical one. The situation is different in the four year junior middle school environment, not directly leading to higher education access, which has generally a more technical and professional orientation. A further five year junior middle school track offers opportunities with vocational, technical, and professional orientation. The minimum compulsory schooling in Germany (not including three years of schooling during professional/ vocational/ technical apprenticeship) is nine years. Students transferring from the latter two middle school tracks into a higher education access track do not generally have opportunities to continue vocational & technical subjects during the last two/three years of secondary schooling.
As a result, China and Germany have cohorts of students prepared in vocational & technical subjects leaving senior middle school with the option of entering higher technical education. In both countries, students from non-technical tracks can also qualify for higher vocational & technical education. In China all students have to pass national examinations to obtain placement options within the Chinese higher education system. The United States and New Zealand students who have completed secondary schooling obtain access to the different types of higher education on the basis of choice and general scholastic achievement. Prior exposure to technical or vocational skills training is not required to enter higher technical education. In Germany, as in China, students with some technical training at the middle school level tend to enroll in higher technical education institutions, but prior technical education is not a requirement for admission.
Generally, in all education systems there is no direct connection between skills based vocational & technical subjects and higher education options in this area.

4.2 Position and Function of Higher Vocational & Technical Education

Post-secondary education in the United States does not have an easily distinguishable or identifiable higher vocational & technical education environment. The United States structure has a variety of post-secondary educational institutions with different missions, yet no clearly identified vocational & technical sector. Several States that are interested in attracting and maintaining goods production as part of their regional economy may have vocational & technical education options integrated in their higher education system. One example is the State of Tennessee which operates two higher education systems, the University of Tennessee system, and the system operated by the Tennessee Board of Regents, the latter established in 1972 also including 27 regionally distributed Tennessee Technology Centers providing certificates and diplomas for workforce development. Although operated by a higher education system, it is not clear how these centers address higher vocational & technical education aspects.
Among the more than 4000 accredited United States institutions of higher education there are some that could be considered technically oriented, frequently carrying the name 'Technical Institute'. But most of those are baccalaureate institutions, i.e. universities by definition, offering general four year Bachelor degrees and post-graduate degrees in many areas, including technical ones.

In comparison, higher vocational & technical education has a special place in China, New Zealand, and Germany. In China, three year Vocational & Technical Colleges and three and four year Technical Colleges can easily be identified as the major location of higher vocational & technical education. In New Zealand Institutes of Technology and Polytechnics, (and to some degree Industry Training Organizations) provide higher vocational & technical education through two and three year curricula, the latter being similar to Bachelor degrees in New Zealand universities in learning content and scholastic achievement. In Germany, in general terms, the primary location of higher technical education, other than that provided by research level Technical (Engineering) Universities are the Fachhochschulen (universities of applied sciences), which teach predominantly at the diploma, bachelor and master's level, and also the applied science environments of 'Gesamthochschulen' (comprehensive universities). But also 'Fachschulen' (professional schools) and 'Berufsakademien' (professional academies) provide higher vocational & technical education through multi-year (two or three year) curricula. It needs to be mentioned that much skills based but also advanced vocational & technical education in Germany occurs outside the higher education framework. Content and achievement of these vocational, technical, or professional education opportunities would warrant formal inclusion into higher education by standards in other educational cultures. Therefore, higher technical education in China, New Zealand, and Germany is well positioned at the end of secondary schooling and occupies well defined positions in the respective national higher education systems.

United States institutions providing post-secondary, but not specifically higher vocational & technical education, are Associate Colleges, commonly called Community Colleges. Public Associate Colleges provide to a significant degree vocational, technical and professional training through credit and non-credit courses. For example, Honolulu Community College in the State of Hawaii teaches technical courses for apprentices in auto mechanics, sponsored by trade unions. In addition, Associate Colleges provide a significant fraction of remedial non-credit courses and opportunities for adult education. The highest terminal degree offered by Associate Colleges is the two-year Associate degree. Course content and accomplishments are not always equivalent to that of higher vocational education in other cultures.

Public and private Associate Colleges however, have an additional and very important function, namely to teach at university level up to two years of required and elective courses that allow students, provided their achievements are high, to seamlessly transfer into universities. This access role is unique to US higher education and is an important part of the Associate College mission. In comparison and as part of their present specific focus, Vocational & Technical Colleges and Technical Colleges in China, Technical Institutes and Polytechnics in New Zealand, and Universities of applied science and other higher technical education academies in Germany do not have a mission based role of providing access to other forms of higher education such as universities, though in some cases vocational & technical credit can be applied towards achieving university bachelor degrees via self-study pathways or through adult and continuing higher education.

From this analysis one can derive that the higher vocational & technical education role in the US must therefore be partially or completely covered by four year baccalaureate and comprehensive master's degree institutions, i.e. four year colleges, master's universities, and sometimes even research universities. Predominantly publicly funded United States institutions at all levels have an obligation to respond to workforce education and workforce development needs of their states. In general these institutions accept their regional role and provide for the majority of professional education needed regionally for public and private enterprises. The majority of public four year higher education institutions in the US have therefore mission elements that should address professional, vocational, and technical education.

4.3 Diversity of Approaches

One of the key questions arising from the diversity of vocational & technical education approaches is where most effectively to locate higher technical education within an educational pathway and where to position higher vocational & technical education within a system of higher education. Due to increasingly rapid progress of technology and science, the additional question emerges and is becoming highly important how education providers will be evolving their curricula to follow these developments in a timely fashion. One general answer lies in the mission of higher education institutions.

The missions of research universities are clearly defined across many education cultures by the 'scholarship of discovery' paradigm, which means 'research' and includes (but is not limited to) 'commitment to knowledge for its own sake, to freedom of inquiry, and to following, in a disciplined fashion, an investigation wherever it may lead' (Boyer, 1997). Such a paradigm has proven to develop science and technology well, but this does not apply to all areas of knowledge production. The missions of other components of higher education systems are well defined in some education cultures but not in others.

Table 3 provides a brief overview over some macroscopic data on higher vocational & technical education. The data are described and explained in the chapter text, again indicating that the complexity of national higher vocational & technical education environments cannot be compared without difficulty.

In China, the development of higher vocational & technical education through independent, local, and university associated vocational & technical colleges is a logical consequence of its

	PR CHINA	GERMANY	NEW ZEALAND	USA
POPULATION (M)	1.329	82	4	300
HIGHER V/T INSTUTUTIONS	872	213	19 (52)^	1.086*
HIGHER V/T ENROLMENT (M)	5.957	0.56	0.162	6.370
STUDENTS/INSTITUTION	6830	2630	8520 (3115)^	5865
TOTAL HE ENROLMENT (M)	13.33	1.94	0.503	13.33*
% V/T STUDENTS	44	29	39	48

Table 3. Higher Vocational & Technical Institutions in 2004. (*public sector institutions only, ^number of campuses, (M) Million; data references are provided in the text)

social and economic development based on goods production and services in addition to the primary sector, and the increasing knowledge and information content in these macroscopic economic sectors (Dai, 1991a; Dai, 1991 b; Cheung, 1996). Policy encouraged the mission of higher vocational & technical education in supporting regional and local industrial development through devolving oversight over establishment and curricular development of Vocational & Technical Colleges to provincial governments. The construction of this sector is a significant and important part of the changes in the higher education system of China. Over the last decade the number of higher vocational & technical education institutions grew from about 100 through over 800 (not including 175 post-secondary technical colleges), and the number of students enrolled from 1.17 million to more than 6 million. Two other key factors of interest are that the 5.96 million students enrolled in higher vocational technical schools in 2004 represent 44% of all college students in China (13.33 million), and the 2.37 million of new vocational technical enrolments of 2004 represent 53.1% of all new college recruits (4.46 million) (Zhou, 2006). These trends remained unchanged over the last few years.

In New Zealand, the Tertiary Education Strategy of 2007 emphasizes the need for mission clarification of the different parts of the higher education system, indicating that it has to be achieved through investment policies and implementation (Ministry for Tertiary Education, 2007; Tertiary Education Commission, 2007). While some emphasis is placed on mission differentiation between universities, the mission based contribution of Institutes of Technology and Polytechnics (ITPs) is defined as achieving economic competitiveness via the continuous development of a productive and skilled workforce. The key potential of Technical Institutes and Polytechnics is that, as publicly owned institutions, they can address regional industry support at increasing levels of accomplishment. For comparison, 2004 overall enrolment in ITPs was 191,884 students, in universities and colleges of education 162,322 students, in Wānanga (provide higher education in a Maori cultural context) 69,768, and in Private Training Establishments (PTE) 78,917 students. It means that enrolment in dedicated vocational & technical institutions of higher learning constitutes 39.42% of total enrolment (Education Statistics of New Zealand, 2004). Total enrolment in vocational & technical education may be higher, depending on vocational & technical enrolments in Wānanga and PTE.

In the United States all public research universities, master's universities and colleges have missions that require them to pay attention to workforce development and education within the framework of their course offerings, in part following their heritage as Land-grant institutions, but their university culture, modeled after that of research universities, delivers them less well suited and inclined to make this a major effort. Frequently university industry cooperation is not valued and workforce development needs not reflected in curricula and mode of delivery of education. Associate Colleges, on the other hand, are limited to a two year education that can and does commit to flexible workforce education and workforce development needs, but the depth of education achieved does not always fit knowledge society's need for advanced higher vocational & technical education. This gap may increase due to growing sophistication of products and services.

The task of vocational or technical education at universities and the tension between liberal and vocational education has been with United State colleges since the curricular reforms of the mid-nineteenth century which originated at Brown and Harvard universities (Bastedo, 2005). With the first Morrill Act of 1879 the development of public universities received significant support. Curricular issues were determined by public needs but the tensions between vocational/professional and liberal education were inherited. Lisa R. Latucca writes (Latucca, 2006): "In the late 1800s, as demand for specialization in the United States rose along with more call for practical studies, the emphasis on liberal education in college and university curriculum decreased but did not disappear. Even in the land grant institutions established in the late 1800s, founded with the explicit mission of educating the citizenry of individual states in agriculture and technical fields, liberal education remained a significant component of higher education." This tension provides even today the basis for important curricular debates.

The public part of the US higher education system in 2005 enrolled about 77% of all college students (13.334 million). In 2005, public Associate Colleges enrolled 6.474 million students, public master's universities enrolled 4.277 million students, and public research universities enrolled 2.583 million students (National Center for Education Statistics, 2006). Associate Colleges as non-baccalaureate institutions train a large fraction of students in vocational & technical areas, but they do not provide higher vocational & technical education. This type of education in the American system is, as derived previously, supposed to be delivered by baccalaureate level and higher institutions. It is, however, difficult to quantitatively assess how many students pursue a higher 'vocational & technical' education without content analysis of bachelor degrees. The overall analysis therefore suggests that there is a need for improved knowledge about higher vocational & technical education for advanced workforce development.

In Germany, 102 universities which include research universities, comprehensive universities and technical universities enrolled in 2004 about 1.38 million students. Only a small fraction of these students is engaged in higher vocational & technical education in applied and professional areas. It is yet to be seen if the changes of the Bologna process bring more vocational & technical education into German universities. Of course, technical universities play a special role. The enrolment in 213 universities of applied science was 0.56 million (Statistisches Bundesamt Deutschland, 2005). This means that about 29% of total formal higher education system enrolment is engaged in higher vocational, technical, and professional education. Absolute and relative engagement and enrolment numbers in universities of applied science indicate that a significant fraction of higher vocational & technical education of Germany's advanced workforce occurs formally outside of the formal higher education system. It indicates that for higher vocational & technical education to be successful does not require it to become a part of a formal/classical higher education system.

5. Role and Development of Higher Vocational/Technical Education

5.1 Current Developments

When goods production and service providing sectors of economies were predominantly resource based, skills based vocational & technical training of a workforce was of importance for success and profitability. Therefore, traditional vocational & technical education was not part of higher education. In many education cultures its location was in compulsory secondary education and its post-schooling position in industrial apprenticeship and related educational environments was very close to the industries in need.

This historical and current proximity to enterprise and economy is an advantage that higher vocational & technical education has and should maintain. It is a strategic asset both for industries and for higher vocational & technical education institutions. One, but by far not the most important reason is, that research and even comprehensive universities missions are frequently centered around general and research education, which creates cultures that are not well prepared to deliver flexible, fast changing curricula, and curricula that can support the dramatic changes occurring in major sectors of developing and mature economies.

For many traditional industries the material resource base cannot change much (although there are new materials and new knowledge about materials). Knowledge and information will accelerate change in their way of operation in many dimensions, including advancing production technologies and modes, high responsiveness and flexibility in the consumer or demand–supply domain, responses to integrated environmental and workplace safety concerns, or larger issues such as sustainability and in particular global warming and climate change. Workforces will adapt to more complex equipment, production and distribution schemes through higher levels of flexibility obtained through education. Management will require and expect that their advanced demands in compliance and advancement of corporate goals in this complex modern environment will be understood and carried by all employees. As these changes are likely to be continuous and sometimes 'disruptive' with no 'steady state' anywhere in sight, workforce education needs to be providing a good foundation upon which continuous need based and flexible education can be built on. Higher vocational & technical colleges with well defined missions including a forward orientation will be best suited to address this need.

The development of higher vocational & technical education in all countries considered is at a cross roads of development and could alleviate much of the concerns if mission based differentiation of higher education would become one of the arguments. Hence, the development of higher vocational & technical education as a respected part of higher education systems or a respected education trajectory outside of those systems could avoid mission stretch of classical higher education providers.

The vocational & technical colleges in China have had a significant success as demonstrated by the growth in numbers and in enrolment as indicated previously: From 1998 to 2004 the number of vocational/technical colleges grew by more than a factor of eight from 101 to over 872, and enrolment increased by a factor of almost six from 1.17 Million to 5.97 Million students (Zhou, 2006). This constitutes a desirable and significant growth in overall post-secondary education for China, a major outcome of this development is the contribution it has made to the strong growth of goods production in China.

The same drivers for a highly qualified workforce are at work in the United States, especially as production outsourcing is not viewed favorably any more, and opportunities for goods production are considered essential for a balanced economy. The Carl D. Perkins Vocational and Technical Education Act of 1998 (Public Law 105-332, 1998) understands the significance of vocational & technical education and reflects the knowledge based changes, and provides support for pre-baccalaureate programs. Yet for higher vocational & technical education productive sector demands do not have a direct and immediately obvious addressee. Associate Colleges would be the appropriate place for advanced and flexible workforce development, but other than Vocational and Technical Colleges in China, Institutes of Technology and Polytechnics in New Zealand, and Universities of Applied Science in Germany, they are restricted to two year degrees that do not allow them attainment at higher vocational & technical education. There is a strong movement to allow Community Colleges to teach 4-year applied science and technical degrees, and many drivers of economic development would see this as absolutely necessary. But current rules of accreditation agencies, such as the Western Association of Schools and Colleges (WASC) only allow one four year degree per Associate College; otherwise these colleges would have to comply with the full set of requirements for a university, a condition that would create the typical university attitudes not conducive for higher vocational & technical education. The States of Florida and Texas have created policies to allow Associate Colleges to teach more than one four year degree. So far, predominantly professional degrees are under development. The advancement of Associate Colleges or institutions such as the Tennessee Technology Centers towards the development of three or four year higher vocational & technical programs and degrees could be a key to workforce development through flexible regional industry orientation, desirable in the currently fast changing economic environment.

The role of Institutes of Technology and Polytechnics in New Zealand, through the recent Tertiary Education Strategy (Ministry of Education, 2007), is similarly well defined as that of Vocational & Technical Colleges in China. For the workforce needs of the country they serve a distinct and essential role apart from and in parallel to universities and Industry Training Organizations. Other than higher vocational & technical institutions in China but separate from universities they have the ability to teach three and four year bachelors as well as post-graduate degrees, including the master's degree, in applied technical subjects. This provides Institutes of Technology and Polytechnics an additional dimension of flexibility and prepares them well to knowledge growth and workforce education demands of the future. An additional interesting development occurred in New Zealand in 2001, when the then Auckland Institute of Technology received university status through an act of parliament, to become Auckland University of Technology (AUT). The development of AUT's programs could become a model case for higher vocational & technical education if economy orientation and flexibility in delivery and content prevail.

The attainment of university status of Fachhochschulen as universities of applied sciences is a clear indication of the importance of higher vocational & technical education for the German goods production and services based industries. However, outside of the official higher education system there are many other and diverse institutions that provide higher vocational & technical education. These are positioned even closer to industry and professions, yet with content requirements similar to those of universities of applied science. In general, the developments in Germany in recognizing the increased knowledge, information content, and student attainment in non-university higher vocational & technical education, and its potential recognition through appropriate degrees, provides another approach of accommodating real needs of economic development through practical solutions. Although this German approach has traditional roots it is innovative in creating spaces for recognized higher vocational & technical education outside formal/classical higher education systems. This aspect could have model character and function for countries that want to develop a strong higher vocational & technical education environment without embracing the university as the provider model.

5.2 Transfer and Continuing Education Function

Knowledge in all four macro-economic sectors changes fast and so does knowledge obtained through specialized formal education. By necessity therefore higher vocational & technical institutions in all academic cultures need to focus on being a major resource for lifelong education in their area. The advantage of such institutions is their regional distribution, resulting in close proximity to regional enterprises and their integration with and availability to their communities. This is demonstrated very clearly in the case of

Tennessee where the 27 Tennessee Technology Centers are regionally well distributed, and in Hawaii, where two of the public and all four of the private non-profit universities are concentrated on the by far most populous island, yet public Community Colleges cover five (of a total of six) main islands. Vocational & technical Colleges in China, Institutes of Technology and Polytechnics in New Zealand, and Community Colleges in other US States, also have a wider distribution than universities.

US Associate Colleges in addition to vocational and remedial training of students have the opportunity to engage in a more academically oriented Associate program, for which staff resources and courses are available. During this program students can acquire credit that is directly applicable as transfer credits into Bachelors degree programs at universities. This credit can be gained in courses fulfilling general education requirements and frequently also in discipline oriented courses. Therefore, in Hawaii, students on islands not served by universities can obtain up to two years of university credit before they have to relocate to four year institutions or to distance education modes delivered by four year institutions to complete their bachelor degree education. For periodical retraining and refresher courses in the main subject areas of vocational & technical education, the regional distribution and the engagement with regional economic needs make higher vocational & technical institution a desirable provider of continuous education.

It is obvious that, due to curricular constraints and the lack of higher vocational & technical bachelor degree education, Associate College students that aim at transfer to universities are not likely to be engaged in vocational & technical education. The transfer mission of the community colleges therefore is addressing at present different student populations. However, the concept of 'transparency', i.e. the advancement of talented students from skills based to higher vocational and technical education, from basic diplomas to the most advanced available in vocational & technical education should be given serious consideration as an opportunity for future development. In developing and designing higher vocational & technical education opportunities a student trajectory from skills training to the highest degree of a technical university could be constructed as a means to reach deep into the talent pool for technical innovation.

5.3 Future Developments

Future development of higher vocational & technical education will significantly be influenced by the need for higher levels of knowledge required in all four economic sectors as well as in the field of knowledge itself as a result of knowledge and information potential growth. In addition, there is a unique and growing capacity of enterprises and vocational technical institutions to create new and advanced knowledge outside of the realm of basic and applied research at comprehensive and research universities. Innovation and scholarship in this knowledge and information capability driven vocational & technical environment will have still to be explored, defined and developed in an adaptive process of continuous advancement. But there is no doubt about the capacity as well as need for innovation in the vocational & technical education and research environment. Some theoretical foundations have been provided in 'Scholarship Reconsidered' (Boyer, 1997) though developed on research not specifically addressing higher vocational & technical education. Descriptors and definitions provided include the creation of new intellectual understanding arising from the act of application and the interaction between theory and practice, which both are applicable to higher vocational & technical education. This type of scholarship has produced new knowledge outside of the realm of university/research institute bound discovery. It can be argued that higher vocational & technical institutions are places where practice based creation of new knowledge and innovation has an opportunity to develop significantly and as the main direction of advanced work of its faculty and students.

The availability of three or four year higher education degrees at Vocational Technical Colleges in China and Institutes of Technology and Polytechnics in New Zealand is taking into account the effects of knowledge growth and information capability growth. The availability of four year degrees and Master's degrees at New Zealand and in German vocational/technical institutions within or outside the official higher education system, providing for the opportunity of higher levels of education in applied and economy related fields, reflects the presence of the scholarship of application as well at the heritage of close cooperation with industries. It also provides incentives for other higher vocational & technical education cultures to consider the establishment of advanced degrees outside of traditional university settings.

6. Conclusion

Higher vocational & technical education has been a major factor for economic advancement of developed and developing countries. Its establishment and growth as a separate part of higher education systems or a separate system is based on its special kind of scholarship and its heritage of being in close connection with economic development. The educational paradigm of higher vocational & technical education provides for larger flexibility and better responsiveness to local and regional industrial needs than the research paradigm of universities. The work of higher vocational & technical education is different in content and direction from that of mainstream universities but has equal requirements in mastering knowledge and scholarship of application.

Knowledge and information potential growth is in the process of transforming the goods production and services sector of all economies either through the knowledge content of products and services, through information technology innovations embedded into products and services, or into production and delivery processes. These advancements will place high demands on the development of higher vocational & technical institutions. As a result and as one opportunity for development, their degree structure will have to respond gradually and with flexibility allowing higher degrees to be developed and awarded under the premise that institutions of higher vocational & technical education are able to maintain industry and community connection through this development process.

The countries compared all show specific strength in their higher vocational & technical education. The clarity of mission and the immensely successful implementation of this segment of the higher education system in China, the flexibility of breadth, depth in level and content, and delivery of the New Zealand Institutes of Technology and Polytechnics and the German higher vocational/technical institutions provide concepts for the further development of higher vocational & technical education as a branch of higher education. The access functionality of American Associate Colleges from distributed entry points via 'transparent' pathways to highest levels of attainment in higher education, provide an important design principle to amplify the impact of higher vocational & technical education development. Altogether, higher vocational & technical education development is an integral part of the advances all of higher education has to make to address societal needs for the future.

7. References

Bastedo, M.N. (2005) Curriculum in Higher Education. The Historical Roots of Contemporary Issues. In: Altbach, P.G., Berdahl, R.O., & Gumport, P.J. (eds.) American Higher Education in the Twenty-First Century. Social, Political, and Economic Challenges. Second Edition, Johns Hopkins University Press, ISBN 0-8018-8035-1, Baltimore, MD

Boyer, E.L. (1997) Scholarship Reconsidered, Priorities of the Professoriate, The Carnegie Foundation for the Advancement of Teaching, Jossey-Bass Publishers, ISBN-0-7879-4069-0, Wiley New York

Castells, M. (2000a) The Rise of the Network Society (The Information Age: Economy, Society and Culture), Vol. 1, Blackwell Publishers, ISBN 0-631-22140-9, Oxford, UK

Castells, M. (2000b) End of Millenium, Blackwell Publishers, ISBN 0-631-22139-5, Oxford, UK

Castells, M. (2004) The Power of Identity (The Information Age: Economy, Society and Culture), Vol. 2, Blackwell Publishers, ISBN 1-4051-0713-8, Oxford, UK

Cheung, E. (1996) Higher Vocational Education in China in Response to the Changing Needs of the Labor Market beyond 2000, Industry and Higher Education, 10(4), 261-263

Dai, S. (1991a) The Development of Higher Vocational and Technical Education in China, Chinese Education, 24 (1), 8-26

Dai, S. (1991b) Vocational Universities can Develop into Institutions combining Vocational and Technical education, Chinese Education, 24(2), 21-34

De Raeve, A. (2007) "Mo TIV", Cross Fertilization between Industry and Education, Proceedings of International Technology, Education and Development Conference 2007, 6p. , IATED, ISBN 84-611-4517-8, Valencia, Spain, March 2007

Duderstadt, J.J. (2000) A University for the 21st Century, The University of Michigan Press, ISBN 0-472-11091-8, Ann Arbor, Michigan

Dyson, E.; Gilder, G.; Keyworth, G.; & Toffler, A. (1994) Cyberspace and the American Dream: A Magna Carta for the Knowledge Age, PFF Classisc Publications, Progress and Freedom Foundation, Washington D.C.

Englert, P.A.J. (2007) International Postgraduate Education through Collaborative and Joint Degree Programs, Proceedings of International Technology, Education and Development Conference 2007, 8p. , IATED, ISBN 84-611-4517-8, Valencia, Spain, March 2007

Ernst, D. (2005) The New Mobility of Knowledge: Digital Information Systems and Global Flagship Networks, In: Latham, R. & Sassan S. (eds.) Digital Formations: IT and New Architectures in the Global Realm, Princeton University Press, ISBN 0-691-11987-0, Princeton, USA

Ernst, D. (2006) Innovation Offshoring: Asia's Emerging Role in Global Innovation Networks, East-West-Center Special Reports No. 10, East West Center, ISBN 978-0-205-2, 48 p., Honolulu, USA

Farrell, D. (2003). The Real New Economy. Harvard Business Review, 105-112

Grossmann, W.D. (2001) Entwicklungsstrategien in der Informationsgesellschaft, Mensch, Wirtschaft, und Umwelt, Springer, ISBN 3-540-67800-X, Berlin, Germany

International Association of Universities IAU (2008), World Higher Education Data Base - WHED 2008, 10th edition, Palgrave, Macmillan's Global Academic Publishing, ISBN-13: 978 14-0399-260-4, Hampshire, UK

Katz, R.N. (1999) Competitive Strategics for Higher Education in the Information Age, In: Katz R.N. & Associates (eds.), Dancing with the Devil: Information technology and the New Competition in Higher Education, Jossey-Bass, ISBN 0-7879-4695-8, San Francisco

Lattuca, L.R. (2006) Curricula in International Perspective, In: Forest, J.F. & Altbach, P.G. (eds.) Springer Handbooks on Education: International Handbook of Higher Education, Part 1, Springer, ISBN 10-4020-4011-3 (HB)

McCormick, A.C. & Zhao, X.M. (2005) Rethinking and Reframing the Carnegie Classification, Change, (Sept. / Oct.), 51-57

Ministry of Education, Data Management and Analysis Division (2005) Education Statistics of New Zealand for 2004, http://www.educationcounts.govt.nz/publications/ece/2507, Wellington, New Zealand

Ministry of Education (2007) Tertiary Education Strategy 2007 - 10, Incorporating: Statement of Tertiary Education Priorities 2008 - 10, Office of the Minister for Tertiary Education, Wellington, New Zealand

Moazzem, K.G. & Das Shimon , S.R. (2007) Technological Restructuring in the Apparel Sector of Bangladesh in View of MFA Phase Out, Proceedings of International Technology, Education and Development Conference 2007, 8p., IATED, ISBN 84-611-4517-8, Valencia, Spain, March 2007

OECD Publishing (2008) Global Competition for Talent, Mobility of the Highly Skilled, ISBN 9-7892-6404-7740, Paris, France

Office of the Minister for Tertiary Education (2006) Tertiary Education Strategy 2007 - 12, Incorporating: Statement of Tertiary Education Priorities 2008 - 10, Office of the Minister for Tertiary Education (New Zealand), ISBN 0-478-13612-9, ISBN 0-478-13613-7 internet, Wellington, New Zealand

Pine, B.J.; Gilmore, J. (1999) The Experience Economy. ISBN 0-87584-819-2, Harvard Business School Press, Boston

Pucel, D.J. (2001) Beyond Vocational Education: Career Majors, Tech Prep, Schools within Schools, Magnet Schools & Academies, Eye on Education, Inc., ISBN 1-930556-04-7, Larchmont, New York

Romer, P.M. (1990) Endogenous Technological Change, Journal of Political Economy, 98, S71-S102

Statistisches Bundeamt Deutschland (2005), Hochschuldaten, November 2005

Stern, S.; Porter, M.E. & Fuhrman, J.L. (2000) The determinants of national innovative capacity, NBER Working Paper No. w7876

Tertiary Education Commission (2007) Investment Guidance 2008 -2010, ISBN, Wellington, New Zealand

UNESCO Institute for Statistics (2006) Global Education Digest 2006, Comparing Education Statistics around the World, ISBN 92-9189-028-6, Montreal, Canada

US Department of Education, National Center for Education Statistics (2008) Fast Facts http://nces.ed.gov/fastfacts

US Government (1998) Carl D. Perkins Vocational and Technical Education Act, Public Law 105-332

Zhou, J. (2006) Higher Education in China, Thomson Learning, ISBN 981-254-364-3, Singapore

26

The Role of Diaspora Entrepreneur in the Advancement of Science and Technology: Knowledge Economy Perspective

Mervat Hatem Sharabati-Shahin
Department of Science and Technology Studies
Faculty of Science, University of Malaya
Malaysia

1. Introduction

The industrial society brought with it a profound socioeconomic change that transformed the economy in many countries from largely rural societies engaged in agriculture to owner-centered societies engaged in the manufacture of goods (Al-Hawamdeh & Hart, 2002). Trends in world economy have clearly shifted towards a knowledge economy. In this instance, economic development calls more upon intangibles, i.e. brains, rather than tangibles, i.e. muscles, and productivity calls upon ideas, information and adaptive thinking. In view of this rising globalised knowledge economy, trans-national migrants are playing an increasing role contributing to demographic changes and answering to the competition amongst nations for skilled knowledge nomads.

Brain drain refers to the phenomenon of emigration of trained and talented individuals to other nations. This human capital flight is observed to have two key trajectories of migration: Firstly, the flow of brains from the developing nations to the developed nations, and secondly, from developed nations to developing nations. The first type of emigration is largely superior in numbers, to the latter. Emigrational trajectories can be characterised by divers push factors and pull factors, respectively, from countries of origin and to recipient countries. Conflict, health hazards, troubled economy or a difficult political situation, contribute substantially to this flight. There is also the search for greener economic pastures and opportunity for intellectual recognition or simply the prospect to exercise capacities that may not find a demand or appreciation in the country of origin.

The phenomenon of migration of people differs from country to country, from time to time, and from mechanism to mechanism. For example, the emigration trajectory may have resulted from brain overflow, resulting in turn in brain spill over absorbed into foreign markets. The migration of this surplus brain constitutes an overflow and can, if strategically coordinated, provide solutions for the brain exporting country. Another example is the brain exchange, a temporary phenomenon whereby brain drain is compensated by corresponding brain gain. This could be in the form of exchange of scholars, researchers and/or scientists.

This international migration could thus profit developing nations through the economic network benefits created. The resource loss through brain drain could be converted into a long-term resource profit for the developing country. Within this perspective, the emigrated intellectual, skilled, technological elites would remain an invaluable resource for the development of their home country. Their contribution to economic development would be substantial through platforms of the knowledge economy, and *via* knowledge networks of global knowledge societies.

The question is how does Diaspora conserve and maintain these bonds? Skilled immigrants, scientists, entrepreneurs, technopreneurs and intellectuals may play a strong role in science and technology. Saxenian (1999) expressed the significant role of diaspora fostering science and technology driven innovation and economic progress in countries. The most powerful Diaspora mechanism could be defined by different degrees of connectivity, mobility, and interdependence of trans-national knowledge networks.

This chapter aims at highlighting the strong relationships between Diaspora Knowledge Entrepreneurial networks, Mother country and the host country in order to have win-win relationship, based on a strong supporting platform of Science, Engineering, Technology & Innovation (SET&I). This would in turn strengthen the STE&I platform rendering it an enabled and enabling platform.

The structure of this chapter is as follows: the second section discusses the diaspora, the definition and the impact of the diaspora that may play on the origin country and host country, also the rationale for thinking about how to make the diaspora take forward steps to be a part of the development. The third section discusses the entrepreneur and the main characteristics that are needed in order to have a quality entrepreneur especially among the diaspora. The fourth section discusses the diaspora Entrepreneur as a catalyst for the development under the umbrella of knowledge economy. The fifth section discuses science and technology as a core for the development, with a concentration view about the university and their linkages with industry and how diaspora can take this step to foster such a relationship. The seventh and last section introduces the framework that could be applied within many countries and especially needed in medium and low income countries, taking the most important elements; which is believed to make a development by enhancing science and technology within these countries.

2. Diaspora

2.1 Diaspora Definition, causes and facts

Diaspora refers to people or ethnic population that leaves their traditional ethnic homelands and being dispersed throughout other parts of the world. Influenced by push factors pull factors, this dispersion may have been a consequence of force or a consequence of reason. Either way, the Diaspora may retain reasons for bond with his/her country of origin.

More and more people choose to live outside their countries of birth. It was reported (IOM, 2006) that in 2005 migrants comprised 3.0 percent of the global population. There was an estimated 191 million migrants worldwide in 2005, up from 176 million in 2000. Illegal immigration is recorded by IOM to be the most rapidly growing form of human migration. Developed economies, particularly in the EU and US, face new challenges as well as opportunities in managing their immigration policies.

The countries hosting the largest number of international migrants in order of their Mother country, percentage of the worlds as expressed by IOM, (2006), migrant stock are: United States (20.0%), Russian Federation (7.6%), Germany (4.2%), Ukraine (4.0%), France (3.6%), India (3.6%), Canada (3.3%), Saudi Arabia (3.0%), Australia (2.7%) and Pakistan (2.4%).
Migration is rising in many OECD countries with temporary movement rising and foreign-born workers meeting skill shortages in rich countries. Statistics as reported by (UNDP, 2005), show that so many people in low and middle-income countries wish to migrate to more successful states, and that high-income countries, which have less than 20 per cent of the global labour force, now accommodate over 60 per cent of the world's migrants. Migrants who move from lower to higher income economies are often able to gain an income that is 20 or 30 times higher than they would be able to gain at home.
The type of policies a country offers will determine the type of immigrants or brains it attracts. Because workplaces encourage integration; countries must ensure that there are readily available jobs and housing. These two things give people a stake in society (Mehta, 2007).
Factors that encourage the migrant to move away from the home country are termed push factors. These may influence the individual on a temporary basis or, if related to discriminatory factors may conclude in permanent migration as seen in figure.1. Unstable politics-economic conditions and conflict are the main characteristics for such countries.
There are also factors that encourage an individual to consider migrating to a host country. These factors are termed pull factors. For example, in many industrialized states, the increasing competitiveness of the global economy has placed new pressures on both private and public sector employers to minimize costs and to maximize the use of cheap and flexible labour - precisely the kind of labour that migrants, whether they have moved in a regular or irregular manner, are able to provide. From another perspective, we can also witness the migration of large companies in search of cheaper labour force.

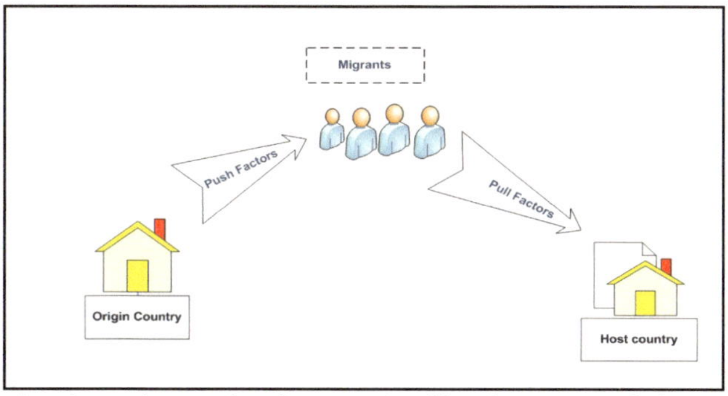

Fig. 1. Emigrational trajectories can be characterised by diverse push factors and pull factors, respectively, from countries of origin and to recipient countries

2.2 Diaspora and Country of Origin Development

Since Diaspora is any people or ethnic population that leaves their traditional ethnic homelands, being dispersed throughout other parts of the world and influenced by push factors or pull factors, the Diaspora may retain reasons for bond with his/her country of origin. The most obvious of these reasons would be family and a sense of 'national consciousnesses'. The Diaspora individual may safeguard links with family and friends, and also retain positive attitudes towards the home country. He may also harbour a strong responsibility in contributing towards economic stability in the home country.

Lowell and Gerova (2004); and Johnson and Sedaca, (2004) represent some bonds between the diaspora and their origin countries like remittances, business investment, and knowledge transfer mechanisms undertaken by Diaspora. Orozco, (2004) mentioned that Diaspora impact on the origin country can be coined as the five Ts: tourism, transportation, telecommunications, trade, and the transmission of monetary remittances. Workers' remittances are an important source of income for many developing countries. Orzoco reports in Lowell paper (2004) that workers' remittances are the second-largest source of external funding for developing countries. While living costs are usually much higher in countries of destination, most migrants can still earn enough to support themselves and send remittances home to members of their household and community.

An excellent example of the mechanism used by Diaspora to participate in the development of the home country can be observed in the case of immigrants in America's high-tech Silicon Valley. A large number of the foreign-born entrepreneurs in Silicon Valley have business relations in their countries of origin. This linkage is often catalyzed by industry - university interactions. Another notable case is the Taiwanese Diaspora, which played a crucial role in developing the country's electronics industry.

These positive attitudes towards the home or origin country could however be dampened by a number of factors. Alienating circumstances of flight, or ethnic-religious discrimination in home country notwithstanding, factors that could prevent or inhibit their enthusiasm to remain in contact with the home country could include a negative attitude of home government towards Diaspora or political rejection of Diaspora by the home Government. Then again, an overly enthusiastic 'welcome' by the home Government via Return Programmes and the re-injection of knowledge Diaspora into the local knowledge platform could provoke a negative reaction by the local knowledge nomads, forcing the once Diaspora to again take flight.

Hence, how do and how could Governments facilitate this conservation of bonds between Diaspora and Home? A number of significant experiments are underway around the world to make effective use of Diasporas. The Swiss government has created a consulate (the Swiss House) in Cambridge, Massachusetts, to promote interactions between the Swiss in the Boston area and their counterparts at home. Swiss House was created in recognition of the importance of the area as the world's leading knowledge centre, especially in the life sciences. In addition to Harvard University and MIT, the Boston area is home to more than 50 colleges and universities and a cluster of biotechnology firms (UN Millennium project, 2005).

More and more attention is turning to possible opportunities that would enable developing countries to build international partnerships with the Diaspora. However, before even considering brain gain or spill-over mechanisms from Diaspora to home country, would it not be wise for the Government to firstly facilitate integration of Diaspora into the host country? This could be achieved through Government to Government understandings and efforts towards securing legal status in the host country; access to information, employment and banking facilities; access to welfare and pensions from home country and from host country; and, freedom of movement within host country. This would empower the Diaspora individual for participation in the reconstruction or development of the home country. Moreover, economic incentives or lack of disincentives for remittances and investments in home country could further encourage the Diaspora - Home interaction. These interactions would require stable pathways or platforms. University - Industry linkages as an example of a pathway or mechanism that diaspora may play a strong role in, could provide a sustainable, flexible conduit for techno-entrepreneurs or knowledge nomads. These University - Industry linkages could be defined by different degrees of connectivity, mobility, and interdependence of trans-national knowledge networks. University-Industry linkages and the role that diaspora may take a place in such linkages will be discussed in a separate section in this chapter.

3. Diaspora Entrepreneur

Economic development, being a choice, is willed within an economy. It is strategically planned, pronounced and implemented, then closely monitored. Economic development occurs when local leaders choose to identify their comparative advantages, choose to invest in these and choose to draw out clear and realistic timelines of development. This thus enables individuals and industries to better compete. In the new century, the comparative advantage of an economy lies in the abundance as well as the quality of entrepreneurs instead of merely traditional inputs, such as labour and capital (Ming, 2005).

3.1 Who is Entrepreneur?

Trying to define Entrepreneur is not easy, although many have tried (Skrzeszewski, 2006).
An *Entrepreneur* as Ming (2005) states has become, in the new economic era that features advancement in technology, one element of economic development. Entrepreneurship is recognized as a major economic force, a major source of business and job development, and it has been identified as an effective tool for community and individual growth and change (Skrzeszewski, 2006). Entrepreneurs are usually the key actors in recognition, exploration and exploitation of new opportunities (Madsen and Fisker, 2004), guided by experience, knowledge, intuition, and a desire for freedom (Skrzeszewski, 2006). Hirich *et al.*, (2008) defined Entrepreneur as behaviour that comprises firstly, of initiative taking, secondly, of the organizing and recognizing of social and economic mechanisms to turn resources and situations to practical account, and thirdly, of the acceptance of risk or failure.
In the new century, the comparative advantage of an economy lies in the abundance as well as **quality of Entrepreneurs** instead of traditional inputs; such as labour and capital (Ming, 2005). Skrzeszewski, (2006) stated that Entrepreneurship in the nonprofits sector (for example, libraries) is based on increasing the organizational capacity to achieve goals rather than to make a profit.
Entrepreneurs can be motivated by money and profit, but they can also be motivated by a desire to bring about social, organizational, or community change. An Entrepreneur is different from a businessman as business investment is not the only sector that an entrepreneur can engage. Because entrepreneurship is an attempt to fill human needs, it is a more dependable source of solutions to societal problems or issues than are government-driven solutions based on political or bureaucratic need (Skrzeszewski, 2006) as seen in figure.2.
Entrepreneurship thrives on globalisation, it is allowed to thrive by national and international deregulation, and it is driven by the IT related communications revolution. In spite of all difficulties that are facing the Entrepreneur, Entrepreneurship is presently the

most effective method for bridging the gap between science and marketplace, creating new enterprise and bringing new products and services to the market (Hirich et al, 2008). Entrepreneurs, be they local or diaspora, have become a key element of economic development, success and sustainability.

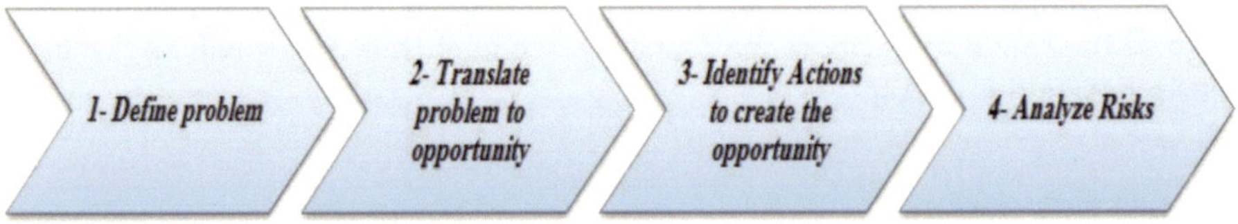

Fig. 2. The Models_ From Problems to Opportunities Adopted from (Skrzeszewski, 2006)

3.2 Diaspora Entrepreneur

The UN Millennium Goals Project (2005) mentions that globalizing forces such as connectivity, mobility, and interdependence have made it possible for Diaspora communities to strengthen their research and business connections to their countries of origin. These three elements should thus also catalyse Diaspora Entrepreneurship, in particular techno-entrepreneurship which allows technical trans-national spill over and propagation of knowledge intensity.

Houghton and Sheehan (2000) clearly state that knowledge has always played an important role in all economies, and this use of knowledge has been increasing since the Industrial Revolution. They go on to argue that, although there is nothing new about knowledge playing a role in economy, but the degree of incorporation of knowledge and information into economic activity is now so great that it is inducing quite profound structural and qualitative changes in the operation of the economy and transforming the basis of competitive advantage.

3.3 Knowledge Entrepreneur

Skrzeszewski (2006) states that a knowledge entrepreneur can be defined as follows:

"A knowledge entrepreneur is someone who is skilled at creating and using intellectual assets for the development of new ventures or services they will lead to personal and community wealth creation or to improved and enhanced services. The Knowledge Entrepreneur must have sufficient personal knowledge capital to be able to create value and/or wealth through the use of the knowledge capital"

Intellectual assets are intellectual material -knowledge, information, intellectual property, experience- that can be put to use to create wealth. It is, as Skrzeszewski emphasizes, the sum of everything everybody in a company knows that gives it a competitive edge. These knowledge assets include skills, experience, expertise, culture, and awareness. However, to be useful in a practical sense, knowledge assts must also be formalized, organized, shared, and utilized in some productive way as depicted in (Figure.2) which provides a theoretical basis for the knowledge base of the entrepreneur (Skrzeszewski, 2006).

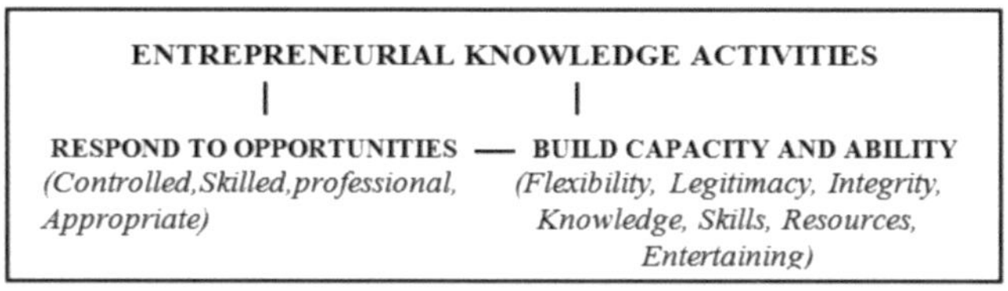

Fig. 3. Knowledge Entrepreneur Model
Source: (Skrzeszewski, 2006)

4. Diaspora Entrepreneurs A Catalyst for A Global Knowledge Economy

According to the United Nations Development Programme (UNDP), the proportion of the world's population living in poverty has fallen faster in the past 50 years than in the previous 500 years. Nonetheless, the gap between the rich and the poor continues to grow forcing an ever widening division between living standards in richer and poorer parts of the globe. In 1975, UNDP reported a per capita Gross Domestic Product (GDP) in high-income countries as 41 times greater than that in low income countries and eight times greater than that in middle-income countries. UNDP reports that today, high income countries have per capita GDPs that are 66 times those of low-income countries and 14 times those of middle-income countries.

4.1 Knowledge Economy

The industrial society brought with it a profound socioeconomic change that transformed the economy in many countries from largely rural societies engaged in agriculture to owner-centered societies engaged in the manufacture of goods (Al-Hawamdeh & Hart, 2002). Trends in world economy have clearly shifted towards a knowledge economy. In this instance, economic development calls more upon intangibles, i.e. brains, rather than tangibles, i.e. muscles, and productivity calls upon ideas, information and adaptive thinking. In view of this rising globalised knowledge economy, trans-national migrants are playing an increasing role contributing to demographic changes and answering to the competition amongst nations for skilled knowledge nomads.

'Knowledge Economy' refers to the overall economic structure that is emerging, whereby the balance between knowledge and resources has shifted so far towards the former that knowledge has become perhaps the most important factor determining the economic development and thus the standard of living. Today's most technologically advanced economies are truly knowledge-based (World Development Report, 1999). As such, today's most technologically advanced economies are truly dependent on their knowledge nomads.

Sheehan and Tegart (1998) identify the rise in knowledge intensity of economic activities, and the increasing globalization of economic affairs as the two defining forces from which emerges the Knowledge Economy. The rise in knowledge intensity is being driven by the combined forces of the information technology revolution and the increasing pace of technological change. This increasing knowledge intensity involves both the increasing knowledge intensity of individual goods and services, and the growing importance of those goods and services in the economy. Hence, knowledge intensity and globalization are not only two forces, but two interdependent forces influenced by existing degrees of connectivity and mobility of the knowledge nomad.

Hargreaves and Shaw (2004) explain that Knowledge economies work best when they are developed in conjunction with knowledge societies. These are societies that recognize their knowledge elites and uphold the emergence of potential elites, promoting mechanisms geared towards spin-off benefits and social dividends for the broader civil society. This is accomplished without 'burn-out' of the knowledge elite, or hindering his process for continual exploration and expression. Diaspora techno-entrepreneurs, whether being temporary or permanent Diaspora, weave themselves through trans-national knowledge societies.

Hence, the basis of a knowledge economy is a learning society (Hargreaves and Shaw, 2004). Economic success and a culture of continuous innovation depend greatly on sustaining a continual education and innovation process. According to OECD, successful knowledge economies rely on four sources of innovation: Scientific and technical knowledge; Interactions and incentives to innovate among users and doers; Decentralized modular patterns of innovation within a coordinated system; and, Widespread application of information and communication technologies, in education.

4.2 The Entrepreneurial Network

Burt (2000) provides a comprehensive account about Network theory with entrepreneurship perspectives. He submits that a player (Entrepreneur) with a network rich in information enjoys a number of benefits from: i) contacts established in the places where useful bits of information are available, ii) a reliable flow of information to and from those places. Burt (2000) explains that networks could be modelled in two different routes. The first route describes the networks as the actor accesses people with specific resource, creating a correlation with the actor. The second route involves the networks themselves which are seen as a resource, because they allow the actor better access, better timing and better chance for referrals. The first line describes the networks as a conduit, while the second line describes how networks are themselves a form of social capital (Burt, 2000). An understanding of the two routes is vital since Diasporas originate from different countries with different characteristics.

4.3 Knowledge Entrepreneur Network

Al-Hawamdeh & Hart (2002) have noted that the essence of the Knowledge-based Economy is the capacity to absorb, process, and apply knowledge or intellectual property and translate it into a key source of competitive advantage together with the basic factors of production, which continue to be important in the Knowledge-based Economy. The emphasis is toward intellectual capital or knowledge as a source of value and wealth creation (Al-Hawamdeh & Hart, 2002). So the richer country will be the country with high numbers of Intellectuals and educated people. Ultimately, the basis of a knowledge economy is a learning society (Hargreaves and Shaw, 2004). Economic success and a culture of continuous innovation depend greatly on sustaining a continual education and innovation process.

There is no doubt that brain drain is a big problem, but it can act as a safety valve to relieve the pressure of a pressing problem rather than to resolve it. As mentioned by Borta (2007) the safety valve happens for the reasons that migration affords the skilled workers with individual exits such as: it facilitates the export of the unemployment problem for skilled workers; and it alleviates the pressure to change the structural barriers to improving the business climate in order to return the benefits also to the origin country. Generally, by attracting highly educated workers, recipient countries could first and foremost expect a positive impact on economic output in both absolute and in per capita terms. Clearly, an increase in the population generates positive outcomes on supply capacity and demand, which will result in output gains (Borta, 2007). The core issue is how the Diaspora could play a win-win role facilitating development in both directions, toward the origin country, and from the recipient country.

Let us look at the impact of brain drain on origin countries. Brain drain economic impact on each origin country depends on many circumstances—among them the skills and former employment of migrants, the history of migration (the existence and location of a large Diaspora), the sectors affected, patterns of trade and production, the investment climate, and the size and geographical location of the country. Origin countries may face both favourable and unfavourable consequences from brain drain. Typically, migrants are better educated, younger, and more mobile than the majority in their country of origin. That's why origin countries may not only lose an important amount of their well-educated domestic work force, but also some of their innovative and motivated youth. Considerable out-migration could lead to both a brain drain and a youth drain also from poorer countries. Borta (2007) mentioned that in some instances, highly-skilled emigration has a negative impact on living standards of those left behind and on growth. This is because: (a) those left behind in the home country may suffer because they lose the prospect for training and mutually beneficial exchanges of ideas; (b) the provision of key public services with positive externalities, such as education and health, may be damaged; (c) opportunities to achieve economies of scale in skill-intensive activities may be reduced; (d) society loses its return on high-skilled workers educated at public expense; and (e) the price of technical services may rise. This means, that if highly educated workers would stay in their countries, they could help to improve governance, improve the quality of debate on public issues, encourage education of children, and strengthen the administrative capacity of the state—contributions that would be impaired in the case of brain drain. However, due to the ongoing debate about brain drain impacts on origin countries, many studies have emphasized some potential gains from brain drain occurrence.

The return of skilled workers to their home country is a positive occurrence because they may be more efficient than foreigners in transferring knowledge back home because of their understanding of local culture, but most of the studies show that most of people who are leaving their home lands looking for better situations rarely returning back, other studies from IOM indicate that thirty percent of students who are studying overseas return back to their home lands. In the case of countries facing dangerous situations such as war or conflict, the Diaspora may be restricted re-entrance into their origin countries. The concern related to this group of people is that they may carry a deep feeling towards their origin countries and are burdened with the incapacity to channel assistance or to participate in origin country development.

Two key notions were discussed in detailed by (Kuznetsove *et al.*,2003), in order to include the Diaspora as a part of the development; (1) Open migration chains are sequences of educational or job opportunities, which allow a migrant to move to progressively complex educational and job tasks necessary to work in the global environment. (2) Diaspora networks (or expatriate networks) are the locus of concerted action by expatriates to

promote their collective interests or to help them engage in their home countries. *The question is what would we expect from Diaspora?*
It is well known that expatriates have played a critical role in accelerating technology exchange and foreign direct investment in the economies of India, China and Israel. They have frequently taken the role of pioneer investors at a time when major capital markets regarded these economies as too risky (Kuznetsove *et al.*, 2003).
The networks utilized by migrants vary considerably depending on local histories of migration, national conditions and communal socio-cultural traits (Wong et al., 2007). There has been shown to be qualitative variation in types of networks used by different occupational classes (Wong *et al.*, 2007). High occupational groups, for instance, rely more on networks of colleagues or organizations and less on kin-based networks than unskilled workers. In any case, 'The forms and characteristics of these networks may depend on their composition - friends, relatives, kin, acquaintances, professional colleagues, etc.,' Meyer (2001) observes, 'but the result is similar: most positions are acquired via connections (Wong et al., 2007).
Hence, we could expect Diaspora to play a strategic and systematic role in technology exchange, in facilitating direct foreign investment, and also in the identification and penetration into reliable knowledge and business networks.
Another important question is, how do we attract Diaspora, or otherwise, how do we play the Brain Gain Game? Since the onset of the 1990s, skilled labour migration has been a burgeoning and ever developing field of research. Here, skilled migrants - most broadly defined as those in possession of a tertiary degree or extensive specialized work experience - include architects, accountants and financial experts, engineers, technicians, researchers, scientists, chefs, teachers, health professionals, and - increasingly - specialists in information technology (IT, including computing professionals, computing engineers, managers, sales reps, etc.) (Wong *et al.*, 2007) It would be these areas and fields of expertise that we would need to focus on.
According to Kuznetsov and Sabel (2006), in this 21st century marketplace, knowledge is recognized to be the most important factor in economic development; the richer countries compete to attract and retain the world's best-trained minds in many ways. The more influential "pull" factors of professional migration are envisaging effective policies that stimulate R&D activities and increase direct investment, offering attractive postgraduate training and research opportunities, and recruiting younger graduates and professionals (Borta, 2007). University is obviously a critical factor in the "Brain gain" game. Their linkages to industries, local or global, would determine the intellectual drive and momentum for innovation.

5. Science, Technology and Innovation

The knowledge economy is founded on a learning society. Investment in science, technology, and innovation education **has thus become the most critical source of economic transformation** in newly industrial countries. This transformation that is equally dependent on access to information, intellectual development and knowledge nomad mobility. These can only be achieved if the knowledge networks are in place. Only then can the nation foster an infrastructure of linkages among and between firms, universities and government and thus gains competitive advantage through quicker information diffusion and product deployment.

5.1 Science and Technology for development

Science is a driver of **technology** and economic prosperity. Certainly in the twentieth century, science and technology have been linked. The clear example is the tight link between advances in nuclear science, atomic weapons, and nuclear generation of electric power. Basic science can be perceived as a vast reservoir upon which creators of technology can draw for ideas and knowledge.

In today's reality, most advances are only made possible by complementary advances in other enabling sciences and technologies. All science and technology advances rely on excellence in and developments made in the basic sciences, especially those of physics, chemistry, and biology. Therefore, excellence in the basic sciences must be maintained to support S&T advances in all disciplines and to support the development of applications.

Today the initialize S&T (for science and technology) is common in policy papers and journal articles; the two are thought of as a continuum. Michael Porter (1991) believes that part of government's role in stimulating innovation is to invest in basic research as well as in educational systems and infrastructure, although he clearly states that such investment must be consciously advanced and specialized.

Science and technology exert a growing influence on society and the economy. Scientific achievements continue to expand the frontiers of knowledge and increasingly contribute to the technological progress that affects how people live and work.

Scientific advances and technological change are important drivers of recent economic performance. The ability to create, distribute and exploit knowledge has become a major source of competitive advantage, wealth creation and improvements in the quality of life. Science, technology and innovation are now seen as keys to improving economic performance and social well-being. However, if governments want to obtain the benefits from this transformation they will have to put the right policies in place. Limits on public spending, increased competition and globalization, changes in the drivers of the innovation process, and a better understanding of the role played by science and technology in economic performance and societal change, have led governments to sharpen their policy tools (OECD, 2000).

The inherent function of the scientific endeavour is to carry out a comprehensive and thorough inquiry into nature and society, leading to new knowledge. This new knowledge provides educational, cultural and intellectual enrichment and leads to technological advances and economic benefits. Promoting fundamental and problem-oriented research is essential for achieving endogenous development and progress. UN, (2002) in its publications also confirms that, Governments, through national science policies and in acting as catalysts to facilitate interaction and communication between stakeholders, should give recognition to the key role of scientific research in the acquisition of knowledge, in the training of scientists and in the education of the public. Scientific research funded by the private sector has become a crucial factor for socio-economic development, but this cannot exclude the need for publicly-funded research. Both sectors should work in close collaboration and in a complementary manner in the financing of scientific research for long-term goals.

Science is an engine for development. Today, more than ever, science and its applications are indispensable for development. All levels of government and the private sector should provide enhanced support for building up an adequate and evenly distributed scientific and technological capacity through appropriate education and research programs as an indispensable foundation for economic, social, cultural and environmentally sound development. This is particularly urgent for developing countries. Technological development requires a solid scientific basis and needs to be resolutely directed towards safe and clean production processes, greater efficiency in resource use and more environmentally friendly products. Science and technology should also be resolutely directed towards prospects for better employment, improving competitiveness and social justice. Investment in science and technology aimed both at these objectives and at a better understanding and safeguarding of the planet's natural resource base, biodiversity and life-support systems must be increased. The objective should be a move towards sustainable development strategies through the integration of economic, social, cultural and environmental dimensions.

Science and Technology needs, however, to also be enabled, that is to be nurtured and strengthened. This can only be achieved through education and capacity building. Investment in science, technology, and innovation education has been one of the most critical sources of economic transformation in the newly industrial countries. Such investment should be part of a larger framework to build capacities worldwide. The one common element of the East Asian success stories is the high level of commitment to education and economic integration within the countries. This strategy was a precursor to what have come to be known as knowledge societies (World Bank, 2002).

The **industrial** sectors that invested more in research and performed more innovative activity are those that employed a larger share of higher skilled workers … increased up skilling is thus not merely a consequence of some labour-based technological shock. Economic success and a culture of continuous innovation depend on the capacity of workers to keep learning themselves and from each other. According to OECD, successful knowledge economies rely on four sources of innovation: Scientific and technical knowledge; Interactions and incentives to innovate among users and doers; decentralized modular patterns of innovation within a coordinated system; and, Widespread application of information and communication technologies, including in education.

5.2 Diaspora and University-Industry Linkages

Firms can acquire knowledge and technology from many external sources. Mueller (2006) explains these sources include competing firms, research organizations, government laboratories, industry research associations, and universities. Universities are unique in terms of their potential. **Not only can a firm obtain knowledge and technology, but it can also recruit graduates and faculty to serve as employees and consultants**. While much of inter organizational literature focuses on the collaboration between two or more industrial firms, we concentrate on industrial firm and university collaboration.

Knowledge spill over allows other economic actors to exploit the newly created knowledge as well as resulting in an acceleration of economic growth (Mueller, 2006).

Regions with a high level of entrepreneurship and university-industry relationships experience, has greater productivity and economic growth, this is what Mueller (2006) mentions as a results of the econometric analysis.

So, **University** have to spot a formal relationship with the industry, even for bilateral benefits. The last 20 years or so have seen a growing demand for universities to be beneficial to their environment in a more direct and immediate way than before. University-industry co operation gained increased attention in different western economies in the 1980s as

Geisler (1993) mentioned. Governments, universities and industry were developing different models in technology transfer. More funding was targeted into university-industry cooperation. In addition, university-industry relations were seen as critical for innovation, new product commercialization and industrial competitiveness (Geisler, 1993). Knowledge networks consist of groups of expert institutions working together on a common concern, strengthening each other's research and communications capacity, sharing knowledge bases and developing solutions that are made available for use by others outside the network (Cole *et al.*, 2001).

5.3 University networks for sustainable development

Government policies, in terms of science and technology, industry, and education, will need new emphasis in a knowledge based economy. The term technology is used broadly in business and science to refer to the process of transforming basic knowledge into useful application (Day & Schomaker, 2000). Science might be thought of *know-what* and technology as *know-how*, while markets or business focus on *know-where* and *know-how* (Day & Schomaker, 2000). The central workforce in the knowledge society will consist of highly specialized people (Al-Hawamdeh & Hart, 2002); these people could be gained from the diaspora. Emigrated intellectual, skilled and technological people are an invaluable resource for the development of their respective home countries. Their contributions to economic development are substantial through platforms of the knowledge economy, and *via* knowledge networks.

The position of the university consortium in the centre of the auto-learning society and with the responsibility to be hub in development processes may seem a bit pretentious. However, no other institution has the potential to fill this role equally well. Universities offer the academic space necessary to critically assess research results and address overarching issues such as democracy, social responsibility and corruption, regardless of religious, political or national backgrounds. Few, if any other institutions are able to offer similar conditions for free and unbiased discussion of development and progress. Universities can establish bonds and partnerships across technological, commercial, cultural, religious and political borders to the benefit of students, faculty and society. Taking the role as development hub is possibly a challenge that universities should face more willingly and consciously than in the past. Figure.4 may help to challenge the habits and existing paradigms and devise new paths for development.

There may be other stakeholders involved than those shown in figure 4, for example, other research institutions in both recipient and donor countries. However, universities and university consortia seem indispensable in the auto-learning context, because they are responsible for education of future decision-makers in the society. The question is not university participation as such, but what approach and type of partnership to establish and how to include local and international university networks to the mutual benefit of each participating country.

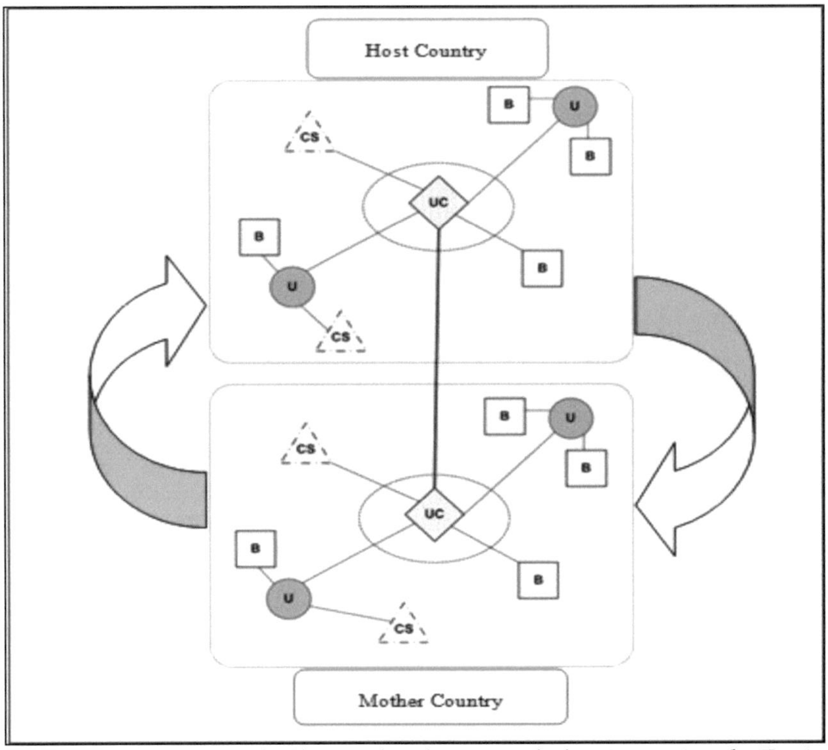

Fig. 4. University consortia (UC) as development hubs in national, Regional and international partnerships consisting of private and public Enterprises (B) as well as civil society (CS) U is individual university. Adopted from (Hansen and Lehmann, 2006).

Knowledge is recognized as a crucial element of economic growth in addition to physical capital and labour (Mueller, 2006). Also Hansen and Lehmann (2005) argued that, Universities educate decision-makers of tomorrow in both public and private sectors. To do this they are dependent on a bottom up supply of students and the national primary and secondary education systems must be maintained and tuned accordingly. It is also necessary for universities to have well-developed contacts to business and other groups in society in order to be able to identify needs for research as well as competencies and numbers of graduates to fill present and future positions. In doing so, universities are obviously indispensable partners in what could be identified as a bottom-up and demand-driven development process. Universities, however, must also be independent institutions in terms of defining areas of research that they consider important for the sake of seeking new knowledge and understanding, even in the absence of any immediate applicability or demand from government, business or civil society. This freedom of choice is important in a long term perspective because of the inherent uncertainty associated with scientific research: we cannot know for sure which parts of what we know or learn today will also be valuable tomorrow. Additionally, open science and open access to knowledge facilitates independent replication of scientific results; enhances the generalization of results; avoids excessive duplication of research; increases the possibility for useful ideas, products and technologies; and realizes for these reasons the social value of knowledge (Foray, 1997).

This may run counter to other criteria such as political correctness or immediate technological or economic relevance. But free research and inherent learning and education are necessary degrees of freedom in any democratic and innovative society and must be fostered and supported by governments and universities. Also recent empirical studies as quoted in Mueller (2006), (Plummer and Acs, 2005; Acs and Varga and Schalk, 2004) have shown that knowledge spill over positively affect technological change and economic growth.

On this background, international university networking is necessary in order to create structured bases for education and research and promote auto-learning societies (enhanced NIS). In a global context, university networking is one important contribution to capacity building with the aim of achieving sustainable development of human and material resources. This viewpoint is in accordance with recent statements by the World Bank regarding tertiary education as an indispensable means of constructing and maintaining knowledge economies and democratic societies (World Bank, 2002). It is also in harmony with the Union of Industries and Confederation of Employers in Europe, which expresses the need of business as a driving force towards sustainable development (UN, 2002). And, it is in good accordance with the results of the World Summit in Johannesburg in 2002.

6. A framework for middle and low income countries

Government policies, in terms of science and technology, industry, and education, will need new emphasis in a knowledge based economy. The term technology is used broadly in business and science to refer to the process of transforming basic knowledge into useful application (Day & Schomaker, 2000).

Science might be thought of *know-what* and technology as *know-how,* while markets or business focus on *know-where* and *know-how* (Day & Schomaker, 2000). The central workforce in the knowledge society will consist of highly specialized people (Al-Hawamdeh & Hart, 2002); these people could be gained from the diaspora. Emigrated intellectual, skilled and technological people are an invaluable resource for the development of their respective home countries. Their contributions to economic development are substantial through platforms of the knowledge economy, and *via* knowledge networks. The core issue is how the Diaspora could play a win-win development in both directions, toward the origin country, and from the recipient country. Bridgstock *et al,* (1998) stated that Science is always the product of human activity; this is one reason why it is important to study science, Technology and society. Different societies and different cultures need to build bridges or even as called by many scientists the highways between these different societies. The knowledge entrepreneur who has these unique opportunities can build these bridges, since he carries his nationality within his blood, and stay in the host country where he gains the new knowledge and serves as a new blood in the host country.

Many networks could be created, even without waiting for policy to mobilize them, while these networks could be more efficiently and more precisely to the needs on the origin country if the entrepreneur takes the step to create networks.

The phenomenon of migration of people differs from country to country, from time to time, and from mechanism to mechanism. For example, the emigration trajectory may have resulted from brain overflow, resulting in turn in brain spill over absorbed into foreign markets. The migration of this surplus brain constitutes an overflow and can, if strategically coordinated, provide solutions for the brain exporting country. Another example is the brain exchange, a temporary phenomenon whereby brain drain is compensated by corresponding brain gain. This could be in the form of exchange of scholars, researchers and/or scientists especially from middle and low income countries.

This international migration could thus profit developing nations through the economic network benefits created. The resource loss through brain drain could be converted into a long-term resource profit for the developing country. Within this perspective, the emigrated intellectual, skilled, technological elites would remain an invaluable resource for the development of their home country. Their contribution to economic development would be substantial through platforms of the knowledge economy, and *via* knowledge networks of global knowledge societies.

Knowledge networks consist of groups of expert institutions working together on a common concern, strengthening each other's research and communication capacity, sharing knowledge bases and developing solutions that are made available for use by others outside the network (Cole et al., 2001).

IOM, (2006) noted that, a successful co-operation means, to some degree, overcoming these differences. The network approach suggests that a long-term relationship between organizations is a cumulative process that produces means of difference reduction. The elements that emerge in relationship are described as bonds. Mattsson (1985) classifies the bonds between inter organizational exchange as follows: Technical bonds, Time related bonds, Knowledge related bonds, Social bonds, Economic bond and Legal bonds. Also, several models have been tested or used. They may be unsuitable in certain countries and communities that have less stable political and/or economic landscapes. For countries where a sizeable proportion of their populations are residing abroad, there should be a model or a strategy to harness the potentials of the Diaspora through, for example, the establishment of knowledge Entrepreneurial networks, in order to obtain win-win relationship for all parties.

The framework proposes to create diaspora Entrepreneurs through opportunities of funding and support. This Entrepreneur will be the core that would connect all elements of the framework together, inside origin country or the Diaspora.

The framework addresses Binary Economy which envisages any individual to have his own capital assets and labour. The criteria for selecting the **project and economic sector** that receives government support should include job creation potential, the degree of forward and backward linkages, export potential, and the ability to survive.

There is an obvious call on medium and low income countries to **consolidate and build on the institutional science, engineering and technology capacity for greater economic benefit** in a multi-disciplinary approach. **Mobility** of researchers and access to **training facilities** for senior and especially young scientists is thus fundamental.

International co-operation in science, technology and innovation is indispensable for medium and low income countries in this context in different directions:

- To absorb knowledge from around the world for the development of a sound science and technology base and domestic innovative capacity,
- To assimilate the know-how through learning by doing and learning by research (including management skills),

- To enable diaspora to produce innovative products (material or immaterial) for the international market, meeting international standards and, thus, ensuring sustainable development.

Employment generation programs can also be jointly established, provided they are designed in ways that make them contribute to social and economic development.

The collapse of barriers to the flow **of goods and services, capital and labor** has not always been orderly and has proceeded at different speeds in different parts of the world. But it is now virtually **universal in scope**. Also with reduced transport costs, **location is becoming less important** and political and economic stability, a well-trained labor force, and strong institutional underpinnings are emerging as the key drivers of prosperity. **No** meaning for **borders**, nothing can stop the development if there is a strong brain force behind all these.

Diaspora entrepreneur as seen in figure 5, can be an important source of investment for the origin country economy. Diaspora entrepreneur can play an important role in reconnecting the medium and low income countries economy to the whole world. **Embassies** represent the government in each country.

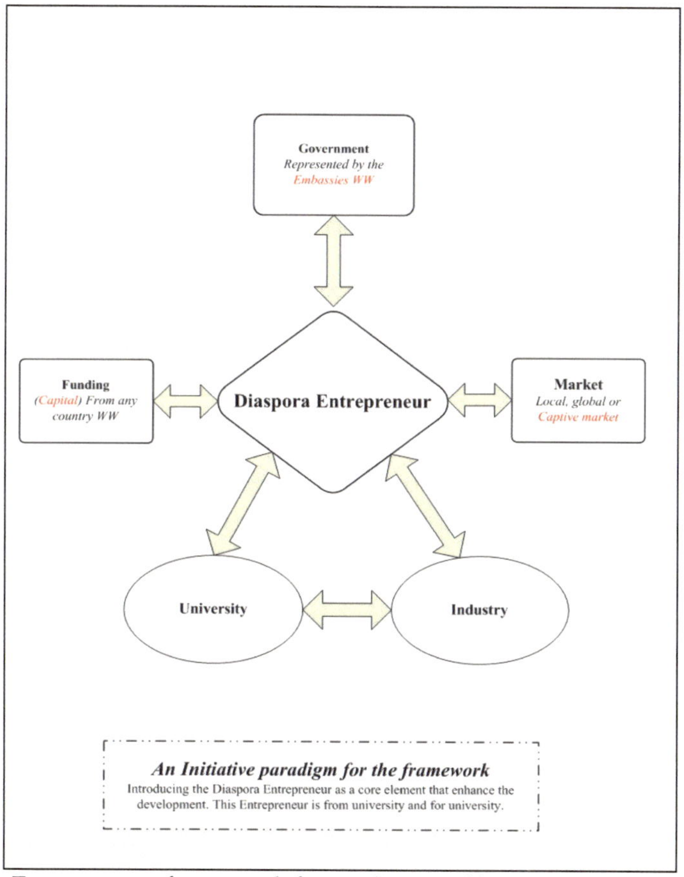

Fig. 5. Diaspora Entrepreneur framework for medium and low income countries.

Their role would include naming the policy, giving Legitimacy, monitoring the project, enhancing research, helping in finding funds, etc. As Diaspora is found all over the world, it gives this framework a unique opportunity or strength. That is, the ***Framework for University-Industry Relationships for the Advancement of Science and Technology as an Enabled and Enabling Force in medium and low income countries*** can be applied in any country in the world that hosts the Diaspora community.

7. Conclusion and future research

This study aims at building a framework for stronger relationships between Diaspora Entrepreneur and the origin country, based on a strong supporting platform of Science, Engineering, Technology & Innovation (SET&I). Within this context, Science and Technology are perceived as an enabling platform. However, before being so, this platform must be enabled.

The framework that emerges from this study is hoped to be applied for medium and low income countries and by diaspora. It is deeply believed that many benefits would materialize, in the form of spin-offs, spill-over, and many other relations.

Since human resource is the capital resource, then the framework must start at this point and end at this point. Hence, diaspora Entrepreneurship worldwide is the goal; Embassies are the vehicle, and entrepreneur in the Diaspora, the catalysts.

Many Diaspora students around the world carry in their hearts a deep hope to return home, to create and to reap opportunities in the homeland. This hope is carried by this the framework. Connecting with these diaspora students becomes essential.

This study is a part of an ongoing research about Palestinian diaspora focusing on the impact of knowledge Entrepreneurial networks as a driving force in economic development. Such a strategy was created in order to help the Palestinian diaspora to be connected to Palestine, since the majority of the Palestinian people (more than 50%) reside outside Palestine.

If developing countries wish to move forward on a strategy that can be implemented, then this strategy would need to be flexible, adaptable and feasible in its requirements. The strategy of harnessing the talents of diaspora must be seen as integral to the overall efforts of developing the economies of these countries. Without political commitment, these efforts will flounder. We are confident that the issues presented in this chapter underscore the potentials as well as challenges involved in tapping the diaspora networks.

8. References and Bibliography

Al-Hawamdeh, S., & Hart, T. L. (2002) *Information and Knowledge Society* Singapore: McGraw-Hill Education

Borta, O. (2007). BRAIN DRAIN CONTROVERSY *Linköping University Department of Management and Economics, Master thesis*, Linköping, Sweden.

Bridgstock, M., Burch, D., Forge J., Laurent, J., & Lowe, I. (1998). Science, Technology and Society United Kingdom: Cambridge University Press.

Burt, R. (2000). The Network Entrepreneur in R. Svedberg, *Entrepreneurship: the social science view* (pp. 281-331). UK: Oxford University Press.

Cole, V., Buckler, C., Creech, H., and Willard, T. (2001), hidden assets: Young Professionals in Knowledge Networks, *International Institute for Sustainable Development*. Canada.

Day, G. S., & Schomaker, P. J. (2000) A different Game in G. S. Day, & P. J. Schomaker, *Wharton on Managing Emerging Technologies* (pp. 1-23). New Jersey: John Wiley & Sons, Inc.

Foray, D. (1997), Generation and distribution of technological knowledge: incentives, norms, and institutions. *In: C. Equistar, Editor, Systems of innovation. Technologies, Institutions and Organizations*, Pinter, London.

Geisler, E. (1993), Editorial: On the Importance of University-Industry-Government Cooperation: A Global Perspective, *International Journal of Technology Management, Vol. 8, Nos. 6/7/8*, pp. 435-438.

Hansen, J., and Lehmann, M. (2006), Agents of change: universities as development hubs, *Journal of Cleaner Production*, Vol. 14 (2006), pg. 820-829.

Hargreaves, A. and Shaw, P. (2004), Knowledge and Skill Development in Developing and Transitional Economies, *An analysis of World Bank/DfID Knowledge and Skills for the Modern Economy Project*. Retrieved from http://siteresources.worldbank.org/EDUCATION/Resources/278200-1126210664195/1636971-1126210694253/ DFID_WB_KS_FinalReport_7-31-06.pdf on 23/10/2007.

Hisrich, R., Peters, M., and Shepherd, D., (2008), Entrepreneurship, 7th edition. *Singapore; McGraw-Hill companies, Inc.*

Houghton, J. *and* Sheehan,P. (2000), A Primer on the Knowledge Economy, *Centre for Strategic Economic Studies,* Victoria University, February 2000.

IOM (2005), Costs and benefits of International Migration. International Organization for Migration , Vol. 3, pp. 1-479.

IOM (2006), "Engaging Diasporas as Development Partners for Home and Destination Countries: Challenges for Policymakers", *International Organization for Migration*, Geneva.

Kuznetsov, Y., & Sabel, C. (2006). Global Mobility of Talent from a Perspective of New Industrial Policy Open Migration Chains and Diaspora. *UNU-WIDER* , 1-22.

Kuznetsov, Y., Nemirovsky, A., & Yoguel, G. (2003). Argentina's Renaissance as a Knowledge Economy: Role of the Diaspora of Highly Skilled. *World Bank Institute* , 2-38.

Lowel, B. L., & Gerova, s. G. (2004). DIASPORAS AND ECONOMIC DEVELOPMENT: STATE OF KNOWLEDGE. *World Bank Publications*, 1-35.

Lowell, B. L. (2001). Policy Responses to the International Mobility Of Skilled Labour. *International Migration Papers; International Labour Office,* Geneva.

Madsen, H., & Fisker, S. (2004). Entrepreneurshio in the Knowledge -Intensive sector: Influential Factors at the start -up and realy growth Phase. *13th Nordic Conference on Small Business Research.* Denmark: NCSB 2004 Conference. Retrived on 1/12/2008 from: http://web.bi.no/forskning/ncsb2004.nsf/pages/index.

Malinin, P., and Toivonen, T. (1998), University Roles in University-Industry CO-operation, Proceedings of the *Academic and Industrial Cooperation in Space Research,* European Space Agency, November 4-6, 1998, 169-175.

Mehta: (*world economy forum*, 2007), [online] December 2006, http://www.weforum.org/en/knowledge/Industries/KN_SESS_SUMM_18522?url=/en/knowledge/Industries/KN_SESS_SUMM_18522

Millennium Development Goals Occupied Palestinian Territory, 2005, Progress Report. Website: www.publications.parliament.uk/pa/cm200607/cmselect/cmintdev/114/114i.pdf
Ming, W.H.,(2005), Entrepreneurship and Economic Development: A Case Study of Taiwan , [online], Retrieved on march, 2007:http://www.usasbe.org/conference/2005-icsb/2005_ICSB_Program.pdf
Mueller, P. (2006), Exploring the knowledge filter: How Entrepreneurship and University-Industry relationships drive economic growth, *Research Policy*, issue 35, October 2006, p1499-1508.
OECD (1996), *Technology and Industrial Performance*, OECD Paris.
OECD (2000), Science, Technology and Innovation in the New Economy, Policy Brief, September 2000, *OECD publications* 2000, website: http://www.oecd.org/findDocument/0,2350,en_2649_201185_1_119696_1_1_1,00.html
OECD (2004), Science and Innovation Policy: Key Challenges and Opportunities, *Policy Brief*, January 2004, retrieved from http://www.oecd.org/dataoecd/24/11/25473397.pdf on 2/4/2007.
Porter, M.E. 1998. Clusters and the new economics of competition, *Harvard Business*, Review 76 (6): 77-90.
Porter, Michael E. (1991). The Competitive Advantage of Nations, In Strategy: Seeking and Securing Competitive Advantage. *Cynthia A. Montgomery and Michael E. Porter (Eds), Boston: Harvard Business School Press*.
Saxenian, A. L. (1999). Silicon's New Immigrant Entrepreneurs. *Public Policy Institute of California*.
Sheehan, P. And Tegart, G. (1998), Working *for the Future: Technology and Employment in the Global Knowledge Economy*, Victoria University Press.
Skrzeszewski, S. (2006). *The Knowledge Entrepreneur*. UK: Scarecrow Press, INC.
The World Bank Group (WB) (2002), Constructing knowledge societies: new challenges for tertiary education, *World Bank*, Washington.
UNDP (2005). Worker Remittance as an Instrument for Development, Panama: *United Nations Development Program*, http://www.undp.org/surf-panama/docs/migrant_remittance.doc
UNESCO, (2002), UNESCO's Strategic Objectives for Education, 2002-2007 http://portal.unesco.org/education/en/ev.php-URL_ID=22824&URL_DO=DO_TOPIC&URL_SECTION=201.html
Wong, P.-K., Ho, Y.-P., & Singh, A. (2007). Towards an "Entrepreneurial University" Model to Support Knowledge-Based Economic Development: The Case of the National University of Singapore. *World development* , Vol. 35, No. 6, pp. 941-958.
World Bank. (1999)*World Development Report 1998/99: Knowledge for Development*. Washington: World Bank. Available: http://www.worldbank.org/wdr/wdr98/contents.htm [1999, 9 August].

Exploratory investigation into preservice teachers' career-goal contents and their relationships with class participation motivation in higher education in South Africa

Byron Brown [1] and Ntonghanwah Forcheh [2]
[1] *Faculty of Education, University of Fort Hare South Africa*
[2] *Department of Statistics, University of Botswana Botswana*

1. Introduction

There is a pattern of low student enrolment in teacher education programmes in many countries (CEPD, 2005; HSRC, 2003; Kassiem, 2007; Nilsson, 2003a; Nilsson, 2003b; Sikkes, 2001; Siniscalco, 2002; UNESCO, 2003). Although the low enrolment trend is apparent, there is evidence that it is not uniform; indeed, it is more chronic in some subject areas than in others (HSRC, 2003; Kassiem, 2007). The trend has been blamed, however, for the shortage of teachers in many nations (Commonwealth Secretariat, 2002:1-12; Crouch & Perry, 2003:477; Kassiem, 2007). It seems the slump in interest in the teacher education field is taking place at a time when global demand for teachers is on the increase (Kassiem, 2007:2; Nilsson, 2003a:8; Nilsson, 2003b:10). Already, there is recognition of the strategic importance adequate supply of teachers is for achieving the education targets set in both the Dakar Framework for Action and the Millennium Development Goals (Dakar, 2000; UN, 2003).
But in interviews with higher education managers, Sikkes (2001:28), found that getting people to opt for studies in teacher training is a challenge for faculties and schools of education in countries, not only in Africa but in Europe and South Asia. There are clear evidences of such reluctance among grade 12 learners in South Africa (DoE, 2001; HSRC, 2003), although regional countries like Botswana is experiencing a contrasting response (TSM, 2006:5). The general thrust in much of these evidences is that the students who enter higher education are more motivated to pursue non-teaching related careers; they are less enthused to pursue teaching related careers (DoE, 2001; HSRC, 2003).
In countries rocked by dwindling student aspirations to opt for programmes in the teacher education field and with teacher shortage, the state of motivation and types of goals being pursued by the few students who have actually entered these programmes, are often ignored. But their motivational level has crucial implications for classroom practices (Schunk, 2004). We do not know much or understand in-depth how, for instance, the goals that a preservice teacher seeks to pursue in the teaching career is related to his/her motivation to engage in activities at the classroom level in pursuit of those goals. Most of the previous research on post-grade 12 student motivation, certainly within the African context,

has focused more on the demotivation to entry into the teacher education field, the potential stock of new entrants to teacher education and the teaching profession (CEPD, 2005:8; HSRC, 2003:477), and on the various problems linked to the low enrolment in teacher education programmes. For example, Kassiem (2007:1) argued that the disinterest in teacher education is a result of the poor image of teaching as a profession in the society. According to Kassiem (2007), the poor image has created apathy for teacher education and discouraged enrolment.

While there is merit in Kassiem's perspective, I assert that the argument is also skewed and problematic. Focusing mainly on why people *do not* opt for education programmes in higher degree institutions creates an exclusion of the debate surrounding, for instance, the career related goal-pursuit and motivation to engage in the learning and teaching process among those who have actually entered, and how these goals may have been shaped by social context s. In contexts where there is teacher shortage and apathy for teacher education, generally, understanding these dynamics is crucial if student participation at the classroom level is to be maximized. The purpose of the chapter is to present evidence from a research which investigated, in the African country of Botswana, with historically different patterns of enrolment into teacher education programmes, the nature of preservice teachers' career-related goals and their relationship with the motivation of these preservice teachers to participate in class in pursuit of those goals.

2. The context: Botswana

Two reasons informed the decision to use Botswana preservice teachers. First, unlike many other regional African countries, Botswana is often seen as a stable country economically, with reports of over-supply of teachers (TSM, 2006); second, student enrolment into teacher education programmes in the country has steadily increased over the last decade (TSM, 2006). Teaching is perceived in Botswana as a stable and financially viable profession (Tabulawa, 2005). For instance, since 1993 in South Africa, while faculties and schools of education, have experienced significant declines in enrolments (Crouch & Perry, 2003:477), Botswana's experience, over the same period, has been much different. Average enrolment rate into teacher education programmes increased and, according to one report, students seeking training to become professional teachers are now more likely to be turned away or placed on waiting list (TSM, 2007:4). These contrasting experiences in enrolment trends between Botswana and South Africa would perhaps allow the researcher to frame a sense of the underpinning motivation and goals driving people into teaching in Botswana, contrary to global trends in the teaching profession.

3. Goal-framing and Self-determination theory

3.1 Self-determination theory

Within the African and European educational settings, a large number of studies suggested the types of goals that students often frame and pursue in higher education, or in teaching as a career, vary (DoE, 2001; Houle, 1961; HSRC, 2003; Ryan, Sheldon, Kasser, & Deci, 1996). One theory that helps clarify and describe differences in these goals is the self-determination theory (Deci & Ryan, 2000).

Self-determination theory (SDT) is an empirically verified theory of motivation. To Deci and Ryan (2000:227), SDT is built on the assumption that students, whether in higher education or elsewhere, are intrinsically motivated toward learning, growth, intellectual challenges, and well-being. Within this framework therefore, individuals pursue goals for the satisfaction of three basic needs of competence, relatedness, and autonomy, which are essential for psychological growth and well-being (Deci & Ryan, 2000:229). In SDT's framework, autonomy concerns the basic need to experience one's behaviour as volitional (Goodenow, 1993). The need for competence is the need to experience satisfaction in exercising and extending one's capabilities (Deci & Ryan, 2000). Finally, the need for relatedness concerns feeling connected with significant others. It is for these needs satisfaction, according to the SDT, that goals are framed (Elliot & Thrash, 2002). This pursuit can be deliberate or accidental.

The notion that goal-directed behaviour is linked to psychological needs satisfaction informs this research. Needs give goal-directed behaviours psychological potency (Goodenow, 1993). An important aspect of the everyday life of most university preservice teachers involves completing coursework and being successful in their studies. For many of these students, the completion of those works represents the antecedent to realizing the career goals that they frame. The quality of the psychological potency underpinning the goal-directed behaviour should have a bearing on the way students pursue these goals. Thus, when goals are being pursued, concerns have to be given to whether basic needs are being satisfied. Deci and Ryan (2000:229) concluded that the fulfillment versus the thwarting of goal-directed behaviours bears inherent consequences. But the effects of these consequences depend on the nature of the goal itself. The SDT is adopted in this research to clarify the nature of goals. It is also adopted because, unlike other theoretical perspectives, it posits a conceptual distinction between goal-types and motivation (Deci & Ryan, 2000:227). It is this distinction that makes the framing of hypotheses possible, for instance, between preservice teachers' goal-pursuit and their class participation behaviours (Vansteenkiste, Simons, Lens, Soenens, & Matos, 2005:483).

3.2 Aspects of goal framing

According to the SDT theory, one way to describe differences between goals is to state that the goal is either intrinsic or extrinsic (Deci & Ryan, 2000). Intrinsic goals reflect people's natural growth tendencies (Kasser, 2002). These goals, scholars (Vansteenkiste, Simons, Lens, Soenens, et al, 2005:483) have claimed, create an 'inward orientation', which manifests, for instance, in concerns for affiliation, community contribution, health, and self-development. When intrinsic goals are framed, they are directed at the satisfaction of basic needs essential for growth and well-being. In contrast, extrinsic goals, research suggested, create an 'outward orientation' (Vansteenkiste, Simons, Lens, Soenens, et al, 2005:484). They tend to orientate individuals toward engaging in interpersonal comparisons (Sirgy, 1998:227), obtaining contingent approval and acquiring external signs of self-worth and success (Kasser, Ryan, Couchman, & Sheldon, 2004:11). Williams, Cox, Hedberg, and Deci (2000:1756) report that extrinsic goals manifest in concerns for financial success, rewards, prestige, image, status, physical attractiveness, power, and publicity. The classification of goals as intrinsic versus extrinsic suggests that some goals are expected to be more closely linked to basic need satisfaction than others. But the concept of intrinsic and extrinsic goal, within the SDT framework, specifies the contents of the goal (Deci & Ryan, 2000:244).

Previous studies on goal-content found differential effects for intrinsic versus extrinsic goal. Sheldon, Ryan, Deci, and Kasser (2004:475) report that people's goal content (intrinsic vs. extrinsic) and their motives (autonomous vs. controlled) have independent effects on personal adjustment. In analysis of the effects of goal contents on certain life-related variables, Deci and Ryan (2000:245) found that when people value intrinsic aspirations, they

tend to be more autonomous in pursuing them, whereas there is a tendency for people to be controlled in their pursuit of extrinsic aspirations. These evidences indicate that different goal contents can result in different behavioural and affective consequences.
Previous researches have also investigated the effects of different goal contents from an individual difference perspective. These have been used to classify people in terms of the degree to which a person focuses on the attainment of intrinsic rather than extrinsic goals (Vansteenkiste, Simons, Lens, Soenens, & Matos, 2005:484). But it seems that not only the individual but also the social environments can be classified in terms of the types of goals that they promote or emphasized (Kasser & Ahuvia, 2002). This means some social contexts such as the home or school environments might encourage and reinforce the pursuit of intrinsic goals while others focus on the pursuit of extrinsic goals. In a set of experimental field study of college students, Vansteenkiste, Simons, Lens, Sheldon, and Deci (2004) investigated the effects of the goals promoted by the classroom environments on students learning. They (2004:246) found that presenting the learning material as serving the attainment of an extrinsic goal (financial success) undermined academic achievement, persistence, and deep processing of the learning material, compared with intrinsic goal framing.
Although the result of these studies on intrinsic versus extrinsic goal contents reveal a reasoned picture, it needs to be noted that these goals were framed in relation to students' in-class academic achievements, rather than in respect of a teaching career. Hence, since social environments can shape the goals framed people frame, am important focus of this research was to explore the career goal contents being pursued by the preservice teachers in their current contexts.

4. Motivation in context

4.1 Dimensions of motivation

To Schunk (2004:177), motivation represents a basic dimension by which people make sense of their own or others' behaviour. It concerns drive, direction, persistence, and all aspects of activation and intention (Goodenow, 1993). There is a prevailing view in the field of motivation that humans initiate and persist at behaviours to the extent that they believe the behaviours will lead to desired goals (Kasser & Ahuvia, 2002; Sagiv & Schwartz, 2000). Motivation then is a behaviour sustaining phenomenon, linking people's goal pursuit with attainment and basic needs satisfaction. This research is informed by this broad interpretation of motivation because it draws attention to a conceptual link between goal and motives, which is crucial in the context of this investigation.
There are different types of motivation, according to Deci and Ryan (2000:227), which reflects different levels of self-determination. The two broad strands used to categorise motivation types are labeled intrinsic and extrinsic. But the concept of intrinsic versus extrinsic goals is conceptually different from the classical motivational constructs above of intrinsic and extrinsic motivation. Vansteenkiste, Simons, Lens, Soenens, et al (2005:483) explain that whereas the former reflects the differential contents (or what) of goals that preservice teachers can pursue, the latter pertains to preservice teachers' motives or reasons for pursuing particular goals. Motivation then represents the 'process' (or why) of goal pursuits (Deci & Ryan, 2000:227). This distinction between intrinsic versus extrinsic goal and intrinsic versus extrinsic motivation allows us, for instance, to see that a student could establish intrinsic goals (e.g. for self development) for opting for teacher education related career but relies on extrinsic motivation (e.g. only does classwork that will be grades) in

pursuit of these goals. It means that the goals for entering teacher training and the motivation that energise preservice teachers in their daily engagement in school activities may be one characterised by tension. There is implication in such tension for class participation and instructional leadership.

But in the broad discourse on motivation, for instance, intrinsic motivation, which is seen as '...engaging in an activity for its own sake and the experience of pleasure and satisfaction derived from participation' (Goodenow, 1993:21), is fully self-determined or autonomous; it is an innate quality which does not result from an internalisation of ambient values and regulations (Deci & Ryan, 2000:239). However, extrinsic motivation, which is seen as '...engaging in an activity as a means to an end rather than for its intrinsic qualities', varies in its relative degree of autonomy. Based on this analysis, Vansteenkiste, Simons, Lens, Soenens, et al (2005:484) concluded that behaviours which are extrinsically motivated are guided by the pursuit of an outcome that is separate from the activity. This bimodal view of motivation informs this research because it provides the basis for clarifying the main variables.

Empirical researches on motivation, within the SDT framework, have isolated three types of extrinsic motivation. These have been labeled: (a) external regulation (e.g. when a students engages in an activity to comply with reward, constraints or other externally pressuring demand); (b) introjected regulation (e.g. when a student engages in an activity to meet internally pressuring feelings of guilt, shame, and self-aggrandization); and (c) identified regulation (e.g. when a student identifies with the personal importance of the activity and engages in it with a sense of volition and willingness) (Deci & Ryan, 2000:237). External and introjected regulations, collectively, create a form of controlled motivation because when students engaged in activities for these reasons/motives, their actions are said to be relatively controlled (Vansteenkiste, Lens, Dewitte, De Witte, & Deci, 2004:345). However, identified regulation bears close qualities with intrinsic motivation because it induces action that results from one's choice based on one's assessment of its importance (Vansteenkiste, Lens, Dewitte, De Witte, & Deci, 2004:345). The combining of identified regulation and intrinsic motivation to form an autonomous motivation composite have been reported (Vallerand, Fortier, & Guay, 1997).

It is possible that a student could have no motivation for pursuing a goal; that is, an absence of intrinsic or extrinsic drives (Deci & Ryan, 2000:237). Deci and Ryan (2000:237) claim that the condition of no motivation (called 'amotivation') pertains to a person's lack of intentionality. SDT researchers (Pelletier, Dion, Tuson & Green-Demers, 1999:2481) found that students are likely to be amotivated when they lack either a sense of efficacy or a sense of control with respect to desired outcomes. Goodenow (1993:24) reports that amotivated students experience feelings of incompetence and expectancies of uncontrollability. There is evidence to suggest that the different forms of extrinsic motivation and amotivation have different behavioural consequences (Deci & Ryan, 2000:237). Amotivation, for instance, can be an impediment to both goal attainment and efforts to increase preservice teacher participation in the learning and teaching process.

4.2 Internalisation of extrinsic motivation

Extrinsic Motivation has been extensively researched and it is shown that this type of motivation can be internalized (Deci & Ryan, 2000:236). Numerous theories utilize the concept of internalization as a central process in socialization (Meissner, 1988), providing differing perspectives that range from internalization being something that gets done to individuals by the socializing environment (e.g., Mead, 1934) to something that represents the individual's active transformation of external regulations into inner values (Ryan, 1993). SDT proposes that, like intrinsic motivation, internalization is an active, natural process in which individuals attempt to transform socially sanctioned mores or requests into personally endorsed values and self-regulations (Deci & Ryan, 2000). It is the means through which individuals assimilate and reconstitute formerly external regulations so the individuals can be self-determined while enacting them. When the internalization process functions optimally, people will identify with the importance of social regulations, assimilate them into their integrated sense of self, and thus fully accept them as their own.

4.3 Goal-contents and motivation

The relationships between goal contents and motivation have been explored by some researchers, but these have mainly been in relation to certain life goals and well-being. Carver and Baird (1998:290) assessed the relative importance participants placed on the aspiration for wealth (extrinsic goal), and also the strength of their autonomous reasons (intrinsic motivation) and the strength of their controlled reasons (extrinsic motivation) for pursuing wealth. They found that autonomous reasons for pursuing wealth were positively related to self-actualisation, but controlled reasons for pursuing wealth were negatively related to self-actualisation. In other words, the extrinsic goal was in tension with the intrinsic motivation. Vansteenkiste, Simons, Lens, Soenens, et al (2005:485) theorized that because intrinsic goals are more closely lined with people's inner-growth tendencies, learning in the service of such goal is more likely to prompt a deep and task-oriented commitment toward learning. They tested this hypothesis on a sample of early adolescents and found that the effects of intrinsic versus extrinsic goals on learning were mediated by task involvement: linking learning to intrinsic goal content yielded greater task engagement. The degree of task involvement is a crucial indictor to judge preservice teachers' progress and pace of pursuit of their career goals. The evidence seems to suggest that an anticipation of greater task involvement from preservice teachers, whose learning is linked to intrinsic goal contents. But educators would need to know preservice teachers' goal contents in order to be in a position to make such link. Furthermore, although the evidence is suggesting that when people's goal contents (e.g. intrinsic) are similar in nature to their motives (e.g. intrinsic) for engaging in an activity, their task commitment to the activity increases (Deci & Ryan, 2000), it is possible that among preservice teachers the school environments in which they entered could promote a type of motivation which stand in contrast to the goal contents that they are pursuing. These possibilities lead this research to explore whether preservice teachers' career-related goal contents for entering teacher training are consistent with the motivation that they seek to engage in class activities in pursuit of those goals.
But for student-teachers in training, their career goals may be seen as constituting long-term goals; that which they are striving to accomplish later in life (Ryan & Connell, 1989:749). Researchers have examined the effects of goal attainment proximity on behaviours (Schunk, 2004; Sheldon & Kasser, 1995). Sheldon and Kasser (1995:531) indexed the strivings (i.e. relatively short-term, semester-long, goals) of undergraduate students and their reasons for pursuing each striving, and the helpfulness of each striving for attainment of intrinsic versus extrinsic life-goals (i.e. long-term aspirations). They found, inter alia, that the extent to which the students believed that each striving would lead to the attainment of long-term goal intrinsic goals was positively related to well-being, as against unrelated to well-being for extrinsic goals; these extrinsic goals were however related to controlled orientations. In other words, the progress that preservice teachers make toward the attainment of extrinsic related life-goals can be controlled. The incremental strivings show that students quite often

make a deliberate connection between what they do in class and their personal aspirations, which sometimes have no direct link with each other.

4.4 Motivation and class participation

Motivating students to achieve in traditional classroom environments is a topic of practical concern to instructional designers, and of theoretical concern to researchers. Important variables that have been identified as motivators for student effort are perceived importance, usefulness, and the value of engaging in a task (Schunk, 2004). Student perceptions of their ability to accomplish the task, that is, their self-efficacy, has been found to affect effort and achievement (Bandura in Schunk, 2004:289). Task characteristics such as task difficulty can be instrumental in providing cues as to the efficiency of effort. If the effort expenditure is perceived as a waste of energy or as unnecessary for success, learners will not be motivated to exert sufficient mental effort. In other words, their participation would be low. Also, learner preconceptions about the effort required by a learning task influence the effort expenditure (Cennamo, 1993). These preconceptions are influenced not only by task characteristics, but also by characteristics of the learner (Woolfolk, 2004).

The present research does not relate the attainment of goal contents to well-being variables as previous research have focused upon; it, instead, investigated the interaction between the goal-contents and the motivation itself, which is an unexplored issue in the broader research context in Africa. The specific issues investigated are outlined in the research problems below.

5. The present research

The present research was developed around the following research problems:

1. What are the contents of the main career goals being pursued by the preservice teachers in training? What factors do they perceived to influence the framing of these goals?
2. What motivational expectations do preservice teachers have or seek for participating in classroom activities in pursuit of their career goal attainment?
3. Are there significant relationships between the contents of preservice teachers' main career gaols and the forms of motivation which they have/seek for engaging in class activities in pursuit of those goals? (what are the implications for class participation?)

The questions posed above address the link between and consequences of goal-framing and motivation in the classroom, which are critical issues in motivational research and in instructional leadership in schools.

5.1 Method

5.1.1 Combined-methods design

The study adopted a combined-methods design; this results from a merger of the quantitative and the qualitative approaches (Brown, 2004:74). Within this paradigm, aspects of both the quantitative and qualitative techniques are applied on a phased basis (Saunders, Lewis and Thornhill, 2007:340). Creswell (in De Vos 1998:360) developed a dominant-less-dominant framework for carrying out research using the mixed paradigm; this framework guided this study. The quantitative phase dominated, while the qualitative phase was less-dominant. This is because the investigation was built around testing the relationships between the goal-contents and motivation types (*cf. problem statement 3*). A small qualitative investigation was done as a follow-up to solicit clarification on the results of the quantitative phase. This facilitated a holistic view and strengthened the internal validity of the design. A survey design was adopted in the quantitative phase because the researchers wanted to include a large number of preservice teachers; a semi-structured interview was used in the qualitative phase since it was a follow-up investigation.

5.1.2 Research participants

College students in Botswana comprised the sample for this research. The research participants were pursuing a Diploma in teaching. Participants were in different years of study, ranging from year 1 to year 3. Preservice teachers were selected from across the different year groups in order to have a broad mix of goal framing. In the cohort, there were 123 preservice teachers who participated. These participants were selected purposive. These were taken from the main teacher training institution in the North Eastern region of the country. The sample of preservice teachers consisted mainly of females (60.2%); this was consistent with the wider college population; age range from 20 to 25 years, $M = 21$ years. All preservice teachers were pursuing programmes leading to qualification to teach at the intermediate (junior secondary) phase.

5.1.3 Instruments

Two separate instruments (questionnaire and interview schedule) were used to collect data; each was influenced by the design adopted above (*cf. mixed-method design*).

<u>Questionnaire</u>

A self-administered questionnaire was used to collect data for the quantitative phase. The questionnaire was developed in the English language by the researcher and consisted of three sections, as follows: Section one covered demographic data (e.g. gender, age, and year group). Section two had one open-ended type measure which asked participants to list their *main* career goal which they intend to pursue in teaching. Participants also had to specify the perceived factors which caused them to choose these goals. The open-ended measure was adopted to allow participants to reflect on their life-history and consider possible influences. The measure allowed for the collection of 'rich' qualitative data, which would not have been possible had participants been asked to respond to predetermined statements.

Section three had 20 statements, measuring preservice teachers' class participation behaviours and motivation. The statements were developed from an indepth review of the literature, and included three dimensions of class participation as follows: lesson attendance, study-hard, class involvement preparation, and modes. Each measure of participation was phased to reflect one of the following forms of motivation: intrinsic motivation; extrinsic motivation. Three different forms of extrinsic motivation, based on the SDT, were incorporated: external regulation, identified regulation, and introjected regulation. Participants rated on a 5-point Likert scale ranging from 1 (strongly disagree) to 5 (strongly agree) their class participation and motivation behaviours.

Five scholars who specialized in the area of pedagogy checked whether the draft questionnaire appeared to be a suitable measure of the aspects being measured and whether the constructs were accurately captured. The instrument was also pilot tested to ensure that all relevant factors were included in each of the sections. Thus, content and face validity were addressed.

Interview schedule

The qualitative follow-up data was collected via interviews. This was designed to gain clarification on a single theme which emerged from the quantitative data: that is, the influences on preservice teachers' goal framing. A semi-structured interview facilitated the asking of probing questions.

5.1.4 Procedure

To gain access to students in the different sites, the researcher used the Programme Coordinators as gatekeeper (Brown & Schulze, 2002:4). For the quantitative data collection, the researcher asked the Programme Coordinators in the institution to recruit fellow colleagues to administer the questionnaire. As many preservice teachers as possible were asked to participate. Participants responded to the questionnaire during one of their scheduled lecture sessions.

Questionnaires were given to all preservice teachers who volunteered. They were asked to complete the instrument on the spot. This was to ensure maximum return. They were instructed to consider each statement carefully and use as much time as they needed to provide complete responses. In cases where the written responses were unclear or irrelevant, a decision was taken to exclude them. The researcher judged that a response was irrelevant where it deviated from providing answers to the research questions, or was illegible. Eight of the questionnaires fell into this category. Follow up interviews arrangements were made during the administration of the questionnaires. This was done by research assistants recruited on both research sites specifically for this exercise.

Data from the questionnaire was analysed using various tests: Chi-Square Tests. The main method of data analysis used for the qualitative data was thematic content analysis. This entailed identifying, coding and categorizing patterns in the data (Corbin & Strauss, 1990; Miles & Huberman, 1994). The results of these analyses are presented in the sections below.

Trustworthiness of the findings was addressed by means of Guba's model of trustworthiness (Brown & Schulze, 2002:5). This model includes: (a) truth value, (b) applicability or the degree to which the findings can be applied to other contexts or with other groups, (c) consistency or whether the findings would be consistent if the enquiry was replicated, and (d) neutrality or the freedom from bias in the research procedures and results. These dimensions were addressed through (a) triangulation of methods (b) prolonged engagement in the research setting to establish good rapport, and (c) the analysis of interviews transcripts with external coder to ensure peer examination.

6. Results

6.1 Quantitative results

Result 1: *The contents of the main career goals being pursued by the preservice teachers in training*

Goal-contents	**Frequency**	**% Responses**
Intrinsic goal contents		
Community contributions	10	8.13
Affiliation related	8	6.5
Health-related	0	0.0
Self-development	0	0.0

Extrinsic goal contents		
Financial success	62	50.41
Status/prestige	38	30.89
Publicity	5	4.07
Power	0	0.0
Personal image	0	0.0
Total	123	100

Table 1. The contents of preservice teachers' main goals for entering teacher

The intrinsic and extrinsic goal-contents that emerged from the main career goals of preservice teachers are shown in Table 1. The intrinsic goal-contents measured included self-development, improvement in personal health, quest for affiliation, and community contribution; the extrinsic goal-contents measured included financial success, personal status/prestige, publicity, power, personal image.

Intrinsic goals were not popular (14.63%). Table 1 shows that less than one tenth (8.13%) of the preservice teachers considered making contributions to the community as the main goal pursuing in teaching. Community contribution meant: "…imparting knowledge, skills and values to the younger generation; contributing to the achievement of Botswana vision 2016 pillar of building an educated/informed nation; building/serving the nation; and contributing to society by replacing dying and retiring teachers." Even fewer preservice teachers (6.5%) had the pursuit of affiliation-related aspirations (e.g. the desire to work with and enjoy being among young children), as a main career goal.

However, Table 1 shows, in contrast, that the majority (85.37%) of the preservice teachers had extrinsic-related goals as a main aspiration to pursue in teaching. Over one-half percent (50.41%) of preservice teachers had the pursuit of financial success (i.e. to earn a good salary; earn a living and take care of family) as a main career goal. A smaller percentage (30.89%) were mainly in pursuit of status-related career aspirations (e.g. for the qualification/certification to become teacher; to gain employment; to enhance personal social status). The status-related goals also included the benefits associated with teaching, such as the holidays, job security, loans, promotions, flexible working hours, and accommodation.

Other extrinsic forms of career goals with contents linked to personal *publicity* (e.g. to please or satisfy family members or past teachers), and to *power* and personal *image* were not popular as a main career goal to pursue in teaching (see Table 1).

Result 2: *Preservice teachers' motivational expectations to participate in classroom activities*

Table 2 shows responses to class participation behaviours. Measures of participation were linked to specific types of motivation. Class participation was defined in terms of the following four aspects: lesson attendance, study-hard, involvement preparation and modes.

Participation behaviours and motives	**% Responses**		
	***Agree**	**Sometimes**	**Disagree**
Lesson attendance:			
I attend lessons to get *grades* to pass my modules to qualify as teacher	85.4	10.5	4.1
I attend lessons to learn; i.e. because I *enjoy* learning /	65.9	21.1	13.0

academic work			
I attend lessons in order to be in the *company of friends*	40.5	47.0	12.5
I often only attend some lessons because the duration of my training to become a qualified teacher is too long	18.7	11.4	69.9
Involvement preparation:			
I always read related lesson materials before lessons to learn more so that I can participate (i.e. ask questions, engaged in discussion, make presentation)	39.1	38.2	22.7
Study-hard:			
I study hard for *grades*	78.0	7.0	15.0
I study hard (i.e. frequently rehearse and practice learning tasks; spend time thinking about and linking old and new learning; completing coursework)	68.3	25.2	6.5
I *study-hard* to finish my schooling in order to start working	60.2	12.1	27.7
I study hard for the *sake of learning*, i.e. because its fun & I love learning	55.3	24.4	20.3
I study hard because it gives me time to be with my friends	20.3	12.7	67.0
Involvement modes:			
I prefer to participate in more than just note-taking and listening to lectures when I attend lessons	77.3	14.5	8.2
I participate in class only when I want to *avoid the negative* consequences of not doing so	65.0	15.4	19.6
I participate in class (i.e. ask questions, engage in discussion, make presentation)	64.3	30.0	5.7
I participate in class because I *enjoy* learning more	44.1	34.0	21.9
I participate in class only when I know the *tasks will be graded*	38.2	15.5	46.3
I participate in class only when I am *called upon*	30.0	25.2	44.8
I *prefer* classes which allow me to participate	27.0	44.0	29.0
I participate in class because I get the chance to *help* others	24.4	11.2	64.4
Participating in class has little/no immediate benefits to me so I *do not* bother to prepare to take part	14.6	15.5	69.9
Valuing and Internalising:			
Although I do not find learning experiences enjoyable, I freely choose to work hard because these experiences are important to reach a valued goal in my life	78.1	13.0	8.9

Table 2. Distribution of preservice teachers' class participation and motivation behaviours

Table 2 shows a mixed response to the different dimensions of class participation. While the majority (85.4%) of preservice teachers agreed that they attended lesson for academic grades to pass their modules to qualify as teacher, there were others (10.5%) who only did so sometimes, or disagreed (4.1%) to doing so. Over one-half (65.9%) of the preservice teachers attended lessons for the sake of learning, or because they found it enjoyable, but fewer (21.1%) indicated that they did so sometimes, or disagreed to doing so for those motives (13.0%). However, a high proportion agreed that they sometimes (47.0%) or always (40.5%) attended lessons to be with friends. The duration of the training programme influenced the attendance pattern of some of the preservice teachers (see Table 2).

Table 2 also shows that perceptions about class participation planning varied. Few (22.7%) preservice teachers disagreed that they prepare themselves (i.e. read lesson materials) for class participation prior to the lesson. Those who agreed only did so sometimes (38.2%), or always (39.1%).

Over one-half (64.3%) of the student cohort agreed they participated (i.e. ask questions, engage in discussion, make presentation) in class; but few (30.0%) did so sometimes or disagreed (5.7%) to doing so. The majority of those who participated did so to avoid the negative consequences of not participating (65.0%), or only when they know the tasks would be graded (38.2%), when called upon (30.0%), or because they enjoy learning (44.1%). But there were a high proportion of preservice teachers who disagreed to participating for these motives (see Table 2).

Over one-half (68.3%) of the preservice teachers agreed that they study hard, that is, frequently rehearse and practise learning tasks, spend time thinking about and linking old and new learning, completing their coursework. The majority of those who study hard did so for grades (78.0%), to quickly finish their training (60.2%), because of finding learning fun/enjoyable (55.3%). Few preservice teachers study hard because of friendship motives (20.3%); in fact, the majority (69.9%) disagreed they study hard for friendship motives (see Table 2).

In addition, more than three-quarters (78.1%) of the preservice teachers did not find their learning experiences in the school enjoyable, but they freely chose to work hard because they perceived the learning experiences were important to reach a valued goal in their life.

Motivation classification	**Motive indicators**
Intrinsic motivation	Enjoy learning / academic work
	Learning for its sake
Extrinsic motivation	
• *External regulation*	Grades to pass
	Training duration
	Friends' company
	To finish schooling to start working
	To avoid negative consequences
	When called upon

• *Identified regulation*	To help others
	Perceived benefits
	Free choice

Table 3. Motivation classification and motive indicators for participating in class

Table 3 shows the motivation classification and the various indicators of motives for which the preservice teachers participated in class. Preservice teachers who indicated that they participated in class for the sake of learning and or for the enjoyment of learning or academic work (cf. Table 2) had an inward orientation for their actions. These motives reflect intrinsic motivation (see Table 3).

In Table 3, preservice teachers who indicated that they participated in class for grades, friends' company, to avoid negative consequences, only when called upon, to finish schooling, or motives linked to the duration of the training period had an outward orientation for their actions. These reflect the extrinsic motivation of external regulations (i.e. engaging in an activity to comply with reward, constraints or other externally pressuring demand).

However in Table 3, preservice teachers who indicated that they participated in class to help others, or out of free choice, or because of perceived benefits reflect the extrinsic motivation of identified regulation (i.e. when the personal importance of the activity is identified and one engages in it with a sense of volition and willingness).

The data reported in Tables 1 to 3 was further measured to explore how they influence class participation and other variables. To test these hypotheses, Chi Square tests were conducted. Significant relationships are reported in Tables 4 and 5a-5e.

Result 3: *Significant relationships between the contents of preservice teachers' main career goals and the forms of motivation which they have/seek for engaging in class activities in pursuit of those goals*

Participation behaviours and motivation types	**df**	**Categories of goal-contents**							
		Intrinsic-related goals		**Extrinsic-related goals**					
		Community contributions		*Financial success*		*Status/Prestige*		*Publicity*	
		X^2	*p-value*	**X^2**	*p-value*	**X^2**	*p-value*	**X^2**	*p-value*
External regulation: Attend lessons to get grades to pass my modules to qualify as teacher	2	3.08	0.215	**11.29** **	**0.004**	**6.13** *	**0.047**	0.81	1.078
External regulation: Participate in class only when the tasks will be graded	2	**7.06** *	**0.029**	0.14	0.93	3.77	0.152	4.60	0.082

External regulation: Often only attend some lessons because the duration of my training to become a qualified teacher is too long	**2**	0.26	0.878	4.39	0.111	**8.00** *	**0.018**	2.78	0.210
Identified regulation: I always read related lesson materials before lessons to learn more so that I can participate (i.e. ask questions, engage in discussion, make presentations)	**2**	2.37	0.306	**7.11** *	**0.029**	5.68	0.059	1.36	0.416
Identified regulation: I participate in class (i.e. ask questions, engage in discussion, make presentation)	**2**	1.23	0.542	3.96	0.138	**6.43** *	**0.04**	2.13	0.202

* **X^2** Critical value for *df* = 2 is 5.99 at the 0.05 level of significance; ** **X^2** Critical value for *df* = 2 is 9.21 at the 0.01 level of significance

Table 4. Significant relationships between the contents of main career goals for entering teacher training and motivation for class participation

Table 4 shows the various motivations for class participation behaviours that associated significantly with preservice teachers' main career goal-contents. Five behaviours showed significant associations with the different goal-contents:

- Behaviours that were motivated by the external regulation of 'attendance to lessons to get grades to pass the modules and qualify as teachers' associated significantly with the extrinsic goal-contents of financial success (X^2=11.29; p=0.004), and status/prestige (X^2=6.13; p=0.047), respectively;
- Behaviours that were motivated by the external regulation of 'participation in class only when the tasks would be graded' associated significantly with the intrinsic goal-content of making community contributions (X^2=7.06; p=0.029);
- Behaviours that were motivated by the external regulation of 'often only attending some lessons because the duration of training to become a qualified teacher is too long' associated significantly with the extrinsic goal-content of status/prestige (X^2=8.00; p=0.018);
- Behaviours that were motivated by the identified regulation of 'always reading related lesson materials before lessons to learn more so as to participate in class' associated significantly with the *extrinsic* goal-content of financial success (X^2=7.11; p=0.029);
- Behaviours that were motivated by the identified regulation of 'participating in class (i.e. ask questions, engage in discussion, make presentation)' associated significantly with extrinsic goal-content of status/prestige (X^2=6.43; p=0.04).

These relationships were further investigated for behavioural differences, and the results are displayed in Table 5a to 5e.

Motivation type in participation behaviours	Career goals to pursue in teaching					
	Extrinsic		*Non-extrinsic*		*Total*	
	N	*%*	*N*	*%*	*N*	*%*
External regulation: I attend lessons to get grades to pass my modules to qualify as teacher						
Agree	97	**89.0**	8	57.1	105	**85.4**
Disagree/Sometimes	12	11.0	6	42.9	18	14.6
Total	109	100.0	14	100.0	123	100.0

Table 5a. Behavioural differences between preservice teachers who ranked extrinsic and those who ranked non-extrinsic career goals as main goal to pursue in teaching

Attendance to lessons for external regulation related motivation (i.e. to get grades to pass the modules and qualify as teachers) is significantly associated with two types of extrinsic goal-contents: financial success and status/prestige, respectively (cf. Table 4). Table 5a shows that the majority (85.4%) of preservice teachers who agreed that they attended lesson for academic grades were pursuing extrinsic goal-contents. This means that those preservice teachers who ranked financial success and status/prestige related career goals as their main goal pursuing in teaching were significantly *more* motivated to attend lessons to get grades to pass the modules and qualify as teachers than those who did not rank these as primary goals.

Motivation type in participation behaviours	Career goals to pursue in teaching					
	Extrinsic		*Non-extrinsic*		*Total*	
	N	*%*	*N*	*%*	*N*	*%*
External regulation: Often only attend some lessons because the duration of my training to become a qualified teacher is too long						
Agree	8	11.1	15	29.4	23	18.7
Sometimes	11	15.3	3	5.9	14	11.4
Disagree	53	**73.6**	33	**64.7**	86	**69.9**
Total	72	100.0	51	100.0	123	100.0

Table 5b. Behavioural differences between preservice teachers who ranked extrinsic and those who ranked non-extrinsic career goals as main goal to pursue in teaching

Attendance to only some lessons because of the perceived duration of the teacher training programme (external regulation) is significantly associated with the extrinsic goal-content of status/prestige (cf. Table 4). Table 5b shows however that the majority (69.9%) of preservice teachers disagreed to this class participation behaviour; the larger proportion (73.6%) of those who disagreed were pursuing extrinsic career goal-contents. This means that those preservice teachers who ranked status/prestige related career goals as their main goal pursuing in teaching were significantly *less likely* to become demotivated to attend lessons or to attend only some lessons because of the training duration time-span.

Motivation type in participation behaviours	**Career goals to pursue in teaching**					
	Extrinsic		*Non-extrinsic*		*Total*	
	N	%	N	%	N	%
Identified regulation: Participate in class (i.e. ask questions, engage in discussion, make presentation)						
Agree	50	**69.4**	29	**56.9**	79	**64.2**
Sometimes	21	29.2	16	31.4	37	30.1
Disagree	1	1.4	6	11.8	7	5.7
Total	72	100.0	51	100.0	123	100.0

Table 5c. Behavioural differences between preservice teachers who ranked extrinsic and those who ranked non-extrinsic career goals as main goal to pursue in teaching

Class involvement mode (i.e. ask questions, engage in discussion, and make presentations), which is a form of extrinsic motivation (i.e. identified regulation), is significantly associated with the extrinsic goal-content of status/prestige (cf. Table 4). Table 5c shows that the majority (64.2%) of preservice teachers who agreed that they participated in class were pursuing extrinsic career goal-contents. This means that those preservice teachers who ranked status/prestige related career goals as their main goal pursuing in teaching were significantly *more* motivated to ask questions, engage in discussion, and make presentation than those who did not rank these as primary goals.

Motivation type in participation behaviours	**Career goals to pursue in teaching**					
	Extrinsic		*Non-extrinsic*		*Total*	
	N	%	N	%	N	%
Identified regulation: Always read related lesson materials before lessons to learn more so as to participate (i.e. ask questions, engage in discussion, make presentations)						
Agree	38	34.9	10	**71.4**	48	**39.0**
Sometimes	44	40.3	3	21.5	47	38.2
Disagree	27	24.8	1	7.1	28	22.8
Total	109	100.0	14	100.0	123	100.0

Table 5d. Behavioural differences between preservice teachers who ranked extrinsic and those who ranked non-extrinsic career goals as main goal to pursue in teaching

Preparing to participate in class (always read related lesson materials before lessons to learn more), which is a form of extrinsic motivation (identified regulation), is significantly associated with extrinsic goal-contents linked to financial success (cf. Table 4). Table 5d shows that the majority (71.4%) of preservice teachers who disagreed that they prepare them for class participation were pursuing non-extrinsic career goal-contents. This means that those preservice teachers who ranked financial success related career goals as their main goal pursuing in teaching were significantly *less likely* to feel motivated to read related lesson materials and prepare themselves before the lessons than those who did not rank these as primary goals.

Motivation type in participation behaviours	**Career goals to pursue in teaching**					
	Intrinsic		***Non-intrinsic***		***Total***	
	N	%	N	%	N	%
External regulation: Participate in class only when the tasks will be graded						
Agree	24	37.5	23	**39.0**	47	**38.2**
Sometimes	5	7.8	14	23.7	19	15.4
Disagree	35	**54.7**	22	37.3	57	**46.3**
Total	64	100.0	59	100.0	123	100.0

Table 5e. Behavioural differences between preservice teachers who ranked intrinsic and those who ranked non-intrinsic career goals as main goal to pursue in teaching

Preparation to participate in class for external regulation related motives (i.e. only when the tasks will be graded), which is a form of extrinsic motivation, is significantly associated with the intrinsic goal-content of community contribution (cf. Table 4). Table 5e shows that about the same proportion of preservice teachers who were pursuing intrinsic goal contents (37.5 percent) and those pursuing non-intrinsic goal contents (39.0%) agreed to that they participated in class for external regulation related motives. But more (54.7%) preservice teachers who were pursuing intrinsic (community contributions) career goal disagreed. This means that preservice teachers who ranked community contributions related career goals as their main goal pursuing in teaching were significantly *less likely* to participate in class only when they know the tasks will be graded than those who did not rank these as primary goals.

Discussion

The Self-Determination Theory (SDT) provides a framework for distinguishing between goal contents and motivation. Informed by the SDT framework, this research investigated the career goal contents and motivation among preservice teachers in the African state of Botswana. It provides, within the context of the cohort studied, a better understanding of the preservice teachers' career goal types and motivational issues.

The evidence shows that the preservice teachers were in pursuit of a diverse range of career goals, which were predominantly extrinsic in nature for the majority of trainees (research problem 1). This was evident, for instance, in the ranking of extrinsic related goal contents by over three quarters (85.37%) of the preservice teachers as their main career goals for pursuit in teaching. In fact, the pursuit of intrinsic related goals was unpopular as a main career goal. Of all the extrinsic goals considered in the research, those related to financial success, social status/prestige, and personal publicity were most important for the majority of preservice teachers. One explanation for the prevalence of these extrinsic related goals seems to be the socioeconomic standing of teaching, generally, in the Botswana society. Teaching is perceived in Botswana as a stable and financially viable profession (*cf. Botswana context section*). Botswana's government use of financial and other incentives over the years to attract migrant/expatriate teachers to, and to promote teaching career in, that country may have also added to the notion of financial viability of teaching (*cf. Botswana context section*). This explanation points to the influence of social environment on preservice teachers' goal framing (*cf. aspects of goal framing*).

The extrinsic emphasis in the preservice teachers' main career goals, it should be noted, reflects an instrumental view of teaching. This view suggests, for instance, that for preservice teachers, the value of teaching lies in what they can obtain from their job as teachers. This outward orientation in the preservice teachers' goal pursuit is in contrast with the few preservice teachers who ranked intrinsic goal-contents (to develop affiliation; make community contributions) as their main goals for pursuit in teaching. For these few preservice teachers, it appears that they hold a caring, socio-romantic view of teaching. The desire to help others through teaching (i.e. make contributes to community) implies that the seriousness, and societal value, of education is also recognised. But this desire may merely be reflective of the collectivist cultural nature of the local populace in Botswana (Hofstede in Poole 1999:75).

SDT isolates external, identified, and introjected regulations as three main types of extrinsic motivation (*cf. motivation section*). This research found evidence of two of these types of extrinsic motivation underpinning class participation behaviours among the preservice teachers. Indeed, the majority of preservice teachers participated in class (i.e. attend lessons, study-hard, read related material before lessons in order to prepare to ask questions, engage in discussion and, or, make presentations) predominantly for external regulation (academic grades, being with friends, to avoid negative consequences, be called upon) and identified regulation (judging the importance of the activity and choosing, volitionally, to act) related forms of motivation (research problem 2). This finding is consistent with previous research, which reported support for the extrinsic motivational focus of college students, with grades (external regulation) being a powerful motivator for performance in academic work (*cf. goal framing and self-determination theory*). In post-modern societies, it is argued, the measurement of academic progress is based largely on extrinsic standards. The expectation of extrinsic motivation in order to participate in scholastic activities may thus be a learnt behaviour, grounded in the social nature of schools. This explanation is plausible because, among the preservice teachers with intrinsic goals, there were those who had extrinsic motivation to participate in class (*cf. Table 5e*).

The external and identified regulations expected by the preservice teachers represent contrasting forms of extrinsic motivation. Based on the SDT, people engaged in an activity for external regulation motives when they act to comply with reward, constraints, or other externally pressuring demand, whereas, for identified regulation motives, action is based on the person's judgement and volitional choice regarding the value of the activity. While the evidence of external and identified regulations draws attention to the need to use motivation as a resource to maximize student class participation behaviour, which is a critical issue in instructional leadership, it also reveals important power mechanisms. For instance, external regulations generate a form of control motivation. When preservice teachers engaged in class for these reasons, their actions are not autonomous. In other words, the progress that preservice teachers make toward the attainment of their career goals can be controlled, or frustrated, at the classroom level by virtue of how the teacher manipulates the dispensation of externally regulated forms of extrinsic motivation. This is a pertinent point because significant relationships emerged in this study between various forms of extrinsic motivation and class participation behaviours (*cf. Table 4*).

Previous researches conducted within the SDT framework reported a natural tendency of people to internalise values and regulations, especially when they understand or grasp the meaning or rationale behind those regulations, and have an ability to enact it (*cf. Deci and Ryan, 2000:238*). Support for this argument is found in this research. There are indications of internalisation of regulation because although a significant number of the preservice teachers did not often find their learning experiences enjoyable, many chose freely to work-hard, academically, because they recognized that the activities were important for them to achieve certain goals that they have set in life (*cf. Table 2*). These actions suggest that the preservice teachers might have judged the importance of the class participation activity, and participated volitionally. Such behaviours are typical of individuals motivated by identified regulations. The perceived internalisation of identified regulations (extrinsic motivation) is unsurprising considering that preservice teachers are outwardly orientated in their main career goals (*cf. Table 1*).

But while many of the preservice teachers participated in class for different forms of extrinsic motivation, there were a few who appeared intrinsically motivated to participate in as far as attending lessons and study hard was concerned) (*cf. Table 1*). However, the intrinsic nature of there motivation is questioned. The SDT suggests that identified regulation bears some of the qualities of intrinsic motivation (*cf. dimension of motivation section*). The theory also suggests that when regulations are internalised, they prompt actions in ways that seem intrinsically driven (*cf. self-determination theory section*). It is argued therefore that the few preservice teachers who reported intrinsic motivation to participate in class might have done so by virtue of internalising extrinsic regulations, than anything else. It is conceivable that those preservice teachers who internalised regulation, volitionally, and who perceived the personal benefits of their actions, would report more instances of finding the activity enjoyable or fun, than others who did not (*cf. Internalisation section*). Since many of the preservice teachers (78.1%) were driven by identified regulation for participating in class in terms of study-hard (*cf. Table 1 and 2*), it is possible that these preservice teachers were among those reporting intrinsically driven motivation to participate in class. But of course this perspective is speculative, and requires further investigation to clarify the nature of the claim.

Nevertheless, in contrast to the above class participation motivation behaviours, the study found no evidence of amotivation or participation for introjected regulation-motives (feelings of shame, guilt, remorse, self-aggrandization). This is understandable given that the preservice teachers were generally adults (*cf. research participants*), who are often less susceptible to peer pressure (Kroger, 2000:79).

A key finding of this research, however, is the emergence of significant relationships between the contents of preservice teachers' main career goals and the motivation that they seek to participate in class activities in pursuit of these goals (research problem 3). The research found significant relationships between three main types of career goal-contents (financial success, social status/prestige, and community contributions) and two forms of extrinsic motivation (external regulation and identified regulation) (*cf. Table 4*). These relationships have important implications for preservice teachers' class participation behaviours. For instance, preservice teachers who ranked extrinsic goals related to financial success and social status/prestige as their main career goals for pursuit in teaching were significantly *more* motivated to participate in class for extrinsic motivation (i.e. attend lessons to get grades to pass the modules and qualify as teachers) than those who did not rank these as primary goals. In other words, the goal contents and the motivation types are both extrinsic in nature. This similarity is unsurprising given the outward orientation of the majority of preservice teachers. But it may be a result of the nature of preservice teachers' social (societal and school) environments, where the extrinsic aspects of teaching are often emphasized.

At the same time, 'financial-success' goal seekers placed parameters on how they participated in class. Indeed, they were significantly *less likely* to feel motivated to prepare (i.e. read related lesson materials before the lessons) to participate in class, compared with other preservice teachers who did not rank the pursuit of financial success as a primary goal (*cf. Table* 4). It means therefore that these 'financial-success' goal seekers were not particularly interested in engaging in class activities for its sake. Participation in the learning process was pursued for its end-gains, which confirms what other studies such as Schunk (2004:275) have predicted. This is typical of extrinsically motivated individuals.

In contrast to the financial success goal seekers, the social status/prestige goal seekers wanted to be more altruistic in their class participation. In other words, preservice teachers who ranked the pursuit of social status/prestige as their main career goal were significantly *more* motivated to participate in class by asking questions, engaging in discussion, and making presentation, than those who did not rank these as primary goals. These altruistic behaviours are symbolic of active class participation, which is vital for educative learning and teaching. But the SDT posits that goals are framed and pursued to satisfy specific needs (*cf. Self-determination theory*). Since the seeking of social status/prestige reflects, within the SDT framework, needs linked to relatedness - feeling connected to others - it means a desire to satisfy relatedness needs at the classroom level may explain the participation mode preferred by preservice teachers who were in pursuit of social status/prestige goals. In other words, their behaviours may be directed at obtaining external signs of worth and approval, which is typical of individuals seeking to establish a social posture among peers.

Furthermore, it is noteworthy that asking questions, engaging in discussion, and making presentations are indicative of identified regulation. Identified regulation is extrinsic in nature. Since volition is inherent in identified regulations, it seems that the social status/prestige goal oriented preservice teachers recognised the value and benefits of participating in class through these altruistic modes. Perhaps it is for this reason that these preservice teachers were significantly *less likely* to get demotivated to attend lessons generally, or to attend only some lessons because of the training duration time-span (*cf. Table* 4).

While it is evident that the majority of preservice teachers were in pursuit of extrinsic goal-contents and sought extrinsic motivation in the process of this pursuit, the study found evidence of significant relationship, in one case, between extrinsic motivation and intrinsic goal contents (*cf. Table* 4). The intrinsic goal-content was the desire to make a contribution to the community (i.e. to replace dying/retiring teachers; impart knowledge/skills to the younger generation; build an educated/informed nation). This goal significantly associated with the extrinsic motivation of external regulation (i.e. participate in class only when the tasks will be graded) (*cf. Table* 4). Consistent with expectations, the nature of this relationship was negative. This means preservice teachers who ranked community contributions related career goals as their main goal were significantly *less likely* to participate in class only when they knew the tasks would be graded. In other words, these preservice teachers would participate in class regardless of whether the tasks would be graded or not. Task-grading was unimportant in determining their class participation. But

these may not so much be a unique group of preservice teachers in the cohort, but rather may be those who had internalized regulations.
Finally, while it is clear that the preservice teachers were in pursuit of different career goals and sought motivation to participate in class, there were a variety of issues, related to how the goals were framed, that emerged. It was therefore necessary to qualitatively explore with a small group of preservice teachers, the factors which they perceived to influence the career goals that they set.

6.2 Qualitative results

The following main findings emerged as influential in the goal-contents pursued by the preservice teachers.

- Socio-economic concerns

Among the ten preservice teachers interviewed, socio-economic issues were major influential factors. In fact, for all the teachers, socio-economic considerations were the common thread binding the ideas shared. The socio-economic features were variously expressed. This view was captured in the comments of one preservice teacher:

> *I want to my family…I was looking [for] a stable income job because we grew up poor and I am the only one in the family who has gone to college [tertiary school] so I have to first think of them and how to help them…there is a lot of pressure on you when you come out of those circumstances [poor situations].*

The desire to support the family is evident as an influence. This desire can be seen as anything but misplaced for individuals who grew up in poverty conditions. In the African cultural context, this is often an expectation of families of their siblings. But many of the preservice teachers appeared to have had influences on their goal-contents from their own internalised ambition to improve their personal financial stature. A typical comment among all the student-teachers was:

> *…I think teachers earn a good salary [so] when I left secondary schools I though it would be the sort of work to do…it [teaching] is the kind of work that would allow me to become independent and acquire my own things…I can make a decent living and I need to develop myself that way.*

The economic influences on the career goals that the preservice teachers pursued are evidence that forces within the environment do impact the goal contents that a person pursues.

- Service

It appears that the disposition to be of service to others also had a role in the nature of the goal contents that the preservice teachers pursued. There was clear sense of altruism. This is the view expressed by one preservice teacher:

> *…We have many expatriate [migrant] teachers in our school…government is paying them a lot of money…I want to reduce the dependence on these [migrant] teachers…the best way for me to do this is to become a teacher, that is my view. And the other thing is HIV/AIDS; many teachers are dying from AIDS, we have to replace them.*

Some preservice teachers derived their career goals out of desires to be of service to the nation.

> *...Nation building is important to me...I have to think about how I can contribute to improving the nation because the government is sending us to school for free...many other countries don't do that...I had our vision 2016 pillars in mind when I consider teaching...I would say it influenced my choice because we want to become an educated and informed nation. I want to help in this.*

The desire to service is clearly portrayed in these comments. But it seems the altruism was shaped in, and by, steep nationalistic forces. This is a further reflection of goals being shaped by the social environment in which one finds him/her self.

7. Implications and conclusions

This research establishes that there were a variety of specific career goals being pursued by the preservice teachers. With a few exceptions, the preservice teachers maintained an extrinsic focus in both their goal-contents pursued and class participation motives. Indeed, in an environment of global teacher shortage caused in some cases by poor compensation, new entrants into teacher education in Botswana pursued extrinsic career goals, linked to financial success, social status/prestige, and publicity. The relatively stable social-economic teaching environment in which the teachers work appears to profoundly shape the nature of the preservice teachers' goal-contents and the motivation to pursue same.

The evidence in this study confirms the existence of two types of extrinsic motivation, namely: external and identified regulations. The expectation of extrinsic motivation for participating in scholastic activities appears to be learnt behaviour, grounded in the social nature of schools and the way academic standards are measured. The internalisation of regulations, that is extrinsic motivation, seems a practice sustaining class participation among the preservice teachers.

A number of significant relationships emerged between the goal-contents of preservice teachers' main career goals and the different types of motivation that preservice teachers seek in order to engage in class activities in pursuit of those goals. In all but one of the significant relationships, the goal-contents and motivation types were the same, largely being extrinsic in nature. Preservice teachers' general reliance on extrinsic motivation to participate in class can be problematic. While it draws teacher-trainer's attention to an approach to maximized class involvement, it also reveals opportunities for teacher-trainers to control, or even frustrate, preservice teachers' behaviours in the learning context because aspects of extrinsic motivation are indicative of control motivation. When preservice teachers engaged in class for control motivation forces, their actions are not autonomous.

Three main types of career goal-contents (financial success, social status/prestige, and community contributions) and two forms of extrinsic motivation (external regulation and identified regulation) showed significant relationships. The seeking of social status/prestige reflects, within the SDT framework, needs linked to relatedness - feeling connected to others, which suggested that a desire to satisfy relatedness needs at the classroom level underlies social status/prestige goals seekers' class participation modes.

The pursuit of goals for extrinsic motives further holds implications for teaching and personal adaptation. The Literature on SDT (*cf. Deci & Ryan, 2000*) indicates that if people did not experience satisfaction from learning for its own sake (but instead needed to be prompted by external reinforcements) they would be less likely to engage the domain-specific skills and capacities they inherited, to develop new potentialities for adaptive employment, or both. They would thus be ill prepared for new situations and demands in the physical world, and moreover, they would be less adaptable to the extremely varied cultural niches into which a given individual might be born or adopted. It means therefore that teacher-trainers should try to get preservice teachers to shift from the extrinsic motivation emphasis to more intrinsic focus for class participation by offering the extrinsic motivator initially, and work subsequently toward building the preservice teachers' pride in their participatory efforts and accomplishments (intrinsic motivator).

8. Further research

The following issues should be further researched:

- Why Botswana entrants into teacher education programmes are so extrinsic in their goal pursuit; exploring this would further facilitate the identification of causal relationships.
- This study draws attention to the possibility of the internalisation of extrinsic motivation, especially various regulations. The nature, extent and mechanism facilitating internalisation of extrinsic motivation would be a new direction to expand this research.
- The goal contents and motivation across different countries should be explored comparatively. This would expand the goal-motivation knowledge base and allow different aspects of the SDT to be tested.

9. Reference

Brown, B. & Schulze, S. 2002. The development of working relationships between indigenous and expatriate teachers. *Journal of the Botswana Educational Research Association, 10 (1):3-20.*

Brown, B. 2004. Teacher migration to Botswana: implication for human resources management in education. D.Ed. Thesis. Pretoria: UNISA

Brown, B. 2006. Teacher migration and quality education in southern Africa: what lessons for the Caribbean? *Journal of Arts, Science and Technology, 12, 5-20.*

Carver, C., & Baird, E. 1998. The American dream revisited: is it what you want or why you want it that matters? *Psychological Science,* 9, 289-292.

Cennamo, K. S. 1993. Learning from video: Factors influencing learners' preconceptions and invested mental effort. *Educational Technology Research and Development, 41*(3), 33-45.

CEPD. 2005. Teacher education in South Africa: proposal for research and development programme. Center for Education Policy Development. Pretoria. February 2005

Commonwealth Secretariat. 2003. Teacher mobility and loss in Commonwealth member states - a study commissioned by the Commonwealth Secretariat. Oxford Center for Comparative and International studies in Education: University of Oxford.

Corbin, J. & Strauss, A. 1990. *Basics of qualitative research: grounded theory, procedures and techniques*. Newbury Park: Sage.

Crouch, L., & Perry, H. 2003. Teacher shortage. In HSRC. 2003.*Human resources development review: education, employment, and skills in South Africa.* Cape Town: HSRC Press

De Vos, A.S. 1998. Combined quantitative and qualitative approach. In: A.S. De Vos, H. Strydom, C.B. Fouche, M. Poggenpoel, E. Schurink, & W. Schurink. (eds.). 1998. *Research at grassroots: a primer for the caring profession.* Pretoria: Van Schaik.

Deci, E., & Ryan, R. 2000. The 'what' and 'why' of goal pursuits: human needs and the self-determination of behaviour. *Psychological Inquiry,* 11(4): 227-268.
DoE. 2001. *National plan for higher education*. Ministry of Education. Pretoria.
Elliot, A., & Thrash, T. 2002. Approach-avoidance motivation in personality: approach and avoidance temperaments and goals. *Journal of Personality and Social Psychology,* 82, 804-818.
Goodenow, C. 1993. Classroom belonging among early adolescents: relationships to motivation and achievements. *Journal of Early Adolescence,* 13, 21-43.
Houle, C. 1961. *The inquiring mind.* Madison: University of Wisconsin Press.
HSRC. 2003.*Human resources development review: education, employment, and skills in South Africa.* Cape Town: HSRC Press
Kasser, T., & Ahuvia, A. 2002. Materialistic values and well-being in business students. *European Journal of Social Psychology,* 32, 137-146.
Kasser, T., Ryan, R., Couchman, C., & Sheldon, K. 2004. Materialistic values: their causes and consequences. In T. Kasser & A. Kanner (Eds.). *Psychology and consumer culture: the struggler for a good life in a materialistic world,* (pp. 11-28). Washington: American Psychological Association.
Kassiem, A. 2007. Educators feel crunch of teacher shortage. IOL Bulletin. [online]. url: http://www.iol.co.za/index.php?from=rss_South+Africa&set_id=1&click_id=13&art_id=vn20070520235116644C994448. accessed: 18th August 2007.
Kroger, J. 2000. *Identity Development: Adolescence through adulthood.* Thousand Oaks: Sage Publications.
Mead, G. H. 1934. *Mind, self, and society*. Chicago: University of Chicago Press.
Meissner, W. W. 1988. *Treatment of patients in the borderline spectrum*. Northvale, NJ: Jason Aronson.
Miles, M.B. & Huberman, A.M. 1994. *Qualitative data analysis: an expanded sourcebook.* Thousand Oaks: Sage.
Nilsson, P. 2003a. Teacher demand and supply in Africa. Education International Working Papers, No. 12: Education for all. Brussels: Education International.
Nilsson, P. 2003b. Teacher demand and supply in South Asia. Education International Working Papers, No. 12: Education for all. Brussels: Education International.
Pelletier, L., Dion, S., Tuson, K., & Green-Demers, I. 1999. Why do people fail to adopt environmental behaviours? Towards a taxonomy of environmental amotivation. *Journal of Applied Social Psychology,* 29, 2481-2504.
Ryan, R. M. 1993. Agency and organization: Intrinsic motivation, autonomy and the self in psychological development. In J. Jacobs (Ed.), *Nebraska symposium on motivation: Developmental perspectives on motivation,* vol 40, pp 1–56. Lincoln: University of Nebraska Press.
Ryan, R., & Connell, J. 1989. Perceived locus of causality and internalisation: examining reasons for acting in two domains. *Journal of Personality and Social Psychology,* 57, 749-761.
Ryan, R., Sheldon, K., Kasser, T., & Deci, E. 1996. All goals are not created equal: an organismic perspective on the nature of goals and their regulation. In P.M. Gollwitzer & J.A. Bargh (Eds.). *The psychology of action: linking cognition and motivation to behaviour,* (pp. 7-26). New York: Guilford.
Sagiv, L., & Schwartz, S. 2000. Value priorities and subjective wellbeing: direct relationships and congruity effects. *European Journal of Social Psychology,* 30, 177-198.

Saunders, M., Lewis, P., & Thornhill, A. 2007. *Research methods for business students*, 4th ed., Harrow, Prentice-Hall

Schunk, D. 2004. *Learning theories: an educational perspective*. Ohio: Pearson

Sheldon, K., & Kasser, T. 1995. Coherence and congruence: two aspects of personality integration. *Journal of Personality and Social Psychology*, 68, 531-543

Sheldon, K., Ryan, R., Deci, E., & Kasser, T. 2004. The independent effects of goal contents and motives on well-being: its both what you pursue and why you pursue it. *Personality and Social Psychology Bulletin*, 30, 475-486.

Sikkes, M. 2001. The teacher shortage: how to get new talent into needy classrooms. *Dossier of Education International Magazine (May 2001).*

Sinsicalco, M. 2002. *A statistical profile of the teaching profession*. Geneva: ILO/UNESCO.

Sirgy, M. 1998. Materialism and quality of life. *Social Indicator Research*, 43, 227-260.

Tabulawa, R. 2005. PBRS is bad news for teachers and education. *The Botswana Gazette*, June 10, 8

TSM. 2006. Report on the state of teacher supply and demand in Botswana. Teaching Service Management, Gaborone, Government Printer

TSM. 2007. Report on the status of applicants to Teacher Education Colleges in Botswana. Teaching Service Management, Gaborone, Government Printer

UN. 2003. Millennium development goals. [Online]. Available url: www.un.org/millenniumgoals/index.html. Accessed: 5th March, 2003.

UNESCO. 2003. *Annual statistical yearbook*. [Online]. Available url: www.qesdb.cdie.org/ged/index.html. Accessed: 26th August, 2003.

UNESCO. 2005. Global monitoring report. Paris.

Vallerand, R., Fortier, M., & Guay, S. 1997. Self-determination and persistence in a real-life setting: toward a motivational model of high school dropout. *Journal of Personality and Social Psychology*, 72, 1116-1176.

Vansteenkiste, M., Lens, W., Dewitte, S., De Witte, H., & Deci, E. 2004. The 'why' and 'why not' of job search behaviours: their relation to searching, unemployment experience, and well-being. *European Journal of Social Psychology*, 34, 345-363.

Vansteenkiste, M., Simons, J., Lens, W., Sheldon, K., & Deci, E. 2004. Motivating learning, performance and persistence: the synergistic role of intrinsic goal-content and autonomy-supportive context. *Journal of Personality and Social Psychology*, 87, 246-260.

Vansteenkiste, M., Simons, J., Lens, W., Soenens, B., & Matos, L. 2005. Examining the motivational impact of intrinsic versus extrinsic gaol framing and autonomy-supportive versus internally controlling communication style on early adolescents' academic achievement. *Child Development*, 76(2):483-501

Williams, G., Cox, E., Hedberg, V., & Deci, E. 2000. Extrinsic life goals and health risk behaviours among adolescents. *Journal of Applied Psychology*, 30, 1756-1771.

Woolfolk A 2004. *Educational psychology*. 9th edition. Boston: Allyn & Bacon.

World Bank. 2003. *Accelerating progress towards Education for All (EFA): the fast track initiative.* Brussels.

Automatic Classification of Language Learner Sentences into Native-Like or Non-Native-Like Based on Word Alignment Distribution

Katsunori Kotani[1], Takehiko Yoshimi[2], Takeshi Kutsumi[3] and Ichiko Sata[3]
[1]*Kansai Gaidai University,* [2]*Ryukoku University,* [3]*Sharp Corporation*
Japan

1. Introduction

The recent advancement of natural language processing techniques has brought about significant development in computer-assisted language learning and teaching. For instance, Lee et al. (2007) proposed a computer-based evaluation system for writing proficiency of English as a second language (ESL) learners. The basic technique employed is statistical linguistic models for machine translation (MT) evaluation (Corston-Oliver et al. 2001, Kulesza & Shieber 2004, Gamon et al. 2005). The evaluation method of Lee et al. (2007) automatically classifies English sentences produced by EFL learners either into native-like or non-native-like sentences by analyzing morphological and syntactic features. This evaluation method is intuitively correct, because sentences judged as native-like should be adequate and fluent, but, on the contrary, sentences regarded as non-native-like must involve some unnatural expressions.

The classifier of Lee et al. (2007), however, is difficult to identify what makes sentences judged as non-native-like unnatural. Since this classifier just examines the morphological and syntactic features such as dependency relation of subject-verb, we could find typical morphological and syntactic patterns in non-native-like sentences. From pedagogical viewpoint, this identification of (non-)native-likeness may help language teachers identify what problems a learner has. A classification-based evaluation method could more directly reveal a learner's problems if a classifier examines specific linguistic features concerning with a learner's problems. Then, we developed an automatic classifier that examines the existence/absence of linguistic problems in learner sentences. Among various learner problems, the first language influence is seen as a critical problem that language learners and teachers have to face (Ellis 1994). Therefore, we focused on the influence of learners' first language in the target language.

Since the influence of the first language often takes the form of word-for-word translation, our classifier examines whether learner sentences involve unnatural literal translation based on word alignment distribution. Word alignment distribution shows word-level correspondence between learner sentences and sentences conveyed the relevant meaning in a learner's first language. Word alignment technique is one of the natural language processing techniques, and word alignment distribution is available with a word aligner, e.g., GIZA++ (Och & Ney 2003).

The goal of this paper is to address a writing proficiency evaluation method for learners of Japanese as a second language (JSL) whose first language is English. As we will see below, there are various linguistic differences between Japanese and English. The differences can be seen in lexical, syntactic and discourse levels. The validity of our classifier will be examined. It will be shown that our system can correctly classify approximately 80% of JSL learner sentences.

We will further examine the adequacy of our classifier. First, we will examine the adequacy of our word-alignment-based classifier by comparing our classifier with a classifier using syntactic features. The result showed that our classifier achieved higher classification accuracy than classifiers based on parsing information features. Secondly, we will investigate whether the classification results reflect the learner proficiency. The proper classification results should exhibit the decrease of the classification accuracy for sentences produced by learners with higher writing proficiency, because these learners can write native-like sentences. Thus, the classification task becomes more difficult for sentences written by proficient learners. The experiment result showed that the classification results exhibited statistic significant difference ($p<.05$) between learners who marked more than 50 points of human evaluation scores and learners with less than 50 points. Given these findings, we concluded that word alignment-based classification techniques can be used for evaluating the writing proficiency of foreign language learners.

2. Related Studies

In this section, we review related studies on (i) classification-based MT evaluation (Corston-Oliver et al. 2001, Kulesza & Shieber 2004, Gamon et al. 2005, Paul et al. 2007), (ii) word alignment-based MT evaluation (Blatz et al. 2004, Lin & Gidea 2007) (iii) classification-based evaluation of foreign language learner sentences (Lee et al. 2007) and (iv) Computer-assisted language assessment (Chapelle 2008).

First, let us review studies on classification-based MT evaluation (Corston-Oliver et al. 2001, Kulesza & Shieber 2004, Gamon et al. 2005, Paul et al. 2007). These studies constructed classifiers for MT that distinguish between MT-like sentences and human translation (HT)-like sentences, assuming that good MT sentences should be similar to HT sentences. This idea is intuitively understandable, as poor MT sentences can be easily distinguished from HT sentences, but good MT sentences are often mistaken for HT sentences. Hence, these studies treated evaluation of quality of MT sentences as a classification problem.

Corston-Oliver et al. (2001) used decision trees (Quinlan 1992) with both perplexity and linguistic features of Spanish-to-English MT sentences and HT sentences. A perplexity-based classifier yielded an accuracy of 74.7%, a linguistic feature-based classifier showed an accuracy of 76.5%, and a classifier using both features achieved the best classification accuracy of 82.9%.

Kulesza & Shieber (2004) constructed a classifier for Chinese-to-English MT sentences using well-known machine learning algorithms, Support Vector Machines (SVMs) (Vapnik 1998). This classifier examined the following classification features: (i) n-gram precision of MT sentences compared with HT sentences, the length of MT sentences and HT sentences, and (iii) the word error rate of MT sentences. Their classifier yielded an accuracy of 64.4%.

Gamon et al. (2005) developed an SVM classifier based on linguistic features. Classification features included subcategorization properties and semantic properties such as finiteness or argument structures. This classifier showed a classification accuracy of 77.6% for English-to-French MT sentences.

Paul et al. (2007) developed a classifier with decision tree algorithms employing evaluation scores obtained with other automatic MT evaluation metrics including BLEU (Papineni et al. 2001), NIST (Doddington 2002) and METEOR (Banerjee & Lavie 2005). Unlike the other classifiers (Corston-Oliver et al. 2001, Kulesza & Shieber 2004, Gamon et al. 2005), this method requires a lot of manual evaluation results for MT evaluation scores.

By contrast, our classifier as well as the other classifiers (Corston-Oliver et al. 2001, Kulesza & Shieber 2004, Gamon et al. 2005) needs parallel corpora, which are more easily obtained than manual MT evaluation results. As we mentioned above, our classifier could identify learner problems more directly than classifiers based on the general linguistic features (Corston-Oliver et al. 2001, Kulesza & Shieber 2004, Gamon et al. 2005, Paul et al. 2007)

Secondly, we will review research on word alignment MT evaluation (Blatz et al. 2004, Lin & Gildea 2007), which is similar to our classifier. As we will see below, our classifier employs word alignment distribution between learner sentences and sentences written in a learner's first language. Our classifier uses alignment features differently from the way these previous methods employed.

Blatz et al. (2004) used word alignment results for evaluating MT sentences. Under their method, contiguities of aligned words are taken as classification features. Liu & Gildea (2007) also constructed a classifier that employs source sentence-related features. Under this approach, alignment features were used to identify overlapping words for counting in their metric: words were counted only if the words were aligned to corresponding words in source sentences. By contrast, our approach uses aligned pairs and non-aligned words directly as classification features, as explained in the following section.

Thirdly, we will review research on classification-based evaluation of learner sentences. Lee et al. (2007) constructed a classifier for sentences written by EFL learners. Interestingly, this study employed MT sentences for training a classifier instead of EFL learner sentences, because MT sentences are more cheaply available than learner sentences. Lee et al. (2007) showed that MT sentences can be used as an alternative language data to learner sentences. As an experiment result showed, a classifier trained with EFL learner sentences yielded a classification accuracy of 66.4%, while a classifier based on MT sentences achieved the similar classification accuracy of 59.0%. From this experiment result, we determined to employ MT sentences in training a classifier for sentences written by JSL learners, as explained in Section 4.1.

Last, we will introduce research on the advantage of computer-based evaluation for language learners. Chapelle (2008) pointed out major contributions of computer-based evaluation methods. According to Chappelle (2008), one of the advantages of computer-based evaluation methods can be seen in that it is a computer-adaptive test that can assess learner proficiency more effectively than non-adaptive tests can. Given this advantage, we will modify our classifier so that it assesses learner sentences more adoptively.

3. Classification Features

Good, natural sentences should differ from word-for-word translation, whereas unnatural learner sentences often causes from word-for-word translation. For instance, an English nominal modifier "some" can convey the existential meaning of an entity as in Sentene (1a). A literal translation of this nominal modifier makes a sentence unnatural as seen in a JSL learner's sentence (1b). In Japanese, the existential meaning of an entity is often expressed using an existential verb "i-ta (exisited)" as in Sentence (1c). Sentence (1c) is clearly natural, while Sentence (1b) is perfectly grammatical but less natural. The unnaturalness of Sentence (1b) is due to the word-for-word translation of the English nomial modifier "some" to Japanese nominal modifier "ikuraka-no (some)."

(1) a. Some students came.
b. Ikuraka-no gakusei-wa ki-ta
some-GEN student-TOP come-PST
'Several students came.'
c. Ki-ta gakusei-mo i-ta
come-PST student-also exist-PST
'Some students came.'

(GEN: genitive Case marker, PST: past tense marker, TOP: topic marker)

As Example (1) illustrates, the influence of the first language can be seen in the literal translation. In order to identify words derived from word-for-word translation, we decided to examine word alignment distribution between JSL learner sentences and sentences conveying inteded meaning in a learner's first language, i.e., English. This is because literally translated words are more easily aligned than non-literally translated words. Literal translation maintains lexical features such as part of speech, but, on the other hand, non-literal translation usually lacks parallel lexical features, as seen in Example (1).

Let us consider another example of unnatural word-for-word translation. Sentence (2a) is literally trasnlated into Sentence (2b). Sentence (2b) is grammatical but unnatural as a Japanese sentence. Though Sentence (2c) is not literal translation, this sentence is perfectly natural.

(2) a. Today the sun is shining. (original sentence)
b. Kyoo taiyoo-wa kagayai-teiru (MT)
today the-sun-TOP shine-BE-ING
'Today the sun is shining.'
c. Kyoo-wa seiten-da (HT)
today-TOP fine-BE
'It's fine today.'

(BE: copular verb, ING: gerundive verb form)

Here, we examined whether word alignment distribution differs between a literally traslated sentence and a non-literally translated sentence. The word alignment distribution of Sentence (2b) and Sentence (2c) is automatically derived with our experimental word aligner, described in Section 4.

Table 1 shows the word alignment distribution of Sentence (2b) and Sentence (2c). Note that "align(A, B)" means that an English word "A" and a Japanese word "B" compose an aligned pair, "non-align_eng(C)" means that an English word "C" remains unaligned, and "non-align_jpn(D)" means that a Japanese word "D" remains unaligned. As shown in Table 1, the rate of alignment and non-alignment varies based on whether or not a sentence is literally translated. That is, more aligned words are observed in Sentence (2b), i.e., a non-native-like sentence, and more non-aligned words appear in Snentece (2c), i.e., a native-like sentence. Thus, non-aligned words should create a sense of naturalness, while aligned words would make a sentence unnatural.

Classification-based writing evaluation should not only classify learner sentences into native-like or non-native-like sentences, but also identify linguistic problems that arise from the influence of a learner's first language in the form of literal translation. The difference between a non-native-like sentence (2b) and a native-like sentence (2c) can be drwan with the alignment distribution of these sentences as shown in Table 1. The English words "today" and "is" are aligned with the relevant Japanese words in both sentences. By contrast, the other words exhibit the different alignment distribution. Whilie the words "sun" and "shining" are aligned with Japanese words in Snetnece (2b), these words are remained unalinged in Sentence (2c). From this result, examining alignment distribution could reveal linguistic problems in learner sentences arising from literal translation.

Unnatural sentence (2b)	Natural sentence (2c)
align(today, kyoo [today])	align(today, kyoo-wa [today-TOP])
align(is, teiru [BE-ING])	align(is, da [BE])
align(sun, taiyoo [sun])	non-align_jpn(seiten [fine])
align(shining, kagayai [shine])	non-align_eng(the)
non-align_jpn(wa [TOP])	non-align_eng(sun)
non-align_eng(the)	non-align_eng(shining)

Table 1. Alignment Distribution of Example (2)

4. Experiment

4.1 Designs

The goal of this experiment is to validate our classification-based evaluation method for JSL learners. In this experiment, we constructed the following two types of classifiers using word alignment distribution as classification features: (i) a classifier based on non-aligned words and (ii) a classifier based on both aligned and non-aligned words.

Classifiers were constructed with SVMs that have high generalization performance (Vapnik 1998). SVMs were carried out with TinySVM (a software implemented as a packaging tool available at the following URL: http://chasen. org/~taku/software/TinySVM/). The first order polynomial was taken as the type of kernel function, and the other settings were taken as the default settings.

The classifiers were trained with a parallel corpus of HT and MT instead of a learner corpus. Although various learner corpora have been distributed (The National Institute for Japanese Language 2001, Izumi et al. 2004), the amount of data they contain is not as large as first language corpus. In addition, what we need for training a classifier based word alignment distribution is a parallel corpus. The data size of parallel learner corpus further decreases. Then, we decided to employ MT data as learner data, because MT sentences are similar to learner sentences, in that, both sentences involve some linguistic problems. This alternative use of MT data as learner data was investigated in Lee et al. (2007), and it is suggested that MT data can be used as an alternative data to learner data.

Training data consisted of Reuters' articles in English and expert Japanese translations of the original articles, i.e., HT, (Utiyama & Isahara 2003). Duplicates of sentences and translations were deleted if they appeared repeatedly in the corpus. MT data was obtained by operating machine translation systems over this corpus. The translation systems are state-of-art systems commercially supplied in Japan (MT-α and MT-β). A total of 25,800 example sentences were obtained (12,900 HT sentences and 12,900 MT sentences).

Word alignment distributions were provided with an experimental word aligner between the source English sentences and Japanese translation sentences (MT and HT). This tool segments Japanese sentences into word-units before aligning English and Japanese words. Word alignment process is performed using a bilingual dictionary/thesaurus and a dependency analyser. The alignment results consisted of aligned pairs and non-aligned words. Each alignment instance was taken as a classification feature.

Our classifiers were evaluated with a learner corpus. Test data was taken from a JSL corpus (The National Institute for Japanese Language 2001). This corpus consists of essays written by JSL learners and the corresponding English sentences. Classification accuracy of our classifiers was examined with 689 sentences. Then, the validity of our classifiers was further investigated by examining the relation between human evaluation results and classification accuracy. This examination was carried out with 279 sentences out of the 689 learner sentences. The fluency of the 279 sentences was evaluated by three native Japanese speakers. This evaluation was carried in 100-point scale. Then, the test sentences were divided into higher and lower at the 50-point. The higher group consists of 63 sentences (22.6%), and the lower group is made up of 216 sentences (77.4%).

In this experiment, we first examined the robustness of our classifier against MT of training data by comparing the classification accuracies of classifiers trained with MT-α and MT-β. Secondly, we examined our classifiers with JSL learner data. Classifiers tested are constructed with either aligned features or both non-aligned & aligned features. Thirdly, we compared our word-alignment-based classifiers with classifiers based on syntactic features. Last, we investigated whether the classification results can reflect the learner proficiency.

4.2 Results and Discussion

Before reporting the experiment results, we shall briefly report the word alignment distribution in MT and HT data. Table 2 shows the distribution of aligned pairs and non-aligned words in the training data. The alignment rate of MT data was higher than that of HT data, as more aligned pairs appear in MT data. The alignment rates between HT (the control sample) and both MT data were analyzed with a one-way ANOVA test and Tukey's test, and a statistic significant difference was observed between HT and MTs. ($F(3, 56)=616.10$, $p<.01$). Therefore, it is evident word alignment distribution differs between HT and MT.

	N	Aligned pairs (%)	Non-aligned words (%)	Alignment rate (%)
MT-α	518894	37.1	62.9	59.0
MT-β	537460	36.4	63.6	57.3
HT	568259	24.1	75.9	31.7

Table 2. Alignment Distributions of MT & HT

Hereafter, we will report the experiment results. First, we examined the robustness of our classifier against MT of training data by comparing the classification accuracies of classifiers trained with MT-α and MT-β. We evaluated the classifiers in a five-fold cross validation test. Table 3 shows the mean classification accuracy in the five trials. As both the classifiers marked rather high classification accuracy, it is suggested that our classifier is robust against machine translation systems.

	Mean classification accuracy (%)
MT-α-based classifier	99.7
MT-β-based classifier	99.8

Table 3. Mean Classification Accuracy

Secondly, we examined our classifiers using JSL learner sentences as test data. Classifiers tested are constructed with either aligned features or both non-aligned & aligned features. Table 4 shows the classification accuracy of the two types of classifiers. Any type of classifiers marked high classification accuracy (more than 70%). The highest classification accuracy (approximately 80%) was yielded by non-aligned-based classifier trained with MT-α. Given this classification accuracy, our classifier is tenable for classifying learner sentences.

	MT-α (%)	MT-β (%)
Non-aligned-based classifier	79.1	71.8
Aligned & non-aligned-based classifier	72.5	77.6
Mean classification accuracy	75.8	74.7

Table 4. Classification Accuracy

Thirdly, we compared our word-alignment-based classifier with a classifier using syntactic features. Lee et al. (2007) employed parsing results such as (i) context-free grammar rules used for parsing sentences, (ii) parsing scores, and (iii) co-occurrence relations between a verb and its subject/object noun. Then, we constructed a classifier using Japanese syntactic parsing information extracted with a dependency parser Cabocha. We regarded phrase dependency relation as classification features. The dependency relation shows part-of-speech information of a modifier and a modifiee. Although this syntactic dependency relation does not precisely reproduce the experimental conditions of Lee et al. (2007), we consider that this comparison would suggest the validity of our method because these features correspond to the classification features (i) and (iii) used by Lee et al. (2007).

Table 5 shows the classification accuracy of parsing information-based classifiers for 279 learner sentences. The classification accuracy of our classifiers (shown in Table 4) is much higher than the accuracy of the parsing information-based classifiers. From this result, it is suggested that learner sentences can be identified more properly by word-alignment-based classifiers than the parsing information-based classifiers.

	Classification accuracy (%)
Classifier trained by MT-α	43.7
Classifier trained by MT-β	37.6

Table 5. Classification Accuracy of Parsing Information-based Classifier

Last, we investigated whether the classification results can reflect the learner proficiency. If the classifiers are tenable, the classification accuracy should decrease for sentences written by learners with high writing proficiency. This is because a proficient learner can write sentences similar to sentences written by native speakers.

In this experiment, the classification accuracy was compared between sentences written by less proficient learners and the ones written by more proficient learners. The learner proficiency was determined by human evaluation score (more/less than 50 points).

Table 6-9 show the classification accuracy of non-aligned-based classifiers and that of aligned & non-aligned-based classifiers trained with MT-α and MT-β. The classification accuracy decreases for more proficient learner sentences, except for the accuracy of a non-aligned-based classifier trained with MT-β. The difference of classification accuracy was statistically analyzed by the chi-square test, and the statistically significant decrease ($p<.05$) was observed for the classification results of an aligned & non-aligned-based classifier trained with MT-α. (Table 7) Therefore, it is clear that our classifier can account for learner proficiency. This is another piece of supporting evidence that our classifier is tenable as a writing evaluation method.

Learner sentence	Correct	Incorrect	Classification accuracy (%)
Less proficient learner sentence	58	5	92.1
More proficient learner sentence	198	18	91.7

Table 6. Human Assessment and Non-aligned-based Classification Accuracy (MT-α)

Learner sentence	Correct	Incorrect	Classification accuracy (%)
Less proficient learner sentence	61	2	96.8
More proficient learner sentence	188	28	87.0

Table 7. Human Assessment and Aligned & Non-aligned-based Classification Accuracy (MT-α)

Learner sentence	Correct	Incorrect	Classification accuracy (%)
Less proficient learner sentence	56	7	88.9
More learner sentence	198	18	91.7

Table 8. Human Assessment and Non-aligned-based Classification Accuracy (MT-β)

Learner sentence	Correct	Incorrect	Classification accuracy (%)
Less proficient learner sentence	58	5	92.1
More proficient learner sentence	189	27	87.5

Table 9. Human Assessment and Aligned & Non-aligned-based Classification Accuracy (MT-β)

5. Conclusion

In this paper we constructed classifiers for JSL learner sentences based on word alignment distribution for evaluating writing proficiency from viewpoint of the first language influence. Our classifiers were trained with MT data, and evaluated with JSL learner sentences. Though the classification results vary depending on word alignment features, any type of classifiers marked more than 70% classification accuracy. The highest classification accuracy (approximately 80%) was yielded with a classifier based on non-alignment feature trained by MT-α.

We further examined the adequacy of our word-alignment-based classifier by comparing our classifiers with classifiers using syntactic features. Our classifiers achieved higher classification accuracy than parsing information-based classifiers.

In addition, we evaluated our classifier by examining whether classification results reflect learner proficiency. Our classifiers were tested with 279 JSL learner sentences that were evaluated as more/less than 50 points in human evaluation scores. The classification accuracy showed the statistic significant decrease ($p<.05$) for more proficient learner sentences.

From these results we conclude that a word alignment-based classifier is tenable as an evaluation method for JSL learner writing proficiency.

Even though the experiment results demonstrated the validity of word alignment-based classifiers, there are remaining problems to be solved. First, we have to examine to what extent MT and learner sentences are similar. In this paper, the similarity of MT and learner sentences is assumed based on research of the previous study (Lee et al. 2007). Second, we will compare classification-based evaluation results not only in two classes (more proficient learner sentence & less proficient learner sentence), but also in more classes, e.g., 5 classes for examining the distinctiveness of our classifier. Thirdly, we will examine to what extent our classification-based evaluation method can reveal the first language influence. Last, our classification-based evaluation method has to be implemented on a computer language learning system.

6. References

Banerjee, S. and A. Lavie. 2005. METEOR: An automatic metric for MT evaluation with improved correlation with human judgement. In Proceedings of the 43th Annual Meeting of the Association of Computational Linguistics (ACL) Workshop on Intrinsic and Extrinsic Evaluation Measures for Machine Translation and/or Summarization. 65-72.

Blatz, J., E. Fitzgerald, G. Foster, S. Gandrabur, C. Goutte, A. Kulesza, A. Sanchis, and N. Ueffing. 2004. Confidence estimation for machine translation. Final Report, JHU /CLSP Summer Workshop.

Chapelle, C. A. 2008. Utilizing technology in language assessment. In Encyclopedia of Language and Education: Language Testing and Assessment Shohamy, E. and N. H. Hornberger (eds.) Heidelberg: Springer-Verlag.

Corston-Oliver, S., M. Gamon, and C. Brockett. 2001. A machine learning approach to the automatic evaluation of machine translation. In Proceedings of the 39th Annual Meeting of the Association for Computational Linguistics (ACL01). 148-155.

Doddington, G. 2002. Automatic evaluation of machine translation quality using n-gram co-occurrence statistics. In Proceedings of the second international conference on Human Language Technology Research (HLT). 138-145.

Ellis, R. 1994. The Study of Second Language Acquisition. Oxford University Press, Oxford.

Gamon, M., A. Aue and M. Smets. 2005. Sentence-level MT evaluation without reference translations: Beyond language modelling. In Proceedings of the 10th the European Association for Machine Translation Conference (EAMT05). 103-111.

Izumi, E., K. Uchimoto, and H. Isahara. 2004. The overview of the SST speech corpus of Japanese learner English and evaluation through the experiment on automatic detection of learners' errors. In Proceedings of the International Conference on Language Resources and Evaluation (LREC-04), 1435-1439.

Kulesza, A. and S. M. Shieber. 2004. A learning approach to improving sentence-level MT evaluation. In Proceedings of the 10th International Conference on Theoretical and Methodological Issues in Machine Translation (TMI04). 75-84.

Lee, J., M. Zhou, and X. Liu. 2007. Detection of non-native sentences using machine-translated training data. In Proceedings of the 2007 Human Language Technology Conference of the North American Chapter of the Association for Computational Linguistics (NAACL HLT07). 93-96.

Liu, D. and D. Gildea. 2007. Source-language features and maximum correlation training for machine translation evaluation. In Proceedings of the 2007 Human Language Technology Conference of the North American Chapter of the Association for Computational Linguistics (NAACL HLT07). 41-48.

Och, F. J. and H. Ney. 2003. A systematic comparison of various statistical alignment models. Computational Linguistics 29(1): 19-51.

Papineni, K. A., S. Roukos, T. Ward, and W.-J. Zhu. 2001. Bleu: A method for automatic evaluation of machine translation. Technical Report RC22176 (W0109-022), IBM Research Division, Thomas J. Watson Research Center.

Paul, M., A. Finch, and E. Sumita. 2007. Reducing human assessment of machine translation quality to binary classifiers. In Proceedings of the 11th International Conference on Theoretical and Methodological Issues in Machine Translation (TMI 2007). 154-162.

Quinlan, J. 1992. C4.5: Programs for Machine Learning. Morgan Kaufmann, San Mateo, CA.

The National Institute for Japanese Language. 2001. Contrastive Linguistic Database for Japanese Language Learners' Written Language.

Utiyama, M. and H. Isahara. 2003. Reliable measures for aligning Japanese-English news articles and sentences. In Proceedings of the 41st Annual Meeting of the Association for Computational Linguistics (ACL). 72-79.

Vapnik, V. 1998. Statistical Learning Theory. Wiley-Interscience, New York.

Analysis of the Students' Socio-Demographic Profile

Oto Težak
Centre for Higher Education, REVIVIS Ptuj
Slovenia

1. Introduction

The paper describes statistical analysis of the students' profile. The Centre for higher education Ptuj (Revivis Ptuj) was established to encourage tertiary education in a specific region of the Republic of Slovenia. The aim of the Centre is to offer different study programs, the so-called guest study programs, to the local population as well as to establish a new high school. Students in the Centre for higher education were analyzed to get information for support of the high school education progress and quality as well as student centered curriculum development. The aim of the research was to find out a socio-demographic profile of students, a dynamic of students' profile variables and if the analyzed students have their own particularities of the selected indicators. Some indicators of interest were proposed, analyzed and compared with the profile of students from the nearby university. Supported by this research, the decisions regarding the high education development in our particular region were made.

Methods of descriptive statistics and statistical analyzes (Montgomery and Runger, 2003; Knežević, 2006) were used. The unit of the analysis was a student. Statistical socio-demographic and pedagogic variables of the students in the study centre were gathered by the use of a questionnaire. The sampling procedure used was random sampling. An analysis was made by descriptive statistic methods as well as by statistical inference methods where chi-squared test was performed.

The analyses comprised data of the students of the Centre for higher education in Ptuj, situated in the north-eastern part of Slovenia. Significant socio demographic indicators were emphasized and analyzed. Among proposed indicators were: gender, age, distance from the school, parents' education, final school result, an alternative to a selected study place, international students' exchange, employment status during the study, employment chances after the study, place of living, type of dwelling, preferred study form, etc. The questionnaire should be constantly updated with regards to experiences and new requirements.

The present paper introduces a two step-approach. In the first step is done a longitudinal evaluation of the indicators. In this particular example data from the academic years 2006/07 (Težak, 2007) and 2007/08 (Težak, 2008) were analyzed.

In the second step a comparison between students' profiles is done. Valuable data for comparison can be found in (Evroštudent SI, 2007; Eurostudent III, 2008). In this particular example a comparison between undergraduate and graduate students of tourism at Centre for higher education and students of the nearby university (Flere, 2005), was done. The research was a part of a development process of a new tourism study course; therefore the research comprised only students of tourism programs.

2. Methodological Remarks

The purpose of the research is to establish some students' socio-demographic and pedagogical profile indicators. Also, two research hypotheses are set. The first is: "The structure of the students' answers is similar for the study year 2006/07 and 2007/08". The second research hypothesis is: "The structure of the students at the Centre for higher education is similar to the structure of the students at the University of Maribor".

Survey results of the students profile can be found at the web pages for Slovenia (Evrošudent SI, 2007) and for other European countries (Eurostudent III, 2008), but they cannot describe our potential students in details. In the academic year 2007/08 we performed a survey of the students' profile as well as in the study year before (Težak, 2007; Težak, 2008). The purpose of the survey is to define some indicators of student's life, as well as to put the findings into broader social circumstances.

The unit of the analysis is a student. The research instrument used was a standardized questionnaire completed by students. The sampling procedure used was random sampling.

To test the first hypothesis, the universe consisted of students who attended lectures of all study programs performed at the Centre for higher education Ptuj. The sample numbers are n1 = 41 units and n2 = 83 units, for the successive academic years respectively. Described are characteristics such as: student's gender and age profile, family status of student, social background and a source of income, students' mobility and employment possibilities.

The second hypothesis comprised students who attended lectures of undergraduate and graduate study programs of tourism, performed at the Centre for higher education in Ptuj, n1 = 61 units. The second source of data are students of the University of Maribor, n2 = 1209 units. Questionnaires differ in the number of parameters. In the research we compared parameters such as: gender, age profile, place of living, family status of students, social background and a source of income, students' mobility and employment possibilities etc.; only some will be presented here.

An analysis was made by descriptive statistics as well as by statistical inference methods.

Tabular form and graphs were used for the survey data presentation. Chi-squared test was performed for statistical inference. We chose the significance level $\alpha = 0.05$. Figures represent relative frequencies. Tables contain absolute frequencies.

3. Research Results and Discussion

In this section are presented some of the most specific or interesting results of the survey, according to our opinion. Complete survey can be found in already mentioned data sources.

The first hypothesis gives us longitudinal evaluation of the students' profile parameters. Let us set and test hypothesis for some parameters.

3.1 Gender

Gender	2006_7	2007_8	2006_7(%)	2007_8(%)
female	28	54	68,29	65,06
male	13	29	31,71	34,94
total	41	83	100,00	100,00

Table 1. Gender of the student

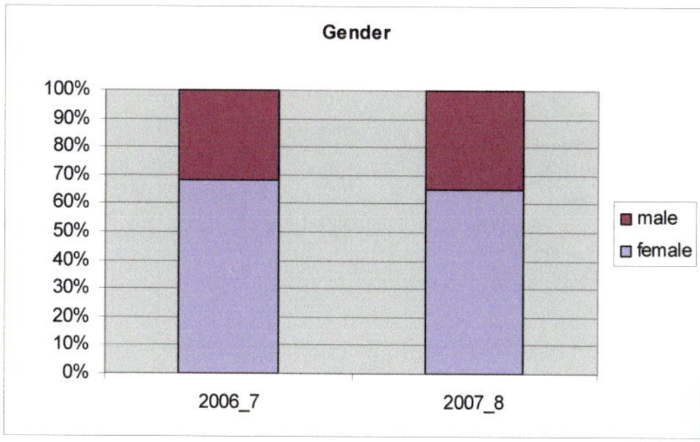

Fig. 1. Gender of the student

H_0: the structure of the answers is similar for both years.
H_a: the structure of the answers is not similar.
$\alpha = 0.05$. DF=1.
Chi-squared test, $p = 0.72$. H_0 is accepted.
The structure of the answers is similar for both years.

3.2 Age

Age	2006_7	2007_8	2006_7(%)	2007_8(%)
<21	4	24	9,76	28,92
22-25	14	17	34,15	20,48
26-30	11	18	26,83	21,69
>31	12	24	29,27	28,92
total	41	83	100,00	100,00

Table 2. Age of the student

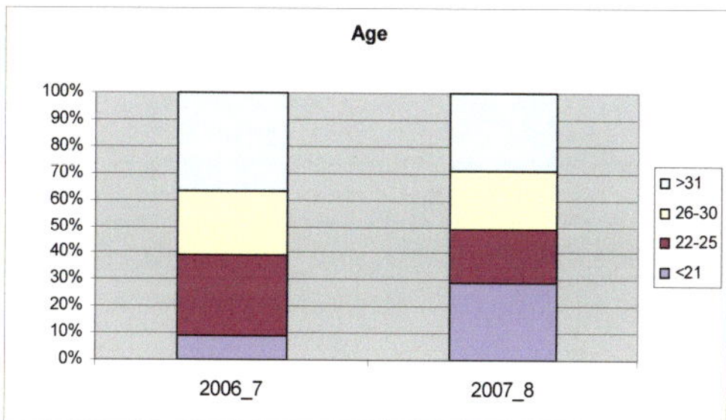

Fig. 2. Age of the student

H_0: the structure of the answers is similar for both years.
H_a: the structure of the answers is not similar.
$\alpha = 0.05$. DF=3.
Chi-squared test, $p = 0.08$. H_0 is accepted.
The structure of the answers is similar for both years.

3.3 Distance From the School

Distance	2006_7	2007_8	2006_7(%)	2007_8(%)
<5 km	12	17	29,27	20,48
5-30 km	20	44	48,78	53,01
>30 km	9	22	21,95	26,51
total	41	83	100,00	100,00

Table 3. Distance from the school

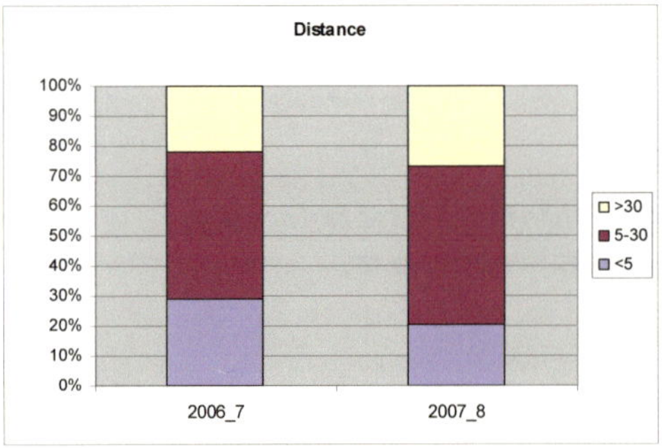

Fig. 3. Distance from the school

H_0: the structure of the answers is similar for both years.
H_a: the structure of the answers is not similar.
$\alpha = 0.05$. DF=2.
Chi-squared test, $p = 0.55$. H_0 is accepted.
The structure of the answers is similar for both years.

3.4 Parents Education

Parents education - mother	2006_7	2007_8	2006_7(%)	2007_8(%)
primary and less	7	9	17,07	10,98
middle	28	48	68,29	58,54
high and more	6	25	14,63	30,49
total	41	82	100,00	100,00

Table 4. Parents education - mother

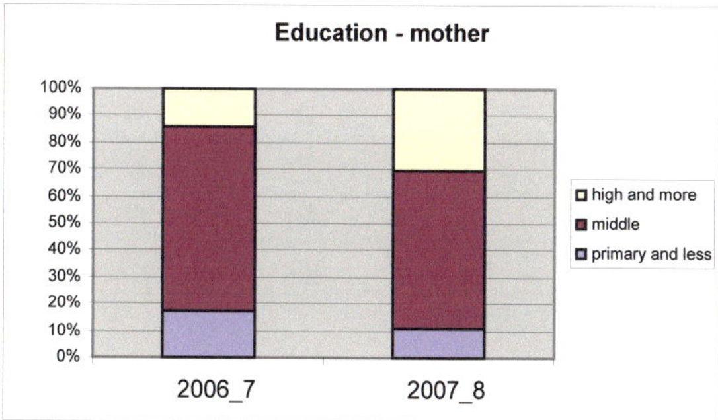

Fig. 4. Parents education - mother

H_0: the structure of the answers is similar for both years.
H_a: the structure of the answers is not similar.
$\alpha = 0.05$. DF=2.
Chi-squared test, $p = 0.14$. H_0 is accepted.
The structure of the answers is similar for both years.

Parents education - father	2006_7	2007_8	2006_7(%)	2007_8(%)
primary and less	6	4	15,00	4,82
middle	27	55	67,50	66,27
high and more	7	24	17,50	28,92
total	40	83	100,00	100,00

Table 5. Parents education - father

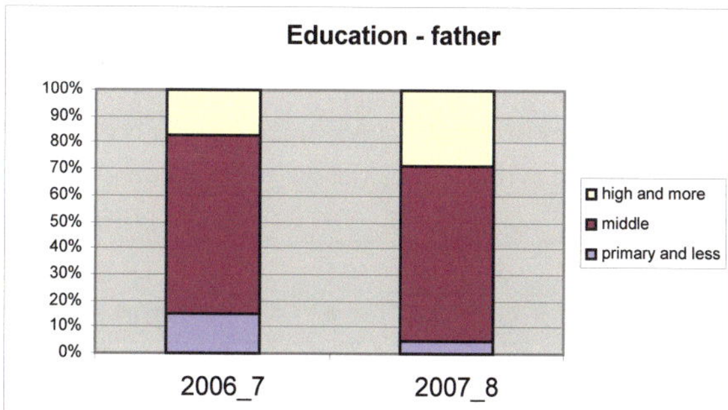

Fig. 5. Parents education - father

H_0: the structure of the answers is similar for both years.
H_a: the structure of the answers is not similar.
$\alpha = 0.05$. DF=2.
Chi-squared test, $p = 0.09$. H_0 is accepted.
The structure of the answers is similar for both years.

3.5 Final Secondary School Result

Final school success	2006_7	2007_8	2006_7(%)	2007_8(%)
excellent	4	6	10,00	7,23
very good	15	27	37,50	32,53
good and less	21	50	52,50	60,24
total	40	83	100,00	100,00

Table 6. Secondary education final result

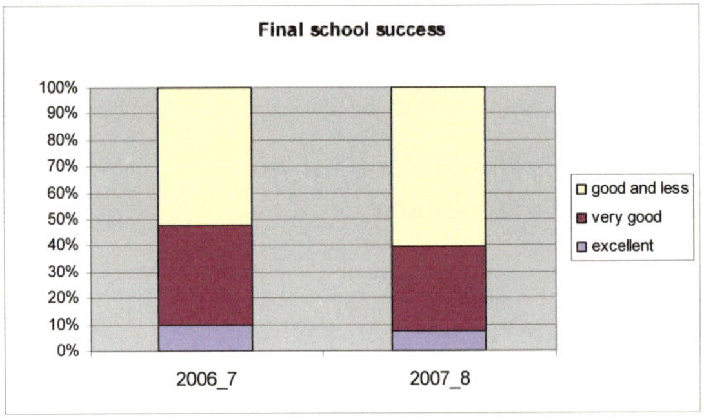

Fig. 6. Secondary education final result

H_0: the structure of the answers is similar for both years.
H_a: the structure of the answers is not similar.
$\alpha = 0.05$. DF=2.
Chi-squared test, $p = 0.69$. H_0 is accepted.
The structure of the answers is similar for both years.

3.6 Alternative to Choose a Study Place

Alternative for study	2006_7	2007_8	2006_7(%)	2007_8(%)
easy elsewhere	13	37	32,50	50,00
hard elsewhere	22	32	55,00	43,24
can not study	5	5	12,50	6,76
total	40	74	100,00	100,00

Table 7. Alternative to choose a study place

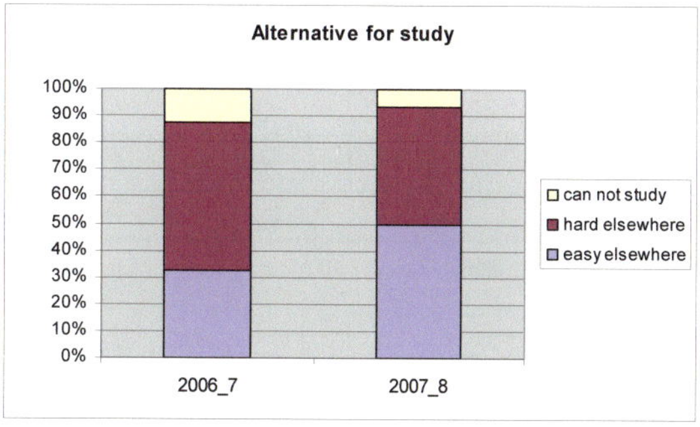

Fig. 7. Alternative to choose study place

H_0: the structure of the answers is similar for both years.
H_a: the structure of the answers is not similar.
$\alpha = 0.05$. DF=2.
Chi-squared test, $p = 0.17$. H_0 is accepted.
The structure of the answers is similar for both years.

3.7 International Student Exchange Intention

International exchange	2006_7	2007_8	2006_7(%)	2007_8(%)
yes	15	33	38,46	47,14
no	24	37	61,54	52,86
total	39	70	100,00	100,00

Table 8. International student exchange intention

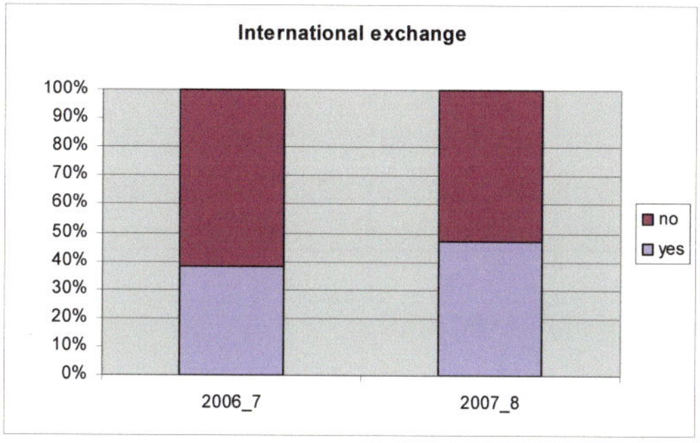

Fig. 8. International student exchange intention

H_0: the structure of the answers is similar for both years.
H_a: the structure of the answers is not similar.
$\alpha = 0.05$. DF=2.
Chi-squared test, $p = 0.38$. H_0 is accepted.
The structure of the answers is similar for both years.

3.8 Employment Status During the Study

Employment in time of study	2006_7	2007_8	2006_7(%)	2007_8(%)
employed	26	59	65,00	86,76
not employed	14	9	35,00	13,24
total	40	68	100,00	100,00

Table 9. Employment status during the study

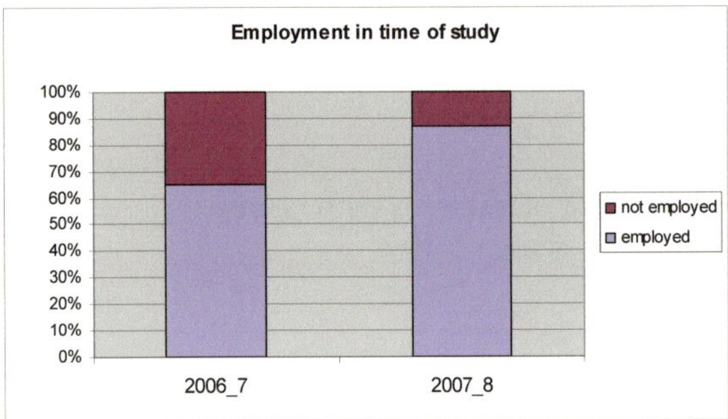

Fig. 9. Employment status during the study

H_0: the structure of the answers is similar for both years.
H_a: the structure of the answers is not similar.
$\alpha = 0.05$. DF=1.
Chi-squared test, $p = 0.008$. H_0 is rejected.
The structure of the answers is not similar for both years.

3.9 Employment Chances After the Study

Employment after study	2006_7	2007_8	2006_7(%)	2007_8(%)
easily	16	33	39,02	40,74
difficult	17	36	41,46	44,44
not know	8	12	19,51	14,81
total	41	81	100,00	100,00

Table 10. Employment chances after the study

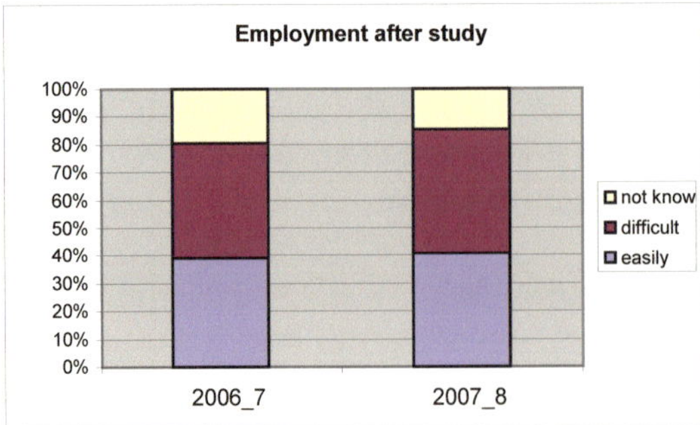

Fig. 10. Employment chances after the study

H_0: the structure of the answers is similar for both years.
H_a: the structure of the answers is not similar.
$\alpha = 0.05$. DF=2.
Chi-squared test, $p = 0.8$. H_0 is accepted.
The research $\chi 2$ tests show that students responses have similar structure for gender, age, distance from the school, parents education, final school success, alternative to choose study place, vision about international student exchange and employment chances after study. We cannot say the same for employment status during the study period. We can conclude that we have got some parameters of our students' socio-demographic profile.
The second research step will compare students at the Centre for higher education Ptuj and students at the University of Maribor which is only 30km away.

3.10 Gender

Gender	Ptuj	UMb	Ptuj (%)	Umb (%)
female	45	702	73,77	58,06
male	16	507	26,23	41,94
total	61	1209	100,00	100,00

Table 11. Gender of the student

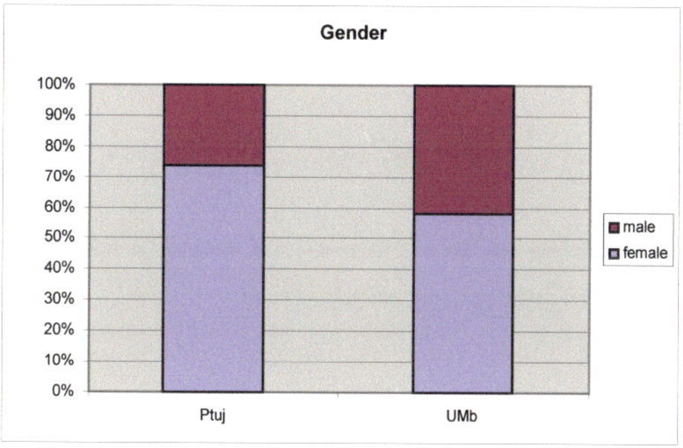

Fig. 11. Gender of the student

H_0: the structure of the students at the Centre for higher education is similar to the structure of the students at the University of Maribor.
H_a: the structure of the students at the Centre for higher education is not similar to the structure of the students at the University of Maribor.
$\alpha = 0.05$. DF = 1.

$\chi^2_{crit} = 3.84$. $\chi^2 = 5.91$.

Statistical conclusion: H_0 is rejected and we accept H_a. There are differences between students of both educational centers.
The gender structure shows that students in Ptuj count more women than their peers in Maribor. According to the structure of persons employed in the tourism industry one should expect even a greater number of women-students. Basing ourselves on the survey results we can conclude that students in Ptuj range among managing staff and that is why the ratio of women-students does not prevail.

3.11 Age

Age	Ptuj	UMb	Ptuj (%)	Umb (%)
<19	11	254	18,03	21,01
20-21	13	508	21,31	42,02
22-23	7	363	11,48	30,02
24-25	6	60	9,84	4,96
>26	24	24	39,34	1,99
total	61	1209	100,00	100,00

Table 12. Age of the student

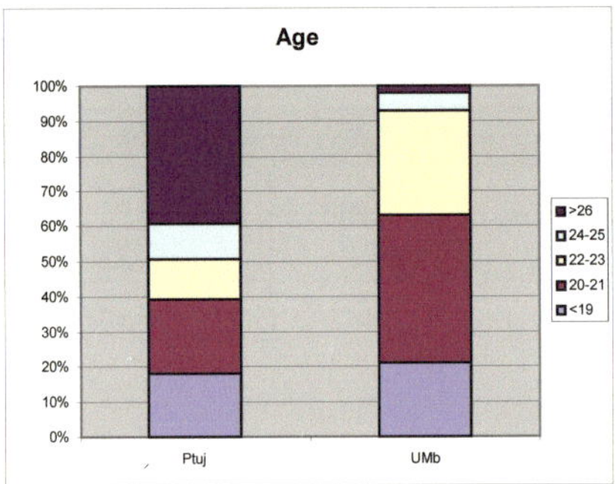

Fig. 12. Age of the student

H_0: the structure of the students is similar to the structure of the students at the University of Maribor.
H_a: the structure of the students at the Centre for higher education is not similar to the structure of the students at the University of Maribor.
$\alpha = 0.05$. DF = 4.

$\chi^2_{crit} = 9.49$. $\chi^2 = 472.39$.

Statistical conclusion: H_0 is rejected and we accept H_a. There are differences between students.
The age parameter shows huge differences between the groups of Ptuj and Maribor students. Ptuj students are much older which leads to a conclusion that those who are studying already work in the tourism sector.

3.12 Place of Living

Place of living	Ptuj	UMb	Ptuj (%)	Umb (%)
school city	23	193	37,70	15,96
another city	27	411	44,26	34,00
rural settlement	11	605	18,04	50,04
total	61	1209	100,00	100,00

Table 13. Place of living

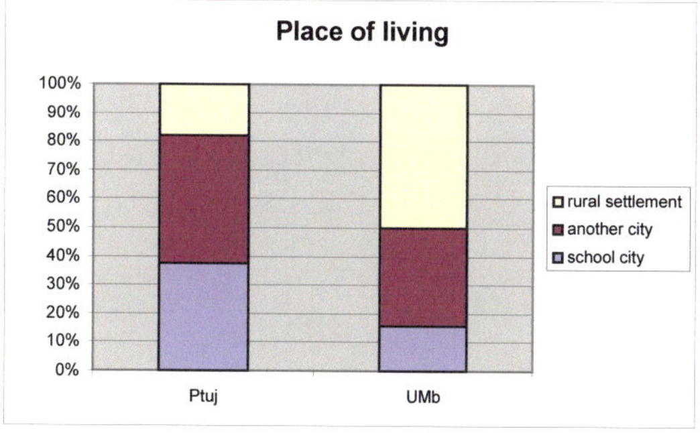

Fig. 13. Place of living

H_0: the structure of the students is similar to the structure of the students at the University of Maribor.
H_a: the structure of the students at the Centre for higher education is not similar to the structure of the students at the University of Maribor.
$\alpha = 0.5$. DF = 2.

$\chi^2_{crit} = 5.99$. $\chi^2 = 30.18$.

Statistical conclusion: H_0 is rejected and we accept H_a. There are differences between students.
The permanent address parameter equally shows significant differences between both groups of students. It could be deduced that students in Ptuj mostly belong to the leading staff from urban environment. On the other hand in Maribor half of the students come from the urban environment in comparison with Ptuj where as much as 80% of all students are from urban environment.

3.13 Parents Education

Parents education - mother	Ptuj	UMb	Ptuj (%)	Umb (%)
less than primary	0	30	0,00	2,48
primary	5	182	8,20	15,05
middle	36	713	59,02	58,97
higher	8	133	13,11	11,00
high	10	145	16,39	11,99
graduate	2	6	3,28	0,50
total	61	1209	100,00	100,00

Table 14. Parents education - mother

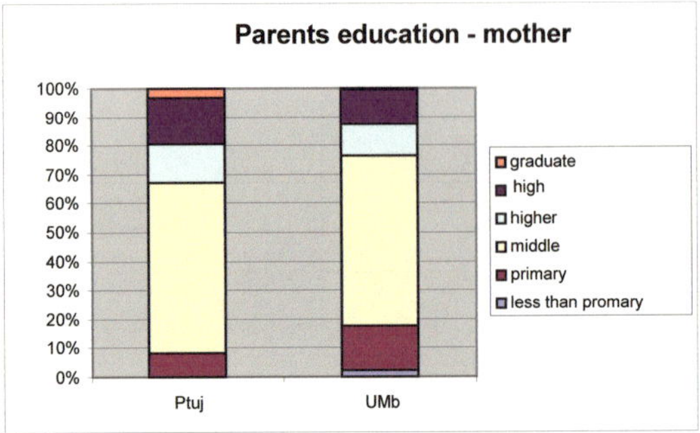

Fig. 14. Parents education - mother

H_0: there is no difference between students at the Centre for higher education and students at the University of Maribor.
H_a: there are differences between students.
$\alpha = 0.05$. DF = 5.

$\chi^2_{crit} = 11.07$. $\chi^2 = 134.66$.

Statistical conclusion: H_0 is rejected and we accept H_a. There are differences between students, concerning mothers' education.
The educational level of mothers shows higher level in Ptuj which can be ascribed to the older age of Ptuj students in general, and consequently their parents, who might have finished their formal education, are older too. University students are younger and some of their parents are planning to proceed with their own studies. Another established fact is that 80% of Ptuj students come from urban environment where the level of education is generally higher, which holds true of Ptuj students.

Parents education -father	Ptuj	UMb	Ptuj (%)	Umb (%)
less than primary	0	36	0,00	2,98
primary	2	145	3,28	11,99
middle	37	737	60,66	60,96
higher	13	146	21,31	12,08
high	7	133	11,48	11,00
graduate	2	12	3,28	0,99
total	61	1209	100,00	100,00

Table 15. Parents education - father

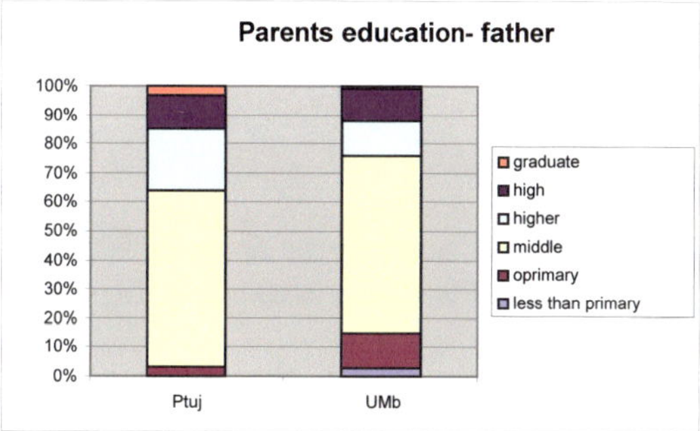

Fig. 15. Parents education - father

H_0: there is no difference between students at the Centre for higher education and students at the University of Maribor.
H_a: there are differences between students.
$\alpha = 0.05$. DF = 5.

$\chi^2_{crit} = 11.07$. $\chi^2 = 89.46$.

Statistical conclusion: H_0 is rejected and we accept H_a. There are differences between students, concerning fathers' education.
The conclusion is the same as the one regarding the educational level of the mother. It also conditions the higher educational level of the father as the age level of students in Ptuj is higher. The urban environment and consequently different academic experiences of students' parents also speak for their higher formal education.
The findings were put into broad social circumstances. It was shown, that there is a statistically significant difference between populations of students of the Centre for higher education and students of the nearby university. Students attending courses at the higher education Centre clearly reflect characteristic structure of employed staff in the middle professional position. They are also characterized by their origins in a relatively poor region and by their specific needs.

4. Conclusion

Results of the research give us an important aspect of and quantitative data for making decisions regarding higher education development in our region. The analyze shows that students at the Centre for higher education are statistically different from students of the nearby university regarding some analyzed parameters. However, we have got a profile of a student in our region. This was the purpose of the research. Students' needs are different and a new curriculum development has to consider this fact to better suit students' needs and to encourage higher education quality in our region.
With permanent students' profile and study outcomes observation, we will be able to make better student policy and study conditions for the students. Consecutively we will offer more effective study to students as well as students' outcomes will be better. This gives sense to our efforts to encourage quality higher education in the region. The similar analysis of the students' socio-demographic profile is going to be done as an international joint project between Centre for higher education in Ptuj and Faculty of Education of the

University of St. Kliment Ohridski. The initial questionnaire with nineteen questions will be updated to show additional parameters that are important for the particular university.

5. References

Flere, S. et al. (2005). *Social Profile of Students in Slovenia 2005,* University of Maribor, Slovenia, Maribor, http://www.studentska-org.si/files/2006-02-profil-studentov-2005.pdf

Knežević, M. (2006). *Statistika z uporabo računalnika.* University of Primorska, Turistica - Faculty of Tourism Studies, Slovenia, Portorož

Montgomery, D.C.; & Runger, G. C. (2003). *Applied statistics and probability for engineers,* John Wiley & Sons, Inc., ISBN 0-471-20454-4, USA, NY

Research report (2007). *Evroštudent SI 2007,* MVZT, Slovenia, Ljubljana http://www.avantis.si/eurostudent/rezultati-2007/media/evrostudent.si.2007.pdf

Research report (2008). *Eurostudent III.* http://www.eurostudent.eu/download/Summary Eng.pdf

Težak, O. (2007). *Profile of the student 2006/07,* Research report, (in Slovene), Revivis Ptuj, Slovenia, Ptuj

Težak, O. (2008). *Profile of the student 2007/08,* Research report, (in Slovene), Revivis Ptuj, Slovenia, Ptuj